NEW!

6th edition

BABY

BARGAINS

SECRETS

to saving 20% to 50% on babyfurniture, equipment, clothes, toys, maternity wear and much, much more!

Denise & Alan Fields
Authors of the Best-seller
Bridal Bargains

Copyright Page, Credits and Zesty Lo-Cal Recipes

Saxophone, lead guitar and breast-feeding by Denise Fields
Drums, rhythm guitar and father stuff by Alan Fields
Congas on "Grandparents" by
Max & Helen Coopwood, Howard & Patti Fields
Cover/interior design and keyboard solo by Epicenter Creative
Screaming guitar solos on "(Let's Go) Perego" by Charles & Arthur Troy
Additional guitar work on "Diaper Changing Blues" by Todd Snider
Backing vocals on "(She's Got A) LATCH Car Seat" by Ric Ocasek
Band photography by Moses Street

*This book was written to the music of the Barenaked Ladies,
which probably explains a lot.*

Distribution to the book trade by Publisher's Group West, Berkeley, CA 1-800-788-3123. Thanks to the entire staff of PGW for their support.

To order this book, call 1-800-888-0385. Or send $17.95 plus $3 shipping to Windsor Peak Press, 436 Pine Street, Boulder, CO 80302. Questions or comments? Please call the authors at (303) 442-8792. Or fax them a note at (303) 442-3744. Or write to them at the above address in Boulder, Colorado. E-mail the authors at authors@babybargains.com.

Learn more about this book online at www.BabyBargains.com

Library Cataloging in Publication Data

Fields, Denise
Fields, Alan
    Baby Bargains: Secrets to saving 20% to 50% on baby furniture, equipment, clothes, toys maternity wear and much, much more/ Denise & Alan Fields
    544 pages.
    Includes index.
    ISBN 1-889392-19-7
    1. Child Care—Handbooks, manuals, etc. 2. Infants' supplies—Purchasing—United States, Canada, Directories. 3. Children's paraphernalia—Purchasing—Handbooks, manuals. 4. Product Safety—Handbooks, manuals. 5. Consumer education.
    649'.122'0296—dc20. 2006.

We miss you Dee Dee.

Version 6.1

CONTENTS

Chapter 1

"IT'S GOING TO CHANGE YOUR LIFE"

Chapter 2

NURSERY NECESSITIES: CRIBS, DRESSERS & MORE

Chapter 3

BABY BEDDING & DECOR

Chapter 4

THE REALITY LAYETTE: LITTLE CLOTHES FOR LITTLE PRICES

Chapter 5

MATERNITY/NURSING CLOTHES

Chapter 6

FEEDING: BREASTFEEDING, BOTTLES, HIGH CHAIRS

to be comfortable. They can't even distinguish between the liberals and conservatives on "Meet the Press," so how would they ever be able to tell the difference between Baby Gucci crib bedding and another less famous brand that's just as comfortable, but 70% less expensive? Our focus is on making your baby happy—at a price that won't break the bank.

2 **YOUR BABY'S SAFETY IS MUCH MORE IMPORTANT THAN YOUR CONVENIENCE.** Here are the scary facts: 67,000 babies per year are injured (and 49 deaths are caused) by juvenile products, according to government estimates. Each chapter of this book has a section called "Safe & Sound," which arms you with in-depth advice on keeping your baby out of trouble. We'll tell you which products we think are dangerous and how to safely use other potentially hazardous products.

3 **MURPHY'S LAW OF BABY TOYS SAYS YOUR BABY'S HAPPINESS WITH A TOY IS INVERSELY RELATED TO THE TOY'S PRICE.** Buy a $200 shiny new wagon with anti-lock brakes, and odds are baby just wants to play with the box it came in. In recognition of this reality, we've included "wastes of money" in each chapter that will steer you away from frivolous items.

4 **IT'S GOING TO COST MORE THAN YOU THINK.** Whatever amount of money you budget for your baby, get ready to spend more. Here's a breakdown of the average costs of bringing a baby into the world today:

The Average Cost of Having a Baby

(based on industry estimates for a child from birth to age one)

Crib, mattress, dresser, rocker	$1500
Bedding / Decor	$300
Baby Clothes	$500
Disposable Diapers	$600
Maternity/Nursing Clothes	$1200
Nursery items, high chair, toys	$400
Baby Food / Formula	$900
Stroller, Car Seat, Carrier	$400
Miscellaneous	$500
TOTAL	**$6300**

The above figures are based on buying name brand products at regular retail prices. We surveyed over 1000 parents to arrive at these estimates.

Bedding/Decor includes not only bedding items but also lamps, wallpaper, and so on for your baby's nursery. Baby Food/Formula assumes you'd breastfeed for the first six months and then feed baby jarred baby food ($400) and formula ($500) until age one. If you plan to bottle-feed instead of breastfeed, add another $500 on to that figure.

Sure, you do get an automatic tax write-off for that bundle of joy, but that only amounts to about $3100 this year (plus you also get an additional $1000 child care tax credit, depending on your income). But those tax goodies won't nearly offset the actual cost of raising a child. And as you probably realize, our cost chart is missing some expensive "extras" . . . like medical bills, childcare, saving for college and more. Here's an overview of what can add to the tab:

◆ *Medical/adoption bills.* Yes, for most couples, conceiving a child is free (although some may argue about that). But not everyone is that lucky—fertility treatments for the estimated 10% to 15% of couples who can't conceive naturally can run $10,000 to $20,000 a try (although there are less expensive treatments out there as well). Only a handful of states require health insurance policies to cover infertility—hence, the vast majority of couples who face this challenge do so without insurance and must pay those costs out of pocket. Or if their insurance covers infertility, it may just pay for the infertility *diagnosis* but not treatments. Bottom line: it is not uncommon for couples to spend upwards of $40,000 on infertility treatments (again, check with your doctor for less expensive alternatives).

Besides the normal prenatal visits to the doctor, the biggest medical bill is for the birth—about $7090 for a "normal" delivery at a hospital. The same study (Expenditures on Children by Families, 2003 annual report by the US Dept. of Agriculture) pegs the cost of a Caesarean at $11,450. Medical bills for first year routine check-ups and immunizations can cost $2500 or more. Yes, insurance typically picks up most of those costs, but there are many children (15% of the total births this year) that are born without any coverage. So, if you have insurance, count yourself among the lucky.

Couples who adopt a baby typically face fees and expenses that range from $15,000 to $30,000. Check out this great website, www.costs.adoption.com, for cost details for all types of adoptions. There is a $10,000 federal tax credit that offsets some adoption expenses—check with your tax preparer for details (see IRS publication 968, "Tax Benefits for Adoption"). One bargain for parents who are considering an overseas adoption: some airlines now offer adopting parents a break on airfares. Several airlines offer 50% or more discounts off full coach fares (the fares adopting parents have to use, as most adoptions are done on short notice). The baby's one-way fare back home is also discounted. Always ask your airline if they have an adoption fare deal.

◆ **Child Care.** According to the Department of Agriculture, the average cost of childcare for a three to five-year old child is $1800 per year. But those costs seemed low to us—our research on child care costs (detailed in chapter later in this book) revealed family daycare runs $4000 to $10,000 and center care can cost up to $13,000 per year. What about a nanny? Most run $10,000 to $20,000 in average cities, but that depends on whether they are live-in or not. In high cost cities like New York or San Francisco, childcare costs for families can top $30,000 a year.

◆ **Housing.** Those neighborhoods with the best schools aren't cheap. The government estimates the average middle-class family with one child will spend an *extra* $60,120 on shelter until the child is 18. The average annual cost of housing one child is $2620 to $5620, according to government estimates.

◆ **Transportation.** Yes, a brand new minivan today tops $20,000 and some models approach $35,000. All those trips to daycare (and later, the mall) add up—the government says average parents will spend $25,110 to transport a child to all those required activities until the age of 18.

◆ **And more.** Additional expenses that parents face include health care (the government says even the average, healthy child can rack up $13,230 in medical bills for the first 18 years), clothing (if you think baby clothes are pricey, check out the $10,430 bill the average kid racks up in clothes until age 18), and education (private school, anyone?).

The bottom line. If you're still with us, let's see what the government says is the GRAND TOTAL of expenses to raise a baby to age 18. Are you sitting down? Try $178,590. And that's for middle class Americans. More affluent parents spend $261,270. Yes, there are economies of scale if you add more children—but there's a limit to the savings. On average, each additional child costs just 24% less than a single child. (Source: 2003 Annual Report, Expenditures on Children by Families, US Dept of Agriculture).

But wait! The government leaves two critical costs out of its equation: saving for college and lost wages from a parent who stays at home. Let's look at both:

◆ **College.** Price college tuition lately? Even if you forget about Harvard, the cost of attending a state school today is staggering. And with college costs expected to continue to rise in the future, you'll have to put away $375 each month for baby's college fund if you start at birth to pay for the average state school's four-year program (tuition plus room and board). Wait longer to get started and the costs rise rapidly. T Rowe Price (www.troweprice.com) has an excellent free "college planner" feature on their web site that lets you compare savings plans for public versus private schools. Fidelity also has a college cost calculator that is easy to use (fidelity.com; go to Retirement & Guidance and then College Planning).

◆ **Lost wages.** Having a baby is a financial double-whammy—not only are your expenses rising, but your income drops. Why? At least one parent will have to take off time to care for the baby. Yes, lost wages could be a short six-week maternity leave . . . or the next 18 years for a stay-at-home parent.

Hence, when you add in saving for college and lost wages for a stay-at-home parent for 18 years, the cost of raising an average middle class child to age 18 will run $1,455,581. Amazing, eh?

(Source: the above numbers are from the 2003 "Expenditures on Children by Families" by the US Dept of Agriculture and US News & World Report's "The Cost of Children", March 30, 1998; updated using 2005 dollars).

Reality Check: Does it Really Cost that Much to Have a Baby?

Now that we've thoroughly scared you enough to inquire whether the stork accepts returns, we should point out that children do NOT have to cost that much. Even if we focus just on the first year, you don't have to spend $6300 on your baby. And that's what this book is all about: how to save money and still buy the best. Follow all the tips in this book, and we estimate the first year will cost you $3985. Yes, that's a savings of over $2300!

Now, at this point, you might be saying "That's impossible! I suppose you'll recommend buying all the cheap stuff, from polyester clothes to no-name cribs." On the contrary, we'll show you how to get *quality* name brands and safe products at discount prices. For example, we've got outlets and catalogs that sell all-cotton baby clothing at 20% to 40% off retail. You'll also learn about web sites that sell car seats and strollers for 40% off. And much more. Yes, we've got the maximum number of bargains allowed by federal law.

A word on bargain shopping: when interviewing hundreds of parents for this book, we realized bargain seekers fall into two frugal camps. There's the "do-it-yourself" crowd and the "quality at a discount" group. As the name implies, "do-it-yourselfers" are resourceful folks who like to take second-hand products and refurbish them. Others use creative tricks to make homemade versions of baby care items like baby wipes and diaper rash cream.

While that's all well and good, we fall more into the second camp of bargain hunters, the "quality at a discount" group. We love discovering a hidden factory outlet that sells goods at 50% off. Or finding a great web or mail-order source that discounts name-brand baby products at rock bottom prices. We also realize savvy parents save money by not *wasting* it on inferior goods or useless items.

While we hope that *Baby Bargains* pleases both groups of bargain hunters, the main focus of this book is not on do-it-yourself projects. Books like the *Tightwad Gazette* (check your local library for a copy) do a much better job on this subject. Our main emphasis will be on discount web sites, catalogs, outlet stores, brand reviews and identifying best buys for the dollar.

What? There's No Advertising in This Book?

Yes, it's true. This book contains zero percent advertising. We have never taken any money to recommend a product or company and never will. We make our sole living off the sales of this and other books. (So, when your friend asks to borrow this copy, have them buy their own book!) Our publisher, Windsor Peak Press, also derives its sole income from the sale of this book and our other publications. No company recommended in this book paid any consideration or was charged any fee to be mentioned. (In fact, some companies probably would offer us money to leave them *out* of the book, given our comments about their products or services).

As consumer advocates, we believe this "no ads" policy helps to ensure objectivity. The opinions in the book are just that—ours and those of the parents we interviewed.

We also are parents of two small children. As far as we know, we are the only authors of a consumer's guide to baby products that actually have young kids. We figure if we actually are recommending these products to you, we should have some real world experience with them. (That said, we should disclose that our sons have filed union grievances with our company over testing of certain jarred baby foods and that litigation is ongoing.)

Of course, given the sheer volume of baby stuff, there's no way we can test everything personally. To solve that dilemma, we rely on reader feedback to help us figure out which are the best products to recommend. We receive over 100 emails a day from parents; this helps us spot overall trends on which brands/products parents love. And which ones they want to destroy with a rocket launcher.

Finally, we enlist readers to test new products for us, evaluating items on how they work in the real world. One bad review from one parent doesn't necessarily mean we won't recommend a product; but we'll then combine these tests with other parent feedback to get an overall picture. (If you'd like to volunteer to be a product tester, sign up for free e-newsletter on our web site BabyBargains.com. Also check the message boards on our site for postings about product tests).

What about prices of baby products? Trying to stay on top of this is similar to nailing Jell-O to a wall. Yet, we still try. As much as we can confirm, the prices quoted in this book were accurate as of the date of publication. Of course, prices and product features can change at any time. Inflation and other factors may affect the actual prices you discover in shopping for your baby. While the publisher makes every effort to ensure their accuracy, errors and omissions may exist. That's why update this book with every new printing—make sure you are using the most recent version (go to BabyBargains.com and click on Which Version?).

Our door is always open—we want to hear your opinions. Email us at authors@BabyBargains.com or call us at (303) 442-8792 to ask a question, report a mistake, or just give us your thoughts. Finally, you can write to us at "Baby Bargains," 436 Pine Street, Suite 700, Boulder, CO 80302.

What about the phone numbers listed in this book? We list contact numbers for manufacturers so you can find a local dealer near you that carries the product (or request a catalog, if available). Unless otherwise noted, these manufacturers do NOT sell directly to the public.

So, Who Are You Guys Anyway?

Why do a book on saving money on baby products? Don't new parents throw caution to the wind when buying for their baby, spending whatever it takes to ensure their baby's safety and comfort?

Ha! When our first son was born in 1993, we quickly realized how darn expensive this guy was. Sure, as a new parent, you know you've got to buy a car seat, crib, clothes and diapers . . . but have you walked into one of those baby "superstores" lately? It's a blizzard of baby stuff, with a bewildering array of "must have" gear,

What you need, when

Yes, buying for baby can seem overwhelming, but there is a silver lining: you don't need ALL this stuff immediately when baby is born. Let's look at what items you need quickly and what you can wait on. This chart indicates usage of certain items for the first 12 months of baby's life:

	MONTHS OF USE				
ITEM	BIRTH	3	6	9	12+
Nursery Necessities					
Cradle/bassinet	▨				
Crib/Mattress	▨▨▨▨▨				
Dresser	▨▨▨▨▨				
Glider Rocker	▨▨▨▨▨				
Bedding: Cradle	▨				
Bedding: Crib	▨▨▨▨▨				
Clothing					
Caps/Hats	▨				
Blanket Sleepers	▨▨▨▨▨				
Layette Gowns	▨				
Booties	▨				
All other layette	▨▨▨				
Around the House					
Baby Monitor	▨▨▨▨▨				
Baby Food (solid)			▨▨▨		
High Chairs			▨▨▨		
Places to Go					
Infant Car Seat	▨▨				
Convertible Car Seat*			▨▨▨		
Carriage Stroller	▨▨				
Umbrella Stroller			▨▨▨		
Front Carrier	▨▨▨				
Backpack Carrier			▨▨▨		
Safety items		▨▨▨▨			

*You can use a convertible car seat starting immediately with that first ride home from the hospital. However, it is our recommendation that you use an infant car seat for the first six months or so, then, when baby grows out of it, buy the convertible car seat.

gadgets and gizmos, all claiming to be the best thing for parents since sliced bread.

Becoming a parent in this day and age is both a blessing and curse. The good news: parents today have many more choices for baby products than past generations. The *bad* news: parents today have many more choices for baby products than past generations.

Our mission: make sense of this stuff, with an eye on cutting costs. As consumer advocates, we've been down this road before. We researched bargains and uncovered scams in the wedding business when we wrote *Bridal Bargains*. Then we penned an exposé on new homebuilders in *Your New House*.

Yet, we found the baby business to be perilous in different ways—instead of outright fraud or scam artists, we've instead discovered some highly questionable products that don't live up to their hype—and others that are outright dangerous. We were surprised to learn how most juvenile items face little (or no) government scrutiny, leaving parents to sort out true usefulness and safety from sales hype. In addition, in recent years new "discount" baby product web sites have failed to live up to their own promises of prompt delivery and customer service.

So, we've gone on a quest to find the best baby products, at prices that won't send you to the poor house. Sure, we've sampled many of these items first hand. But this book is much more than our experiences—we interviewed over 1000 new parents to learn their experiences with products. Our message boards have over 15,000 members, buzzing with all sorts of product feedback and advice. We also attend juvenile product trade shows to quiz manufacturers and retailers on what's hot and what's not. The insights from retailers are especially helpful, since these folks are on the front lines, seeing which items unhappy parents return.

Our focus is on safety and durability: which items stand up to real world conditions and which don't. Interestingly, we found many products for baby are sold strictly on price . . . and sometimes a great "bargain" broke, fell apart or shrunk after a few uses. Hence, you'll note some of our top recommendations aren't always the lowest in price. To be sensitive to those on really tight budgets, we try to identify "good, better and best" bets in different price ranges.

First Time Parent 101

As a first-time parent, it's easy to get confused by all the jargon in the world of parenting books. But since you've never had a baby before, you may wonder how we define basic terms like "newborn," "infant," "toddler," "sleep deprivation" and so on. So, here's a quick primer:

◆ **Newborn.** As you'd expect, these are very young bambinos just recently born. Most folks define a newborn as a baby under four weeks or so in age.

◆ **Infant/baby.** We generally refer to children under age two as babies or infants.

◆ **Toddler.** For purposes of our books (*Baby Bargains* and *Toddler Bargains*—see below for more detail), we define a toddler as a child who is age two to five. As the name implies, these are young children who are just learning to walk. Okay, obviously most babies do this before age two. Some books define "toddler hood" as age 18 months to three years. "Toddler" clothes are typically for children age one to three. Confused yet? The point: there isn't one single definition of "toddler." We use it to describe the slew of products for older children (booster car seats, potty seats, etc).

◆ **Sleep deprivation.** See "newborn."

We get questions: the Top 5 Questions & Answers

From the home office here in Boulder, CO, here are the top five questions we get asked here at *Baby Bargains*:

1 **DO YOU HAVE A BOOK FOR OLDER CHILDREN? WHY DOESN'T BABY BARGAINS COVER PRODUCTS FOR OLDER CHILDREN LIKE POTTIES, TOYS OR BICYCLES?** *Baby Bargains* focuses on products for babies age birth to two. We did this to a) keep this book from becoming 800 pages long and b) to maintain our sanity. We realize there is a whole universe of products out there that parents buy for older kids. So, to help out those parents of toddlers, we have published a separate book called *Toddler Bargains* (ToddlerBargains.com). This book focuses on products for toddlers age two to five. Which topics are covered in which book? *Baby Bargains* covers infant and convertible car seats, while *Toddler Bargains* covers booster seats. Likewise, the baby book has a detailed section on high chairs and strollers—the toddler one focuses on kitchen boosters and double strollers, plus joggers (which are used more when a child is older). Go online to ToddlerBargains.com to read a detailed table of contents for that book. Also: check out our newest book, *Baby 411*—the ultimate FAQ for new parents. See the back of this book for more details.

2 **HOW DO I KNOW IF I HAVE THE CURRENT EDITION?** We strive to keep *Baby Bargains* as up-to-date as possible. As such, we update it periodically with new editions. But if you just borrowed this book from a friend, how do you know how old it is? First, look at the copyright page. There at the bottom you will see a version number (such as 6.0). The first number (the 6 in this case) means you have the 6th edition. The second number indicates the printing—every time we reprint the book, we make minor corrections, additions and changes. Version 6.0 is the initial printing of the 6th edition, version 6.1 is the first reprint of the sixth edition and so on.

So, how can you tell if your book is current or woefully out-of-date? Go to our web page at www.BabyBargains.com and click on "Which version?" There we will list what the most current version is. (One clue: look at the book's cover. We note the edition number on each cover. And we change the color of the cover with each edition). We update this book every two years (roughly). About 30% to 40% of the content will change with each edition. Bottom line: if you pick up a copy of this book that is one or two editions old, you will notice a significant number of changes.

3 **WHAT IF I SEE A NEW PRODUCT IN STORES? HOW CAN I FIND INFO ON THAT?** First, make sure you have the latest edition of *Baby Bargains* (see previous question). If you can't find that product in our latest book, go to our web page at www.BabyBargains.com. There you will find a treasure trove of information. First, check out the archives of our free e-newsletter to read past news articles on the latest products. Second, search the "Message Boards" section to see if other readers have tried out the product and reported to us on their experiences. If that doesn't work, post a query to the Message Boards for other parents to respond to. Of course, you can email us with a question as well (see the How to Contact Us page at the back of this book). Be sure to sign up for our free e-newsletter to get the latest news on our book, web page, product recalls and more. All this can be done from BabyBargains.com. (A note on our privacy policy: we NEVER sell reader email addresses or other personal info).

Even though we have a treasure trove of FREE stuff on our web page, please note that we do not post the entire text of *Baby Bargains* online (hey, we have to make a living somehow). If a friend gives you a ten year-old edition of this book, you can't go online and just download all the changes/updates for free. We appreciate your purchase of the most recent edition of this book.

4 **I AM LOOKING FOR A SPECIFIC PRODUCT BUT I DON'T KNOW WHERE TO START! HELP!** Yep, this book is 500+ pages long and we realize it can be a bit intimidating. But you have a friend in the Index—flip to the back of the book to look up just about anything. You can look up items by category, brand name and more.

If that doesn't work, try the Table of Contents. We sort the book into major topic areas (strollers, car seats, etc). In some chapters, we have "also known as" boxes that help you decode brand names that might be associated with other companies (for example, Eddie Bauer car seats are made by Cosco).

Don't forget the handy Telephone/Web Site Directory in the back of the book as well. You can pop to any company's web page to find more details about a product we review in *Baby Bargains*.

5 **WHY DO YOU SOMETIMES RECOMMEND A MORE EXPENSIVE PRODUCT THAN A CHEAPER OPTION?** Yes, this is a book about bargains, but sometimes we will pick a slightly more expensive item in a category if we believe it is superior in quality or safety. Sometimes it makes sense to invest in better-quality products that will last through more than one child. And don't forget about the hassle of replacing a cheap product that breaks in six months.

To be sure, however, we recognize that many folks are on tight budgets. To help, we offer "Good, Better, Best" product suggestions that are typically sorted by price (good is most affordable, best is usually more expensive). Don't torture yourself if you can't afford the "best" in every category; a "good" product will be just as, well, good.

Another note: remember that our brand reviews cover many options in a category, not just the cheapest. Don't be dismayed if we give an expensive brand an "A" rating—such ratings are often based on quality, construction, innovation and more. Yes, we will try to identify the best values in a category as well.

Why does our advice sometimes conflict with other publications like *Consumer Reports*? See the box on the next page for more on this.

Let's Go Shopping!

Now that all the formal introductions are done, let's move on to the good stuff. As your tour guides to BabyLand, we'd like to remind you of a few park rules before you go:

1 **NO FEEDING THE SALESPEOPLE.** Remember, the juvenile products industry is a $6.34 BILLION DOLLAR business. While all those baby stores may want to help you, they are first and foremost in business to make a profit. As a consumer, you should arm yourself with the knowledge necessary to make smart decisions. If you do, you won't be taken for a ride.

2 **KEEP YOUR PERSPECTIVE INSIDE THE VEHICLE AT ALL TIMES.** With all the hormones coursing through the veins of the average pregnant woman, now is not the time to lose it. As you visit

Baby Bargains versus Consumer Reports

First off, let us say right here and now that we are BIG fans of *Consumer Reports* (CR) magazine. The magazine (and now web site) are the gold standard of consumer journalism.

That said, we often get deluged with email from readers when CR reviews and rates a baby product category. Many folks ask us why we at *Baby Bargains* sometimes come to different conclusions than *Consumer Reports*.

First, understand that we have different research methods. *Consumer Reports* often lab tests products to make sure they are safe and durable. At *Baby Bargains*, we rely on parent/reader feedback to make our recommendations. Yes, we do hands-on inspections of products and meet with manufacturers at trade shows to demo the latest gear, but the reader feedback loop is our secret sauce.

Not surprisingly, most of the time we actually agree with *Consumer Reports*. In recent articles on strollers in CR and in our book, we both picked the same three of four brands as best. Yet, sometimes there are differences—we might pick a model as a "best bet" that CR thinks is only a second runner-up. And vice versa. We suppose you can chalk up the differences in ratings to different research methods.

Another issue: out of date reports. We love CR, but sometimes they are WAY behind when it comes to reviewing baby products. Since they don't focus on baby products, it can be YEARS between reports for certain categories. Models and brands change very quickly in this industry. Trying to compare a five year old report in a CR back issue with a current edition of this book isn't very helpful.

Of course, we don't take everything *Consumer Reports* says as the gospel truth. They (like us) make mistakes; we always try to verify results if CR determines a product is unsafe. In cases where we differ with CR, we'll point that out in our book and on our web site.

baby stores, don't get caught in the hype of the latest doo-dad that converts a car seat to a toaster.

3 **HAVE A GOOD TIME.** Oh sure, sifting through all those catalogs of crib bedding and convertible strollers will frazzle your mind. Just remember the goal is to have a healthy baby—so, take care of yourself first and foremost.

What's New in This Edition?

Wow, is it really the sixth edition of this book? When we first published *Baby Bargains* in 1994, we didn't realize how this would take on a life of its own. We are grateful to our loyal readers for not only supporting this book, but also giving it as a gift to their friends and recommending it to strangers.

Along the way, we've tried to listen to you to improve the book. And one message comes through loud and clear: MORE! You want more name brand reviews of cribs, strollers, car seats and, well, more. So, in this edition, we have expanded our name-brand reviews of those categories, adding dozens of new offerings in just about every chapter. As always, we've updated the book to include the most current models, including the latest scoop on car seats and strollers.

First, check out our crib chapter ("Nursery Necessities"). You'll note over a dozen new crib maker reviews, including the latest brands sold in both chain stores and specialty boutiques. In the wake of some baby stores that have gone bankrupt, we have new advice on how to protect yourself when ordering nursery furniture.

The "Feeding" chapter now includes brand name reviews and ratings for breast pumps, as well as detailed advice on bottle feeding and solid foods. The "Around the House" chapter includes the latest ratings and reviews of bathtubs and baby monitors, plus now incorporates our baby proofing tips (this was in a separate chapter in previous editions). Be sure to read our top 10 list of baby products that should be banned!

Read about new car seats from Chicco and Compass and then check out the newest rage: tri-wheel strollers. We've got the latest info on hot models from makers like Valco and Zooper. Then we'll look at several new stroller brands on the market, including BumbleRide, Chariot and i'coo. Plus we have expanded coverage on the stroller everyone is buzzing about, the Bugaboo.

New this year, we have upgraded our web site to include more Bonus Material (go to BabyBargains.com and click on Bonus Material). You'll find advice on announcements, how to introduce your pet to the new baby and other extras. Also online: extra reviews of smaller crib makers that didn't fit in the book, plus detailed baby proofing tips and bottle feeding advice.

Also new online: parent reviews of baby products. This new section of our web site lets parents sound off on what they really think about that new stroller or car seat. While on our site, be sure to sign up for our free e-newsletter for breaking news updates about product recalls and more.

Of course, we've kept the features you love about *Baby Bargains*, including those handy comparison charts that sum up our picks and our ever-popular baby registry at-a-glance (Appendix B). Don't forget the handy phone/web directory (Appendix D) in the back of the book. We also have updates for our Canadian readers (Appendix A) and a section on recommendations for parents of twins (Appendix C).

So, buckle your seat belts and secure all loose items like sunglasses and your sanity. We're off to Baby Gear Land.

CHAPTER 2

Nursery Necessities: Cribs, Dressers & More

Inside this chapter

How can you save 20% to 50% off cribs, dressers, and other furniture for your baby's room? In this chapter, you'll learn these secrets, plus discover smart shopper tips that help clarify all those confusing crib options and features. Then, you'll learn which juvenile furniture has safety problems and where to go online to find the latest recall info. Next, we'll rate and review over 30 top brands of cribs, focusing on quality and value. Finally, you'll learn which crib mattress is best, how to get a deal on a dresser, and several more items to consider for your baby's room.

Getting Started: When Do You Need This Stuff?

So, you want to buy a crib for Junior? And, what the heck, why not some other furniture, like a dresser to store all those baby gifts and a changing table for, well, you know. Just pop down to the store, pick out the colors, and set a delivery date, right?

Not so fast, o' new parental one. Once you get to that baby store, you'll discover that most don't have all those nice cribs and furniture *in stock*. No, that would be too easy, wouldn't it? You will quickly learn that you have to *special order* much of that booty.

To be fair, we should note that in-stock items vary from shop to shop. Some (especially the larger chain stores) may stock a fair number of cribs. Yet Murphy's Law says the last in-stock Futura Crib with that special chartreuse trim was just sold five minutes ago. And while stores may stock a good number of cribs, dressers are another story—these bulky items almost always must be special-ordered.

Most baby specialty stores told us it takes four to six weeks to order many furniture brands. And here's the shocker: some imported cribs can take 12 to 16 weeks. Or longer. Making matters worse is the practice by most European furniture makers of shutting down for two weeks in July and again at Christmas. It's hard to believe that it takes so long for companies to ship a simple crib or dresser—we're not talking space shuttle parts here. The way it's going, you'll soon have to order the crib *before* you conceive.

Obviously, this policy is more for the benefit of the retailer than the consumer. Most baby stores are small operations and they tell us that stocking up on cribs, dressers and the like means an expensive investment in inventory and storage space. That's understandable, but it makes the nursery furniture shopping process more daunting for consumers. Why you can't get a crib in a week or less is one of the mysteries of modern juvenile product retailing that will have to be left to future generations to solve. What if you don't have that much time? There are a couple of solutions: some stores sell floor models and others actually keep a limited number of styles in stock. Discounters also stock cribs—the only downside is that while the price is low, often so is the quality.

Here's an alternate idea submitted by a reader: don't buy the crib until *after* the baby is born. The infant can sleep in a bassinet or cradle for the first few weeks or even months, and you can get the furniture later. (This may also be an option for the superstitious that don't want to buy all this stuff until the baby is actually born.) The downside to waiting? The last thing you'll want to do with your newborn infant is go furniture shopping. There will be many other activities (such as sleep deprivation experiments) to occupy your time.

So, when should you make a decision on the crib and other furniture for the baby's room? We recommend you place your order in the sixth or seventh month of your pregnancy. By that time, you're pretty darned sure you're having a baby, and the order will arrive several weeks before the birth. (The exception: if your heart is set on an imported crib, you may have to order in your fourth or fifth month to ensure arrival before Junior is born).

First-time parent question: so, how long will baby use a crib? Answer: it depends (and you thought we always had the answer). Seriously, most babies can use a crib for two or three years. Yes, some babies are out of the crib by 18 months, while others may be pushing four. One key factor: when does baby learn they can climb out of the crib? Once that happens, the crib days are numbered, as you can understand. Of course, there may be other factors that push baby out of a crib—if you are planning to have a second child and want the crib for the new baby, it may be time to transition to a "big boy/girl" bed. We discuss more about the transition out of a crib (as well as reviewing toddler and twin beds) in our book *Toddler Bargains*. See the back of this book for more info on that title.

Cribs: Sources to Find

This year, more than 1.2 million households plan to buy infant/nursery furniture, according to a survey by Furniture Today. That translates into $4 billion in sales of infant and youth bedroom furniture—yes, this is big business. In their quest for the right nursery, parents have five basic sources for finding a crib, each with its own advantages and drawbacks:

1 **BABY SPECIALTY STORES.** Baby specialty stores are pretty self-explanatory—shops that specialize in the retailing of baby furniture, strollers, and accessories. Some also sell clothing, car seats, swings, and so on. Independents come in all sizes: some are small mom and pop stores; others are as large as a chain superstore. A good number of indie retailers have joined together in "buying groups" to get volume discounts on items from suppliers—these groups include Baby Furniture Plus (www.babyfurnitureplus.com), Baby News (www.BabyNewsStores.com), NINFRA (www.ninfra.com) and USA Baby (www.USAbaby.com). The web sites for those four groups have store locators so you can find a specialty store near you.

Like other independent stores, many baby specialty shops have been hard hit by the expansion of national chains like Babies R Us. Yet, those that have survived do so by emphasizing service and products you can't find at the chains. Of course, quality of service can vary widely from store to store . . . but just having a breathing human to ask a question of is a nice plus. The problems with specialty stores? Consumers complain the stores only carry expensive brands. One parent told us the only baby specialty store in her town doesn't carry any cribs under $500. We understand the dilemma faced by mom and pop retailers—in order provide all that service, they have to make a certain profit margin on furniture and other products. And that margin is easier to get on high-end goods. That's all well and good, but failing to carry products in entry-level price points only drives parents to the chains.

Another gripe with some indie stores: some shops can be downright hostile to you if they think you are "price-shopping" them. A reader said she found this out when comparing Ragazzi and Morigeau furniture in her town. "When I asked to price cribs and dressers at two baby stores, I met with resistance and hostility. At one store, I was asked if I was a 'spy' for their competition! The store managers at both baby stores I visited said they didn't want people to comparison shop them on price, yet both advertise they will 'meet or beat' the competition's prices." Crazy as it sounds, the only way to write down prices at some stores is to have a friend distract the sales help (Hey, look over there! A naked basketball team crossing the street!).

The bottom line: despite the hassles, if you have a locally owned baby store in your town, give them a shot. Don't assume chains always have lower prices and better selection.

2 **THE CHAINS.** There are two types of chains that sell baby products: specialty chains like Babies R Us that focus on juvenile products and general discounters like Wal-Mart, Target, and K-Mart that have baby departments. We'll discuss each more in-depth later in this chapter. The selection at chains can vary widely—some carry more premium brands, but most concentrate on mass-market names to appeal to price-conscious shoppers. Service? Fuggedaboutit—often, you'll be lucky to find someone to help you check out, much less answer questions.

3 **DEPARTMENT STORES.** Traditional department stores like Sears still have baby departments that carry clothing and some gear; most furniture and nursery items are delegated to department store catalogs. Prices aren't typically as low as the discounters, but occasional sales sometimes bring bargains.

4 **THE WEB/MAIL-ORDER CATALOGS.** You can mail order many items for baby, but furniture is somewhat tricky. Why? Shipping bulky items like cribs and dressers is prohibitively expensive. There's also the risk of damage from shipping. But that doesn't keep some companies and catalogs from trying: JCPenney (800-222-6161) has a catalog with nursery items and, yes, you can even buy a crib or dresser via the mail. Baby product web sites like Pottery Barn Kids also sell a limited number of cribs. Be careful of exorbitant shipping charges for cribs; Pottery Barn adds a whopping $120 shipping charge onto a crib that is already $700. Other sites refuse to ship furniture items to Alaska, Hawaii, Canada or military (APO) addresses. As a result of shipping costs and challenges, most mail order catalogs and web sites concentrate more on selling nursery accessories—glider rockers, changing tables, decor, etc. And if you find a crib for sale online, it will usually be a more obscure brand (like Delta, Angel Line or Million Dollar Baby's DaVinci line—all of these are reviewed later in this chapter).

5 **REGULAR FURNITURE STORES.** You don't have to go to a "baby store" to buy juvenile furniture. Many regular furniture stores sell name-brand cribs, dressers and other nursery items. Since these stores have frequent sales, you may be able to get a better price than at a juvenile specialty store. On the other hand, the salespeople may not be as knowledgeable about brand and safety issues.

Parents in Cyberspace: What's on the Web?

There are an amazing number of sites out there where you can look at cribs and get safety information. Unfortunately, actually BUYING a crib or dresser online is another matter. As we discussed above, the sheer bulk and weight of furniture typically limits mail-order options to a few peripheral items like glider-rockers, bassinets and the like. This section covers some of the bigger sites that sell baby furniture online. But first, let's discuss a good site to learn about crib safety.

Danny Foundation

Web site: www.dannyfoundation.org

What it is: The best source for crib safety info.

What's cool: Founded in 1986, the Danny Foundation's mission is to educate parents about crib dangers and to warn the public about the millions of unsafe cribs still in use or storage. You can read the latest recalls with cribs and portable play yards (which often have a bassinet feature) on the site. Danny Foundation's excellent crib safety checklist is a must read. Sample: below is a sketch from the site that illustrates all the hazards that old cribs may include such as cut outs and corner posts (Figure 1).

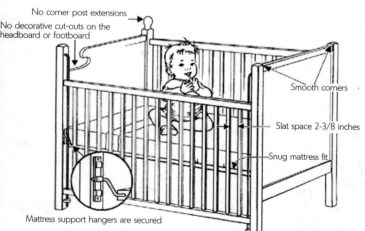

Figure 1. Crib safety points from the Danny Foundation's web site.

◆ **Sites that sell baby furniture.** The best selection of Dutailier rocker-gliders and ottomans has to be on **Baby Catalog** (www.babycatalog.com), the online offshoot of a Connecticut store and catalog. We love the prices, and if you use the search function or brand name option it will get you to the rocker-gliders fast.

The smallish collection of cribs on **Baby Style** (www.babystyle.com) runs from $236 to $700. On the plus side, we loved the "Nursery Collections" section on Baby Style. Here the site features cribs, bedding, lamps and other décor accessories for a complete look. Very cool . . .even if you don't buy anything the ideas are interesting.

Burlington Coat Factory's **Baby Depot** (www.coat.com) has over a dozen different styles of cribs available on their site, mostly by Delta (see review later). Prices are affordable ($140 to $400) and shipping is reasonable (about $30, depending on the style). But we have been put off by the site's nutty organization that requires you to sift through several menus and sub-menus to actually see products.

The **Pottery Barn Kids** catalog is online at PotteryBarnKids.com. While cribs are available from PBK, we found them very overpriced. And the added shipping charge can make them even more outrageous. PBK's cribs are made overseas and sold as their own private label brand; it's hard to get a read on their quality, but most parents who've bought PBK kids are satisfied.

One final bit of advice: check our web site BabyBargains.com (click on Bonus Material) for detailed info on the best baby gear web sites. We have general online shopping tips, specific site comments and more.

What Are You Buying?

While you'll see all kinds of fancy juvenile furniture at baby stores, focus on the items that you really need. First and foremost is a crib, of course. Mattresses are typically sold separately, as you might expect, so you'll need one of those. Another nice item is a dresser or chest to hold clothes, bibs, washcloths, etc. A changing table is an optional accessory; some parents just use the crib for this (although that can get messy) or buy a combination dresser and changing table. Some dressers have a removable changing table on top, while others have a "flip top": a hinged shelf that folds up when not in use.

So, how much is this going to cost you? Crib prices start at $100 for an inexpensive crib at a discounter like Wal-Mart. The mid-range for cribs is probably best typified by what you see at Babies R Us and Baby Depot—most of their cribs are in the $200 to $400 range. Specialty stores and catalogs carry many Italian and other imported nursery furniture . . . these "better" cribs tend to run $400 to $600. And what about the top end? We'd be remiss not to mention the wrought iron cribs by Corsican, which top $1000 to $1500.

Surprise! The vast majority of cribs don't come with mattresses; those are sold separately. Fortunately, mattresses for cribs aren't that expensive. Crib mattresses start at about $40 and go up to $200 for fancy varieties. Later in this chapter, we'll have a special section on mattresses that includes tips on what to buy and how to save money.

Dressers and changing tables (known in the baby business as case pieces) have prices that are all over the board. At the low end are the "ready to assemble" dressers from Sauder (reviewed later in this chapter) that sell for just $120 to $200. Name brand, already-assembled dressers run $400 to $700 in most styles, while top-of-the-line designer cases pieces can push $1000.

Where to change baby? If you have room for a separate changing table, these run $70 to $200. If space is tight, a better solution may be to buy a dresser that has a changing area on top—these styles run $400 to $800.

So, you can see that a quest for a crib, mattress, dresser, and/or changing table could cost you as little as $300 or more than $1000.

 More Money Buys You . . .

Here's a little secret expensive crib makers don't want you to hear: ALL new cribs (no matter what price) sold in the U.S. or Canada must meet federal safety standards. Yes, the governments of both the U.S. and Canada strictly regulate crib safety and features—that's one reason why most cribs have the same basic design, no matter the brand or price. So, whether you buy a $100 crib special at K-Mart or a $700 Italian design at a posh specialty boutique, either way you get a crib that meets federal safety requirements.

Now, that said, when you spend more money, there are some perks. The higher the price tag of the crib (generally), the fancier the design (thicker corner posts, designer colors, etc.) And more expensive cribs tend to have quieter drop-sides (cheap cribs can be noisy when you raise or lower the side rail). Another perk when you spend more: pricey cribs are likely to convert into a twin or double bed. Lower-price cribs are just, well, cribs.

Some extras have dubious value, however—take the under-crib storage drawer. Often seen on cribs that run $300 or more, this feature appeals to parents who have a storage crunch in their home (you can put blankets, extra clothes in the drawer). The problem? The drawer doesn't have a top. So, anything inside will be a dust magnet.

Safe & Sound

Here's a fact to keep you up at night: cribs are the third-biggest cause of injuries and deaths among all nursery products. In the latest year for which statistics are available, over 10,000 injuries and 16 deaths were blamed on cribs alone.

Now, before you get all excited, let's point out that old cribs cause the vast majority of injuries related to cribs. Surprisingly, these old cribs may not be as old as you think—some models from the 1970s and early 1980s have caused many injuries and deaths. (Safety standards for cribs were first enacted in 1973 then again in 1976; these rules were revised in 1982 and again in 1999). Nearly all *new* cribs sold in the United States meet the current safety standards designed to prevent injuries. In fact, the annual death rate for cribs (16) is dramatically below that in the 1970's, when nearly 200 children died each year from crib hazards.

These facts bring us to our biggest safety tip on cribs:

◆ ***Don't buy a used or old crib.*** Let's put that into bold caps: **DON'T BUY A USED OR OLD CRIB.** And don't take a hand-me-down from a well-meaning friend or relative. Why? Because old cribs can be death traps—spindles that are too far apart, cutouts in the headboard, and other hazards that could entrap your baby. Decorative trim (like turned posts) that looks great on adult beds are a major no-no for cribs—they present a strangulation hazard. Other old cribs have lead paint, a dangerous peril for a teething baby.

Another hazard to hand-me-down cribs (regardless of age): missing parts and directions. It only takes one missing screw or bolt to make an otherwise safe crib into a danger. Without directions, you can assemble the crib wrong and create additional safety hazards. So, even if your friend wants to give/sell you a recent model crib, you could still have problems if parts or directions are missing.

It may seem somewhat ironic that a book on baby bargains would advise you to go out and spend your hard-earned money on a new crib. True, we find great bargains at consignment and second-hand stores. However, you have to draw the line at your baby's safety. Certain items are great deals at these stores—toys and clothes come to mind. However, cribs (and, as you'll read later, car seats) are no-no's, no matter how tempting the bargains. And second hand stores have a spotty record when it comes to selling safe products. A recent report from the CPSC said that a whopping two-thirds of all U.S. thrift/second-hand stores sell baby products that have been recalled, banned or do not meet current safety standards (specifically 12% of stores stocked old cribs). Amazingly, federal law does not prohibit the sale of cribs (or other dangerous products like jackets with drawstring hoods, recalled playpens or car seats) at second hand stores.

Readers of the first edition of this book wondered why we did not put in tips for evaluating old or hand-me-down cribs. The reason is simple: it's hard to tell whether an old crib is dangerous just by looking at it. Cribs don't always have "freshness dates"—some manufacturers don't stamp the date of manufacture on their cribs. Was the crib made before or after the current safety standards went into effect in 1999? Often, you can't tell.

Today's safety regulations are so specific (like the allowable width for spindles) that you just can't judge a crib's safety with a cursory examination. Cribs made before the 1970's might contain lead paint, which is difficult to detect unless you get the crib tested. Another problem: if the brand name is rubbed off, it will be hard to tell if the crib has been involved in a recall. Obtaining replacement parts is also difficult for a no-name crib. Another important point: in 1999, new rules for cribs went into effect that mandated slat attachment strength (in the 1990's, several crib models were recalled because the slats fell out).

What about floor model cribs? Is it safe to buy a crib that has been used as a floor sample in a baby store? Yes—as long as it is in good working condition, has no broken parts, etc. Floor model cribs CAN take a tremendous amount of abuse from parents, who shake them to check stability and so on. As a result, the bolts that hold the crib together can loosen. Obviously, that can be fixed (just have the store tighten the bolts) . . . and as a result, we think floor model cribs are fine. That isn't what we mean by avoiding a "used" crib!

What if a relative insists you should use the "family heirloom" crib? We've spoken to dozens of parents who felt pressured into using an old crib by a well-meaning relative. There's a simple answer: don't do it. As a parent, you sometimes have to make unpopular decisions that are best for your child's safety. This is just the beginning.

◆ **Cribs with fold-down railings or attached dressers.** Most cribs have a side rail that drops to give you access to an infant. However, a few models have fold-down railings—to gain access to the crib—the upper one-third of the railing is hinged and folds down. These are also called swing gate cribs (see picture above).

What's the problem? Actually, there are two problems. First, the folding rail can be a pinch point (see Baby's Dream review later in this chapter for details on a recall that addressed this very issue). While Baby's Dream has fixed their fold-down rail, we're still leery of other brands that have this type of rail release.

The second problem: toddlers can get a foothold on the hinged rail to climb out of the crib, injuring themselves as they fall to the floor. It's much harder for a child to climb out of a crib with a traditional drop side.

Attached dressers pose a similar problem. Children can climb onto the dresser and then out of the crib. One mother we interviewed was horrified to find her ten month-old infant sitting on top of a four-foot-high dresser one night. Unfortunately, there are no federal safety standards that apply to attached dressers. It's clear to us there is a risk here.

So what's the appeal of these cribs? We're not sure what the appeal of the fold-down rail is . . . there really is no advantage. As far as the attached dressers, we can see how space-crunched nurseries would cry out for this solution. But we say resist the call.

◆ **Stripped screws.** Cheap cribs often have screws that attach directly to the wood of the headboard. The problem? The screws can strip over time (especially if the crib is set up several times) and that can weaken the crib's support . . . which is very dangerous. If you ever discover you are not able to tighten the screws or bolts used to hold your crib together, immediately stop using it. When you are crib shopping, look at how the mattress support is attached to the headboards—look for metal screwed into metal.

◆ **Forget about no-name cribs.** In the past, a few less-than-reputable baby stores imported cheap no-name cribs from foreign countries whose standards for baby safety are light years behind the U.S. Why would stores do this? Bigger profits—cheap imports can be marked up big-time yet sold to unsuspecting parents at prices below name-brand cribs. Take the Baby Furniture Outlet of Marathon, Florida. These scam artists imported cribs and playpens that grossly failed to meet federal safety standards. From the construction to the hardware, the cribs were a disaster waiting to happen. As a result, 19 babies were injured, and the Consumer Products Safety Commission permanently banned the items in 1987. Sold under the "Small Wonders" brand name at the Baby Furniture Outlet (and other outlets nationwide), parents were undoubtedly suckered in by the "outlet" savings of these cheap cribs. Instead of recalling the cribs, the company declared bankruptcy and claimed it couldn't pay to fix the problem. (By the way, this company is not related to Baby Furniture Outlet of Canada, which is mentioned later in this chapter).

There is one exception to our advice to avoid no-name cribs—JCPenney's catalog sells several "private label" cribs that are made exclusively for Penney's and sold under names like Domusindo and Bright Future. Penney's has strict standards that make these cribs a decent buy, despite their lack of a brand name.

◆ **Watch out for sharp edges.** It amazes us that any company today would market a baby furniture item with sharp edges. Yet, there are still some on the market. We've seen changing tables with sharp edges and dressers with dangerous corners. A word to the wise: be sure to check out any nursery item carefully before buying—look in less-than-obvious places, like the bottom edges of a dresser or the under-crib drawer.

◆ **Be aware of the hazards of putting a baby in an adult bed.** Co-sleeping (where a baby sleeps in an adult bed) has been linked to 122 deaths of babies from 1999 to 2001, says the Consumer Products Safety Commission. Of those deaths, many were caused when a child's head became entrapped between the bed and another object (a headboard, footboard, wall, etc). Other deaths were caused by falls or suffocation in bedding. We are alarmed by these statistics and urge any parent who is considering co-sleeping to consult with a pediatrician before going forward. (For the record, we should note that a product we recommend later in this book, the Arm's Reach Co-sleeper, is safe since a baby doesn't actually sleep in the adult bed when using this product.)

◆ **Some Italian cribs can make bumper tying a challenge.** Those thick corner posts on Italian cribs sure look pretty, but they can create problems—using a bumper pad (a bedding item discussed in the next chapter) on these cribs can be darn near impossible. Why? Many bumper pads have short ties that simply don't fit around thick corner posts. And other cribs have solid headboards or footboards—this prevents the tying of a bumper. We'll discuss bumpers in the next chapter (our position: they're optional) . . . but if you decide you want to use them, be sure to get a crib that is bumper-compatible.

◆ **When assembling a crib, make sure ALL the bolts and screws are tightened**. A recent report on *Good Morning America* pointed out how dangerous it can be to put your baby in a miss-assembled crib—a child died in a Child Craft crib when he became trapped in a side rail that wasn't properly attached to the crib. How did that happen? The parent didn't tighten the screws that held the side rail to the crib. All cribs (including the Child Craft one here in question) are safe when assembled correctly; just be sure to tighten those screws! A smart safety tip: check your crib once a month to make sure all screws and bolts are firmly attached.

◆ **What about the finish?** Some crib makers are now touting "non-toxic water-based finishes" for their cribs. Example: on an eco-baby web site, we saw a $720 crib that is "hand rubbed with pure beeswax and tung oil." The implication: older oil-based finishes for baby furniture are somehow dangerous. Really? We've seen no evidence that a baby that sleeps in a crib finished/painted with an oil-based product is somehow at risk for health problems. In 1978, the federal government required ALL cribs to be finished with *non-toxic* materials. Of course, there is no requirement that the finish be water-based or oil-based—each is equally safe in our opinion. While we realize some eco-sensitive parents might shell out extra for the water-based finish, we don't see a problem or a reason to spend more.

◆ **Recalls: where to find information**. The U.S. Consumer Product Safety Commission has a toll-free hotline at (800) 638-2772 and web site (www.cpsc.gov) for the latest recall information on cribs and other juvenile items. Both are easy to use—the hotline is a series of recorded voice mail messages that you access by following the prompts. You can also report any potential hazard you've discovered or an injury to your child caused by a product. Write to the U.S. Consumer Products Safety Commission, Washington, D.C. 20207 or file a complaint online at cpsc.gov. FYI: The CPSC takes care of all juvenile product recalls, except for car seats—that's the purview of the National Highway Traffic Safety Administration (nhtsa.gov).

A great "all-in-one" site for recalls is www.Recalls.gov. Also: consider subscribing to our free e-newsletter. We send out updates on product recalls and other news to our readers on a periodic basis. Go to BabyBargains.com and click on "E-Newsletter" to subscribe.

Smart Shopper Tips

Smart Shopper Tip #1
Beware of "Baby Buying Frenzy."

"I went shopping with my friend at a baby store last week, and she just about lost it. She started buying all kinds of fancy accessories and items that didn't seem that necessary. First there was a $50 womb sound generator and finally the $200 Star Trek Diaper Changing Docking Station. There was no stopping her. The salespeople were egging her on—it was quite a sight. Should we have just taken her out back and hosed her down?"

Yes, you probably should have. Your friend has come down with a severe case of what we call Baby Buying Frenzy—that overwhelming emotional tug to buy all kinds of stuff for Junior—especially when Junior is your first child. Baby stores know all about this disease and do their darnedest to capitalize on it. Check out this quote from *Juvenile Merchandising* (October 1993) advising salespeople on how to sell to expectant parents: "It's surprising how someone who is making a purchase (for baby) sometimes can be led into a buying frenzy." No kidding. Some stores encourage their staff by giving them bonuses for every additional item sold to a customer. Be wary of stores that try to do this, referred to in the trade as "building the ticket." Remember what you came to buy and don't get caught up in the hype.

Smart Shopper Tip #2
The Art and Science of Selecting the Right Crib.
"How do you evaluate a crib? They all look the same to me. What really makes one different from another?"

Selecting a good crib is more than just picking out the style and finish. You should look under the hood, so to speak. Here are our eight key points to look for when shopping for a crib:

◆ **Mattress support.** Look underneath that mattress and see what is holding it up. You might be surprised. Some lower-end cribs use cheap vinyl straps. Others use metal bars. One crib we saw actually had a flimsy piece of MDF (a wood composite) holding up the mattress. What's best? We like a set of metal springs, which provides solid mattress support and a springy surface to stand on when Junior gets older. Second bet: a wood slat platform. Some crib makers (notably Pali) have gone to this. Why? The soaring cost of steel is the main reason; wood is now cheaper.

◆ **Ease of release.** Most cribs have at least one side that lowers down so you can pick up your baby. There are five types of crib rail releases:

FOOT-BAR. You release the crib drop side by lifting up the side rail while depressing a foot bar. This used to be the most common rail release type. But many crib makers have abandoned the foot-bar in recent years for alternatives like the knee-push (see below). The negatives to the foot-bar seemed to spell its doom—some parents found the foot-bar release awkward, requiring them to balance on one foot while lowering the rail with one hand. Another negative: the foot-bar release required exposed hardware (rods, springs, etc.) that was noisy and unattractive. While we think there is no safety concerns with the foot-bar release or exposed hardware, Canada has banned the use of the foot bar release. Million Dollar Baby and Angel Line (see reviews later) are two of the few holdouts still using the foot-bar release.

2 KNEE-PUSH. By lifting the side rail and pushing against it with your knee, the drop side releases. We first saw this release on more expensive cribs imported from Europe or Canada, but in recent years nearly all crib makers have turned to this type of release. This is probably the quietest release, although that can vary from maker to maker. Another plus: the hardware is often hidden inside the crib posts, so there are no rods and springs like the foot-bar release. We should note that one version of the knee-push rail has exposed plastic brackets on the crib posts. The Italian crib makers are more likely to have the completely hidden hardware.

3 DOUBLE TRIGGER. This release is used on low-price cribs from makers like Storkcraft and Delta. The drop side is released by simultaneously pulling on two plastic triggers on either side of the rail. Crib makers that use this type of release tout its safety (only an adult can release the rail) and the lack of exposed hardware like that used on foot-bar releases. However, we see two major drawbacks: first, you need *two* hands to operate the release, not really possible if you have a baby in your arms (unless you can grow extras!). Also, the double trigger release uses plastic hardware that can be a problem if you live in a dry climate. Why? The wood posts can shrink, causing the plastic hardware to crack.

4 FOLD DOWN/SWING-GATE. Rarely used in the market today, the fold-down rail release does what it sounds like— instead of lowering, the rail has a hinge that allows the top portion to fold down. The biggest user of the fold-down release is Baby's Dream. As we'll discuss later, we're not big fans of fold-down rails—we believe the rail gives an opportunity for larger toddlers to gain a foothold to climb out of the crib.

5 STATIONARY. This is the latest rage with crib design—side rails that don't move at all! Child Craft started this trend with their Millennium crib (also called the Crib and Double Bed), which was such a hot seller that other crib makers quickly copied it. The advantage to this design: there are no moving parts to break and these cribs seem much more stable/solid than other models. The downside: for shorter parents, it can be a long reach to put a sleeping infant down on the mattress when set in its lowest position. Our advice: try these cribs out in the store before buying.

◆ **Hardware: hidden or exposed?** Crib rail releases have hardware that enables the side to drop. Less expensive cribs have exposed hardware—either a rod/cane that the side rail slides up and down on or plastic brackets. More expensive cribs have "hidden" hardware, which is tucked inside the headboard and footboard. Is there a difference in safety or durability? No, it often boils down to an aesthetic decision—some parents like hidden hardware because it gives the crib a cleaner, sleeker look. Hidden hardware does have another benefit over exposed hardware: it tends to be quieter. The trend over the last few years has been a move toward hidden hardware. Now you can find hidden hardware on cribs from as little $200 at Baby Depot. And don't forget about the trend toward stationary drop sides—these cribs have no hardware at all!

One safety note: some crib headboards have an exposed plastic track where the rail slides up and down—even if they have hidden hardware. This is a safety hazard in our opinion, as little fingers can get caught in the track. The safest option is a hidden track.

◆ **Mattress height adjustment.** Most cribs have several height levels for the mattress—you use the highest setting when the baby is a newborn. Once she starts pulling up, you adjust the mattress to the lowest level so she won't be able to punt herself over the railing. You have two choices when it comes to this topic: bolt/screws or a hooked bracket. The first system requires you to loosen a bolt or screw that connects a strap to each of the four posts. Then you lower the mattress and screw the bolt back to the post. The only problem with the bolt/screw method: cheap cribs use uncoated bolts that over time can strip the holes on the post, weakening the support system. The bolt/screw is used on cribs with knee-push or double trigger rail releases. The alternative is the hooked brackets—the mattress lies on top of springs, anchored to the crib frame by hooked brackets. Some makers use this system on their cribs with foot-bar releases. Yet, as we mentioned, those makers are phasing out the foot-bar release and, with it, the hooked bracket hardware.

◆ **How stable is the crib?** Go ahead and abuse that crib set up in the baby store. Knock it around. The best cribs are very stable. Unfortunately, cheap models are often the lightest in weight (and hence, tend to wobble). Cribs with a drawer under the mattress are probably the most stable, as are those with stationary side rails. Unfortunately, all this extra stability comes at a price—models with these features start at $400 and can go up to $500 or $600. Keep in mind that some cribs may be wobbly because the store set them up incorrectly. Check out the same model at a couple of different stores if you have stability concerns.

◆ **Check those casters.** Metal casters are much better than plastic. We also prefer wide casters to those thin, disk-shaped wheels. You'll be wheeling this crib around more than you think—to change the sheets, to move it away from a drafty part of the room, etc. One solution: if you find a good buy on a crib that has cheap casters, you can easily replace them. Hardware stores sell heavy-duty metal casters for $10 to $20—or less.

◆ **How easy is it to assemble?** Ask to see those instructions—most stores should have a copy lying around. Make sure they are not in Greek. The worst offenders in the "lousy assembly directions department" are the importers (from Asia and Europe). Poorly translated directions and incomprehensible illustrations can frustrate even the most diligent parent. Even worse: instructions that are OMITTED altogether. This occasionally happens with furniture that is imported from Europe. Yes, this problem would be solved if manufacturers put their instructions online as a back up . . . but few do.

◆ **Compare the overall safety features of the crib.** In a section earlier in this book, we discuss crib safety in more detail.

◆ **Which wood is best?** Traditionally, cribs were made of hardwoods like maple, oak, ash and cherry. Crib makers considered these woods superior since they were more durable and easier for them to stain/paint. In the last couple of years, however, the latest craze is pine furniture—and pine has also come to baby cribs. The problem? Pine is a softwood that tends to nick, scratch and damage. Of course, not all pine is the same. North American pine is the softest, but pine grown in cold climates (Northern Europe, for example) is harder. Hence, the pine you're most likely to see used in baby furniture is hardwood pine.

So, which wood is best? To be honest, it doesn't really matter much. The traditional hardwoods like oak and maple are fine. Italian crib makers use beech wood (a European hardwood), while Canadian makers often use birch. Again, each is fine. The only wood we would shy away from would be ramin, a wood from Asia that's often called the a poorman's mahogany. Ramin doesn't have the durability of other hard woods, but is so cheap you'll see it on promotional cribs sold at rock-bottom prices.

Of course, dressers are another subject that we'll cover later in this chapter. Wood choices (including man-made substitutes like MDF) are more of a factor in that decision than with cribs. And if you want your furniture to match, you may want to read the section on dressers before making a crib decision.

Another note: some stores and web sites tout "cherry" cribs when they are actually referring to the finish, not the actual wood. It may be a "cherry" stain, but the wood is probably not.

◆ **Consider other special needs.** As we noted above, noisy crib railing release mechanisms can be a hassle—and this seems especially so for short people (or, in politically correct terms, the vertically challenged). Why? Taller folks (above 5′ 8″) may be able to place the baby into a crib *without* lowering the side rail (when the mattress is in the highest position). Shorter parents can't reach over the side rail as easily, forcing them to use the release mechanism more often than not. Hence, a quieter release on a more expensive brand might be worth the extra investment.

Disabled parents also may find the foot bar difficult or impossible to operate. In that case, we recommend a crib that has a knee-push rail release, described earlier.

Smart Shopper Tip #3
Cyber-Nursery: Ordering furniture online

"We don't have any good baby stores nearby, so I want to order furniture online. How do you buy items sight unseen and make sure they arrive in one piece?"

As we've mentioned, ordering furniture via the web/mail can be tricky. Damage from shipping and exorbitant costs have convinced many retailers to not offer this service. Yet, other web sites, mail-order catalogs and even eBay sellers have figured out how to ship nursery furniture across the country without breaking the bank—or the furniture itself.

First, deal with an established seller that has a good customer service track record. We review several companies in this chapter that sell online—stick with the ones with the best reputations when buying furniture via the mail. You want a company that *specializes* in selling furniture online, not a general baby products web site that also sells a few dressers among their car seats, strollers and baby monitors. If you buy from an eBay seller, make sure they have a good track record based on their online feedback. Do a search of the message boards on our web site to make sure other parents have been happy.

JCPenney used to have a good reputation when it came to mail order furniture, but in recent years we have started receiving more and more complaints about them—late deliveries, damaged shipments, etc. Pottery Barn attracts its fair share of complaints as well.

One key factor to consider: does the mail-order source or web site actually stock the merchandise? Or will they have your furniture drop-shipped direct from the manufacturer? We like the former—these companies seem to know how to better pack a dresser for shipment cross country. Drop shipments usually generates more consumer complaints. Why? You have two companies involved with the transaction and if something goes wrong, one usually blames the other (for faulty packaging, etc). The consumer, caught in the cross fire, can end up the loser. See the following email from the real world for an example of how a dresser purchase went wrong for one reader.

Consider spending extra for insurance. And make sure you get all shipping costs and delivery details in writing. Will the items be delivered to your door if you live on the third floor of an apartment building? Does delivery include set-up? Confirm the details.

 Wastes of Money

I **LOW QUALITY "BABY" FURNITURE THAT WON'T LAST.** Baby furniture stores (both chains and independents) are sometimes guilty of selling very poor quality furniture. Take a dresser, for exam-

---

E-MAIL FROM THE REAL WORLD
Spending $385 for a $50 dresser.

A reader in Ohio shared this bad experience with shopping for a dresser online:

"I ordered a three drawer combo dresser from BabyUniverse. com. It had all of the things suggested in your book and was $385 (the Rumble Tuff line around here was $700 for the same thing). The manufacturer is Angel Line. The item arrived with split wood on the corner, a knob missing, a missing wall strap and one of the drawers didn't shut completely and was crooked. I called Baby Universe and they said I had to contact the manufacturer directly to get the problem resolved. It took four calls and the best I could get was another knob and drawer sent to me with corners that did not fit together. So, I essentially paid $400 for something that looks like it was $50 at a garage sale."

ple. Many dressers made by juvenile furniture companies have stapled drawers, veneer construction (instead of solid wood), cheap drawer glides and worse. Now, that wouldn't be so bad if such dressers were low in price. But often you see such dressers going for $500 and up in baby stores—it's as if you are paying a premium to merely match the color of your crib. While we don't see a problem buying low-end "disposable" furniture at a good price (IKEA is a prime example), paying a fortune for a poorly-made dresser seems ridiculous. In this chapter, we will point out brand names that provide more quality for the dollar. Look for solid wood construction, dove tail drawers, smooth drawer glides if you want that dresser to last.

2 UNDER-CRIB DRAWERS. It sounds like a great way to squeeze out a bit more storage in a nursery—the drawer that slides out from under a crib. Getting a crib with such a feature usually costs an extra $100 or $150. The problem? These drawers do NOT have tops . . . therefore anything kept in there will get dusty in a hurry. So that nixes storing extra blankets or clothes. We say skip the extra expense of an under-crib drawer.

3 SURPRISE COSTS WITH "CONVERTIBLE" CRIBS. Convertible to what, you might ask? Manufacturers pitch these more expensive cribs as a money-saver since they are convertible to "youth beds," which are smaller and narrower than a twin bed. But, guess what? Most kids can go straight from a crib to a regular twin bed with no problem whatsoever. So, the youth bed business is really a joke. Another rip-off: some manufacturers sell cribs that convert to adult-size beds. The catch? You have to pay for a "conversion kit," which will set you back another $30 to $200. And that's on top of the hefty prices ($400 to $600) that many of these models cost initially. (There is good news to report on the price front, though. In the past year or so, several crib makers have rolled out new, lower-price convertible cribs. We'll discuss such models later in this chapter in the manufacturer reviews). Another negative to convertible cribs: if you have more than one child, you'll have to buy another crib, because the older child is using the "convertible" crib frame for their bed.

4 CRADLE. Do you really need one? A newborn infant can sleep in a regular crib just as easily as a cradle. And you'll save a bundle on that bundle of joy—cradles run $100 to $400. Of course, the advantage of having the baby in a cradle is you can keep it in your room for the baby's first few weeks, making midnight (and 2 am and 4 am) feedings more convenient. If you want to go this way, consider a bassinet instead of a cradle (bassinets are baskets set on top of a stand, while cradles are miniature versions of cribs that rock). We priced bassinets at only $40 to $180, much less than cradles. Is it worth the extra money? It's up to you, but our baby slept in his crib from day one, and it worked out just fine. If the distance between your room and the baby's is too far and you'd like to give a bassinet a try, see if you can find one at a consignment or second-hand store. Or consider a playpen with bassinet feature like the Graco Pack N Play. We'll discuss good buys on bassinets later in this chapter; playpens like the Pack N Play are reviewed in Chapter 7, Around the House.

5 **CRIBS WITH "SPECIAL FEATURES."** Some stores carry unique styles of cribs and that might be tempting for parents looking to make a statement for their nursery. An example: round cribs. The only problem: special cribs like this may require additional expenses, such as custom-designed mattresses or bedding. And since few companies make bedding for round cribs, your choices are limited. The best advice: make sure you price out the total investment (crib, mattress, bedding) before falling in love with an unusual brand.

6 **CHANGING TABLES.** Separate changing tables are a big waste of money. Don't spend $70 to $200 on a piece of furniture you won't use again after your baby gives up diapers. A better bet: buy a dresser that can do double duty as a changing table. Many dressers you'll see in baby stores are designed with this extra feature—just make sure the height is comfortable for both you and your spouse. Other parents we interviewed did away with the changing area altogether—they used a crib, couch or countertop to do diaper changes.

Top 8 Things No One Tells You About Buying Nursery Furniture

◆ *Our store may disappear before your nursery furniture arrives.* It's a sad fact: baby stores come and go. Most retailers that close do so reputably—they don't take special orders for merchandise they can't fill. A handful are not so honest . . . they take deposits up until the day the landlord padlocks their door. Our advice: always charge your purchase to a credit card. If the store disappears, you can dispute the charge with your credit card and (most likely) get your money back. Another red flag: stores that ask for payment up front on a special order. The typical deal is half down with the balance due upon delivery. Stores that are desperate for cash might demand the entire purchase price upfront. Be suspicious. Another piece of advice: keep a close eye on what's going on with your furniture maker. How? Subscribe to our free e-newsletter, read our blog or surf our message boards at BabyBargains.com. We've seen it all over the years—strikes, floods, fires, port shutdowns and more. You name it, it can happen to the factory that makes your furniture. When we get whiff of a problem, we send out the news to our readers via our e-newsletter, blog or on our message boards. That way you can switch to another brand if you've haven't placed an order yet . . . or formulate a plan B if your furniture is caught by a delivery delay.

◆ *Never assume something in a sealed box is undamaged.* Always OPEN boxes and inspect furniture before taking it out of a store. Yes, that is a hassle, but we've had numerous complains about boxed furniture that someone has driven 50 miles home, only to discover a major gash or other damage. Or the wrong color is in the right box. Or a major piece is missing. A word to the wise: inspect it BEFORE going home.

◆ *If it is in stock, BUY IT.* Let's say you see a crib that is in stock, but the matching dresser is on back order. Do you get the crib now and wait on the dresser? Or special order both? Our advice: if an item is sitting there in a store (even if it is a floor sample), it is ALWAYS better to take the in-stock item now. Will the stain match since the furniture will be from two different batches? Mis-matched finishes are rare and usually not an issue. Most furniture makers make their cribs in one factory and their case pieces in another; hence the dye lot thing is not relevant. Even if there is a slight difference in coloration, you probably won't put the dresser right next to the crib anyway. And you'll use the crib for two to four years, but the dresser for much longer—so if there is a slight color difference, you won't notice it when you've long put away the crib!

◆ *Your special order merchandise will be backordered until 2011, despite our promise to get it to you before your baby is born.* Almost all furniture today is imported . . . we are not talking from close-by countries like Canada or Mexico. Nope, odds are your furniture will be made in China, Eastern Europe or South America. And a myriad of problems (labor strikes, port shutdowns, Latvian Independence Day) can delay the shipment of your nursery furniture. Our advice: ORDER EARLY. If the furniture store says it will take six weeks, plan on 12. Or 15.

◆ *Just because the crib maker has an Italian name doesn't mean your furniture is made in, say, Italy.* Not long ago, you had domestic makers of cribs (Child Craft, Simmons) and the imports, most of which were from Italy. As we mentioned above, nearly all cribs are imported today, most from China and Eastern Europe, but some from South America and Canada. And yes, the Italians are still major players in the crib business. Here's where it gets confusing: sometimes the very same brand will import furniture from different countries. Sorelle, for example, started out as an Italian importer. Today, Sorelle still sells some cribs from Italy, but now also imports cribs and dressers from Brazil and Latvia (Eastern Europe). Ditto for Bonavita, which now supplements its Italian imports with a few collections from Vietnam. And even Ragazzi, the high-end Canadian crib maker now has an imported line from Chile under the separate brand Bambino. An important point: don't assume you are getting a crib made in Italy because the brand has an Italian name.

Bottom line: key on the brand's reputation for quality and customer service, not so much the country the crib is made in. Yes, Italian-made cribs are still considered the gold standard in the biz. But we've seen great quality cribs from Brazil, Eastern Europe and yes, even China. Because of currency exchange rates, these other cribs will be a better value than Italian cribs. In the reviews in this section, we will give you our opinion about a brand's quality and customer service. We consider the furniture's construction and safety in assigning our ratings as well.

◆ *That special mattress we insist you buy isn't necessary.* Some baby stores are trying a new tactic to sell their pricey in-house brand of crib mattress: scaring the pants off new parents. We've heard all the stories—only OUR mattress fits OUR crib, a simpler foam mattress is DANGEROUS for your baby and so on. Please! Government standards require both cribs and mattresses to be within standard measurements. Yes, fancy boutiques might make their mattress a bit larger to give a tighter fit . . . but that doesn't mean a regular mattress won't work just as well (and safely). It's no wonder stores push the in-house mattress—it can cost $250 or more. Our advice: save your money and get a plain crib mattress for half the price at another store.

◆ *Just because we say this item is discontinued does NOT mean you can't find it anywhere else.* This is especially true for chain stores—just because Babies R Us says the crib you've fallen in love with is now discontinued, that does NOT mean you can't find it from another store. That's because chains discontinue items all the time . . . and not just because the manufacturer is discontinuing it. Chains replace slow moving merchandise or just make way for something new. Meanwhile, the very same furniture (or for that matter, any baby gear) is sold down the street at another store.

cribs

◆ *This beautiful sleigh style crib will make it impossible to tie a crib bumper.* Cribs with solid panel ends (like sleigh styles) are hip these days . . . but if you want to use a bumper, you may be disappointed. That's because many crib makers forget to design these cribs with any place to tie a bumper; and a poorly attached bumper is a safety hazard. (More on bumpers and whether you really need one in the next chapter). Cribs with very thick corner posts also make it hard to tie a bumper (cribs from Natart, Petite Cheris, and Bonavita are often guilty of this design flaw). Our advice: if in doubt, take a bumper from another crib and try to tie it on the style you want.

 Money Saving Secrets

1 **CHECK OUT REGULAR FURNITURE STORES FOR ROCKERS, DRESSERS, ETC.** Think about it—most juvenile furniture looks very similar to regular adult furniture. Rockers, dressers, and bookcases are, well, just rockers, dressers, and bookcases. And don't you wonder if companies slap the word "baby" on an item just to raise the price 20%? To test this theory, we visited a local discount furniture store. The prices were incredibly low. A basic three-drawer dresser was $60. Even pine or oak three-drawer dressers were just $129 to $189. The same quality dresser at a baby store by a "juvenile furniture" manufacturer would set you back at least $400, if not twice that. We even saw cribs by such mainstream names as Bassett at decent prices in regular furniture stores. What's the disadvantage to shopping there? Well, if you have to buy the crib and dresser at different places, the colors might not match exactly. But, considering the savings, it might be worth it.

2 **FORGET THE DESIGNER BRANDS.** What do you get for $600 when you buy a fancy crib brand like Bellini or Ragazzi? Safety features that rival the M-1 tank? Exotic wood from Bora Bora? Would it surprise you to learn that these cribs are no different than those that cost $180 to $300? Oh sure, expensive cribs typically come in designer colors. But take a good look at these cribs—except for fancy styling, they are no better than cribs that cost half as much.

3 **CONSIDER MAIL ORDER.** Say you live in a town that has one baby shop. One baby shop that has sky-high prices. What's the antidote? Try mail order. JCPenney and Sears sell such famous (and quality) name brands as Child Craft and Bassett. Granted, they don't sell them at deep discount prices (you'll find them at regular retail). But this may be more preferable than the price-gouging local store that thinks it has a license from God to overcharge everyone on cribs and juvenile furniture. You can also check the web sites mentioned in this chapter for quotes on cribs and other nursery items. One note of caution: be sure to compare delivery costs and policies. See the box "E-Mail from the Real World" about a story on this subject earlier in this chapter. (One important note: Sears does NOT have a catalog; some Sears' stores carry juvenile furniture. You can also buy nursery furniture from Sears.com).

4 **SHOP AROUND.** We found the same crib priced for $100 less at one store than at a competitor down the street. Use the manufacturers' phone numbers and web sites (see later in this chapter) to find other dealers in your area for price comparisons. Take the time to visit the competition, and you might be pleasantly surprised to find that the effort will be rewarded.

E-MAIL FROM THE REAL WORLD
Get all the details on delivery
before you mail-order furniture

A mom-to-be in Chicago discovered Sears was a much better deal than JCPenney for her nursery furniture. Here's her story:

"While I was searching for baby furniture, I thought JCPenney's would be a good choice. The catalog gave me a large selection to choose from and it would be less time consuming than hitting all the little shops. So, I put in an order for a crib and mattress and a four-drawer dresser. The prices on the furniture were pretty good (about $150 less than in other stores). However, the furniture has to be shipped directly from the warehouse to your home. Shipping and handling would have been $110 and the shipping company would only drop off the material at the front door—not into the home (or, in our case, a second floor apartment!) I could hardly believe it! If I had to spend over a hundred dollars extra on shipping, I would rather spend it on a higher quality crib and dresser than on shipping and handling. Hence, the search continued.

"Next I went to Sears where they had a 'Sculptured' series Child Craft crib and matching flip-top dresser. The prices were reasonable, you could pick the delivery day (including Saturdays) and they would deliver for just $25! They had these items in stock, so we got it in two days. Even if it did have to be shipped from the main warehouse, however, we would still only be charged the $25 fee and would have to wait at most four weeks. Needless to say, we bought the crib and dresser at Sears!"!"

5 **GO NAKED.** Naked furniture, that is. We see an increasing number of stores that sell unfinished (or naked) furniture at great prices. Such places even sell the finishing supplies and give you directions (make sure to use a non-toxic finish). The prices are hard to beat. At a local unfinished furniture store, we found a three-drawer pine dresser (23″ wide) for $100, while a four-drawer dresser (38″ wide) was $175. Compare that to baby store prices, which can top $300 to $600 for a similar size dresser. A reader in California e-mailed us with a great bargain find in the Bay Area: "Hoot Judkins" has three locations (Redwood City, Fremont, Millbrae; www.hootjudkins.com) that sell unfinished furniture. She found a five-drawer dresser in solid pine for just $260 and other good deals on nursery accessories. Another idea: Million Dollar Baby (see review later in this chapter) is one of the few crib makers to offer unfinished crib models (Jenny Lind, M0301). While unfinished cribs are somewhat rare, naked furniture stores at least offer affordable alternatives for dressers, bookcases, and more.

6 **HEAD TO CANADA.** A weak Canadian dollar has created some incredible cross-border bargains. Thanks to NAFTA, it's now even easier to shop in Canada—there are no duties or taxes. The best deals are on juvenile furniture actually made in Canada (as opposed to imported from Asia). If you want to explore this tip, first start by calling a Canadian manufacturer to find the names of both U.S. and Canadian dealers (the numbers/web sites are in our manufacturer review section later in this chapter). Then compare prices over the phone or email.

What if you don't live near Canada? Can you just call up a Canadian baby shop and have a crib shipped to the U.S.? Well, you *used* to be able to do this a few years ago. Since then, Canadian crib makers have cracked down on this practice, fearing that cross-border shipping was cutting into their lucrative sales to U.S. baby retailers. As a result, only a few brands (such as Morigeau/Lepine) permit their Canadian retailers to ship across the border.

Also, we should note Dutailier (the glider/rocker company reviewed later in this chapter) has stopped cross-border discounting. Does that mean you can't find Dutailier at a discount? No, you just have to use the U.S.-based web sites to find deals. Among the best: BabyCatalog.com. This site usually has great pricing and free ground shipping on many models. Another good source for deals on glider rockers: Target. The discount chain carries Dutailier rocker gliders for as little as $199 in Super Targets and online (target.com).

7 **GO FOR A SINGLE INSTEAD OF A DOUBLE.** Cribs that have a single-drop side are usually less expensive ($50 to $100 cheaper) than those with double-drop sides. Sure, double-drop side cribs are theoretically more versatile (you can take the baby out from either side), but ask yourself if your baby's room is big enough to take advantage of this feature. Most small rooms necessitate that the crib be placed against a wall—a double-drop side crib would then be a tad useless, wouldn't it?

8 **SKIP THE SLEIGH CRIB.** Lots of folks fall in love with the look of a sleigh-style crib, which looks like, well, a sleigh. The only problem? Most sleigh cribs have solid foot and headboards. All that extra wood means higher prices, as much as $100 to $300 more than non-sleigh crib styles. If you have your heart set on a sleigh style, look for one that doesn't have solid wood on the ends.

9 **CONSIDER AN AFFORDABLE CONVERTIBLE CRIB.** Now, the key word here is "affordable." Earlier in this chapter, we derided most "convertible" cribs for their high prices and expensive conversion kits. And then there is the whole issue of whether you really want a crib to morph into a twin bed. But we realize that many parents like the convertible concept, so let's talk about how to get a deal. Good news: several companies (among them Munire, Child Craft/Legacy and Sorelle) have rolled out affordable convertible cribs. Walk into Babies R Us and you'll find convertible cribs around $500 . . . that buys you a decent crib that converts to a toddler bed and then to a real-size double bed with the addition of simple bed rails. One tip: make sure the design has a true headboard and shorter footboard (many low-end convertible cribs cheat on this point by having the same size head and foot boards). That looks much better when converted to a double bed.

10 **TRY CRAIGSLIST.ORG.** What is Craigslist? This popular online classified site has versions for three dozen cities, with a special "for sale" section for baby/kids stuff. Use Craigslist to find a local

---

"Exclusive" cribs hard to price shop

When you visit a local baby store and see a particular crib style, you might think you can price shop this furniture online, or at least, at another store across town. But sometimes it isn't that easy. That's because juvenile furniture makers sometimes make "exclusive" cribs and dresser styles for certain groups of baby stores like NINFRA's Baby Express group or the USA Baby stores. These exclusive models aren't sold to other stores or online. In fact, you can't even look them up on a manufacturer's web site. The reason is clear: baby stores know you can't price shop the crib.

family that is unloading unneeded nursery furniture, gear and other items (but beware of used cribs, as we've discussed earlier). Other sites that have similar classified ads include ShopLocal.com, SetUp.com, LiveDeal.com and Cairo.com. Most of the sites don't charge a fee for text-based ads.

Baby Superstore Reviews: The Good, Bad & Ugly

There's good news and bad news when it comes to shopping for baby. Good news: there are an amazing number of stores to shop for baby gear. Bad news: there are an amazing number of stores to shop for baby gear.

And as a first-time parent, you probably have never been in these stores (except for that time you bought a gift for a pregnant co-worker). Walking into a baby superstore for the first time can give even the most levelheaded mom or dad-to-be a case of the willies. It is a blizzard of pacifiers, strollers, cribs and more in a mind-numbing assortment of colors, features and options. So, as a public service, here's our overview of the major players in the baby store biz.

Babies R Us

To find a store near you, call 888-BABYRUS. Over 200 locations.
What's Cool: Gotta love the selection in this chain, which includes everything from diapers to car seats, cribs to clothes. Unlike some competitors who carry lesser-known brands, Babies R Us (BRU) actually carries good-to-better brand names like Peg Perego strollers, Britax car seats and more. Some of the best buys are their in-house brands for diapers and wipes. What about the rest of the prices? Yes, you can find better deals on the web or at Wal-Mart, but Babies R Us is generally competitive. Their return policy is more customer-friendly than that of Target or Baby Depot. In recent years, BRU has expanded its private label and "exclusive" brand products, including bedding and décor by Wendy Bellissimo, furniture by Chris Madden (Bassett) and so on. The attempt is to give BRU stores more brand cache, similar to what Target has done with its in-house designers. What about BRU's baby registry, which is the largest in the country? Reviews on that are mixed, as we'll note below.

Needs work: Did someone say service? Unfortunately, that's not Babies R Us' strong suit. Our reader email is filled with stories of inconsistent service at BRU, and our own personal experiences echo that sentiment. Sometimes we find helpful, friendly salespeople who can give you basic facts about products. On other visits, however, we're lucky to find someone to check us out, much less answer questions.

Now, in a past edition of this book, we compared the IQ of *some* Babies R Us sales associates to that of a rutabaga. As a result, we received angry letters from rutabagas nationwide, including one pointed missive from the Rutabaga Anti-Discrimination League (RADL). But seriously, Babies R Us has told us they are trying to improve service. One area of improvement could be to stop the miss-information that some BRU sales associates give out to parents. Example: When Babies R Us drops a product, some sales associates erroneously tell customers "the manufacturer has discontinued it." Yes, that sometimes is true—but more often than not, you can still find that product somewhere else . . . just not at BRU. Other complaints about Babies R Us center on snafus with special order items, especially furniture and glider-rockers. Some of this is a lack of communication between corporate and the stores; other times, it is an error at the store level.

Yes, mistakes can happen at any store, chain or not. The key is how the store deals with/fixes the problem. Most of the time, Babies R Us does the right thing and takes care of the customer.

Web: www.babiesrus.com Babies R Us' web site is actually run by Amazon—and that's been a blessing and a curse. On the up side, Amazon's easy-to-use interface and consumer product reviews win kudos from most parents. You can return online purchases to BRU stores, which is a nice plus. The problem? The inventory online often doesn't match what is in the stores . . . and vice versa. And don't expect the lowest prices here—you can often find the same items for less elsewhere online. We should finally note, at press time, Babies R Us and Amazon were embroiled in a legal dispute regarding how Amazon handles the online store for BRU. While Amazon and BRU are bound by a ten-year agreement that runs to 2010, we wouldn't be surprised to see the partners going their separate ways in coming years.

Baby Depot (Totally for Kids)
To find a store near you, call 800-444-COAT. 360 locations.
What's Cool: The Burlington Coat Factory has 360 locations, but only 250 have "Baby Depot" departments. The company also operates two freestanding baby stores (one is called Totally 4 Kids; the other Super Baby Depot—check their web site at www.coat.com for a store locator, which also tells you which location has what). Baby Depot's strength is its low prices, often lower than competitors like Babies R Us and even Wal-Mart. Yes, a Baby Depot department is smaller than a Babies R Us store, but we're always amazed at the top-quality brands they sell, including Combi, Peg Perego and Chicco. Baby Depot's furniture selection is also impressive—crib brands include Child Craft, C & T (Sorelle), Generation 2, Storkcraft

and more. Baby Depot also has added a maternity section and carries a small but decent layette selection. Also at Baby Depot: a national gift registry that offers a 5% rebate of purchases made for you by friends. And look for Burlington's in-store magazine with coupons for select items.

Needs work: "Inconsistent" would be a charitable way to describe the Baby Depot experience. Some Baby Depots have the ambience of a decrepit warehouse, while others are bright and cheerful. Obviously, much of the blame for this can be pinned on parent Burlington Coat Factory, which doesn't seem to have a clue about marketing strategy and hence operates in widely disparate loca-

E-Mail from The Real World
The world's worst return policy?

Baby Depot's draconian no-cash refund policy draws harsh criticism from our readers:

"Add yet another dissatisfied Baby Depot customer to your list. I was aware of their awful return policy, but somehow, I lost my mind, and we ordered a Simmons crib from them anyway. Four weeks after we ordered, we get a message saying that our order was in at Baby Depot. But when we went to the store to pick it up not only could they not find the crib we had ordered, but our order had been listed as "combo unit", not a crib, and had been marked as "picked up" on the same day that we ordered it. So not only did we have to wait for 30 minutes while the lone salesperson in that department searched for our item, we have to find some way to spend $50 of store credit at a store we never want to set foot in again."

"We bought a car seat at Baby Depot, got it home, and opened the box only to discover that the wrong car seat was in the box! We took it back to Baby Depot, and were told that we could be issued a store credit, but that's it. They don't give refunds. We were also told the model we wanted had been discontinued. After the rude treatment we received at the store, I am not inclined to purchase anything else there."

A word to the wise: make sure you REALLY want an item before buying it at Baby Depot. And check carefully for any damage (open boxes, confirm the right thing is in the box, etc.) before giving them your money.

tions (outlet malls, power centers, free standing stores, etc). Our last visit to Baby Depot was disappointing—the drone of the harsh florescent lights was only matched by the apathetic sales help and disorganized aisles. And watch out for Baby Depot's return policy, which is among the worst in North America. Basically, there are no cash refunds—if you buy something that doesn't work or breaks, that's tough. All you get is store credit. And, generally, there are no returns after 14 days. As a result of that return policy, quite a few of our readers boycott Baby Depot. At a bare minimum, we would recommend passing on Baby Depot's gift registry. As a side note, we did have an employee of Baby Depot email us with some "inside" info on the return policy. She told us if you have a miscarriage or stillbirth, Baby Depot will give you a cash refund on returned purchases—but only if you go through their corporate headquarters. Wow, how considerate! (See the previous page email from the real world for more on Baby Depot's return policy.)

Web: www.babydepot.com. Burlington's web site has come a long way in the last year or so. Besides the standard store locator, you can shop from several "baby" categories, like Nursery, Baby Travel, Maternity and more. But we still found the site very hard to use—you have to click through numerous menus just to get to something to buy. There are lots of online coupons for Baby Depot and Burlington. Check the box in Chapter 7 for coupon sources.

The Discounters: Target, Wal-Mart, K-Mart

What's Cool: Any discussion of national stores that sell baby items wouldn't be complete without a mention of the discounters: Target, Wal-Mart, K-Mart and their ilk. In recent years, the discounters have realized one sure-fire way to drive traffic—discount toys and baby stuff in order to get parents to buy other higher-margin items. As a result, you'll often see formula, diapers and other baby essentials at rock-bottom prices. And there are even better deals on "in-house" brands.

Of all the discounters, we think Target is best (with one big caveat—their draconian return policy, see below for a discussion). Target's baby department is just a notch above Wal-Mart and K-Mart when it comes to brand names and selection. Yes, sometimes Wal-Mart has lower prices—but usually that's on lower-quality brands. Target, by contrast, carries Perego high chairs and a wider selection of products like baby monitors. The best bet: Super Targets, which have expanded baby products sections.

Needs work: If you're looking for premium brand names, forget it. Most discounters only stock the so-called mass-market brands: Graco strollers, Cosco car seats, Gerber sheets, etc. And the baby departments always seem to be in chaos when we visit, with items strewn about hither and yon. K-Mart is probably the worst when it comes to organization, Wal-Mart the best. We like Target's selection (especially of feeding items and baby monitors), but their prices are somewhat higher than Wal-Mart. What about service? Forget it—you are typically on your own.

While we do recommend Target, we should warn readers about their return policy. Once among the most generous, Target now requires a receipt for just about any return. A raft of new rules and restrictions greet customers (sample: exchanges now must be made for items within the same department). This has understandably ticked off a fair number of our readers, especially those who have unfortunately chosen to register at Target for their baby gifts. Among the biggest roadblocks: Target won't let you exchange duplicate baby gifts if you don't have a gift receipt (and there are numerous other rules/restrictions as well). Of course, your friends may forget to ask for a gift receipt or throw it away. And watch out: gift receipts have expiration dates; be sure to return any item before that date.

After receiving a fair amount of consumer complaints about this, Target now allows returns of registry gifts without a gift receipt IF the item is listed on your registry. The rub: you will get the lowest sales price in the last 90 days, not necessarily what your guest paid for it. That's a special gotcha for new parents—many baby products and clothes go on sale frequently, rendering your gift almost worthless on an exchange. This and other beefs with Target have spawned many complaints about their registry and even a web site (target-sucks.com).

Our advice: think twice about registering at Target. While we get complaints about all baby registries (even industry leader Babies R Us), be sure to read the fine print for ANY baby registry before signing up. Ask about returns and exchange policies, including specifically what happens if you have to return/exchange a duplicate item without a gift receipt.

Web: Each of the major discounters sells baby products online. Here's an overview of each site:

◆ **WalMart.com:** This redesigned site is easy to use, complete with a "baby" tab at the entry page. Moving into the Nursery category, we noticed the site had a smattering of furniture, bedding and other products for sale. We like the detailed info for each product, including weight, dimensions, shipping info and more. They've also beefed up their selection. For example, they only had one infant car seat when we first reviewed this site . . . but now feature 30 models. We're pleased with the improvements and the prices are usually pretty competitive.

◆ ***Kmart.com***: K-Mart's online outpost is a winner—we liked the bright graphics and easy navigation. Kmart has fixed some of the problems with this site that we noted in our last edition . . . navigation is easier and categories are logically organized. The selection of items (notably monitors) was not as good as WalMart.com.

◆ ***Target.com*** has probably the coolest looking web site of all the discounters—click on the "baby" section and then select from categories like furniture, safety or strollers. Like the store, Target.com focuses on more stylish and better-quality goods than their discount competition. Sample: the $299 rocker-glider deal from Shermag, which we'll discuss more in depth later. A handy drop-down menu on most pages lets you sort items by price, brand and more. Most cool feature: Target lets consumers rate and review products, a la Amazon. Often, you'll find out more about a product in the user reviews than is provided in Target's own descriptions.

Specialty Chains: More Baby Stores To Shop!

Inspired by the success of Pottery Barn Kids, several chains have ventured into the nursery business. An example: Room & Board (web: www.RoomandBoard.com), an 11-store chain with locations in California, Colorado, Illinois and Minnesota. Their well-designed web site has a nursery section with a couple of cribs ($400 to $450), dressers and accessories. Quality is good and prices are reasonable, say our readers who've ordered from them.

And that's just the beginning. Bombay Company of Ft. Worth, Texas opened their first Bombay Kids store in 2002 and at the end of 2004 had 47 total. Pier 1 Imports, also of Ft. Worth, acquired the CargoKids chain in 2001 and plans to roll out 300 more stores in the next decade. Finally, Crate & Barrel has begun to launch Land of Nod stores (four plus an outlet store at the time of this writing) that feature their funky nursery furniture and bedding.

One of the most promising new entrants into the field is Buy Buy Baby, which is run by the sons of the family that founded the Bed, Bath & Beyond chain. Yes, they only have handful of locations in New York and DC metro areas (check www.BuyBuyBaby.com for locations), but they are expanding. Readers rave about Buy Buy Baby's selection, service and prices, so if there's one near you, check it out. And BuyBuyBaby.com's web site carries a small selection of the store's offerings for online shoppers.

What's driving this is a boom in babies, especially to older moms and dads. Tired of the cutesy baby stuff in chain stores, many parents are looking for something more sophisticated and hip. Of course, it remains to be seen what this means for bargain shoppers. On one hand, more competition is always good—having a wide diversity of places to buy nursery furniture and accessories is always a plus. On the downside, most of these chains are chasing that "upscale" customer with outrageously priced cribs and bedding. "As much as parents love the furniture at Pottery Barn Kids, some wince at the prices," said the *Wall Street Journal* in a recent article on this trend. And we agree—you gotta love the PBK look, our goal in life is to try to find that same look . . . at half the price!

Baby gift registries disappoint

The Internet age was supposed to make this so easy—just register for gifts at a baby store and the computers do the rest. Need to change something? Stores promised you could create/change your registry via the web. Sounds so easy . . . but not so fast. Baby gift registries generate a big number of complaints, judging from our reader email. The gripes: duplicate gifts, out of stock items, backorders and other frustrations. And it doesn't seem to matter the size of the registry—we hear complaints about small retailers' registries and those of the big chains and web sites.

With Babies R Us, parents complain that they can't see their entire registry online (the web site only has a partial listing; you to have to physically go into a store and print out the entire list to see it all). BRU's web site doesn't immediately update items that have been bought, which leads to more duplicate gifts. And some parents complain the registry is poorly organized, failing to group together logical items like safety or feeding items in the same category.

And here's a major caveat: an gift certificate bought at a Babies R Us store can NOT be used online at Babiesrus.com—which is frustrating, as some items are sold online and not in the stores. Memo to Babies R Us: better coordinate your registry, online site and stores, pronto!

There is similar frustration over at Pottery Barn for new parents—if you want to use a gift certificate for an online or telephone purchase at Pottery Barn Kids, you must MAIL the certificate in and cool your heels for a two to three week processing period. How convenient.

We don't know what the problem is here. Perhaps retailers should take their web programmers out back, give them 30 lashes and withhold the Starbucks for a week. Until baby stores can figure out how to de-bug their registries, we urge caution with all baby gift registries.

NURSERY NECESSITIES

Outlets

There are dozens of outlets that sell kids' clothing, but when it comes to furniture the pickings are slim. In fact, we found just a handful of nursery furniture outlets out there. Here's a round up:

Child Craft has a strange arrangement for their outlet stores. First, there is the "official" (and only) Child Craft factory outlet. Then there are two semi-official outlets (Kiddie Kastle and Baby Boudoir, discussed below) that are operated by CC dealers in Kentucky and Massachusetts.

First, the official outlet: located in the Tanger Outlet center in Seymour, IN (exit 50A), the Child Craft Outlet (812) 524-1999 sells only first-quality merchandise including discontinued pieces. While there is little damaged merchandise, some of the pieces are "off color." Prices are discounted 30% to 70%—cribs start at $129 and most are $200 to $400.

A reader who scoped out the outlet for us said she was a little disappointed with the selection (none of the fancier models were in the outlet at the time she visited) but the "prices were terrific." She also pointed out that a nearby Child Craft dealer in Louisville, KY (Kiddie Kastle) was so miffed at the official outlet that they convinced the manufacturer to let them open their own Child Craft Outlet. The **Kiddie Kastle Warehouse Outlet** is at a different location than the main store (502-499-9667) and is only open limited hours (mainly Fridays, Saturdays and Sundays—call first). But the deals are great— "the selection is small but there are some very desirable models." She found a cherry sleigh crib (original $600) for just $350. And the same outlet also carries bedding at very good prices.

Live in the Northeast? Check out **Baby Boudoir Outlet,** an off-shoot of a baby store in New Bedford, MA. (800-272-2293, 508-998-2166) that is also authorized by Child Craft to sell their discontinued furniture at wholesale prices or below. The Baby Boudoir Outlet has 1000 cribs in stock at any one time at prices that start at $59 and up (most are $150 to $300). The store also carries glider rockers, bedding and other baby products at 30% to 70% off retail. FYI: There is both a Baby Boudoir store and a warehouse outlet—you want to visit the outlet for the best deals. The outlet is around the corner from the main store. Of course, Baby Boudoir sells more than just Child Craft—they also sell discontinued Sorelle cribs (30% to 70% off) and certain discontinued Munire styles, as well as factory seconds from such bedding lines as Kids Line, Lambs & Ivy and more.

Along the same lines, **Baby Furniture Warehouse**, with stores in Reading and Braintree, MA (781-942-7978 or 781-843-5353; web: www.BabyFurnitureWarehouse.com, see below), is a Ragazzi outlet that specializes in selling overstock and discontinued cribs. You can save up to 30% off Ragazzi's regular retail prices here—cribs run $299 to $599 and case pieces are also available. One special we noticed was a $569 Ragazzi crib with under crib drawer marked down to $329.

Pottery Barn Kids has several outlets for their kids catalog, including Memphis, TN (901-763-1500) and Dawsonville, GA (706-216-6456) as well as San Marcos, TX. A reader found some good deals there, including a changing table for $99 (regularly $199) and a rocker for $199 (down from $700). The outlet also carries the PBK bedding line at good discounts. A reader in Georgia said the PBK outlet there features 75% off deals on furniture and you can get a coupon book at the foot court for an additional 10% discount. "The best time to shop is during the week—they run more specials then," she said. "And bring a truck—they don't deliver." One final tip: call AHEAD before you go (check outbound.com for locations and contact numbers for a PBK outlet near you). The selection of nursery furniture (which by the way, rarely includes cribs or twin beds—but they have other accessory items) can vary widely from outlet to outlet . . . some may have no stock during certain months.

Bassett sells its cribs and nursery furniture from its namesake outlet in Bassett, Virginia (276) 629-6446. A reader recently visited the outlet for a good selection of cribs.

Finally, don't forget that **JCPenney** has 15 outlet stores nationwide. The stores carry a wide variety of items, including children's and baby products (always call before you go to confirm selection). Check out the web site Outlet Bound (www.outletbound.com) for a current listing of locations.

Hotel cribs: hazardous at $200 a night?

Sure, your nursery at home is a monument to safety, but what happens when you take that act on the road? Sadly, many hotels are still in the dark ages when it comes to crib safety. A 2000 survey by the CPSC found unsafe cribs in a whopping 80% of hotels and motels checked by inspectors. Even worse: when the CPSC invited hotel chains to join a new safety effort to fix the problem, only the Bass Hotel chain (Inter-Continental, Holiday Inn, Crowne Plaza) agreed to join. That chain pledged to have their staffs inspect all cribs, making sure they meet current safety standards. We urge other hotels to join this effort, as research shows children under age two spend more than seven MILLION nights per year in hotels and motels. And if you find yourself in a hotel with your baby, don't assume the crib you request is safe—check carefully for loose hardware, inadequate size sheets and other problems.

The Name Game:
Reviews of Selected Manufacturers

Here is a look at some of the best-known brand names for cribs sold in the U.S. and Canada. There are over 100 companies in the U.S. that manufacture and/or import cribs, but, because of space limitations, we can't review each one. We decided to concentrate on the best and most common brand names. If you've discovered a brand that we didn't review, feel free to share your discovery by calling or emailing us (see our contact info at the end of the book).

How did we evaluate the brands? First, we inspected samples of cribs at stores and industry trade shows. With the help of veteran juvenile furniture retailers, we checked construction, release mechanisms, mattress supports, and overall fit and finish. Yes, we did compare styling among the brands but this was only a minor factor in our ratings (we figure you can decide what looks best for your nursery).

Readers of previous editions have asked us how we assign ratings to these manufacturers—what makes one an "A" vs. "B"? The bottom line is quality *and* value. Sure, anyone can make a high-quality crib for $500 or $800. The trick is getting that price down to $300 or less while maintaining high quality standards. Hence, we gave our highest ratings to manufacturers that make high-quality cribs at prices that don't break the bank.

What about the crib makers who got the lowest ratings? Are their cribs unsafe? No, of course not. ALL new cribs sold in the U.S. and Canada must meet minimum federal safety standards. As we mentioned earlier in this chapter, a $100 crib sold at Wal-Mart is just as safe as a $700 designer brand sold at a posh boutique. The only difference is styling, features and durability—more expensive cribs have thick wood posts, fancy finishes, features like "hidden hardware" on the rail release, under-crib storage drawers and durability to last through two or more kids.

Brands that got our lowest rating typically have had a problem with recalls in previous years. Some were fined by the CPSC for failing to report injuries or problems with their products. That doesn't mean that their current production cribs are unsafe; but we were troubled enough by their past track record to assign that lower rating.

Ratings here *only apply to cribs*; many of these manufacturers also make dressers and other furniture pieces. Later in this chapter, we'll discuss our brand recommendations for these items.

Please note: we've included phone numbers and web sites in this section so you can find a local dealer. These manufacturers do NOT sell directly to the public, unless otherwise noted. Most web sites will feature a selection of cribs, if not the entire line.

The Ratings

A **EXCELLENT**—*our top pick!*
B **GOOD**— *above average quality, prices, and creativity.*
C **FAIR**—*could stand some improvement.*
D **POOR**—*yuck! could stand some major improvement.*

AFG Furniture. *This crib brand is reviewed on our free web site, BabyBargains.com (click on Bonus Material).*

Alta Baby *180 Vreeland Rd., West Milford, NJ 07480. Call (888) 891-1489 for a dealer near you. Web: www.altababyweb.com.* Alta is the newest Italian crib maker to debut in the U.S., launching nationwide back in 2002. Like other Italian cribs, Alta's styles feature solid beech wood construction, hidden hardware, knee-push rail releases and under crib drawers. Alta Baby cribs are JPMA certified. The cribs look much like those of Pali, Sorelle and Bonavita—basic styling with just a handful of finish options. Yes, there are a few accessories (Alta has a line of crib bedding as well as changing tables) and a handful of matching dressers. Yet, the prices are rather high: $600 for a crib? Yea, you can find these online for less (we saw prices ranging from $400 to $550 using froogle.com) . . and in fact, that might be the best thing about Alta Baby. With few other Italian crib brands sold online, this might be your best option if you live in the boonies and still want this look. So, what's the bottom line on Alta Baby? "Nice but not spectacular," said a retailer and we agree. The prices are too high, considering the lack of innovative styling or features. If you find one of these cribs on sale, we say go for it. But we'd be hard pressed to get excited about an Alta Baby crib at full retail. ***Rating: B-***

Amby Baby Motion Bed *Call 1-866-519-2229 for a dealer near you. Web: www. AmbyBaby.com* Invented by an Australian dad for his colicky daughter, the Amby baby hammock is just that—a hammock that is designed as a safe sleep environment to replace a bassinet, cradle or even crib. It looks like a swing, with a wide base (18") and comes with a mattress, pair of sheets, frame, spring and cross bar. The basic  version runs $215, while a couple of more deluxe versions (which include accessories like a mosquito net and more sheets) can cost up to $282. So, should you get one? Well, we agree with the science behind this idea—a cocooned environment like a hammock mimics the womb, which soothes colicky babies. So, is it safe? Yes, we think it is—the exception would be preemies. We don't recommend a baby hammock for preemies (despite the fact the company sells an accessory to better accommodate smaller infants). If you have a preemie, discuss your baby's sleeping arrangement with your pediatrician. And, while Amby says you can use the hammock up to 59 lbs with a second spring (the first spring that comes with the unit is good up to 29 lbs), we suggest you transition your baby out of the hammock around three months of age. Why? First, that's when colic usually ends (it starts around three weeks and can continue until three months. For more about colic, which affects 15% of babies, see our other book *Baby 411*). Second, around three to four months of age, babies become more aware of their surroundings and that's why most pediatricians suggest that is the right time to transition a baby out of a cradle or bassinet (or in this case, a hammock). After four months, babies start to establish a permanent sleep routine. A crib would be best then. Why? Babies need to roll over and learn how to pull themselves up—something that can't be done in a hammock. Yea, Amby dismisses this concern by saying baby can learn these developmental milestones during the daytime on the floor, but considering how much time a baby spends in a "sleep environment," that seems a bit misguided. The take home message: if you have a history of colic in your family or your baby develops colic, consider the Amby Baby Motion Bed hammock (after consulting with your pediatrician first). Use it until around three months. No, Amby does NOT cure colic, but it could help lessen it. ***Rating: A***

Angel Line *17 Peak Place, Sewell, NJ 08080, Call (800) 889-8158 or (856) 863-8009 for a dealer near you. Web: www. angelline.com* This low priced line offers good quality even though the styling is rather boring. Their entry-level Jenny Lind-style crib sells for $130, but other more contemporary styles are in the $200

Who Is Jenny Lind?

You can't shop for cribs and not hear the name "Jenny Lind." Here's an important point to remember: Jenny Lind isn't a brand name; it refers to a particular *style* of crib. But how did it get this name? Jenny Lind was a popular Swedish soprano living in the 19th century. During her triumphal U.S. tour, it was said that Lind slept in a "spool bed." Hence, cribs that featured turned spindles (which look like stacked spools of thread) became known as Jenny Lind cribs. All this begs the question—what if today we still named juvenile furniture after famous singers? Could we have Britney Spears cribs and Jessica Simpson dressers? Nah, bad idea.

to $400 range. Typical of the plain vanilla styling is the Angel II crib with curved headboard and single drop side (all Angel Line models have single drop sides). Available finishes are natural, white, maple, white wash, oak and cherry. As for the quality, we liked the overall construction (they use a spring mattress platform, for example) and large casters. One negative: many of Angel Line's cribs featured exposed rail hardware and a foot-bar rail release mechanism, which most of their competition has abandoned in recent years. On the plus side, Angel Line is one of the few crib brands you can buy online (do a quick search for Angel Line cribs on froogle.com). In the past year, Angel Line has rolled out new styles including an Italian-style line of cribs with hidden hardware on the rail releases and under-crib storage drawers for $350. Angel Line (whose parent is Longwood Forest Products) also makes canopy cribs, changing tables, cradles, rockers and high chairs, all made in Taiwan. The company's detailed web site features extensive info on their cribs (even size and weight), as well as thumbnail pictures of each model (which can be enlarged for viewing). ***Rating: B-***

A.P. Industries *346 St. Joseph Blvd., Laurier Station, Quebec, Canada, Call (800) 463-0145 or (418) 728-2145. Web site: www. apindustries.com* Quebec-based crib maker A.P. Industries (also known as Generations) offers stylish cribs and case pieces, which are available in nine different collections. All the items are made in Quebec of solid birch (except one, made of beech). Sample price: $500 to $600 for a crib with hidden hardware and a knee-push rail release. We thought A.P had the best look of all the Canadian cribs we reviewed (the 20 finish options provide more choice than most crib makers), although the rail release does make a rather loud "click" when it is locked into position, at least on one model we tested. Another plus: A.P. makes some very affordable dressers; a reader spied an A.P. hi-low dresser for just $309 at Baby Depot. Despite all the positives, we should note a few problems with A.P. Deliveries and customer service reviews for this brand have been mixed. The production glitches of a few years ago seem to be ironed out now, which is good. Customer service has been up and down—in a past edition, we complained about the rude way A.P. treated parents calling with a problem. That also seems to have been addressed, as the last report we had from a parent was much more positive. So we will tick up A.P.'s rating this time out. ***Rating: B+***

Babee Tenda *See box on page 54-55.*

Baby Trilogy Corner Cribs *This crib brand is reviewed on our free web site, BabyBargains.com (click on Bonus Material).*

Baby's Dream *PO Box 579, Buena Vista, GA 31803, Call (800) TEL-CRIB or (912) 649-4404 for a dealer near you. Web: www. babysdream.com* Baby's Dream has come a long way since we first reviewed them. In the late 90's, the company was fined for failing to report problems with their folding rail release (also called a drop gate). Not only were 13,000 defective cribs recalled, but the company was also cited for hiding the problem from safety regulators. As you might guess, we took a dim view of this and rated Baby's Dream accordingly.

Babee Tenda's "safety" seminar: Anatomy of a Hard Sell

We got an interesting invitation in the mail during our second pregnancy—a company called "Babee Tenda" invited us to a free "Getting Ready For Baby" safety seminar at a local hotel. The seminar was described as "brief, light and enjoyable while handing out information on preventing baby injuries." Our curiosity piqued, we joined a couple dozen other expectant parents on a Saturday afternoon to learn their expert safety tips.

What followed was a good lesson for all parents—beware of companies that want to exploit parents' fears of their children being injured in order to sell their expensive safety "solutions." Sure enough, there was safety information dispensed at the seminar. The speaker started his talk with horrific tales of how many children are injured and killed each year. The culprit? Cheap juvenile equipment products like high chairs and cribs, he claimed. It was quite a performance—the speaker entranced the crowd with endless statistics on kids getting hurt and then demonstrated hazards with sample products from major manufacturers.

The seminar then segued into a thinly veiled pitch for their products: the Babee Tenda high chair/feeding table and crib. The speaker (really a salesperson) spent what seemed like an eternity trying to establish the company's credibility, claiming Babee Tenda has been in business for 60 years and only sells its products to hospitals and other institutions. We can see why—these products are far too ugly and expensive to sell in retail stores.

How expensive? The pitchman claimed their crib retailed for $725—but is available for you today at the special price of $489! And what about the high chair/feeding table (which converts into a walker, swing, etc.)? It "regularly" sells for $450, but we'll give you a special deal at $298!

We found Babee Tenda's sales pitch to be disgusting. They used misleading statistics and outright lies to scare parents into thinking they were putting their children in imminent danger if they used

Well, there is good news: the company has replaced its management and cleaned up its act. While you still see the folding rail on many of their model, the company re-designed the hinge and it's now safe. The company's new managers have also beefed up quality and lowered prices, which have contributed to the strong growth of the brand in recent years.

Baby's Dream's line consists of stationary side models, folding rails (drop gates) and traditional knee push rail releases. All models are JPMA certified and most feature spring mattress platforms . . .

---

store-bought high chairs or cribs. Many of the statistics and "props" used to demonstrate hazards were as much as 20 years old and long since removed from the market! Even more reprehensible were claims that certain popular juvenile products were about to be recalled. Specifically, Babee Tenda's salesperson claimed the Evenflo Exersaucer was "unsafe and will be off the market in six months," an accusation that clearly wasn't true.

The fact that Babee Tenda had to use such bogus assertions raised our suspicions about whether they were telling the truth about their own products. Sadly, the high-pressure sales tactics did win over some parents at the seminar we attended—they forked over nearly $800 for Babee Tenda's items. Since then, we've heard from other parents who've attended Babee Tenda's "safety seminars," purchased the products and then suffered a case of "buyer's remorse." Did they spend too much, they ask?

Yes, in our opinion. While we see nothing wrong per se with Babee Tenda's "feeding table" (besides the fact it's god-awful ugly), you should note it costs nearly four times as much as our top recommended high chair, the very well made Fisher Price Healthy Care. (At some seminars, the price for the feeding table is $400, but you get a free car seat with your purchase. Whoopee). There's nothing wrong with the crib either—and yes, Babee Tenda, throws in a mattress and two sheets. But you can find all this for much less than the $500 or so Babee Tenda asks.

A new twist to the Babee Tenda pitch: their invitations in 2004 carried a line that their seminar is sponsored "in conjunction with the Consumer Product Safety Commission and the National Highway Traffic Safety Administration." Whoa, sounds official! Except it isn't true—the CPSC or NHTSA have nothing to do with Babee Tenda's seminar . . . they warned Babee Tenda to stop this deceptive practice after we brought it to their attention.

So, we say watch out for Babee Tenda (and other similar companies like Babyhood, who pitches their "Baby Sitter" in hotel safety seminars). We found their "safety seminar" to be bogus, their high pressure sales tactics reprehensible and their products grossly overpriced.

some have under crib drawers and most convert to adult beds. The majority of crib styles are in the $300 to $500 range. The cribs and other furniture are milled in Chile and finished in Baby's Dream's factory in Georgia. In the past year, Baby's Dream branched out into bedding, acquiring the Cotton Tale bedding line.

Quality is excellent and retailers tell us the deliveries and customer service of this brand is better than most in the industry. No, we still aren't wild about the folding rail releases, but there are plenty of other styles here to choose from. So we will give Baby's Dream a much better rating this time out, reflecting their improvements. **Rating: A**

Babi Italia This is a special brand made by Bonavita for chain stores. See the Bonavita review later in this section for more info.

Babies Love by Delta See the review of Delta later in this section.

Bambino See *Ragazzi*.

Bassett *3525 Fairystone Park Hwy, Bassett, VA 24055. Call (276) 629-6000 for a dealer near you. Web: www.bassettfurniture.com* Pop into chains stores like Babies R Us and you'll see Bassett's offerings. The brand has teamed with lifestyle guru Chris Madden (who has a show on HGTV) and designer Pamela Scurry to give its nursery furniture some pizzazz that was lacking in past years. An example: a Chris Madden 2-in-1 crib for $400 that has a stationary rail and converts to a full size bed. We also spied a Pamela Scurry crib in antique white for $370 with a matching canopy kit for $130. The legs were sculpted (nice touch) and a matching dresser was $550 with glass knobs. That little bit of bling is what separates Bassett from the low-end Jardine stuff you see at BRU. As for quality, we'd say it is above average for the cribs—most are made of wood from New Zealand and Australia, although other parts are made in such diverse places as Indonesia and Slovenia. Final assembly is in the U.S. at Bassett's factory in Virginia. As for rail releases, it's all over the board—some Bassett cribs have the old-style foot bar releases with exposed hardware, while newer models have hidden hardware and knee-push releases. While we like the cribs, the case pieces are another story. A hi-lo dresser we recently saw had drawer glides that were sticky—and the drawers themselves are stapled, not dove tailed. You're supposed to spend $560 for this? So while we give Bassett a good rating for their improved design mojo and overall crib quality, we say skip the dressers. **Rating: B+**

Bella D' Este See *Jardine*.

Bellini *Call (805) 520-0974, (800) 332-BABY or (516) 234-7716 for a store location near you. Web: www.bellini.com* This baby store chain's claim to fame is Italian cribs—long before they became com-

Certifications:
Do they really matter?

As you shop for cribs and other products for your baby, you'll no doubt run into "JPMA-Certified" products sporting a special seal. But who is the JPMA and what does its certification mean?

The Juvenile Products Manufacturers Association (JPMA) is a group of over 400 companies that make juvenile products, both in the United States and Canada. Twenty years ago, the group started a testing program to help weed out unsafe products. Instead of turning this into a propaganda effort, they actually enlisted the support of the Consumer Products Safety Commission and the American Society of Testing and Materials to develop standards for products in several categories: carriages/strollers, cribs, play yards, high chairs, safety gates, portable hook-on chairs, and walkers (which we think are dangerous, but more on this later).

Manufacturers must have their product tested in an independent testing lab and, if it passes, they can use the JPMA seal. To the group's credit, the program has been so successful that the JPMA seal carries a good deal of credibility with many parents we interviewed. But does it really mean a product is safe? Well, yes and no.

First, as with any product, you must carefully follow instructions for assembly and use. Second, realize the testing program and standards are voluntary. Since certification can cost $10,000 or more, some smaller manufacturers claim they can't afford to test their products. Hence, you will often see the JPMA seal on cribs and baby gear from larger baby companies, not the smaller importers.

One important point to remember: ALL cribs sold in the U.S. must meet government safety standards. Yes, the JPMA certification rules for cribs are slightly stricter than the government's rules, but the difference is negligible. And most of the JPMA's standards for other products (like high chairs, strollers, etc.) are merely labeling requirements. For more info on the JPMA program or to get a list of certified products, you can call (856) 439-0500 or check out their web site at www.jpma.org. A safety brochure (in both English and Spanish) is available online.

monplace in the market, Bellini was hawking them from their 50 boutiques on the East and West coasts. Most cribs in Bellini run $600 and up (the prices have crept upward in recent years, due to unfavorable currency exchange rates). Yes, today you can find a similar look from Sorelle (C&T at Babies R Us) or Babi Italia for 40% less . . . so what's the appeal of Bellini? Fans cite great customer service, but detractors of Bellini say it can be inconsistent (each Bellini is independently owned). One reader complained the finish on her $800 dresser started to chip off after six months; and the store's owner wouldn't replace the item (although they did try to repair it). That was the exception to the rule, however. Most parents we've interviewed say they are happy with their Bellini furniture and the chain's service. And we are happy the company has ditched their double trigger rail release in favor of a hidden hardware, knee push design. Bellini scored a coup in 2004, when one of their models (the Isabella) topped *Consumer Reports* rankings for cribs. CR especially liked Bellini's safety (excellent) and ease of use (which ranked very good). One caveat: the question of crib mattresses. Readers tell us some Bellini salespeople try to convince parents to buy a special (and expensive) Bellini mattress, claiming that regular mattresses don't fit Bellini cribs. Hogwash. Bellini's cribs are within the same standards that all cribs must meet to be JPMA certified . . . yes, the Bellini mattress is slightly larger than other crib mattresses (the chain claims it gives a tighter fit). But that doesn't mean a regular crib mattress won't fit their cribs! Given how expensive Bellini's mattresses are (up to $229), it's no wonder some salespeople push it. Bottom line: while we have upped Bellini's rating from our last edition, the lingering question over their mattress sales tactics brings the brand up a bit short in our book. ***Rating: B-***

Berg *(908) 354-5252. Web: www.bergfurniture.com.* In business since 1984, Berg branched out into juvenile furniture in the late 90's. The company offers several different crib models. Solid pine cribs (made in Russia) run $349 to $449, while convertible cribs (that convert to twin beds; made in the U.S.) run $649 to $849. That is pricey, but the convertible models do include the conversion kit. We liked the hidden hardware on the knee-push rail releases, but the attached dressers on their "Crib N Beds" were a turn-off (for safety reasons, as we discussed earlier). Speaking of dressers, we noticed Berg's offerings feature screwed drawers (no dovetail) and lack a smooth glide. Despite that, readers who've bought Berg furniture have been very happy with the quality, according to our research. One caveat: Berg's pine groupings. Berg uses a soft pine, which is susceptible to nicks and scratches. As a result, Berg's pine furniture in baby stores often looks beaten up. . . obviously, this is less of an

cribs

issue in a nursery, as long as you're careful. Or just skip the pine groups and get a different Berg style! We are raising Berg's rating this time out, reflecting the positive feedback of late. ***Rating: A-***

Bonavita *125 Jackson Ave., Edison, NJ 08837. Call (888) 266-2848 or (732) 346-5150 for a dealer near you. Web site: www. bonavita-cribs.com, www.babiitalia.com.* Bonavita has had its ups and downs in the past decade. The company's claim to fame was their Italian-imported cribs, which won wide audience in both chains and specialty stores in the 1990's. Bonavita sells its furniture under the Babi Italia and Issi brands in Babies R Us and Europa in Baby Depot. In specialty stores, Bonavita uses its own brand name.

Despite their success in the 90's, Bonavita has stumbled in the past few years. As the euro rose, Bonavita's furniture became more and more expensive. While other competitors like Sorelle reacted by importing furniture from Eastern Europe and Brazil, Bonavita only belatedly came to the realization that its prices were too high. Forays into manufacturing (at one point, Bonavita made its own dressers in a plant in Virginia) were also unsuccessful, amid quality complaints and other snafus. All this added up to a rough past year, as Bonavita faced a warehouse of unsold inventory, a cash crunch and credit problems.

Bonavita now says it is in a midst of a turnaround. One major change: 80% of Bonavita's furniture is imported today from Vietnam and Thailand (the balance is still made in Italy, mostly cribs). An entry-level crib made in Vietnam that you'd see in a chain store sells for $250 to $300. A pine collection that is sold in specialty stores goes for $500 to $600 for a crib and $500 for a combo dresser.

How's the quality? This has been hard to pin down in recent years. We've always thought Bonavita's Italian cribs (even the low-end ones sold in chain stores) were a good value. Yet we weren't impressed with the first round of Vietnam-imported furniture Bonavita did a year ago. The quality has improved as Bonavita worked out the kinks with those suppliers. Inconsistency has haunt-ed Bonavita over the years, but to be fair, other importers (Sorelle) have also faced similar problems. Yet the bar in this industry contin-ues to be raised by new and old competition: Munire has out-flanked Bonavita on design and even old-line manufacturers like Ragazzi have shifted to lower-cost imports (Bambino) with more skill than Bonavita. Sorelle now sells many of its cribs via online sites, even drop-shipping for e-tailers. . . . Bonavita is a no-show when it

Rug Burn: How to save on nursery rug prices

Yes, it's always exciting to get that new Pottery Barn Kids cata-log in the mail here at the home office in Boulder, CO. Among our favorites are those oh-so-cute rugs Pottery Barn finds to match their collections. But the prices? Whoa! $300 for a puny 5′ 8′ rug! $600 for an 8′ by 10′ design! Time to take out a second mortgage on the house. We figured there had to be a much less expensive alternative out there to the PBK options. To the rescue, we found **Fun Rugs** by General Industries (www.funrugs.com; 800-4FUN-RUGS). This giant kids' rug maker has literally hundreds of options to choose from in a variety of sizes. Fun Rugs makes matching rugs for such well-known bedding lines as California Kids and Olive Kids. Now, their web site lets you see their entire collection, but you can't order direct from Fun Rugs. Instead, go to one of their dealers like **American Blind & Wallpaper** (**RugsUSA** (www. RugsUSA.com) and **NetKidsWear** (www.netkidswear.com search for rugs). All of those web sites sell Fun Rugs at prices that are sig-nificantly below similar rugs at PBK. Example: a 5′ by 8′ log cabin quilt design rug is only $155; PBK's price is $300 for a similar size rug. We found most of those web sites sell rugs for 40% less than PBK or posh specialty stores.

comes to e-commerce.

Customer service has also been a sore point for Bonavita. Again, the story here is one of ups and downs. Readers of past editions of our book may remember stories of customer service lapses and safety recalls (a 2003 recall involving crib side rail slats that came loose was especially troubling). Well, things are better as of this writing—the number of angry emails about Bonavita has dropped in the past year, to the company's credit. Yet, if you ask baby store retailers who their favorite furniture suppliers are (based on customer service, delivery reliability, etc), most would not name Bonavita.

So, all in all, we give a mixed review to Bonavita. Kudos to their affordable cribs and generally good quality. But if you decide to buy this line for your nursery, be sure to deal with a store that has a good customer service reputation in case there are any snafus. One tip: be sure to check the box BEFORE leaving the store to make sure nothing is damaged. ***Rating: B***

Why do all Italian cribs look alike?

Walk into a baby store to look at Italian cribs and you'll be hard pressed to tell any difference between the brands. Except for the finish color, the cribs look identical. Why is that? First, understand that most Italian cribs are made by just a handful of manufacturers. All these crib makers are located in the same region of Italy; in fact, they are clustered right across the street from one another. Second, while manufacturers like Pali and Bonavita assemble their own cribs, they buy many component pieces (like side rails) from the same supplier. That's why the rail releases on Italian cribs are nearly identical. Finally, consider the wood used to make the cribs—nearly all the manufacturers use 100% Italian beech. (No wonder things look so alike!).

Where this gets confusing is the brand names. Most Italian manufacturers (with the exception of Pali) do not directly export to the U.S. and Canada. They sell their wares to importers like Bellini, Sorelle, Mondi and Bonavita. Then those importers sometimes slap different model names on cribs sold in discount stores or specialty stores (Bonavita's cribs in Babies R Us go under the name Babi Italia or La Jobi; in specialty stores, the same importer as Bonavita).

That's not to say there are no differences between the Italian crib brands. Often, the importers have different track records for delivery and customer service (we'll note who is better in this chapter). And some importers have been more aggressive than others to target the entry-level price points at stores like Babies R Us. But if you wonder why all the Italian cribs look alike, there's your answer.

Bridgeport Cosco makes wood cribs under this name and Jardine. See Jardine for a full review. (See Cosco's review for contact information and web site).

Bratt Décor PO Box 20808, Baltimore, MD 21209. Call (888)-24-BRATT or (410) 327-4600 for a dealer near you. Web: www.brattdecor.com. Well, at least you have to give this company bonus points for creativity—they made their name with cribs like the "Casablanca Plume" crib that was topped with (and we're not making this up) ostrich feathers. That (and the $1050 price tag) enabled Bratt Décor to earn a distinguished place on our list of the most ridiculous baby products in a previous edition of this book. In the past year, Bratt has expanded their line to include a series of wood cribs in various "vintage" and whimsical looks. Their Heritage Four Poster Crib with Stars is a take-off of a 1940's design with four finials that can be changed from stars to bunnies, flowers, planes or balls. Price: $700. All in all, we've noticed Bratt Décor's prices have drifted downward in recent years—gone are most of the $1000+ options, replaced by cribs

E-MAIL FROM THE REAL WORLD
Leg got stuck in crib slats

"Yesterday, my nine month old somehow wedged his leg between two slats of the crib. I heard him scream shortly after I put him to bed for his afternoon nap and found his leg entrapped up to the thigh. I couldn't pull the slats apart and get his leg out myself, so I called 911. A police officer was able to pull the slats apart just enough so I could gently guide by son's leg back through. I took him to the doctor and he's fine, other than a bruise on his leg. Any tips on how we can avoid this in the future?"

Crib slats are required by federal law to be a certain maximum distance apart (2 3/8"). This is done to prevent babies from getting their heads trapped by the crib spindles or slats, a common problem with cribs made before 1973 when the rule was enacted. Of course, just because baby can't get a head stuck in there doesn't mean an arm or leg can't be wedged between the slats. A solution: Trend Lab makes a "Crib Shield System" ($30) and "Breathable Crib Bumper" ($20 to $25) that uses Velcro to attach to a crib (it is compatible with most, but not all cribs). It is made of breathable mesh and is sold online at BabiesRUs.com and OneStepAhead.com. Does everyone need this? No—it is rather uncommon for baby to get their arms or legs wedged in the slats. But if you do discover this is a problem, that is one answer!

that now sell for $600 to $900. What parents seem to like here is the style and colors of the cribs (Bratt Décor is one of the few crib makers out there today that does a navy blue or bright red finish). Bratt Décor also has matching accessories such as nightstands, mirrors, bookcases and other decorative options. All in all, we'll give Bratt Décor thumbs up for style—but you're going to pay for it. **Rating: B**

Bright Future *See the JCPenney catalog (800) 222-6161, web: www.jcpenney.com.* This is a private label brand made for JCPenney and imported from Asia. A recent Penney's catalog featured a single drop side crib for $200. The cribs are similar to other low-end brands in quality; on the plus side, the newer models have knee-push release rails and spring mattress supports. The styling is rather plain; don't look for any fancy features like under-crib drawers or cutting-edge looks from Bright Future. On the upside, Penney's cribs have a good reputation for safety and durability. The company dispatches its own representative to suppliers to make sure quality is up to snuff. Yet, you get what you pay for here—a low-end crib at a decent price. You sacrifice things like a spring mattress platform on the older models (a reader who bought a Penney's sleigh crib reported the mattress platform was made of plywood). Nonetheless, this might make a good secondary crib for grandma's house. One major caveat about Penney: while the quality and safety is good, we have received an increasing number of complaints about order snafus at Penneys: late deliveries, backorder nightmares, the wrong style shipped—you name it. As a result, we are lowering the rating for this brand this time out. **Rating: C-**

C&T International This company is the same as Sorelle; see their review later in this section.

Canalli *Web: www.canallifurniture.com* This furniture is made by Munire (see review later) and sold in a small number of stores in New Jersey and New York, most notably the Crib & Teen City chain (www.cribteencity.com). A handful of Canalli cribs are imported from Golden Baby in Italy, the same manufacturer that supplies Sorelle (reviewed later).

Cara Mia *146 Needham St #6, Lindsay, Ontario Canada K9V 4Z6 Call (877) 728-0342 or (705) 328-0342 for a dealer near you. Web: www.CaraMiaFurniture.com.* These affordable cribs (most are $249 to $500, although one entry-level style is only $150) are sold in specialty stores and touted as "European crafted." This apparently has a better ring than "Made in Slovenia in the former Yugoslavia." Cara Mia makes a wide variety of crib styles, from traditional drop sides to stationary rail models. Among their best models is "Tammy," a knock-off of Child Craft's Millennium convertible crib with stationary side rail. Cara Mia's price: $450, about a $100 less than Child Craft. Other Cara Mia cribs feature hidden hardware and knee push rail releases (although one style still has exposed hardware). Delivery is six to eight weeks on average, which is rather zippy in this industry. As for the wood, most styles are solid beech with a selection of nice finishes. Optional under crib drawers add another $50 or so to most styles (although Cara Mia's newer styles now include the drawer). How about the quality? Most folks are happy with Cara Mia's cribs, although we did get a complaint from one mom whose crib rail slats separated one day when she was pulling up the side rail. Fortunately, the baby wasn't in the crib at the time, but this incident raises questions about Cara Mia's quality control. Cara Mia's dressers aren't that impressive either . . . most are made with MDF and feature very plain styling at too-high prices. FYI: Cara Mia also makes cribs sold under the names Mother Hubbard's Cupboard and Nini Scott. These are the same as Cara Mia's offerings, just a different name. **Rating: B-**

Chanderic Call 800-363-2635 or819-566-1515 for a dealer near you. Web: www.shermag.com It's been a rough couple of years for Canadian furniture makers—a falling U.S. dollar has made their products more expensive, just as the competition from Asian imports has intensified. The result: some companies have gone out of business (Status) while others have retrenched or been sold (EG). Canadian furniture behemoth Shermag has been buffeted by the same forces and has tried to diversify—their "Chanderic" line is an attempt to crack the middle to upper end of the nursery market. When Chanderic debuted in 2003, we weren't that impressed . . . they had just a handful of styles and prices seemed high. Well, the line has expanded and now includes five collections (a total of 12 cribs). The cribs are imported from Croatia, while the case goods are made in Canada. We liked the birch wood and expanded color choices; all the cribs feature hidden hardware and good stability. Yet, the prices are still on the high side: $450 to $500 for a regular crib or $600 to $700 for a convertible style. The dressers feature all wood drawers with dovetail joints and wall straps to prevent tipping. Yes, the quality is higher than the Chinese imports, but not as good as Munire or Pali. However, we will give Chanderic bonus points for their emphasis on safety—unlike other crib makers whose styles with solid headboards make tying a crib bumper impossible, Chanderic's styles are more bumper-friendly. One final note of caution on Chanderic/Shermag: as we were going to press, the company's stock was sinking fast on news of slumping sales and profits. Part of that was due to labor disputes (now resolved) that slowed

cribs

shipments last year, but we are still a bit wary of the company's financial position. Subscribe to our e-newsletter for any updates to this situation. ***Rating: B+***

Child Craft *PO Box 444, Salem, IN 47167. Call (812) 883-3111 for a dealer near you. Web: www.childcraftind.com* It's been a rough year or two for Child Craft, the Indiana-based crib maker that traces its roots back to 1910. A major flood devastated Child Craft's warehouse and offices in May 2004 and that just about wiped out the company, which was under-insured. The company was able to struggle back and is now shipping again . . . but as you can imagine in any industry, the moment you stand still, your competition will blow by you. Such is the case with Child Craft (and its sister brand Legacy). When the company stopped shipping for most of the latter half of 2004, other brands like Munire and Jardine zoomed by. As a result, the brand is still struggling—Child Craft used to be sold at Babies R Us, but on a recent visit we just saw one style there (and that was on clearance). Legacy has also lost market share in specialty stores. All this is too bad: Child Craft/Legacy had a good reputation for quality, safety and value, even as they switched from domestic production to importing in recent years (most items are made in Eastern Europe and Asia, although some final assembly still occurs in Indiana). Child Craft pioneered the stationary rail bed with their "Crib N Double" bed style (an affordable $400). Legacy is basically the same as Child Craft, just fancier finishes and detailing (and higher prices). So, will Child Craft/Legacy survive and make it to their 100th anniversary in 2010?

E-MAIL FROM THE REAL WORLD
Tricks from the sale floor

Reader Jennifer Gottlieb shared an interesting story about a trick some baby stores use to convince parents to buy more expensive cribs:

"Here's an interesting tidbit we heard recently and wanted to pass along: A guy in our childbirth education class works at a baby furniture store, and let us in on a marketing ploy. Evidently, some stores purposely loosen the screws on the floor models of less expensive cribs so that when you're checking them out they seem more rickety than their pricey counterparts. This makes most nervous parents naturally turn to the cribs that appear to be more solid—not to mention expensive!"

It's hard to say but we hope they do. A couple final notes on Child Craft: don't forget about Child Craft's outlet stores in Indiana, Kentucky and Massachusetts (see the outlet section earlier in this chapter for details). And kudos to Child Craft for their commitment to safety—CC now tests all their case goods with 50-pound weights hanging from a top drawer. That would prevent a climbing toddler from tipping a dresser over. Child Craft even adds weight to the bottom of their case goods to make sure they pass this 50 pounds test. And all CC dressers include drawer glides that have safety bumps to prevent them from coming all the way out plus a tip restraint that attaches to the wall to prevent tipping. **Rating: A**

Childesigns *This company went out of business in 2005. An archived review of their furniture is on our web site BabyBargains (click on bonus material).*

Chris Madden See Bassett.

Concord *This crib brand is reviewed on our free web site, BabyBargains.com (click on Bonus Material).*

Corsican Kids 2417 E. 24th St, Los Angeles, CA 90058. Call (800) 421-6247 or (323) 587-3101 for a dealer near you. Web: www. Corsican.com. Looking for a wrought iron crib? California-based Corsican Kids specializes in iron cribs that have a vintage feel, with detailed headboard and footboard decoration. Before you fall in love with the look, however, be sure to turn over the price tag. Most Corsican Kids iron cribs sell for a whopping $1000 to $2000! Yes, you can choose from a variety of cool finishes like pewter and antique bronze but these prices are hard to swallow. And there are some downsides to wrought iron cribs: first, they are darn noisy when raising or lowering the side rail. And Corsican's drop-sides are those exposed (rod/cane) hardware foot bar releases that most of the market long abandoned (most parents find knee push easier to use). So, it's a mixed review for these guys. Yes, they are cool to look at but the practical drawbacks of wrought iron cribs (as well as the stratospheric prices) scores only an average rating in our book. **Rating: C+**

Cosco 2525 State St., Columbus, IN 47201. Call (800) 544-1108 or (812) 372-0141 for a dealer near you. Web: www.coscoinc.com. The Cosco name has just about disappeared from the crib market, as parent Dorel has concentrated on their Jardine line for the Babies R Us chain. It's no wonder—Cosco must translate as "recall" in Canadian. The company suffered through several high-profile recalls (and sadly, injuries and deaths) due to their poorly made

Co-sleepers

If you can't borrow a bassinet or cradle from a friend, there is an alternative: the **Arm's Reach Bedside Co-Sleeper** (call 800-954-9353 for a dealer near you; web: www.armsreach. com). This innovative product is essentially a bassinet that attaches to your bed under the mattress and is secured in place. The three-sided co-sleeper is open on the bedside. The result: you can easily reach the baby for feedings without ever leaving your bed, a boon for all mothers but especially those recuperating from Caesarean births. Best of all, the unit converts to a regular playpen when baby gets older (and goes into a regular crib). You can also use the co-sleeper as a diaper changing station. The cost for the basic model? $150 to $230, which is a bit pricey, considering a plain playpen with bassinet feature is about $100 to $120. But the unique design and safety aspect of the Arm's Reach product may make it worth the extra cash layout.

In recent years, Arm's Reach has rolled out several variations on its co-sleeper. The "Universal" model ($190 to $230) is re-designed to fit futons, platform and European beds. The removable sidebar and new liner can also be positioned at the top level of the play yard to create a four-sided freestanding bassinet. New in the past year is the "Mini-Bassinet Co-Sleeper," which does not convert to a playpen and sells for around $140 to $160. New this year, a sleigh-style wooden co-sleeper. This version retails for $290 to $330.

If you like the functionality of a co-sleeper but not the look, there is good news. Arm's Reach web site (see above; click on accessories) now sells 13 floor-length liners in various colors.

Of course, Arm's Reach isn't the only co-sleeper on the market. The **Baby Bunk** (www.BabyBunk.com) is a wood co-sleeper that is either purchased for $200 to $300 or rented by the month. That's right, you can rent one for just $30 a month (with a $50 refundable deposit) in case you want to see if this is for you. That might be the best bargain of all when it comes to co-sleepers! Baby Bunk also sells a series of accessories for their co-sleepers, including sheets, mattresses, bumpers and more.

While we like the co-sleeper, let us point out that we are not endorsing the concept of co-sleeping in general. Co-sleeping (where baby sleeps with you in your bed) is a controversial topic that's beyond the scope of this book. Consult your doctor and other parenting books for more pros/cons on co-sleeping.

cribs in the 1990's. And we weren't that impressed with the Chinese-made Jardine line (see review below), which features poor quality and unimpressive detailing. So, we don't recommend this brand, no matter what they are calling it today (the exception: Jardine, which is designed by Cosco for Babies R Us—see review later in this section). Sure, there is a $109 "2 in 1" Cosco crib sold at Wal-Mart now, but we say skip it. **Rating: F**

DaVinci *See Million Dollar Baby later in this chapter for contact info.* DaVinci is the online name for Million Dollar Baby (MDB), reviewed later in this section. Million Dollar Baby uses the different name for its cribs sold online to avoid offending its regular retail stores. Basically, DaVinci cribs are just a re-packaged version of MDB's cribs—same styles, same finishes. Hence, like MDB, you'll see two price groups of DaVinci. The lower price ones (under $200) are imported from Asia and feature foot bar releases, and simple styling. The upper-end DaVinci cribs are similar to MDB's "Reflections" line. Styles like the Leonardo are $400 to $500 and feature knee push rail releases. And despite the Italian sounding name, most of these cribs are NOT made in Italy (a few models are made of Italian parts, but final assembly is in the U.S.). As for quality, we give DaVinci the same rating as MDB since they are basically the same thing. Most parents are happy with their DaVinci cribs, although we noted some of the pine models can scratch/ding very easily. You can find DaVinci cribs online at BabyUniverse.com and BabyCenter.com. **Rating: C+**

Delta *114 West 26th St, New York, NY 10001. Call (212) 736-7000 for a dealer near you. Web: www.deltaenterprise.com.* Imported from Indonesia, Delta (also known as Delta Luv and Babies Love by Delta) is sold in chain stores like Wal-Mart, Sears and Target, as well as online. Delta scored a coup recently when one of their basic Jenny Lind cribs (style 4750-1) scored a top ranking from *Consumer Reports*. And we agree—it's a good value for $110. In fact, most Delta cribs are low in price, about $130 to $240 on average. So, what is Delta's quality like? Well, our biggest beef with Delta is the cheap-o wood mattress platform. Delta claims its wood design is better for your baby's back than the spring platform you see in other brands, but we remain unconvinced. On the plus side, Delta has eliminated the double trigger rail releases on most of its models; more now have knee push releases (although the hardware is still exposed). Also good: all Delta cribs feature hardwood construction, heavy-duty furniture-style casters and easy assembly (all models ship pre-assembled from the factory and require no tools to set up). Yes, the styling of Delta is very plain (especially the dressers) but they have introduced a few models with carved headboards that add a bit more pizzazz to the line. Also new: a Baby Snoopy line of furniture (cribs, bassinets) and strollers. Basically, the Snoopy line is the same as the Delta furniture, just with a picture of, well, Snoopy on the headboard. If you decide to go with a Delta crib, leave plenty of time however. The president of one major baby product web site told us Delta is perennially back-ordered, as the company struggles to keep up with production. The bottom line on Delta: this is a good crib for grandma's house. That aforementioned Jenny Lind style for $110 is a deal; or go for the Delta Fold-A-Way crib for $100. Each can be set up quickly without tools. Finally, we should mention that in the past year, Delta has purchased Simmons (see review later). **Rating: B-**

Domusindo Web: www.domusindo.com Imported from Indonesia exclusively for JCPenney's catalog, Domusindo cribs are affordably priced ($200 to $300) and feature decent quality, features and styling. The downside? Most Domusindo cribs have wood mattress platforms (not springs) and exposed hardware. That's a bit behind similarly priced competitors at Babies R Us. As for safety, we are impressed with Penney's track record and quality assurance programs. Penney's actually sends inspectors into their supplier's plants to make sure things are being assembled correctly and rigorously makes sure its cribs meet safety standards. Hence, while we probably would be a bit nervous about other cribs imported from Indonesia, Penney's Domusindo's cribs are worthy of recommendation. That said, as we noted earlier in the Bright Future (a Penney's private label) review, we have received an increasing number of complaints about Penney's customer service. Late deliveries, back order nightmares and so on. As a result, we are knocking down this brand's rating. If you decide to order any nursery furniture from JCPenney, make sure you have plenty of time before the baby arrives . . . and an iron stomach. **Rating: C-**

Dorel Dorel is the parent of Cosco, which also sells their cribs under the names Bridgeport and Jardine. See the Cosco review for Dorel, Bridgeport and Cosco cribs; Jardine is reviewed separately later.

ducduc For a dealer near you, call 212-226-1868. Web: ducducnyc.com Looking for high-style nursery furniture? Got $1500 to spend on a crib? Like orange? If you answered yes to those questions, then take a look at ducduc, a New York-based design company that aims to  give the nursery biz a shot of glam. The result is a group of five nursery collections (and matching linens) that are rather retro in design . . . and oddly, heavy on orange as a design accent. "A new aesthetic, a new generation" is the theme and we will give ducduc points on creativity—the pieces emphasize lacquered veneers and contrasting colors, a fusion between the Brady Bunch and a European cable access show. We suppose this is going to appeal to hipsters in San Francisco or Soho, but it's hard imagine the rest of the country going wild over ducduc. How's the quality? This line is so new (it launched in 2005) that we haven't heard from any parents who've bought it yet, although the samples we saw at a trade show appeared to be well-made. And they better be at these prices. Check it out at stores like Design Within Reach. *Rating: B*

EA Kids. See Ethan Allen below

EG Furniture *See Petite Cheris.*

Ethan Allen *(888) EAHELP1; web: ethanallen.com.* You gotta love the EA Kids catalog, which is available in any of Ethan Allen's 300 stores nationwide, but the prices! Whoa! A basic crib, $700 to $800. An armoire, $1350. A three-drawer dresser, $780. Even when EA puts this stuff on "sale," the prices are hard to swallow if you haven't won the lottery recently. That said, readers who've bought Ethan Allen furniture for their nursery sing their praises for quality and durability. "We found their furniture isn't much more expensive than Morigeau or Ragazzi, but is much better quality. I'm confident the EA furniture we purchased will last for a very long time." Point well taken. The downside? We've heard several complaints from readers about late deliveries . . . most of that was due to a 2004 fire at their crib supplier. Yea that might have been a fluke, but a word of caution: if you plan to order EA furniture, leave plenty of time (double their estimated delivery time frame). So we'll give this line a "B" rating—great quality, style and features—if you can afford it. *Rating: B*

Evenflo *For a dealer near you, call (800) 233-5921. Web: www.evenflo.com.* Evenflo just sells a few crib models, but since they are sold in chain stores you might see them. A basic Jenny Lind style crib is available in white or oak and runs about $120 to $140 at places like Sears (you can see them online at Sears.com). We weren't impressed with the quality of the crib, which had a foot bar release with exposed hardware. In the last year, Evenflo has introduced a couple of Jenny Lind models with double-trigger releases—again, not very impressive. Finally, we should note that Evenflo has withdrawn from the foldaway mini-crib market after recalling 364,000 cribs in 2003 for a safety defect. We recommended these fold-away cribs in a previous edition of our book, so if you have one sitting in your home or grandma's house, you need to call (800) 582-9359 (web: www.portablewoodcrib.com) for an upgrade kit that will fix the problem. *Rating: C*

cribs

Bait and Switch with Floor Samples

Readers of our first book, *Bridal Bargains*, may remember all the amazing scams and rip-offs when it came to buying a wedding gown. As you read this book, you'll notice many of the shenanigans that happen in the wedding biz are thankfully absent in the world of baby products.

Of course, that doesn't mean there aren't ANY scams or rip-offs to be concerned about. One problem that does crop up from time to time is the old "bait and switch scheme," this time as it applies to floor samples of baby furniture. A reader in New York sent us this story about a bait and switch they encountered at a local store:

"We ordered our baby furniture in August for November delivery. When it all arrived, the crib was damaged and both the side rails were missing paint. We were suspicious they were trying to pass off floor samples on us—when we opened the drawer on a dresser, we found a price tag from the store. The armoire's top was damaged and loose and the entire piece was dirty. There was even a sticky substance on the door front where a price tag once was placed. Another sign: both the changing table and ottoman were not in their original boxes when they were delivered."

The store's manager was adamant that the items were new, not floor samples. Then the consumer noticed the specific pieces they ordered were no longer on the sales floor. After some more haggling, the store agreed to re-order the furniture from the factory.

Why would a store do this? In a down economy, a store's inventory may balloon as sales stall. The temptation among some baby storeowners may be to try to pass off used floor samples as new goods, in order to clear out a backlog at the warehouse. Of course, you'd expect them to be smarter about this than the above story—the least they could have done was clean/repair items and make sure the price tags were removed! But some merchants' dishonesty is only matched by their stupidity.

Obviously, when you buy brand new, special-order furniture that is exactly what you deserve to get. While this is not an everyday occurrence in the baby biz, you should take steps to protect yourself. First, pay for any deposits on furniture with a credit card—if the merchant fails to deliver what they promise, you can dispute the charge. Second, carefully inspect any order when it arrives. Items should arrive in their original boxes and be free of dirt/damage or other telltale signs of age. If you suspect a special-order item is really a used sample, don't accept delivery and immediately contact the store.

Fisher Price This line of cribs is made by Storkcraft, reviewed later in this chapter.

Forever Mine *This mail-order furniture company is reviewed on our web site (BabyBargains.com; click on bonus material).*

Generation 2 This was the parent company of Childesigns, which is now out of business.

Golden Baby This crib is imported from Italy by C&T International. This company is reviewed under their main trade name, Sorelle, later in this section. Golden Baby cribs are sold at Babies R Us. There are very few differences between Golden Baby and Sorelle cribs.

Graco *Rt. 23, Main St., Elverson, PA 19520. For a dealer near you, call (800) 345-4109, (610) 286-5951. Web: www.gracobaby.com.* Graco markets a couple of cribs under their own name (Wal-Mart carries one style), but they are made by Simplicity (see review later).

Issi See Bonavita earlier in this chapter.

Jardine *(See Cosco's review for contact information and web site).* Jardine is Cosco/Dorel's major offering in Babies R Us and it's been quite a success—judging from the large number of models at BRU and the low prices, this line seems to be a hit. Jardine (and its sister brand Bella D'Este) is imported furniture from China and offers a variety of price points, from a basic $200 drop-side crib to $300 for a stationary model and $479 for a "Lifetime" crib under the Bella D'Este imprint. The latter converts to a full size bed. First, the good news: all Jardine cribs feature spring platforms, good stability and a variety of matching dressers and accessories. We've got to give it to Jardine—for the money, they give you a good amount of style. But what about the quality? The cribs are OK (the exposed bolts are the only clue that these are cheap Chinese imports), but the case goods are another story. Jardine's dressers have drawers that don't fit well and glides that are rough; some models have stapled drawers and other sloppy construction touches. Jardine's glider-rockers are great deals ($140 to $240) but again, inferior in quality to Dutailier and Shermag. And don't get us started on Cosco/Dorel's safety track record for cribs, as we discussed previously. So, it's a mixed bag for Jardine/Bella D'Este: the cribs aren't bad, but the case goods stink. ***Rating (cribs): B+ Rating (dressers, glider rockers): F***

Jenny Lind This is a generic crib style, not a brand name. We explain what a Jenny Lind crib is in the box on page 52.

Jesse. See Natart.

JCPenney. See Bright Future.

Kinderkraft This brand was sold at Babies R Us but is now out of business.

La Jobi This is the parent company for Babi Italia and Bonavita. See their review earlier in this section.

Land of Nod *Web: www.landofnod.com* This popular catalog offers two cribs last we looked: an Arts & Crafts maple design for $799 and a Jenny Lind for $329. Quality is good, but we noticed one model had exposed hardware on the knee-push rail release . . . for $800? Coordinating dressers ran $600 to $800. The look is very contemporary, as most of the furniture lacks any frou-frou detailing. No, not a bargain but the feedback we hear from parents on this catalog is positive. **Rating B**

Legacy *See Child Craft for contact and web info.* This is the upscale part of Child Craft, sold in specialty stores. See Child Craft's review earlier in this chapter. The main difference between Child Craft and Legacy is styling (the latter being more fancy and expensive). Both Legacy and Child Craft use knee-push rail release mechanisms (although Legacy has hidden hardware; Child Craft is exposed).

Li'l Angels. *This crib brand is reviewed on our free web site, BabyBargains.com (click on Bonus Material).*

Little Miss Liberty *This crib brand is reviewed on our free web site, BabyBargains.com (click on Bonus Material).*

Luna *Call 888-346-5862 for a dealer near you. Web: www. lunaproducts.com* Canadian crib maker Luna has limited distribution in the U.S., but we liked their offerings. The company's dozen crib styles feature knee-push rail releases and solid beech construction (except for two models). Most styles feature a metal mattress support and half the line has an optional under-crib drawer. We were a bit surprised to see the exposed crib rail release hardware, as that is a bit behind the times. Nonetheless, we thought the quality was above average—the company also makes a couple of convertible cribs, dressers, cradles and more. Luna's more simple styles retail in the $400 range while models with under crib drawers are in the $500 range. **Rating: B**

E-Mail from The Real World
IKEA fans love ready-to-assemble furniture

A European furniture superstore with stylish furniture at down-to-earth prices, IKEA has 27 stores in the U.S., most of which are on the East and West Coast (plus Chicago and Houston). For a location near you, call 610-834-0180 or web: www.ikea.com. IKEA has a special baby/kids section called "Children's IKEA", a 5000 square foot area that showcases IKEA's nursery and kids' furniture as well as accessories. While our readers applaud IKEA's prices, they are mixed on the quality. Here's a sampling:

"We outfitted our entire nursery for just $300 at IKEA. The crib was $109; a basic dresser with changing tabletop was $179. The beauty of Ikea is that many of the furnishings come flat-packed, ready to take home and assemble yourself—don't fret, though, each piece comes with easy-to-follow, logical instructions. Only drawback: IKEA furniture isn't for traditionalists. Most items are made of beech, wood veneer or laminate and particleboard. Despite this, they are very durable and of high quality."

"IKEA is a great place for changing tables—the model we purchased (DIKTAD) was $219 and very sturdy. It can be screwed into the wall so it won't tip over if baby decides to climb up the drawers. Another great feature: it has a flip-top shelf."

"We love Ikea but their $79 crib has no drop sides and the mattress height can not be adjusted, so it is a bit of a problem for short parents (they have since added other affordable cribs with height adjustment). Ikea does have a lovely crib with a drop side (double trigger mechanism) and adjustable height but it's priced at around $179. They have a nice selection of inexpensive dressers, though."

Another reader wasn't impressed with IKEA's quality:
"We looked at the Ikea crib, as one of your readers did, and found it substandard—plastic hardware, shaky and thin particle board construction. Hard to imagine it even lasting through one baby."

Our advice: before you make a special trip to IKEA, first pre-shop their catalog. This 39-page publication has a special section on kids' items. IKEA's web site also features children's furniture and accessories. If you browse the catalog or web site before you visit the store, you'll have a better idea of the offerings, prices and styles.

MIBB This Italian crib maker withdrew from the U.S. market in 2002.

Million Dollar Baby *855 Washington Blvd., Montebello, CA 90640. Call (323) 728-9988 for a dealer near you. Web: www.milliondollarbaby.com* Hong Kong entrepreneur Daniel Fong started Million Dollar Baby (MDB) in 1989 and was one of the first successful importers of cribs from Asia. MDB got its start selling low-end $99 cribs to discounters, but over time has broadened its line to include convertible cribs and more upscale resellers (you'll find their Jenny Lind crib at Land of Nod, for example). MDB was one of the first crib importers to embrace the internet, although the cribs are sold under an alias (DaVinci) so as to not offend their retail customers. An example: the DaVinci Emily pine crib sold on BabyCenter.com for $350. So, how's the quality? We've never been big fans of this company, which is probably a legacy of their earlier low-end cribs. Their newer convertible cribs get much better marks from consumers and retailers, although the styling in this line is a bit behind the rest of the market. The biggest issue with MDB: their Asian pine is softer (and more prone to damage) than other pine cribs on the market. We wish MDB had more hardwood groupings in their line and less pine. On the plus side, Million Dollar Baby does offer crib styles (the Alpha and Jenny Lind) in an unfinished option, which is a boon for parents who want to paint/finish a crib themselves for a small savings. How is MDB's customer service? We've heard mixed reports. Some consumers tell us stories of delivery delays and emails that don't get answered. Yet retailers report they get better response, with quick turn around for replacement parts. All in all, we give this brand an average rating.
Rating: C+

Mondi *This crib brand is reviewed on our free web site, BabyBargains.com (click on Bonus Material).*

Morigeau/Lepine *3025 Washington Rd., McMurray, PA 15317. Call (800) 326-2121 or (724) 941-7475 or (970) 845-7795 for a dealer near you Web: www.morigeau.com* Based in Quebec, Canada, this family-run juvenile furniture company has been in business for over 50 years. Like other Canadian manufacturers, Morigeau/Lepine's specialty is stylish cribs and dressers that look like adult furniture. The quality is above average, but you're going to pay for it—cribs run $500 to $700 and a simple dresser can run $600 to $900. What do you get for those bucks? Solid wood construction (Morigeau even runs its own sawmill to process the maple and birch it uses in the furniture), drawers with dovetailed joints and cribs with completely hidden hardware and self-lubricating nylon tracks. Safety-wise, Morigeau's dressers have side-mounted glides with safety stops. We also liked the fact that most of Morigeau's dressers are oversized with 21" deep drawers to give you extra storage. The styling of the line is quite sophisticated—in fact, this is probably the most "adult" looking baby furniture on the market today. In the past year, Morigeau has introduced a new value line called the 8000 series with more affordable price points (a crib for $399; a combo hi-low dresser for $499). FYI: this line is made of MDF (most of Morigeau's line is solid wood). We should also note that Morigeau's sister line is "Lepine," a smaller collection of cribs at slightly lower prices (cribs are $450 to $660). All in all, we liked Morigeau—the prices are high, but the quality is there. Perhaps the biggest beef we've heard about Morigeau is their slow delivery; some retailers gripe it can take forever to get in special order items. Complaints about late delivery increased last year and as a result, we recommend leaving extra time in ordering—because of these concerns, we've dropped Morigeau's rating a bit in this edition. And another small negative: some parents do not like the Morigeau rail release, which latches with a loud click. That bugs some, but not others—try it out in the store first. **Rating: B+**

Mother Hubbard's Cupboard *Call (416) 661-8201 for a dealer near you. Web: www.mhcfurniture.com* This Canadian-based maker of dressers and case goods now imports cribs from Bulgaria. One static-side crib we saw at a recent trade show had impressive quality—the price was $529, not bad for a crib that converts to a full-size bed. Mother Hubbard also sells a handful of cribs made by Cara Mia (reviewed earlier) for about $600. The company finishes all its cribs in house to make sure they match their dressers. **Rating: A**

Munire *For a dealer near you, call 973-574-1040. Web: www.MunireFurniture.com* Although the brand name is new to the retail scene, Munire has been making juvenile furniture since 1987 for other companies. Their most notable customer is Crib & Teen City in New Jersey, which sells Munire furniture under its Canalli label. We visited Munire's factory in New Jersey and were impressed with their highly automated production process. Munire's claim to fame is their all-wood construction, unlike other juvenile furniture makers that use veneers and MDF. The drawers on the dressers are dovetailed and there are other little quality details. As for prices, Munire is more than the cheap stuff you see at Babies R Us but not as pricey as high-end Ragazzi. Yet, when you factor in the quality, we think Munire is a good value for the dollar. Most cribs are around $500, while dressers are in the $450 to $600 range. While most of Munire's offerings are made in New Jersey, we should also note the company is importing some pieces from Brazil and Mexico (from the latter, Munire now offers an entry-level collection called Majestic with a crib that starts at $400). The lower-price Mexican made furniture does have some veneers and does not feature the dovetail drawers, which we think is a mistake—if Munire wants to stake out a quality reputation in the market, it shouldn't muddy its brand with cheaper imports. We should note that Munire has struggled as it ramped up the Mexican plant; as a result, we heard reports of delays and long delivery lead times for the Majestic line.

Munire's rapid rise in the baby furniture market was a bit of a surprise. While some of their success can be attributed to the afore-mentioned quality and good customer service (despite the delivery snafus with the Majestic line), there was also a bit of luck and good timing. Munire debuted just as Legacy/Child Craft was hit by a mas-sive flood, which knocked them offline for several months. With a major competitor hobbled, Munire got a big head start in their effort to launch a national brand (it is now in 125 stores nationwide). Munire's challenge will now be to manage the company's rapid growth and maintain the same quality . . . and that quality should extend to imported items as well. So, overall, we will recommend Munire. Since similar quality furniture runs about 20% to 30% more than Munire's prices, the brand is a decent value. ***Rating: A***

Natart *240 Rue Pratte, Princeville, Quebec, Canada G6L 4T8. Call (819) 364-3189 for a dealer near you. Web: www.natartfurniture. com* Natart—a company in desperate need of a catchier name—is one of a number of Quebec-based nursery furniture makers to come to the U.S. market in recent years (Natart debuted in 2001). The emphasis is on a stylish look with high quality (and often, high prices). Sample: like the look of Pottery Barn's sleigh crib but not the $800 price tag? Natart makes a similar style called the Logan that is $700. Not much of a deal, eh? Yes, but we noticed that price includ-ed the conversion kit at a USA Baby store, while PBK wanted anoth-er $80 bucks for their conversion kit. All in all, you get the PBK look at 20% less. Other Natart cribs are less expensive, including some models that retail for $550 (a reader even spied them on sale for as little as $300 at one store). Matching dressers are pricey, most in the $700 range. While the prices are high, you're getting quality for the dollar—take a look at the dressers. Made in Canada, the dressers have dovetail drawers and stabilizer bars for a smooth glide. All the cribs have hidden hardware for the knee-push rail releases. Delivery is eight to ten weeks. ***Rating: A-***

Pacific Rim Woodworking *For a dealer near you, call 541-342-4508. Web: pacificrimwoodworking.com* How times have changed—not more than 15 years ago, if you wanted nursery fur-

eBay for cribs: 3 smart shopper tips

When you think of eBay, you might think of folks selling stuff they cleared out of an attic or garage. But surprisingly, eBay sellers hawk many BRAND NEW items . . . including cribs. At last glance, we noticed over 200 cribs for sale including some steals starting at just $100. So should you buy your crib this way? Before you start bidding, consider these caveats:

◆ *What exactly are you buying?* eBay lets just about any crib be listed online—even those that are clearly "antiques" that don't meet current safety standards. Most of the time, however, the cribs sold are imported from Canada, Asia or Europe. The best eBay sellers identify the brand names in the listings. Other eBay sellers aren't so honest—they list a crib as an "exclusive" with no brand name. If you email them, they might reveal their source . . . odds are it is a Canadian crib that isn't sold here in the U.S. Or a crib imported from Asia. A key question: is the crib JPMA-certified? At least then you know the crib will meet a certain level of safety. While all cribs sold in the U.S. must by law meet federal safety standards, eBay is like the Wild West of Baby Products . . . it's hard to say whether some of those obscure cribs really meet the standards or not. A word to the wise: make sure the crib is BRAND NEW in a box and meets safety standards.

◆ *Beware shipping charges—and damage!* As we have discussed earlier in this chapter, very few retailers attempt to sell cribs online or via catalogs. The expense of shipping a crib that can weigh 100 pounds or more is simply prohibitive. Of course, that doesn't keep eBay sellers from trying—you will have to pay a hefty shipping charge ($50 to $100) on top of some sales and that can turn a bargain into a bad deal. And let's not forget about damage. Shipping anything this heavy is risky—if not packed correctly, a crib can be easily damaged in transport. Make sure the item is insured. And check the seller's track record to see if others have complained about shipping damage.

◆ *Is the crib really new?* Some eBay items are returned stock, discontinued items or worse. Most honest sellers will report damage—but if a crib has been sitting in a hot warehouse somewhere for the last five years, we'd pass.

So, let's review. If you find a crib on eBay, consider bidding IF: the crib is brand new, a name brand that is JPMA certified or reviewed in this book, has no damage, reasonable shipping and the seller has a good standing on eBay for taking care of problems like shipping damage. As always, compare prices in a local store and factor in shipping/insurance before bidding.

niture that was made in the USA, you didn't have to look far. There were probably a dozen or more domestic nursery furniture companies sold in stores as recently as the 1990's. But that was then and now, with the glut of imported furniture from Asia, domestic furniture makers are few and far between. Among the few survivors is Pacific Rim Woodworking, an Oregon-based company that still makes cribs, dressers and twin beds in the U.S. The look here is clean and contemporary. The "Arts & Crafts" crib (pictured above) is made from solid maple (as are all Pacific Rim's pieces) and has a single drop side with spring mattress platform. The price? About $600. No, not a tremendous bargain, but we liked the quality here: all Pacific Rim's dressers are hard wood (no veneers) and other little details are similarly impressive. We wish the crib hardware was hidden (at this price point, you'd expect that), but environmentally-inclined parents will probably be more impressed by Pacific Rim's commitment to use "green certified" lumber. That probably explains why we occasionally see Pacific Rim's cribs sold in eco-catalogs. The company has only about 50 retail dealers nationwide, so if you want to take a peek at their offerings, you may have to do a bit of searching. Bottom line: this is a good option if you want a domestically-made crib and nursery furniture. The plain maple finish and look won't appeal to everyone, but we give Pacific Rim a thumbs up. ***Rating: B***

Pali *For a dealer near you, call (877) 725-4772. Web: paliitaly.com* Italian furniture maker Pali had its ups and downs over the last few years, but the company still makes great cribs. Yes, Pali can still get behind in production (requiring customers to cool their heels for up to 12 weeks for certain crib styles). But the cribs are among the best on the market—all feature knee push rail releases with hidden hardware and solid beech wood construction. Pali's mattress platform is a series of wood slats, a switch from the spring mattresses of the past (we suspect the rising cost of steel has something to do with the switch—nonetheless, we think Pali's mattress support is good quality). Most Pali cribs are in the $400 to $600 range, although one model even tops $800. New this year is a fancy Jenny Lind style crib with a funky, antiqued finish for $480 (sold at Buy Buy Baby). A specialty store version of the Jenny Lind Pali crib is about $600. Also new: Pali will import a line of pine cribs and dresses that are made in Brazil. Brazilian cribs will sell for $480, a dresser $500 to $550 and an armoire for $700. This marks a big change for Pali, which for years has stuck with its Italian-made cribs (the dressers have been made in Canada among other countries).

Another major change at Pali: the company will debut a warehouse and distribution center in Montreal. This should dramatically improve the delivery times for cribs and Pali's other furniture, which in past years could stretch out for months. FYI: you won't find Pali sold online or in chain stores; it's only at specialty stores. The only exceptions: the Buy Buy Baby chain and one web site (Cloud9web.com). One note of caution: beware of Pali's assembly instructions, which are apparently written in 16th century Latin. Our advice: have the store assemble the crib for you. ***Rating: A-***

Pamela Scurry *See Bassett.*

Petite Cheris *For a dealer near you, call 800-363-9817 or 450-772-2403. Web: dutailier.com or egfurniture.com* Petite Cheris is the new brand name for Dutailier's furniture offerings. A brief bit of history: Dutailier started as a glider rocker company (see info later in this chapter). In 2004, Dutailier purchased Canadian crib maker EG and re-branded the new combined furniture line aimed at specialty stores as "Petite Cheris." (Dutailier still sells its goods in chain stores under the Dutailier name). Dutailier plans to phase out the EG name, but at press time, we noticed the EG web site is still up and the company hasn't added furniture to its main site. While EG's cribs and dressers were made in Canada, we should point out that the Petite Cheris line now features imports from China and Romania. A sample convertible crib we checked out was $600 to $650—nicely styled, but pricey. Petite Cheris now has 17 case good collections that are available in 28 colors. It's hard to get a quality read on this line—as Petite Cheris phases out the Canadian made items and imports more goods, we're a bit leery about giving this line a recommendation until we see more of a track record when it comes to deliveries and customer service. So, while we like the coordinated looks with Dutailier's glider rockers, we give Petite Cheris an average rating. ***Rating: C+***

PJ Kids *This company went out of business in 2005. We have an archived review of PJ Kids on our web site (click on Bonus Material) in case you discover some of their furniture for sale second-hand.*

Pottery Barn Kids *(800) 430-7373 or www.potterybarnkids.com.* PBK has been a trend-setter over the last few years, combining classic looking furniture with their own bright bedding and accessories . . . many other retailers have copied the PBK look, so something must be clicking here. Yet, we remain unimpressed with the high prices—most PBK cribs are $500 to $700. Imported from Asia as their own private label, PBK's cribs are good quality, have hidden hardware and knee-push releases . . . but you can find the same looks/quality elsewhere for $200 to $300 less. And watch out for the shipping charges Pottery Barn slaps on their cribs—as much as $100 or more, on top of the already high prices. Bottom line: use this catalog for décor items like bedding or lamps and order the furniture elsewhere. **Rating (crib quality only): A-**

Ragazzi 8965 Pascal Gagnon, St. Leonard, Quebec H1P 1Z4. Call (514) 324-7886 for a dealer near you. Web: www.ragazzi.com Ragazzi is like the Lexus of the nursery furniture market—expensive, stylish, exclusive, and, did we mention expensive? Sold only in 150 specialty stores nationwide, Ragazzi is the French-Canadian crib maker known for its adult styling, multiple finish choices (two dozen at last count) and excellent quality. Founded by the son of an Italian carpenter, Ragazzi started out in 1972 making TV consoles (of all things), then segued into cribs and juvenile furniture in 1991. Retailers love Ragazzi's snappy delivery and customer service, among the more reliable in the biz. Yet like other Canadian crib makers, Ragazzi has been bruised by the weak economy and increased competition from Asian imports in recent years. To address today's more price-sensitive market, Ragazzi will break with tradition and import a new line from Chile this year, dubbed Bambino. We saw the new furniture at a trade show recently and thought it was competitively priced (a three drawer Bambino chest in pine is $550; the same look in Ragazzi is more like $800 and up). Yes, the Bambino finishes will be more limited (five at last count), but at least Ragazzi is attempting to hit a lower price point. Since Bambino is so new, we don't have much feedback on their deliveries and quality. As for Ragazzi, parents we've interviewed are generally happy . . . and they better be for these prices! A simple Ragazzi crib can run $600 to $700—add in a dresser and changing table and some parents spend $2000 or more on their Ragazzi nurseries. Ragazzi's rail release is among the quietest on the market and the dressers feature dovetailed drawers. The only gripe we hear about Ragazzi is their "distressed" finishes—we've had several parents complain the stain wasn't evenly applied on some pieces, creating a sloppy look. That was the exception to the rule, however. Overall, we will give Ragazzi a slightly higher rating this time out. We still think other brands like Pali and Sorelle offer better value (and some say Bellini with its stores has better service), but Ragazzi is closing the gap. **Rating: B+**

Relics Furniture 607 Washington Ave N, Minneapolis, MN 55401. For a dealer near you, call 612-374-0861. Web site: www.relicsfurniture.com. Minneapolis furniture maker Relics specializes in antique looking furniture that has been "distressed" for a retro feel. Relics cribs are actually made by another company that specializes in commercial cribs; Relics finishes and distresses the cribs to fit their collection. While styles are limited, Relics does offer ten color options, including a "fire truck" red and an ivory "French cream." Matching case goods, including a changer are also available. Quality is OK. While we loved the look, the prices are going to limit Relic's appeal—a crib with hidden hardware and knee-push drop side is $789. A spindle crib with exposed hardware and foot bar release is $649. The changer with three drawers is $1325. If you're going to drop that much money, we'd go for one of their funky finishes. You can find a white or ivory crib for much less elsewhere. ***Rating: B***

Sauder *Web: www.sauder.com.* We mentioned this brand of RTA (ready-to-assemble) furniture in our *Toddler Bargains* book as an inexpensive option for dressers and wanted to include a quick mention here. Some readers were surprised that we'd recommend Sauder, given their past reputation for cheap, particle board/laminate offerings that were poor quality and prone to damage. But they've improved the line lately and we do recommend you consider it as an option, especially if you are a do-it-yourselfer who wants to finish the furniture (Sauder offers both finished and unfinished options). Yes, you do have to assemble the furniture and that can be a hassle. But the prices are amazing—you'll see Sauder at Wal-Mart, Lowe's and other stores. We're talking (at Wal-Mart) a hi-low combo dresser for $198, five-drawer chest for $169 and armoire for $165. For unfinished options, Lowe's offers a four-drawer chest for just $122. If you go this route, be sure to get the ALL WOOD Sauder furniture (the Sand Castle for Kids collection at Wal-Mart is an example). And see it before you buy to make sure it is what you expect. ***Rating: A-***

Simmons *Web: www.simmonsjp.com.* Here's a sad story about the fall of an American company. Simmons Juvenile was once one of the country's biggest nursery furniture makers, selling cribs and dressers to many generations of parents. Started in 1917 by Thomas Alva Edison to provide wooden cabinets for one of his recent inventions (the phonograph), Simmons morphed into a furniture company that also made mattresses. The company spun off its juvenile division in the 1980's (just to confuse you, there is still a Simmons company that makes mattresses). Then the company began its slow decline. Simmons made a couple major mistakes, chief among them a decision in the 1990's to concentrate on selling its furniture in chain stores (forsaking the independent stores that built its business over the decades). Yet the company never adapted to the changing nursery furniture market, which soon became flooded with low-cost imports from Asia. Simmons stuck to making its cribs and dressers in plants in Wisconsin and Canada.

By 2004, the company's deteriorating fortunes prompted the management to sell their crib mattress biz back to Simmons and then shutter the Wisconsin plant. Simmons sold the rights to their name to Delta, which plans to market Simmons as a separate division aimed at specialty stores. Ironic, no? We saw Delta's first Simmons collections at a trade show and were not impressed—$800 for a beech crib with burl wood inserts at the headboard? Another collection featured a $700 crib and dresser. All the furniture is imported from China. So the jury is out on the new Simmons. Will Delta be able to pull off a better-quality furniture line in a crowded specialty store market? One thing is for sure: watch Delta slap the Simmons name on a wide variety of low-price baby gear, from strollers to high chairs. FYI: Delta plans to extend the Simmons brand to strollers, high chairs and play yards, as well as other baby products. **Rating: C**

Simplicity (800) 448-4308. Web: www.simplicityforchildren.com This Pennsylvania-based crib importer seemingly came out of nowhere in the past year to be a major player in the low-end crib biz. Yes, they have been around since the 80's, but now they've traded a low profile of importing private label cribs for other companies like Graco for a more visible brand under the name Simplicity. You'll see Simplicity in chains like Target, Wal-Mart and Baby Depot. All the cribs are imported from China and Indonesia. Simplicity sells both wood and metal cribs, as well as bassinets, dressers, changing tables and other baby gear (such as swings, bed rails and gates). A typical offering: in Wal-Mart a wood Simplicity crib runs $129 and features an under crib drawer and mattress spring support platform. Other Simplicity models run $200 to $300. We found the quality of the cribs to be good, although the features are all over the board—some cribs have hidden hardware; others are exposed. Most styles come with drawers but the lack of a spring mattress support in some models is disappointing. And while we liked the cribs, the case pieces are "RTA"—ready to assemble and not as impressive quality-wise. A 2005 safety recall involving a crib that was a suffocation risk was also troubling. **Rating: B**

Sorelle 46 Whelan Rd, East Rutherfod, NJ 07073. Call 201) 531-1919. Web: www.sorellefurniture.com for a dealer near you. Sorelle is the main brand for C&T, an importer that has been in the market since 1977 (FYI: Sorelle cribs are sold under the name Golden Baby or C&T at Babies R Us and Baby Depot). Sorelle started out as an Italian importer, but in recent years, the company has begun importing cribs from Brazil and Latvia (in addition to Italy). Case pieces are made in all those locales, as well as Canada. A good example of the line: the popular Rita crib sold at Baby Depot for $200—that's a great value for a birch crib with hidden hardware, knee push rail release and under crib drawer. Other Sorelle models run $250 to $400, which is competitive. We should note that Sorelle now uses a wood slat mattress support on some models—yes we prefer spring platforms, but Sorelle's wood support is an acceptable alternative. All in all, we think Sorelle's cribs are excellent and the value is hard to beat. The negative? Sorelle has struggled to ship goods on time, forcing some parents to wait ten to 16 weeks for special orders. A warehouse move in 2004 exacerbated that problem, but shipments are back to normal as we go to press. Another caveat: while we like Sorelle's quality, we have seen an increasing number of complaints about Sorelle's service (or lack thereof) in recent months. Consumers complained to us about the difficulty of getting parts shipped and other service snafus. As a result, we've dropped Sorelle's rating by a half grade. Some of these glitches may be growing pains, but we have high expectations for top-rated crib companies in this book . . . and Sorelle missed the mark in the past year. *Rating: B+*

Stanley/Young America Call 888-839-6822 for a dealer near you. Web: www.stanleyfurniture.com Here's a trend in the baby biz: adult furniture makers extending their lines into the nursery. Witness Stanley, the big furniture company and its new Young America Baby collection. This line debuted in 2003 and now features a dozen styles with sculpted headboards and other high-end details. In our last report, we complained about Stanley's prices (initially, cribs were priced at $700 or so). There is good news to report on that front: Stanley has dropped their prices this year, with cribs ranging from $500 to $600. Yeah, that's still pricey but now at least Stanley is in the ballpark. And the quality of this line makes it worth a look-see—we liked the thoughtful design touches like a full bed that can be adjusted in height to allow for under-bed storage drawers. You'll find dove-tail construction with the dressers, anti-tipping restraints on most pieces and more. The cribs have hidden hardware, solid construction with two dowels for stability and spring mattress platforms. All in all, Stanley has both standard cribs (seven styles in 12 finishes) and convertible options (four styles in 17 finishes). You'll find this brand in regular furniture stores. Bottom line: it is pricey but the quality may make it worth the investment. *Rating: B+*

Status This Canadian crib maker folded in 2003.

Stokke/Sleepi Call (877) 978-6553 for a dealer near you. Web: www. stokkeusa.com. This Norwegian company (produced stoke-ah) debuted in the U.S. with their KinderZeat toddler chair (reviewed in *Toddler Bargains*). Their latest import: the Sleepi crib "system" that morphs from a bassinet to a crib, then a toddler bed and finally two chairs. Its compact, rounded shape is very European, as is the price: about $700 to $800 if you want the full conversion (that price includes a mattress). A separate changing table (the Care) converts to a play table and desk for $400. As with all these funky European products, you'll have to buy specially made bedding with limited choices ($20 for a sheet; $250 to $350 for a set). This is a niche product that appeals to urban parents who have little room in their apartments (the crib is smaller than traditional cribs and can fit through a standard door-way); beyond that, we can't see a mass audience for the Sleepi crib at these prices. On the plus side, the few parents who have purchased it tell us they love it. *Rating: B-*

Sleepi™

From Bassinet...

To Sleepi Crib...

To Toddler Bed...

To Junior Bed...

To Two Sleepi Chairs

Storkcraft *11511 No. 5 Road, Richmond, British Columbia, Canada, V7A4E8. For a dealer near you, call (604) 274-5121. Web: www.storkcraft.com* Unlike other Canadian crib makers that concentrate on the upper-end markets, Storkcraft's cribs are priced for the rest of us. Most are in the $150 to $250 range (although a few reach $400) and are sold in such places as Babies R Us and other chain stores. Manufactured in Mississauga, Ontario (just outside Toronto), Storkcraft has three collections. The entry-level "Fisher Price" brand cribs sell for $130 to $200 and feature very simple styling, painted MDF construction (not solid wood) and wood mattress platforms (no springs). The middle-price cribs (Cribs Collection, $100 to $250) feature mixed species of wood and a bit more fancy styling (as well as spring mattress platforms). The top-end "Stages" cribs are convertible models ($200 to $400), most of which feature stationary side rails. All Storkcraft cribs with moveable rails now feature knee-push rail release (gone are the foot-bar rail releases). The hardware on Storkcraft is exposed, which is a bit behind the times. FYI: These cribs are sold at Wal-Mart, K-Mart, JCPenney and USA Baby in the U.S. (in Canada, you can find them in Sears, the Bay, Wal-Mart and Zellers). *Rating: B*

Today's Baby *This crib brand is reviewed on our free web site, BabyBargains.com (click on Bonus Material).*

Vermont Precision *249 Professional Dr., Morrisville, VT 05454. For a dealer near you, call (802) 888-7974. Web: www.vtprecision.com* This children's furniture veteran launched a crib line in 1998, winning kudos from our readers. Their handcrafted cribs boast solid wood (maple) construction that exceeds Pali and Ragazzi in quality and stability, according to recent customers we've interviewed. The cribs use the knee-push rail release and all the hardware is concealed. But the prices are steep: a crib from Vermont Precision will set you back $500 to $750. A combo maple and cherry crib this year nears $800. That's a bit steep, considering the competition. And all the cribs are only single-drop sides. But this is really an heirloom-quality piece of furniture, so some readers have felt the high price was worth it. Vermont Precision has limited distribution (about 30 stores nationwide), so it may take searching if you want to check them out. Finally, we should note that Vermont Precision had a recall in 2002 for about 1000 cribs for defective side rail slats. Vermont Precision said they made changes to their production process to fix this problem, but we were a bit disappointed that a $700 crib would have this problem. **Rating: B-**

Vox *This crib brand from Poland is reviewed on our free web site, BabyBargains.com (click on Bonus Material).*

Westwood Design *For a dealer near you, call 908-719-4707. Web: www.westwoodbaby.com* New kid on the block Westwood Design was started in 2005 by several veteran nursery furniture executives who partnered with an adult furniture company for distribution expertise. The result is Westwood, a company that imports all its designs from China, Vietnam and Thailand. All the cribs are static (no moveable drop sides) and will retail for $420 to $600. The dressers are made of pine, Italian beech and Asian hardwoods and veneers—a pine six drawer would retail for about $450 to $500. As you can see from the prices, Westwood is positioning itself to compete with the likes of Munire, Pali and Sorelle . . . the question is, will the quality match up with the price? Design-wise, Westwood is going for a more traditional look—not as fancy as Munire or over the top as ducduc. We did like the samples we saw at a recent trade show, which featured thoughtful design points like dressers that had adjustable heights. Yet the company is still in the formative stages as we go to press—we haven't heard any reports from retailers or parents who've actually purchased the line yet. So we'll take a wait and see approach with this line until we get a better picture of their track record. **Not rated yet.**

Brand Recommendations: Our Picks

Good. On a tight budget? A basic single drop-side crib like the Storkcraft "Sandra" sold online for $100 at Walmart.com is a good bet. Another model we like: Child Craft's 10171 (see picture) is sold on Target.com for $199. Again, nothing fancy, but it will do the trick!

Better. Want to step up a bit in style? Consider an Italian import from Pali or Sorelle (which also imports cribs from Brazil). Each features all beech wood construction and hidden hardware rail releases that are a bit quieter than domestic makers. A basic Sorelle crib (also sold under the name Golden Baby or C&T) is about $200 to $400 and is sold at chain stores like Babies R Us. Pictured is the Sorelle Nina crib ($280). A step-up in price and style is Pali ($400 to $500 for an entry-level model), which is only sold at specialty stores.

Best. The choices here are mind-boggling . . . you have your pick of over a dozen brands. Who's got the very best quality? Munire, Ragazzi and Bellini would be the top picks, followed closely by Natart, Pali and Legacy. The advantage to Bellini would be their own stores, which may be convenient if you have one near by. If not, a good specialty store will most likely carry Munire, Ragazzi or Pali. Hard to go wrong with any of these.

A convertible crib is more expensive to start, but you actually get two products—a crib that later converts to a full-size bed. Baby's Dream probably has among the best selection in this category, but most of the top brands now carry convertible models. These models will set you back $400 to $600, depending on the finish. Pictured above is the Infinity collection from Baby's Dream, both as a crib and then converted to a bed.

Grandma's house. If you need a secondary crib for Grandma's house, consider a foldaway crib from Delta for $100 (pictured). Or Delta's simple Jenny Lind style for $110 can be assembled without any tools.

CRIB RATINGS

NAME	RATING	COST	WHERE MADE?
ALTA BABY	B-	$$$	ITALY
ANGEL LINE	B-	$ TO $$	TAIWAN
A.P. INDUSTRIES	B+	$$$	CANADA
BABY'S DREAM	A	$$ TO $$$	CHILE/USA
BASSETT	B+	$$	ASIA/USA
BELLINI	B-	$$$	ITALY
BERG	A-	$$ TO $$$	RUSSIA/USA
BONAVITA/BABI ITALIA	B	$$ TO $$$	ITALY/ASIA
BRATT DECOR	B	$$$	ASIA
CARA MIA	B-	$ TO $$$	SLOVENIA
CHANDERIC	B+	$$$	CROATIA
CHILD CRAFT	A	$$ TO $$$	ASIA/USA
CORSICAN KIDS	C+	$$$	USA
COSCO	F	$	ASIA
DELTA	B-	$ TO $$	ASIA
DOMUSINDO	C-	$$	ASIA
DUCDUC	B	$$$	ASIA
EVENFLO	C	$	ASIA
JARDINE	B+ (CRIBS)	$$ TO $$$	ASIA
LUNA	B	$$$	CANADA
MILLION $ BABY	C+	$ TO $$$	ASIA/USA
MORIGEAU/LEPINE	B+	$$$	CANADA
MOTHER HUBBARD	A	$$$	BULGARIA
MUNIRE	A	$$$	USA/MEXICO/BRAZIL
NATART	A-	$$$	CANADA
PACIFIC RIM	B	$$$	USA
PALI	A-	$$$	ITALY
PETITE CHERIS	C+	$$$	ASIA
RAGAZZI	B+	$$$	CANADA/CHILE
SIMMONS	C	$$ TO $$$	ASIA
SIMPLICITY	B	$ TO $$	ASIA
SORELLE	B+	$$ TO $$$	ITALY/BRAZIL/LATVIA
STANLEY	B+	$$$	USA
STOKKE/SLEEPI	B-	$$$	NORWAY
STORKCRAFT	B-	$ TO $$	CANADA
VERMONT PRECISION	B-	$$$	USA

RATING: Our opinion of the manufacturer's quality and value.

COST: $=under $200, $$=$200-400, $$$=over $400.

WHERE MADE? Where the cribs parts are made; in many cases, final assembly may be in the U.S. In those cases, we note the country of origin as "Asia/USA."

RELEASE: How does the crib drop-side release? For a discussion of the different releases, see the section earlier in this chapter. Note that the release type may vary by model within the same manufacturer's line.

HARDWARE: This refers to the hardware that operates the crib drop-side,

A quick look at some top crib brands:

RELEASE	HARDWARE	STABILITY	WARRANTY
KNEE-PUSH	HIDDEN	EXCELLENT	25 YEARS
FOOT-BAR**	EXPOSED	AVERAGE	6 MONTHS
KNEE-PUSH	HIDDEN	EXCELLENT	1 YEAR
FOLD-DOWN/KNEE PUSH	HIDDEN	EXCELLENT	1 YEAR
FOOT-BAR/KNEE-PUSH	EXPOSED	AVERAGE	1 YEAR
KNEE-PUSH	HIDDEN	EXCELLENT	NONE
KNEE-PUSH	HIDDEN	GOOD	1 YEAR
KNEE-PUSH	HIDDEN	EXCELLENT	1 YEAR
FOOT-BAR/KNEE-PUSH	VARIES	GOOD	2 YEARS
KNEE-PUSH	VARIES	AVERAGE	1 YEAR
KNEE-PUSH	HIDDEN	EXCELLENT	1 YEAR
KNEE-PUSH	EXPOSED	EXCELLENT	15 YEARS
FOOT-BAR	EXPOSED	AVERAGE	1 YEAR
KNEE-PUSH	EXPOSED	AVERAGE	1 YEAR
KNEE-PUSH	EXPOSED	AVERAGE	1 YEAR
KNEE-PUSH	HIDDEN	GOOD	5 YEARS
FOOT-BAR/DOUBLE TRIGGER	EXPOSED	AVERAGE	N/A
KNEE-PUSH	EXPOSED	GOOD	N/A
KNEE-PUSH	EXPOSED	GOOD	5 YEARS
KNEE-PUSH	VARIES	AVERAGE	1 YEAR
KNEE-PUSH	HIDDEN	EXCELLENT	1 YEAR
KNEE-PUSH	HIDDEN	EXCELLENT	1 YEAR
KNEE-PUSH	HIDDEN	EXCELLENT	1 YEAR
KNEE-PUSH	HIDDEN	EXCELLENT	1 YEAR
KNEE-PUSH	EXPOSED	EXCELLENT	N/A
KNEE-PUSH	HIDDEN	EXCELLENT	1 YEAR
KNEE-PUSH	HIDDEN	EXCELLENT	1 YEAR
KNEE-PUSH	HIDDEN	EXCELLENT	15 YEARS
KNEE-PUSH	HIDDEN	GOOD	1 YEAR
KNEE-PUSH	VARIES	AVERAGE	5 YEARS
KNEE-PUSH	HIDDEN	EXCELLENT	1 YEAR
KNEE-PUSH	HIDDEN	EXCELLENT	1 YEAR
SWING GATE	HIDDEN	GOOD	90 DAYS
KNEE-PUSH	EXPOSED	AVERAGE	N/A
KNEE-PUSH	HIDDEN	EXCELLENT	1 YEAR

whether it is concealed or exposed.

STABILITY: Our opinion of a crib's stability based on hands-on inspection. "Average" is an acceptable rating; "good" is better and "excellent" is tops.

WARRANTY: Some companies don't have written warranties. Several crib makers told us they "stand behind their cribs and will replace parts if they break," but that's not in writing and there are no time guidelines. Our position: if it isn't in writing, there is no warranty.

While most of Baby's Dream models have a fold-down rail release, a few have the knee-push drop-sides.

Do it by Mail: Mail-Order
Sources for Cribs and Baby Furniture

JCPenney

To order call: (800) 222-6161
Web: www.jcpenney.com

JCPenney has been selling baby clothes, furniture, and more for over 90 years. Their popular mail-order catalog and web site has a plethora of nursery furniture offerings.

Last we looked, Penney offered over 30 styles of cribs, most with matching dressers and other accessories. Prices start at $169 for a basic crib, but most styles are $200 to $400 with some convertible models hitting the $500 price point.

Penney's web site is easy enough to use (click on a crib and you'll see matching accessories), but there are a few frustrations. It would be great to sort the results by price or best sellers—instead you can just look by category or brand. Speaking of brands, most Penney's cribs are made by Dorel/Cosco, Storkcraft or their own private label (Bright Future, Domusindo). Frustratingly, Penney's often omits the manufacturer name, so you don't quite know what you are buying (calling won't help, as the phone reps don't know either).

So, what is the quality of Penney's furniture? Penney's has an excellent safety track record for their in-house cribs and nursery furniture. Penneys sends inspectors into its Asian plants to make sure everything is up to spec. Overall, parents we interviewed were pleased with the quality and durability of Penney's nursery offerings.

While Penney's catalog is a good place to start researching juvenile furniture, actually ordering from the catalog can be an exercise in frustration. First, consider Penney's customer service. Don't ask any detailed questions of the reps—all the info they have is the same that is in the catalog or web site. For additional details, Penney's customer service reps must email their warehouse and then they'll call you back . . . within three weeks! Whoa, that's fast.

Then, let's talk about ordering. Talk with three different reps and you'll get three different shipping quotes. Once you place the order, Penney's may change the shipping fee; if so, they'll call you. Finally, consider how long it takes to get most items—Penney's can take six weeks or more to ship some items.

As we noted in the crib brand reviews above, we've received a steady stream of complaints about Penney's in the past year—late deliveries, back order snafus and customer service headaches. As a result, we urge ordering from Penney's as a last resort. If you live in a remote area of the U.S. with no baby stores within 100 miles, this might be your only option. Otherwise, we'd skip Penney's.

POTTERY BARN KIDS

To order call: (800) 430-7373.
Web: www.potterybarnkids.com

You've got to give Pottery Barn credit for their excellent kid's catalog—it's rare that one catalog can actually influence an entire industry. But that's exactly what happened when this smartly designed book landed in parents' mailboxes in 1998—the "Pottery Barn" look suddenly spread from mail order to baby stores and beyond. Even Penney's has been trying to make their baby catalog more hip in response to PBK.

So, what's all the fuss about? PBK smartly mixes stylish looks (patchwork quilts; denim accents) with upscale furniture and accessories to create contemporary layouts that don't scream "baby." The best bets: those cute rugs, lamps and other accessories. And we generally found the bedding to be high quality (see review in the next chapter). But what about the furniture? Grossly overpriced, we're sad to say. What are these guys thinking? A sleigh crib for $800? Plus $100 shipping? The huge mark-ups on these items are obscene. Our advice: go to a specialty store or chain like Babies R Us and buy the same furniture at 30% to 40% less.

One little trick to getting a deal at Pottery Barn: their regular stores sometimes sell the same stuff you see at Pottery Barn Kids stores, but at lower prices. A reader who fell in love with a $50 laundry hamper in the kid's catalog was surprised to see the same hamper in a natural finish in Pottery Barn's regular store. Price? $27.49 on sale. Sometimes we wonder if you slap the word "baby" on an item, the price doubles.

So, it's a mixed review for PBK—love the look, but the furniture is a no go. Use this catalog as design inspiration for your nursery, even if you decided to buy items elsewhere. And we wish PBK didn't have to be so secretive as to who makes their cribs—we noticed the catalog omits any details on this and operators refuse to say when asked.

Bassinets/Cradles

A newborn infant can immediately sleep in a full size crib, but some parents like the convenience of bassinets or cradles to use for the first few weeks. Why? These smaller baby beds can be kept in the parents' bedroom, making for convenient midnight feedings.

What's the difference between a bassinet and a cradle? Although most stores use the terms interchangeably, we think of bassinets as small baskets that are typically put onto a stationery stand (pictured at top right). Cradles, on the other hand, are usually made of wood and rock back and forth.

A third option in this category is "Moses baskets," basically woven baskets (bottom right) with handles that you can use to carry a newborn from room to room. (A web site with a good selection of Moses baskets is Babies Boutique, www.babiesboutique.com).

As for prices, we noticed a Badger Basket bassinet (a rather common brand, www.badgerbasket.com) runs about $40 at chain stores like Target, but that price doesn't include the "soft goods" (sheets, liners, skirts and hoods). Models that include soft goods typically run closer to $90 and up to $180.

Cradles, on the other hand, run about $100 to $400 but don't need that many soft goods (just a mattress, which is usually included, and a sheet, which is not). Moses baskets run $100 to $250.

So, which should you buy? We say none of the above. As we mentioned at the beginning of this section, a newborn will do just fine in a full-size crib. If you need the convenience of a bassinet, we'd suggest skipping the ones you see in chain stores. Why? Most are very poorly made (stapled together cardboard sheets, etc) and won't last for more than one child. One reader said the sheets with her chain store-bought bassinet "were falling apart at the seams even before it went into the wash" for the first time. And the function of these products is somewhat questionable. For example, the functionality of a Moses basket, while pretty to look at, can be easily duplicated by an infant car seat carrier, which most folks buy anyway.

Instead, we suggest you borrow a bassinet or cradle from a friend. . . or buy a portable playpen with a bassinet feature. We'll review specific models of playpens in Chapter 7, but basic choices like the Graco Pak 'N Play run $60 to $200 in most stores. The bassinet feature in most playpens (basically, an insert that creates a small bed area at the top of the playpen) can be used up to 15 pounds, which is about all most folks would need. Then, you simply remove the bassinet attachment and voila! You have a standard size playpen. Since many parents get a playpen anyway, going for a model that has a bassinet attachment doesn't add much to the cost and eliminates the separate $100 to $200 expense of a bassinet. (See the next chapter for a discussion of bassinet sheets).

Another way to save: check out second-hand stores and garage sales. Just make sure the bassinet or cradle is in good repair and not missing any pieces. Most parents use these items for such a short period of time that there is little wear and tear.

Of course, you can also go for the Arm's Reach Co-Sleeper (reviewed earlier) as an alternative to the bassinet as well.

Mattresses

Now that you've just spent several hundred dollars on a crib, you're done, right? Wrong. Despite their hefty price tags, most cribs don't come with mattresses. So, here's our guide to buying the best quality mattress for the lowest price.

Safe & Sound

Babies don't have the muscle strength to lift their heads up when put face down into soft or fluffy bedding—some have suffocated as a result. The best defense: buy a firm mattress and DO NOT place your baby face down in soft, thick quilts, wool blankets, pillows, or toys. (Futon mattresses are also a no-no). Never put the baby down on a vinyl mattress without a cover or sheet since vinyl can also contribute to suffocation. In addition, you should know that several studies into the causes of Sudden Infant Death Syndrome (SIDS) have found that a too-soft sleep surface (such as the items listed above) and environmental factors (a too-hot room, cigarette smoke) are related to crib death, though exactly how has yet to be determined. Experts therefore advise against letting infants sleep on a too-soft surface. Another important tip: make sure you put your baby to sleep on her back. See the box on the next page for more tips on preventing SIDS.

Another point to remember: while mattresses come in a standard size for a full-size crib, the depth can vary from maker to maker. Some mattresses are just four inches deep; others are six. Some crib sheets won't fit the six-inch thick mattresses; it's unsafe to use a sheet that doesn't snugly fit OVER the corner of a mattress and tuck beneath it.

Mattresses should fit your crib snugly with no more than two finger's width between the mattress and all sides of the crib. Since most cribs and mattresses are made to a standard size, this is usually not a major problem. However, we occasionally hear about imported, obscure-brand cribs that are too large or too small for a standard American-size crib mattress. In that case, you may need to either return the crib or get a specialized mattress from the manufacturer that fits the crib correctly.

Smart Shopper Tips

Smart Shopper Tip #1
Foam or Coil?
"It seems the choice for a crib mattress comes down to foam or coil? Which is better? Does it matter?"

Yes, it does matter. After researching this issue, we've come down on the foam side of the debate. Why? Foam mattresses are lighter than those with coils, making it easier to change the sheets

8 tips to lower the risk of SIDS

Sudden Infant Death Syndrome (SIDS) is the sudden death of an infant under one of year of age due to unexplained causes. Sadly, SIDS is still the number one killer of infants under age one—over 2000 babies die each year.

So, what causes SIDS? Scientists don't know, despite studying the problem for two decades. We do know that SIDS is a threat during the first year of life, with a peak occurrence between one and six months. SIDS also affects more boys than girls; and the SIDS rate in African American babies is twice that of Caucasians. Despite the mystery surrounding SIDS, researchers have discovered several factors that dramatically lower the risk of SIDS. Here is what you can do:

Put your baby to sleep on her back. Infants should be placed on their back (not side or tummy) each time they go to sleep. Since the campaign to get parents to put baby to sleep on their stomachs began in 1992, the SIDS rate has fallen by 50%. That's the good news. The bad news: while parents are heeding this message, other care givers (that is, grandma or day care centers) are less vigilant. Be sure to tell all your baby's caregivers that baby is to sleep on their back, never their tummy.

Encourage tummy time. When awake, baby should spend some time on their tummy. This helps prevent flat heads caused by lying on their backs (positional plagiocephaly). Vary your child's head position while sleeping (such as, turning his head to the right during one nap and then the left during the next nap). Minimize time spent in car seats (unless baby is in a car, of course!), swings, bouncer seats or carriers—any place baby is kept in a semi-upright position. A good goal: no more than an hour or two a day. To learn more about plagiocephaly, go online to www.plagiocephaly.org.

Forget gadgets. Special mattresses, sleep positioners, breathing monitors—none have been able to reduce the risk of SIDS, says the American Academy of Pediatrics. Just put baby to sleep on her back.

Use a pacifier. Consider giving baby a pacifier, which has been

in the middle of the night when Junior reenacts the Great Flood in his crib. Foam mattresses typically weigh less than eight pounds, while coil mattresses can top 20 or 30 pounds! Another plus: foam mattresses are less expensive, usually $100 to $150. Coil mattresses can be pricey, with some models running $200+.

We get quite a few calls from readers on this issue. Many baby stores only sell coil mattresses, claiming that coil is superior to foam. One salesperson even told a parent that foam mattresses aren't safe for babies older than six months! Another salesperson actually told a parent they should expect to replace a foam mattress two to three times during the two years a baby uses a crib. Please! We've

shown in studies to reduce the rate of SIDS. Why? Scientists don't know exactly, but some speculate pacifiers help keep the airway open. Okay, we should acknowledge that pacifiers are controversial—key concerns include breastfeeding interference, tooth development and ear infections. But if you introduce the pacifier after breast-feeding is well-established (around one month), there are few problems. Stop using the pacifier after one year (when the SIDS risk declines) and there are no ill dental effects. While pacifiers do increase the risk of ear infections, ear infections are rare in babies when the risk of SIDS is highest (under six months old). Bottom line: Use pacifiers at the time of sleep starting at one month of life for breastfed babies. If the pacifier falls out once the baby is asleep, don't re-insert it. Stop using pacifier once the risk of SIDS is over (about a year of life).

Don't smoke or overheat the baby's room. Smoking during pregnancy or after the baby is born has shown to increase the risk of SIDS. Keep baby's room at a comfortable temperature, but don't overheat. Use a sleep sack or swaddle baby with a blanket.

Bed sharing: bad. Room sharing: good. Why does bed sharing increase the risk of SIDS? Scientists say the risk of suffocation in adult linens (pillows, etc) or entrapment between bed frame and mattress, or by family members is a major contributor to SIDS. That said, room sharing (that is, having baby in the same room as the parents either in a bassinet or a product like the Arm's Reach Bedside co-sleeper) is shown to reduce the rate of SIDS. Again, researchers don't know exactly why, but it's possible parents are more attuned to their baby's breathing when baby is nearby.

No soft bedding. Baby's crib or bassinet should have a firm mattress and no soft bedding (quilts, pillows, stuffed animals, etc). Bumpers are optional—we will discuss this topic in the next chapter.

Make sure all other caregivers follow these instructions. Again, you might be vigilant about back-sleeping . . . but if another caregiver doesn't follow the rules, your baby could be at risk. Make sure your day care provider, grandma or other caregiver is on board.

consulted with pediatricians and industry experts on this issue and have come to the conclusion that the best course is to choose a *firm* mattress for baby—it doesn't matter whether it's a firm coil mattress or a firm foam one. What about the claim that foam mattresses need to be replaced constantly? In the ten years we've been researching this topic, we've never heard from one parent whose foam mattress had to be replaced!

What's going on here? Many baby stores try to make up for the thin profit margins they make on cribs by pitching parents to buy an ultra-expensive mattress. The latest rage are so-called "2 in 1" mattresses that combine foam *and* coil (foam on one side; coil on the other). These can run $200 or more! While these mattresses are nice, they are totally unnecessary. A $100 foam mattress will do just as well.

So why all the pressure to get the fancy-shmancy double dip mattress? Such mattresses cost stores just $40 at wholesale, yet they sell for $200 or more!

One caveat to foam: In 2005, California passed new flammabil-

Is SIDS linked to second-hand mattresses?

We're big fans of second-hand and hand-me-down products for baby as a money-saver—except when it comes to old cribs and car seats. And based on a new study from Scotland, we're going to add crib mattresses to that list.

According to a study published in the *British Medical Journal* (November 2, 2002), Scottish researchers said "babies who sleep on a second-hand mattress seem to be at a higher risk of sudden infant death syndrome (SIDS)" than those that don't. The lead author of the study, Dr. David Tappin, compared 131 children who died of SIDS between 1996 and 2000 with 278 healthy infants. The babies that died of SIDS were "roughly three times as likely as other children to have regularly slept on a mattress that was previously used by another child," according to a Reuters article on the study. The association was stronger if the mattress was from another home.

So, why might this be the case? Researchers don't know if it is really the mattress that is causing the problem, but some speculate that "toxic bacteria might grow in the mattress after it becomes repeatedly soaked with milk, urine or saliva. Such bacteria might contribute to illness or death of the second child," the article stated.

While more research needs to be done on this issue, we'll come down on the side of safety—use a NEW mattress for your child, not a hand-me-down. And even though the problem seems to be worse with second-hand mattresses from another home, we'd recommend a new mattress for your baby's future siblings as well.

ity rules that essentially outlaw foam crib mattresses (that's because the new standard is so strict, only coil mattresses and perhaps a handful of foam ones could ever pass). Does that mean foam mattresses are dangerous? No, not in our opinion or that of federal safety regulators. Unfortunately, however, the new California rules will spell the end of MOST foam crib mattresses, as many manufacturers will stop selling them. But there is good news: Colgate (see brand recommendations later) has figured out a way to engineer their foam mattresses to meet the new standard and will continue to sell a few foam models (including their top-rated Classica I), albeit at prices about $20 higher than before.

Bottom line: foam mattresses are the best deal, but can be hard to find. As a result, we'll recommend mattresses in both the coil and foam categories just in case the baby stores near you only stock coil.

Smart Shopper Tip #2
Coil Overkill and Cheap Foam Mattresses

"How do you tell a cheap-quality coil mattress from a better one? How about foam mattresses—what makes one better than the next?"

Evaluating different crib mattresses isn't easy. Even the cheap ones claim they are "firm" and comparing apples to apples is difficult. When it comes to coil mattresses, the number of coils seems like a good way to compare them, but even that can be deceiving. For example, is a 150-coil mattress better than an 80-coil mattress?

Well, yes and no. While an 80-coil mattress probably won't be as firm as one with 150 coils, it's important to remember that a large number of coils do not necessarily mean the mattress is superior. Factors such as the wire gauge, number of turns per coil and the temper of the wire contribute to the firmness, durability and strength of the mattress. Unfortunately, most mattresses only note the coil count (and no other details). Hence, the best bet would be to buy a good brand that has a solid quality reputation (we'll recommend specific choices after this section).

What about foam mattresses? The cheapest foam mattresses are made of low-density foam (about .9 pounds per cubic foot). The better foam mattresses are high-density with 1.5 pounds per cubic foot. Easy for us to say, right? Once again, foam mattresses don't list density on their packaging, leaving consumers to wonder whether they're getting high or low density. As with coil mattresses, you have to rely on a reputable brand name to get a good foam mattress (see the next section for more details).

One good, basic test for crib mattress firmness: take the mattress between your two hands and push your hands together. Okay, that sounds silly but you'll notice some differences in firmness right away!

Smart Shopper Tip #3
Flatulent foam mattresses?

"I read on the 'net that some foam mattresses have an out-gassing problem. Is this true?"

We've noticed that several eco-catalogs and web sites have raised concerns that standard crib mattresses are a possible health hazard. One even went on to say that such mattresses are "unhealthy combinations of artificial foams, fluorocarbons, synthetic fibers and formaldehyde, all materials that give off toxic fumes." The solution? Buy *their* organic cotton crib mattress for a whopping $650 and your baby won't have to breathe that nasty stuff.

Hold it. We checked with pediatricians and industry experts and found no evidence that such a problem exists. While it is possible that a foam or coil mattress might give off a few vapors when you first take it out of the packaging, there's no ongoing fume problem in our opinion. There are also no medical studies linking, say, lower SAT scores to kids who slept on foam mattresses as babies. While it is possible that a few children who have extreme chemical sensitivities might do better on "organic" mattresses, it's doubtful such products will make any difference to the vast majority of infants. We think it's irresponsible of such eco-crusaders to raise bogus issues intended to scare parents without providing corresponding proof of their claims.

What about mattresses that are hypoallergenic with special anti-microbial covers? These all-natural, organic mattresses are again pitched to parents as the ultimate safe place for baby to sleep. Even regular "conventional" crib mattress makers are jumping on the bacteria hysteria wagon by coating their mattress covers with Microban and other additives. Yet there are no studies showing these mattresses give babies a better night sleep, stop sicknesses or prevent allergies. If your baby develops severe allergies (which is rare for infants), then we can see a reason for attempting to outfit a nursery with such pricey special products. But for the vast majority of parents, these mattresses are a waste of money.

Here are a few more shopping tips/myths about crib mattresses:

◆ **What's the best way to test a crib mattresses' firmness?** Test the center of the mattress (not the sides or corners)—place the palm of one hand flat on one side of the mattress and then put your other hand on the opposite side. The greater the pressure needed to press your hands together, the more firm the mattress.

◆ **Are all crib mattresses the same size?** No, they can vary a small amount—both in length/width and thickness. Most coil mattresses are 5" to 6" in depth. What's the best thickness? It doesn't matter, but 5″ should be fine. Remember the safest crib mattress is the one that snugly fits your crib—you shouldn't be able to fit more than two fingers between the headboard/side rails and the mattress. A tip: the mattress should be CENTERED on the crib mattress platform, not jammed up to one side or the other!

◆ **All foam mattresses look alike—what separates the better ones from the cheaper options?** Test for firmness (see above). The more firm, the better. Another clue: weight. A slightly heavier foam mattress usually means they used a better-quality foam to make the product. Finally, look at the cover: three layers of laminated/reinforced vinyl are better than a single or double layer. Anti-bacterial covers are also a worthwhile feature. What about quilted covers? They are a waste of money, in our opinion.

E-Mail from The Real World
Colic remedy turns mattress into magic fingers.

Colic, that incessant crying by young infants at night, can drive parents to distraction. A mom in Tennessee writes about one solution she found:

"After several relatively sleepless nights with our two-week old infant, I found a product called the Sleep Tight Infant Soother. This product basically makes sleeping in the crib similar to riding in the car. A vibration device attaches underneath the mattress and you can either get a sound box for the crib, which plays white noise, or get a 90-minute cassette tape. If you opt for the sound box, the price is $129; it is $89 if you go for the cassette tape. The product has a 15-day trial period and can be ordered online at www.colic.com or by calling 1-800-NO COLIC. The FDA has approved it as a medical device so insurance may reimburse the cost."

One caution: a recent study by researchers at the University of California, San Francisco warned against exposing babies to continuous white noise, which may damage the auditory region of the brain. The study, which appeared in an April 2003 issue of the journal Science (www.hhmi.org/news/chang.html), convinced us to recommend AGAINST white noise generators for infants. Hence, you could use the above product just for the vibration and not the sound component.

Top Picks: Brand Recommendations

When it comes to mattresses, it's best not to scrimp. Go for the best mattress you can afford. Besides, the price differences between the cheap products and the better quality ones are often small, about $50 or less.

◆ **Foam Mattresses.** Our top brand recommendation for foam mattresses is **Colgate** (call 404-681-2121 for a dealer near you; web: www.colgatekids.com). This Georgia-based company makes a full line of foam mattresses. Among the best of Colgate's offerings is the "Classica," a group of five-inch foam mattresses with varying firmness. The Classica I was top-rated by *Consumer Reports* and is available in discount stores and mail order catalogs like Baby Catalog of America (1-800-PLAYPEN; web: www.babycatalog.com) for $120. New this year is the Visco-Elastic Classic I, which has memory foam. It runs $160 to $180. Of course, just about any Colgate foam mattress will do the trick; the company has several different models but we found little difference among them.

FYI: Colgate is eliminating their least expensive foam mattresses, which used to start at $50 or so. Why? The new California flammability rules (discussed earlier) have forced the company to re-engineer their mattresses . . . Colgate decided to make that investment on their more expensive foam models.

A final note on Colgate: it can be hard to find a Colgate foam mattress, as the brand is not sold in chain stores. Instead, the company concentrates on independent juvenile retailers—check their web site for the current list of dealers.

◆ **Coil Mattresses.** We liked the **Simmons** Super Maxipedic 160 coil mattress for $100 at Babies R Us as a best buy for the dollar. Also good: **Serta's** Perfect Comfort mattress (117 coils) for $80 (again at Babies R Us). We also liked the Evenflo's "Serta" line, sold at Baby Depot and other stores for $60 to $110.

If you can find the Colgate brand, they too make a decent coil mattress—a 150-coil model is about $100. Another Colgate best buy in the coil mattress category: the Little Aristocrat I for $69.

Yes, most major crib makers also have mattress lines, most notably Child Craft and Pali. Prices typically run $150 to $250. Are they any better than the Sealy or Simmons coil mattresses found in chain stores? No. Save your money and get a basic mattress.

What about those fancy vibrating mattresses? Kolcraft makes a "Tender Vibes" mattress for $130 to $170 that features 150 coils, a vibrating feature and an automatic timer that turns off the vibration after 15 minutes. Is this necessary? Unless you have a history of colic (that never-ending crying that afflicts some babies) in your family, it's overkill. Nothing wrong with it, but save your money and get a regular non-vibrating mattress.

Bottom line: there isn't much difference between coil mattress brands—each does a good job. Stick with the ones at 150 coils (80 is too little; 250 is overkill).

Still can't decide between foam or coil? Well, Colgate has a solution—a "2 in 1" mattress that is half foam and half coil. The company suggests the extra-firm foam side for infants. When your baby reaches toddler hood, you flip the mattress over to the coil side. The price: $140. As we pointed out earlier, the "2 in 1" mattress isn't something we'd recommend (it really isn't necessary), but we realize some parents will consider it.

Dressers & Changing Tables

Now that you've got a place for the baby to sleep (and a mattress for her to sleep on), where are you going to put all those cute outfits that you'll get as gifts from Aunt Bertha? The juvenile trade refers to dressers, changing tables, and the like as "case pieces" since they are essentially furniture made out of a large case (pretty inventive, huh?).

Of course, a dresser is more than just a place to store clothes and supplies. Let's not forget that all too important activity that will occupy so many of your hours after the baby is born: changing diapers. The other day we calculated that by our baby's first birthday, we had changed over 2400 diapers! Wow! To first-time parents, that may seem like an unreal number, but babies actually do go through 70 to 100 diapers a week for the first six months or so. That translates into ten to 15 changes a day. So, where you are going to change all those diapers? Most parents use the dresser top, but we'll also discuss changing tables in this section.

 ### What are You Buying

DRESSERS. As you shop for baby furniture, you'll note a wide variety of dressers—three drawer, four drawer, armoires, combination dresser/changing tables, and more. No matter which type you choose, we do have three general tips for getting the most for your money. First, choose a dresser whose drawers roll glide easily—that's usually because they have two tracks on either side of the drawer. Cheap dressers have drawers that simply sit on a track at the bottom center of the drawer. As a result, they don't roll out as smoothly and are prone to coming off the track.

Our second piece of advice: look at the drawer sides—the best furniture makers use "dove-tailed" drawer joints (they look like interlocking fingers) where the side panel meets the front of the drawer. Cheaper drawers are merely stapled together.

Take a second to look at the dresser . . . do the drawers or doors fit? Or is it askew? It's amazing to see cheap dressers in chain stores whose sloppy construction is obvious.

What about wood substitutes like medium density fiberboard (MDF)? MDF by itself isn't necessarily good or bad. It really depends on the overall construction (drawer glides, joints, etc.), not so much the wood content. Yes, some high-price furniture makers tout their "all wood" construction (where even the sides and backs of the dressers are wood), but that might be overkill. How often will you be looking at the back of your child's dresser anyway? While you should avoid dressers made of cheap laminate, we've seen several good MDF dressers that were impressive.

2 **CHANGING AREA.** Basically, you have two options here. You can buy a separate changing table or a combination dresser/changing table. As mentioned earlier, we think a separate changing table is a waste of money (as well as a waste of space).

A better option is the combo package, a dresser and changing table all rolled into one. These come in two varieties: hi-low (also called combo units; see picture at right) and regular chests with add-on changing areas. Hi-low dressers are a popular option. These dressers (also called "combo" or "castle" units)  were pioneered by Rumble Tuff, reviewed later in this section. The two-tier design of these dressers provides a convenient space to change diapers while not looking like a diaper-changing table. Most parents keep diaper-changing supplies in the upper drawer, while the lower dresser functions as clothing storage, etc. Combo dressers start at $500 and range up to $700. As an option, some manufactures offer a hutch that attaches to a dresser to give you shelf space.

Let's say you're on a really tight budget. What should you do? Forget the diaper changing station altogether! Some mothers we interviewed just change their baby in the crib or on a countertop.

A hip new alternative is the chiffarobe, which is a combination dresser and armoire (that is, a place to hang clothes). In the past year, we noticed more furniture companies rolling out chiffarobes, which are low enough to change a baby on top (you add a changing pad with no skid bottom for $20 and poof! Instant changing area).

Where do you keep the diaper changing supplies? Well, you can use a drawer in the combo or chiffarobe. Or, a rolling storage cart is another solution (cost: about $25 in many catalogs and stores; we saw one for $18 at the Container Store 800-733-3532; web: www.containerstore.com; Sam's Club has a plastic "six drawer mini chest" for $24). One disadvantage to changing baby in the crib: if you have a boy, he could spray the crib sheets, bumper pads, and just about anything else in the crib with his little "water pistol." Hence, you might find yourself doing more laundry. If you have back problems, leaning over into the crib to change a diaper may also be uncomfortable.

One mom sent us an e-mail with a solution to the changing table dilemma—she bought a "Rail Rider," changing table that fits across a crib and can be removed when the baby is sleeping. For $32, it did the trick. Made by Burlington Basket Company (for a dealer near you, call 800-553-2300 or 319-754-6508) and sold online at BabyCenter.com, the Rail Rider does have a few drawbacks: it doesn't fit all cribs and shorter folks find it more difficult to use.

Safe & Sound

Safety doesn't stop at the crib—also consider the nursery's other furniture items when baby-proofing.

◆ **Anchor those shelves.** A nice bookcase (whether on the floor or on top of the dresser) can become a tip-over hazard as the baby begins pulling up on objects. The best advice is to attach any shelves to a wall to provide stability.

◆ **Baby proof the diaper station.** If your diaper changing area has open shelves, you may have to baby proof the bottom shelves. As the baby begins to climb, you must remove any dangerous medicines or supplies from easily accessible shelves.

◆ **Choose a dresser that doesn't have drawer pulls.** Those little knobs can make it easy for baby to open the drawers—and it's those open drawers that can be used as a step stool to scale the dresser. A good tip is to buy a dresser without drawer pulls; a few styles have drawers with grooves that let you open them from below (Rumble Tuff, for example). While this isn't totally baby proof, it reduces the attraction for baby. Another good tip: anchor the dresser to the wall. In case baby does find a way to climb it, at least the unit won't tip over.

◆ **Air out all that new nursery paint, furniture and decor.** A University of Maryland School of Medicine study suggests new parents should air out freshly painted or wallpapered rooms before baby arrives. New furniture and mattresses also "out-gas" fumes, so consider ventilating the nursery when they arrive as well. How much ventilation? The study suggested four to eight weeks of open window ventilation, which seems a bit excessive to us. But it makes sense to do some air-out of the nursery before baby arrives. Another idea: look for environmentally friendly paints that have lower out-gas emissions. If you install new carpet in the house, leave during the installation and open the windows (and turn on fans) for two days.

◆ **Stay away from wicker.** Sure, those wicker storage baskets and other accessories look nice . . .but watch out. Most wicker is treated with gasoline before it's painted. When the weather warms up, the fumes from wicker furniture can be noticeable. Wicker is great for other parts of the house or an outside deck—but we say skip it for the nursery.

Our Picks: Brand Recommendations

As previously noted in this chapter, many of the crib makers also manufacture "case pieces" (dressers, armoires, etc). For contact information on these brands, refer to the reviews earlier in this chapter. Here's a round up:

Good. The dressers from brands like **Bassett** and **Child Craft** are good entry-level options and widely available in chains like Babies R Us and Baby Depot. A simple four-drawer dresser from Bassett

E-MAIL FROM THE REAL WORLD
Antique bargains

A reader reminds us that antique stores can be great sources for baby furniture.

"You might remind readers not to overlook the local antique store when shopping for nursery furniture. We found a great English dresser from the 1930s with ample drawer and cupboard space for $325 that has a lot more character than anything we've seen in baby stores, plus it can be easily moved to another room/use when our baby outgrows it.""

is $300 to $400; the same item from Child Craft is $400 to $500 (both available at Babies R Us). Hi-low combo dressers are a bit more ($540 to $600) but do offer more flexibility. As for quality, Simmons is probably a notch or two ahead of other brands on the lower-end. The only bummer: most drawers in this price range lack dovetail joints and feature plain styling.

Better. If you're looking for better quality and more style, check out the offerings from brands like **Sorelle** and **Pali**, as well as the Canadian importers **Ragazzi** and **Morigeau**. We thought the dressers imported from Brazil by Sorelle represented decent value and styling a notch above what you find from other brands (note the bun feet on several models). Sorelle's prices are in the $400 to $600 range for case goods . . . step up in price to the $600 and $800 range and you'll find the more adult styling by Pali, Ragazzi and Morigeau. Yea, these dressers cost 30% more than what you see in chain stores, but you are getting much better quality for the dollar.

Best. Our top pick for juvenile furniture is a tie between **Munire** (reviewed earlier) and **Rumble Tuff**. Rumble who?

Rumble Tuff is an small Utah-based company that doesn't even make cribs—they concentrate solely on case pieces (dressers, book-shelves and more). Rumble Tuff (for a dealer near you, call 800-524-9607 or 801-226-2648; web: www.rumbletuff.com) is also a best buy—their prices are often 10% to 25% less than the competition. Their strategy is to knock-off the big guys, making similar furniture styles in the exact same finishes as the crib makers so everything will match. (Well, to be fair, they don't match EVERY last finish offered by crib makers, but darn close).

Rumble Tuff's claim to fame is their popular combo dresser. This unit combines a three-drawer dresser/changing table and a taller base cabinet and drawer. Price: $500 to $600, depending on the finish. These combo units have proven so popular that other furniture makers have knocked them off. In fact, Simmons and Child Craft have tried to match Rumble Tuff on price for their combo units, but you'll note that the competition is still much higher when you look at accessories like book shelves, desks and so on.

All in all, Rumble Tuff makes 30 different pieces, in both contemporary and traditional finishes. The quality is a cut above what you find in chain stores: all of Rumble Tuff's drawers feature roller bearings. Every dresser is made of solid wood like maple and oak (except for the sides and tops, which are veneers). Best of all, the furniture comes in 20 different colors; you can mix and match color accents for knobs or tops to your heart's content.

While the drawer sides are not solid wood, we found the overall construction to be good. We bought a Rumble Tuff dresser and bookshelf unit and have been very happy—it matched our Child Craft crib exactly and we saved over $100.

One caveat to Rumble Tuff: the brand can be difficult to find, as their distribution is spotty in places like New England. Go to their web site to find a list of dealers.

As we mentioned earlier, **Munire** is a newcomer to the juvenile furniture market but offers impressive quality at prices that won't break the bank. We're talking ALL wood dressers, with prices starting at $400 for their budget line made in Mexico to $500 to $700 for the styles made in Munire's New Jersey plant. Best of all, customer service and delivery times from Munire are excellent.

Another brand to consider: Readers write to us to say **Camelot Furniture** of Anaheim, Calif. (for a dealer near you, call 714-283-4194) has some great deals on dressers and other case pieces. "The infant and case pieces by Camelot gave me the most bang for the buck, not to mention a perfect match in color for my Pali crib," says a reader. Yes, it's made of laminate but the drawer glides have a lifetime warranty and the prices are great—$479 for an armoire, $198 for a bookshelf.

Finally, a reader recommended an excellent source for dressers from Canada: **Mother Hubbard's Cupboard** (416) 661-8201. This Toronto-based furniture maker offers a four-drawer dresser for $399 to $499 and an armoire for $599; quality is very good. The reader was especially pleased that the Mother Hubbard dresser she was considering matched her crib's finish.

Yet Even More Nursery Stuff

Just because to this point you have spent an amount equivalent to the gross national product of Peru on baby furniture doesn't mean you're done, of course. Nope, we've got four more items to consider for your baby's room:

1 ROCKER-GLIDER. We're not talking about the rocking chair you've seen at grandma's house. No, we're referring to the high-tech modern-day rockers that are so fancy they aren't mere rockers—they're "glider-rockers." Thanks to a fancy ball-bearing system, these rockers "glide" with little or no effort.

Is a glider-rocker a waste of money? Some parents have written to us with that question, assuming you'd just use the item for the baby's first couple of years. Actually, a glider-rocker can have a much longer life. You can swap the cushions after a couple of years (most makers let you order these items separately) and move the glider-rocker to a family room. Making this transition even easier is the trend toward all upholstered gliders (earlier models had exposed wood; the newer ones are all fabric). Yep, they are more expensive, but they can go from the nursery to the family room in a single bound.

Here is an overview of the biggest players:

◆ **Best Chair** *Call 812-367-1761 for a dealer near you. Web: www.bestchair.com* This Indiana-based rocking chair maker just entered the baby biz in 2002, although they trace their roots to the 1960's. We were very impressed with their quality and offerings. Basically, Best specializes in upholstered chairs with over 100+ fabric choices. Delivery is four weeks and prices are reasonable for an all-upholstered look: most are $400 to $500. A matching ottoman is $200. Best is only sold in specialty stores. **Rating: A**

◆ **Dutailier** *Call 800-363-9817 or 450-772-2403; web: www. dutailier.com* Quebec-based **Dutailier** is to glider-rockers what eBay is to online auctions—basically, they own the market. Thanks to superior quality and quick delivery, Dutailier probably sells one out of every two glider rockers purchased in the U.S. and Canada each year.

Dutailier has an incredible selection of 45 models, seven finishes, and 80 different fabrics. The result: over 37,000 possible combinations. All wood is solid maple or oak and features non-toxic finishes. You have to try real hard to avoid seeing Dutailier—the company has 3500 retail dealers, from small specialty stores to major retail chains.

Prices for Dutailier start at about $400 for a basic model (although you can occasionally find them for less online). Of course, the price can soar quickly from there—add a swivel base, plush cushions or leather fabric and you can spend $600. Or $1000.

If we had to criticize Dutailier on something, it would have to be their cushions. Most are not machine washable (the covers can't be zipped off and put into the washing machine). As a result, you'll have to take them to a dry cleaner and pay big bucks to get them looking like new. A few of our readers have solved this problem by sewing slipcovers for their glider-rockers (most fabric stores carry pattern books for such items). Of course, if the cushions are shot, you can always order different ones when you move the glider-rocker into a family room.

It can take 10-12 weeks to order a custom Dutailier rocker (more for leather options), but the company does offer a "Quick Ship" program—a selection of 17 chair styles in two or three different fabric choices that are in stock for shipment in two weeks. We have received occasional complaints about how long it takes to order a Dutailier—one reader special-ordered a Dutailier from

Babies R Us, only to find out some weeks later that the fabric they wanted was discontinued (Dutailier "forgot" to tell Babies R Us, who, to their credit, tried to fix the problem immediately). Other readers complain about fabric backorders, which cause more delays in delivery. Our advice: make sure the store double checks the order with Dutailier.

While Dutailier's web site lacks a product catalog, this is one of those products that is easy to research (and buy) online. Several sites carry the brand at a discount, including BabyCatalog.com—the entire Dutailier line (both wood and metal) is on that site and some models have free ground shipping. An additional site that has a great selection of Dutailier is Rocking Chairs 100% (web: rocking-chairs.com; 800-4-ROCKER), a web site offshoot of the San Rafael, CA store of the same name. The site is easy to navigate, with thumbnails of different models and little color chips for available colors. Unfortunately, Dutailier prohibits this site from listing prices online, so you have to email for a quote.

So, who's got the very best deals on Dutailier? At the moment, we'd have to give the crown to Target. At both their Super Target locations and online (target.com), you can get a Dutailier for just $199 to $229. Yes, Target only carries one or two styles, so your choices are limited. If you want a discount on a Dutailier you saw online or at another store, check out the above mentioned sources like BabyCatalog.com.

An optional accessory for glider rockers is the ottoman that glides too. These start at $80 at discounters like Target, but most cost about $160. We suggest forgetting the ottoman and ordering an inexpensive "nursing" footstool (about $30 to $40 in catalogs like Motherwear 800-950-2500 or on line). Why? Some moms claim the ottoman's height puts additional strain on their backs while breastfeeding. While the nursing footstool doesn't rock, it's lower height puts less strain on your back. (That said, we should note that some ottoman fans point out that once their mom/baby get the hang of nursing, that gliding ottoman is a nice luxury).

One safety note: don't leave an older child sitting in a glider-rocker. Many can be tipped over by a toddler when they climb out of it. (Hint: some glider rockers have a lever that locks it in position when not in use). ***Rating: A***

◆ ***Brooks*** *Call 800-427-6657 or 423-626-1111 for a dealer near you.* Tennessee-based Brooks has been around for 40 years, but only entered the glider-rocker business in 1988. Their glider-rockers retail for $169 to $399, while the ottomans are $100-$150. Unlike Dutailier, all their fabrics are available on any style chair. Brooks chairs feature solid base panels (Dutailier has an open base), which the company touts as more safe. While we liked Brooks' styles and fabrics, one baby storeowner told us he found the company very disorganized with poor customer service. **Rating: B**

◆ **Jardine** (see review earlier in this chapter). This line, manufactured in China by Cosco, sells bargain basement glider rockers at Babies R Us. We've seen Jardine glider rockers for as little as $100 on sale, but most run $140 to $240. The quality is disappointing—these chairs don't rock as easily as a Dutailier or Shermag. We say pass on this one. **Rating: D**

◆ **Shermag/Conant Ball** In the U.S., call 800-363-2635 for dealer near you or 800-556-1515 Canada. Web: www.shermag.com. We saw this brand at chain stores and the prices can't be beat. Sample: Target.com sells a Shermag glider AND ottoman for just $179 to $299 total. Yes, you read that right—prices

start at $179. A similar Shermag (see picture above) available from BabiesRUs.com is $199—again, including ottoman! Okay, what's the catch? First, these styles are a bit smaller in size than other glider-rockers—they fit most moms fine, but those six-foot dads may be uncomfortable. The color choices are also limited (just one or two, in most cases). And you should try to sit in these first to make sure you like the cushions (no, they aren't as super comfy as more expensive options but most parents think they're just fine).

Of course, Shermag offers many more styles and options than just those rock-bottom deals at Target and elsewhere. We noticed other Shermag gliders were $300 to $350 while ottomans were an extra $150 or so. What's Shermag's quality like compared to Dutailier? Frankly, we couldn't tell much of a difference—both are excellent. We give Dutailier a slight edge overall for its wide variety of offerings, but Shermag is a close second. **Rating: A-**

◆ **Relax-R**. Relax-R was sold to new owners last year and their status is up in the air, yet we still notice their gliders sold online (we suppose this is left-over stock). Yes, Relax-R offerings were unique (one model even had heated massage), but since we are unclear about their future direction, we say pass. **Not recommended**

◆ **Towne Square** Call 800-356-1663 for a dealer near you; web: www.gliderrocker.com. Hillsboro, Texas-based Towne Square has a lifetime warranty for all its glider-rockers. They feature a "long-glide" rocking system that has no ball bearings that can wear out. Towne Square's gliders sell for $300 to $500. Their "nursing ottoman" is low to the ground at a height that the manufacturer claims is "ideal for nursing" and gives you control over the chair's rocking motion. Like Brooks, Towne Square gliders feature solid sides as a safety measure (to keep little hands out of the rocking mechanism). As for looks, we'd put Towne Square in the "very traditional" category style-wise—if you want a contemporary look, this probably isn't for you. FYI: in late 2004, Dutailier acquired Towne Square. We're not sure what changes Dutailier plans for the company, which will function as a separate brand for the time being. ***Rating: B***

◆ ***And more ideas.*** What about plain rocking chairs (without cushions)? Almost all the glider-rockers we recommend above can be ordered without cushions. Of course, just about any furniture store also sells plain rocking chairs. We don't have any preference on these items—to be honest, if you think you want a rocker, we'd go for the glider-rocker with cushions. Considering the time you'll spend in it, that would be much more comfortable than a plain rocking chair with no padding.

2 **CLOSET ORGANIZERS.** Most closets are a terrible waste of space. While a simple rod and shelf might be fine for adults, the basic closet doesn't work for babies. Wouldn't it be better to have small shelves to store accessories, equipment and shoes? Or wire baskets for blankets and t-shirts? What about three more additional rods at varying heights to allow for more storage? The solution is closet organizers and you can go one of two routes. For the do-it-yourself crowd, consider a storage kit from such brands as Closet Maid (call 800-874-0008 for a store near you; web: www. closetmaid.com), Mill's Pride (800-441-0337; web: www.mill-spride.com). Closet Maid's web site (closetmaid.com) is particularly helpful, with a useful "Design Selector" and how-to guide. Two catalogs that sell storage items include Hold Everything (800) 421-2264 web: www.holdeverything.com and the Container Store (800) 733-3532 web: www.containerstore.com.

What if you'd rather leave it to the professionals? For those parents who don't have the time or inclination to install a closet organizer themselves, consider calling Closet Factory (call 310-715-1000 for a dealer near you; web: www.closetfactory.com) or California Closets (call 888-36-9709 for a dealer near you; web: www.californiaclosets.com). You can also check your local phone book under "Closets" for local companies that install closet organizers. Professionals charge about $400 to $500 for a typical closet.

While a closet organizer works well for most folks, it may be especially helpful in cases where baby's room is small. Instead of buying a separate dresser or bookshelves, you can build-in drawer stacks and shelves in a closet to squeeze out every possible inch of storage. Another idea: a deep shelf added to a closet can double as a changing area.

We invested in a closet organizer for our youngest child's room and were more than pleased with the results.

3 STEREO. During those sleep deprivation experiments, it's sure nice to have some soothing music to make those hours just whiz by. Sure, you could put a cheap clock radio in the baby's room, but that assumes you have decent radio stations. And even the best radio station will be somewhat tiring to listen to for the many nights ahead. Our advice: buy (or register for) one of those CD/cassette boom box radios that run $100 to $300 in most electronics stores.

4 DIAPER PAIL. Well, those diapers have to go somewhere. We'll review our top picks for diaper pails in Chapter 7, Around the House. A safety note on this subject: many basic diaper pails come with "deodorizers," little cakes that are supposed to take the stink out of stinky diapers. The only problem: many contain toxic chemicals that can be poisonous if toddlers get their hands on them. There are some non-toxic options available now like the Citrus Circles Diaper Pail Deodorizer. Find it at www.babyminestore.com.

5 A CUTE LAMP. What nursery would be complete without a cute lamp for Junior's dresser? A good web site for this is BabyCenter.com, which has a decent selection of lamps and nightlights.

The Bottom Line:
A Wrap-Up of Our Best Buy Picks

For cribs, you've got two basic choices: a simple model that is, well, just a crib or a "convertible" model that eventually morphs into a twin or full size bed. For a basic crib, Child Craft's 10171 is a hardwood design with single-drop side for just $200 (see picture earlier in this chapter) at Target.com or Babies R Us. In a similar vein, Graco/ Simplicity's Aspen 3-in-1 crib is $130 at Wal-Mart.

Look for a crib that has hidden hardware and a quiet rail release—and check under the hood to look at the mattress support.

We like metal springs or wood slats; avoid the cheap "posture" board made of MDF. Safety wise, see if the crib is JPMA-certified and watch out for cribs with fancy detailing that can snag clothing. Choose a crib made of hard wood that will resist scratches and nicks (stay away from pine for that very reason).

If a convertible crib makes sense to you, look at Baby's Dream or Munire. Their models run $400 to $600. Yep, it costs more money up-front but you get a crib that converts to an attractive looking full-size bed.

The best mattress? We like the foam mattresses from Colgate ($120 for the Classica I). Or, for coil, go for a Simmons Super Maxipedic 160 coil mattress at Babies R Us for $100.

Where to buy a crib and other nursery furniture? Our readers say chains like Babies R Us and Baby Depot have the lowest prices, but the web can be a great source for discounts on non-bulky items like rocker gliders. For design inspiration, consider the Pottery Barn Kids catalog for ideas (but few deals).

Dressers and other case pieces by Munire and Rumble Tuff were great deals—the latter brand offers dressers that exactly match the finishes of fancier brands, but at prices 10% to 25% less than the competition. We liked Rumble Tuff's three-drawer combo unit that combines a changing table and a dresser for $500 to $600. Finally, we recommend the Dutailier and Shermag brands of glider-rockers. At $200 to $300, their basic models are well made and stylish. A matching ottoman runs $110 to $180.

So, let's sum up some of our recommendations:

Child Craft single drop-side crib	$200
Simmons 160 coil mattress	$100
Munire dresser	$500
Shermag glider-rocker	$180
Miscellaneous	$200
TOTAL	$1180

By contrast, if you bought a Bellini crib ($600), a 200-coil mattress ($200), a Ragazzi dresser ($750), a fancy glider-rocker ($500), separate changing table ($200) and miscellaneous items ($200) at full retail, you'd be out $2450 by this point. Of course, you don't have any sheets for your baby's crib yet. Nor any clothes for Junior to wear. So, next we'll explore those topics and save more of your money.

CHAPTER 3
Baby Bedding & Decor

Inside this chapter

H ow can you find brand new, designer-label bedding for as much as 50% off the retail price? We've got the answer in this chapter, plus you'll find nine smart shopper tips to help get the most for your money. We'll share the best web sites and mail-order catalogs for baby linens. Then, we'll reveal nine important tips that will keep your baby safe and sound. Finally, we've got reviews of the best bedding designers and a must-read list of seven top money-wasters.

Getting Started: When Do You Need This Stuff?

Begin shopping for your baby's linen pattern in the sixth month of your pregnancy, if not earlier. Why? If you're purchasing these items from a baby specialty store, they usually must be special-ordered—allow at least four to eight weeks for delivery. If you leave a few weeks for shopping, you can order the bedding in your seventh month to be assured it arrives before the baby does.

If you're buying bedding from a store or catalog that has the desired pattern in stock, you can wait until your eighth month. It still takes time to comparison shop, and some stores may only have certain pieces you need in stock, while other accessories (like wall hangings, etc.) may need to be special ordered.

Sources

There are six basic sources for baby bedding:

1 **BABY SPECIALTY STORES.** These stores tend to have a limited selection of bedding in stock. Typically, you're expected to choose the bedding by seeing what you like on sample cribs or by looking through manufacturers' catalogs. Then you have to special-order your choices and wait four to eight weeks for arrival. And that's the main disadvantage to buying linens at a specialty store: THE WAIT. On the upside, most specialty stores do carry high-quality brand names you can't find at discounters or baby superstores. But you'll pay for it—most specialty stores mark such items at full retail.

2 **DISCOUNTERS.** The sheer variety of discount stores that carry baby bedding is amazing—you can find it everywhere from Wal-Mart to Target, Marshall's to TJ Maxx. Even Toys R Us sells baby bedding and accessories. As you'd expect, everything is cash and carry at these stores—most carry a decent selection of items in stock. You pick out what you like and that's it; there are no special orders. The downside? Prices are cheap, but so is the quality. Most discounters only carry low-end brands whose synthetic fabrics and cheap construction may not withstand repeated washings. There are exceptions to this rule, which we'll review later in this chapter.

3 **DEPARTMENT STORES.** The selection of baby bedding at department stores is all over the board. Some chains have great baby departments and others need help. For example, JCPenney carries linen sets by such companies as NoJo and Cotton Tale (see the reviews of these brands later in this chapter), while Foley's (part of the May Department Store chain) seems to only have a few blankets and sheets. Prices at department stores vary as widely as selection; however, you can guarantee that department stores will hold occasional sales, making them a better deal.

4 **BABY SUPERSTORES.** The superstores reviewed in the last chapter (Babies R Us, Baby Depot, etc.) combine the best of both worlds: discount prices AND quality brands. Best of all, most items are in stock. Unlike Wal-Mart or Target, you're more likely to see 100% cotton bedding and better construction. Yet, the superstores aren't perfect: they are often beaten on price by online sources (reviewed later in this chapter). And superstores are more likely to sell bedding in sets (rather than a la carte), forcing you to buy frivolous items.

5 **THE WEB.** If there were a perfect baby product to be sold on-line, it would have to be crib bedding and linens. The web's full-color graphics let you see exactly what you'll get. And bedding is lightweight, which minimizes shipping costs. The only bummer: you can't feel the fabric or inspect the stitching. As a result, we recommend sticking to well-known brand names when ordering online.

6 **MAIL-ORDER CATALOGS.** In the last few years, there's been a marked increase in the number of catalog sellers who offer baby linens, and that's great news for parents. Catalogs like Pottery Barn Kids, Land's End and Company Kids offer high quality bedding (100% cotton, high thread counts) at reasonable prices. Best of all, you can buy the pieces a la carte (eliminating unnecessary items found in sets) while at the same time, mixing and matching to your heart's content. If you want "traditional" bedding sets, JCPenney's catalog won't disappoint. We'll review these and more catalogs later in this chapter.

Parents in Cyberspace: What's on the Web?

Burlington Coat Factory Direct (Baby Depot)
Web site: www.bcfdirect.com
What it is: The online version of discounter Burlington Coat Factory's Baby Depot.
What's Cool: This site offers good discounts (about 20% to 30%) on bedding from such famous names as Lambs & Ivy, Laura Ashley by Sumersault, CoCaLo and more. Best of all, you can order a la carte if you don't want a complete set—each page lists a plethora of matching accessories for each grouping plus you can click on thumbnail swatches for a closer look. Finally, Baby Depot lets you know how long each item takes to ship and the shipping costs are reasonable.
Needs work: We were a bit disappointed with the navigation on this site in our last edition and it hasn't improved. It takes a tremendous number of clicks to see all the bedding offerings. We had to navigate through four menus to get to the bedding list (go first to Baby, then Nursery). Even more confusing: the site mixed in general categories like "boy" and "girl" or "florals" and "bears" with specific manufacturers like Glenna Jean.

Baby Bedding
Web site: www.babybedding.com
What it is: The online outpost for bedding manufacturer Carousel.
What's cool: Carousel used to sell its line of bedding exclusively through retail stores at about $250 to $300 per set. Several years ago, however, they decided to sell directly to the public via their web site, Baby Bedding. The prices have taken a huge drop as a result. For example, their four-piece Summer Plaid used to sell for

$254. Online it's a modest $189. Can't beat those prices for an all cotton bedding line (overall, prices for a set run $125 to $225). And best of all, Carousel doesn't do this half way: the web site offers free fabric swatches other goodies. Looking for quality portacrib sheets or matching cradle sheets? How about rocking chair pads and high chair pads? They've got them. Lastly, Baby Bedding has an outlet store near Atlanta; check the web site for their latest schedule (it was open to the public only on the third Saturday of the month last we checked).

Needs work: The folks at Baby Bedding have made some nice improvements over last edition. They now show the price for a four-piece set under each picture. The pictures are bigger as well. This site isn't going to win any awards for design innovation but it's pretty simple to use.

Baby Universe

Web: www.babyuniverse.com
What it is: The web's largest selection of bedding.
What's cool: Over 75 bedding brands are here; best of all, you can buy many designs in a set or a la carte (including extra fabric). The site is easy to navigate and includes helpful hints, which note when matching twin bedding sets are available for a certain pattern. We liked the ability to search by gender, nursery theme or brand name. The shop by theme section included 30 choices under animal, 108 for floral & lace, etc. We saw lots of free shipping offers on this site when we last visited.
Needs work: The site has few negatives to report. FYI: Some bedding items are special order—leave six weeks or more.

◆ *Other web sites to check out:* Don't forget manufacturers' web sites—one of the best is *Brandee Danielle's* (www.brandeedanielle. com). Their entire catalog is online so you can surf to your heart's content. Since most baby stores only carry a few patterns from any one manufacturer, it's informative to see the *entire* collection.

For parents looking for accessories and bedding with a Beatrix Potter theme, check out *Country Lane* (www.countrylane.com). This site sells 750 different accessories and bedding pieces available in the Beatrix Potter line. They also have Pooh themed merchandise and Precious Moments. The discounts are up to 40% off.

 ## What Are You Buying?

Walk into any baby store, announce you're having a baby, and stand back: the eager salespeople will probably pitch you on all types of bedding items that you MUST buy. We call this the "Diaper Stacker Syndrome," named in honor of that useless (but expensive) linen item that allegedly provides a convenient place to store diapers. Most parents aren't about to spend the equivalent of the Federal Deficit on diaper stackers. So, here's our list of the absolute necessities for your baby's linen layette:

◆ **Fitted sheets**—at least three to four. This is the workhorse of your baby's linens. When it comes to crib sheets, you have three choices: woven, knit and flannel. Woven (also called percale) sheets are available in all cotton or cotton blend fabrics, while knit and flannel sheets are almost always all cotton. As to which is best, it's up to you. Some folks like flannel sheets, especially in colder climates. Others find woven or knit sheets work fine. One tip: look for sheets that have elastic all-around the edges (cheaper ones just have elastic on the corners). See the "Safe & Sound" section for more info on crib sheet safety issues.

If you plan to use a bassinet/cradle, you'll need a few of these special-size sheets as well . . . but your choices here are pretty limited. You'll usually find solid color pastels or white. Some specialty linen manufacturers do sell bassinet sheets, but they can get rather pricey. And you may find complete bassinet sets that come with all the linens for your baby. Just be sure to check the fabric content (all cotton is best) and washing instructions. By the way, one mom improvised bassinet sheets by putting the bassinet mattress inside a king size pillowcase. You may want to secure the excess fabric under the mattress so it doesn't un-tuck.

◆ **Mattress Pads/Sheet Protector.** While most baby mattresses have waterproof vinyl covers, many parents use either a mattress pad or sheet protector to protect the mattress or sheet from leaky diapers. A mattress pad is the traditional way of dealing with this problem and is placed between the mattress and the crib sheet. A more recent invention, the sheet protector, goes on top of the crib sheet.

A sheet protector has a waterproof vinyl backing to protect against leaking. And here's the cool part: it Velcro's to the crib's posts, making for easy removal. If the baby's diaper leaks, simply pop off the sheet protector and throw it in the wash (instead of the fitted crib sheets). You can buy sheet protectors in most baby stores or catalogs. See an "Email from the Real World" on the next page for information on sheet savers.

◆ **A Good Blanket.** Baby stores love to pitch expensive quilts to parents and many bedding sets include them as part of the package. Yet, all babies need is a simple cotton blanket. Not only are thick quilts overkill for most climates, they can also be dangerous. The latest report from the Consumer Product Safety Commission on Sudden Infant Death Syndrome (SIDS) concluded that putting babies face down on such soft bedding may contribute to as many as 30% of SIDS deaths (that's 900 babies) each year in the U.S. (As a side note, there is no explanation for the other 70% of SIDS cases, although environmental factors like smoking near the baby and a too-hot room are suspected). Some baby bedding companies have responded to these concerns by rolling out decorative flannel-backed blankets (instead of quilts) in their collections.

But what if you live in a cold climate and think a cotton blanket won't cut it? Consider crib blankets made from fleece (a lightweight 100% polyester fabric brushed to a soft finish) available in most stores and catalogs. For example, Lands End sells a polar fleece crib blanket for $18. Of course, polar fleece blankets are also available from mainstream bedding companies like California Kids (reviewed later in this chapter). Or how about a "coverlet," which is lighter than a quilt but more substantial than a blanket? Lightweight quilts (instead of the traditional thick and fluffy version) are another option for as little as $70 in mail order catalogs.

Finally, we found a great product to keep baby warm and avoid a blanket altogether. Halo Innovations (www.halosleep.com), the manufacturer of a crib mattress reviewed in the last chapter, also makes a product called the SleepSack. This "wearable blanket" helps baby avoid creeping under a blanket and suffocating. Available in three sizes and fabrics, the SleepSack is $25. A portion of the sale price goes to the SIDS Alliance. Kiddopotamus also has a couple options: the BeddieBye Zip-Around Safety Blanket for $14 to $16 and the Swaddle Me infant wrap for $13.

◆ **Bumper Pads.** In a previous edition of this book, we called bumper pads "an important safety item." We've since changed our mind and now consider them to be an optional accessory that we don't necessarily recommend. Why the change of heart? All the warnings about SIDS and soft bedding (see previous section) that no soft bedding should be in a crib, even if bumpers are designed as a "safety item." The CPSC "recommends that infants under 12 months be put to sleep in a crib with no soft bedding of any kind under or on top of the baby." Note the CPSC doesn't specifically say anything about banning bumpers but some safety experts have extrapolated their warning to include crib bumpers.

As you would guess, that warning didn't sit well with crib bedding makers, who felt bumpers were getting a bad wrap. The industry's trade association (the JPMA) asked the CPSC to examine

bedding

E-Mail from The Real World
Sheet savers make for easy changes

Baby bedding sure looks cute, but the real work is changing all those sheets. Karen Naide found a solution:

"One of our best buys was 'The Ultimate Crib Sheet.' I bought one regular crib sheet that matched the bedding set, and two Ultimate Crib Sheets. This product is waterproof (vinyl on the bottom, and soft white cotton on the top) and lies on top of your regular crib sheet. It has six elastic straps that snap around the bars of your crib. When it gets dirty or the baby soils it, all you have to do is unsnap the straps, lift it off, put a clean one on, and that's it! No taking the entire crib sheet off (which usually entails wrestling with the mattress and bumper pads)... it's really quick and easy! While the white sheet may not exactly match your pattern, it can only be seen from inside the crib, and as you have so often stated, it's not like the baby cares about what it looks like. From the outside of the crib, you can still see the crib sheet that matches your bedding. Anyway, I think it's a wonderful product, and really a must."

*The **Ultimate Crib Sheet** is made by Basic Comfort (call 800-456-8687 for a store near you; web: www.basiccomfort.com). It sells for $18 and is available at Babies R Us or we've seen it for as little as $15 on other baby web sites . FYI: older versions of the Ultimate Crib Sheet generated a few complaints. Some of our readers report that their children were able to get under the Ultimate Crib Sheet as they got a bit older. This scary scenario can be avoided by using their new, improved version with snaps on the ends, not just the sides.*

Of course, there are several other companies that sell similar sheets; we've seen them in general catalogs like One Step Ahead and Baby Catalog of America.

*One of the coolest new products we found was the **Quick Zip** crib sheet from Clouds and Stars (www.cloudsandstars.com). Here's how it works: the sheet base covers the bottom of the mattress and stays in place. The top of the sheet is secured via a plastic zipper. Baby's diaper leaks at two in the morning, you zip off the top of the sheet and zip on a spare. No lifting of the mattress (except when you first set it up) and no untying bumpers. The white or ecru sheet sets are $35 and additional top sheets are $17.50. They even make a version for portacribs. Hand painted and custom sheets are available for a bit more.*

the data on infant injuries and deaths due to bedding in order to better determine if bumpers were the culprit. The CPSC released a report in 2004 which found that 94 infant deaths between 1995 and 2003 were caused by bedding . . . but here's the rub: in most cases, the authorities didn't specify exactly WHICH bedding item caused the death. In a third of the cases, the "sleep environment was cluttered with adult sized blankets, quilts and pillows." The bottom line: the CPSC concluded "although bumper pads and stuffed toys were mentioned as being in the crib in some of the other deaths, there was insufficient detail to conclude these were the causative agents in the infants' deaths."

Now that clears it up, doesn't it?

One important point for this study: the CPSC excluded any SIDS deaths from their examination of crib bumpers, for reasons unknown. Yet it stands to reason that if you want to decide whether bumpers are safe or dangerous, you should include ALL the data (both SIDS and other deaths due to bedding).

Making this even more confusing for parents: *Consumer Reports* has entered this debate, sparking a feud between the magazine and the CPSC and JPMA. *Consumer Reports* takes the position that bumpers (and all soft bedding items) are dangerous and should never be used. The JPMA, however, says that in essence bumpers are fine.

Here's the take-home message: bumpers are OPTIONAL. If your baby starts banging into the side of her crib (or gets her arms/legs stuck), then go buy an affordable set of bumpers. If you choose to purchase bumpers, don't buy the ultra-thick or pillow-like bumpers. Instead choose firm bumpers that are made to properly and securely fit the crib (that means no overlapping sections or wide gaps between the ends at the corner sections). We recommend bumpers with ties on the top and bottom, which let you more securely attach them to a crib. Check to see if you can machine-wash them—thinner bumpers can be popped into a washing machine, while ultra-thick bumpers may have to be dry-cleaned. Some parents are concerned that the chemical residue from dry-cleaning might be harmful to their baby. (As a side note, federal law requires the fill in bumpers be 100% polyester).

Another alternative: the so-called breathable bumper. One such brand is the CribShield, which we will review later.

Also: we'll have more comments on the safety aspects of bumpers in the Safe & Sounds section later in this chapter.

More Money Buys You . . .

Baby bedding sets vary from as little as $40 in discount stores up to nearly $1000 in specialty stores. The basic difference: fabric quality and construction. The cheapest bedding is typically made of 50/50 cotton-poly blends with low thread counts (120 threads per inch). To mask the low quality, many bedding companies splash cutesy licensed cartoon characters on such low-end bedding. So what does more money buy you? First, better fabric. Usually, you'll find 100% cotton with 200 thread counts or more. Better quality bedding sets include more substantial bumpers with more ties. Some may even have slipcovers removable for easy cleaning. Cheap quality crib sheets often lack elastic all the way around and some shrink dangerously when washed (see Safe and Sound next for details). Beyond the $300 price point, you're most likely paying for a designer name and frilly accessories (coordinating lamp shade, anyone?).

As a side note, we've noticed many of the manufacturers who made only all-cotton bedding sets are adding some blends to keep prices down. Patch Kraft and Cotton Tale are a couple brands we've noticed who are adding a bit of cotton-poly to their designs. Sheets and most bumpers are still typically all cotton, but you may find accent fabrics on quilts and bumpers that are blends. We still recommend these manufacturers as long as the sheets are all cotton.

Safe & Sound

While you might think to cover your outlets and hide that can of Raid, you might not automatically consider safety when selecting crib sheets, comforters, and bumpers. Yet, your baby will be spending more time with these products than any others. Here are several safety points to remember:

◆ Make sure the crib sheets snugly fit the mattress.
One quality sign: check to make sure the sheet's elastic extends around the entire sheet (cheaper quality crib sheets only have elastic on the ends, making a good fit more difficult to achieve). Another problem: shrinkage. Never use a sheet that has shrunk so much it no longer can be pulled over the corners of the mattress. Unfortunately, some sheets shrink more than others. Which ones shrink least? In a past edition of this book, we printed the results of a Good Housekeeping (GH) test of various crib sheets as a guide. But we've omitted it from this edition. Why? First, the last test was five years ago and we think the results may be out of date. Second, we found GH's last test produced results that were inconsistent with their first test back in 1998. The results were more confusing than helpful. If you are curious, you can read the results of the tests

on our web site (BabyBargains.com, click on "Bonus Material").

So, what do we recommend now? For any crib sheet you buy, be sure to wash it several times according to the directions and see if it correctly fits your crib. If not, return it to the store.

If you are not convinced that a standard crib sheet is the answer, consider a special crib sheet that is designed NOT to come off the mattress. Example: The **Stay Put** safety sheet (www.babysheets. com) which works like a pillowcase on your mattress. Another option to consider: "pocket" sheets wrap around the crib mattress and close easily with Velcro. You can find these on **Baby-Be-Safe** (www.baby-be-safe.com). **J. Lamb** (www. jlambandfriends.com) makes a 100% cotton, 200 thread count Safety Sheet with "Stay-Put" elastic safety bands (see picture). Four colors are available; there's even a "chemical free" version. Price: about $15 at BuyBuyBaby.com, JCPenney (under the Bright Future label), Sears (Little Wonders label) and Baby News stores.

◆ **Recent studies of Sudden Infant Death Syndrome** (SIDS, also known as crib death) have reported that there is an increased incidence of crib death when infants sleep on fluffy bedding, lambskins, or pillows. A pocket can form around the baby's face if she is placed face down in fluffy bedding, and she can slowly suffocate while breathing in her own carbon dioxide. The best advice: put your infant on her back when he or she sleeps. And don't put pillows, comforters or other soft bedding or toys inside a crib.

In 1999, the Consumer Product Safety Commission issued new guidelines regarding SIDS and soft bed linens. The CPSC now recommends that parents not use ANY soft bedding around, on top of, or under baby. If you want to use a blanket, tuck a very thin blanket under the mattress at one end of the crib to keep it from moving around. The blanket should then only come up to baby's chest.

Sheets with All Around Elastic

Here is a partial list of manufacturers who make their crib sheets with elastic all around the sheet:

Amy Coe	Circo
Cotton Tale	Gerber
Hoohobbers	Lands End
Patch Kraft	

Safest of all: avoid using any blankets in a crib and put baby in a blanket sleeper (basically, a thick set of pajamas) and t-shirt for warmth. (More on blanket sleepers in the next chapter). See the picture at right for an example of the correct way to use a blanket.

Finally, one mom wrote to tell us about a scary incident in her nursery. She had left a blanket hanging over the side of the crib when she put her son down for a nap. He managed to pull the blanket down and get wrapped up in it, nearly suffocating. Stories like that convince us that putting any soft bedding in or near a crib is risky.

◆ **Beware of ribbons and long fringe.** These are possible choking hazards if they are not attached properly. Remove any questionable decoration.

◆ **If you decide to buy bumper pads,** go for ones with well-sewn ties at the top *and* bottom (at least 12 to 16 total). Ties should

E-MAIL FROM THE REAL WORLD
Lack of Bumper Ties Cause a Scare for Parents

Nicole Morely of Chicago wrote to tell us of a frightening incident with borrowed bedding that did not have ties on the bottom of the bumper. (Keep in mind, there is no requirement for bumpers to have ties top and bottom. We recommend it highly, however.)

"We were spending the holidays with grandparents who bought a crib and borrowed bedding so that our five-month-old would sleep comfortably. We failed to check the crib bumpers for ties at the top and bottom and woke up in the middle of the night to shrieking—we found our baby's head and arms trapped under the crib bumper! Scary and unbelievable! Fortunately, we got there in time. I can't believe that so many manufacturers still make them that way. We've called nearby stores and all the bumpers they sell only tie at the top. The one our daughter was trapped under is Classic Pooh made by Red Calliope. I can't imagine that it doesn't happen more often!

be between seven and nine inches in length. That's the industry's voluntary standard for safety—ties that are too short can't be tied correctly around a crib post. If ties exceed nine inches, they can be a strangulation hazard.

We should note that while that's the standard, our investigation of baby bedding found many manufacturers exceed the limit—one even had ties that were 14″ in length! In their defense, expensive bedding makers claim their customers put their bedding on high-price Italian cribs, whose thick corner posts require longer ties. We think that's a weak excuse—14″ is too long, even for cribs with the thickest posts. If you buy bumpers with ties that exceed 9″, we recommend cutting off any excess length after you install them on the crib. (See the previous chapter's Safe & Sound section for a discussion of Italian cribs and bumper pads).

A related issue to the length of the ties is their location: some companies have ties ONLY on the top of bumpers. In this case, we've had many reports of babies scooting under the bumper and getting trapped (see our Email from the Real World below). If you fall in love with bedding that has ties only on the top, consider adding additional ties yourself. Just be sure to sew them on securely. A chart later in this chapter will compare the tie length and location among different brands.

As we noted earlier, make sure the bumpers fit well with no overlapping and no gaps at the ends. And avoid bumpers that are too thick and fluffy. They pose the same kind of risk as pillows. Look for firm, flat bumpers. Before you decide to use bumpers, read the section earlier in this chapter for the latest research on bumper safety.

◆ *Remove bumper pads immediately when your child starts to pull up or stand.* Why? Bumpers make a great step stool that lets baby launch herself out of the crib! This usually happens around six months of age.

◆ *Never use an electric blanket/heating pad.* Babies can dangerously overheat, plus any moisture, such as urine, can cause electric shock.

◆ *Avoid blankets that use nylon thread.* Nylon thread melts in the dryer and then breaks. These loose threads can wrap around your baby's neck, fingers or toes or break off and become a choking hazard. Cotton thread is best.

◆ *Look out for chenille.* It's the hip new thing and sort of like the shag carpeting of fabric—chenille is all over the market (sweaters, blankets, etc.) and now it has come to baby products. At a recent trade show, we saw many bedding manufacturers who had chenille groupings. Some use it as an accent on bumpers, while others have chenille blankets. Yet, some safety advocates wonder if this trim is safe for baby's bedding—with some chenille, you can actually pull out fibers from the fabric backing with little effort. And that might be a choking hazard for baby.

◆ **Travel.** Now that you've created a safe nursery at home, what about when you travel? Parents who frequently travel are often frustrated by hotels, which not only have unsafe cribs (see previous chapter) but also questionable sheets. At one hotel, we were given queen size bed sheets to use in a crib! A solution: one reader recommended bringing a crib sheet from home. That way you know your baby will be safe and sound. (When you reserve a crib find out if it is a portable crib or a standard crib so you know what size sheet to bring.) Check with some of our recommended safety sheet manufacturers listed above and consider buying their port-a-crib versions for travel.

◆ **All linens should have a tag** indicating the manufacturer's name and address. That's the only way you would know if the linens were recalled. You can also contact the manufacturer if you have a problem or question. While this is the law, some stores may sell discounted or imported linens that do not have tags. Our advice: DON'T buy them.

 Smart Shopper Tips

Smart Shopper Tip
Pillow Talk: Looking for Mr. Good Bedding

"Cartoons and more cartoons—that seemed to be the basic choice in crib bedding at our local baby store. Since it all looks alike, is the pattern the only difference?"

There's more to it than that. And buying baby bedding isn't the same as purchasing linens for your own bed—you'll be washing these pieces much more frequently, so they must be made to withstand the extra abuse. Since baby bedding is more than just another set of sheets, here are nine quality points to look for:

1 RUFFLES SHOULD BE FOLDED OVER FOR DOUBLE THICKNESS— INSTEAD OF A SINGLE THICKNESS RUFFLE WITH HEMMED EDGE.
Double ruffles hold up better in the wash.

2 **COLORED DESIGNS ON THE BEDDING SHOULD BE PRINTED OR WOVEN INTO THE FABRIC, NOT STAMPED** (like you'd see on a screen-printed t-shirt). Stamped designs on sheets can fade with only a few washings. The problem: the pieces you wash less frequently (like dust ruffles and bumpers) will fade at different rates, spoiling the coordinated look you paid big money for. In case you're wondering how to determine whether the design is printed rather than stamped, printed fabrics have color that goes through the fabric to the other side. Stamped patterns are merely applied onto the top of the fabric.

3 **MAKE SURE THE PIECES ARE SEWN WITH COTTON/POLY THREAD, NOT NYLON.** Nylon threads will melt and break in the dryer, becoming a choking hazard. Once the thread is gone, the filling in bumpers and quilts can bunch up.

4 **CHECK FOR TIGHT, SMOOTH STITCHING ON APPLIQUÉS.** If you can see the edge of the fabric through the appliqué thread, the work is too skimpy. Poor quality appliqué will probably unravel after only a few washings. We've seen some appliqués that were actually fraying in the store—check before you buy.

5 **HIGH THREAD-COUNT SHEETS.** Unlike adult linens, many packages of baby bedding do not list the thread count. But, if you can count the individual threads when you hold a sheet up to the light, you know the thread count is too low. High thread-count sheets (200 threads per inch or more) are preferred since they are softer and smoother against baby's skin, last longer and wear better. Unfortunately, most affordable baby bedding has low thread counts (80 to 120 thread counts are common)—traditionally, it's the design (not the quality) that sells bedding in the baby biz. But there is good news on this front: there are several upstart brands (reviewed later) that are actually touting high thread counts for their sheets.

Another telltale sign of a quality sheet is the elastic. The best sheets will have elastic that encircles the entire sheet.

6 **FEEL THE FILLING IN THE BUMPER PADS.** If the filling feels gritty, it's not the best quality. Look for bumpers that are firm when you squeeze them (Dacron-brand filling is a good bet).

7 **THE TIES THAT ATTACH THE BUMPER TO THE CRIB SHOULD BE BETWEEN SEVEN AND NINE INCHES IN LENGTH.** Another tip: make sure the bumper has ties on both the top and bottom and are securely sewn. For more discussion on this issue, see "Safe & Sound" earlier in this chapter.

8 **THE DUST RUFFLE PLATFORM SHOULD BE OF GOOD QUALITY FABRIC**—or else it will tear. Longer, full ruffles are more preferable to shorter ones. As a side note, the dust ruffle is sometimes referred to as a crib skirt.

9 **REMEMBER THAT CRIB SHEETS COME IN DIFFERENT SIZES**— bassinet/cradle, portable crib, and full-size crib. Always use the correct size sheet.

Wastes of Money/Worthless Items

"I have a very limited budget for bedding, and I want to avoid spending money on stuff that I won't need. What are some items I should stay away from?"

It may be tempting to buy every new fad and matching accessory. And you'll get a lot of sales pressure at some stores to go for the entire "coordinated" look. Yet many baby-bedding items are a complete waste of money—here's our list of the worst offenders:

1 **DIAPER STACKER.** This is basically a bag (in coordinating fabric, of course) used to store diapers—you hang it on the side of changing table. Apparently, bedding makers must think stacking diapers on the shelf of your changing table or storing them in a drawer is a major etiquette breach. Take my word for it: babies are not worried if their diapers are out in plain sight. Save the $30 to $50 that bedding makers charge for diaper stackers and stack your own.

2 **PILLOWS.** We are constantly amazed at the number of bedding sets that include pillows or pillowcases. Are the bedding designers nuts, or what? Haven't they heard that it's dangerous to put your baby to sleep on a pillow? What a terrible safety hazard, not to mention a waste of your money. We don't even think a decorative pillow is a good idea—what if another caretaker puts your baby to sleep in her crib and forgets to remove the decorative pillow? Forget the pillow and save $20 to $30.

3 **SETS OF LINENS.** Sets may include useless or under-used items like those listed above as well as dust ruffles and window valances. Another problem: sets are often a mixed bag when it comes to quality. Some items are good, while others are lacking. Many baby stores or even chains will sell bedding items a la carte.

That way you can pick and choose just the items you need—at a substantial savings over the all-inclusive sets.

4 CANOPIES. Parents-to-be of girls are often pressured to buy frilly accessories like canopies. The emphasis is on giving her "everything" and achieving a "feminine" look for your nursery. Don't buy into it. The whole set-up for a canopy is going to be more expensive (you'll need a special crib, etc.)—it'll set you back $75 to $175 for the linens alone. And enclosing your baby's crib in a canopy won't do much for her visual stimulation or health (canopies are dust collectors).

5 ALL-WHITE LINENS. If you think of babies as pristine and unspoiled, you've never had to change a poopy diaper or clean spit-up from the front of an outfit. We're amazed that anyone would consider all-white bedding, since keeping it clean will probably be a full-time job. Stick with colors, preferably bright ones. If you buy all-white linens and then have to go back to buy colored ones, you'll be out another $100 to $200. (Yes, some folks argue that white linens are easier to bleach clean, but extensive bleaching over time can yellow fabric.)

6 TEETHING PADS FOR CRIB RAILS. Most new, name brand cribs will already have plastic teething guards on the side rails, so adding pads (cost: $20 extra) is redundant. One storeowner pointed out that if your baby has nothing better to teeth on than the crib railing, he is spending too much time in the crib anyway.

7 HEADBOARD BUMPERS. Whatever side you come down on in the bumper debate (some parents think they're a good safety item; others worry about the suffocation risk), there is a certain bumper that definitely is a waste of money—the headboard bumper. This bumper is designed to cover the entire headboard of the crib. Regular bumpers are just a six to nine-inch tall strip of padding that goes around the crib . . . and that's all you need if you want bumpers. Headboard bumpers are more expensive than regular bumpers, running another $25 to $100, depending on the maker. Skip them and save the money.

8 SLEEP POSITIONERS. These $10 to $20 blocks of foam are supposed to hold baby in place on their side or back, but they are unnecessary. The current recommendation is to put baby to sleep on her back . . . and nearly all infants will stay right there through out the night until they reach six months of age (when they are strong enough to roll over on their own). Positioners are a waste

Cyber bedding deals: Overstock.com

What happens when those high-flying dot-coms crash down to earth? Liquidators move in to sell their warehouses stuffed with unsold goods. Since they pay pennies on the dollar, these liquidators can turn around and sell you the goods at substantial discounts and still make a buck. And how do liquidators sell distressed inventory from dot-coms? The Internet, of course. Case in point: Overstock.com, the premier liquidator of dot-coms. This company has an excellent web site that sells brand-new merchandise at 50% off and more. We've seen $40 to $70 designer four-piece sets of all-cotton crib bedding sets (original retail $150), as well as crib mobiles for $34 (originally $56), toys, baby clothes, shoes and more. To see what's available for babies at Overstock.com, go to "Home & Garden" department (then Bedding & Bath, Bedding and then Crib Sets). Selection does vary from time to time..

Figure 2: Why pay $150 for this designer crib set when you can snag it on OverStock.com for just $39? The deals on bedding make this site a great bargain find.

of money. (One exception to this piece of advice: the Sleep Shaper System we discussed in the last chapter on page 95; this crib wedge that prevents positional plagiocephaly, a deformation of the skull. That product is been proven in clinical studies to be effective).

Money Saving Secrets

1 **IF YOU'RE ON A TIGHT BUDGET, GO FOR A GOOD BLANKET AND A NICE SET OF HIGH THREAD-COUNT SHEETS.** What does that cost? A good cotton blanket runs $10 (even fancy fleece ones are only $15), while a fitted sheet runs $10 to $20. Forget all the fancy items like embroidered comforters, duvet covers, window valances, diaper stackers and dust ruffles. After all, your baby won't care if she doesn't have perfectly coordinated accessories.

2 **DON'T BUY A QUILT.** Sure, they look pretty, but do you really need one? Go for a nice cotton blanket, instead—and save the $50 to $200. Better yet, hint to your friends that you'd like receiving blankets as shower gifts.

3 **SKIP EXPENSIVE WALL HANGINGS—DO DECOR ON THE CHEAP.** One of the best new products we've discovered for this is Wall Nutz (www.wallnutz.com). These innovative iron-on transfers let you create paint-by-number masterpieces in your baby's room. Paint a six-by-eight foot mural or just add some decorative borders. Cost: $30 (plus the cost of paints).

Of course, crafts stores are another great source for do-it-yourself inspiration. Michaels Arts & Crafts (800-MICHAELS; web: www.michaels.com) sells stencils and supplies for nursery decor.

4 **MAKE YOUR OWN SHEETS, DUST RUFFLES AND OTHER LINEN ITEMS.** Think that's too complicated? A mom in Georgia called in this great tip on curtain valances—she bought an extra dust ruffle, sewed a curtain valance from the material and saved $70. All you need to do is remove the ruffle from the fabric platform and sew a pocket along one edge. I managed to do this simple procedure on my sewing machine without killing myself, so it's quite possible you could do it too. A good place for inspiration is your local fabric store—most carry pattern books like Butterick, Simplicity and McCalls, all of which have baby bedding patterns that are under $10. There are other pattern books you can purchase that specialize in baby quilts—some of these books also have patterns for other linen items like bumpers. Even if you buy good quality fabric at $10 per yard, your total savings will be 75% or more compared to "pre-made" items.

5 **SHOP AT OUTLETS.** Scattered across the country, we found a few outlets that discount linens. Among the better ones Garnet Hill and Carousel (also known as www.babybedding-gonline.com)—see their reviews in this chapter. Another reader praised the Pottery Barn Outlet. They have six locations at the time of this writing. You can find a listing of them on OutletBound.com. The discounts start at 50% and only get better from there. They have bedding and other furniture on sale.

6 **DON'T PICK AN OBSCURE BEDDING THEME.** Sure, that "Exploding Kiwi Fruit" bedding is cute, but where will you find any matching accessories to decorate your baby's room? Chances are they'll only be available "exclusively" from the bedding's manufacturer—at exclusively high prices. A better bet is to choose a more common theme with lots of accessories (wall decor, lamps, rugs, etc.). The more plentiful the options, the lower the prices. Winnie the Pooh is a good example, although you'll find quite a few accessories for other common themes like Noah's Ark, teddy bears, rocking horses, etc.

7 **GO FOR SOLID COLOR SHEETS AND USE THEMED ACCESSORIES.** Just because you want to have a Beatrix Potter-themed nursery doesn't mean you have to buy Beatrix Potter *bedding*. A great money-saving strategy: use low-cost solid color sheets, blankets and other linen items in the crib. Get these in colors that match/compliment theme accessories like a lamp, clock, poster, wallpaper, rugs, etc. (Hint: register for these items, which make nice shower gifts). You still have the Beatrix Potter look, but without the hefty tag for Beatrix Potter bedding. Many of the mail-order catalogs we review later in this chapter are excellent sources for affordable, solid-color bedding. Another bonus: solid color sheets/linens from the catalogs we recommend are often much higher quality (yet at a lower price) than theme bedding.

8 **SURF THE WEB.** Earlier in this chapter, we discussed the best web sites for baby bedding deals. Later in this chapter you'll find additional mail-order sources for bedding on a budget. The savings can be as much as 50% off retail prices. Even simple items like crib sheets can be affordably mail ordered. Next up: the best outlets for saving on baby bedding.

Outlets

GARNET HILL

Location: Historic Manchester Outlet Center, Manchester, Vermont. (802) 362-6198.

Love the look of the Garnet Hill bedding catalog but think the prices are hard to swallow? Then check out their outlets in New

Hampshire and Vermont, which feature first-quality overstock items from the current catalog like flannel sheets, quilts, blankets, children's clothing and more. The savings is 30% to 50%.

THE INTERIOR ALTERNATIVE

Locations: 8 locations, most of which are in the East, Midwest and South. Call (413) 743-1986 for a location near you.

Looking for fabric to decorate your baby's room or do-it-yourself bedding projects, but shocked at retail fabric prices? Then seek out the Interior Alternative, a fantastic fabric outlet. We visited their Dallas location and were amazed at the deals—literally THOUSANDS of bolts of fabric in just every imaginable pattern. If you like Waverly patterns, you'll find them here for just $8 a yard (half of retail). There's also wallpaper, borders, upholstery, pre-made curtain valances (for just $20) and more. Everything here is factory seconds, but we couldn't see any flaws. If you buy the entire bolt, take another 10% off.

The Name Game:
Reviews of Selected Manufacturers

Here are reviews of some of the brand names you'll encounter on your shopping adventures for baby bedding. Note: we include the phone numbers, web sites and addresses of each manufacturer—this is so you can find a local dealer near you (most do not sell directly to the public, nor send catalogs to consumers). We rated the companies on overall quality, price, and creativity, based on an evaluation of sample items we viewed at retail stores. We'd love to hear from you—tell us what you think about different brands and how they held up in the real world by emailing authors@BabyBargains.com.

The Ratings

A EXCELLENT—*our top pick!*
B GOOD— *above average quality, prices, and creativity.*
C FAIR—*could stand some improvement.*
D POOR—*yuck! could stand some major improvement.*

Amy Coe *For a dealer near you, call (203) 221-3050. Web: www.amycoe.com.* Designer Amy Coe turned her hobby of collecting vintage fabrics into a business when she launched her eponymous baby bedding line in 1993. The result is a linen collection with a flair for nostalgia: Coe takes fabrics that replicate patterns from the 1930's to the 1950's and crafts a full line of bedding items.

Coe has two lines: one for specialty stores (Amy Coe) and another for Target (amy coe). While both play off the same design inspiration, as you might expect, there are some major differences. The Amy Coe in specialty stores features more sumptuous fabrics and (no surprise) bigger price tags. The more expensive line runs $300 to $400 for a set and accessories are pricey too (chenille throws for $110, flannel blankets for $40 and so on). Quality is high and most fabrics are all cotton.

At Target, you get a more muted version of Amy's designs, although the fabric is still all-cotton and the sheets boast 200 thread counts and all-around elastic. Sheets run just $9, bumpers $40 and blankets $20. How's the quality? Coe's first offering for Target was a smash hit, but something happened with the second collection. We noted many buyers complained about the sheets shrinking and other quality snafus (we speculate that Target switched manufacturers for the coe line at some point). Opinions were definitely mixed on this line. Some parents told us they were very happy and had no shrinkage; others complained about too-short bumper ties on one collection (which oddly wasn't a problem for other collections). One tip: read the user reviews for the specific bedding you want on Target's web site before buying—you'll see when parents think there is a quality glitch. ***Rating (Target version): B (Specialty stores version): A-***

Baby Basics. See Carter's.

Affordable Artwork

Framed artwork for baby's room has to be very expensive, right? Nope, not if you buy a framed print from Creative Images (call 800-784-5415 or 904-825-6700 for a store near you; web: www.crimages.com). This Florida-based company sells prints, growth charts, wall hangings and more at very affordable prices—just $20 to $80. Each print is mounted on wood and laminated (no glass frame) so baby can enjoy it at eye-level (just sponge it off if it gets dirty). Best of all, there are hundreds of images in any theme to choose from: Pooh, Beatrix Potter, Noah's Ark, plus other collections of animals, sports and pastels. Check out their web site for samples.

Baby Gap *Web: www.babygap.com* Baby Gap jumped into the bedding biz in 2005 with six cute collections that are sold a la carte on their web site. A 200 thread count sheet goes for $24 (or two for $35), a bumper is $78, crib skirt $58 and quilt $88. So, a four-piece ensemble would be about $250. That's on the high end of baby bedding, as you might guess—so does Gap deliver on the quality? Mostly, yes. We like the sheets with all-around elastic and the matching fleece and cashmere blankets are divine. The only downside? The embroidery on such items as the crib skirts is low quality—the threads from the design came loose after a washing, complains one mom who emailed us. If you get this brand, you might stick with the non-embroidered patterns. All in all, we liked the Baby Gap crib bedding. Whether the look is for you (the line is heavy on baby-ish pastels) is up for debate, but the quality is pretty good. **Rating: A-**

Baby Martex This brand is distributed by CoCaLo. See their review later in this section.

BananaFish *For a dealer near you, call (800) 899-8689 or (818) 727-1645. Web: www.bananafishinc.com* "Sophisticated" and "tailored" is how we'd describe this California-based bedding maker. BananaFish's emphasis is on all-cotton fabric with adult-like finishes (such as pique) and muted color palettes. It's not cheap—prices range from $240 to $400 at retail for a four-piece set. Quality is high. FYI: You can see most of the collection at BabyUniverse.com **Rating: B**

Beatrix Potter This brand was a license by Crown Craft (see review later in this section), but the company no longer makes it. We still see a few closeout sets online for this brand, however.

Beautiful Baby *For a dealer near you, call (903) 295-2229. Web: www.bbaby.com.* Next to Nava's (reviewed later), this is probably the most over-the-top bedding in the market today. There's nothing subtle about Beautiful Baby's linens, which feature satin, lace and tulle. The bumpers are so huge they're like king-size pillows sewn together (okay, that's an exaggeration, but trust us, they are BIG) but they do have the most bumper ties of any manufacturer (26). Good news, though, you can customize the bumper thickness. As we noted earlier, thinner bumpers are safer, in our opinion. In fact, you can custom change just about anything in this line. Another plus: their sheets all have safety straps, an added feature we applaud. With over 1300 fabrics to choose from, Beautiful Baby says it takes four to six weeks to ship most orders. Prices are high:

bedding

LICENSE TRANSLATOR

Who makes what brand of bedding

One of the hottest trends in crib bedding is licensed characters—just about every cartoon character imaginable has been licensed to one of the big bedding makers for use in juvenile bedding. But how can tell you tell who makes what? Here is a list of popular licensed characters and their bedding makers:

LICENSE	SEE BEDDING MAKER
BABY GUND	LAMBS & IVY
BABY BLASS	QUILTEX
BABY LOONEY TUNES	GERBER
BABY MARTEX	COCALO
BEATRIX POTTER	NOJO
EDDIE BAUER	CROWN CRAFTS
HELLO KITTY	QUILTEX, LAMBS & IVY
J. GARCIA	QUILTEX
LAURA ASHLEY	SUMERSAULT
MY FIRST THOMAS	QUILTEX
OPBABY!	CROWN CRAFT
OSH KOSH B'GOSH	COCALO
PRECIOUS MOMENTS	CROWN CRAFTS, QUILTEX
RAGGEDY ANN & ANDY	SPRINGS
SESAME STREET	RIEGEL/MT. VERNON MILLS
SNOOPY	LAMBS & IVY
SUZY'S ZOO	GERBER
TODD PARR	QUILTEX
WAVERLY BABY	CROWN CRAFTS
WINNIE THE POOH	CROWN CRAFTS

expect to shell out $400 to $800 for a four-piece set, although all the pieces are priced individually. Most but not all fabrics are 100% cotton. Bottom line: this line isn't cheap, but if you're looking for bedding you can customize with an over-the-top style, this is the brand for you. ***Rating: B***

Bedtime Originals This brand is made by Lambs & Ivy. See their review later in this section.

Blueberry Lane *Call (413) 528-9633 for a dealer near you. Web: www.blueberrylanehome.com.* Designer Diane Sorrell uses textured blends to give Blueberry Lane's baby bedding a unique look. Quality is good; the bedding is sewn in North Carolina and Massachusetts. Blueberry Lane offers "total room concepts" that pair bedding with coordinating hand-painted furniture pieces and window treatments. Prices for the bedding run $350 to $520 for a four piece set. One bummer: their web site is for retailers only so consumers can't look at their offerings online. **Rating: B+**

Blue Moon Baby *For a dealer near you, call (626) 455-0014. Web: www.bluemoonbaby.com.* In business for seven years, California-based Blue Moon Baby specializes in chenille bedding.

The Marketing of Baby Linens: Dangerous Impressions?

Flip through any bedding catalog or web site and you'll see decked-out cribs, stuffed with sumptuous linens. Some linen companies like Baby Martex even use long ago recalled cribs (with dangerous corner posts) to market "antique" looking patterns. Yet, in their haste to market their products, baby linen makers may be sending a wrong (and dangerous) message to parents—that it's OK to put soft bedding items like pillows, comforters and the like in cribs. Safety advocates clearly warn against this, but it still amazes us to see bedding brochures with many offending items loaded into cribs, some of which are missing a drop-side (in order to show the merchandise more clearly, of course). The reason why this happens is obvious: linen manufacturers make fat profits off of such "decorative" accessories. And what better way to sell such items for baby than to deck out cribs? But we wonder if this sends the wrong message to parents—some folks may think that's how their crib *should* look. Yeah, many bedding makers include warning labels (in six-point type) that says you shouldn't put such items in a crib—but that's usually in the fine print if it exists at all. All bedding makers should eliminate this practice at once.

By the way, in 2000, retailers including JCPenney, Sears, Babies R Us, Target, IKEA and Lands End promised the CPSC they would discontinue displaying soft bedding in cribs including quilts and pillows. In a spot check of Sears' and JCPenney's online catalogs, we continued to see quilts draped over crib railings as we went to press. On a recent visit to our local Babies R Us, we also noted they are continuing to drape crib rails with quilts. So much for promises.

Their four collections feature chenille in a variety of patterns and designs for both boys and girls. One of the best bets: The Cowboy Collection with its red bandanna trim and denim accents, along with a chenille cowboy. For girls, the Cotton Tail collection featured cute pink bunnies that are sure to draws ooh's and aah's from grandparents. Blue Moon Baby also sells coordinating furniture, stuffed animals and other decorative accents. Prices are about $400 for a three-piece set which includes bumper, skirt and quilt (Blue Moon Baby doesn't sell sheets). The fabric is all cotton. We thought the quality was very good and we really like the unique designs— no one else is doing sculptured chenille designs. However, the use of chenille in baby bedding is quite controversial. See the Safe and Sound section earlier in this chapter. Another downside: the price is rather high for what is just a three-piece set of bedding. Blue Moon Baby also makes bassinet bedding in four designs. Because of the controversy over chenille, we're going to give this line a lower rating this year. And we are disappointed that Blue Moon Baby's web site is still "coming soon." ***Rating: C***

Brandee Danielle *For a dealer near you, call (800) 720-5656, (714) 957-1240. Web: www.brandeedanielle.com.* Despite its feminine-sounding name, Brandee Danielle is one of the few makers that designs bedding with strongly "boyish" themes. One pattern, "Sports Fan," even featured a series of vintage sport equipment illustrations for the sport fan. In recent years they've added some new feminine patterns like "Baby Lilac" to round out their selection. Also unique: Brandee Danielle still sews all its bedding in-house (most use outside contractors). The bedding is widely available at specialty shops. Prices are $200 to $400 for a four-piece set. Even at that price level, it's a pretty good buy; most of the fabrics are 100% cotton. FYI: Brandee now has both top and bottom ties to their bumpers (in the past, it was top only). One negative to Brandee Danielle: many of their bedding items must be "hand washed" according to the washing instructions. But we noted many parents have ignored that advice and just washed items like sheets on the gentle cycle with no harm. New this year, the company's "BD Baby" line echoes Wendy Bellissimo's simple embroidery designs. Also new: Brandee Danielle Vintage, which features several "greatest hits" patterns of the past. ***Rating: A-***

California Kids *For a dealer near you, call (800) 548-5214, (650) 637-9054.* One of our favorite bedding lines, California Kids specializes in bright and upbeat looks. In the past few years, they've added more girl-oriented themes as well as a line of coordinating drawer pulls. Look for their Waverly prints and matching rugs plus new sports-themed groupings. The quality is excellent; everything is 100% cotton and made in California. Prices run $250 to $350 for a five-piece set (the average is about $300). With an amazing array of options (60+ patterns were available at last count), California Kids is available in specialty stores and upper-end department stores. Available accessories include wall hangings, lampshades and fabric by the yard. While we like the designs, again these guys don't have a web site. It's time to get with the program! **Rating: A**

Carousel We discussed this brand earlier under BabyBeddingOnline. com. In short, sets are an affordable $125 to $225 and fabrics are 100% cotton. You can also buy a la carte pieces. Bumpers have ties on the top and bottom and are not over-stuffed. Sheets are 200 plus thread count. And best of all, it can all be ordered online, with UPS tracking and more. So, overall, we recommend Carousel—good designs, great quality and affordable prices. **Rating: A**

Carter's *Made by Riegel. Call (800) 845-3251 or (803) 275-2541 for a dealer near you. Web: www.carters.com or www.parentin-formation.com.* Carter's is one of the biggest names in baby products—you'll find clothes, high chairs, strollers and even bedding sporting the name. One reason: clever design, which explains the runaway success of the John Lennon Real Baby collection. The collection (which also includes coordinating clothing and accessories) is based on a series of drawings Lennon made for his youngest son, Sean. We were impressed with the quality of this whimsical bedding—100% cotton, 200-thread count with sewn appliqués. That's not what we expect from a brand known for its affordable sleepers. And, amazingly enough, the price isn't that high—a four-piece set of Lennon baby is $140-$160.

If you don't like the Lennon look, Carter's has another bedding line: Baby Basics, a mix and match coordinates line in 100%, 200-thread count cotton; a set runs about $60 while individual sheets are about $11. Baby Basics is sold at Babies R Us (both in their stores and online). Other sets are sold at Baby Depot.

We are impressed with the improvements to the Carter's line. We think the Baby Basics are an amazing value (although the bumpers are a bit skimpy) and the flexibility of buying just what you need is terrific. The line is also available just about everywhere including at their outlet stores. **Rating B+**

Celebrations *Call (310) 532-2499 for a dealer near you. Web: www.baby-celebrations.com.* Celebrations specializes in feminine, sophisticated looks—patchwork motifs, eyelet laces, chenille trim and layered dust ruffles. The all-cotton linens range from $300 to $590.

Quality is excellent; we noticed the bumpers sported ties on the top and bottom (16 total). Most fabrics are all cotton. In recent years, Celebrations has branched out into matching accessories and now sells hand-painted lamps, cradle sets, wall hangings and more. This line is only sold in specialty stores. ***Rating: B+***

Circo *Available at Target (web: target.com)* Target's in-house brand of crib bedding gets mixed reviews from parents—readers say they love the prices ($8 to $12 for a sheet) and the cute prints, but quality is a mixed bag. Yes, it is all-cotton and the sheets feature elastic all-around, but some complain of shrinkage and thin thread counts. Our advice: buy a sheet or two to test out on your own before investing much in this brand. ***Rating: B***

CoCaLo *Call (714) 434-7200 for a dealer near you. Web: www.cocalo.com.* You could say baby bedding runs in the family at CoCaLo. Owner Renee Pepys Lowe's mother (Shirley) founded Nojo in 1970 and Renee worked at the family business before it was sold to Crown Crafts a few of years ago. Since then, Renee has branched out on her own, launching the CoCaLo line in 1999 (the name comes from the first two letters of Renee's daughters, Courtenay and Catherine Lowe). CoCaLo is made up of four lines: Osh Kosh, Baby Martex, an eponymous collection and Kimberly Grant, which CoCaLo acquired in 2002 and is reviewed separately later in this section. The lowest priced (and largest) group is Osh Kosh, ranging from $180 to $250 for a four-piece set. Unfortunately, not all of this collection is all-cotton (some sets are blends). CoCaLo has their own line of bedding that features extra long ruffles for $200 to $300 per set and includes a pastel patchwork motif (although we noticed CoCaLo has de-emphasized their own brand in recent years). Design-wise, the Osh Kosh line features their trademark denim look in most groupings, while CoCaLo is more whimsical, in brighter hues. Baby Martex (priced around $200 at Babies R Us and up to $300 at specialty stores) is simpler with checks, plaids and seersucker looks, although one grouping also showcased vintage floral prints. Quality-wise, we were impressed with Baby Martex and Kimberly Grant (which are all cotton) compared with the Osh Kosh sets, some of which are cotton-poly blends. We'd stick with the 100% cotton selections. FYI: CoCaLo designs a couple of collections for the Stokke round crib. New this year, CoCaLo is showing a "Luxury" line of bedding, replete with satin and crushed velvet for $180 to $200 for a five-piece seat. ***Rating: B+***

Company Kids This bedding is sold via mail order in the Company Store catalog. See the "Do it By Mail" section later in this chapter for details. ***Rating: A***

Cotton Tale *Call (800) 628-2621 or (714) 435-9558 for a dealer near you. Web: www.cottontaledesigns.com.* Now owned by crib-maker Baby's Dream, Cotton Tale is one of our favorite bedding lines for one reason: originality. There are no licensed cartoon characters or trendy fabrics like chenille here. Instead, you'll see hand-painted looks in beautiful soft pastels, all made in the U.S. We loved the whimsical animal prints and the feminine touches. Best of all, Cotton Tale's prices are affordable—most range from $200 to $350 with an average of $275 for a four piece set. Most of the fabrics are 100% cotton, although a few patterns have satin trim that is a blended fabric. We were also impressed with Cotton Tale's "Safe & Sound" bedding system, a revolutionary and somewhat controversial solution to the concern over bumpers. The system includes a "safety bumper" that eliminates the gap between bumper and mattress and a safety crib sheet with more elastic and deeper corner pockets for a snug fit. Best of all, the Safe & Sound bedding is affordable—$120 for an all-cotton three piece set (bumper, sheet, dust ruffle). Sheets sell separately for $16 (there are six different patterns available in the Safe & Sound line). Cotton Tale also sells a "safety sleep sack" that eliminates the need for a blanket for $28. Yep, this has been controversial—we point this out because some baby stores have balked at carrying it, worrying that the name implies all other bedding (especially those with regular bumpers) is not safe. As we discussed previously, there is no clear consensus on the safety of bumpers in cribs. But we're proud of Cotton Tale for coming up with a solution that enables parents to still have bumpers without the worry of entrapment. So, we'll give this line a big thumbs up for their innovative designs and beautiful patterns. FYI: Cotton Tale bedding is available just about everywhere. . . even in the JCPenney catalog and Babies R Us. **Rating: A**

CribShield & Breathable Bumper *Made by Trend-Lab. Call 866-873-6352 for a dealer near you. Web: www.cribshield.com* Here's a mom-invented product that is a simple solution to babies who get their arms or legs caught in the crib spindles: a "breathable" bumper made of mesh that velcros on to the crib. Unlike other thicker bumpers, this one allows for airflow and baby can't get trapped between it and the mattress. And it's affordable: $20 to $25 and available in stores or online (Wal-Mart.com carries it). FYI: The company makes two versions of the product: one is the Breathable Bumper (11" tall) and the other is the CribShield. The latter covers the entire crib from bottom rail to top rail, while the bumper is just a bumper. Detractors of these products say it doesn't fit all cribs (given the wide variety of models out there, that isn't a big surprise) and older babies can rip it off the crib. (It can only be used up to nine months of age, as recommended by the manufacturer). Yes, we see the last point . . . but this is a good solution for most folks. FYI: Don't rush out and get this product before baby is born. Only AFTER your baby develops a habit of getting arms or legs stuck in the crib spindles (only a small percentage will do that), do we recommend getting this product! **Rating: A**

Crown Crafts *Call (800) 421-0526 or (714) 895-9200 for a dealer near you. Web: www.CrownCraftsInfantProducts.com.* Baby bedding behemoth Crown Crafts seems to have snapped up every possible character license you can imagine. Their current line up includes Eddie Bauer Baby, opbaby!, Disney, Winnie the Pooh, Karen Neuburger, Precious Moments, Nojo, Waverly and more. Depending on the brand, sets run $40 to $140 and are sold at chain stores like Target (which has the company's Classic Pooh as an exclusive), Babies R Us, Baby Depot and other chains. In the past, we knocked Crown Craft's emphasis on cartoon characters instead of quality. And there is still room for improvement here (we noted the company's high end sets have bumpers with both top and bottom ties; the cheaper sets just have top ties). But we noticed the company has made a renewed effort to improve quality, particularly with the Nojo line ($100 to $270). Most of Crown Crafts' sheets are 100% cotton, which is better than in years past when the sheets could be blends. Bottom line, you get what you pay for with this manufacturer. Stick with the better quality sets (Nojo, Eddie Bauer) and avoid the cheap-o character-theme sets (Disney Baby). **Rating: C+**

Eddie Bauer. Once only available in their catalog, this bedding now is sold exclusively at Babies R Us and is made by Crown Craft (see above). Prices are high for the quality, which is average.

Fisher Price. This was made by Crown Craft, but they have since dropped the license. We still see some of this bedding on clearance online.

Fleece Baby *Web: www.fleecebaby.com* So, you live in a part of the country where winter is colder than (fill in your own punch line here)? Given all the warnings about soft bedding and heavy quilts, how do you keep baby warm during those cold winter months? One solution is fleece baby sheets. Invented by a mom, Fleece Baby makes a wide variety of crib sheets, blankets, play yard sheets and more . . . all of 100% polar fleece. Crib sheets run $30 to $35 and are sold online at BabyCenter.com and various other sites. We had a reader road test the play yard version of the Fleece Baby sheet and she gave it two thumbs up. The only concern: after washing, the sheet lost a bit of its softness, but still overall it was a winner. ***Rating: A***

Gerber *For a dealer near you, call (800) 4GERBER Web: www.gerber.com.* While Gerber offers some cute patterns in their bedding line and they're available almost everywhere, the bedding's quality leaves much to be desired. One reader emailed us this typical story: "I bought several of the Gerber Everyday Basics knit sheets. They fit my 5" thick Sealy mattress well when I bought them, they were super soft, and had elastic all the way around for safety. BUT THEN . . . I washed them on the delicate cycle in cold water and dried them on low/delicate as instructed in the package, and they shrunk so much I couldn't even get them on the mattress anymore!" Other parents complained about colors that faded after just a couple washes and bumpers that lost their form as well. Gerber's biggest licenses are Suzy's Zoo and Baby Looney Tunes. And yes, the prices are cheap— a three-piece set of Baby Looney Tunes from Babies R Us is a mere $40. But the designs are screen printed on low quality cotton/poly fabrics. We can't recommend this brand. ***Rating: D***

Glenna Jean *For a dealer near you, call (800) 446-6018 or (804) 561-0687. Web: glennajean.com* We liked Glenna Jean's designs—as long as you stick with non-appliquéd patterns. The quality and sewing construction of the appliqués just wasn't very impressive. Glenna Jean is big on teddy bear designs and accessories, but they've brightened their color schemes of late. A four-piece set starts at $150 and averages $280 per set. We like their pretty, textured fabrics and denim patchwork designs. Overall, the best bets in the Glenna Jean line are the 100% cotton patchwork and floral print designs (only certain groupings are all-cotton; the rest are blends). FYI: this bedding is sold and often discounted deeply all over the Internet. Be sure to do a search to see what deals are available. One final caveat: Glenna Jean bumpers only have ties on the top, instead of both top and bottom as we prefer. ***Rating: B-***

Hoohobbers *For a dealer near you, call (773) 890-1466. Web: www.hoohobbers.com.* The quality of this brand was impressive—all of the comforters are made duvet-style with Velcro enclosures. The result: it's easy to remove the cover for washing. Even the bumpers feature zippered covers. Hoohobbers' dozen designs tend to have interesting color combinations in both brights and pastels. Prices for all their four-piece collections are $375; that's expensive, but everything is 100% cotton and well constructed (the sheets feature all-around elastic, for example). The good news is you can see and buy any of their patterns on their web site. All bedding is made at

Hoohobbers' Chicago factory. Finally, we should mention Hoohobbers' bassinets and Moses baskets come in coordinating fabrics as well. In fact, the company makes a wide range of accessories including furniture, bouncer seat covers and more. **Rating: B+**

Koala Baby *Available exclusively at Babies R Us.* Koala Baby is Babies R Us' attempt at establishing an in-house brand of bedding. A six-piece set sells for $150 to $170 and includes the quilt, bumper, sheet, dust ruffle, diaper stacker and valance. They also offer four piece sets for about $100. The designs are all made in China and come in three designs. So what's the downside? Quality, for one. As one reader put it "This brand is TERRIBLE!!!! I washed the fitted sheet before putting it on my crib mattress and it shrunk about 6" in length! I wouldn't recommend these sheets to anyone." Another reader knocked the Koala Baby dust ruffle she bought, which was very poor quality and didn't wash well. While the concept is admirable (private-label bedding at affordable prices), it seems that Babies R Us has missed with their Koala Baby line. **Rating: D+**

KidsLine *151 W. 135th St., Los Angeles, CA 90061. Call (310) 660-0110 for a dealer near you. Web: www. Kidslineinc.com.* Kidsline has been on a roll in recent years, designing sets with luxury touches while keeping prices affordable (most Kidsline sets are $100 to $200 for a six-piece set). New in the past year are several sets that incorporate denim, either as an accent or patchwork design. We also liked the mixed textures (faux suede, fleece, silver threads). How's the quality? Well, reviews on this vary. Some of KidsLine's sheets do not have elastic all-around, which is not impressive. Shrinkage is also a problem. Other parents, however, say they have been happy with their KidsLine bedding. So it is a mixed review for this brand—nice designs, but a bit iffy on the quality. FYI: as we were going to press, we noticed KidsLine was acquired by Russ Berrie and Co., a maker of plush animals and baby gifts. **Rating: B**

Kimberly Grant *Call (714) 546-4411 for a dealer near you. Web: www.kimberlygrant.com.* If you're looking for bedding designs that are a bit more low key and not too cutesy, Kimberly Grant is a great option. Now produced by CoCaLo (see review above), Grant continues to create sophisticated looks (floral prints, plaids) using luxe fabrics (velvets, satins, cotton), all in a warm palette. Prices run $389 to $529 for a four-piece set. Pricey but good quality. **Rating: A-**

Lambs & Ivy *For a dealer near you, call (800) 345-2627 or (310) 839-5155. Web: www.lambsivy.com* Barbara Lainken and Cathy Ravdin founded this LA-based bedding company in 1979. Their specialty: cutesy baby bedding that is sold in discount and mass market stores (you'll also see them sold in JCPenney's catalog and on many web sites). This year they've added some whimsical looks along with vintage prints and licensed characters. In fact, they've expanded their Snoopy license to include three options now. Quality of the Snoopy line is actually good. Instead of using stamp printing, Lambs & Ivy uses photo-quality heat transfer technology. This is a clever way of achieving a nicer look without big cost (you have to see the bedding in person to note the difference). Prices are still reasonable at $120 to $285 for a four-piece set. Bedtime Originals, a sub-line of Lambs & Ivy, is lower in price (around $50 for a three piece set) and quality. We'd rank the overall quality of Lambs & Ivy a bit ahead of other mass-market bedding brands. Yes, most of the fabrics are blends (50-50 cotton/poly), but the stitching and construction is a cut above. **Rating: B+**

Little Bedding This is a sub-line of Crown Crafts. See their review earlier in this section.

Lands End This bedding is sold via mail order in the Lands End catalog. See the "Do it By Mail" section later in this chapter for details. **Rating: A**

Laura Ashley This is a licensed line of Sumersault. See their review later in this section.

Luv Stuff Call (800) 825-BABY or (972) 278-BABY for a dealer near you. Web: www.luvstuffbedding.com. Texas-based Luv Stuff's claim to fame is their unique, hand-trimmed wall hangings, which match their custom bedding. You can mix and match to your heart's content (all items are sold a la carte). The quality is high: the company's exclusive fabrics are mostly 100% cotton and high-thread count, plus all their collections are made in-house in Texas. As you might expect, however, all this quality isn't free—a four-piece ensemble (sheet, comforter, bumper, dust ruffle) runs $400 to $500. And Luv Stuff's bumpers aren't very consumer friendly—they are surface clean (with a mild detergent) or dry-clean only. Despite this, we liked the brand's unique and bold styles. This bedding is a tour de force of color and contrast. **Rating: B**

Martha Stewart Web: www.kmart.com. This brand was sold in K-Mart stores but is now on hiatus. We weren't wild about their previous offerings, quality-wise. **Rating: C**

Mr. Bobbles Blankets Web: www.MrBobblesBlankets.com We

love the Graco Pak N Play and other playpens for their convenience . . . with one exception: those darn cheap sheets! The sheets that come with most playpens are easily pulled off by active babies and the thin, low-thread count cotton makes them a cold place for baby during winter months. To the rescue comes Mr. Bobbles Blankets, which besides the namesake blankets, also makes a No-Slip Play Yard Sheet for $19. We had a reader give this product a test-run and the verdict was positive. Made of 100% cotton flannel, the "very soft" sheets come in "cute fabrics" and "held up well after several washings," said our reviewer. And true to its claims, it does not slip off the mattress—the sheet is designed like a pillow sham so it doesn't easily pull off the corners. FYI: Another no-slip playpen sheet our readers like is by Kushies, the brand better known for their cloth diapers. Kushies' fitted flannel playpen sheet is $8. **Rating: A**

Nava's Designs For a dealer near you, call (818) 988-9050. Web: www.navasdesigns.com. Okay, Warren Buffet is your uncle . . . and he wants to give you a gift of baby bedding. Who you gonna call? Try Nava's, the most over-the-top bedding on the market today. The fabrics in this line are simply amazing—damask, silk dupioni, matte lasse and so on. Owner Nava Shoham has been designing nurseries since 1986 and her credits include numerous celebrities such as (and we are not making this up) Slash's nursery. Yes, Slash from Guns N Roses. Fill in your own joke here. So, how much does this cost? Are you sitting down? Nava's bedding runs $800 to $1000 for a set. And, yes, some of the fabrics have to be dry-cleaned. But seriously, we dare you to find more sumptuous bedding on the market. We decided to raise Nava's rating this year . . . making it 20 years in this biz by selling these linens at these prices, well, that's an achievement in its own right. **Rating: B**

NoJo See Crown Craft.

OshKosh B'Gosh See CoCaLo.

Pali This bedding is made by Glenna Jean; see review earlier.

Patchkraft Call (800) 866-2229 or (973) 340-3300 for a dealer near you. Web: www.patchkraft.com Patchkraft has one of the best web sites of any bedding manufacturer. They have done a terrific job of showcasing their extensive bedding line with clear thumbnails and enlargements that even include a swatch of fabric in many cases. While there is no substitute for feeling the fabric first-hand, the site helps you picture how these well made, mostly 100% cotton bedding collections look in real life. Besides the web site, we were also impressed with Patchkraft owner Paula Markowitz's commitment to safety. All the bumpers feature ties on the top and bottom and the company provides detailed safety and care instructions to its customers. We also liked the fact that Patchkraft has eliminated the comforter from some of its sets (instead, they substitute a flannel blanket; the quilt is now an optional accessory). You do have to pay for all that quality at prices ranging from $300 up to $500 for a four-piece set, but it is a good brand if you want to splurge. New in recent years are lightweight velour fabrics and flannels among the patchwork designs. They've also added a wallpaper line in addition to borders. Our only gripe: we wish Patchkraft had more entry-level options below $300 (they have two as of this writing). FYI: Dmart2000.com carries this brand, with prices starting at $200. Despite the prices, we'll give Patchkraft our highest rating based on safety, quality and design. **Rating: A**

Picci *Imported by Inglesina. Web: www.picci.it* And now for something completely different. Stroller maker Inglesina decided to bring Italian bedding maker Picci to the U.S. after sensing there was a niche for high-end bedding made in Europe. And that points up an oddity of the baby market here: many European-made products are a big hit here (Baby Bjorn, Perego strollers), but bedding is not among them. Why? Part of the blame is that what sells well in Europe for nurseries (garish colors, frilly treatments like canopies) just doesn't translate well across the Atlantic. To solve that dilemma, Inglesina hired an American designer to do Picci USA . . . but the linens are still made in Italy with the same high-quality fabrics and detailing. The result is impressive. In a market stuffed with cheaply-made imports from Asia, Picci actually pulls off a line with a high-end feel that still has an American design sensibility. The only caveat are the prices: $270 and up for a set. Some of the silk and embroidered groups can top $500. But we give Picci bonus points for creativity and quality. **Rating: B+**

Pine Creek *Call (503) 266-6275 for a dealer near you. Web: www.pinecreekbedding.com* Oregon-based Pine Creek Bedding has come back to their signature look with more flannel options, while offering sets with a new vintage feel. Look for old-fashioned graphics and soft colors. All the fabrics are 100% cotton. Considering the quality, we thought Pine Creek's prices were reasonable at $280 to $360 for a four-piece set. Pine Creek also sells accessories like lampshades and curtain valances, plus fabric is available by the yard. FYI: A related web site, www.comfortlines.com carries the entire Pine Creek line. So if you don't have a retailer near you, you'll find even accessories like wallpaper here. **Rating: A-**

Pitter Patter *For a dealer near you, call 505-751-9067 Web: www.pitterpattercollections.com* Taos, New Mexico-based Pitter Patter has a unique take on baby bedding. Their Hawaiian themed nursery linens are designed by independent artists, so many of the patterns and designs are one-of-a-kind. We loved the embroidered accents and playful prints. And yes, you can get a fabric-covered surf board as an accessory. Quality is high, but the price is as well—this might be a suggestion for grandma to buy. A four piece set runs $520 to $600 and features all cotton and some linen-cotton blends. And Pitter Patter offers one of the few (only?) crib bedding collections made from hemp, which some eco-parents laud for its environmentally-friendly and hypo-allergenic qualities. The hemp sets are $700, so you may need to whip out the Sierra Club American Express Platinum to pay for that. All in all, we liked Pitter Patter. It's refreshing to see a newcomer like Pitter Patter offer a different twist on baby bedding. ***Rating: B+***

Pooh Classic Pooh and Disney Pooh bedding are made by Crown Crafts subsidiary Red Calliope; see review below.

Pottery Barn See review later in this chapter. ***Rating: C***

Quiltex *For a dealer near you, call (800) 237-3636 or (212) 594-2205. Web: www.quiltex.com* Quiltex is famous for their licensed bedding items, including Hello Kitty, Precious Moments and Thomas the Tank Engine. Style-wise, we'd put Quiltex into the "cutesy, babyish" category—the groupings are heavy on the pastel colors and frilly ruffles. Unfortunately, most of the line is blends (50/50 cotton-poly fabric). The quality of the Quiltex designs is middle-of-the-road: some appliqué work leaves a bit to be desired, while other designs are merely stamped on the fabric. Their prices ($140 to $190 for a four-piece set) are a bit more reasonable. ***Rating: C-***

Red Calliope *See Crown Craft.*

Sleeping Partners *Call (212) 254-1515 for a dealer near you. Web: www.sleepingpartners.com* Sleeping Partners' mojo is embroidered bedding sets—their simple animal-theme designs echo that of Wendy Bellissimo . . . nice but pricey. How pricey? We noticed a simple four-piece set was $400 online (Sleeping Partners is sold on sites like BabyUniverse.com and in some stores like Buy Buy Baby), although we noticed a few sites had prices starting in the $200 range. It's all cotton and washes well, but beware: some of the bumpers are DRY CLEAN ONLY. Whoops, that just shot down their rating by an entire letter grade. ***Rating: C+***

Sumersault *Call (800) 232-3006 or (201) 768-7890 for a dealer near you.* Web: www.sumersault.com Owner Patti Sumergrade imports beautiful fabrics from Europe to create this top-shelf bedding line. We loved the plaids and whimsical fabrics, all done with a sophisticated spin. Compared to other lines, Sumersault leaves most of the cutesy touches to optional wall hangings. A four piece set retails for $325 to $400. FYI: Sumersault also makes the Laura Ashley Mother and Child bedding collection, which sells for $250 to $400 for four pieces. New this year are touches of embroidery and a few mixed-texture sets, which were winners design-wise. Overall, the quality of Sumersault is excellent. ***Rating: A***

Sweet Kyla *Call 800-265-2229 for a dealer near you.* Web: www.sweetkyla.com Canadian bedding maker Sweet Kyla has popped up stateside in USA Baby Stores among other outlets. We liked their take on crib bedding, which often uses mixed textures (a touch of faux suede, for example) and patchwork motifs. Most fabrics are all-cotton and customer service and delivery is excellent. Readers who have purchased this line have been impressed with the quality. Sets are around $220 to $260 or you can order pieces a la carte. You can also buy their fabric by the yard. One parent who bought this brand for her son's nursery raved about their excellent fabric, saying the sheets in particular were "very soft and cozy." ***Rating: A-***

Sweet Pea *Call (626) 578-0866 for a dealer near you.* You gotta like Sweet Pea . . . their fun and funky fabrics are imported from places like the Vatican (which we didn't realize exported anything other than Popes). Sweet Pea's 100% cotton bedding features a variety of very-adult finishes including jacquards, satins and even crushed velvets. If you don't like the damask-woven fabric, consider a floral chintz that looks like Laura Ashley on acid. One impossibly over-the-top design featured mix-and-match cabbage roses, corded piping trim and ribbon accents. Unfortunately, the prices are also over-the-top: five piece sets *start* at $400 and can top $1000. Ouch. While the quality is high, the prices are way out of the ballpark. ***Rating: B***

Waverly See Crown Crafts review earlier in this section.

Wendy Bellissimo Baby N Kids *Call (818) 348-3682 for a dealer near you.* Web: www.wendybellissimo.com. Hot-shot young designer Wendy Bellissimo hawked her pricey bedding at specialty boutiques until 2004, when she abruptly shifted gears to partner with Babies R Us. Now a BRU exclusive, Bellissimo has expanded her horizons beyond bedding to include all sorts of décor accessories, diaper bags, mobiles and more. As for the bedding, the designs look much the same as before: the typical Bellissimo look is a simple block pattern with a touch of embroidery or chenille. But the prices! $300 for a five-piece set that's sewn in China? While we thought the look was a notch above what is normally sold at BRU, we were unimpressed with the crib sheet, which seemed thin and low in thread count. And the first reviews on Amazon for this bedding have been similarly mixed to downright hostile (several folks knocked the bedding for low quality). Take your $300 and buy a better quality bedding set from any of the above-mentioned designers. **Rating: C-**

◆ **Other brands to consider: Simmons** (the crib maker) also makes bedding ranging from $130 to $280. The designs are simple with patchwork accents in some cases. They have quite a wide range of accessories to go with each collection and they are discounted heavily on the web and in chain stores.

For folks living in those ice cold climates who want to add a bit of island chic to their baby's room, check out **Uhula.com**. Their Hawaiian themed bedding (also very popular in Hawaii as you can imagine) will have you imagining warm beaches and cool island breezes in no time. We love this site's laid back style and the patterns are like nothing you'll find anywhere else.

Riegel (800) 845-3251 or (803) 275-2541 (web: www.parentinformation.com) made by Mt. Vernon Mills is a big player in the bedding market—but you might not recognize the name. Riegel is the company behind the in-store bedding brands at discounters like Target and Wal-Mart. The company also sells two collections under their own name, makes the Carter's Lennon Baby (reviewed earlier, ($150 for a four-piece 100% cotton 200 thread count set) and the Carter's Coordinates ($60 for four pieces in 100% cotton). Finally, Riegel manufacturers Sesame Street crib bedding for $40 for a four-piece set. While the Carter's line is good quality, the Sesame Street and Riegel collections are poly/cotton blends intended for mass-market discount stores. **Springs** (call 212-556-6300 for a dealer near you; web: www.springs.com) has three patterns available in their collection. Wamsutta Baby is a standout with 100% cotton sheets and matte lasse finish on the coverlet and bumpers. Entry-level bedding sets sell in Wal-Mart for $40 and go up to $100 for a four-piece set.

New on the upper-end bedding scene is **Bebe Chic** (201) 941-5414 (www.bebechic.com), a New Jersey-based designer who says their bedding combines "old world charm (with) soft textures, jacquards and quilted solids." Their prices: $200 to $300 for a comforter, $40 to $60 for a single sheet. Available in Bellini stores.

Continued on page 146

BEDDING RATINGS

NAME	RATING	COST
AMY COE	A-/B	$ TO $$$
BABY GAP	A-	$$
BANANA FISH	B	$$
BEAUTIFUL BABY	B	$$$
BLUEBERRY LANE	B+	$$$
BRANDEE DANIELLE	A-	$$
CALIFORNIA KIDS	A	$$
CAROUSEL	A	$ TO $$
CARTERS	B+	$
CELEBRATIONS	B+	$$ TO $$$
COCALO	B+	$ TO $$
COMPANY KIDS	A	$
COTTON TALE	A	$$
CROWN CRAFTS	C+	$ TO $$
GERBER	D	$
GLENNA JEAN	B-	$ TO $$
HOOHOBBERS	B+	$$
KOALA BABY	D+	$
KIDSLINE	B	$ TO $$
KIMBERLY GRANT	A-	$$ TO $$$
LAMBS & IVY	B+	$ TO $$
LANDS END	A	$
LUV STUFF	B	$$$
NAVA'S DESIGNS	B	$$$
PATCHKRAFT	A	$$ TO $$$
PICCI	B+	$$ TO $$$
PINE CREEK	A-	$$
PITTER PATTER	B+	$$$
POTTERY BARN	C	$$
QUILTEX	C-	$
SLEEPING PARTNERS	C+	$$$
SUMERSAULT	A	$$ TO $$$
SWEET KYLA	A-	$$
SWEET PEA	B	$$$
WENDY BELLISSIMO	C-	$$

KEY

* N/A. In some cases, we didn't have this information by press time.
COST: Cost of a four-piece set (comforter, sheet, dust ruffle/bed skirt, bumpers) $=under $200; $$=$200 to $400; $$$=over $400
FIBER CONTENT: Some lines have both all-cotton and poly/cotton blends—these are noted with the word "Mix."

Fiber Content	Bumper Ties	Tie Length
100% cotton	Top/Bottom	10"
100% cotton	Top/Bottom	*
100% cotton	Top	6"
100% cotton	Top/Bottom	8"
100% cotton	Top/Bottom	*
Mix	Top/Bottom	7"
100% cotton	Top/Bottom	10"
100% cotton	Top/Bottom	*
100% cotton	Top/Bottom	*
100% cotton	Top/Bottom	9"
Mix	Top/Bottom	6.5"
100% cotton	Top/Bottom	*
100% cotton	Top	7.5"
Mix	Varies	8"
Poly/Cotton	*	*
Mix	Top	10"
100% cotton	Top	6"
100% cotton	Top	*
Mix	Top/Bottom	7" to 9"
100% cotton	Top/Bottom	6.5"
Poly/cotton	Top	10"
100% cotton	Top/Bottom	*
100% cotton	Top	11"
100% cotton	Top/Bottom	14"
100% cotton	Top/Bottom	9"
100% cotton	Top/Bottom	*
100% cotton	Top/Bottom	8"
100% cotton	Top/Bottom	*
100% cotton	Top/Bottom	*
Poly/cotton	Top	7"
100% cotton	Top/Bottom	10"
100% cotton	Top	7"-9"
Mix	Top	9.5"
100% cotton	Top/Bottom	10"
100% cotton	Top/Bottom	*

Bumper Ties: refers to the location of bumper ties, top and bottom or top only.
Tie Lengths: the length of the bumper ties; these are approximate estimates and may vary from style to style.

Do It By Mail

Here's an overview of several catalogs that offer baby bedding. In most cases, the catalogs carry private label merchandise (with the exception of JCPenney and Baby Catalog, which sell name brands). In general, we find that the bedding from most mail-order catalogs is very high quality and unique in design. Another big plus: you can find affordable basic items like solid color sheets and blankets.

BABY CATALOG OF AMERICA

Call (800) PLAYPEN or (203) 931-7760; Fax (203) 933-1147.
Internet: www.babycatalog.com
Accept: all major credit cards
Order by mail or visit the Baby Club of America Warehouse Outlet, 719 Campbell Ave., West Haven, CT 06516.

How can you get name-brand bedding at a big discount? Unfortunately, most catalogs sell bedding at full retail and baby stores are loath to discount fancy brands.

Well, here's the good news: Baby Catalog of America is a one-stop source for brand new bedding, linen, decor and other accessories at prices 20% to 50% off retail. And we're not talking about just the low quality bedding brands either. Baby Catalog of America sells a wide variety of premium brands, including Sumersault and Patch Kraft.

What about accessories? You can find lamps, wall decor, and other nursery items at good prices too

If those prices weren't low enough, Baby Catalog will give you another 10% off each purchase if you buy an annual membership ($25). And that's just the beginning: the catalog also sells strollers, car seats, accessories and more. The only caveat to using this catalog and web site is we don't recommend using their baby registry. We've received many complaints from past readers about this service.

COMPANY KIDS

To Order Call: (800) 323-8000
Web: www.companykids.com
Shopping Hours: 24 hours a day, seven days a week.
Or write to: 500 Company Store Rd., La Crosse, WI 54601.
Credit Cards Accepted: MC, VISA, AMEX, Discover.

A subsidiary of the Company Store, Company Kids now offers a complete catalog catering to the bedding whims of parents and little ones alike. Basically, Company Kids offers a selection of quilts for infants, which can then be paired with sheets in solids or checks. There are also some bedding sets (sold a la carte with matching bumpers, sheets and dust ruffles) as well. Duvets are also available.

Sheets run $12 to 15 each while comforters are about $59 each. Not a bad deal at all for 100% cotton percale or knit bedding fabrics.

Bottom line: we think Company Kids sells high quality baby bedding at great prices. We also liked their web site, which is easy-to-navigate and features clearance items for even bigger savings. If you're in the vicinity of The Company Store's outlet store, don't miss it. One reader found the prices amazing including sheets at only $5.

GARNET HILL

To Order Call: (800) 622-6216; In Canada, call (603) 823-5545.
Shopping Hours: 24 hours a day, seven days a week.
Or write to: Garnet Hill, 231 Main St., Franconia, NH 03580.
Credit Cards Accepted: MC, VISA, AMEX, Discover.
Outlet: Historic Manchester Outlet Center, Manchester VT (802) 362-6198.

If you want to spend the big bucks on bedding, check out Garnet Hill. This catalog makes a big deal out of its "natural fabric" offerings, and they do sell products we haven't seen elsewhere. But you'll pay for the privilege.

Garnet Hill sells woven and knit crib bedding. Unfortunately, they've scaled back their crib bedding options since our last edition. While they offer a few crib size quilts, they only have one set that comes with a bumper and the other items are just fitted sheets. The Pixie Chix percale crib sheet is one example for $25. The quality is high: all sheets are 200 thread count. One reader emailed her thoughts on Garnet Hill's sheets: "A big thumbs up," she said, adding "even though the price was high, the sheets were very high quality and soft." She wasn't as thrilled with their bumper pads, which only have ties at the top and the filling "got a bit munched in the washing machine."

The catalog's patchwork quilts ($78 to $98) are quite beautiful.

GRAHAM KRACKER

To Order Call: (800) 489-2820; Fax: (915) 697-1776
Web: www.grahamkracker.com; Credit Cards Accepted: MC, VISA.

This mail order company specializes in custom bedding. You can mix and match your own selections from 108 different fabrics or you can provide your own fabric. The price? A whopping $495 for a five-piece set, which includes a headboard bumper and baby pillow (don't use this in the crib, please!). But, everything is 100% cotton and there are all sorts of matching accessories. Most of the choices are bright, cheerful colors, but not too cutesy. Shipping time is two to three weeks.

THE LAND OF NOD

To Order Call: (800) 933-9904. Web: www.landofnod.com
Shopping Hours: Mon-Fri 7:30am to 9:00pm, Weekends 9am to 5pm
Or Write to: PO Box 1404, Wheeling, IL 60090
Credit Cards: MC, VISA, AMEX, Discover.

This stunning catalog (now owned by Crate & Barrel) features attractive layouts of baby's and kid's rooms, replete with cute linens and accessories. Even if you don't buy anything, the Land of Nod is a great place to get decorating ideas.

Crib bedding is sold a la carte and some designs only have the quilt, bed skirt and bumpers available. A four-piece set runs $218 to $270, while a single sheet can cost $20. The prices are still very good, maybe even a bit less than last time. We loved the color palette, which ranged from patchwork denim to bright pastels. Check out the whimsical lamps and other accessories, including their cool Nod Chair and Ottoman.

LANDS' END

To Order Call: (800) 345-3696; Web: www.landsend.com
Shopping Hours: 24 hours a day, seven days a week.
Or write to: Lands' End Inc., 1 Lands' End Lane, Dodgeville, WI 53595.
Credit Cards Accepted: MC, VISA, AMEX, Discover.
Retail Outlets: Lands' End has 20 outlet stores, mostly in the Midwest and Northeast—call the number above for the nearest location to you.

Lands' End changes their options so frequently, it's tough to nail them down for you. While they've always made great quality, 100% sheets with all around elastic, you never know what colors and fabrics they'll have. For example, a recent visit netted only two options, both of cotton knit fabric. Sold in sets of two sheets, they range from $34 to $36. Solid color sheets come in pink, blue, gold and white. The one pattern option available had blue and gold stars on a white background.

While the offerings change each season, Land's End designs have tended toward the simple, with no cartoons or appliqués to clutter up the basic look. Another bonus: Lands' End web site has fantastic overstock deals, posted twice weekly.

POTTERY BARN KIDS

To Order Call: (800) 430-7373. Web: www.potterybarnkids.com

Shopping Hours: 24 hours a day, seven days a week.
Or write to: P.O. Box 379909, Las Vegas, NV, 89137.
Credit Cards Accepted: MC, VISA, AMEX.
Outlet Stores: Jeffersonville, OH (740) 948-2004, Dawsonville, GA (706)
216-5211 or (706) 216-6465, Memphis, TN (901) 763-1500.

No catalog has shaken up the baby bedding and décor business in recent years like the Pottery Barn Kids (PBK) catalog. Their cheerful baby bedding, whimsical accessories and furniture have overrun the rest of the industry. PBK isn't cutesy-babyish or overly adult. It's playful, fun and bright. And hot. We get more questions about this catalog than any other.

So let's answer a few of those questions. PBK's bedding is 100% cotton, 200-thread count. The sheets have 10" corner pockets and they *used* to have elastic that went all the way around the edge. We're disappointed to say that they now only make their crib sheets with elastic on the ends. And that elastic is the source of frustration among some parents we talked to—one PBK customer said she had to exchange several sheets after the elastic popped off or simply wore out after only one washing.

Several readers have also complained about the bumpers, which are knocked as "thin and insubstantial." One reader wrote saying "they are very thin and my child can get his arms and legs out of the slats of the crib because the bumpers smush down so easily!" Another reader complained that the ties kept pulling off her bumper.

Prices for quilts range from $59 to $79, bumper sets are $59 to $69, sheets are $14 to $16 and dust ruffles are $35 to $49. While the prices are affordable, the nagging quality issues give us pause to recommend PBK's crib bedding. On the plus side, frequent sales make more expensive items like lamps and rugs even more affordable. The best deal: PBK's outlet stores. One reader saw sheets on sale for $8, duvet covers for $15 and even a crib for $175 at the outlet (see above for locations).

What really seems to be PBK's strong suit is accessories. The catalog is stuffed with so many rugs, lamps, storage options and toys, you can shop one place for a complete look.

So, it is a mixed bag for PBK: kudos to this retailer for shaking up the staid baby bedding biz. But poor quality gives us pause in recommending this brand, unless you get an unbelievable deal at their outlet store.

◆ **Other Catalogs to Consider**. Here are several other catalogs that carry basic linens and supplies:

The Right Start (800) 548-8531, web: www.rightstart.com

One Step Ahead (800) 274-8440, web: www.onestepahead.com
Baby Universe Web: www.babyuniverse.com
JcPenney (800) 222-6161. Web: www.jcpenney.com

The Bottom Line:
A Wrap-Up of Our Best Buy Picks

For bedding, we think Cotton Tale and Lambs & Ivy combine good quality at a low price. If you can afford to spend more, check out the offerings from Patchkraft, Sumersault, and California Kids. And if money is no object, try Nava's. Of course, there's no law that says you have to buy an entire bedding set for your nursery—we found that all baby really needs is a set of sheets and a good cotton blanket. Catalogs like Lands' End and Company Store sell affordable (yet high-quality) basics like sheets and blankets. Instead of spending $300 to $500 on a bedding set with ridiculous items like pillows and diaper stackers, use your creativity to decorate the nursery affordably and leave the crib simple.

And if you fall in love with a licensed cartoon character like Pooh, don't shell out $300 on a fancy bedding set. Instead, we recommend buying solid color sheets and accessorizing with affordable Pooh items like lamps, posters, rugs, etc.

Who's got the best deals on bedding? If it's a set you desire, check out web sites like Baby Depot (www.coat.com) for discounts of 20% to 40%. If you're lucky to be near a manufacturer's outlet, search these stores for discontinued patterns.

Let's take a look at the savings:

Company Kids cotton fitted sheets (three)	$45
Fleece coverlet blanket (Company Kids) or sleep sack	$20
Miscellaneous (lamp, other decor)	$100

TOTAL	**$165**

In contrast, if you go for a designer brand and buy all those silly extras like diaper stackers, you could be out as much as $800 on bedding alone—add in wall paper, accessories like wall hangings, matching lamps and you'll be out $1100 or more. So, the total savings from following the tips in this chapter could be as much as $900 to $1000.

Now that your baby's room is outfitted, what about the baby? Flip to the next chapter to get the lowdown on those little clothes.

CHAPTER 4

The Reality Layette:
Little Clothes for Little Prices

Inside this chapter

What the heck is a "onesie"? How many clothes does your baby need? How come such little clothes have such big price tags? These and other mysteries are unraveled in this chapter as we take you on a guided tour of baby clothes land. We'll reveal our secret sources for finding name brand clothes at one-half to one-third off department store prices. Which brands are best? Check out our picks for the best clothing brands for your baby and our nine tips from smart shoppers on getting the best deals. Next, read about the many outlets for children's apparel that have been popping up all over the country. At the end of this chapter, we'll even show you how to save big bucks on diapers.

Getting Started:
When Do You Need This Stuff?

◆ **Baby Clothing.** You'll need basic baby clothing like t-shirts and sleepers as soon as you're ready to leave the hospital. Depending on the weather, you may need a bunting (a snug-fitting, hooded sleeping bag of heavy material) at that time as well.

You'll probably want to start stocking up on baby clothing around the seventh month of your pregnancy—if you deliver early, you will need some basics. However, you may want to wait to do major shopping until after any baby showers to see what clothing your friends and family give as gifts.

Be sure to keep a running list of your acquisitions so you won't buy too much of one item. Thanks to gifts and our own buying, we had about two thousand teeny, side-snap shirts by the time our baby was born. In the end, our son didn't wear the shirts much (he grew out of the newborn sizes quickly and wasn't really wild about them anyway), and we ended up wasting the money we spent.

◆ **Diapers.** How many diapers do you need for starters? Are you sitting down? If you're going with disposables, we recommend 600 diapers for the first six weeks (about 14 diapers a day). Yes, that's six packages of 100 diapers each (purchase them in your eighth month of pregnancy, just in case Junior arrives early). You may think this is a lot, but believe us, we bought that much and we still had to do another diaper run by the time our son was a month old. Newborns go through many more diapers than older infants because they feed more frequently. Also, remember that as a new parent, you'll find yourself taking off diapers that turn out to be dry. Or worse, you may change a diaper three times in a row because Junior wasn't really finished.

Now that you know how many diapers you need, what sizes should you buy? We recommend 100 newborn-size diapers and 500 "size one" (or Step 1) diapers. This assumes an average-size baby (about seven pounds at birth). But remember to keep the receipts—if your baby is larger, you might have to exchange the newborns for size one's (and some of the one's for two's). Note for parents-to-be of multiples: your babies tend to be smaller at birth, so buy all newborn diapers to start. And double or triple our recommended quantity!

If you plan to use a diaper service to supply cloth diapers, sign up in your eighth month. Some diaper services will give you an initial batch of diapers (so you're ready when baby arrives) and then await your call to start up regular service. If you plan to wash your own cloth diapers, buy two to five dozen diapers about two months before your due date. You'll also probably want to buy diaper covers (6 to 10) at that time. We'll discuss cloth diapers in depth later in this chapter.

Even if you plan to use disposable diaper, you should pick up one package of high-quality cloth diapers. Why? You'll need them as spit-up rags, spot cleaners and other assorted uses you'd never imagined before becoming a parent.

 *Sources*

There are ten basic sources for baby clothing and diapers:

BABY SPECIALTY STORES. Specialty stores typically carry 100% cotton, high-quality clothes, but you won't usually find them affordably priced. While you may find attractive dressy clothes, play clothes are typically a better deal elsewhere. Because the stores themselves are frequently small, selection is limited. On the upside, you can still find old-fashioned service at specialty stores—and that's helpful when buying items like shoes. In that case, the extra help with sizing may be worth the higher price.

As for diapers, you can forget about it—most specialty baby stores long ago ceded the diaper market to discounters and grocery stores (who sell disposables), as well as mail-order/online companies (who dominate the cloth diaper and supply business). Occasionally, we see specialty stores carry an offbeat product like Tushies, an eco-friendly disposable diaper. And some may have diaper covers, but the selection is typically limited.

2 **DEPARTMENT STORES.** Clothing is a department store's bread and butter, so it's not surprising to see many of these stores excel at merchandising baby clothes. Everyone from Sears to Nordstrom sells baby clothes and frequent sales often make the selection more affordable.

3 **SPECIALTY CHAINS.** Our readers love Old Navy (see money-saving tips section) and Gap Kids. Both sell 100% cotton, high-quality clothes that are stylish and durable. Not to mention their price adjustment policies. One reader told us that if you buy an item at Gap/Old Navy and it goes one sale within seven days, you get the new price. Old Navy's selection of baby clothes is somewhat limited compared to Gap Kids. Other chains to check out include Gymboree, and Talbots for Kids. All are reviewed later in this chapter.

4 **DISCOUNTERS.** Wal-Mart, Target and K-Mart have moved aggressively into baby clothes in the last decade. Instead of cheap, polyester outfits that were once common at these stores, most discounters now emphasize 100% cotton clothing in fashionable styles. Even places like Toys R Us now stock basic layette items like t-shirts, sleepers and booties.

Target has vastly expanded their baby clothes with their in-store brand, Cherokee. Not only have they expanded, but also the quality is terrific in most cases. We shop Target for all cotton play clothes and day care clothes. They seem to last pretty well with the active play our kids indulge in.

Diapers are another discounter strong suit—you'll find both name brand and generic disposables at most stores; some even carry a selection of cloth diaper supplies like diaper covers (although they are the cheaper brands; see the diaper section later in this book for more details). Discounters seem to be locked into an endless price battle with warehouse clubs on baby items, so you can usually find deals.

5 **BABY SUPERSTORES.** Both Babies R Us and Baby Depot carry a decent selection of name-brand clothing at low prices. Most of the selection focuses on basics, however. You'll see more Carter's and Little Me than the fancy brands common at department stores. We've noticed in recent years that places like Babies R Us have "dumbed-down" their clothing section, trading fancy dress clothes and brands for more staples at everyday low prices. In that respect, Babies R Us has ceded the hip, stylish market to specialty chains like Gap Kids.

Diapers are a mixed bag at superstores. Babies R Us carries them, but Baby Depot doesn't. When you find them, though, the prices are comparable to discounters. We've seen diapers priced 20% to 30% lower at Babies R Us than grocery stores.

6 **WAREHOUSE CLUBS.** Members-only warehouse clubs like Sam's, Costco and BJ's sell diapers at rock-bottom prices. The selection is often hit-or-miss—sometimes you'll see brand names like Huggies and Pampers; other times it may be off-brands. While you won't find the range of sizes that you'd see in grocery stores, the prices will be hard to beat. The downside? You have to buy them in "bulk," huge cases of multiple diaper packs that might require a forklift to get home.

As a side note, we've even seen some baby clothes at warehouse clubs from time to time. We found very good quality blanket sleepers at Sam's for $8 each during one visit. Costco has also greatly improved their kids clothing offerings in recent years. We love Costco's 100% cotton pajamas for toddlers at $10 a pair (compare at $36 a pair in catalogs). Costco also has infant-size play clothes and sleepers at bargain prices.

7 **MAIL-ORDER.** There are a zillion catalogs that offer clothing for infants. The choices can be quite overwhelming, and the prices can range from reasonable to ridiculous. It's undeniably a great way to shop when you have a newborn and just don't want to drag your baby out to the mall. Another mail order strength: cloth diapers and related supplies. Chains and specialty stores have abandoned these items, so mail order suppliers have picked up the slack. Check out "Do it By Mail" later in this chapter for the complete low-down on catalogs that sell clothing and diapers.

8 **THE WEB.** Baby clothing sales on the 'net have been somewhat slow to take off. We suspect this might have to do with the glut of mail order catalogs that vie for parents' attention, as well as the fact that clothing's relative low prices make the discounts less dramatic. As for diapers, several web sites have popped up in recent years to offer discount disposables. And the web is a great source for cloth diapers and supplies. We'll discuss the best web sites for all these items later in the chapter.

9 **CONSIGNMENT OR THRIFT STORES.** You might think of these stores as dingy shops with musty smells—purveyors of old, used clothes that aren't in great shape. Think again—many consignment stores today are bright and attractive, with name brand clothes at a fraction of the retail price. Yes, the clothes have been worn before, but most stores only stock high-quality brands that are in excellent condition. And stores that specialize in children's apparel are popping up everywhere, from coast to coast. Later in this chapter, we'll tell you how to find a consignment store near you.

10 **GARAGE/YARD SALES.** Check out the box on the next page for tips on how to shop garage sales like the pros.

Baby Clothing

So you thought all the big-ticket items were taken care of when you bought the crib and other furniture? Ha! It's time to prepare for your baby's "layette," a French word that translated literally means "spending large sums of cash on baby clothes and other such items, as required by Federal Baby Law." But, of course, there are some creative (dare we say, sneaky?) ways of keeping your layette bills down.

At this point, you may be wondering just what does your baby

CPSC Issues Thrift Shop Warning

Do second-hand stores sell dangerous goods? To answer that question, the Consumer Product Safety Commission randomly surveyed 301 thrift stores in 2000, looking for recalled or banned products like clothing with drawstrings (an entanglement and strangulation hazard). The results: 51% of stores were selling clothing (mostly outerwear) with drawstrings at the waist or neck. This is particularly disturbing since 22 deaths and 48 non-fatal accidents since 1985 have been attributed to drawstrings. If you buy clothing at a consignment or thrift store or from a garage sale, be sure to avoid clothes with drawstrings. Another disturbing finding: about two-thirds of the stores surveyed had at least one recalled or banned product on the shelves.

need? Sure you've seen those cute ruffled dresses and sailor suits in department stores—but what does your baby *really* wear everyday?

Meet the layette, a collection of clothes and accessories that your baby will use daily. While your baby's birthday suit was free, outfitting him in something more "traditional" will cost some bucks. In fact, a recent study estimated that parents spend $12,000 on clothes for a child by the time he or she hits 18 years of age—and that sounds like a conservative estimate to us. That translates into a $20 *billion* (yes, that's billion with a B) business for children's clothing retailers. Follow our tips, and we estimate that you'll save 20% or more on your baby's wardrobe.

Garage & Yard Sales
Eight Tips to Get The Best Bargains

It's an American institution—the garage sale.

Sure you can save money on baby clothes and products at an outlet store or get a deal at a department store sale. But there's no comparing to the steals you can get at your neighbor's garage sale.

We love getting email from readers who've found great deals at garage sales. How about 25¢ stretchies, a snowsuit for $1, barely used high chairs for $5? But getting the most out of garage sales requires some pre-planning. We interviewed a dozen parents who call themselves "garage sale experts" for their tips:

1 CHECK THE NEWSPAPER FIRST. Many folks advertise their garage sales a few days before the event—zero in on the ads that mention kids/baby items to keep from wasting time on sales that won't be fruitful.

2 GET A GOOD MAP OF THE AREA. You've got to find obscure cul-de-sacs and hidden side streets.

3 START EARLY. The professional bargain hunters get going at the crack of dawn. If you wait until mid-day, all the good stuff will be gone. An even better bet: if you know the family, ask if you can drop by the day *before* the sale. That way you have a first shot before the competition arrives. One trick: if it's a neighbor, offer to help set-up for the sale. That's a great way to get those "early bird" deals.

4 DO THE "BOX DIVE." Many garage sale hosts will just dump kids clothes into a big box, all jumbled together in different sizes, styles, etc. Figuring out how to get the best picks while three

Parents in Cyberspace: What's on the Web?

Bella Kids

Web: www.bellakids.com

What it is: Site with domestic and European baby clothing.

What's cool: Organized by season, boy/girl and age, this site is easy to navigate. They carry brands from Zutano, Cozy Toes, Mulberribush and more. Although prices are quite high, the clothes are excellent quality and they offer up to 50% off sale items. Free shipping is another plus.

---

other moms are digging through the same box is a challenge. The best advice: familiarize yourself with the better name brands in this chapter and then pluck out the best bets as fast as possible. Then evaluate the clothes away from the melee.

5 CONCENTRATE ON "FAMILY AREAS." A mom here in Colorado told us she found garage sales in Boulder (a college town) were mostly students getting rid of stereos, clothes and other junk. A better bet was nearby Louisville, a suburban bedroom community with lots of growing families.

6 HAGGLE. Prices on big-ticket items (that is, anything over $5) are usually negotiable. Another great tip we read in the newsletter *Cheapskate Monthly*—to test out products, carry a few "C" and "D" batteries with you to garage sales. Most swings and bouncing seats use those type batteries, so you want to make sure they're working before you buy.

7 DON'T BUY A USED CRIB OR CAR SEAT. Old cribs may not meet current safety standards. It's also difficult to get replacement parts for obscure brands. Car seats are also a second-hand no-no—you can't be sure it wasn't in an accident, weakening its safety and effectiveness. And watch out for clothing with drawstrings, loose buttons or other safety hazards.

8 BE CREATIVE. See a great stroller but the fabric is dirty? And non-removable so you can't throw it in the washing machine? Take a cue from one dad we interviewed. He takes dirty second-hand strollers or high chairs to a car wash and blasts them with a high-pressure hose! Voila! Clean and useable items are the result. For a small investment, you can rehabilitate a stroller into a showpiece.

Needs work: Well, they're darned expensive. But if you're looking for items you saw in magazines like Baby Talk, check them out. They often list where an outfit was advertised or promoted. And they do have a sale section.

Patsy Aiken

Web: www.patsyaiken.com or www.chezami.com
What it is: The only source now for this well-liked brand.
What's cool: We've always loved Patsy Aiken's clothes, but their distribution used to be limited to fancy baby boutiques. The good news: their site now sells the entire collection online. The US-made clothes are all 100% cotton with amazing embroidery, appliqué and smocking. You'll find adorable lambs, sailboats, and more in pale pastels. They also offer beautiful holiday outfits for those family portraits. Prices average around $25 to $30 for a typical bubble, dress or pantsuit. Not cheap but the quality is terrific. This is a great site for grandmas looking for that perfect shower gift.

Since they've decided to discontinue selling their line in stores, they've added a new method of buying their designs. Called Chez Ami it's a take off on the old Tupperware parties. You get a group of your friends together and have a Patsy Aiken clothing party. Check out the web site for more details.
Needs work: Now on the site, you have to download a PDF of their catalog. Its better than the old thumbnails, but we'd recommend signing up for their mailed catalog. It'll be easier to use.

One of a Kind Kid

Web: www.oneofakindkid.com, see Figure 1 on the next page.
What it is: Discount outlet offering deals on high-quality kids clothes.
What's cool: This site specializes in the upper-end clothes you see in Nordstrom and Neiman Marcus. We saw brands like Hartstrings, Skivvydoodles and Funtasia among others. One of a Kind Kids sells many their clothes at 70% off, a great deal only topped by the flat $6 shipping fee. New items appear weekly so checking back frequently is a good idea.
Needs work: Unfortunately, the site notes that many of the items on their site are "one of a kind." This means if you see something you like, you may have to order it on the spot. While the thumbnails of the clothes are expandable, their tiny size makes it hard to get a quick read on what's available.

◆ *Other great sites. Preemie.com* (www.preemie.com) is a wonderful oasis for parents of preemies. You'll find items like hospital shirts, basics, sleepwear, caps and booties. Not to mention, they have a selection of diaries and books as well as preemie announce-

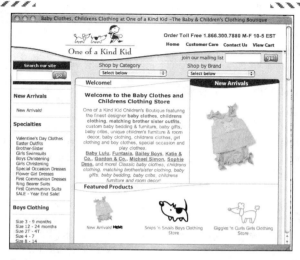

Figure 1: Great prices, high-quality brands and flat fee shipping make OneOfAKindKid.com a winner.

ments. If you've got a preemie, this is the site for you.

While **SuddenlyMommies** (www.suddenlymommies.com) does not have a huge selection of baby wear, it sure is cute stuff. All white with colorful ribbon borders, the outfits are generally all cotton and include booties, pants sets, diaper covers, dresses and more. Prices are a bit high. For example, a short-sleeve cotton knit dress is $33.

Kid Surplus (www.kidsurplus.com) is another discounter/close-out store. They've expanded their layette to include Zutano, Lil' Jellybean and Flap Happy. We also saw sleep sacks and Goldbug socks and slippers.

We'd be remiss if we didn't also mention **eBay** (web: www. ebay.com) in this section. Their baby area is often stuffed with great deals on baby clothes. One tip: look for listings that say NWT—that's eBay-speak for "New With Tags." Obviously, these items are worth the most, yet often still sell for 50% off retail. EBay has just about everything it comes to baby clothes, from basic items to luxury goods. When we recently appeared on the NBC Today Show, we showed off several eBay deals on high-end baby apparel. A producer for the show snagged a Geisswein jacket made from Austrian felted wool. The jacket retails for a whopping $225 in boutiques. We bought it on eBay for $122, a savings of over $100. (Of course, we'd never spend $100+ on a winter jacket for our child, but if you have to that Geisswein look, eBay is da bomb).

Of course, remember our mantra: never pay retail. You don't have to pay full retail for these clothes online. A great way to save is to use web coupons. See the box in the Chapter 7 ("Coupon deals cut the cost of online shopping") for a list of sites that catalog the best web deals.

What Are You Buying?

Figuring out what your baby should wear is hardly intuitive to first-time parents. We had no earthly idea what types of (and how many) clothes a newborn needed, so we did what we normally do—we went to the bookstore to do research. We found three-dozen books on "childcare and parenting"—with three-dozen different lists of items that you *must* have for your baby and without which you're a very bad parent. Speaking of guilt, we also heard from relatives, who had their own opinions as to what was best for baby.

All of this begs the question: what do you *really* need? And how much? We learned that the answer to that last, age-old question was the age-old answer, "It depends." That's right, nobody really knows. In fact, we surveyed several department stores, interviewed dozens of parents, and consulted several "experts," only to find no consensus whatsoever. So, in order to better serve humanity, we have developed THE OFFICIAL FIELDS' LIST OF ALMOST EVERY ITEM YOU NEED FOR YOUR BABY IF YOU LIVE ON PLANET EARTH. We hope this clears up the confusion. (For those living on another planet, please consult our *Baby Bargains* edition for Mars and beyond).

Feel free to now ignore those lists of "suggested layette items" provided by retail stores. Many of the "suggestions" are self-serving, to say the least.

Of course, even when you decide what and how much to buy for your baby, you still need to know what *sizes* to buy. Fortunately, we have this covered, too. First, recognize that most baby clothes come in a range of sizes rather than one specific size ("newborn to 3 months" or "3-6 months"). *We recommend you buy "3-6 month" sizes (instead of newborn) so your child won't grow out of his clothes too quickly.* Stay away from newborn to three-month sizes unless you are having multiples. If you have a premature baby or an infant who is on the small side (parents of multiples, take note), we have identified a couple of catalogs that specialize in preemie wear. And, if on the other hand, you deliver a 10-pounder, make sure you keep all receipts and labels so you can exchange the clothes for larger sizes—you may find you're into six-month sizes by the time your baby hits one month old! (Along the same lines, don't wash *all* those new baby clothes immediately. Wash just a few items for the initial few weeks. Keep all the other items in their original packaging to make returns easier).

Ever wonder how fast your baby will grow? Babies double their birth weight by five months . . . and triple it by one year! On average, babies grow 10 inches in their first year of life. Given those stats, you can understand why we don't recommend stocking up on "newborn" size clothes.

Also: remember, you can always buy more later if you need them. In fact, this is a good way to make use of those close friends and relatives who stop by and offer to "help" right after you've suffered through 36 hours of hard labor—send them to the store!

We should point out that this layette list is just to get you started. This supply should last for the first month or two of your baby's life. Also along these lines, we received a question from a mom-to-be who wondered, given these quantities, how often do we assume you'll do laundry. The answer is in the next box.

The "Baby Bargains" Layette

◆ **T-Shirts.** Oh sure, a t-shirt is a t-shirt, right? Not when it comes to baby t-shirts. These t-shirts could have side snaps, snaps at the crotch (also known as onesies or creepers) or over-the-head openings. If you have a child who is allergic to metal snaps (they leave a red ring on their skin), you might want to consider over-the-head t-shirts. As a side note, you have to wait until your baby's umbilical stump falls off (don't ask; this

E-Mail from The Real World
How Much Laundry Will I Do?

Anna Balayn of Brooklyn, NY had a good question about baby's layette and laundry:

"You have a list of clothes a new baby needs, but you don't say how often I would need to do laundry if I go with the list. I work full time and would like to have enough for a week. Is the list too short for me?"

Our answer: there is no answer. Factors such as whether you use cloth or disposable diapers (cloth leaks more; hence more laundry) and how much your baby spits up will greatly determine the laundry load. Another factor: breast versus bottle-feeding. Bottle-fed babies have fewer poops (and hence, less laundry from possible leaks). An "average" laundry cycle with our layette list would be every two to three days, assuming breast feeding, disposable diapers and an average amount of spit-up.

usually happens in a week or two) until you can use the snap-at-the-crotch t-shirts.

By the way, is a onesie t-shirt an outfit or an undergarment? Answer: it's both. In the summer, you'll find onesies with printed patterns that are intended as outfits. In the winter, most stores just sell white onesies, intended as undergarments.

HOW MANY? T-shirts usually come in packs of three. Our recommendation is to buy two packages of three (or a total of six shirts) of the side-snap variety. We also suggest buying two packs of over-the-head t-shirts. This way, if your baby does have an allergy to the snaps, you have a backup. Later you'll find the snap-at-the-crouch t-shirts to be most convenient since they don't ride up under clothes.

◆ **Gowns**. These are one-piece gowns with elastic at the bottom. They are used as sleeping garments in most cases. (We'll discuss more pros/cons of gowns later in this chapter.)

HOW MANY? This is a toss-up. If you want to experiment, go for one or two of these items. If they work well, you can always go back and get more later.

◆ **Sleepers**. This is the real workhorse of your infant's wardrobe, since babies usually sleep most of the day in the first months. Also known as stretchies, sleepers are most commonly used as pajamas for infants. They have feet, are often made of flame-retardant cloth and snap up the front. While most are made of polyester, we've seen an increase in the numbers of cotton sleepers in recent years. Another related item: cotton long johns for baby. These are similar to sleepers, but don't have feet (and hence, may necessitate the use of socks in winter months).

One parent emailed us asking if she was supposed to dress her baby in pants, shirts, etc. or if it was OK to keep her daughter in sleepers all day long. She noted the baby was quite comfortable and happy. Of course, you can use sleepers exclusively for the first few months. We certainly did. As we've said all along, a comfortable baby is a happy parent!

HOW MANY? Because of their heavy use, we recommend parents buy at least four to six sleepers.

◆ **Blanket Sleepers.** These are heavyweight, footed one-piece garments made of polyester. Used often in winter, blanket sleepers usually have a zipper down the front. In recent years, we've also seen quite a few fleece blanket sleepers, their key advantage being a softer fabric and a resistance to pilling.

HOW MANY? If you live in a cold climate or your baby is born in the winter, you may want to purchase two to four of these items. As an alternative to buying blanket sleepers, you could put a t-shirt on underneath a sleeper or stretchie for extra warmth. (Note: we've upped the recommended quantity of blanket sleepers from past editions of this book. Why? Safety advocates are increasingly worried about any soft bedding/blankets in a crib. So, using a blanket sleeper to keep baby warm in the winter and not using a blanket is a more preferred alternative).

Another option is a new product: the sleep sack. A couple manufacturers, Halo (www.halosleep.com) and Kiddopatomus (www.kiddopatomus.com) have these new wearable blankets. Typically make of lightweight fleece, they are worn over t-shirts or light sleepers (see picture of the Halo at right).

◆ **_Coveralls_**. One-piece play outfits, coveralls (also known as rompers) are usually cotton or cotton/poly blends. Small sizes (under 6 months) may have feet, while larger sizes don't.

HOW MANY? Since these are really play clothes and small infants don't do a lot of playing, we recommend you only buy two to four coveralls for babies less than four months of age. However, if your child will be going into daycare at an early age, you may need to start with four to six coveralls.

◆ **_Booties/socks_**. These are necessary for outfits that don't have feet (like gowns and coveralls). As your child gets older (at about six months), look for the kind of socks that have rubber skids on the bottom (they keep baby from slipping when learning to walk).

HOW MANY? Three to four pairs are all you'll need at first, since baby will probably be dressed in footed sleepers most of the time.

◆ **_Sweaters_**. HOW MANY? Most parents will find one sweater is plenty (they're nice for holiday picture sessions). Avoid all-white sweaters, since they show dirt much faster.

◆ **_Hats_**. Believe it or not, you'll still want a light cap for your baby in the early months of life, even if you live in a hot climate. Babies lose a large amount of heat from their heads, so protecting them with a cap or bonnet is a good idea. And don't expect to go out for a walk in the park without the baby's sun hat either.

HOW MANY? A couple of hats would be a good idea—sun hats in

summer, warmer caps for winter. We like the safari-style hats best (they have flaps to protect the ears and neck).

 ◆ **Snowsuit/bunting.** Similar to the type of fabric used for blanket sleepers, buntings also have hoods and covers for the hands. Most buntings are like a sack and don't have leg openings, while snowsuits do. Both versions usually have zippered fronts. FYI: Snowsuits and buntings should NOT be worn by infants when they ride in a car seat. Why? Thick fabric on these items can compress in an accident, compromising the infant's safety in the seat. So how can you keep your baby warm in an infant car seat? Check out Chapter 7 (Car Seats)—we'll discuss several car seat cover-ups/warmers that keep baby toasty without compromising the safety of the seat.

HOW MANY? Only buy one of these if you live in a climate where you need it. Even with a Colorado winter, we got away with layering clothes on our baby, then wrapping him in a blanket for the walk out to a warmed-up car. If you live in a city without a car, you might need two or three snowsuits for those stroller rides to the market.

◆ **Kimonos**. Just like the adult version. Some are zippered sacks with a hood and terry-cloth lining. You use them after a bath.

HOW MANY? Are you kidding? What a joke! These items are one of our "wastes of money." We recommend you pass on the kimonos and instead invest in good quality towels.

 ◆ **Saque Sets**. Two-piece outfits with a shirt and diaper cover.

HOW MANY? Forget buying these as well. We'll discuss later why saque sets are a waste of money.

 ◆ **Bibs**. These come in two versions, believe it or not. The little, tiny bibs are for the baby that occasionally drools. The larger versions are used when you begin feeding her solid foods (at about six months). Don't expect to be able to use the drool bibs later for feedings, unless you plan to change her carrot-stained outfit frequently.

HOW MANY? Skip the drool bibs (we'll discuss why later in this chapter under Wastes of Money). When baby starts eating solid foods, you'll need at least three or four large bibs. One option: plastic bibs for feeding so you can just sponge them off after a meal.

 ◆ **Washcloths and Hooded Towels**. OK, so these aren't actually clothes, but baby washcloths and hooded towels are a necessity. Why? Because they are small and easier to use . . . plus they're softer than adult towels and washcloths. HOW MANY? At first, you'll probably need only three sets of towels and washcloths (you get one of each per set). But as baby gets older and dirtier, invest in a few more washcloths to spot clean during the day.

 ◆ **Receiving Blankets**. You'll need these small, cotton blankets for all kinds of uses: to swaddle the baby, as a play quilt, or even for an extra layer of warmth on a cold day.

HOW MANY? We believe you can never have too many of these blankets, but since you'll probably get a few as gifts, you'll only need to buy two or three yourself. A total of seven to eight is probably optimal.

What about the future? While our layette list only addresses clothes to buy for a newborn, you will want to plan for your child's future wardrobe as well. For the modern baby, it seems clothes come in two categories: play clothes (to be used in daycare situations) and dress-up clothes. Later in this chapter, we'll discuss more money-saving tips and review several brands of play and dress-up clothes.

 ## More Money Buys You . . .

Even the biggest discounters now offer good quality clothing. But with more money you tend to get heavier weight cottons, nicer fasteners, better quality embellishments and more generous sizing. At some point, however, considering how fast your little one is growing, you'll be wasting money on the most expensive clothes out there.

 ## Safe & Sound

Should your baby's sleepwear (that is, the items he'll wear almost non-stop for the first several months of life) be flame retardant? What the heck does "flame retardant" mean anyway?

According to the Consumer Product Safety Commission (CPSC), items made of flame retardant fabric will not burn under a direct flame. Huh? Doesn't "flame retardant" mean it won't burn at all? No—that's a common myth among parents who think such clothes are a Superman-style second skin that will protect baby against any and all fire hazards.

Prior to 1996, the CPSC mandated that an item labeled as sleepwear be made of "flame retardant fabric." More often than not, that meant polyester because the alternative (untreated cotton fabric) DOES burn under direct flame. While there are a few companies that make cotton sleepwear that is chemically treated to be fire retardant, the prices of such items were so high that the de facto standard for children's sleepwear for many years was polyester.

Then the government changed its mind. The CPSC noticed that many parents were rebelling against the rules and putting their babies in all-cotton items at bedtime. After an investigation, the CPSC revised the rules to more closely fit reality.

First, pajamas for babies nine months and under were totally exempt from the flame-retardancy rules. Why? Since these babies aren't mobile, the odds they'll come in contact with a fire hazard that would catch their clothes on fire is slim. What if the whole house catches fire? Well, the smoke is much more dangerous than the flames—hence, a good smoke detector in the nursery and every other major room of your house is a much better investment than fire retardant clothes.

What about sleepwear for older babies? Well, the government admits that "close-fitting" all-cotton items don't pose a risk either. Only flowing nightgowns or pajamas that are loose fitting must meet the flame retardancy rules today.

If you still want to go with "flame retardant" baby items, there are a couple of options beyond plain polyester. The Lands' End catalog now sells "Polar Fleece" pajamas for babies and young children ($20). The fabric, while polyester, is specially woven to breathe and be more comfortable. Another option: some catalogs listed later in this chapter sell cotton pj's treated to be flame retardant.

Finally, one last myth to dispel on this topic: does washing flame-retardant clothing reduce its ability to retard flames? Nope—fabrics like polyester are *naturally* flame retardant (that is, there is no magic chemical they've been doused with that can wash out in the laundry). What about those expensive treated all-cotton clothes? We don't think that's a problem either. While we haven't seen any evidence to the contrary, we think those companies that sell these pricey items would be drummed out of business in a heartbeat if the flame-retardancy of their clothes suddenly disappeared after a few spins in the rinse cycle.

There is one exception to the laundry rule: if you do choose to buy flame-retardant clothing, be sure to avoid washing such clothing in soap flakes. Soap flakes actually add a flammable chemical residue to clothes. And so do dryer sheets and liquid softeners. For more advice on washing baby clothes, see the following box.

What about other safety hazards with children's clothing? Here are a few more to consider:

◆ **Check for loose threads.** These could become a choking hazard, or the threads could wrap around fingers or toes, cutting off circulation. Be careful about appliqués as well. "Heat-welded" plastic appliqués on clothes can come off and cause choking. Poorly sewn appliqués can also be a hazard.

◆ *Avoid outfits with easy-to-detach, decorative buttons or bows—these may also be a choking hazard.* If you have any doubts, cut the decorations off.

◆ *Watch out for drawstrings.* In recent years, most manufacturers have voluntarily eliminated such drawstrings. But if you get hand-me-downs or buy second-hand clothes, be sure to remove any strings.

Laundry Conundrum: What's Best for Baby's Clothes?

Ever since Dr. Spock's best-selling tome on taking care of baby, most parenting authors have advised washing baby's clothes and linens in mild soap or detergents. The implication is that baby's skin is delicate and could be irritated by harsh chemicals.

Yet, it helps to take a second to talk about just WHAT we are washing our clothes, hands and hair with these days. Until World War II, most soaps were made of animal or vegetable products. After the war, new synthetic "detergents" debuted, which were chemical compounds that cleaned better and cost less than soap. Detergent use skyrocketed, while soaps languished. Today nearly all products we think of as "soap" are really detergents.

Over the past 20 years, we've seen an explosion in personal care detergents, including soft soaps, bath gels, anti-bacterial liquids, hair products and more. In the nursery, just look at the huge use of baby wipes (which contain alcohol and crude detergents) instead of the washcloths of old. At the same time, however the number of children with severe eczema has climbed sharply, from the single digits in the 1950's to nearly 20% today. That's right, one out of five children today suffers from severe eczema.

Is it possible the high-tech detergents we use today to wash our skin, clothes and dishes are contributing to the eczema epidemic? While there is no scientific data to prove this link, researchers in England have been actively studying this for the past decade. Dr. Michael Cork, a dermatologist at Sheffield University, suggests detergents strip the fat between cells, making the skin more susceptible to conditions like eczema.

Unfortunately, there is no known cure for childhood eczema, which can be painful in its most severe form. It is often treated with

One Size Does Not Fit All

A six month-size t-shirt is a six-month-size t-shirt, right? Wrong. For some reason, baby clothing companies have yet to synchronize their watches when it comes to sizes. Hence, a clothing item that says "six-month size" from one manufacturer can be just the same dimensions as a "twelve-month size" from another. All this begs the question: how can you avoid wide-spread confusion? First, open packages to check out actual dimensions. Take your baby along and hold up items to her to gauge whether they'd fit. Second, note whether items are pre-shrunk—you'll probably have to ask the salesperson or catalog representative (if not, allow for shrinkage). Third, don't key on length from head to foot. Instead, focus on the length from neck to crotch—a common problem is items that seem roomy but are too tight in the crotch. Finally, forget age ranges and pay more attention to labels that specify an infant's size in weight and height, which are much more accurate. To show how widely sizing can vary, check out the following chart. We compared "six-month" t-shirts from six major clothing makers plus three popular catalogs, Hanna Anderssen, Lands' End and Talbot's Kids. Here's what these six-month t-shirts really trans-lated to in terms of a baby's weight and height:

What a six month t-shirt really means

MAKER	WEIGHT	HEIGHT
BABY GAP	17-22 LBS.	27-29"
CARTER'S LAYETTE	12-18 LBS.	25"
GYMBOREE	17-21 LBS.	25-27"
HANNA ANDERSON	14-21 LBS.	26-30"
HEALTH-TEX	13-17 LBS.	25-28"
LANDS' END	19-22 LBS.	27.5-29"
LITTLE ME	12-16 LBS.	24-27"
OSHKOSH	16.5-18 LBS.	27-28.5"
Talbot's Kids	13-17 lbs.	24-27"

Here's another secret from the baby clothing trade: the more expensive the brand, the more roomy the clothes. Conversely, cheap items usually have the skimpiest sizing. What about the old wives' tale that you should just double your baby's age to find the right size (that is, buying twelve-month clothes for a six-month old?). That's bogus—as you can see, siz-ing is so all over the board that this rule just doesn't work.

steroid creams, which may have harmful long-term side effects.

So, what should new parents do? First, look at your family's history of eczema and other skin diseases. If you DO have a family history of eczema, we'd suggest going on a detergent-free diet for your household. Why the entire house? That's because baby will be touching your hair, clothes and sheets and those of your family as well. It's not enough to wash your baby's clothes in non-detergent soap. The entire family will have to sign on to this. See below for specific suggestions of detergent-free products.

Even if you have no such history in your family, consider using the mildest soaps or detergents for your baby: products like Cetaphil, Ivory and Dove bar soap among other options. Stick with laundry products that are dye and fragrance free as well. No, you don't have to use Dreft—any perfume and dye-free mild detergent will do. And consider a second rinse cycle—this helps remove detergent residue. Finally, if you use bleach in the laundry add some distilled vinegar to the rinse cycle to remove some of the odor and help clothes last longer.

In our family, we've had success removing detergents from our house, where our youngest son suffers from severe eczema. We noticed a sharp improvement in his skin after banishing detergents. Here are our tips for families with severe skin allergies:

◆ **Wash baby's clothes** in pure soap. We use **Cal-Ben's Seafoam Liquid** laundry soap, which is made from natural soap (web: www.CalBenPureSoap.com). Another source for traditional soap flakes is www.soap-flakes.com. You may also find other pure soaps in natural food stores. Read the labels carefully, however, since some items still contain detergents and others may have allergenic fruit or vegetable ingredients. Do not use fabric softeners, drier sheets or other laundry products.

◆ **Hair and skin** should be washed with Dove bar soap (Ivory and Cetaphil are fine too; no liquid soaps). Never use bubble baths, oils or kid's shampoo. For hand soap in the kitchen and bath, we use Cal-Ben's Seafoam liquid soap or the bar soap mentioned above. Yes, that means everyone in the house. We chucked our old shampoo and use a pure soap shampoo (Cal Ben's Gold Star shampoo) as well. Stay away from anti-bacterial soaps. They can cause painful flair ups for eczema sufferers. Wash hands frequently to avoid germs and follow with a good emollient moisturizer.

◆ **Dishes.** Yes, babies can be exposed to detergent residue by handing cups or dishes. Again, we use a Cal-Ben product (Seafoam Dish Glow) to wash our dishes.

A few caveats to this: pure soap products are hard to find and expensive—we order ours from the web site mentioned above, although some natural food stores carry these brands as well.

And, true enough, soap does NOT clean as well as detergent, especially in the laundry. That said, we are willing to put up with this hassle in order to see improvement in our son.

We understand this is quite a commitment—having mom or dad give up a favorite shampoo or hair gel isn't fun. But remember, baby is running her hands through your hair and touching your skin. Even a small detergent residue can cause a reaction in some kids.

While we follow this detergent-free diet and it seems to be offering huge relief for our son's eczema, we realize it may just be part of the puzzle. Some kids have eczema that is triggered by a food allergy . . . and drier times of the year (winter, for example) can aggravate the skin, even in a detergent-free house. More research has to be done in this issue. Someday we hope science is able to positively link eczema with environmental factors, then we as parents can take positive steps so our children don't have to suffer.

Smart Shopper Tips

Smart Shopper Tip
Tips and Tricks to Get the Best Quality
"I've received several outfits from friends for my daughter, but I'm not sure she'll like all the scratchy lace and the poly/cotton blends. What should she wear, and what can I buy that will last through dozens of washings?"

Generally, we recommend dressing your child for comfort. At the same time, you need clothes that can withstand frequent washings. With this in mind, here are our suggestions for baby clothing:

1 **SEE WHAT YOUR BABY LIKES BEFORE INVESTING IN MANY GARMENTS.** Don't spend $90 on fancy sweaters, only to find baby prefers cotton onesies.

2 **WE GENERALLY RECOMMEND 100% COTTON CLOTHING.** Babies are most comfortable in clothing that breathes.

3 **IF YOU DISCOVER YOUR CHILD HAS AN ALLERGY TO METAL SNAPS** (you'll see red rings on his skin), consider alternatives such as shirts that have ties. Another option is a t-shirt that pulls on over the head. Unfortunately, many babies don't like having anything pulled over their heads. Another alternative for allergic babies: clothes with plastic snaps or zippers.

4 IN GENERAL, BETTER-MADE CLOTHES WILL HAVE THEIR SNAPS ON A REINFORCED FABRIC BAND. Snaps attached directly to the body of the fabric may tear the garment or rip off.

5 IF YOU'RE BUYING 100% COTTON CLOTHES, MAKE SURE THEY'RE PRE-SHRUNK. Some stores, like Gymboree (see review later in this chapter), pre-wash their clothes to prevent shrinkage. With other brands, it's hard to tell. Our advice: read the label. If it says "wash in cold water" or " tumble dry low," assume the garment will shrink (and hence buy a larger size). On the other hand, care instructions that advise "washing in warm water and tumble dry" usually indicate that the garment is already preshrunk.

6 GO FOR OUTFITS WITH SNAPS AND ZIPPERS ON BOTH LEGS, NOT JUST ONE. Dual-leg snaps or zippers make it much easier to change a diaper. Always check a garment for diaper accessibility—some brands actually have no snaps or zippers, meaning you would have to completely undress your baby for a diaper change! Another pet peeve: garments that have snaps up the back also make diaper changes a big hassle.

7 BE AWARE THAT EACH COMPANY HAS ITS OWN WARPED IDEA ABOUT HOW TO SIZE BABY CLOTHES. See the box "One Size Does Not Fit All" earlier in this chapter for more details.

8 BEWARE OF APPLIQUÉS. Some appliqué work can be quite scratchy on the inside of the outfit (it rubs against baby's skin).

9 KEEP THE TAGS AND RECEIPTS. A reader emailed us her strategy for dealing with baby clothes that shrink: until she has a chance to wash the item, she keeps all packaging, tags and receipts. If it shrinks, she returns it immediately.

 Wastes of Money

Waste of Money #1
Clothing that Leads to Diaper Changing Gymnastics
"My aunt sent me an adorable outfit for my little girl. The only problem: it snaps up the back making diaper changes a real pain. In fact, I don't dress her in it often because it's so inconvenient. Shouldn't clothing like this be outlawed?"

It's pretty obvious that some designers of baby clothing have never had children of their own. What else could explain outfits that snap up the back, have super tiny head, leg and arm openings, and snaps in inconvenient places (or worse, no snaps at all)? One mother we spoke with was furious about outfits that have snaps only down one leg, requiring her baby to be a contortionist to get into and out of the outfit.

Our advice: stay away from outfits that don't have easy access to the diaper. Look instead for snaps or zippers down the front of the outfit or on the crotch. If your baby doesn't like having things pulled over his head, look for shirts with wide, stretchie necklines.

Waste of Money #2
The Fuzz Factor

"My friend's daughter has several outfits that aren't very old but are already pilling and fuzzing. They look awful and my friend is thinking of throwing them out. What causes this?"

Your friend has managed to have a close encounter with that miracle fabric known as polyester. Synthetics such as polyester will often pill or fuzz after washing, making your baby look a little rag-tag. Of course, this is less of a concern with sleepwear—the flame retardancy of polyester fabric outweighs the garment's appearance.

However, when you're talking about a play outfit, we recommend sticking to all-cotton clothes. They wash better, usually last longer, and generally look nicer—not to mention they feel better to your baby. Cotton allergies are rare, unlike sensitivities to the chemicals used to make synthetic fabrics. You will pay more for all-cotton clothing, but in this case, the extra expense is worth it. Remember, just because you find the cheapest price on a polyester outfit doesn't mean you're getting a bargain. The best deal is not wasting money on outfits that you have to throw away after two washings.

If you get polyester outfits as gifts, here's a laundry tip: wash the items inside out. That helps lessen pilling/fuzzing. And some polyester items are better than others—polar fleece sweatshirts and pajamas are still made of polyester, but are softer and more durable.

Waste of Money #3
Do I Really Need These?

"My mother bought me a zillion gowns before my baby was born, and I haven't used a single one. What the heck are they for?"

"The list of layette items recommended by my local department store includes something called a saque set. I've never seen one, and no one seems to know what it is. Do I really need one?"

....

clothes

"A kimono with matching towel and washcloth seems like a neat baby gift for my pregnant friend. But another friend told me it probably wouldn't get used. What do you think?"

All of these items come under the heading "Do I Really Need These?" Heck, we didn't even know what some of these were when we were shopping for our baby's layette. For example, what in the world is a saque set? Well, it turns out it's just a two-piece outfit with a shirt and diaper cover. Although they sound rather benign, saque sets are a waste of money. Whenever you pick up a baby under the arms, it's a sure bet her clothes will ride up. In order to avoid having to constantly pull down the baby's shirt, most parents find they use one-piece garments much more often than two-piece ones.

As for gowns, the jury is still out on whether these items are useful. We thought they were a waste of money, but a parent we interviewed did mention that she used the gowns when her baby had colic. She believed that the extra room in the gown made her baby more comfortable. Other parents like how gowns make diaper changes easy, especially in the middle of the night. Finally, parents in hot climates say gowns keep their infants more comfortable. So, you can see there's a wide range of opinions on this item.

There is no question in our minds about the usefulness of a baby kimono, however. Don't buy it. For a baby who will only wear it for a few minutes after a bath, it seems like the quintessential waste of your money (we saw one Ralph Lauren baby kimono for $39. And that was on sale). Instead, invest in some good quality towels and washcloths and forget those cute (but useless) kimonos.

Waste of Money #4
Covering Up Those Little Piggies
"I was looking at baby shoes the other day and I saw a $43 pair of Merrell JungleMoc Juniors! This must be highway robbery! I can't believe babies' shoes are so expensive. Are they worth it?"

Developmentally, babies don't need shoes until after they become quite proficient at walking. In fact, it's better for their muscle development to go barefoot or wear socks. While those expensive Merrells might look cute, they're really a waste of time and money. Of course, at some point, your baby will need some shoes. See the following box for our tips on how to buy babies' first shoes.

Waste of Money #5
To Drool or Not to Drool
"I received a few bibs from my mother-in-law as gifts. I know my

baby won't need them until she's at least four to six months old when I start feeding her solids. Plus, they seem so small!"

What you actually received was a supply of drool bibs. Drool bibs are tiny bibs intended for small infants who drool all over everything. Or infants who spit-up frequently. Our opinion: they're pretty useless—they're too small to catch much drool or spit-up.

When you do buy bibs, stay away from the ones that tie. Bibs that snap or have Velcro are much easier to get on and off. Another good bet: bibs that go on over the head (and have no snaps or

Baby Needs a New Pair of Shoes

As your baby gets older, you may find she's kicking off her socks every five minutes. And at some point she's going to start standing, crawling and even walking. So what's a parent to do? You need something that will stay on and protect her feet as she moves through these milestones. Here are some suggestions:

First, look for shoes that have the most flexible soles. You'll also want fabrics that breath and stretch, like canvas and leather—stay away from vinyl shoes. The best brands we found were recommended by experienced parents. Reader Teri Dunsworth wrote us about Canadian-made **Robeez** (800) 929-2649 or (604) 435-9011; web: www.robeez.com. (See picture at right). "They are the most AWESOME shoes—I highly recommend them," she said in an email. And Teri wasn't the only one who loves them. Our email has been blitzed by fans. Robeez are made of leather, have soft, skid-resistant soles and are machine washable. They start at $26 for a basic pair. Another reader recommended New Zealand-made **Bobux** shoes ($25.50 at www.bobuxusa.com). These cute leather soft soles "do the trick by staying on extremely well," according to a reader. Finally, another reader recommended **Scootees** (www. scootees.com). These slippers "really stay on babies' feet!" And they only cost $11.

What about shoes for one or two year olds? We've found great deals at Target, where a wide selection of sizes and offerings was impressive. Another good source: Gap Kids/Baby Gap. Their affordable line of sneakers are very good quality. Parents have also told us they've had success with Babies R Us' in-house brand; others like Stride Rite shoes, which are often on sale at department stores. If none of these stores are convenient, consider the web or mail order—see the Do It By Mail section later in this chapter for possibilities. We discuss how to get more deals on shoes for toddlers in our *Toddler Bargains* book. See back of this book for details..

Velcro). Why? Older babies can't pull them off by themselves.

Stay away from the super-size vinyl bibs that cover the arms, since babies who wear them can get too hot. However, we do recommend you buy a few regular-style vinyl bibs for travel. You can wash them off much more easily than the standard terry-cloth bibs. As for sources of bibs, many of the catalogs we review in this book carry such items. Readers have recommended the long sleeve bib from A Better Bib (www.abetterbib.com). Made of soft, breathable fabrics, these bibs run $15.

As a side note, many readers wrote to us to disagree with the idea of blowing off drool bibs. They claim that their babies are like water faucets stuck in the "on" position and a bib was a necessity. If you have a leaker, consider using larger bids that can also be used later when you begin solid foods. We still think the tiny drool bibs are a waste of money even in these cases.

Waste of Money #6
The Dreft Syndrome

"I see ads in parenting magazines that say an infant's clothes should be washed in special laundry detergent. Is this true?"

See our earlier discussion of this topic, "The Laundry Conundrum."

Money Saving Secrets

1 **REMEMBER THESE TWO STORES: OLD NAVY AND THE CHILDREN'S PLACE.** Old Navy (oldnavy.com): The hip, discount offshoot of the Gap (www.gap.com) was launched in 1994 and now has 700+ stores nationwide. Readers rave about the buys they find at Old Navy (sample: "adorable" 100% cotton onesies for just $4; gripper socks, 3 for $4.50), although most admit the selection is limited. The options change rapidly and Old Navy's sales and clearance racks are "bargain heaven," say our spies. An insider tip to Old Navy and Gap Kids: the stores change out their merchandise every six weeks, moving the "old" stuff to the clearance racks rather quickly. Ask your local Old Navy or Gap Kids which day they do their markdowns (typically it is mid-week).

Here's another tip for folks who shop Old Navy or the Gap regularly: check to see if your recent purchases have been marked down. You may be able to get a refund if items you've bought are marked down even more. One reader emailed us her great deal: "Last month I found a hooded sweatshirt for baby on clearance. It was originally $15 marked down to $10.50. The next week, I went back and the same sweatshirt had been marked down from $10.50 to $1.99. So they refunded me $8.60!" Old Navy only refunds money on markdowns if they occur within seven days of original purchase. However, the Gap gives you up to 14 days to return them. And you don't even have to bring in the item—just the receipt.

The Children's Place (childrensplace.com): With over 680 stores in the US and Canada, the Children's Place is nearly as common as Old Navy. Plus prices are just as good. They offer their clothing in sizes newborn to 4T. One reader wrote: "I found that this chain has really great looking and durable clothes for extremely reasonable prices." She did note that sizes run a bit small, so buy up a size. An example of their offerings: we saw a white, scalloped girls sweater (100% cotton) for a mere $14.50. If you order online, the site offers a flat $5 shipping fee plus you can make returns at their stores.

2 WAIT UNTIL AFTER SHOWERS AND PARTIES TO PURCHASE CLOTHES. Clothing is a popular gift item—you may not need to buy much yourself.

3 STICK WITH BASICS—T-SHIRTS, SLEEPERS, CAPS, SOCKS AND BLANKETS. For the first month or more, that's all you need since you won't be taking Junior to the opera.

E-MAIL FROM THE REAL WORLD
Second-hand bargains easy to find

Shelley Bayer of Connecticut raved about Once Upon A Child, a nationwide chain of resale stores with 100+ locations (call 614-791-0000 for locations; web: www.OnceUponAChild.com).

"We have two locations of Once Upon A Child in Connecticut and I love them! The clothes and toys are of great quality and very affordable. The good thing about these stores is that when you take something in to be sold, they pay you cash. You do not have wait for something to be sold and keep checking your account like a traditional consignment shop."

One caution about second-hand stores—if you buy an item like a stroller or high chair at a resale shop, you may not be able to get replacement parts. One mom told us she got a great deal on a stroller that was missing a front bar ... that is, it was a great deal until she discovered the model was discontinued and she couldn't get a replacement part from the manufacturer.

---

4 **TAKE ADVANTAGE OF BABY REGISTRIES.** Many baby stores offer this service, which helps avoid duplicate shower gifts or too many of one item. This saves you time (and money) in exchanging gifts.

5 **GO FOR THE SALES!** The baby area in most department stores is definitely SALE LAND. At one chain we researched, the baby section has at least some items that are on sale every week! Big baby sales occur throughout the year, but especially in January. You can often snag bargains at up to 50% off the retail price. Another tip: consider buying for the future during end-of-season sales. If you're pregnant during the fall, for example, shop the end-of-summer sales for next summer's baby clothes. Hint: our research shows the sale prices at department stores are often better deals than the "discounted" prices you see at outlets.

6 **CHOOSE QUALITY OVER LOW PRICE FOR PLAYCLOTHES AND BASICS.** Sure that polyester outfit is 20% cheaper than the cotton alternative. HOWEVER, beware of the revenge of the washing machine! You don't realize how many times you'll be doing laundry—that play outfit may get washed every couple of days. Cheap polyester clothes pill or fuzz up after just a few washings—making you more likely to chuck them. Quality clothes have longer lives, making them less expensive over time. The key to quality is thicker or more heavyweight 100% cotton fabric, well-sewn seams and appliqués, and snaps on reinforced fabric bands.

7 **FOR SLEEPWEAR, TRY THE AFFORDABLE BRANDS.** Let's get real here: babies pee and poop in their sleepers. Hence, fancy designer brands are a money-waster. A friend of ours who lives in Texas uses affordable all-cotton onesies as sleepwear in the hot summer months. For the winter here in Colorado, we use thermal underwear, which we've found for as little as $10.50 in Target.

8 **CAN'T RETURN IT?** Did you get gifts of clothing you don't want but can't return? Consign it at a local thrift store. We took a basketful of clothes that we couldn't use or didn't like and placed them on consignment. We made $40 in store credit or cash to buy what we really needed.

9 **SPEAKING OF CONSIGNMENT STORES, HERE IS A WONDERFUL WAY TO SAVE MONEY:** Buy barely used, consigned clothing for your baby. We found outfits ranging from $5 to $7 from high quality designers like Alexis. How can you find a consignment or thrift shop in your area specializing in high-quality children's clothes? Besides looking in the phone book, check out web sites like the National Association of Resale & Thrift Shops (www.narts.com, click on the shopping icon). Here are two tips for getting the best bargains at second-hand stores. First, shop the resale stores in the richest part of town. Why? They are most likely to stock the best brands with steep discounts off retail prices. Such stores also have clothes with the least wear (we guess rich kids have so many clothes they don't have time to wear them all out)! Second: ask the consignment store which day is best to shop. Some stores accept new consignments on certain days; others tell us that days like Tuesday and Wednesday offer the best selection of newly consigned items.

10 CHECK OUT DISCOUNTERS. In the past, discount stores like Target, Wal-Mart and Marshall's typically carried cheap baby clothes that were mostly polyester. Well, there's good news for bargain shoppers: in recent years, these chains have upgraded up their offerings, adding more all-cotton clothes and even some brand names. We've been especially impressed with Target's recent offerings. For basic items like t-shirts and play clothes that will be trashed at day care, these stores are good bets. Wal-Mart sure impressed one of our readers: "I spent $25 for a baby bathing suit in a specialty store, and for a little over twice that (about $60) I bought my daughter's entire summer wardrobe at Wal-mart—shorts, t-shirts, leggings, Capri pants, overalls and matching socks. Some of the pieces were as low as $2.88." And don't forget other discounters like Marshalls, TJ Maxx and Ross Dress for Less. Bargain tip: ask the manager when they get in new shipments—that's when selection is best.

11 CHECK OUT WAREHOUSE CLUBS. Warehouse clubs like Sam's and Costco carry baby clothes at prices far below retail. On a recent visit to Costco we saw Carter's fleece sleepers for only $7 and lightweight sleepers for $5. All cotton play clothes were a mere $10 as were all-cotton pajamas. Even baby Halloween costumes and kids outerwear (raincoats, fleece jackets) are terrific seasonal deals.

12 DON'T FORGET ABOUT CHARITY SALES. Readers tell us they've found great deals on baby clothes and equipment at church-sponsored charity sales. Essentially, these sales are like large garage/yard sales where multiple families donate kids' items as a fund-raiser for a church or other charity.

Outlets

There's been a huge explosion in the number of outlet stores over the last few years—and children's clothing stores haven't been left out of the boom. Indeed, as we were doing research for this section, we heard from many manufacturers that they had even more outlets on the drawing board. Therefore, if you don't see your town listed below, call the numbers provided to see if they've opened any new outlets. Also, outlet locations open and close frequently—always call before you go.

CARTER'S

Locations: Over 140 outlets.
Call (888) 782-9548 or (770) 961-8722 for the location nearest you.

It shows you how widespread the outlet craze is when you realize that Carter's has over 146 outlets in the U.S. That's right, 146. If you don't have one near you, you probably live in Bolivia.

We visited a Carter's outlet and found a huge selection of infant clothes, bedding, and accessories. Sleepers, originally $12, were available for $7, gowns were $5 (regularly $12) and side snap t-shirts were $10 for three (regularly $20).

As for baby bedding, we noted the outlet sells quilts, bumpers, and dust ruffles as well as fitted bassinet sheets and towels at low prices. All Carter's bedding is made by Riegal (see previous chapter for a review of their bedding line).

If you think those deals are great, check out the outlet's yearly clearance sale in January when they knock an additional 25% to 30% off their already discounted prices. A store manager at the Carter's outlet we visited said that they also have two other sales: back-to-school and a "pajama sale." In the past, we noted that all the goods in their outlet stores were first quality. However, they have added a couple "seconds" racks (called "Oops" racks) in most of their stores with flawed merchandise. Our readers report that most seconds have only minor problems and the savings are worth it.

HANNA ANDERSSON

Outlets Stores: Lake Oswego, OR (503) 697-1953; Michigan City, IN (219) 872-3183; Albertville, MN (763) 497-7885; Kittery, ME (207) 439-1992; Lakewood, CO (303) 384-0937; Woodinville, WA (425) 485-7998.

If you like Hanna Anderson's catalog, you'll love their outlet stores, which feature overstocks, returned items and factory seconds. For more information on Hanna Anderson, see "Do It By Mail" later in this chapter.

HARTSTRINGS

Locations: 29 outlets, mostly in the eastern U.S. Call (610) 687-6900.

Hartstrings' outlet stores specialize in first-quality apparel for infants, boys, and girls and even have some mother/child outfits. Infant sizes start at three months and go up to 24 months. The savings range from 30% to 50%.

HEALTH-TEX

Locations: 80 outlets. Call (800) 772-8336 for the location near you.

Health-Tex children's clothing is owned by Vanity Fair Corporation, which also produces such famous brands as Lee jeans, Wrangler, and Jantzen. The company operates over four-dozen outlets under the name VF Factory Outlet. They sell first-quality merchandise; most are discontinued items. Most of the VF outlets carry the Health-Tex brand at discounts up to 70% off retail.

JCPENNEY

Locations: 20 outlets; call (800) 222-6161, Web: www.JCPenney.com

A reader in Columbus, Ohio emailed her high praise for the Penney's outlet there. She snagged one-piece rompers for $5 (regularly $25) and hand-loomed coveralls for $2.99 (compared to $28 in stores). She also found satin christening outfits for both boys and girls for just $5 that regularly sell for as much as $70! The outlet carries everything from layette to play clothes, at discounts of 50% or more. (Hint: the outlet stores also have maternity clothes).

OSHKOSH

Locations: 154 outlets. Call (920) 231-8800 for the nearest location.

OshKosh, the maker of all those cute little overalls worn by just about every kid, sells their clothes direct at over 125 outlet stores. With prices that are 30% to 70% off retail, buying these play clothes staples is even easier on the pocketbook. For example, footed sleepers were $7.70 (regularly $11), and receiving blankets were $18.20 (regularly $24).

We visited our local OshKosh store and found outfits from infant sizes up to size 16. They split the store up by gender, as well as by size. Infant and toddler clothes are usually in the back of the store.

The outlet also carries OshKosh shoes, socks, hats, and even stuffed bears dressed in overalls and engineer hats. Seasonal ensembles are available, including shorts outfits in the summer and snowsuits ($42) in the winter. Some clothes are irregulars, so inspect the garments carefully before you buy.

One complaint: a parent wrote telling us she was disappointed that OshKosh had cheap elastic around the legs and didn't wash well. In her opinion, the quality of Carter's was much better in comparison.

TALBOT'S KIDS

Location: 21 stores, most of which are in the Eastern U.S. and Texas. Call (800) 543-7123 or (781) 740-8888. Web: www.talbots.com

A reader who calls herself a "devoted Talbot's shopper" emailed in her compliments for Talbot's outlet stores, which carry a nice selection of baby and children's clothes that didn't sell in their stores or catalog. "The deals can be fantastic, especially given the quality," she said, adding that you can get on the outlet's mailing list to get notices about additional markdowns. She estimated she saved 40% to 60% on items for her baby. Hint: Talbot's regular stores hold major sales twice a year (after Christmas and the end of June). What doesn't get sold then is shipped to the outlets.

◆ *Other outlets.* A great source for outlet info is **Outlet Bound** magazine, which is published by Outlet Marketing Group ($9 plus $4 shipping, 1-888-688-5382; web: www.outletbound.com). The magazine contains detailed maps noting outlet centers for all areas of the U.S. and Canada, as well as store listings for each outlet center. We liked the index that lists all the manufacturers, and they even have a few coupons in the back.

Outlet Bound also has an excellent web site with the most up-to-date info on outlets in the U.S. and Canada. We did a search on children's clothing outlets (you can search by location, store, brand or product category) and found several additional interesting outlets. These included outlets for Little Me (33 outlets), the Disney catalog outlet (10 locations) and the Oilily catalog (three outlets).

If you can't get enough of the **Gap**, check out their outlet stores (650) 952-4400 (web: www.gap.com). With several locations nationwide, most Gap outlets have a baby/kid's clothing section and great deals (50% off and more).

Yet another outlet: **Pingorama** offers periodic factory sales. Check their web site, (www.pingorama.com, click on the where to buy link) for dates and directions.

Alexis, one of our top rated clothing manufacturers (see below) has an outlet store in Gainesville, GA. Check their web site at AlexisPlaySafe.com for store hours and directions.

Did you discover an outlet that you'd like to share with our readers? Call us at our office at 303-442-8792 or e-mail authors@ BabyBargains.com.

The Name Game:
Our Picks for the Best Brands

Walk into any department store and you'll see a blizzard of brand names for baby clothes. Which ones stand up to frequent washings? Which ones have snaps that stay snapped? Which are a good value for the dollar? We've got the answers, based on extensive parent feedback.

We've broken our recommendations into three areas: best bets, good but not great and skip it. As always, remember most of these manufacturers do not sell directly to consumers (those that do sell online are identified by an asterisk*). The phone numbers and web sites are included so you can locate a retailer near you who carries that brand. Here we go:

Best Bets

ALEXIS	(800) 253-9476	ALEXISUSA.COM
BABY GAP*	(800) GAP-STYLE	BABYGAP.COM
CARTER'S	(770) 961-8722	CARTERS.COM
COZY TOES		COZYTOES.COM
FLAP HAPPY*	(800) 234-3527	FLAPHAPPY.COM
FLAPDOODLES	(302) 731-9793	FLAPDOODLES.COM
GYMBOREE*	(877) 449-6932	GYMBOREE.COM
HARTSTRINGS/KITESTRINGS	(212) 868-0950	HARTSTRINGS.COM
JAKE AND ME*	(970) 352-8802	JAKEANDME.COM
LITTLE ME	(800) 533-5497	LITTLEME.COM
MOTHER-MAID	(770) 479-7558	MOTHERMAID.COM
MULBERRIBUSH (TUMBLEWEED TOO)		MULBERRIBUSH.COM
OSHKOSH B'GOSH*	(800) 692-4674	OSHKOSHBGOSH.COM
PATSY AIKEN*	(919) 872-8789	PATSYAIKEN.COM
PINGARAMA		PINGARAMA.COM
SARAH'S PRINTS*	(888) 477-4687	SARASPRINTS.COM
SKIVVYDOODLES	(212) 967-2918	SKIVVYDOODLES.COM
SWEET POTATOES/SPUDZ	(800) 634-2584	SWEETPOTATOESINC.COM
WES & WILLY		WESANDWILLY.COM
ZUTANO		ZUTANO.COM

Good But Not Great

GOOD LAD OF PHILA.*	(215) 739-0200	GOODLAD.COM
Health Tex**	(800) 5547637	HEALTHTEX.COM
LE TOP	(800) 333-2257	LETOP-USA.COM
TARGET* (LITTLE ME, CLASSIC POOH, HALO, TYKES)		TARGET.COM

Skip It: Gerber, Hanes.

* *Manufacturers who sell direct to consumers.*
***Heathtex's rating is higher than our last edition, thanks to a recent upgrade in quality. One reader wrote to tell us she thought the quality was comparable to Old Navy and the frequent sales at their online store made their clothes an even better bargain.*

 Do it by Mail

CHILDREN'S WEAR DIGEST (CWD)

To Order Call: (800) 242-5437; Fax (800) 863-3395.
Or write to: 3607 Mayland Ct., Richmond, VA 23233.
Web: www.cwdkids.com
Outlet: "CWD Outlet," Gayton Crossing Shopping Center, Richmond, VA.
Also two company stores in Virginia. Call or visit the web site for more info.

If you're looking for name brands, check out Children's Wear Digest (CWD), a catalog that features clothes in sizes 12 months to 14 years for both boys and girls. In a recent catalog, we saw clothes by Sweet Potatoes, Mulberribush, S.P.U.D.Z., Hartstrings, and Sarah's Prints. Unlike other catalogs that de-emphasize brand names, CWD prominently displays manufacturer info.

Children's Wear Digest doesn't offer much of a discount off regular retail, but it does have a selection of sale clothes from time to time with savings of 15% to 25%. A best buy: CWD's web site (www.cwdkids.com) has online bargains, with savings of up to 50% on quite a few items and the latest news on their outlet store.

HANNA ANDERSSON

To Order Call: (800) 222-0544; Fax (503) 321-5289.
Or write to: 1010 NW Flanders, Portland, OR, 97209.
Web: www.hannaandersson.com
Retail Stores: Newport Beach, CA, (949) 759-0153; Santa Clara, CA, (408) 261-2794; Broomfield, CO, (303) 466-5291; Oakbrook, IL, (630) 684-0442; Mall of America, MN, (952) 854-9598; Schaumburg, IL, (847) 413-9110; White Plains, NY, (914) 684-2410; Portland, OR, (503)321-5275; Seattle, WA, (206) 729-1099.
Outlets Stores: Lake Oswego, OR (503) 697-1953; Michigan City, IN (219) 872-3183; Albertville, MN (763) 497-7885; Kittery, ME (207) 439-1992; Lakewood, CO (303) 384-0937; Woodinville, WA (425) 485-7998.

Hanna Andersson says it offers "Swedish quality" 100% cotton clothes. Unfortunately, Swedish quality is going to set you back some big American bucks. For example, a simple coverall with zippered front (called a zipper) was a whopping $36. While Andersson's clothing features cute patterns and attractive colors, it's hard to imagine buying a complete wardrobe at those prices.

These aren't clothes you'd have your baby trash at daycare—Hanna Andersson's outfits are more suitable for weekend wear or going to Grandma's house. One note of caution: while the quality is very high, some items have difficult diaper access (or none at all). Another negative: Hanna Andersson uses "European sizing," which can be confusing. (Yes, there is an explanation of this in the catalog and on the website, but we still found it difficult to follow). Furthermore, some items (like dresses) are cut in a boxy, unstructured way.

On the plus side, we liked their web site (www.hannaandersson.com), which features an online store, sizing info and more. The site has a sale page that offers 20% to 40% off on overstock items; you can quickly glance at the specials by category.

LANDS' END

To Order Call: (800) 963-4816; Fax (800) 332-0103.
Web: www.landsend.com
Or write to: 1 Lands' End Ln., Dodgeville, WI 53595.
Discount Outlets: They also have a dozen or so outlet stores in Iowa, Illinois and Wisconsin—call the number above for the nearest location.

Lands' End children's catalog features a complete layette line—and it's darn cute. The clothes feature 100% cotton "interlock knit," which the catalog claims gets softer with every washing and doesn't pill. Choose from playsuits, onesies, hat/bib sets, even cashmere sweaters and pants—all in sizes birth to 24 months. Most items were $16.50 to $24.50 (cashmere sweater $65). Don't look for fancy dress clothes from this catalog; instead Lands' End specializes in casual playwear basics like sweat pants, overalls and cute caps (for toddlers no doubt).

Lands' End web site is a continuation of the catalog's easy-to-use layout—you can buy items online, find an outlet store and more. Best bet for deals: check the great overstock deals, posted twice weekly.

LL BEAN

To Order Call: (800) 441-5713; Fax (207) 552-3080
Or write to: LL Bean, Freeport, ME 04033; Web: www.llbean.com
Retail store: Freeport, ME

LL Bean used to have a separate site for kids clothes called LL Kids. They have since combined everything into one catalog and reduced the items they carry. They still emphasize outdoor gear: coats, snowsuits, hats, gloves, etc. But they also sell pants and leggings, sleepwear, jumpers and more. Recently, though we only found sleepers available in infant sizes. You might be confused a bit by their sizing as they group infant sizes under their Toddler section. Infant sizes start at 3 months. Prices are not cheap although sales items can be as much as 60% off.

PATAGONIA KIDS

To Order Call: (800) 638-6464; Fax (800) 543-5522.
Web: www.patagonia.com
Or write to: 8550 White Fir St., PO Box 32050, Reno, NV 89523.

Outdoor enthusiasts all over the country swear by Patagonia's scientifically engineered clothes and outerwear. They make clothing for skiing, mountain climbing, and kayaking—and for kids. That's right, Patagonia has a just-for-kids catalog of outdoor wear. In their recent kids' section on line, we found a few pages of clothes for babies and toddlers. They offer synchilla (Patagonia's version of polar fleece) clothes like cardigans ($44-47), coveralls ($36), and baby buntings ($64). We bought our baby a bunting from Patagonia and found that it had some cool features. For example, with a flick of its zipper, it converts from a sack to an outfit with two leg openings, making it more convenient to use. It also has a neck to knee zipper (speeding up diaper changes), flipper hands, and a hood. When your baby's bundled up in this, you can bet she won't get cold.

Other gear for tots includes sets of capilene long underwear ($36), coverall ($48) and interesting accessories like "Baby Pita Pocket" mittens ($18) and assorted hats and booties. The on line store also has a section called "Enviro Action," a series of essays and info on Patagonia's environmental efforts.

The bottom line: this is great stuff. It ain't cheap, but their cold weather gear is unlike that from any other manufacturer in terms of quality and durability.

TALBOT'S KIDS

To Order Call: (800) 825-2687.
Or write to: Talbot's Kids, 1 Talbots Way, Lakeville, MA 02043.
Web: www.talbots.com
Retail stores: 600 stores in the U.S., Canada and the United Kingdom. Talbot's also has 21 outlets—the web site store locator can direct to a store in your area.

Talbot's splashes its bright colors on both layette items for infants (three months to 12 months) and toddlers (up to 4T sizes). For baby, the catalog features a good selection of t-shirts, sleepwear, and overalls. Prices, as you might expect, are moderate to expensive. We saw a cotton cardigans for $28, cotton t-shirts with crotch snaps for $18. Nearly all of Talbot's Kids offerings are 100% cotton. The web site is easy to use.

WOODEN SOLDIER

To Order Call: (800) 375-6002; Fax (603) 356-3530.
Shopping Hours: Monday-Friday 8:30 am to midnight, Saturday and Sunday 8:30 am to 9 pm Eastern Time.
Or write to: The Wooden Soldier, PO Box 800, North Conway, NH 03860.

If you really need a formal outfit for your child, Wooden Soldier has the most expansive selection of children's formalwear we've ever seen. Unfortunately, the prices are quite expensive—a girls' plaid dress with embroidered collar is $54; a boy's suspendered knicker set with shirt is $68. And those are for infant sized clothes!

On the plus side, the *Wall Street Journal* lauded this catalog for its high quality in a recent comparison of girl's holiday dresses from major catalogs. Wooden Soldier continues to expand their casual offerings, which now include overalls, jumpsuits and cotton sweaters.

We're sad to say, Wooden Soldier still doesn't have a web site. Ridiculous and out-dated as it may seem, you'll have to call the company and ask for the catalog to be delivered to you.

◆ *Other catalogs.* Looking for Disney cartoon clothing and accessories? *Disney's* Catalog (800) 237-5751 (web: www.disneydirect.com) has a few infant options. We liked the too-cute Halloween costumes as well as the winter gear. We found the quality from the Disney catalog to be quite good; most items wash and wear well.

Fitigues (www.fitigues.com) sells casual baby clothes at outrageous prices. Yes, the items are made of thermal knit or French terry with velvet trim, but we couldn't see ourselves spending $88 for a mesh summer romper. One plus: the kid's outfits do coordinate with the pricey adult clothes Fitigues offers.

If you need outdoor gear, check out *Campmor* (800) 226-7667 (web: www.campmor.com) or *Sierra Trading Post* (800) 713-4534 (web: www.sierratradingpost.com). Both heavily discount infant and children's outerwear, including snowsuits. Campmor even had some Sarah's Prints PJs for more than %0% off last we looked. They both also have backpacks. Since these items are closeouts, the selection varies from issue to issue.

Our Picks: Brand Recommendations

What clothing brands/catalogs are best? Well, there is no one correct answer. An outfit that's perfect for day care (that is, to be trashed in Junior's first painting experiment) is different from an outfit for a weekend outing with friends. And dress-up occasions may require an entirely different set of clothing criteria. Hence, we've divided our clothing brand recommendations into three areas: good (day care), better (weekend wear) and best (special occasions). While some brands make items in two or even three categories, here's how we see it:

Good. For everyday comfort (and day-care situations), basic brands like Carter's, Little Me, and OshKosh are your best bets. We also like the basics (when on sale) at Baby Gap (Gap Kids) for day-care wardrobes. For great price to value, take a look at Old Navy and Target. As for catalogs, most tend to specialize in fancier clothes.

Better. What if you have a miniature golf outing planned with friends? Or a visit to Grandma's house? The brands of better-made casual wear we like best include Alexis, Baby Gap, Flapdoodles, and Gymboree. Also recommended: Jake and Me, MulberriBush, and Sweet Potatoes. For catalogs, we like the clothes in Hanna Andersson and Talbot's Kids as good brands.

Best. Holidays and other special occasions call for special outfits. We like Patsy Aiken, and the dressier items at Baby Gap. Of course, department stores are great sources for these outfits, as are consignment shops. As for catalogs, check out Wooden Soldier.

Note: For more on finding these brands, check out the Name Game earlier in this chapter. See "Do it By Mail" for more information on the catalogs mentioned above.

Diapers

The great diaper debate still rages on: should you use cloth or disposable? On one side are environmentalists, who argue cloth is better for the planet. On the other hand, those disposable diapers are darn convenient.

Considering the average baby will go through 2300 diaper changes in the first year of life, this isn't a moot issue—you'll be dealing with diapers until your baby is three or four years old (the average girl potty trains at 35 months; a boy at 39 months). Yes, you read that last sentence right . . . you will be diapering for the next 35 to 39 MONTHS.

Now, in this section, we've decided to NOT rehash all the environmental arguments pro or con for cloth versus disposable. Fire up your web browser and you'll find plenty of diaper debate on parenting sites like BabyCenter.com or ParentsPlace.com. Instead, we'll focus here on the FINANCIAL and PRACTICAL impacts of your decision.

Let's look at each option:

Cloth. Prior to the 1960's, this was the only diaper option available to parents. Fans of cloth diapering point to babies that had less diaper rash and toilet trained faster. From a practical point of view, cloth diapers have improved in the design over the years, offering more absorbency and fewer leaks. They aren't perfect, but the advent of diaper covers (no more plastic pants) has helped as well.

Another practical point: laundry. You've got to decide if you will use a cloth diaper service or launder at home. Obviously, the latter requires more effort on your part. We'll have laundry tips for cloth diapers later in this chapter. Meanwhile, we'll discuss the financial costs of cloth in general at the end of this section.

Final practical point about cloth: most day care centers don't allow them. This may be a sanitation requirement governed by state day care regulators and not a negotiating point. Check with local day care centers or your state board.

Disposables. Disposable diapers were first introduced in 1961 and now hold an overwhelming lead over cloth—about 95% of all households that have kids in diapers use disposables. Today's diapers have super-absorbent gels that lower the number of needed diaper changes, especially at night (which helps baby sleep through the night sooner). Even many parents who swear cloth diapers are best still use disposables at night. The downside? All that super-absorbency means babies are in no rush to potty train—they simply don't feel as wet or uncomfortable as babies in cloth diapers.

The jury on diaper rash is still out—disposable diaper users tell us they don't experience any more diaper rash than cloth diaper users.

Besides the eco-arguments about disposables, there is one other disadvantage—higher trash costs. In some communities, the more trash you put out, the higher the bill. Hence, using disposable diapers may result in higher garbage expenses.

The financial bottom line: Surprisingly, there is no clear winner when you factor financial costs into the diaper equation.

Cloth diapers may seem cheap at first, but consider the hidden costs. Besides the diapers themselves ($100 for the basic varieties;

$200 to $300 for the fancy ones), you also have to buy diaper covers. Like everything you buy with baby, there is a wide cost variation with diaper covers. The cheap stuff (like Dappi covers) will set you back $3 to $6 each. And you've got to buy several in different sizes as your child grows so the total investment could be nearly $100. If you're lucky, you can find diaper covers second-hand for $1 to $3. Of course, some parents find low-cost covers leak and quickly wear out. As a result, they turn to the more expensive covers—a single Mother-Ease (see later for more info on this brand) is $9.75. Invest in a half dozen of those covers (in various sizes, of course) and you've spent another $200 to $400 (if you buy them new).

What about laundry? Well, washing your own cloth diapers at home may be the most economical way to go, but often folks don't have the time or energy. Instead, some parents use a cloth diaper service. In a recent cost survey of such services across the U.S., we discovered that most run $600 to $800 a year. While each service does supply you with diapers (relieving you of that expense), you're still on the hook for the diaper covers. Some services also don't provide enough diapers each month. You'll make an average of eight changes a day, so be sure you're getting about 60 diapers a week from your service.

Proponents of cloth diapers argue that if you plan to have more than one child, you can reuse those covers spreading out (and lowering) the cost. You may also not need as many sizes depending on the brands you use and the way your child grows.

So, what's the bottom line cost for cloth diapers? We estimate the total financial damage for cloth diapers (using a cloth diaper service and buying diaper covers) for just the first year is $600 to $800.

By contrast, let's take a look at disposables. If you buy disposable diapers from the most expensive source in town (typically, a grocery store), you'd spend about $600 to $650 for the first year. Yet, we've found discount sources (mentioned later in this chapter) that sell disposables in bulk at a discount. By shopping at these sources, we figure you'd spend $300 to $375 per year (the lowest figure is for private label diapers, the highest is for brand names).

The bottom line: the cheapest way to go is cloth diapers laundered at home. The next best bet is disposables. Finally, cloth diapers from a diaper service are the most expensive.

 Parents in Cyberspace: What's on the Web?

All Together Diaper Company
Web: www.clothdiaper.com

REALITY LAYETTE

What it is: Home of the all-in-one cloth diaper made in house by the All Together Diaper Company.

What's cool: We loved the simplicity of this site. In business since 1990, the All Together Diaper Company sells its own cloth diaper system in various packages. The accompanying FAQ, washing instructions and analysis of diaper costs are really helpful. While some of their price comparisons between cloth and disposable are a bit inaccurate (slanted toward cloth, of course), the information on the cost of home washing was helpful.

What about the diapers? We were impressed with the cool design—the all-in-one system has cotton inside against baby's skin, a waterproof outer shell, adjustable snaps and elastic leg openings. These diapers (the Deluxe) are $8 to $12 each or $84 to $132 per dozen. Less expensive are the Fitted Diapers, which do not have the waterproof shell. Price: $7 to $8.50 each or $72 to $90 per dozen. Packages of diapers do offer some savings: the Deluxe package which includes 30 small diapers, and 24 medium, large and toddler sizes plus 24 Whisper Wraps runs $699 ($6.68 per diaper).

In our last edition we criticized the All Together Diaper Company for a sharp rise in prices. We are pleased to note that as we were going to print, the prices have not changed at all since the last edition.

Needs work: The web site seems to load a bit slowly.

The Baby Lane

Web: www.thebabylane.com
What it is: A comprehensive baby product and information site with a selection of cloth diapers and accessories.
What's cool: This is really the Mother of All Cloth Diaper sites. You'll find offerings from Under the Nile, Bumkins, Kushies, Plushies, Imse Vimse, Bummis and Kissaluv. Kushies Ultras were $9.25 for size small (discounts available for five packs).
Needs work: Unfortunately, this site could use a little more organization. The topics list (in varying type sizes) was rather annoying.

Diapers 4 Less

Web: www.diapers4less.com
What it is: The web site for Diaper Factory Plus, a manufacturer of generic disposable diapers.
What's cool: Even with shipping costs, this site's diapers are about 20% less than any other discount diaper sites. Now you have a couple options with their disposables: Velcro tabs or tape tabs. Both kinds have a cloth like outer covering, elastic leggings, and foam waistband.

So how much, already!? Small (7-14 lbs) size diapers range in price from 20¢ to 22¢ per diaper. You have to buy 4 packs of 64 each for a total of $51. Not bad. In the chart following this section, you'll see this price (which includes shipping) compares well with grocery stores (which of course doesn't usually deliver to your home). Sample packs are available if you want to check out the quality. Note: they will accept unopened packages as returns for refund or exchange.

Needs work: It would be nice if the site had a shipping calculator or chart so you'd know the additional charges before you place your order. And one reader complained that after she ordered a quantity of diapers from Diapers4Less.com, she was notified that they had run out of that size. Apparently, the company knew they did not have stock, yet still charged her credit card. They did not update the site until later to reflect the stock. Hopefully, Diapers4Less has figured out their inventory since then, but we'd suggest confirming they have what you want before you place an order.

Baby Works

Web: www.babyworks.com

What it is: Cloth diapers and a range of other eco friendly baby gear.

What's cool: You'll find diaper covers like Nikkys and Bummis, all-in-one diaper systems, cotton diapers, laundry products, and accessories. We saw the Bumkins all-in-one system for $16 per diaper. We liked all the washing instructions included on each page for the different items. Another nice feature: Baby Works has a recommended layette for cloth diapers and you can order samples.

Needs work: Prices aren't anything to shout about, but the selection is good.

◆ Other sites to consider:

Disposables: We found several more sites that sell disposable diapers on line. Among the best: ***CVS Pharmacy*** (www.cvspharmacy.com), ***Baby's Heaven*** (www.babysheaven.com), and ***Diaper Site*** (www.diapersite.com).

Cloth: Noel Howell, one of our readers, emailed us with great suggestions for sites to help newbee moms interested in using cloth diapers. Diaperpin.com is good for parents still trying to decide whether cloth is for them. Mothering.com is another site with advice on specific brands of cloth diapers. There are also plenty of articles on cloth diapering but be ready to preached at a bit!

Several readers have recommended ***WeeBees.com***. One reader noted, "WeeBees.com has the most wonderful quality, absorbent, affordable diapers that I've seen!" Also check out ***Baby***

J (www.babyj.com). You'll find all-in-ones, folded diapers, wraps, liners and more with such brands as Kushies, Fuzzy Bunz, and Bummis. ***Barefoot Baby*** (www.barefootbaby.com) is another site recommended by readers. Besides their own brand of diapers, they carry Bumkins, Bummis, Cot'n Wrap and Fuzzi Bunz. Check out any of the following web sites as well: ***www.kellyscloset.com, www.jardinediapers.com*** and ***www.babybunz.com***. Reader Sherri Wormstead noted that all three of these sites are competitively priced and have a nice wide variety of supplies. Finally, check out ***Baby Because*** (www.babybecause.com). They carry a huge assortment of folded diapers, all-in-one systems and diaper covers. Samples are available as well as diaper bags and accessories.

Our Picks: Brand Recommendations

Disposables. The evolution of disposable diapers is rather amazing. They started out in the 1960's as bulky and ineffective at stopping leaks. In 40 years, disposables morphed into ultra-thin, super-absorbent miracle workers that command 95% of the market.

And writing about disposable diaper brands is like trying to nail Jell-O to a wall—every five minutes, the diaper makers come out with new features and new gimmicks as they jostle for a piece of the $3.6 billion diaper market. In the 11 years since the first edition of this book came out, the constant innovation in this category is amazing. Before we get to our brand recommendations, consider the three basic types of disposables:

- ◆ *Basic.* These are the cheapest diapers and also the most bulky.
- ◆ *Ultrathin.* Even though they are thinner than basic diapers, they are more absorbent, thanks to high-tech absorbent jells. Most of the diapers sold today are ultrathins.
- ◆ *Premium/Supreme.* As the name implies, these are the most expensive diapers on the market. What do you get for that 25% higher price? Well, some premium diapers have cloth-like outer covers and fancier closures like Velcro.

No matter what brand you try, remember that sizing of diapers is all over the board. The "size two" diaper in one brand may be cut totally different than the "medium" of another, even though the weight guidelines on the package are similar. Finding a diaper that fits is critical to you and your baby's happiness.

Now, let's answer some common questions about disposables:

Q. What makes one brand different from another?

A. Surprisingly, the absorbency of diapers varies little from brand to brand. A *Consumer Reports* test (August 1998) of 8000 diaper changes on 80 babies at a day care center found that of 13 diaper types tested, eight were judged excellent. And three more were "very good." Translation: no matter what brand you choose, you'll probably have a diaper that fits well and doesn't leak. Yes, the premium/supreme diapers scored highest in CR's tests, but the difference between them and the cheaper options was minimal (except for the price, of course).

Besides absorbency, gimmicks and marketing ploys are the only differences between brands. This market goes through fads faster than Madison Avenue. We remember gender-specific diapers, which were on the market for about five minutes. That was more hype than real benefit and now they're gone (we're back to unisex versions). Another fad that came and went: "Pampers Rash Care," a premium diaper which "contains the same active ingredients as many diaper rash creams" to prevent diaper rash. Next week we expect Huggies to come out with a brand that promises higher college entrance test scores (call it Huggies "SAT Boost Supreme").

The latest rage: making diapers that fit babies' development stages. For example, Pampers Cruisers are for active older babies.

Q. What about store brands like Babies R Us and others? Is there much difference?

A. Although store diapers used to be less impressive than name brands, in the last few years they've caught up in terms of cloth like covers, Velcro fasteners and ultra absorbency. And they cost as much as 30% less too.

Q. Do certain brands work better for boys or girls?

A. We used to hear anecdotal evidence from our readers that Huggies were better with boys and Pampers better with girls. In recent years, however, parents tell us there doesn't seem to be a gender difference at all.

Q. How many diapers of each size is a good starting point?

A. Most babies go through 12 to 14 diapers *per day* for the first few months. That translates into about 500 to 600 diapers for the first six weeks. As you read at the beginning of the chapter we recommend buying 100 "newborn" size diapers and 400 to 500 "size one" diapers before baby is born. Caveat: some families have large babies, so keep the receipts just in case you have to exchange some of those newborns for size 1.

So how many do you need of the larger sizes? Starting with a case of each size as you transition to larger diapers is a good idea. There are typically a 100 diapers or more in a case. As you near a transition to a larger size, scale back the amount of smaller size diapers you buy so you don't have any half opened packs lying around.

Finally, remember that as your baby grows, she will require fewer diaper changes. Once you add solid foods to her feeding schedule you may only be doing eight to ten changes a day (we know—eight to 10 a day still seems like a ton of changes; but it will feel much less than baby's first few weeks). Plus you'll be much more experienced about when a diaper really is wet.

Let's break down the diaper choices:

◆ *Huggies.* Huggies is an excellent brand. However, in the last few years, Huggies hasn't added much to their line of diapers. Huggies

Supremes are their top of the line diapers with a fabric-like cover and Velcro closures. They've added a new "soft-knit" let elastic and DRIMAX protective liner to the Supremes for more comfort and leak protection. All Huggies models tout their "baby-shape" design, which implies a better fit than their competitors. Newborn diapers have a fold down waistband for umbilical cord care. Overnights are made to be even more absorbent so babies can actually sleep through the night (and parents too!). A couple specialty diapers round out the options: Huggies Convertibles (can be put on like pants or like a diaper), Preemies and Little Swimmers diapers.

Huggies web site (www.huggies.com) is easy to use with buttons for deals and explanations of each diapering product. A plus: you can use their "Product Chooser" feature to help decide which diapers will work best for your baby. Kimberly Clark, the company that makes Huggies has set up a separate web site called Parentstages (www.parentstages.com). Intended to be more informative and less commercial, the site allows parents to search for advice on health, family, entertainment and more. Ads are kept to a minimum and the emphasis is on information not products.

◆ **Pampers.** Pampers continues to offer a huge line of diapers to cover baby's stages of development and growth. Swaddlers are intended for newborns to size two. Claiming to "swaddle your baby in comfort" these diapers are for very young, inactive babies. Pampers claims they have "grow-with-me" fit—basically extra stretchy sides that can be easily adjusted. For the next stage when babies begin to kick, roll over, crawl and stand, Pampers has introduced their Cruisers. These are supposed to have more elasticity and give for active babies as well as less bulk. They are sized from three to six. Baby Dry diapers are yet another line of diapers in sizes from newborn to toddler. They've added a new closure system as well as cloth like cover to these. Premium diapers are no longer made by Pampers.

Pampers' easy to use web site (www.pampers.com) explains the new offerings pretty well, and there is an easy-to use chart that helps you figure out what's available for your baby at any particular stage. Coupons and deals were not available on the site when we visited.

◆ **Luvs.** Made by the same company that makes Pampers, Luvs are marketed as a lower-price brand. Once again, we didn't see much difference between Luvs and Pampers . . . or Huggies.

Luvs' web site (www.luvs.com) is heavy on Blue's Clues (used to be Barney). After you wade through all the Blue's Clues plugs, you'll note Luvs doesn't offer the swim diapers any more (may be seasonal), but is touting softer covers and tapes.

Eco Friendly Disposables

Is there a diaper that combines the convenience of disposables with the ecological benefits of cloth diapers? Yes—here's an overview of so-called eco-friendly disposables:

Tushies, first invented by a Denver pediatrician in the late 1980's, bills its diapers as a gel-free, latex-free, perfume-free alternative to name brand disposables. Made with non-chlorine bleached wood pulp surrounding an absorbent cotton core, they also offer a new "cloth-like" cover. Tushies mentions that without the gel, their diapers won't "explode" in the swimming pool. The disadvantages to Tushies? They are considerably thicker than regular diapers. And like most "all-natural" versions of consumer goods, Tushies ain't cheap. They sell a case of 160 size small diapers for $54. That's 34¢ per diaper. Compare that to grocery store prices of 17¢ per diaper and warehouse clubs of 13¢ per diaper. By the way, you'll also see a brand of diapers on Tushies site called ***Tender Care***. One reader mentioned they were thinner than Tushies; Tushies' site isn't very helpful in comparing the two brands. Tushies are available in 6000 stores (although not at Sam's, Costco or BJ's) or on line at www.tushies.com.

Nature Boy and Girl was another option for eco friendly disposables and we reviewed them in our last edition. Apparently they are out of business, but we can only hope other options come available for parents who want to avoid the typical disposable from Huggies, et al.

Ultimately, while these products are promising options for parents looking for a natural alternative to mainstream disposables, the price is certainly going to be a factor in getting parents to use them. And there is still an issue of where these diapers will go. Until recycling centers with composting options become available more widely, there's a question as to whether these diapers won't still end up buried under tons of earth and trash waiting to decompose.

◆ ***Store brands***. We've received numerous emails from parents who love store-brand diapers at Target, Wal-Mart, K-Mart and Toys R Us. Even grocery stores are getting into the game with private label diapers at prices to rival the discounters. Generally, these diapers are 20% to 30% cheaper than name brands. In the past, they were inferior in terms of features and quality but no more—most have the same ultrathin design, cloth-like covers and Velcro-closures. Toys R Us and Target's in-house brands received the highest marks from our readers; we noticed *Consumer Reports* liked Walgreens generic brand as well. Yes, there are several other obscure brands of diapers out there (among them Drypers, Dri-

Bottoms, and Fitti), but we didn't receive enough feedback from parents to form an opinion on them.

By the way, we've had the most compliments from readers regarding Wal-Mart's in-store diaper brand, White Cloud. Here's what one mom noted in an email to us: "Even though they seem more 'flimsy' than Luvs, they actually work great! And they are stretchy too, a feature that the premium brands market at a premium price these days."

Cloth Diapers. Ask 100 parents for their recommendations on cloth diapers and you're likely to get 100 different opinions—it seems everyone has their special system or favorite. We did see one common thread amongst cloth diaper devotees: most used a variety of brands/types to make it through the day. Like a well-armed soldier going into battle, the cloth-diapering parent typically has an arsenal of various products, schemes and tactics.

Unfortunately, we don't have space here to review the many brands of cloth diapers, all-in-one systems and covers on the market today. For additional tips on this subject, check our sources above in the Parents in Cyberspace section. A good book on using cloth diapers is *Diaper Changes* by Theresa Rodriquez (M. Evans and Co., publisher; $15). Finally, check out our online message boards on our web site at www.babybargains.com. They have extensive commentary from cloth diaper parents with tips and recommendations.

There are six categories of cloth diapers (plus covers):

◆ *Flat fold diapers.* Sold in stores like Target and Wal-Mart, these are nice for clean-up rags but rather useless for diapers.

◆ *Standard pre-fold diapers.* Common brands: Dundee and Curity. Our verdict: not much more useful than flat-fold diapers. Skip 'em.

◆ *Diaper service diapers.* Yes, you can buy the diapers used by cloth diaper services via mail order or at specialty stores. Used with pins or covers, these diapers come in three sizes (newborn, standard and toddler) and run $25 per dozen. Sometimes these are referred to as Chinese fold. The only bummer: these diapers can be bulky when used on infants under 15 pounds. Hence, most parents use these after a baby is six months old or so.

◆ *Fitted diapers.* The Mercedes of this category is Canada-made "Mother-Ease" (www.mother-ease.com), a brand that has a fanatical following among cloth diaper devotees. Suffice it to say, they ain't cheap but the quality is excellent. Mother-Ease sells both fitted diapers and covers; the diapers run $9 to $10 a pop, while the covers are about $9.75. Before you invest $73 to $375 in one of Mother-Ease's special package deals, consider trying their "introductory offer" (see details below in our money-saving tips section).

Other parents like Kushies (800) 841-5330 (web: www. kushies.com), another Canadian import. (For some reason, Kushies are known as "Kooshies" in the rest of the world). This brand offers several models, which sell for $5 to $7 each.

Another mother recently recommended Kissaluv diapers (kissaluv.com) for their newborn fitted diapers. She told us the price was similar to Mother-ease but she thought the quality was better. One note: all these diapers are sold via mail order only. Yes, you can sometimes find them at second-hand or thrift stores, but most parents buy them from a catalog or on the 'net. Kushies are trying to branch out into retail stores—check your local baby specialty shop.

◆ **Terry flannel diapers.** These are marketed to parents as the ultimate "eco-friendly" choice—terry flannel diapers are typically made of 100% organic cotton. Cost for terry/flannel diapers: about $20 to $35 for six depending on the brand (these diapers are sold via web sites like babynmore.com). Terry flannel diapers can take quite a while to dry and may be overkill for most parents. On the upside, they are contoured and less bulky, which means they fit newborn infants well.

◆ **All-in-one diapers.** As the name implies, these diapers combine a diaper and cover. And they aren't cheap: $8 to $19, depending on the brand. Most moms we interviewed say these diapers are too expensive for everyday use, but their convenience makes them handy for long trips. Once again, Mother-Ease and Kushies are two of the better brands to consider in this category. Other good all-in-one-diapers are made by All Together (801-566-7579, web: www. clothdiaper.com; $8 to $12) and Bumkins (800-338-7581 web: www.bumkins.com; $16 to $18 each). We've also received parental kudos for Indisposables (800-663-1730; www.mylilmiracle.com). Indisposables are cotton diapers starting at about $8.25 each.

◆ **Inserts and liners.** One of the criticisms of cloth diapers (fair or not) is that they leak, especially at night. To help your baby sleep through the night and avoid those 3 am crib changes, consider adding liners or inserts to your cloth diapers. Inserts are additional absorbent pads placed in the strategic crotch area of a regular cloth diaper to soak up any extra wetness. We've seen them for between $2 and $7 per insert on cloth diaper web sites. Liners are flushable, biodegradable paper liners. A three-roll pack on Amazon.com was $25.

◆ **Snappis**. Want to avoid using diaper pins? How about Snappis (we found them on earthbaby.com for $5 each). These fasteners have tiny teeth that grab the diaper and secure it instead of pins. Readers swear by Snappis, especially for babysitters and grandparents.

◆ **Covers.** With the exception of all-in-one cloth diapers, all other cloth diapers typically need covers, which help prevent leaks. The best diaper covers (also called wraps) not only must withstand leaks

E-MAIL FROM THE REAL WORLD
Which cloth diapers work best

Cloth diapering (know as CDing to those hip mammas out there) can be a bit overwhelming when you first decide to take the plunge. Since most parents choose to use disposables, you may not have a network of moms to look to for advice on this subject. So one of our long time readers, Tamara, has a few comments on what worked for her:

"We are currently using a diaper service. I researched and purchased several types of wraps and here is my feedback.

Bummis. These are Canadian and, according to my husband, breathe the most. He is an engineer and actually conducted some weird little test sucking and blowing on the various wraps to determine the ones that breathe the best. My complaint is that their Velcro is too narrow. Our baby is a wiggler and has actually wiggled out of the Bummis a couple of times. They lack leg gussets, which make side leaks and blowouts more frequent. Though size wise they last longer. I ordered these from Born To Love. They cost $7+ dollars depending on the site.

Dappi's. These have a cloth outside and plastic lining material with mesh over it plus a big Velcro band and tabs. These leak less, but poop tends to get caught in the mesh, which is messy. They cost $6.00 a pop at Target.

Diaperaps. Love 'em! My doula told me about them.They have colorful cloth outside and a plastic interior as well as a big Velcro band and tabs, and leg gussets. They are great! Fred Meyer sells them for roughly $11.00 for a 2 pack. They are hard to get hold of here in Seattle area, since they are very popular and sell out quickly. To my delight I discovered you can order these on the web, direct from Diaper Wraps (www.diaperaps.com). They cost $6.25 each plus shipping. The website offers discounts on large orders and package deals. They also sell cloth diapers, training pants, and swim diapers."

but also the washing machine—durability is a key factor.

Earlier in this chapter, we cited the wide variability in diaper cover costs, from the cheapest (Dappi covers at Target or Wal-Mart for $4 to $6) to the most expensive (wool Nikky lambs wool at $19 each). Obviously, most of the cheap diaper covers wear out much quicker than the expensive ones. Realizing that fact, some parents use the cheaper covers when baby is younger and growing rapidly (the faster the growth, the less each cover is used) and switch to more pricey covers when baby is older (say over a year, when growth slows and covers are used for a longer period of time).

As for specific brands, one mom we interviewed didn't like Cottonwraps ("they leaked like crazy"), Ecology Kids (the Velcro wears out too quickly) or Snappiwraps (the elastic also wears out too fast). Bumkins covers got better marks, but they have a vent panel in the back that makes it hard to use. Once again, Mother-Ease received raves for their covers ($9.75 a pop), as did Kushies wraps ($6 each at

E-Mail from The Real World
Cloth diaper laundry tips

Once you make the decision to use cloth diapers, you'll want to research the "art" of cleaning them. Too many harsh chemicals can damage and fade cloth diapers and covers, not enough will leave diapers looking less than pristine. So what's a parent to do? Here's some advice from readers who've experienced lots of diaper cleaning.

Rowan Cerrelli writes:

"I do not like to use chlorine bleach to wash out diapers since they are expensive and the chlorine ruins them. There are some products out there that use natural enzymes to predigest 'stuff' out of the diapers, therefore eliminating the need for bleach. Companies that have these products include Seventh Generation and Ecover. They are also available in natural food grocery stores."

Catherine Advocate-Ross recommends:

"I use Bio-Kleen laundry powder on the diapers. Works great and you need very little."

Bio-Kleen has a web site at www.biokleen.com that explains their products and directs consumers to stores or web sites that carry them. They have an extensive line including liquid as well as powder detergent and stain and odor eliminator. The main ingredient in the line is grapefruit seed and pulp extract.

Kelly Small, from Wallingford, CT emailed us to say:

"I highly recommend OxyClean— it is great on the poop stains!!!"

the www.thebabylane.com). We also heard positive comments about Diaperwraps, although feedback was mixed on Nikki's (some loved them, others said they were overpriced). *Special thanks to readers Sheila Pierson and J. Russel in Baltimore, MD for their insightful emails on this topic. Noel Howell also contributed to this section.*

Wipes. Like diapers, you have a basic choice with wipes: name brand or generic. Our advice: stick to the name brands. We found the cheap generic wipes to be inferior. With less water and thinner construction, store brand wipes we sampled were losers. There is one exception to this rule, however: Costco's Kirkland brand wipes, which many readers have said are fantastic. One mom emailed: "They are not as rigid as Huggies or Pampers, have a lighter scent and are stronger than any other wipe we tried." And the price: $13 for 576 (that's 2.3¢ per wipe).

Finally, Rebecca Parish has some practical advice on cloth diapers: "We (my friends and I) have run across a shortcut that I had not heard about before we attempted cloth diapering. Mainly, we have found it entirely unnecessary to rinse diapers out at all before laundering them. We own a four-day supply of pre-fold diapers and wraps. When our baby poops, we take an extra diaper wipe with us to the toilet, and use it to scrape what easily comes off into the toilet. Then we throw the dirty diaper into our diaper pail, right along with all the other dirty diapers. There's no liquid in the pail for soaking— they just sit in there dry. About every three or four days we throw the entire contents of the diaper pail into the laundry machine, add regular detergent (we use Cheer) and two capfuls of bleach (about 4 teaspoons), and run the machine. The diapers and wraps all come out clean. Just two extra loads of laundry a week (which is nothing compared to the extra loads of clothes we now wash), and no dipping our hands into toilet water. I generally use about five diaper wipes every time I change a messy diaper as it is, so using one extra one for scraping poop into the toilet seems like no big deal.

I think washer technology has improved significantly enough in recent years to allow for this much easier diaper cleaning. We own a fairly new front-loader washer. I don't think the brand name is important; we have a friend who owns a different brand of front-loader, and gets equally good results. However, one of our friends with an older top-loader uses our same system but ends up with stains; she doesn't care but I would. "

Bottom line: new technologies (detergents, additives and washers) have led to great improvements in the cleaning of cloth diapers.

Cloth Diapering 101

If you're considering cloth diapers for your child, you probably have many questions. It's been years since your mom diapered
a baby and the cloth diapers available today are nothing like what
she used. And, odds are, few if any of your friends and neighbors
use cloth either. But there is help. On our web site (BabyBargains.
com), we have extensive message boards including a section
called (appropriately but not subtly) Baby Butts. This board has
detailed discussions of diapering, both cloth and disposable. Look
for a pinned thread at the top of the forum dubbed Cloth
Diapering 101. Here our resident mom experts expound on the
basics of cloth diapering: descriptions of different elements of cloth
diapers, types of covers and even how to successfully wash your
new cloth diapers. It is a detailed treasure trove of advice!

Money Saving Secrets

Here are some tips for saving on disposable diapers (cloth diaper bargain advice is at the end of this section):

1 Buy in bulk. Don't buy those little packs of 20 diapers—look
for the 80 or 100 count packs instead. You'll find the price
per diaper goes down when you buy larger packs.

2 Go for warehouse clubs. Both Sam's (www.samsclub.com)
and Costco (www.costco.com) wholesale clubs sell diapers at
incredibly low prices. For example, Costco sells a 228-count package
of Huggies Step 1-2 for just $29.09 or less than 13¢ per diaper. We
also found great deals on wipes at the wholesale clubs. Another warehouse club is BJ's (www.bjs.com), which has over 100 locations in 16
states, most in the Eastern U.S. By the way, one reader noted that the
size 1-2 diapers she's seeing in warehouse clubs are really size 1. She's
been frustrated with this sizing issue since the size 3 diapers are too
big but there isn't anything in between the 1-2 and the 3 sizes.

3 Buy store brands. As mentioned earlier, many parents find
store brand diapers to be equal to the name brands. And the
prices can't be beat—many are 20% to 30% cheaper. Chains like
Target, Wal-Mart and Toys R Us/Babies R Us carry in-house diaper
brands, as do many grocery stores. Heck, even Sam's stocks a
generic brand of diapers that is 26% cheaper than name brands.

4 **CONSIDER TOYS R US.** You may not have a wholesale club nearby, but you're bound to be close to a Toys R Us (or their sister division, Babies R Us). And we found them to be a great source for affordable name-brand diapers. The best bet: buy in bulk. You can often buy diapers (both name brand and generic) by the case at Toys R Us, saving you about 20% or more over grocery store prices. As you might have noted in the earlier diaper cost comparison, Babies R Us was one of the lowest-priced sources for diapers we found. Don't forget to check the front of the store for copies of Toys R Us' latest catalog. Occasionally, they offer in-store coupons for additional diaper savings—you can even combine these with manufacturer's coupons for double savings.

5 **WHEN BABY IS NEARING A TRANSITION POINT, DON'T STOCK UP.** Quick growing babies may move into another size faster than you think, leaving you with an excess supply of too-small diapers.

6 **DON'T BUY DIAPERS IN GROCERY STORES.** We compared prices at grocery stores and usually found them to be sky-high. Most were selling diapers in packages that worked out to 17¢ per diaper. We should note there are exceptions to this rule, however: some grocery chains (especially in the South) use diapers as a "loss-leader." They'll sell diapers at attractive prices in order to entice shoppers into the store. Also, store brands can be more attractively priced, even at grocery stores.

7 **USE COUPONS.** You'll be amazed at how many coupons you receive in the mail, usually for 75¢ off diapers and 50¢ off wipes. One tip: to keep those "introductory" packages of coupons coming, continue signing up to be on the mailing lists of the maternity chain stores (apparently, these chains sell your name to diaper manufacturers, formula companies, etc.) or online at diaper manufacturers' web sites.

8 **ASK FOR GIFT CERTIFICATES.** When friends ask you what you'd like as a shower gift, you can drop hints for gift certificates/cards from stores that sell a wide variety of baby items—including diapers and wipes. That way you can get what you really need, instead of cute accessories of marginal value. You'd be surprised at how many stores offer gift certificate programs.

9 **FOR CLOTH DIAPER USERS, GO FOR "INTRODUCTORY PACKAGES."** Many suppliers have special introductory deals (Mother-Ease offers one diaper, liner and cover for $17 US; $20 Canadian, which includes shipping). Before you invest hundreds of dollars in one brand, give it a test drive first.

 diapers

The Bottom Line:
A Wrap-Up of Our Best Buy Picks

In summary, we recommend you buy the following layette items for your baby (see chart on next page).

QUANTITY	ITEM	COST
6	T-shirts/onesies (over the head)	$22
6	T-shirts (side snap)	$25
4-6	Sleepers	$64-$96
1	Blanket Sleeper	$10
2-4	Coveralls	$40-$80
3-4	Booties/socks	$12-$16
1	Sweater	$16
2	Hats (safari and caps)	$30
1	Snowsuit/bunting*	$20
4	Large bibs (for feeding)	$24
3 sets	Wash cloths and towels	$30
7-8	Receiving blankets	$42-$48
TOTAL		**$335 to $417**

These prices are from discounters, outlet stores, or sale prices at department stores. What would all these clothes cost at full retail? $500 to $600, at least. The bottom line: follow our tips and you'll save $100 to $300 on your baby's layette alone. (Of course, you may receive some of these items as gifts, so your actual outlay may be less.)

Which brands are best? See "Our Picks: Brand Recommendations" earlier in this chapter. In general, we found that 100% cotton clothes are best. Yes, you'll pay a little more for cotton, but it lasts longer and looks better than clothes made of polyester blends (the exception: fleece outerwear and sleepwear). Other wastes of money for infants include kimonos, saque sets, and shoes.

What about diapers? We found little financial difference between cloth and disposable, especially when you use a cloth diaper service. Cloth does have several hidden costs, however—diaper covers can add hundreds of dollars to the expense of this option although the cost can be spread out among additional children.

For disposables, we found that brand choice was more of a personal preference—all the majors did a good job at stopping leaks. The best way to save money on disposable diapers is to skip the grocery store and buy in bulk (100-diaper packages) from a warehouse club. Diapers from discount sources run about $300 to $375. The same diapers from grocery stores could be $600 or more. Another great money-saver: generic, store-brand diapers from Wal-Mart, Target, K-Mart and like. These diapers performed just as well as the name brands at a 20% to 30% discount.

CHAPTER 5

Maternity & Nursing

Inside this chapter

Love 'em or hate 'em, every mother-to-be needs maternity clothes at some point in her pregnancy. Still, you don't have to break the bank to get comfortable, and, yes, fashionable maternity items. In this chapter, we tell you which sources sell all-cotton, casual clothes at unbelievably low prices. Then, we'll review the top maternity chains and reveal our list of top wastes of money. Finally, you'll learn which nursing clothes moms prefer most.

Maternity & Nursing Clothes

Getting Started:
When Do You Need This Stuff?

It may seem obvious that you'll need to buy maternity clothes when you get pregnant, but the truth is you don't actually need all of them immediately. The first thing you'll notice is the need for a new bra. At least, that was my first clue that my body was changing. Breast changes occur as early as the first month and you may find yourself going through several different bra sizes along the way.

Next, your belly will begin to "swell." Yes, the baby is making its presence known by making you feel a bit bigger around the middle. Not only may you find that you need to buy larger panties, but you may also find that skirts and pants feel tight as early as your third month. Maternity clothes at this point may seem like overkill, but some women do begin to "show" enough that they find it necessary to head out to the maternity shop.

If you have decided to breastfeed, you'll need to consider what type of nursing bras you'll want. Buy two or three in your eighth month so you'll be prepared. You may find it necessary to buy more nursing bras after the baby is born, but this will get you started. As for other nursing clothes, you may or may not find these worth the money. Don't go out and buy a whole new wardrobe right off the bat. Some women find nursing shirts and tops to be helpful while others manage quite well with regular clothes. More on this topic later in the book.

Sources

1 **MATERNITY WEAR CHAINS.** Not surprisingly, there are quite a few nationwide maternity clothing chains. Visit any mall and you'll likely see the names Pea in the Pod, Motherswork, Mimi Maternity, and Motherhood, to mention a few. More on these chains later in the chapter.

2 **MOM AND POP MATERNITY SHOPS.** These small, independent stores sell a wide variety of maternity clothes, from affordable weekend wear to high-priced career wear. Some baby specialty stores carry maternity clothes as well. The chief advantage to the smaller stores is personalized service—we usually found salespeople who were knowledgeable about the different brands. In addition, these stores may offer other services. For example, some rent formal wear for special occasions, saving you big bucks. Of course, you may pay for the extra service with higher prices. While you're shopping at the independents look for lines from manufacturers like Liz Lange, Bella Band and Meet Me in Miami. Readers have been pleased with the quality and style of these brands.

3 **CONSIGNMENT STORES.** Many consignment or thrift stores that specialize in children's clothing may also have a rack of maternity clothes. In visits to several such stores, we found some incredible bargains (at least 50% off retail) on maternity clothes that were in good to excellent condition. Of course, the selection varies widely, but we strongly advise you to check out any second-hand stores.

4 **DISCOUNTERS.** When we talk about discounters, we're referring to chains like Target, Wal-Mart and K-Mart. Now, let's be honest here—these discounters probably aren't the first place you'd think of to outfit your maternity wardrobe. Yet, each has a surprisingly nice selection of maternity clothes, especially casual wear. Later, we'll tell you about the incredible prices on these all-cotton clothes.

5 **DEPARTMENT STORES.** As you might guess, most department stores carry some maternity fashions. The big disadvantage: the selection is usually rather small. This means you'll often find unattractive jumpers in abundance and very little in the way of fashionable clothing. Department stores like Penney's and Sears often have end-of-the-season sales with decent maternity bargains.

6 **WEB/MAIL-ORDER.** Even if you don't have any big-time maternity chains nearby, you can still buy the clothes they sell. Many chains offer a mail-order service, either from printed catalogs or online stores. We also found several mail-order catalogs that have a selection of maternity clothes. In the "Do It By Mail" section of this chapter, we'll give you the run-down on these options.

7 **NON-MATERNITY STORES.** Maternity stores don't have a monopoly on large-size clothes—and you can save big bucks by shopping at stores that don't have the word "maternity" in their name. One of our favorites: Old Navy. Their maternity clothes are both stylish and affordable.

8 **YOUR HUSBAND'S CLOSET.** What's a good source for comfy weekend wear? Look no further than the other side of your closet, where your husband's clothes can often double as maternity wear.

9 **OUTLETS.** Yes, there are several outlets that sell maternity clothes and the prices can be a steal. We'll discuss some alternatives later in this chapter.

10 **YOUR FRIENDS.** It's a time-honored tradition—handing down "old" maternity clothes to the newly pregnant. Of course, maternity styles don't change that much from year to year and since outfits aren't worn for a long time, they are usually in great shape. Just be sure to pass on the favor when you are through with your pregnancy. And if your friend or neighbor is clearly not going to fit in your old maternity clothes (you're six feet tall, she's under 5′5″), don't dump your old gear on her just to get rid of it. You're trying to do someone a favor, not avoid a trip to Good Will.

Parents in Cyberspace: What's on the Web?

Expressiva
Web: www.expressiva.com
What it is: Terrific source for *stylish* nursing clothes.

What's cool: Wow! That's all we could say when we took a look at Expressiva's designs. You really never would know they were nursing clothes. And they don't make you look like a sack of potatoes. Tops, dresses, casual clothes, workout gear, bras and even maternity clothes are available here. Sizes range from extra small to 3X and the site includes hints about sizing for specific outfits. We love the special collection for plus sizes. Three styles of nursing openings are available: vertical, crop top and concealed with zippers or snaps underneath a top layer. Prices are reasonable for the quality. If you want to look good and still offer the best first food for your baby, this is a site to check out.

Motherwear

Web: www.motherwear.com
What it is: The online version of the nursing clothes catalog.
What's cool: "This catalog makes the best clothes for nursing!" gushed one mom in an email to us and we have to agree—this is a great catalog and web site. Prices aren't cheap (a long sleeve nightshirt is $49), but the quality is excellent. And they have a clearance section with additional bargains—that aforementioned nightshirt was last seen marked down to $45 (a 20% savings). Other items were marked down up to 20%. Don't forget to check their weekly specials as well. A cool feature: want to see what the nursing openings look like on each garment? Just click on the little icon on each page and a window pops open with clear photos of each opening. And Motherwear has a satisfaction guarantee and easy return policy.

eStyle

Web: www.estyle.com
What it is: A "lifestyle" retailer targeting pregnant women and new moms with fashions, tips and information.
What's cool: A fast-loading, color-saturated site with easy navigation, it's easy to see why eStyle is a favorite among new and expecting parents. Not only can you shop for maternity fashions, you'll also find tips, calendars, sizing and style suggestions and more. When we last reviewed this site, they carried a plethora of brands including Belly Basics, Diane Von Furstenburg, Belly Beautiful, Michael Stars and more. Now, however, they are focusing on their in-house brand, BabyStyle, All the items we saw were quite stylish.
Needs work: But don't expect cut-rate prices for all that fashion. How 'bout a pair "dobby dock" pants for $74? Remember, you'll only be wearing these for a few months. If you really want to buy something here, check for their specials and deals.

Figure 1: Gap Maternity's web site lets you return items bought online to Gap stores.

eBay

Web: www.ebay.com

What it is: A surprising source of maternity bargains.

What's cool: Here are the deals just one of our readers, Alison Lewis of Winston-Salem, NC found: "I got five long sleeve cotton maternity shirts and two pairs of corduroy pant (mostly Motherhood brand) for a total of $21.50 and the shipping was $4." She notes too that the selection on eBay is "pretty much endless."

Needs work: Expect to find some real duds in the fashion department here. There's bound to be a lot of junk you'll have to sift through to find the jewels. And with eBay raising their fees, good sellers may leave this site for other, less well-known auction sites.

◆ **Other sites:** While most towns only have a handful of maternity stores, the web is teeming with possibilities. **Anna Cris Maternity** (www.annacris.com) sells it's own brand among others.

While most folks know **Gap** as a great place for kids clothes, few realize that Gap also does maternity. While most moms will only be able to find Gap Maternity online (www.gap.com), some BabyGap bricks and mortar stores offer maternity in store as well. You'll find classics like cardigans and jeans as well as stretch shirts, capri pants and more. Check frequently for sale items—they seem to offer more sales than most maternity retailers. Readers have been impressed with the quality of Gap maternity, according to our email. Old Navy, Gap's low price sister chain is also selling maternity on line (www.oldnavy.com). As with other Old Navy clothes, the quality is a bit less but the so are the prices.

Recommended by a reader, **Little Koala** (www.littlekoala.com) sells a decent selection of "natural fiber" maternity clothes including undergarments, plus infant clothes, diaper bags and carries/slings.

Maternity 4 Less (www.maternity4less.com) received yet another reader recommendation, this time for speedy delivery. Our reader reported that they exchanged a pair of maternity pants for her in only a matter of days, not the usual weeks other mail order sources take. They carry the gamut of maternity and nursing clothes and accessories. They also have a section of the site for plus sizes.

For a wide range of styles and sizes (up to 3X plus talls and petites), check out **Mom Shop** (www.momshop.com). With great full size photos and an easy to use site, we think MomShop.com is a top site.

Nursing clothes are where **One Hot Mama** (www.onehotmama.com) got their start, but they have expanded into maternity clothes as well. Either way, they attempt to showcase hip styles from manufacturers like Japanese Weekend. Just don't read the long-winded sermons on nursing from the site's owners.

For our Canadian readers, check out **Thyme Maternity** (www.thymematernity.com), recommended by a reader in Ontario. She thought the styles were more "real world," the sizing was great and prices were reasonable. They no longer offer mail order, but their web site has a directory of stores in Canada. As a side note, another Canadian mom wrote to recommend that her country-women consider going to Buffalo or other US cities to shop for maternity clothes. You've got a good exchange rate (at the time of this writing) and lower taxes.

We could go on and on with all these maternity/nursing web sites, but let's condense it a bit for you. The following are yet more options to check out for maternity and nursing clothing:

Birth and Baby	birthandbaby.com
Mommy Gear	mommygear.com
Fit Maternity	fitmaternity.com
Just Babies	justbabies.com
Liz Lange Maternity	lizlange.com
Mothers In Motion	mothers-in-motion.com
Naissance Maternity	naissancematernity.com
Pumpkin Maternity	pumpkinmaternity.com
Twinkle Little Star	twinklelittlestar.com

What Are You Buying?

What will you need when you get pregnant? There is no short-age of advice on this topic, especially from the folks trying to sell you stuff. But here's what real moms advise you to buy (divided into two topic areas, maternity clothes and then nursing clothes):

Maternity Clothes

◆ **Maternity Bras.** Maternity bras are available just about every-where, from specialty maternity shops to department stores, mail order catalogs and discount chains. More on this topic later in this chapter; look for our recommendations for maternity underwear.

HOW MANY? Two in each size as your bust line expands. I found that I went through three different sizes during my pregnancy, and buying two in each size allowed me to wear one while the other was washed.

◆ **Sleep Bras.** What do you need a bra to sleep in for, you ask? Well, some women find it more comfortable to have a little support at night as their breasts change. Toward the end of pregnancy, some women also start to leak breast milk (to be technical, this is actually colostrum). And once the baby arrives, a sleeping bra (cost, about $10) will keep those breast pads in place at night (to keep you from

Plus-size Maternity Clothing

What's the number one frustration with maternity wear? Finding decent plus-size maternity clothes, say our readers. Some maternity clothing manufacturers think only women with bodies like Cindy Crawford get pregnant. But what to do if you want to look attractive and your dress size starts at 16 or above? Our readers have recommended the following sites:

Baby Becoming	babybecoming.com
JCPenney	jcpenney.com
Maternal Instinct	maternal-instinct.com
MomShop	momshop.com
Motherhood	maternitymall.com
Expressiva	expressiva.com
Plus Maternity	plusmaternity.com

leaking when you inadvertently roll onto your stomach—yes, there will come a day when you can do that again). Some women just need light support, while others find a full-featured bra a necessity.

HOW MANY? Two sleep bras—one to wear while one is in the wash.

◆ **Underpants.** There are two schools of thought when it comes to underpants. Traditional maternity underwear goes over your tummy, while bikini-style briefs are worn under the belly. Some women like the traditional maternity briefs, while others find bikini-style underwear more comfortable. Whichever style you choose, be sure to look for all-cotton fabric, wide waistbands and good construction—repeated washings take their toll on cheap undies. See "Our Picks: Brand Recommendations" later in this section for the best bets.

HOW MANY? We recommend eight pairs. Since you may be wearing them even after your baby is born for a few weeks, get some that will last.

News from Down Under:
Maternity Bras for the Real World

What makes a great maternity bra? Consider the following points while shopping:

◆ *Support—part I.* How much support do you need? Some women we interviewed liked the heavy-duty construction of some maternity bras. For others, that was overkill.

◆ *Support—part II* Once you decide how much support you need, consider the *type* of support you like. The basic choices: under wire bras versus those that use fabric bands and panels. Some moms-to-be liked stretchy knit fabric while others preferred stiffer, woven fabric.

◆ *Appearance.* Let's be honest: some maternity bras can be darn ugly. And what about the bras that claim they'll grow with you during your pregnancy? Forget it—expect to go through several sizes as the months roll along.

◆ *Price.* Yes, the best maternity bras can be pricey. But I've found it doesn't pay to scrimp on underwear like bras and panties. Save money on other items in your maternity wardrobe and invest in comfortable undergarments..

◆ **Maternity belts and support items.** Pregnancy support belts can be critical for some moms. For example, Pam Anderson, one of our readers sent the following email when she was 7 1/2 months along:

"Last week I got the worst pain/cramp that I have ever had in my life. It kept coming and going while I was walking, but it was so bad that I doubled over in pain when it hit. I went to my doctor and she said that the baby was pushing on a ligament that goes between the abdomen and the leg. She recommended that I get a "Prenatal Cradle" from www.aboutbabiesinc.com. I'll tell you what it is the most wonderful purchase I have ever made in my life. It was about $50, but it works wonders. It does not totally eliminate the pain, but it gives enough support that it drastically reduces the pain and even gives me time to change positions so that it does not get worse. I have even found that wearing it at night helps to alleviate the pain at night rolling over in bed."

Your best bet, if you find you need some support, is to check with your doctor as Pam did. Many of these belts are available on general web sites like OneStepAhead.com and BabyCatalog.com.

HOW MANY? Kind of obvious, but one should be enough. And most likely you'll need this late in your pregnancy unless you are carrying multiples.

◆ **Career Clothing.** Our best advice about career clothing for the pregnant mom is to stick with basics. Buy yourself a coordinating outfit with a skirt, jacket, and pair of pants and then accessorize.

Now, we know what you're saying. You'd love to follow this advice, but you don't want to wear the same old thing several times a week—even if it is beautifully accessorized. I don't blame you. So, go for a couple dresses and sweaters too. The good news is you don't have to pay full price. We've got several money-saving tips and even an outlet or two coming up later in this chapter.

At some point, you'll notice that regular clothes just don't fit well, and the maternity buying will begin. When this occurs is different for every woman. Some moms-to-be begin to show as early as three months, while others can wait it out until as late as six months. But don't wait until you begin to look like a sausage to shop around. It's always best to scope out the bargains early, so you won't be tempted to buy outfits (out of desperation) at the convenient—and high-priced—specialty store.

By the way, thanks to trend toward casual office wear, pregnant woman can spend hundreds of dollars LESS than they might have had to five or ten years ago. Today, you can pair a knit skirt with a sweater set for the office. Gone are the days of the power suit, thank goodness.

◆ **Casual Clothes.** Your best bet here is to stick with simple basics, like jeans and cords. You don't necessarily have to buy these from maternity stores. In fact, later in this chapter, we'll talk about less-expensive alternatives. If you're pregnant in the summer, dresses can be a cooler alternative to pants and shorts.

◆ **Dress or Formal Clothes.** Forget them unless you have a full social calendar or have many social engagements associated with your job. Sometimes, you can find a local store that rents maternity formalwear for the one or two occasions when you might need it.

Nursing Clothes

◆ **Nursing Bras.** The one piece of advice every nursing mom gives is: buy a well-made, high quality nursing bra *that fits you*. Easier said than done you say? Maybe. But here are some tips we gleaned from a reader poll we took.

First, what's the difference between a nursing bra and a maternity bra? Nursing bras have special flaps that fold down to give baby easy access to the breast. Access is usually with a hook or snaps either in the middle or on top of the bra near the straps. Readers insist new moms should look for the easiest access they can find. You'll need to be able to open your nursing bra quickly with only one hand in most cases.

Next, avoid under wire bras at all cost. They can cause plugged ducts, a very painful condition. If you sport a large cup size, you'll need a bra that is ultra supportive. Check out Motherhood Maternity bras. Some of our readers told us they have a good selection of large cup sizes. And in most cases, nursing moms require a sleep bra too—some for support, some just to hold nursing pads.

Mothers living near a locally owned maternity shop or specialized lingerie store recommended going in and having a nursing bra fitted to you. One reader reported that "I was wearing a bra at least three cup sizes too small. The consultant fitted me properly and I couldn't believe how comfortable I was!" If you don't have the luxury of a shop full of specialists, the folks at Bravado (www.bravadodesigns.com), Motherwear (www.motherwear.com) and Breast is Best (www.breastisbest.com) have terrific online consultants.

If you plan to nurse, you should probably buy at least two bras during your eighth month (they cost about $30 to $45 each). Why then? Theoretically, your breast size won't change much once your baby is born and your milk comes in. I'd suggest buying one with a little larger cup size (than your eighth month size) so you can compensate for the engorgement phase. You can always buy more later and, if your size changes once the baby is born, you won't have invested too much in the wrong size. If you want more advice on nursing bras, you can check out Playtex's cool web site at www. playtex.com. Click on the apparel section, then "Find the Perfect Fit." "Expectant Moments" is their maternity brand.

How many? Buy one to two bras in your eighth month. After the baby is born, you may want to buy a couple more.

◆ **Nursing Pads.** Readers in our last edition complained that we gave nursing pads short shrift. After all, just about every nursing mom will need some at least at the beginning. So here we are to make up for our past omission! There are two options with nursing pads: disposable and reusable. Common sense tells you that reusable breast pads make the most economical sense, particularly if you plan to have more children. Still, if you aren't a big leaker, don't plan to breast feed for long or just need something quick and easy when you're on the go, disposables are handy.

When we polled our readers, we were surprised to learn that the majority preferred disposables. Those by Lansinoh (www.lansinoh.com; $9 for 60 at www.drugstore.com) were by far the favorite followed by Johnson and Johnson ($5 per 50), Gerber (60 for $5.50) and Curity (66 for $5.49). What's the secret to these disposables? The same type of super absorbent polymer that makes your baby's diapers so absorbent. That makes them super thin too so you aren't embarrassed by telltale "bulls-eyes" in your bra. Moms also love the individually wrapped pads because they can just grab a couple and throw them in the diaper bag on the way out of the house. Interestingly, moms were divided on whether they like contoured or flat pads or those with adhesive strips or without.

While there wasn't one discount source mentioned for disposable breast pads, moms tell us when they see their favorite brands on sale at Wal-Mart, Target or Babies R Us, they snapped up multiple boxes.

For the minority who preferred reusable, washable pads, Medela ($8 per pair), Avent ($6 for three pair) and Gerber ($4 for three pair) made the top of the list. Some moms recommend Bravado's (bravadodesigns.com) Cool Max pads ($16 for five pair) for superior absorption. A few parents have raved about Danish Wool pads (danishwool.com). These soft, felted pads contain natural lanolin, a godsend for moms with sore, cracked nipples. They aren't cheap ($14 to $24 per pair) but we thought them worth the mention. Another pad recommended by a reader is LilyPadz by Lilypadz.com. She told us they are streamlined and reusable, can be worn with or without a bra and cost about $20 per pair.

◆ **Nursing Clothes.** You may not think so (especially at 8 1/2

Reader Poll: Nursing clothes brands

When we polled our readers about nursing clothes we were immediately chastised by at least half the respondents for even considering recommending them. "A waste of money," "ugly!" and "useless" were a few of the more charitable comments from these readers. As many as one third had never even used a single nursing top. They preferred to wear button up shirts or t-shirts and loose tops that they just pulled up. One mom told us "I got pretty good at being discreet in public with my regular clothes and no one was the wiser."

But other moms loved nursing clothes. And their favorites were those from **Motherwear**, the catalog and Internet site we reviewed earlier in this chapter. In our poll over 100 respondents mentioned Motherwear as the best source for well-made, comfortable nursing clothes. The biggest complaint about Motherwear was that their clothes are expensive. Readers suggested checking out the clearance section, visiting their outlet (in Massachusetts), and buying them used from ebay.com. The site offers a discount for parents of multiples too. The next closest company was **One Hot Mama** (www.onehotmama.com) with 17 votes.

Other sites recommended by parents included **Expressiva** (www.expressiva.com), **Birth and Baby** (www.birthandbaby.com) and **Breast Feeding Styles** (www.breastfeedingstyles.com). Breast Feeding Styles received special mention for their easy to use zippered openings.

Regardless of where nursing clothes were purchased, moms were universal in thinking that the best tops have two vertical openings over the breasts. Forget the single center opening! And no buttons either. Too hard, our moms said, to open with one hand while baby is screaming in your ear. Twin sets and cardigan sweaters were the preferred styles. Readers thought they looked least like nursing clothes. And lots of moms thought just having a few nursing camisoles and t-shirts to wear under a regular shirt was the way to go. Finally, several parents recommended the Super Secret Nursing Shirt from One Hot Mama.

Want to make your own nursing clothes? Creative sewers will find great patterns on **Elizabeth Lee's** web site (www.elizabethlee.com) as well as **Mother Nurture** (www.mothernuture.com).

months), but there will come a day when you won't need to wear those maternity clothes. But what if you want to nurse in public after baby is born? Many women swear by nursing clothes as the best way to be discreet, but others do just fine with loose knit tops and button front shirts. Bottom line: one obvious way to save money with nursing clothes is not to buy any. If you want to experiment, buy one or two nursing tops and see how they work for you. By the way, parents of twins found it difficult if not impossible to use a nursing top when nursing both babies at the same time. See the following box for more reader feedback on nursing clothes.

Tracy Guttierez suggested that working moms who are nursing or expressing milk might want to check into getting a nursing camisole or tank top. "I wear them under a regular shirt and don't feel so exposed when I pump at work or nurse in public." Her favorite: a Wal-Mart brand camisole. She thought it was softer than Mimi Maternity or Motherhood Maternity options.

◆ *Nursing Pajamas.* Looking for something comfortable to sleep in that allows you to nurse easily? Check out *Majamas* (www.majamas.com). One of our product testers tried out their cotton/lycra t-shirt with her newborn and thought it was great, worthy of a recommendation. It allowed her to sleep without wearing a nursing bra since it had pockets for holding breast pads and had easy nursing access. Most moms, however, hated nursing gowns and found it much simpler to sleep in pajamas with tops they could pull up or unbutton quickly. By the way, they've added a lot of new styles to their site. Pants, twin sets, and more.

Another option: *Aimee Gowns* (www.aimeegowns.com). The design of these gowns allows you to use breast pads without having to wear a nursing bra to bed. The cost: $40 with a discount if you buy more than one. Three colors are available and sizes run up to extra large.

 ## More Money Buys You . . .

Like any clothing, the more you spend, the better quality fabric and construction you get. Of course, do you really need a cashmere maternity outfit you'll wear for only a few months? Besides fabric, you'll note more designer names as prices go up. For example, Lilly Pulitzer, Nicole Miller and Vivian Tam are making maternity clothes now. You can even buy maternity clothes from Laura Sara M, the designer for Hollywood stars.

Smart Shopper Tips

Smart Shopper Tip #1
Battling your wacky thermostat

"It's early in my pregnancy, and I'm finding that the lycra-blend blouses that I wear to work have become very uncomfortable. I'm starting to shop for maternity clothes—what should I look for that will be more comfortable?"

It's a fact of life for us pregnant folks—your body's thermostat has gone berserk. Thanks to those pregnancy hormones, it may be hard to regulate your body's temperature. And those lycra-blend clothes may not be so comfortable anymore.

Our advice: stick with natural fabrics as much as possible, especially cotton. Unfortunately, a lot of lower-priced maternity clothing is made of polyester/cotton blend fabrics.

Smart Shopper Tip #2
Seasons change

"Help! My baby is due in October, but I still need maternity clothes for the hot summer months! How can I buy my maternity wardrobe without investing a fortune?"

Unless you live in a place with endless summer, most women have to buy maternity clothes that will span both warm and cold seasons. The best bets are items that work in BOTH winter or summer—for example, lightweight long-sleeve shirts can be rolled up in the summer. Cropped pants can work in both spring and fall. Another tip: layer clothes to ward off cold. Of course, there's another obvious way to save: borrow items from friends. If you just need a few items to bridge the seasons (a coat, heavy sweater, etc), try to borrow before buying.

Smart Shopper Tip #3
Petites aren't always petite

"I'm only 5 feet 2 inches tall and obviously wear petite sizes. I ordered a pair of pants in a petite size from an online discounter, but they weren't really shorter in the leg. In fact, I'd have to have the pants reconstructed to actually fit right. What gives?"

Many maternity web sites advertise that they carry a wide range of sizes but in truth you may find the choices very limited. And in some cases, "petite" is really just sizes 2 to 4. Translation: these pants aren't really shorter in the leg. How can you tell without ordering and then having to return items? Your best bet is to try on items before you buy. That's not always easy, of course, especially when ordering online. In that case, check the size charts on each site to be sure they offer *real* petites. And if a manufacturer (like the Gap, for example) makes petites that fit you in their regular clothing, chances are they also will in their maternity line.

Here are our readers recommendations for petite maternity: Kohl's, JCPenney, Old Navy, Gap, Japanese Weekend, Mimi Maternity, and Lands End.

Our Picks: Brand Recommendations for Maternity Undergarments

Thank goodness for e-mail. Here at the home office in Boulder, CO our e-mail (authors@BabyBargains.com) has overflowed with great suggestions from readers on maternity undergarments.

God bless Canada—those Maple Leaf-heads make one of the best maternity bras in the world. Toronto-based **Bravado Designs** (for a brochure, call 800-590-7802 or 416-466-8652; web: www. bravadodesigns.com) makes a maternity/nursing bra of the same name that's just incredible. "A godsend!" raved one reader. "It's built like a sports bra with no under wire and supports better than any other bra I've tried . . . and this is my third pregnancy!" raved another. The Bravado bra comes in three support levels, sizes up to 42-46 with an F-G cup and a couple of wonderful colors/patterns (you can also call them for custom sizing information). Available via mail order, the bra costs $35. Another plus: the Bravado salespeople are knowledgeable and quite helpful with sizing questions. Some of our readers have criticized the Bravado for not providing enough support, especially in the largest sizes. If you have doubts, just try one at first and see if it works for you before investing in several. Our readers have noticed great prices on Bravado Bras at www.sierrablue.com ($31.50 including shipping and free breast pads) as well as on www.WearstheBaby.com ($32 including shipping).

Playtex Expectant Moments was mentioned by our readers as a good choice as well. And they offer sizing advice on their web site at www.playtex.com. You'll find these bras at stores like JCPenney. Medela, as you'd imagine, also has a good following for their bras. Available in a couple styles with a choice of thin or thick straps, they cost about $32.

Finally, one reader recommended a nursing bra she found on line at **iMaternity.com** for those with larger bra sizes:

"As a 36 H the Bravado Bra just didn't do much to stop inertia from taking over! I have to recommend instead a bra found at imaternity.com. On the site it is called the Cotton Under wire Nursing Bra, but the label reads Leading Lady Style #488. It comes in sizes up to or past H and does wonders for me! Just wanted to try to spare someone else the hassle of ordering so many bras at 30$ each in order to find one that gets the job done." (Update: when last we checked the site still had the underwire option but only up to an F. Their Soft Cup bra does go up to an H.) Leading Lady bras are available in many department stores at maternity outlets. Their web site is www.leadinglady.com and they manufacturer quite a wide assortment of bras is a huge range of sizes.

Looking for maternity shorts/tights for working out? One of the best is **Fit Maternity** (www.fitmaternity.com; 800-961-9100). They offer an unbelievable assortment of workout clothes including unitards, tights, swimsuits and more. Also check out their books and work out tapes. On the same subject, the catalog **Title Nine Sports** (www.titleninesports.com; 800-342-4448) offers a few items. Pants are $58 and have a bellyband for extra support. The catalog also carries maternity shorts and bras as well as sports bras, which some women find is a more comfortable alternative to maternity bras. Another site, Raising a Racquet (www.raisingaracquet.com) has active ware for pregnant moms as well.

What about underpants? The best I wore were **Japanese Weekend** (800) 808-0555 (web: www.japaneseweekend.com), a brand available in stores and via mail order (see review later in this chapter). They've changed the styles a bit over the years, but I found them incredibly comfortable *and* durable, standing up to repeated washings better than other brands. Unfortunately, the price has gone up to $36 for two pair ($32 at sites like www.nurturecenter.com). At that price, it's getting tougher to recommend them to our readers. The company also carries tights and nursing bras. Other moms swear by their regular panties and don't see a need to get anything special or new for maternity. You'll find that it's easy to wear bikini underpants below your belly. Other moms have recommended brands from Target, Wal-Mart and Kmart, particularly a brand called Luv Pats.

Our Picks: Brand Recommendations for Nursing Bras, Pads and Clothes

Nursing pads are a passionate topic for many of our readers with disposables beating out reusables as moms' favorites. They loved both **Lansinoh** and **Johnson & Johnson** disposable by an overwhelming number. **Medela**, **Advent** and **Bravado** make great reusable nursing pads.

Bravado is also quite popular as a nursing bra for all but the largest of cup sizes as are **Playtex** and **Medela**. If you need a size larger than DD, consider **Motherhood Maternity's** brand as well as **Leading Lady**. The web is the best place to find bras on deal including **Decent Exposures** (www.decentexposures.com) and **Birth and Baby** (www.birthandbaby.com).

Most moms found that specialized nursing clothes weren't a necessity, but for those who want to try them, nearly everyone recommended **Motherwear** (www.motherwear.com). **One Hot Mama** (www.onehotmama.com) and **Expressiva** (www.expressiva.com) were other stylish sites to consider. Look for discounts on clearance pages or eBay.com.

Wastes of Money

Waste of Money #1
Maternity Bra Blues
"My old bras are getting very tight. I recently went to my local department store to check out larger sizes. The salesperson suggested I purchase a maternity bra because it would offer more comfort and support. Should I buy a regular bra in a larger size or plunk down the extra money for a maternity bra?

We've heard from quite a few readers who've complained that expensive maternity bras they've bought were very uncomfortable and/or fell apart after just a few washings. Our best advice: try on the bra before purchase and stick to the better brands. Compared to regular bras, the best maternity bras have thicker straps, more give on the sides and more hook and eye closures in back (so the bra can grow with you). Most of all, the bra should be comfortable and have no scratchy lace or detailing. I've had luck with the Bravado bra, mentioned earlier in this chapter. Readers tell us that a good sports bra can also be a fine alternative.

Waste of Money #2
Over the Shoulder Tummy Holder
"I keep seeing those 'belly bras' advertised as the best option for a pregnant mom. What are they for and are they worth buying?"

Belly bras provide additional support for your back during your pregnancy. One style envelopes your whole torso and looks like a tight-fitting tank top. No one can argue that, in many cases, the strain of carrying a baby (and the additional weight) is tough even on women in great physical shape. So, if you find your back, hips, and/or legs are giving you trouble, consider buying a belly bra.

However, in our research, we noticed most moms don't seem to need or want a belly bra. The price for one of these puppies can range from $35 to an incredible $55. The bottom line: hold off buying a belly bra or support panty until you see how your body reacts to your pregnancy. Also, check with your doctor to see if she has any suggestions for back, hip, and leg problems.

Waste of Money #3
Overexposed Nursing Gowns/Tops

"I refuse to buy those awful nursing tops! Not only are they ugly, but those weird looking panels are like wearing a neon sign that says BREASTFEEDING MOM AHEAD!"

"I plan to nurse my baby and all my friends say I should buy nursing gowns for night feedings. Problem is, I've tried on a few and even though the slits are hidden, I still feel exposed. Not to mention they're the ugliest things I've ever seen. Can't I just wear a regular gown that buttons down the front?"

Of course you can. And considering how expensive some nursing gowns can be ($35 to $50 each), buying a regular button-up nightshirt or gown will certainly save you a few bucks. Every mother we interviewed about nursing gowns had the same complaint. There isn't a delicate way to put this: it's not easy to get a breast out of one of those teenie-weenie slits. Did the person who designed these ever breastfeed a baby? I always felt uncovered whenever I wore a nursing gown, like one gust of wind would have turned me into a centerfold for a nudist magazine.

And can we talk about nursing shirts with those "convenient button flaps for discreet breastfeeding"? Convenient, my fanny. There's so much work involved in lifting the flap up, unbuttoning it, and getting your baby positioned that you might as well forget it. My advice: stick with shirts you can pull up or unbutton down the front. These are just as discreet, easier to work with, and (best of all) you don't have to add some expensive nursing shirts (at $30 to $50 each) to your wardrobe. See box earlier for more feedback from real moms.

Another tip: if possible, try on any nursing clothing BEFORE you buy. See how easy they are to use. You might be surprised how easy (or difficult) an item can be. Imagine as you are doing this that you have an infant that is screaming his head off wanting to eat NOW, not five seconds from now. You can see why buying any nursing clothes sight unseen is a risk.

Waste of Money #4
New shoes
"Help! My feet have swollen and none of my shoes fit!"

Here's a little fact of pregnancy that no one tells you: your feet are going to swell and grow. And, sadly, after the baby is born, those tootsies won't be shrinking back to your pre-pregnancy size. A word to the wise: don't buy lots of new shoes at the start of your pregnancy. But no need to despair. After your baby is born, you'll likely have a built-in excuse to go shoe shopping!

Another suggestion from reader Gretchen Callison, Rochester, WA: "It is never too early to buy shoes that don't tie! I go to the gym every morning, and it was getting to be a huge ordeal just to get my shoes tied. I bought some slip on shoes at 20 weeks and I still think it's one of the smartest things I've done."

Money-Saving Secrets

1 CONSIDER BUYING "PLUS" SIZES FROM A REGULAR STORE.
Thankfully, fashion lately has been heavy on casual looks . . . even for the office. This makes pregnancy a lot easier since you can buy the same styles in larger ladies' sizes to cover your belly without compromising your fashion sense or investing in expensive and often shoddily made maternity clothes. We found the same fashions in plus-size stores for 20% to 35% less than maternity shops (and even more during sales).

One drawback to this strategy: by the end of your pregnancy, your hemlines may start to look a little "high-low"—your expanding belly will raise the hemline in front. This may be especially pronounced with skirts and dresses. Of course, that's the advantage of buying maternity clothes: the designers compensate with more fabric in front to balance the hemline. Nonetheless, we found that many moms we interviewed were able to get away with plus-size fashions for much (if not all) of their pregnancy. How much can you save? In many cases, from 25% to 50% off those high prices in maternity chains like Pea in the Pod.

2 DON'T OVER-BUY BRAS. As your pregnancy progresses, your bra size is going to change at least a couple times. Running out to buy five new bras when you hit a new cup size is probably foolish—in another month, all those bras may not fit. The best advice: buy the bare minimum (two or three). Or try this idea: bra extenders (three for $3.50 from OneHanesPlace.com or fabric stores). Bra extenders make your bra slightly bigger, which saves on buying new bras.

3 **BUT DON'T SKIMP ON QUALITY WHEN IT COMES TO MATERNI-TY BRAS AND UNDERWEAR.** Take some of the money you save from other parts of this book and invest in good maternity under-wear. Yes, you can find cheap underwear for $3 a pair at discount stores, but don't be penny-wise and pound-foolish. We found the cheap stuff is very uncomfortable and falls apart, forcing you to go back and buy more. Investing in better-quality bras and underwear also makes sense if you plan to have more than one child—you can actually wear it again for subsequent pregnancies. Another obvious tip: if you like bikini style underwear, you may not need to buy spe-cial "maternity" style undies—just use your regular underwear.

4 **CONSIDER DISCOUNTERS FOR CASUAL CLOTHES.** Okay, I admit that I don't normally shop at K-Mart or Target for my clothes. But I was surprised to discover these chains (and even department stores like Sears) carry casual maternity clothes in 100% cotton at very affordable prices. Let's repeat that—they have 100% cotton t-shirts, shorts, pants, and more at prices you won't believe. Most of these clothes are in basic solid colors—sorry, no fancy prints. At Target, for example, I found a 100% cotton white maternity t-shirt (long sleeves) for $12. Jersey pull-on pants were only $20; jeans

Figure 2: A maternity top for just $11? Skirt for $14? Must be Target's maternity department!

were $27. Even a knit skirt was a mere $17. If you buy from one of these discounters, just be sure that you check the fabric and try everything on before you buy. You don't want to have to lug the stuff back to the store. And Target now has maternity apparel from designers like Liz Lange. Our readers say the quality is a bit less than the regular, specialty store version, but the style is good and the prices can't be beat. Don't forget to check Target's sale rack too. One reader found items for as little as $4 on sale.

While the discounters don't carry much in the way of career wear, you'll save so much on casual/weekend clothes that you'll be ecstatic anyway. Witness this example. At A Pea in the Pod, we found a white, cotton-knit top and stretch twill shorts. The price for the two pieces: a heart-stopping $150. A similar all-cotton tank top/shorts outfit from Target was $30. Whip out a calculator, and you'll note the savings is an amazing 80%. Need we say more? Not to mention that nice casual clothes are acceptable for office wear these days anyway.

By the way, don't forget to check out stores like Kohls, Marshall's, Ross and TJ MAXX. One reader told us she found maternity clothes at 60% off at TJ MAXX. Old Navy has added maternity to its web site and many readers have found great, comfortable clothes at good prices. Corrie, a reader from Chicago, did all her maternity shopping on line at Old Navy. She spent a total of $365 for eight pairs of pants, one pair of jeans, eleven sweaters, eight long sleeve tops, three button-down shirts, five sleeveless tops and two cardigans. She notes that works out to less than $10 per piece!

5 RENT EVENING WEAR—DON'T BUY. We found that some indie maternity stores rent eveningwear. For example, a local shop we visited had an entire rack of rental formalwear. An off-white lace dress (perfect for attending a wedding) rented for just $50. Compare that with the purchase price of $175. Since you most likely would need the dress for a one-time wearing, the savings of renting versus buying would be $125.

6 CHECK OUT CONSIGNMENT STORES. You can find "gently worn" career and casual maternity clothes for 40% to 70% off the original retail! Many consignment or second-hand stores carry only designer-label clothing in good to excellent condition. If you don't want to buy used garments, consider recouping some of your investment in maternity clothes by consigning them after the baby is born. You can usually find listings for these stores in the phone book. (Don't forget to look under children's clothes as well. Some consignment stores that carry baby furniture and clothes also have a significant stock of maternity wear.) One web source to find consignment shops is www.narts.org.

7 **FIND AN OUTLET.** Check out the next section of this chapter for the low-down on maternity clothes outlets.

8 **BE CREATIVE.** Raid your husband's closet for over-sized shirts and pants.

9 **SEW IT YOURSELF.** A reader in California emailed in this recommendation: she loved the patterns for nursing clothes by Elizabeth Lee Designs (435-454-3350; web: www.elizabethlee.com). "I would think anyone with a bit of sewing experience could handle any of the patterns, which don't LOOK like nursing dresses or tops." Elizabeth Lee has both a catalog and web site; in addition to patterns, they also sell already-made dresses and tops. Another bonus: the company has one of the largest selections of nursing bras we've seen, including Bravado Bras.

10 **BEG AND BORROW.** Unless you're the first of your friends to get pregnant you know someone who's already been through this. Check around to see if you can borrow old maternity clothes from other moms. In fact, we loaned out a big box after our second baby was born and it has made the rounds of the whole neighborhood. And don't forget to be generous after your baby making days are over too.

11 **CHECK OUT CLEARANCE AREAS IN CATALOGS AND ONLINE.** Many of our most devoted discount shopping readers have scored big deals on their favorite web sites' clearance pages. For example, on Motherwear.com we noticed a "Flyaway Cardigan Dress," regularly marked at $80 but on sale for only $39. Old Navy had some low-rise knit pants marked down $17 and the Gap had a track sweater, regularly $54 for only $30.

12 **WHEN ORDERING MATERNITY CLOTHES FROM JCPENNEY, POOL YOUR ORDERS!** One of our readers noticed that for orders of over $250 you'll only pay a flat shipping fee ($25 in her case) no matter how much more you buy. Then, any returns you have can be taken into the actual bricks and mortar store in your hometown (obviously saving the return shipping charge). And, if you just want to make an exchange of an item for a different size, you can do this in the store at no extra charge as well. Considering how expensive shipping items back and forth could be, the original $25 seems like quite a deal.

Outlets

MOTHERHOOD MATERNITY OUTLETS

Locations: 99 outlets (14 are called Maternity Works). For location info, call (800) 466-6223.

The offspring of the catalog and retail stores of maternity giant Motherhood Maternity (see review later in this chapter), Maternity Works outlets have started springing up in outlet malls across the country. On a recent visit, the outlet featured markdowns from 20% to 75% on the same designs you see in their catalog or retail stores.

MOTHERWEAR

Location: North Hampton, MA (413) 586-2175.

The Motherwear catalog has a factory outlet that is open just Wednesday through Saturday. They sell returned merchandise, seconds, overstock and discontinued items. "Great bargains—worth the trip," says a reader who visited the outlet.

The Name Game: Reviews of Selected Maternity Stores

Usually this section is intended to acquaint you with the clothing name brands you'll see in local stores. But now there is only one giant chain of maternity wear in North America—Mothers Work Inc., which operates stores under three brand names and the Internet, is the 800 pound gorilla of maternity clothes with over 1000 stores in the US, Canada and Puerto Rico. Mothers Work has over a 40% share of the $1.2 billion maternity clothing market in the US. So let's take a look at these three divisions, a new concept they've added, and their Internet site.

◆ **Motherhood.** With 717 stores, Motherhood is the biggest sister in the chain. While most stores are located in malls and power centers, 232 are also leased departments within department stores like Sears. Motherhood carries maternity clothes in the lowest price points. As an example, dresses at Motherhood range from $17 to $69. They also have 106 outlets.

◆ **Mimi Maternity.** Mimi is intended to be the middle price point of the three divisions. Mimi supposed to be a more hip, youthful take on maternity. Here you'll find a more fashion-forward look with dresses in the $40 to $168 price range. They have 121 stores.

◆ **A Pea in the Pod.** Finally, A Pea in the Pod (APIP) is Mothers Works' most expensive division. With dress prices ranging from $150 to $450, you can see what we mean. APIP has only 41 stores and is positioned to be more of a designer boutique. Hence you'll find them in locations like Beverly Hills and Madison Ave.

◆ **Destination Maternity Superstore.** These superstores (check their web site at www.destinationmaternity.com for locations) combine A Pea in the Pod, Mimi Maternity and Motherhood Maternity under one roof. They also include a spa called Edamame Spa offering a wide range of classes with topics like yoga, scrap booking 101 and financial planning. Four stores are operating as of this writing.

Japanese Weekend: Comfort, at a price

Japanese Weekend (JW) is a line of maternity clothing that emphasizes comfort. They are best known for their unusual "OK" belly-banded pants, which have a waistband that circles *under* your expanding tummy for support (rather than cutting across it). In recent years, JW has expanded its line beyond pants to include jumpers, tops, cat suits, nightgowns, and skirts. We really like the simple, comfortable style of the clothes and highly recommend them. For once, a company has created all-cotton clothing for moms-to-be, avoiding the all too common polyester blends. One nice plus: JW will send you a list of stores that carry their clothes (call the above number for more information). In addition, the designer has a company store in San Francisco (415-989-6667). As for JW's web site, they don't seem very committed to making it work. We've received complaints from readers about their customer service. Recently, a reader complained that the casual pants and sweater she purchased pilled horribly after only one day and another pair of pants shrank badly. If you're interested in trying out this brand, consider buying them on eBay or on sale on the 'net. Prices at regular retail are expensive, but we've seen them discounted. *To find a store near you that carries this brand of clothing, call (800) 808-0555, (415) 621-0555, or write to 22 Isis St., San Francisco, CA 94103. You can also ask for a catalog. Web: www.japaneseweekend.com*

◆ **MaternityMall.com.** This is Mothers Works portal, which includes sites for all three chains as well as advice and information for pregnant parents.

All these stores carry mostly merchandise designed in house, exclusively for the different divisions.

Now that you know the basics, what do real moms think of Mothers Works' stores? First and foremost, moms dislike, no, hate their return policy. The policy is pretty basic, once you've bought an item, you have ten days to return it for store credit or exchange only (must have the tags and receipt too). No refunds. What if it falls apart in the wash on day 11? Too bad for you. By the way, if you order an item online from Mother Works web site, you'll find a more generous return policy: *Items can be returned for refund or exchange and you have 30 days to return the clothing.* You cannot return items bought online to the store or vice versa, but at least you get extra time and even the money back with an online return. Our advice, if you see it in the store, try it on and like it, go home and order it online.

And don't forget that some of these chain stores lease space in larger department stores like Marshall Field's and Sears. In those cases, the leased stores have to comply with the same generous

Continued on page 238

Watch out for return policies!

Have you bought a maternity dress you don't like or that doesn't fit? Too bad—most maternity stores have draconian return policies that essentially say "tough!" Most don't accept returns and others will only offer store credit. A word to the wise: make sure you REALLY like that item (and it fits) before you give any maternity store your money. A reader in Brisbane, California emailed us with the most horrific story we've ever heard about maternity stores' return policies.

"I recently visited a Dan Howard (now owned by Mothers Work) maternity store in San Francisco and was shocked to find their return policy stands even when you haven't left their store yet! They overcharged me for a sale item that was miss marked and then said all they could give me was store credit for the difference! I hadn't stepped one foot outside the store! They refused to credit my charge card, so now I'm stuck with a $65 store credit for a place I despise!"

Remember: ALL Motherswork stores (including Mimi and Pea in the Pod) share their appalling return/refund policies.

E-MAIL FROM THE REAL WORLD
Stay fit with pregnancy workout videos

Margaret Griffin e-mailed us with her opinions of several popular workout videos tailored for the pregnant woman. Here are her thoughts:

"As a former certified aerobics instructor, I have been trying out the video workouts for pregnancy. I have only found three videos available in my local stores, but I wanted to rate them for your readers.

"**Buns of Steel 8 Pregnancy Workout** with Madeleine Lewis ($20) gets my top rating. Madeleine Lewis has excellent cueing, so the workout is easy to follow. Your heart rate and perceived exertion are both used to monitor your exertion. There is an informative introduction. And I really like the fact that the toning segment utilizes a chair to help you keep your balance, which can be off a little during pregnancy. Most of the toning segment is done standing. This is a safe, effective workout led by a very capable instructor and I highly recommend it." Available on VHS and DVD (as Buns of Steel: Pregnancy and Post-Pregnancy Workouts; $12).

"A middle rating goes to **Denise Austin's Pregnancy Plus Workout** ($10). Denise has a good information segment during which she actually interviews a physician. She also provides heart rate checks during the workout. However, there are a couple of things about this workout that I don't particularly like. First, during the workout, there are times when safety information is provided regarding a particular move. This is fine and good, but instead of telling you to continue the movement and/or providing a picture-in-a-picture format, they actually change the screen to show the safety information and then cut back into the workout in progress. Surprise! You were supposed to keep doing the movement. Second, Denise Austin is a popular instructor, but I personally find that her cueing is not as sharp as I prefer and sometimes she seems to be a little offbeat with the music. My suggestion is get this video to use in addition to other videos if you are the type who gets easily bored with one workout." Available only on VHS.

"The video I recommend that you skip altogether is the **Redbook Pregnancy Workout** led by Diane Gausepohl. I have nothing positive to say regarding this workout. I did the workout once and immediately retired the tape. The instructor has poor cueing skills and does not keep time with the music well at all. This makes the workout hard to follow. My husband was actually laughing at the instruction, it was so poor. I also don't like the fact that it includes toning exercises that can be done (and are demonstrated) lying on your back. We all know that by the fifth month of pregnancy, the weight of the uterus can restrict the blood flow in the inferior vena cava, so you should not lie flat on your back. Even though these exercises can be modified I think it is better to avoid the temptation altogether. There are plenty of other toning exercises that are effective that do not require you to lie on your back at all. My advice is to skip this video altogether." Available only on VHS.

Yoga is a terrific low impact exercise that does a wonderful job of stretching muscles you'll use while carrying and delivering your child. It's a terrific option for pregnant moms. And it's definitely become one of the most popular exercise options in North America. So it was only a matter of time before our readers began reviewing yoga tapes. Here are some of their comments:

Sheri Gomez, recommended Yoga Zone's video **Postures for Pregnancy** ($15), calling it "wonderful for stretching and preventing back problems. It's beginner friendly and not too out there with the yoga thing." Her only complaint: there is no accompanying music, so she played her own CDs along with the tape. Available only on VHS.

Eufemia Camapagna recommended Yoga Journal's **Prenatal Yoga** with Shiva Rea ($14 to $18). She noted that each segment of the tape is done using three women different stages of pregnancy. "The segments are all accompanied by lovely, relaxing music and the instructor's directions are so clear that you don't even need to look at the TV to know what you need to do!" Another reader, Carolyn Oliner, also complimented this tape: "It's not so much of a traditional yoga work-

out but a great series of poses and stretches that work for pregnant women and leave you feeling warm and stretched and (more gently) exercised." Available on VHS and DVD.

Finally, we should note that pilates has also been adapted for pregnancy exercise. You'll find several options on DVD including **Pilates in Pregnancy, Jennifer Gianni's Fusion Pilates for Pregnancy**, and **Prenatal Pilates**.

Note: Amazon.com is a great source to find these videos. If you have any favorite DVDs or videos, email us your review of them and we'll add them to our collection.

return policy of the department store where they lease space. Good news for you.

As for individual chains, most moms agreed that the quality at Motherhood is poor. Although some readers have praised their maternity and nursing bras, in general, most agree with the following: "I have found the quality to be inconsistent. I've bought shirts that have unraveled within a few months. . . trashy!" The consensus seems to be that if you buy at Motherhood, you should stick to the sale rack and don't expect high quality except for their bras.

Mimi Maternity received better marks from our readers for their clothes. Prices are higher than at Motherhood, but so is the quality. We've received fewer complaints about this division. And many moms liked the more stylish clothing. They sell the Olga line of bras, which many readers liked as well.

A Pea in the Pod is just way too expensive. That's the general feeling among our readers about this store. Most moms don't feel the style of clothing at this chain is anything special. Certainly not to spend $90 for a cotton t-shirt. Considering how short a time a pregnancy is it's a huge waste of money to spend over $150 on a Pea in the Pod shorts outfit. And what about their "legendary" service, as Pea in the Pod likes to tout? It's a joke, say our readers. One mom summed it up best by saying: "For the price that one is paying, one expects a certain degree of customer service and satisfaction, both of which are lacking in this over-priced store. What a complete and utter disappointment!"

Consumer alert: one new mom warned us about giving personal info to a maternity chain when you make a purchase (clerks often will ask you if you want to receive sales notices). The problem: you often end up on a junk mailing lists. In the case of our reader, even though she specifically requested the chain not sell her information to third parties, they did so. Once on those lists, it's tough to stop the junk from arriving in your mailbox.

 ## *Do it By Mail*

JCPenney

*To Order Call: (800) 222-6161. Ask for "Maternity Collection" catalog.
Web: www.JCPenney.com/shopping*

Perhaps the best aspect of Penney's maternity offerings is their wide range of sizes—you can find petites, talls, ultra-talls and women's petites and women's regular sizes. It's darn near impossible to find women's sizes in maternity wear today, but Penney's carries sizes up to 32W.

What most impressed us about Penney's maternity catalog was their career clothes. For example, we saw a nice wrap dress for just $40. This polyester outfit was available in women's and misses sizes.

Most of JCPenney's career wear this time around is separates, giving the option of mixing and matching with pieces you may already have. We saw a wide array of affordably priced cotton maternity shirts and jeans. A selection of nightgowns, swimsuits, nursing shirts and lingerie round out the offerings.

One bargain hint: Penney's has quite a few unadvertised sales and discounts on maternity wear. When placing your order, inquire about any current deals.

LANDS' END

To Order Call: (800) 963-4816, Fax (800) 332-0103. Web: www.landsend.com
Discount Outlets: They also have a dozen or so outlet stores (called "inlets")
in Iowa, Illinois and Wisconsin and Minnesota—call the number above for
the nearest location.

Lands' End purveyor of clothing for middle America, has now made a foray into maternity clothing. With over 60 items in a recent catalog, we think they're making quite an impressive jump into this niche. From pants to tops and sweaters the line is very comprehensive. They've even added swimwear and exercise gear. And don't forget their diaper bags. While the styles aren't exactly cutting edge, you'll find nice, quality basics to fill out your wardrobe. A plus: on the web site you can click on a link to pictures of the belly style for pants and skirts. And they offer free custom hemming as well (a plus for tall and petite moms). Prices aren't ultra cheap, but they aren't over priced either. And you can always return clothes to your local Sears store instead of having to send them through the mail (Sears bought the company a couple years ago).

Nursing fashions in Canada: The Toronto-based Breast is Best catalog sells a wide variety of nursing tops, blouses and dresses as well as maternity wear. For a free catalog and fabric swatches, call (877) 837-5439 toll free or check out their web site online at www. breastisbest.com.

The Bottom Line: A Wrap-Up of Our Best Buy Picks

For career and casual maternity clothes, we thought the best deals were from the Old Navy, the Gap and Motherhood stores (not the other chains like A Pea in a Pod). Compared to retail maternity chains (where one suit can run $200 to $300), you can buy your entire wardrobe from these two places for a song.

If your place of work allows more casual dress, check out the prices at plus-size stores or alternatives like Old Navy. A simple pair of jeans that could cost $135 at a maternity shop are only $35 or less at Old Navy. And if you prefer the style at maternity shops, only hit them during sales, where you can find decent bargains. Another good idea: borrow from your husband's closet—shirts, sweat pants and sweatshirts are all items that can do double-duty as maternity clothes.

For weekend wear, we couldn't find a better deal than the 100% cotton shirts and shorts at discounters like Target, Wal-Mart and K-Mart. Prices are as little as $9 per shirt—compare that to the $80 price tag at maternity chain stores for a simple cotton shirt.

Invited to a wedding? Rent that dress from a maternity store and save $100 or more. Don't forget to borrow all you can from friends who've already had babies. In fact, if you follow all our tips on maternity wear, bras, and underwear, you'll save $700 or more. Here's the breakdown:

1. Career Wear: $240.

Old Navy featured cuffed stretch pants, a blazer and t-shirt for a mere $75. Buy two versions of these in different colors, add a couple nice dresses (another $60) and skirts ($60) and you're set.

2. Casual Clothes: $100.

Five outfits of 100% cotton t-shirts and shorts/pants from Target run $100. Again, JCPenney's sells a five-piece wardrobe set for only $70 to $80. And they offer a huge range of sizes. Don't forget sale items on Gap Maternity as well as Old Navy's maternity line.

3. Underwear: $200 to $300.

We strongly suggest investing in top-quality underwear for comfort and sanity purposes. For example, a Bravado bra is $31 and Japanese Weekend "OK" bikini maternity underwear are three for $26. Some readers have found good deals on affordable underwear at Target or online. Either way, you need eight pairs of underwear, plus six bras, including regular/nursing and sleep bras. One tip: see if you can wear your pre-pregnancy panties . . . this works for some moms, saving the $100 expense in "maternity" underwear.

Total damage: $540 to $640. If you think that's too much money for clothes you'll only wear for a few months, consider the cost if you outfit yourself at full-price maternity shops. The same selection of outfits would run $1200 to $1400.

CHAPTER 6

Feeding

Inside this chapter

How much money can you save by breastfeeding? What are the best options for pumps? Which bottles are best? We'll discuss these topics as well as ways to get discount formula, including details on which places have the best deals. And of course, we'll have tips and reviews on the next step in feeding: solid food. Finally, let's talk about high chairs—who's got the best value? Durability? Looks?

Breastfeeding

As readers of past editions of this book know, we are big proponents of breastfeeding. The medical benefits of breast milk are well documented, but obviously the decision to breast or bottle-feed is a personal call for each new mom. In the past, we spent time in this chapter encouraging breast-feeding . . . but we realize now we are preaching to the choir on this one. Our time is better spent discussing how to save on feeding your baby, no matter which way you go. So, we'll leave the discussion of breast versus bottle to other books (as well your doctor and family). Let's talk about the monetary impact of the decision, however.

Breastfeed Your Baby and Save $500

Since this is a book on bargains, we'd be remiss in not mentioning the tremendous amount of money you can save if you breastfeed. Just think about it: no bottles, no expensive formula to prepare, no special insulated carriers to keep bottles warm/cold, etc.

So, how much money would you save? Obviously, the biggest money-saver would be not buying formula. Even if you were to use the less expensive powder, you would still have to spend nearly

$23 per 28.5-ounce can of powdered formula. Since each can makes 209 ounces of formula, the cost per ounce of formula is about 10¢.

That doesn't sound too bad, does it? Unless you factor in that a baby will down 32 ounces of formula per day by 12 weeks of age. Your cost per day would be $3.25. Assuming you breastfeed for the first six months, you would save a grand total of $546 *just on formula alone*. That doesn't include the expense for bottles, nipples and accessories!

To be fair, there are some optional expenses that might go along with breastfeeding. The biggest dollar item: you might decide to buy a breast pump. Costs for this item range from $60 for a manual pump to $300 for a professional-grade breast pump. Or you can rent a pump for $50 a month (plus a kit—one time cost of about $40).

If $546 doesn't sound like a lot of money, consider the savings if you had to buy formula in the concentrated liquid form instead of the cheaper powder. A 32-ounce can of Similac ready-to-eat liquid costs about $4.99 at a grocery store and makes up only 4 bottles. The bottom line: you could spend over $700 on formula for your baby in the first six months alone!

Of course, we realize that some moms will decide to use formula because of a personal, medical or work situation—to help out, we have a section later in this chapter on how to save on formula, bottle systems and other necessary accessories.

Sources: Where to Find Breast Feeding Help

The basis of breastfeeding is attachment. Getting your new little one to latch onto your breast properly is not a matter of instinct. Some babies have no trouble figuring it out, while many others need your help and guidance. In fact, problems with attachment can lead to sore nipples and painful engorgement. Of course, you should be able to turn to your pediatrician or the nurses at the hospital for breastfeeding advice. However, if you find that they do not offer you the support you need, consider the following sources for breastfeeding help:

LA LECHE LEAGUE (800) LA LECHE or web: www.lalecheleague.org. Started over 35 years ago by a group of moms in Chicago, La Leche League has traditionally been the most vocal supporter of breastfeeding in this country. You've got to imagine the amount of chutzpah these women had to have to buck the bottle trend and promote breastfeeding at a time when it wasn't fashionable (to say the least).

In recent years, La Leche has established branches in many communities, providing support groups for new moms interested in trying to nurse their children. They also offer a catalog full of books and videotapes on nursing, as well as other child care topics. Their famous book *The Womanly Art of Breastfeeding* is the bible for huge numbers of breastfeeding advocates. All in all, La Leche provides an important service and, coupled with their support groups and catalog of publications, is a valuable resource.

2 NURSING MOTHERS' COUNCIL (408) 272-1448, (web: www. nursingmothers.org). Similar in mission to La Leche League, the Nursing Mothers' Council differs on one point: the group emphasizes working moms and their unique needs and problems.

3 LACTATION CONSULTANTS. Lactation consultants are usually nurses who specialize in breastfeeding education and problem solving. You can find them through your pediatrician, hospital, or the International Lactation Consultants Association (703) 560-7330 web: www.iblce.org. Members of this group must pass a written exam, complete 2500 hours of clinical practice and 30 hours of continuing education before they can be certified. At our local hospital, resident lactation consultants are available to answer questions by phone at no charge. If a problem persists, you can set up an in-person consultation for a minimal fee (about $40 to $90 per hour, although your health insurance provider may pick up the tab).

Unfortunately, the availability of lactation consultants seems to vary from region to region. Our research shows that, in general, hospitals in the Western U.S. are more likely to offer support services, such as on-staff lactation consultants. Back East, however, the effort to support breastfeeding seems spotty. Our advice: call area hospitals before you give birth to determine the availability of breastfeeding support. Another good source for a referral to a lactation consultant is your pediatrician.

4 HOSPITALS. Look for a hospital in your area that has breast-feeding-friendly policies. These include 24-hour rooming in (where your baby can stay with you instead of in a nursery) and breastfeeding on demand. Pro-nursing hospitals do not supplement babies with a bottle and don't push free formula samples. Their nurses will also respect your wishes concerning pacifier usage, which is important if you are concerned about nipple confusion.

5 BOOKS. Although they aren't a substitute for support from your doctor, hospital, and family, many books provide plenty of info and encouragement. Check the La Leche League catalog for titles.

FEEDING

6 **THE WEB.** We found several great sites with breastfeeding information and tips. Our favorite was *Medela* (www.medela.com), which is a leading manufacturer of breast pumps. Medela's site features extensive information resources and articles on breastfeeding, as well as advice on how to choose the right breast pump. Of course, you can also get info on Medela's breast pumps and other products, find a dealer near you and more.

The catalog *Bosom Buddies* (www.bosombuddies.com or call 888-860-0041) has a web site with a good selection of breastfeeding articles, product information and links to other breastfeeding sites on the web.

Of course, our message boards are also a good place to find help—we have a special board on feeding where you can ask other moms for advice, tips and support. Hint: use our boards to find a discount web site that has the lowest price on a breast pump you want; there's always lots of discussion on who's the cheapest, got free shipping and more. Go to BabyBargains.com and click on message boards.

7 **YOUR HEALTH INSURANCE PROVIDER.** Contact your health insurance provider as soon as you become pregnant. They often have a variety of services available to policyholders, but you have to ask.

Parents in Cyberspace: What's on the Web?

Medela

Web: www.medela.com

What it is: A treasure trove of info on breastfeeding.

What's cool. Medela's web site is a great example of what makes the 'net so helpful—instead of just a thinly veiled pitch for their products, Medela stuffs their site with reams of useful info, tips and advice. Yeah, you can read about their different breast pumps, but the site is full of general breastfeeding tips, links to other sites and more. "Problems and Solutions" is an excellent FAQ for nursing moms. You'll also find instructions for all their products on line in case you misplace them!

Needs work: Although they've improved the site, you'll find it takes a lot of clicks to get where you want to go. And we'd still like to see approximate retail prices for Medela's products on the site.

MedRhino

Web site: www.breastpumps-breastfeeding.com

What it is: A medical supply company with a selection of breast pumps and accessories.

What's cool: What's not? Here's a site with a huge selection of breast pumps from Medela at discount prices. For example, MedRhino claims the Pump In Style Professional sells for $309 retail, but they sell it for $238. And when you order the Pump In Style, they give you free UPS ground shipping plus a free battery pack. Wow! When you pull up a product you're interested in, the site has clear photos, details on the product and a price grid with retail and sale prices. You'll also find breast shells, pads, storage products and more on the site.

Needs work: The site should sell more brands than just Medela. How about Avent and Ameda Egnell as well?

Nursing Mother Supplies

Web: www.nursingmothersupplies.com

What it is: An extensive nursing supply resource.

What's cool: Not only does this site carry breast pumps and supplies from Medela and Ameda Egnell (among others), they offer support to customers after they buy. Nursing Mothers Supplies offers you an opportunity to contact a counselor for one-on-one help. Prices are discounted a bit (the Purely Yours was $189, regular retail $249), and they offer free shipping for all orders over $100. A portion of sales goes to UNICEF (nice touch). Nursing pillows, storage options (the Mothers Milk Mate is $25), slings, Avent bottles and pads are also available.

Needs work: Not much to complain about here. The site is a bit primitive in design, but it does the job—loads fast, has a shopping cart feature, clear photos, etc. We also like the gentle approach to encouraging breast-feeding. These guys aren't too preachy. Last time we mentioned that they had an excellent online FAQ, but we couldn't locate it this time around.

◆ *Other web sites:* Here are a couple sites with names that speak for themselves: *Affordable-medela-pumps.com*, *Affordable-breast-pumps.com* and *Affordablebreastpumps.com*. Readers have mentioned all three as great sites for pumps from Medela, Ameda, Nurture III and Whittlestone to name a few. *Mother's Milk Breastfeeding Supplies* (Mothersmilkbreastfeeding.com) is owned by a neonatal nurse who's been helping moms for over eight years. And a reader, Cherie Kannarr, thought that *BreastFeeding.com* "is a wonderful site, filled with facts, stories, humor, and support for nursing mothers."

What Are You Buying?

For moms interested in breast-feeding, most eventually approach the issue of what to do when they can't be available to feed their baby. After all, you might want to go out to dinner. Maybe you'll have an overnight trip for your job or just need to get back to work full or part time. Your spouse might even be interested in relieving you of a night feeding (in your dreams; anything's possible). The solution? Pumping milk. Whether you want to pump occasionally or every day, you have a wide range of options. Here's our take on them:

◆ **Manual Expression:** OK, technically, this isn't a breast pump in the sense we're talking about. But it is an option. There are several good breastfeeding books that describe how to express milk manually. Most women find that the amount of milk expressed, compared to the time and trouble involved, hardly makes it worth using this method. A few women (we think they are modern miracle workers) can manage to express enough for an occasional bottle; for the majority of women, however, using a breast pump is a more practical alternative.

◆ **Manual Pumps:** Non-electric, hand-held pumps create suction by squeezing on a handle. While they're cheap, manual pumps are generally also the least efficient—you simply can't duplicate your baby's sucking action by hand. Therefore, these pumps are best for moms who only need an occasional bottle or who need to relieve engorgement.

◆ **Mini-Electrics:** These battery-operated breast pumps are designed to express an occasional bottle. Unfortunately, the sucking action is so weak that it often takes twenty minutes *per side* to express a significant amount of milk. And doing so is not very comfortable. Why is it so slow? Most models only cycle nine to fifteen times per minute—compare that to a baby who sucks the equivalent of 50 cycles per minute!

◆ **Professional-Grade Pumps:** The Mercedes of breast pumps—we can't sing the praises of these work horses enough. In just ten to twenty minutes, you can pump *both* breasts. And professional-grade pumps are much more comfortable than mini-electrics. In fact, at first I didn't think the pump I rented was working well because it was *so* comfortable. The bottom line: there is no better option for a working woman who wants to provide her baby with breast milk.

	Manual	Mini-Elec.	Piston Elec.	Rental*
BREAST PUMPS — *Which pump works best in which situation?*				
Do you need a pump for:				
A missed feeding?	■	◆		
Evening out from baby?	■	◆		
Working part-time.	■	◆		
Occasional use, a few times a week.	■	◆		
Working full-time.			●	●
Premature or hospitalized baby?			●	●
Low milk supply?			●	●
Sore nipples/engorgement?	■		●	●
Latch-on problems or breast infection?			■	●
Drawing out flat or inverted nipples?	■	◆	●	●

Key: ■ = Good ◆ = Better ● = Best
*Rental refers to renting a hospital-grade pump. These can usually be rented on a monthly basis.
Source: Medela.

Today, you have two options when it comes to these pumps: rent a hospital-grade pump (which often is called a piston-electric) or buy a high-end double-pump. As for rental, a wide variety of sources rent breast pumps on a daily, weekly or monthly basis. We called a lactation consultant at a local hospital who gave us a list that included maternity stores, small private companies, and home-care outfits. Another possibility is to call La Leche League (800-LALECHE; web: www.lalecheleague.org) or other lactation support groups for a referral to a company that rents piston electric pumps.

What does it cost to rent a hospital-grade pump? One company we surveyed rented pumps for $60 for one month or $45 per month if you rent for two or more months. In general, we found rental charges ranged from $1 to $3 per day, with the lower rates for longer rentals. You'll also have to buy a kit of the collection bottles, shields, and tubes (this runs about $50 to $60). Medela's Lactina Select (800) 435-8316, White River Concepts Model 9050 (800) 824-6351 and Egnell Elite (800) 323-8750 are all hospital grade pumps available for rental.

What about buying? We will review our picks for pumps next.

Breast Pumps (model by model reviews)

Manual Pumps

AVENT ISIS
Web: AventAmerica.com
Price: $45.
Type: Manual.
Comments: The best manual pump on the market. Our readers love this pump, which Avent claims is as efficient as a mini-electric (it takes about eight to ten minutes to empty a breast). You can buy the Isis by itself, or as part of a kit that includes extra bottles, cooler packs and more ($60 to $75). Yes, there are other manual pumps on the market, but we think the Isis is tops. (One caveat to the Isis, however: a reader recommends going for the model with the reusable bottle, instead of the disposable one. Why? The reader says Avent's bottle liners for the disposable bottles are terrible—you have to double bag to freeze them or they leak). FYI: Avent now sells a version of the Isis that works with their VIA reusable bottles. Overall, the Isis is a winner.
Rating: A

MEDELA HARMONY
Web: Medela.com
Price: $35 to $40.
Type: Manual.
Comments: It has fewer parts to wash than the Avent and is easier to assemble, but the reviews on it are not as universally positive as on the Isis. One mom with larger breasts found this pump worked better for her than the Isis. All in all, a good second bet to the Isis.
Rating: A-

Mini Electric Pumps

EVENFLO COMFORT SELECT SINGLE ELECTRIC BREAST PUMP
Web: Evenflo.com
Price: $38.
Type: Mini-electric.
Comments: It's not nick-named the Evil-Flo for nothing—this one hurts. Yep, it's cheap and that's about the only thing going for it.
Rating: D+

MEDELA DOUBLE SELECT BREAST PUMP
Web: Medela.com
Price: $100 to $130.
Type: Mini electric.
Comments: This new version of Medela's mini electric pump just debuted as we went to press, so we don't have any specific mom feedback yet. But the last version of this model (the Double Ease) performed well. We like the adjustable one-hand suction control feature here.
Rating: A

Professional-Grade Pumps

MEDELA PUMP IN STYLE ADVANCED
Web: Medela.com
Price: $270 to $300.
Type: Professional

The best milk storage options

Once you've decided to express breast milk for your child, you'll need to consider how to store it. Freezer bags are the most common method and most major pump manufactures and bottle makers sell bags. So, who's got the best storage bags? Lansinoh (sold in Target) is the hands-down winner. "They are study, stand on their own and have an excellent double lock seal closure," said one mom. Others echoed that recommendation.

Oddly enough, despite Medela's strong reputable for pumps, their storage bags get much lower marks. "Terrible!" said one mom, saying that while you can attach them to a breast shield directly and pump right into the bag, the bags themselves are "flimsy and use an archaic twist tie method to seal." The bags don't stand on their own—Medela suggests putting them in a coffee cup to stabilize them. Hello?

Other good milk storage bags include the *Gerber Seal N Go*, which fit most bottles including Avent. We also have heard positive results for the Pump-Mate (www.pumpmate.com), a $25 kit of bags and bottles that works with most pumps.

A completely different alternative is *Mothers Milk Mate* (www. mothersmilkmate.com) a $30, ten-bottle storage system with rack. In fact, bottles are probably a better way to go than bags. Why? All those great antibodies in Mom's milk stick to the bags and don't get to baby's mouth. That's why most lactation professionals prefer the hard polypropylene bottles (frosted plastic) for breast milk storage.

Comments: I personally used the Pump In Style for my second child and was impressed—it's a fully automatic double pump that uses diaphragm action to best simulate a baby's sucking motion. Best of all, it's portable (about seven pounds) and is hidden in an attractive black leather bag for discretion.

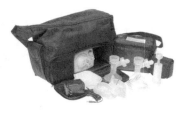

The Pump In Style comes in three different versions: Original ($280), Advanced ($350 retail, pictured left), and the Traveler ($290). What's the difference? All three Pump In Style versions have three suction settings and five pump speeds. The Original and Traveler are much the same, except the latter comes in a back-

pumps

2 **USE THE SHAWL METHOD.** Many women breastfeed in public with a shawl or blanket covering the baby and breasts. While this works well, you must start practicing this early and often with your baby. Otherwise, you'll find that as she gets more alert and interested in her surroundings, she won't stay under the shawl.

3 **FIND ALL THE CONVENIENT REST ROOM LOUNGES IN YOUR TOWN.** Whenever we visited the local mall, I nursed in one of the big department store's lounge areas. This is a great way to meet other breastfeeding moms as well. Of course, not every public rest room features a lounge with couches or comfy chairs, but it's worth seeking out the ones that do. We applaud stores like Babies R Us for having "breastfeeding rooms" with glider-rockers and changing tables for easy nursing.

Another creative alternative: stores will usually let you use a dressing room to breastfeed. Of course, some stores are not as "breastfeeding friendly" as others. New York City, for example, has 10 million people and about seven public rest rooms. In such places, I've even breastfed in a chair strategically placed facing a wall or corner in the back of a store. Not the best view, but it gets the job done.

4 **TRY YOUR CAR.** Yep, the backseat of parked car is a good place to nurse. I found it easier and more comfortable to feed my child there, especially when he started to become distracted in restaurants and stores. The car held no fascination for him, so he tended to concentrate on eating instead of checking out the scenery. I suggest you keep some magazines in the car since you may get bored.

pack for portability. Both have battery packs for mobile use, although we noticed some web sites sell older versions of the Original that lack a battery pack for $200. The new Advanced version has enhanced pumping technology with both let-down and expression modes. It's probably the best bet of the Medela pumps.

What's the disadvantage of the Pump In Styles? Cost for one: it runs about $80 to $100 more than the leading competitor, the Ameda Purely Yours, which is smaller, lighter and has several other attractive features. And Medela has been aggressive in cutting off online discounters that sell its pumps for less than full retail (which of course, has just hurt Medela as rivals like Ameda have surged ahead with lower prices). Yet, we will still give Medela our highest rating for overall quality and features.

Rating: A

FEEDING

AMEDA PURELY YOURS

Web: Ameda.com
Price: $200 for the Carry All version; $220 for the Backpack

Type: Professional.

Comments: It's smaller! It's lighter! And its less expensive—the Ameda Purely Yours has won a large legion of fans for its Purely Yours Pump, which comes in two versions: CarryAll and Backpack. Both weigh about five pounds and have the same number of suction settings (eight) and speeds (nine), but the backpack includes a car adapter (that is optional with the CarryAll). The Ameda has a built-in AA battery pack, versus the Medela, which has a separate battery pack. Best of all, the Ameda is easy to maintain (milk can't get into the tubes, which means less cleaning than the Medela). The downside? Medela is sold in many more retail outlets than Ameda meaning you can get spare parts and supplies easier (although to its credit, Ameda has great customer service).

FYI: The above prices are retail . . .but we've seen Ameda pumps for less online. As we went to press, BabyCatalog.com had the CarryAll version for $137. And the same site sells the Backpack version for $165. **Rating: A**

WHISPER WEAR DOUBLE BREAST PUMP

Web: whisperwear.com
Price: $220
Type: Professional.

Comments: This is the "world's first hands-free pump." Yep, this one has generated much buzz on our message boards, with reviews decidedly mixed. Whisper Wear has cups that mold to each breast and tuck inside a bra. Moms who really like this pump are often commuters, those who need to pump on a long trek to or from the office. But beware: the suction is weaker than Medela's Pump In Style or the Ameda Purely Yours, meaning you have to pump longer to get the same amount of milk. Others complain it is difficult to assemble; it takes some practice to get right. So, it is a mixed bag—some love Whisper Wear and others curse it. "If it works for you," one mom told us, "it's amazing! The ability to use both your hands and wander around is great. I don't think I will use another pump unless I absolutely have to." **Rating: B**

◆ *More pumps.* As we were going to press, Avent debuted a new pump to compete with Medela and Ameda's professional models: the *Avent Isis iQ Duo* ($350). Early feedback from moms was positive, with kudos for the pump's electronic "memory" and light weight.

But, no battery pack or car charger? That's a hefty price premium compared to the Ameda. And we'd be hesitant to recommend the "version 1.0" of any pump, so it is wait and see on this one.

If you've got a spare $1000, check out Medela's new top-of-the-line **Symphony** pump. This model is supposed to simulate baby's two-phase feeding process and can switch between single and double pumping. But the high price (it runs $1200 to $1400) means we've heard from very few moms who've actually used it. Given the cost, this pump is likely to be bought by hospitals and rented to moms.

One reader recommended the **Nurture III** breast pump available on line at www.baileymed.com. Manufactured by Bailey Medical Engineering, it looks a lot like the Purely Yours. But the price is amazing at $115. Quite a deal for a professional pump. **Whittlestone** also makes a breast pump, but we've had little to no feedback about this brand at this point.

Sure, you'll see lots of pumps in the discount stores. While these are all made by reputable companies (First Years, Gerber, Evenflo), we say stick to the quality pumps by Medela, Avent or Ameda.

So, let's sum up our recommendations:

Our Picks: Brand Recommendations

◆ **Manual Pump:** The best manual pump is the Avent "Isis" ($45). Second runner-up is the Medela Harmony.

◆ **Mini Electric Pump:** Medela's new Double Select mini-electric is pricey ($100) but very good quality. Yes, you can find other brands of mini-electric pumps in discount stores for $40 and $50, but we have one word of advice: don't.

◆ **Professional Grade Pump:** You can't go wrong with either, so we'll make it a tie: the Medela Pump In Style ($270 to $350) and Ameda Purely Yours ($137 to $200) are the co-champs. A dark horse choice, especially for commuters, would be the Whisper Wear Double Breast Pump for $220.

Before you buy a pump, we suggest RENTING a hospital-grade pump first for a week or two (or a month). After you decide you're serious about pumping and you're comfortable with the double-pumping action, then consider buying one of your own. Given the hefty retail prices, it makes sense to buy only if you plan to pump for several months or have a second child.

Bottom line: a hospital rental pump is probably best for most moms. But if you need portability and plan to have additional children, investing a good quality pump from Medela or Ameda is worth it.

Introduce the Bottle Early

If you plan to introduce a bottle to your baby so you can go out on the town or back to work, do it around the sixth week of age. Dr. Ari Brown, co-author of the book *Baby 411*, recommends introducing a bottle before the fourth month so baby understands that milk comes in different packages. And keep up bottle feedings perhaps two or three times a week. In our case, we didn't give a bottle consistently, and by the time our son was about four months old, he absolutely refused to take a bottle at all. Oops! That made going out alone to dinner and a movie a lot tougher. A word to the wise: keep up the occasional bottle.

Safe and Sound

In the past editions of this book, we suggested buying a used pump as a way to save. Bad authors—several readers pointed out the health risks to this idea, as a few models (especially Medela) can actually collect milk in the pump mechanism. So, let's state it clearly: DO NOT USE A USED BREAST PUMP. The risk of exposing your baby to any pathogens in the previous user's breast milk is not worth it.

Of course, it is fine to re-use your own breast pump for another child down the road. Just replace the tubing and collection bottles to make sure there are no bacteria left over from previous uses. Or use an Ameda pump, as that model is designed so milk doesn't collect in the tubes or pump mechanism.

Smart Shopper Tip

Smart Shopper Tip #1
When to buy that pump.

"I don't know how long I want to breastfeed. And I'll be going back to work soon after my baby is born. When should I get a pump?"

We'd suggest waiting a bit before you invest in a breast pump or even nursing clothes. Many moms start with breast-feeding, but can't or don't want to continue it after a few weeks. For them investing in a pump would be a waste of money. If you aren't sure how long you want to breast feed, but you'd like to pump some extra bottles of milk anyway, consider renting a hospital grade pump first and try it out before you invest a couple hundred dollars. You can often rent for as little as one month, which will be much cheaper than buying a pump that can run $200 to $300.

Waste of Money

Even Cows Opt for the Electric Kind

"I'm going back to work a couple of months after my baby is born. My co-worker who breastfeeds her baby thinks manual and mini-electrics pumps are a waste of money. Your thoughts?

While they may be useful to relieve engorgement, manual pumps aren't very practical for long-term pumping when you're at work. They are very slow, which makes it hard to get much milk. Mini-electric breast pumps are better but are really best only for occasional use—for example, expressing a small amount of milk to mix with cereal for a baby who's learning to eat solids. The problem with mini-electrics: some are painful and most are too slow.

Your best bet if you plan to do some serious pumping is to rent a piston electric pump. These monsters maintain a high rate of extraction with amazing comfort. A lactation consultant we interviewed said piston electric pumps can empty both breasts in about 10 to 15 minutes—contrast that with 20 to 30 minutes for mini-electrics and 45 minutes to an hour for manual pumps.

As mentioned earlier, the manual pump that received top rating from our readers is the Avent Isis—and even though it is a vast improvement over previous options, it still is a MANUAL pump. It may not work well for moms who plan to work part or full-time and still nurse their baby. That said, one solution is to use two pumps—a mom we interviewed uses a Pump In Style when she's tired (during the evening or night-time) and an Avent Isis at work (it's much quieter; doesn't need electricity, etc).

Money Saving Tips

CONTACT YOUR HEALTH INSURANCE PROVIDER. One reader noted that her insurance provider will pay $50 toward the purchase of a breast pump; yet another reader found her medical insurance covered the entire cost of a $280 pump! You'll have to ask about this benefit; insurance companies aren't always forthcoming with such info. And other insurance providers will only pay for a pump if there is a medical reason (premature birth, etc). You

///

Nursing Extras

Many nursing moms find a nursing pillow makes breastfeeding easier and more comfortable. Our readers have emailed compliments for **My Brest Friend** by Zenoff Products (800-555-5522; web: www. zenoffproducts.com). Okay, it probably qualifies as the Most Stupid Name for a Baby Product Ever award, but it really works—it wraps around your waist and is secured with Velcro. It retails for about $50. Got twins? Check out **EZ-2-NURSE's** pillow (800-584-TWIN; we saw it on www.everythingmom.com). A mom told us this was the "absolute best" for her twins, adding, "I could not successfully nurse my girls together without this pillow. It was wonderful." Cost: $64.

Another idea: Wal-Mart has a breastfeeding collection with **Lansinoh** products (including their amazing nipple cream and breast pads). Check the special displays in the store or on their web site at walmart.com.

///

may have to get a "note from your doctor" to qualify. FYI: Medela has downloadable forms on their web site that are templates to request insurance reimbursement.

2 **CONSIDER EBAY.** Many readers have noted that breast pumps, including Medela's Pump In Style (PIS), are available for sale on eBay.com at huge discounts. We saw one, new in the box, for only $182. Some of them are older models or even used, so you'll need to educate yourself on what you're buying.

3 **DON'T FEEL LIKE YOU HAVE TO BUY THE "TOP BRAND."** There are several manufacturers of breast pumps besides Medela. And our readers say their products work just as great for a lot less money (we discuss these alternative brands later in this chapter). For example, the Ameda Purely Yours pump retails for only $250 retail, while the Medela Pump in Style Advanced is a whopping $320 retail. The Nurture III pump is only $150! We recommend sticking with manufacturers who specialize in breastfeeding. The First Years, for example, makes a ton of other products from spoons to bath tubs as well as breast pumps. We aren't as impressed with the quality of their pumps compared to other brands, however.

Formula

Is there any nutritional difference between brands of formula? According to our research, the answer is no. The federal government regulates the ingredients in baby formula. Hence almost all the commercially available baby formula sold in the U.S. and Canada contains the same basic ingredients . . . usually the only difference is the color of the label on the outside of the can. That's right—the "generic" formula sold at Wal-Mart and Target is no different than pricey Similac.

What does formula cost these days? First realize that formula comes in three different versions: powder, liquid concentrate and ready-to drink. Powder is least expensive, followed by liquid concentrate. Ready-to-drink is the most pricey. A recent check of grocery stores revealed a 27.7-ounce can of powdered Similac with Iron was running about $20. This can makes 190 fluid ounces of formula, so the cost per ounce of formula is 11¢.

Of course, formula makers have tricks to make it difficult to compare prices. Each brand of formula comes in a different size can—Enfamil costs $22, but comes in a can that holds 28.5 oz.

 ## What Are You Buying?

In the past, formula was just formula. You basically had the regular version (with or without iron) and soy (also iron fortified or plain). Now the choices are mind numbing: organic formula, toddler versions, formula with or without ARA additives and more. Here is our overview of some of the newer options:

◆ **Toddler formula.** First created by Carnation ("Follow Up" formula), then copied by other formula manufacturers, "toddler" formulas are intended to be used for older children (typically nine months old and up) instead of regular cows milk or soymilk. Typically, most parents move to whole milk or soymilk when their child reaches one year of age, leaving formula behind forever. In order to hang on to consumers longer, formula manufacturers have developed these toddler formulas. So what's the big difference between baby formula and toddler formula? Carnation adds extra calcium to their formula while Enfamil (Next Step) and Similac (Similac 2) have upped the amount of vitamins C and E as well as iron. We'll comment on the usefulness of these formulas later in this chapter.

◆ **DHA/ARA additives.** Scientists have been researching breast milk for years to find out what makes it the perfect food for our babies. The media has widely reported that the presence of two fatty acids in breast milk (DHA and ARA—also called lipids) may be responsible for the purported difference in IQ levels in breast-fed babies versus those that are formula-fed. As a result, formula companies have added DHA and ARA to their formulas as some kind of a "brain-boost." But the jury is still out on whether these additives really provide any benefit to formula. A 2002 report from the American Council on Science and Health stated that "experts disagree about whether it is necessary to include DHA and ARA in infant formulas to promote optimal brain and visual development."

◆ **Organic formula.** With the boom in all things organic, the formula biz has seen its share of new entrants. In 2003, Horizon Organic (www.horizonorganic.com) debuted Horizon Organic Infant Formula with Iron, a powdered formula made from organic lactose with 27 other vitamins and minerals. Horizon feeds its cows only organic grain and hay grown without fertilizers or insecticides, and they use no growth hormones or antibiotics. We found this brand in Whole Foods Markets, although it may not yet be in every store. A 27.6 oz can runs $35 (that's 17¢ per ounce; 30% more than the cheapest store brand formula bought at a discount store). Horizon's formula is USDA certified organic. By the way, Horizon does not make a soy version.

Baby's Only Organic baby formula (www.babyorganic.com) is manufactured by Nature's One, (www.naturesone.com). The product is made with no genetically engineered organisms, no bovine growth hormones, no antibiotics or steroids, and no insecticides or chemical fertilizers. Available only in a powder, Baby's own comes in regular, soy and a DHA/ADA option. FYI: Baby's Only is marketed as a "toddler" formula for babies 12 months and up. Why? The FDA has a strict certification program for infant formula, which the Baby's Only formula has not gone through. The concern: we fear some parents may give this to younger infants, missing the small disclaimer and "toddler" typeface. We would not feed an infant any formula that was not certified by the FDA.

 ## Safe and Sound

Formula is one of the most closely regulated food items in the US. The Food and Drug Administration has strict guidelines about what can and what cannot go into baby formula. The FDA requires expiration dates, warning labels and so on. So what are the safety hazards you might run up against? Here are a couple:

CONFUSING CANS CONFRONT SOY FORMULA USERS. Soy formula now accounts for 15% of the infant formula market. Yet, a case of mistaken identity has led some parents to nearly starve their infants. Apparently, some parents mistakenly thought they were feeding their babies soy formula, when in fact they were using

Baby Formula Manufacturers: Out of Control?

In the past few editions of this book, we issued a long rant about the marketing tactics of the formula manufacturers. And we still feel that way today. When you check into the hospital to give birth, you start the long promotional parade of formula freebies—most new parents emerge after birth with formula samples, diaper bags emblazoned with formula logos and more. Is this good for parents? For the country?

Considering the fact that breast-feeding rates still trail national goals, we say no. We realize formula makers have the right to market their wares as they see fit . . . but we argue that hospitals and doctors' offices should be no-pitch zones. The subtle and not-so-subtle effect of all the endless formula freebies is to undermine moms who choose to breastfeed. While we realize most moms and dads are intelligent enough to recognize the formula hype as just that, we are concerned that less-educated parents are led to believe that hospitals and doctors are endorsing formula over breast-feeding. And statistics bear that out—moms who are from lower socioeconomic groups are most likely to turn to formula instead of trying breastfeeding.

Nestle, maker of Carnation Good Start formula, deserves special scrutiny. In 2004, Nestle started targeting Hispanic mothers in California with its Nan formula, a leading formula brand in Latin America. Unlike other brands that shun direct consumer marketing, Nestle has run ads in Spanish language magazines and radio, plastering the Nan brand on billboards in Hispanic sections of Los Angeles and handing out free samples at baby fairs.

The key question: is Nestle exploiting a vulnerable population that gets very little or no info on the health benefits of breastfeeding, in order to fatten market share?

Ironically, Nestle does not advertise this brand in countries like Mexico. Why? In 1981, the World Health Organization devised a voluntary code to curb the marketing of formula after allegations that—guess who?—Nestle exploited the world's poor to pitch formula, which was often misused. While the U.S. signed the code, it never passed laws to enforce it. Hence, that's why we have a formula marketing free-fire zone in hospitals, doctors' offices and billboards in the barrio.

As a country, we have to ask ourselves—shouldn't hospitals and doctor's offices be a pitch-free area for formula? And should formula companies be allowed to target vulnerable populations with formula pitches?

formula

soymilk. The problem: soymilk is missing important nutrients and vitamins found in soy formula. As a result, babies fed soymilk were malnourished and some required hospitalization. Adding to the confusion, soymilk is often sold in cans that look very similar to soy formula. The government has asked soymilk makers to put warning labels on their products, but some have still not complied. If you use soy formula, be careful to choose the right can at the grocery store.

Another concern: low-iron formula. A myth among some parents is that the iron in standard formula causes constipation—it does not, says Dr. Ari Brown, a pediatrician who co-authored our other baby book, Baby 411. Yes, constipation can be a problem with ALL formulas. But, babies should NEVER be on low-iron formula unless instructed by a pediatrician.

2 EXPIRED FORMULA. Now we realize those cans of formula look like they could survive a nuclear attack (they remind us of the "bomb-proof" cans of Hawaiian Punch our moms used to buy in the '70's), but they do have expiration dates on them. And many of our readers have written to tell us that stores don't always remove expired formula from the shelves in a timely manner. That includes grocery stores, discounters and even warehouse clubs. So read the label carefully and check your own stores of formula before you open a can. Also, some formula sold on auction sites has been expired as well. Be sure to ask.

 Money Saving Tips

1 STAY AWAY FROM PRE-MIXED FORMULA. Liquid concentrate formula and ready-to-drink formula are 50% to 200% more expensive than powdered formula. Yes, it is more convenient but you pay big time for that. We priced name brand, ready to drink formula at a whopping 25¢ per ounce.

Guess what type of formula is given out as freebies in doctors' offices and hospitals? Yes, it's often the ready-to-drink liquid formula. These companies know babies get hooked on the particular texture of the expensive stuff, making it hard (if not impossible) to switch to the powdered formula later. Sneaky, eh?

2 CONSIDER GENERIC FORMULA. Most grocery stores and discounters sell "private" label formula at considerable savings, at least 30% to 40%. At one grocery store chain, their generic powdered formula worked out to just 7¢ per fluid ounce of formula, a 30% savings. One great brand of generic formula: BabyMil (800-

344-1358; web: www.StoreBrandFormulas.com), whose formulas are 40% less expensive than national brands. BabyMil sells for $8 a 16 oz can (50¢ per ounce), versus $13 or more for 14.3 oz of Enfamil (91¢ per ounce). BabyMil comes both in regular and soy versions (BabySoy). Hint: BabyMil is sold under a variety of different names, depending on the retailer. Go to the web site www. StoreBrandFormulas.com and click on "Available Across America." Find a grocery store/pharmacy/discounter near you. From there you'll find what BabyMil is called in your area. For example, Wal-Mart sells BabyMil formula as "Parents Choice," while Albertson's call it "Baby Basics" formula. It's the same stuff.

We should note that some pediatricians are concerned about recommending generic formula—doctors fret that such low-cost formula might discourage breastfeeding. Ironic when so many pediatricians hand out all those free samples of formula. We'd love to see them stop accepting samples from Similac, Enfamil and Carnation and start discouraging hospitals from doling them out to moms in the maternity wards.

3 BUY IT ONLINE. Yep, you can buy formula online from eBay. You can save big but watch out—some unscrupulous sellers try to pawn off expired formula on unsuspecting buyers. Be sure to confirm the expiration date before buying formula online. And watch out for shipping charges—formula is heavy and shipping can outweigh any deal, depending on the price you pay. We saw one case of formula go for $53 on eBay. But the $6 shipping charge made the deal less sweet, considering a case would retail in stores for $65!

4 BUY IN BULK. We found wholesale clubs had the best prices on name brand formula. For example, Sam's Club (www.samsclub.com) sells a 2.5-pound (40 oz) can of Enfamil for $24. That is 20% less than grocery stores. And generic formula at wholesale clubs is an even bigger bargain. Costco's Kirkland brand formula was $18 for a 36-ounce can making it only 7¢ an ounce.

5 ASK YOUR PEDIATRICIAN FOR FREE SAMPLES. Just make sure you get the powdered formula (not the liquid concentrate or ready to pour). One reader in Arizona said she got several free cases from her doctor, who simply requested more from the formula makers. OK, we know this sounds hypocritical since we just said we think doctors should take a stand against all the formula giveaways in their offices and hospitals. However, as long as doctors' offices are stuffed with such freebies, you might as well ask for them.

6 SHOP AROUND. Yes, powdered formula at a grocery store can run $20 to $25 for a 28-ounce can (approximately)—but there's no federal law that says you must buy it at full retail. Readers of our book have noticed that formula prices vary widely, sometimes even at different locations of the same chain. In Chicago, a reader said they found one Toys R Us charged $1.20 less per can for the same Similac with Iron ready-to-feed formula than another Toys R Us across town. "They actually have a price check book at the registers with the codes for each store in the Chicagoland area," the reader said. "At our last visit, we saved $13.20 for two cases (about 30% of the cost), just by mentioning we wanted to pay the lower price."

Another reader noticed a similar price discrepancy at Wal-Mart stores in Florida. When she priced Carnation Good Start powdered formula, she found one Wal-Mart that marked it at $6.61 per can. Another Wal-Mart (about 20 miles from the first location) sells the same can for $3.68! When the reader inquired about the price discrepancy, a customer service clerk admitted that each store independently sets the price for such items, based on nearby competition. That's a good lesson—many chains in more rural or poorer locations (with no nearby competition) often mark prices higher than suburban stores.

7 **JUST BUY REGULAR VERSIONS OF FORMULA.** When we say regular formula, we mean the basic formula you've seen on the shelves for years. We think those new lipids enhanced formulas (with DHA and ARA) are a waste of money. Similac's Advance, Nestle's Good Start Supreme with DHA & ARA and Enfamil's Lipil are the top brands with these lipids. These can cost as much as 20% more than basic formula. And as we discussed above, there is no scientific proof that these lipids actually improve brain or eye function. Until we see long-term studies that verify those claims we suggest you save you money and skip those lipid-enhanced formulas. And the same goes for toddler formulas. When your child is ready for whole milk (usually at one year of age, according to most pediatricians), you can switch from formula (about 10¢ per ounce) to milk (about 2¢ per ounce) at a savings of 80%! What about the claim that toddler formulas have extra calcium, iron and vitamins? Nutritionists point out that toddlers should be getting most of their nutrition from solid foods, not formula. That extra calcium can be found in foods as diverse as yogurt and broccoli; iron in red meat and spinach; vitamins in a wide variety of foods. But what if you don't think your child is getting enough of those nutrients? Adding a vitamin and mineral supplement to your child's diet would *still* be less expensive than blowing your money on toddler formulas.

8 **CHECK OUT AMAZON.** Yep, Amazon sells formula (and even diapers) in their health and personal care store. Prices for formula were about 10% to 15% cheaper than full retail and if you order more than $25 (which is pretty easy, considering your typical 2 lb can of formula clocks in at $23.79 on the site), you get free shipping. Compare Amazon's prices with the lowest discount source in your area to see if it makes sense.

9 **JOIN A FORMULA CLUB.** Several formula makers have frequent buyer clubs. Example: Enfamil's Family Beginnings offers up to $60 in checks for purchasing formula, a free diaper bag, free portraits at JcPenney and more. It's free (sign up at Enfamil.com). Bonus savings idea: Sam's Club accepts Enfamil's checks, which lets you stretch those freebies even farther!

Bottles/Nipples

What's the best bottle for baby? Actually, it's not the bottle that's so important but the nipple—how the milk is delivered to baby is more important than the container.

When it comes to nipples, there are a myriad of choices. At the low end, *Playtex* and *Gerber* are available in just about every grocery store in the U.S. and Canada. Mid-price options like *Evenflo* and *Munchkin's* Healthflow (formerly made by Johnson & Johnson) are also widely available. At the high end, brands such as *Avent* and *Dr. Brown* bottle systems are sold in baby specialty stores and chains.

So, which nipple (and bottle) system is best? This is like asking folks to name their favorite Thanksgiving dish—everyone will have a different opinion. For many parents, the bottle/nipple system they start with is the one they stick by. And the low-end options can work just as well as the premium brands.

That isn't to say premium, reusable bottle brands like Avent don't have their advantages. The company claims its nipples are clinically proven to reduce colic, the endless crying that some infants develop around one month of age. Avent says its nipples are better since their shape mimics the breast—and many readers of this book tell us Avent is superior to the com-petition. Avent bottles have wide-mouth openings that are easier to fill (for formula) and easier to clean than competing bottles. Avent uses thicker plastic that seems more substantial; you can definitely re-use these bottles for later children (although the nipples should be replaced after six months of use).

Unfortunately, Avent isn't cheap, costing a third more than other less-expensive bottles and nipples. A 9oz Avent bottle with nipple runs about $5 at Babies R Us, compared to $4.29 for a Playtex bottle (8 oz.) or $3.75 for a Munchkin Healthflow bottle (8 oz.).

Until a couple of years ago, Avent only made reusable bottles, missing out on the one-third of the market that prefers the convenience of disposable nursers. Well, there's good news to report: Avent now sells a disposable bottle that includes their famous nipple and storage bags that clip on the bottle.

In the past year, Avent has released a new bottle system, dubbed VIA. These bottles are a hybrid between reusable bottles and disposables. You can use them up to three times before throwing them away. In the past, you could not use reusable nipples on disposable bottles and vice-versa. However, now you can interchange nipples between VIA bottles and reusable bottles. (FYI: It is appears Avent is phasing out their old disposable line in favor of the VIA).

Remember that many bottles use "proprietary" nipples—hence, an Avent nipple won't work on someone else's bottle. Yes, some manufacturers let you mix and match, but you should check first before assuming compatibility.

One gripe for Avent: If you screw the reusable bottle cap on too tight, it will leak. Many readers complained about this problem, but Avent's web site (www.avent.com) offers tips on how to tighten just enough.

Another high-end bottle recommended by our readers is Dr. Brown's Natural Flow (www.handi-craft.com). Dr. Brown (not related to the Dr. Brown with whom we co-authored *Baby 411*) claims these bottles will eliminate colic and reduce middle ear infections. How? A patented vent system eliminates bubbles and nipple collapse. Invented by a physician from Illinois, our readers universally praise his unique bottle system. It isn't cheap, however. Wal-Mart sells a three pack of the four-ounce bottles for $12.50.

Among the more hip products on the bottle front are the "angled nursers." Munchkin's HealthFlow (starting at $2.50 for a four-ounce bottle) started the trend, which purportedly keeps baby from gulping too much air. The bottle makes it easier for parents to monitor the amount of liquid baby has consumed. Evenflo has introduced a similar product (three nine-oz. bottles for $7) and several other companies have knocked-off the Health Flow in recent years.

Looking for a glass baby bottle? These have become scarce in recent years, although they seem to be making a comeback. Evenflo makes a three pack of glass bottles for $5 to $6 depending on the size.

Of course, there are other bottles out there besides the big brands. A reader recommended a new bottle from a company with the scary name of BreastBottle (www.breastbottle.com). Shaped like, well, a breast, this pricey bottle ($13) is made of soft plastic and is dishwasher safe.

Where can you find bottles at a discount? Readers say Avent bottles at Target are three four-ounce bottles for $10.20, about a 15% discount. The web is another source: DrugStore (www.drugstore.com) has great prices on many Avent items. And many of the general baby product sites carry Avent at a discount as well. Kid Surplus (www.kidsurplus.com) has great prices on Dr. Brown's bottles. You'll find the four-ounce bottle three-pack for $12.

Smart Shopper Tip

Smart Shopper Tip #1
Nipple confusion?

"When I check the catalogs and look in baby stores, I see bottles with all different shaped nipples. Which one is best for my baby? How do I avoid nipple confusion?"

Nipple confusion occurs when a baby learns to suck one way at the breast and another way from a bottle. This happens because the "human breast milk delivery system" (i.e., the breast and nipple) forces babies to keep their sucking action forward in their mouth. The result: they have to work harder to get milk from a breast than from a conventional baby bottle.

So if you want to give an occasional bottle, what bottle is least likely to cause nipple confusion? Unfortunately, the answer is not clear—some parents swear that Avent's nipple is best. Fans of Dr. Brown's bottle say it is best. Others find less expensive options like the Playtex Nurser work just as well.

Are there really that many differences between nipples, besides shape? Not really. All major brands are dishwasher-safe, made of latex and have very similar flow rates. The bottom line: you may have to experiment with different nipples/bottles to find one your baby likes.

What about pacifiers? This is a controversial topic. Some experts argue early use of pacifiers may interfere with breastfeeding. The best advice: try to wait until lactation is firmly established before introducing a pacifier. Which type of pacifier is best? There are two types—regular pacifiers have round nipples, while "orthodontic" pacifiers have flat nipples. There's no consensus as to which type is best—consult with your pediatrician for more advice on this topic.

Bottle Warmers & Sterilizers

When you are a first-time parent, how do you know you will really need an item? Which ones are wastes of money? Take bottle sterilizers and warmers, for example. Will your child die from some bacterial agent if you don't sterilize your baby bottles? Will Junior scream bloody murder if his bottle isn't a perfect 85 degrees Fahrenheit? The answer to both questions is: probably not. In most cases washing baby bottles in the dishwasher cleans them just fine and a room temperature bottle will make a hungry baby just as happy as a warmed bottle of formula or milk. But what if you decide a bottle sterilizer or warmer is needed? Here are our recommendations:

Like the competition in bottles, Avent also seems to win the sterilizer war with their "Sterilizer Express," a new model that is even zippier than their previous sterilizers. The Express comes in a microwave ($30) or electric version ($70) that can sterilize six bottles in just four to six minutes (the lower figure is for the microwave; the higher one for the electric version).

What about bottle warmers? Avent makes a pretty good one, the "Express Bottle and Baby Food Warmer" ($40). It can heat a bottle in four minutes. It also fits baby food jars and all types of baby bottles (not just Avent). However, in general, bottle warmers are unnecessary for most parents—you can skip this purchase.).

Smart Shopper Tip #2
Bottle confusion?
"How many bottles will I need if I formula feed? What nipple sizes do I need? Do I need a bottle sterilizer?"

Yes, the questions about bottles and feeding baby can be rather endless! To help, we've posted to our web site a great email from a mom who's been there, done that. This email actually appeared first as a thread on our message boards, but we thought it was the most comprehensive discussion of bottle-feeding we've ever seen. Since it is eight pages long, however, we didn't have room to reprint it here. Go to Babybargains.com and click on Bonus Material to read it online.

Baby Food

At the tender age of four to six months, you and your baby will depart on a magical journey to a new place filled with exciting adventures and never-before-seen wonders. Yes, you've entered the SOLID FOOD ZONE.

Fasten your seat belts and get ready for a fun ride. As your tour guide, we would like to give a few pointers to make your stay a bit more enjoyable. Let's take stock:

Parents in Cyberspace: What's on the Web?

Looking for a schedule of what foods to introduce when? Earth's Best's web site has a comprehensive chart with suggestions (www.earthsbest.com, click on "baby & toddler nutrition"). Gerber's slick web site (www.gerber.com) also has baby development info (including when to start different stage foods). We also liked Beechnut's site (www.beechnut.com), which includes "suggested menus," "feeding FAQ's" and "making feeding fun." Although it is designed for Canadian parents, Heinz's baby food web site, www.heinzbaby.com contains extensive nutritional advice and other helpful info. Canadians can take advantage of rebate offers and other deals on this site (hopefully, they'll add the rest of North America to the coupon deals soon).

Safe & Sound

1 FEED FROM A BOWL, NOT FROM THE JAR. Why? If you feed from a jar, bacterium from the baby's mouth can find their way back to the jar, spoiling the food much more quickly. Also, saliva enzymes begin to break down the food's nutrients. The best strategy: pour the amount of baby food you need into a bowl and feed from there (unless it's the last serving from the jar). And be sure to refrigerate any unused portions.

2 DON'T STORE FOOD IN PLASTIC BAGS. If you leave plastic bags on the baby's high chair, they can be a suffocation hazard. A better solution: store leftover food in small, Tupperware-type containers.

3 DO A TASTE TEST. Make sure it isn't too hot, too cold, or spoiled. We know you aren't dying to taste the Creamed Ham Surprise from Gerber, but it is a necessary task.

4 **CHECK FOR EXPIRATION DATES.** Gerber's jarred food looks like it would last through the next Ice Age, but check that expiration date. Most unopened baby food is only good for a year or two. Use opened jars within two to three days.

5 **A FINAL WORD OF ADVICE ON FEEDING BABY:** don't introduce nuts (like peanuts or peanut butter) until your child is at least three years old. This advice comes from a nationally known allergist we interviewed who's a specialist in nut allergies. He points out that nut allergies are potentially fatal and lifelong . . and early exposure (before age three) tends to heighten the risk. So the longer you wait to introduce nuts, the better chance you have of avoiding these deadly allergies. FYI: Watch out for foods that are processed on the same production lines as those that process nuts—these can contain trace amounts of nuts, even if they are not listed as an ingredient. You'll see this warning noted on labels.

Smart Shopper Tips

Smart Shopper Tip #1
Tracking Down UFFOs (Unidentifiable Flying Food Objects)
"We fed our baby rice cereal for the first time. It was really cute, except for the part when the baby picked up the bowl and flung it across the kitchen! Should we have bought some special stuff for this occasion?"

Well, unless you want your kitchen to be redecorated in Early Baby Food, we do have a few suggestions. First, a bowl with a bottom that suctions to the table is a great way to avoid flying saucers. Plastic spoons that have a round handle are nice, especially since baby can't stick the spoon handle in her eye (yes, that does happen—babies do try to feed themselves even at a young age). Spoons with rubber coatings are also nice; they don't transfer the heat or cold of the food to the baby's mouth and are easier on the gums. One clever spoon is Munchkin's "White Hot Infant Spoon" (call 800-344-2229 or 818-893-5000 to find a dealer near you; web: www.munchkininc.com). This spoon uses a special coating that changes color when baby's food is too hot (105 degrees or warmer). Now they offer three versions including one with airplane wings for the reluctant eater.

Smart Shopper Tip #2
Avoiding Mealtime Baths

"Our baby loves to drink from a cup, except for one small problem. Most of the liquid ends up on her, instead of in her. Any tips?"

Cups with weighted bottoms (about $5) help young infants to get the hang of this drinking thing. A sipping spout provides an interim learning step between bottle and regular cup. When your baby's older, we've found clear plastic cups to be helpful. Why? Your baby can see out the bottom and not feel like someone has turned out the lights.

No-spill cups are a godsend—Playtex (203) 341-4000 pioneered this category with a cup that doesn't leak when tipped over. Despite the fact that many other companies have jumped into the no-spill cup market in recent years, Playtex's cups are still the gold standard. Also check out Gerber's version—readers praise this no-spill cup as well.

"Toddler" foods a waste of money

When the number of births leveled off in recent years, the baby food companies began looking around for ways to grow their sales. One idea: make foods for older babies and toddlers who have abandoned the jarred mushy stuff! One company warns parents not to feed "adult" foods to babies too early, saying they won't provide "all the nutrition they need." To boost sales in the $1 billion baby food market, Gerber rolled out "Gerber Graduates" while Heinz debuted "Toddler Cuisine," microwaveable meals for kids as old as 36 months. Heck, even Enfamil has rolled out the "EnfaGrow" line of fortified snacks. So, what do nutritionists and doctors think of these foods? Most say they are completely unnecessary. Yes, they are a convenience for parents but, besides that, so-called "toddler foods" offer no additional nutritional benefit. In their defense, the baby food companies argue that their toddler meals are meant to replace the junk food and unhealthy snacks parents give their babies. We guess we can see that point, but overall we think that toddler foods are a complete waste of money. Once your baby finishes with baby food, they can go straight to "adult food" without any problem—of course, that should be HEALTHY adult food. What's best: a mix of dairy products, fruits, vegetables, meat and eggs. And, no, McDonald's French fries don't count as a vegetable.

E-Mail from The Real World
Allergies and Baby Food:
Watch those labels!

If you've noticed you're hearing more and more about food allergies these days, you're not alone. In fact, there has been a distinct rise in the number of food allergies among children according to allergists we've interviewed. But can food allergies be avoided? Maybe. One strategy is to put off feeding the most allergenic of foods to your child. Specifically avoid nuts and shellfish. But what about other foods? Here's a comment from one of our readers:

"You're the first people, other than myself it seems, to be bothered by the fact that baby food manufacturers put corn in their foods. I've been reading the labels (since I have a few food allergies and want to prevent my daughter from the same fate), and I've been noticing that all manufacturers add corn, milk products, strawberries, and other things that babies are advised to avoid during the first year to their foods intended for children under one year old. I was also bothered by the fact that companies have limited choices for 'stage one' foods, then offer stage two foods containing multiple ingredients not available at stage one, such as 'banana, mango, kiwi' blends."

You don't have to go to a baby store to find these items—we've seen many baby feeding accessories in grocery stores.

Smart Shopper Tip #3
Finger Foods

"When can we start giving our baby finger foods? What should we give her that she won't choke on?"

After stage one, the pureed versions of real food, you'll be ready to move on to stage two. And you can do this simultaneously, taking into account your child's maturity. Usually, at around ten to twelve months your baby will be ready to try some finger foods like well-cooked diced carrots. Make sure whatever you feed your baby at this stage is soft and cut up rather small. You can include baby in your meals by cutting up cooked chicken as well as soft veggies and small bits of bread. Parents may still want to feed babies some pureed food, but waiting too long to introduce foods with more texture and flavor can be a mistake. If you're not sure what your baby can handle in the way of chunkier foods, check with your doctor.

Money-Saving Tips

1 MAKE YOUR OWN. Let's be honest: baby foods such as mashed bananas are really just . . . mashed bananas. You can easily whip up this stuff with that common kitchen helper, the food processor. Many parents skip baby food altogether and make their own. One tip: make up a big batch at one time and freeze the leftovers in ice cube trays. Check the library for cookbooks that provide tips on making baby food at home. A reader suggestion: the "Super Baby Food" book ($19.95, published by F. J. Roberts Publishing, web: www.superbabyfood.com). This 590-page book is about as comprehensive as you can find on the subject.

2 BELIEVE IT OR NOT, TOYS R US AND BABIES R US SELL BABY FOOD. If you think your grocery store is gouging you on the price of baby food, you might want to check out the prices at Babies R Us. We found Gerber 1st Foods in a four-pack of 2.5-ounce jars for $2.09—that works out to about 50¢ per jar or about 15% less than grocery store prices. Toys R Us also sells four-packs of assorted dinners from Gerber's 2nd and 3rd Food collections.

3 COUPONS! COUPONS! COUPONS! Yes, we've seen quite a few cents-off and buy-one-get-one-free coupons on baby

E-MAIL FROM THE REAL WORLD
Making your own baby food isn't time consuming

A mom in New Mexico told us she found making her own baby food isn't as difficult as it sounds:

"My husband and I watch what we eat, so we definitely watch what our baby eats. One of the things I do is buy organic carrots, quick boil them, throw them in a blender and then freeze them in an ice cube tray. Once they are frozen, I separate the cubes into freezer baggies (they would get freezer burn if left in the ice tray). When mealtime arrives, I just throw them in the microwave. Organic carrots taste great! This whole process might sound complicated, but it only takes me about 20 minutes to do, and then another five to ten minutes to put the cubes in baggies."

food and formula—not just in the Sunday paper but also through the mail. Our advice: don't toss that junk mail until you've made sure you're not trashing valuable baby food coupons. Another coupon trick: look for "bounce-back" coupons. Those are the coupons put in the packages of baby food to encourage you to bounce back to the store and buy more.

4 BUY DEL MONTE. As noted later in this section, Del Monte's Nature's Goodness baby food is often priced below the competition, sometimes as much as 20%. The only drawback: it isn't available everywhere.

5 SUBSTITUTE COMPARABLE ADULT FOODS. What's the difference between adult applesauce and baby applesauce? Not much, except for the fact that applesauce in a jar with a cute baby on it costs several times more than the adult version. While the adult applesauce isn't fortified with extra vitamins, it probably doesn't matter. Baby will get these nutrients from other foods. Another rip-off: the "next step" foods for older babies. Gerber loves to tout its special toddler meals in its "Graduates" line. What's the point? When baby is ready to eat pasta, just serve him small bites of the adult stuff.

6 GO FOR THE BETTER QUALITY. That's a strange money-saving tip, isn't it? Doesn't better quality baby food cost more? Yes, but look at it this way—the average baby eats 600 jars of baby food until they "graduate" to adult foods. Sounds like a lot of money, eh? Well, that only works out to $300 or so in total expenditures (using an average price of 48¢ to 75¢ per jar). Hence, if you go for the better-quality food and spend, say, 20% more, you're only out another $60. Therefore it might be better to spend the small additional dollars to give baby better-quality food. And feeding baby food that tastes more like the real thing makes transitions to adult foods easier.

The Name Game: Reviews of Selected Manufacturers

Here's a round up of some of the best-known names in baby food. We should note that while we actually tried out each of the foods on our baby, you may reach different conclusions than we did. Unlike our brand name ratings for clothing or other baby products, food is a much trickier rating proposition. We rated the following brand names based on how healthy they are and how much they approximate real food (aroma, appearance, and, yes, taste). Our subjective opinions reflect our experience—always consult with your pediatrician or family doctor if you have any questions about feeding your baby. (Special thanks to Ben and Jack for their help in researching this topic.)

The Ratings

A EXCELLENT—*our top pick!*
B GOOD— *above average quality, prices, and creativity.*
C FAIR—*could stand some improvement.*
D POOR—*yuck! could stand some major improvement.*

Beech-Nut *(800) BEECHNUT; Web: www.beechnut.com* Beech-Nut was one of the first baby food companies to eliminate fillers (starches, sugar, salt) or artificial colors/flavors in its 120 flavors. While Beech-Nut is not organic, the company claims to have "stringent pesticide standards." Our readers generally give Beech-Nut good marks (some like it better than Gerber). The only bummer: it can be hard to find (not every state has stores that carry it). You can search their web page or call their 800-number to check availability. One bonus: Beech-Nut's web site includes on-line coupons and other deals. **Rating: B+**

Del Monte *Web: www.naturesgoodness.com* Heinz spun off its baby food division to Del Monte back in 2003 and the new owner re-christened it Nature's Goodness. We like the fact that Del Monte posts its nutritional labels online and noted the lack of added sugars or starches in most of the line. As for price, Del Monte is priced about 15% to 20% less than Gerber, making it a good deal. Del Monte's 2.5-ounce jar of bananas goes for 38¢ versus a similar Gerber fruit for 45¢ per 2.5 ounces. The feedback from parents on this line is positive; the only drawback is availability—Del Monte's Nature's Goodness isn't in as many stores as Gerber. **Rating: A**

Earth's Best *(800) 442-4221. Web: www.earthsbest.com* Organic food has gone mainstream in the last few years, so there's no surprise you can now buy organic baby food. One of our favorite brands: Earth's Best. Started in Vermont, Earth's Best was sold in 1996 to Heinz, one of the baby food giants. Heinz couldn't figure out what to do with the company and decided to sell it to natural foods conglomerate Hain Celestial (parent of Celestial Tea). Despite all the changes in ownership, Earth's Best still has the largest line of "natural" baby foods on the market—all vegetables and grains are certified to be organically grown (no pesticides are used), and meats are raised without antibiotics or steroids. Another advantage: Earth's Best never adds any salt, sugar or modified starches to its food. And the foods are only made from whole grains, fruits and vegetables (instead of concentrates). Surprisingly, Earth's Best costs about the same as Gerber (around 45¢ to 49¢ for a 2.5 ounce jar). We tried Earth's Best and were generally pleased. Our only complaint: Earth's Best can be hard to find (it's more likely in health food stores like Whole Foods, but we've seen it in some regular grocery stores too). All in all, Earth's Best is a much-needed natural alternative to the standard fare that babies have been fed for far too many years. ***Rating: A***

Gerber *Web: www.gerber.com* Dominating the baby food business with a whopping 70% market share (that's right, three out of every four baby food jars sold sport that familiar label), Gerber sure has come a long way from its humble beginnings. Back in 1907, Joseph Gerber (whose trade was canning) mashed up peas for his daughter, following the suggestion of a family doctor. We imagine those peas looked quite different from Gerber's peas today. Now, thanks to scientific progress, Gerber's peas are put through such a rigorous canning process that they don't even look like peas . . . instead more like green slime. And it's not just the look, have you actually smelled or tasted any of Gerber's offerings? Yuck. Sure it's cheap (about 49¢ for a 2 1/2 ounce jar of Gerber 1st Foods), but we just can't feed our baby this stuff with a clear conscience. On the upside, Gerber offers parents one key advantage: choice. The line boasts an amazing 200 different flavors. Gerber is sold in just about every grocery store on Earth. And we have to give Gerber credit: a few years ago, the company announced it would respond to parents' concerns and reformulate its baby food to eliminate starches, sugars and other fillers. Gerber also rolled out "Tender Harvest," a line of organic baby food to compete with Earth's Best. The new line is made with "whole grains and certified organic fruits and vegetables" (note that Gerber's regular line still uses fruit and vegetable concentrates). Finally, we noticed that Gerber is now packing its first foods in plastic rather than glass. No shattered jars when feeding your squirming baby. While we like the changes Gerber has made, we still have problems with the brand. First, we think their "Graduates" line of "toddler" foods is a waste of money. And their juice line is overpriced compared to others on the market. ***Rating: C***

Heinz See Del Monte.

Naturally Preferred *Web: www.kroger.com* Launched in 2003, Kroger's own in-house brand of baby food is dubbed Naturally Preferred. You'll find it in grocery stores like Ralph's, Fry's, City

Market, King Soopers to name a few. For a complete listing of stores in the Kroger chain, check their website. Like all private label brands, the big draw here is the price. Sample: a four-ounce jar of Naturally Preferred is 50¢, compared to Gerber Tender Harvest at 73¢ for the same size item. However, Naturally Preferred did suffer a recall of some of their products in July of 2004 for glass contamination. The manufacturer, J.R. Wood, noted that there were no injuries associated with the recall.

High Chairs

As soon as Junior starts to eat solid food, you'll need this quintessential piece of baby furniture—the high chair. Surprisingly, this seemingly innocuous product generates over 7000 injuries each year. So, what are the safest high chairs? And how do you use them properly? We'll share these insights, as well as some money-saving tips and brand reviews in this section.

Safe and Sound

1 **MOST INJURIES OCCUR WHEN BABIES ARE NOT STRAPPED INTO THEIR CHAIRS.** Sadly, four to five deaths occur each year when babies "submarine" under the tray. To address these types of accidents new high chairs now feature a "passive restraint" (a plastic post) under the tray to prevent this. Note: some high chair makers attach this submarine protection to the tray; others have it on the seat. We prefer the seat. Why? If it is on the tray and the tray is removed, there is a risk a child might be able to squirm out of the safety belts (which is all that would hold them in the chair). We'll note which high chairs feature submarine guards on the seat versus tray later in the reviews section of this chapter.

FYI: Even if the high chair has a passive restraint, you STILL must strap in baby with the safety harness with EACH use. This prevents them from climbing out or otherwise hurting themselves. Finally, never put the high chair near a wall—babies have been injured in the past when they push off a wall or object, tipping over the chair. This problem is rare with the newest high chairs (as they have wide, stable bases), but you still can tip over older, hand-me-down models.

2 **THE SAFETY STANDARDS FOR HIGH CHAIRS ARE VOLUNTARY.** In a recent report, *Consumer Reports* claimed that not all high chairs meet these voluntary standards. Perhaps the safest bet: look for JPMA-certified high chairs. The JPMA requires a battery of safety tests, including checks for stability, a locking device to prevent folding, a secure restraining system, no sharp edges, and so on.

3 **INSPECT THE SEAT—IS IT WELL UPHOLSTERED?** Make sure it won't tear or puncture easily.

4 **LOOK FOR STABILITY.** It's basic physics: the wider the base, the more stable the chair.

5 **CAREFULLY INSPECT THE RESTRAINING SYSTEM.** Straps around the hips and between the legs do the trick. The cheapest high chairs have only a single strap around the waist. Expensive models have "safety harnesses" with multiple straps.

6 **SOME HIGH CHAIRS OFFER DIFFERENT HEIGHT POSITIONS, INCLUDING A RECLINING POSITION THAT SUPPOSEDLY MAKES IT EASIER TO FEED A YOUNG INFANT.** The problem? Feeding a baby solid foods in a reclining position is a choking hazard. If you want to use the reclining feature, it should be exclusively for bottle-feeding. We do think the recline feature is a plus for another reason, however: it is easier to take baby in and out of the high chair when it is reclined. And when babies start out with solid foods, they may go back and forth between the bottle and solid food during meals. Hence, the recline feature is helpful when they need to take a bottle break.

More Money Buys You

Whether you spend $30 or $200, most high chairs do one simple thing—provide you with a place to safely ensconce your baby while he eats. The more money you spend, however, the more comforts there are for both you and baby. As you go up in price, you find chairs with various height positions, reclining seats, larger trays, more padding, casters for mobility and more. From a safety point of view, some of the more expensive high chairs feature five-point restraint harnesses (instead of just a waist belt). Nearly all high chairs feature the under-tray passive restraint mentioned earlier. As for usability, some high chairs are easier to clean than others, but that doesn't necessary correspond to price. Look for removable vinyl covers that are machine-washable (cloth covers on cheaper chairs are harder to clean). Nearly all high chairs sold today are made of plastic and metal, replacing the wooden high chairs that previous generations of babies used.

Smart Shopper Tips for High Chairs

Smart Shopper Tip #1
High Chair Basics 101

"I was looking at those fancy Italian high chairs and trying to figure out why they are so expensive. And does it matter what color you get? I like the white model best."

The high chair market is basically divided into two camps: the low-end chairs from companies like Graco and Cosco and the Italian imports from Peg Perego and Chicco. The key differences: styling (the Italian chairs admittedly look better) and quality/durability.

Peg Perego's Prima Pappa, for example, became a runaway success, thanks to its stylish looks and compact fold for storage. At $160 to $180, however, the Pappa is TWICE the price of Graco's top-of-the-line high chair. And, as you'll read later, some readers gripe that the Pappa is a nightmare to clean.

There finally is good news to report on the high chair front, however. In the past year, several new competitors have debuted in the market in the "mid" price range (that is, between the $50 Graco chairs and the $160 Peregos) with decent looks AND good features. Examples include Baby Trend, Fisher-Price, Zooper and Combi. We'll discuss each later in this section. Here are some basic features and new trends to keep an eye out for:

◆ **Tray release.** Nearly all high chairs now have a "one hand" tray release that enables you to easily remove the tray with a quick motion. The problem: not all releases are the same. The more expensive chairs generally have a release that's easier to operate. Warning: some models have a one-handed "pull" release that is under the tray. Some kids learn they can kick the release and send the tray flying across the kitchen. We'll review which models have this problem later; check under the tray to make sure the release can't be kicked off! (Note: to address this problem, some manufacturers are adding a "kick-guard" to the release). Other trays have a "push" release button that eliminates the kick issue.

◆ **Snack trays.** Some new high chairs have two trays—a big one for meals and a tiny one for snacks. Why? We have no idea.

◆ **Tray wars.** High chair makers like to battle their competitors by touting the newest gimmick on their trays. Hence, you'll now see trays with cup holders, compartmentalized snack areas and so on.

Do you really need a cup holder? Don't worry—your baby will spill their juice, cup holder or not. The latest trend is dishwasher-safe tray liners or double trays (where one can go in the dishwasher). This is a cool feature that helps with clean up.

◆ *Tray height.* Some parents complain the tray height of Italian high chairs is too high—making it hard for smaller babies to use. A smart tip: take your baby with you when you go high chair shopping and actually sit them in the different options. You can evaluate the tray heights in person to make sure the chair will work for both you and baby. We'll note which chairs have the best/worst tray heights later in our reviews. Generally, a chair with a tray height of less than 8" should work for most babies. A few models have tray heights over 8"—those can be a major problem since a child can't reach the food on the tray.

◆ *Seat depth.* Most chairs have multiple tray positions and reclining seats. But what is the distance between the seat back when it is upright and the tray in its closest position? A distance of 5" to 7" is acceptable. Over 7" and you run the risk that there will be a large gap between your baby and the tray—and all their food will end up in their lap/chair. Again, take your baby with you when shopping for a chair, as smaller babies may be harder to fit. For larger babies, you may able to adjust the tray out a bit to create more room.

◆ *Less convertibility.* Here's an ironic twist: while the rest of the baby products market is awash in "convertible" products, high chairs are moving the other way. Gone are the high chairs that converted into a table and chair set, or some other future use. Parents seem to like high chairs that are just, well, high chairs.

◆ *Washability.* Here's an obvious tip some first-time parents seem to miss: make sure the high chair you buy has a removable washable seat cover OR a seat that easily sponges clean. In the latter category, chairs with VINYL covers trump those made of cloth—vinyl can be wiped clean, while cloth typically has to be washed. This might be one of those first-time parent traps—seats with cloth covers sure look nicer than those made of vinyl. But cloth can't be wiped clean and requires washing—some cloth covers can't be thrown in the dryer either! That means waiting a day or more for a cover to line dry. Nojo does make a high chair cover ($20) that may be a handy option for parents who choose a high chair with a fabric seat pad. You could use the Nojo cover while you're washing and drying the original pad.

Of course, the cloth/vinyl issue becomes somewhat confusing

when you consider some vinyl seats have cloth edging/piping. Our advice: be careful of any seat with cloth edging/piping, as it might be very hard to clean. (Make sure the seat is washable and machine dryable).

What color cover should you get? Answer: anything but white. Sure, that fancy white "leatherette" high chair looks all shiny and new at the baby store, but it will forever be a cleaning nightmare once you start using it. Darker colors and patterns are better. Another tip: avoid high chairs that have lots of cracks and crevices near the tray and seat, which makes cleaning difficult. (This seems to be the Peg Perego Prima Pappa's biggest sin).

Smart Shopper Tip #2
Tray Chic and Other Restaurant Tips

"We have a great high chair at home, but we're always appalled at the lack of safe high chairs at restaurants. Our favorite cafe has a high chair that must date back to 1952—no straps, a metal tray with sharp edges, and a hard seat with no cushion. Have restaurateurs lost their minds?

We think so. People who run restaurants must search obscure foreign countries to find the world's most hazardous high chairs. The biggest problem? No straps, enabling babies to slide out of the chair, submarine-style. The solution? When the baby is young, keep her in her infant car seat; the safe harness keeps baby secure. When your baby is older (and if you eat out a lot), you may want to invest in a portable booster seat. Because these products are designed for kids two and up, we review them in our book *Toddler Bargains*. You'll find all these "next-step" products reviewed and rated in a separate chapter in that book.

The Name Game: Reviews of Selected Manufacturers

Many high-tech high chairs feature height adjustments and extra-large feeding trays. While most are made of plastic and metal, there are still fans out there who like traditional wood chairs. If you want a wood chair, consider offerings from Simmons and Child Craft (yes, they're the same names you saw in Chapter 2 in the crib reviews). Since wood high chairs lack fancy features (you can't adjust the height, they don't fold up, etc.), the majority of high chairs sold in the U.S. and Canada are those reviewed in this section:

The Ratings

A **EXCELLENT**—*our top pick!*
B **GOOD**— *above average quality, prices, and creativity.*
C **FAIR**—*could stand some improvement.*
D **POOR**—*yuck! could stand some major improvement.*

Baby Trend For a dealer near you, call (800) 328-7363, (909) 902-5568, Web: www. babytrend.com. Baby Trend's high chair was one of our top picks in a previous edition of this book, but reader complaints have knocked down its rating this year. Yes, it is a credible knock-off of the Perego and Chicco chairs, yet sells for 40% less (about $90 in most stores). You get all the stan-  dard features you'd expect: five-point harness, four-position reclining seat, three-position tray with one hand release, six height positions, compact fold and casters. And, yes, the Baby Trend high chair has a lower tray than the Perego or Chicco models and is generally easier to use (it requires little assembly, for example). So, what's the beef? The pad is this chair's Achilles' heel. We've received several reports that the cloth pad (which has a reversible vinyl side) fell apart or bunched up after machine washing. Even Baby Trend, in an email to us, admitted the pad "responds best to hand washing." Gee, that's nice—too bad the instructions for the chair say to machine wash the pad on the gentle cycle . . . with no mention of hand washing. Add that to the fact the pad has to be line dried and you have a deal-breaker here. Yes, other parents have had success with this chair—and Baby Trend has tried to improve it by adding memory foam to the seat this year and a double tray. But Baby Trend's customer service stumbles and the pad washing issue have resulted in us knocking down the rating of this high chair by a letter grade. **Rating: B-**

Carter's. This high chair is made by Kolcraft, see review later.

Chicco 4E Easy Street, Bound Brook, NJ 08805. For a dealer near you, call (877) 4CHICCO or (732) 805-9200. Web: www. chiccousa.com Chicco's Polly high chair is the successor to the Mamma, a high chair we only gave a C in our last report. So is the Polly an improvement? Yes, in a nutshell. The Polly comes in three different versions: a basic model for $100, one with a double pad for $120 and

a deluxe model for $130 with extra cushions. The Polly features an adjustable footrest, compact fold, three-position seat recline, seven height positions and removable dishwasher-safe tray. So, how does the Polly differ from the Mamma? Well, the biggest difference is a lower tray, which addresses our biggest gripe with the previous model. The Polly also folds more compactly than the Mamma, which is a nice plus. We also like the re-designed tray, which is easy to take off with one hand and can be hung off the back of the chair on pegs. Even the colors of the Polly are an improvement, ranging from stylish grey and taupe to more whimsical patterns with orange accents. Perhaps our only complaint with Chicco is the price. While Polly is much less than Perego's chairs, you still pay a 30% premium over Fisher-Price's strong offerings in this category. And while the Polly is well designed, we're not sure this chair is 30% better than Fisher-Price's Healthy Care. ***Rating: A-***

Combi *1962 Hwy 160 West #100, Ft. Mill, SC 29708. For a dealer near you, call (800) 992-6624, (803) 802-8416; Web: www. combi-intl.com.* Best known for its strollers, Combi has been trying

Living the High Life

Hook-on chairs and booster seats are close relatives to the familiar high chair. Depending on your needs, each can serve a purpose. Hook-on chairs do exactly what they say—hook onto a table. While some have trays, most do not, and that is probably their biggest disadvantage: baby eats (or spills and throws food) on your table instead of hers. At least they're cheap: about $25 to $40 at most stores. Best use: if your favorite restaurants don't have high chairs (or don't have safe ones) or if you plan to do some road trips with Junior. One caveat: hook-on chairs are only safe when used with tables that have four legs (not pedestals).

Booster seats are more useful. With or without an attached tray, most strap to a chair or can be used on the floor. We used ours at Grandma's house, which spared us the chore of dragging along a high chair or hook-on chair. It's also convenient to do evening feedings in a booster seat in the baby's room, instead of dragging everyone to the kitchen. And you can't beat the price: $18 to $30 at most stores.

Both of these products are reviewed in depth in our *Toddler Bargains* book, as they are most useful for two to four year olds. See the back of this book for details on our other book.

to crack the high chair category but its efforts have met with little success. So the company is back at the drawing board with a new model that should be out by the time you read this: the Breeze. This high chair replaces the Easy Glider, an expensive model that had a full recline and gliding feature—which, of course, is kind of silly for a high chair and explains why the Easy Glider flopped sales-wise. The Breeze, on the other hand, is a more traditional high chair with a three-position recline, washable seat cushion and double tray with toy. Yet when folded, the tray doesn't lay flat but instead sticks out horizontally—that might make the Breeze a bit hard to stash in the pantry when company comes. We do think the price is right ($90), but overall the Breeze is a bit disappointing. It lacks the adjustable footrest you see on other models and the fashion quotient of the Italian models. Since the Breeze just came out as of this writing, we don't have any parent feedback on it yet. FYI: Combi will also debut a high chair model that converts to a table and chair in 2006—the "Transition" will sell for $120. We saw a prototype of this model and think it will only have very limited appeal. ***Rating: C***

Cosco *Web:* www.djgusa.com Like most things Cosco makes, their high chairs define the entry-level price point in this market. The Cosco Simple Start high chair is a bare bones model ($28 at Target and Wal-Mart) and would do the trick for grandma's house—this simple chair has a tray with one-hand release, three-position seat recline and vinyl pad. Nothing too fancy to look at, but how many bells and whistles does Grandma need? A step-up from the Cosco Simple Start is the Safety 1st All-in-One Plus high chair (pictured on the next page) with

License mania

One thing that always confuses parents is all the licensed baby products out there. For example, Kolcraft licenses the names "Carter's" and "Lennon Baby" to put on their high chairs. Cosco does the same with Eddie Bauer and NASCAR and Evenflo with Osh Kosh. Here's a little secret of the baby product biz: licensed products are often IDENTICAL to the same ones made under the manufacturer's own name. At most, there are just different fabric colors or patterns. BUT, you pay for that name—most licensed products are 10% to 30% more expensive than the plain vanilla versions. Whether that premium for a certain color or pattern is worth it is up to you.

a dishwasher-safe insert tray and three height positions. Frankly, we are underwhelmed by Cosco's high chair offerings as a main pick for parents. We note these chairs only have three-point harnesses (most competitors have five-points) and both models lack wheels. Cosco's safety track record in this category is spotty at best, including a big recall of over one million high chairs back in 2000. ***Rating: C-***

Eddie Bauer *Web: www.djgusa.com.* Cosco has had big success with their Eddie Bauer brand in car seats and strollers, so it's no big surprise they decided to bring the name to high chairs. However, we were surprised with their creative offering here: a hybrid wood chair with plastic tray. Yep, in the category of "everything old is new again," Cosco's high chair combines the look of wood with the con-venience of plastic (the tray has a removable

dinner tray, like most competitors). All for $100, which is a great price. So, what are the trade-offs? Well, you can forget about many of the features you'll find in plastic chairs—Eddie Bauer's chair lacks wheels, height adjustments, seat recline and more. Yet, did we men-tion how sweet it looks? Parents who love this chair seem to accept the trade off in features versus aesthetics. We had a mom road test the EB high chair and the verdict was thumbs up—the one-hand adjustable tray and storage compartment (under the seat) is a nice design touch. The downsides? The three-point restraint belts were hard to figure out and adjust. And the slide slats of the seat (exposed wood not covered by any padding) were a food magnet. One future improvement to this chair would be to cover the slats with vinyl or a solid piece of wood on the sides. Also: the cloth cover has to be machine-washed and air dried (we prefer vinyl cov-ers you can wipe clean). Despite the caveats, we will recommend this chair. ***Rating: A-***

Evenflo *1801 Commerce Dr., Piqua, OH 45356. For a dealer near you, call (800) 233-5921 or (937) 415-3300. Web: www.evenflo. com* Evenflo has always been an also-ran in the high chair market, thanks to quality woes and designs that lack pizzazz. The "Envision" is their latest effort for the entry-level price point—for $50, you get seven height adjustments, three recline positions, four-position tray with one-hand release and some extras (a towel rack, vinyl pad and easy fold). Parents have also complained about the Envision's flimsy recline and other quality woes (the pad not holding up after several machine washings, etc).

Evenflo has three upper-end models: the Simplicity, the Discovery and (out by the time you read this), the Majestic. The Simplicity chair features eight height adjustments, four recline positions, snack tray, casters, three-position tray and a dishwasher-safe tray liner. Not a bad deal for $80 to $100, right? Hold it—check out the pad. It's cloth. And while it can be machine washed, it can only be tumbled dry on low for "10 to 15 minutes." That means you'll have to line dry it after that—a major negative in our opinion. Parents also complain that the Simplicity's tray is too high and is a nightmare to clean, among other numerous gripes.

Parents are similarly harsh in their reviews of the Discovery high chair, part of Evenflo's SmartSteps developmental program. The Discovery is similar to the Simplicity, but adds a fancy "DiscoverZone" tray, basically an electronic toy that fits into the top tray. For $100, Evenflo pulls out all the stops with the Discovery, which has eight height adjustments, a double pad (cloth and vinyl), dishwasher-safe tray liner and an elliptical design that gives it a more modern look. Parents we interviewed complained about this chair's tray (too high for small babies) and the seat, which does not sit up straight. As a result, babies have to slump over to reach the tray. All in all this one is a loser.

Evenflo's new Majestic high chair will be more like the Simplicity, with an $80 price tag and a slew of similar features (tray insert, swing-out removable snack tray, foot rest, machine washable pad, four position recline and storage in the base). We saw a prototype of this chair at a trade show and weren't that impressed. We still think Evenflo hasn't addressed the tray height issue and the brand's recent quality woes keep us from recommending this one.
Rating: D

Fisher-Price *636 Grand Ave., East Aurora, NY 14052. For a dealer near you, call (800) 828-4000 or (716) 687-3000. Web: www.fisher-price.com* Folks, we have a winner! After years of fumbling around in this category, Fisher-Price finally has hit a home run with the Aquarium Healthy Care high chair. It features a three-position seat recline, five-point restraint, one-hand  tray removal, dishwasher-safe tray liner, and various height adjustments. All in all, a good value for $90. Parents universally praise this chair for its ease of use and cleanability (yep, those harness straps and toys can be thrown into the dishwasher). The only negative to this chair is the fashion—that bright blue pattern and the ruffles on the chair turn off some. And the Healthy Care requires quite a bit of assembly. Despite that, this is the best bet in the high chair market and we give the Healthy Care our highest rating.

Fisher Price plans a major expansion of high chair offerings this year with a slew of new innovative offerings. First up, the Space Saver, which will be the first high chair that sits on a dining chair (sort of a souped-up booster). This $50 chair will feature a full-size tray, three position recline and it converts to a toddler booster. If you are short of space (think New York City apartment), this might be a great option.

Also new: the Close to Me ($60) features a curved tubular design that lets you pull the chair up closer to the dining table. Fisher Price will also market a fancier version of this chair called the Easy Clean for $80 that will feature a pad that easily pulls off for washing and an adjustable tray with three heights.

So what do we think of all these new models? Well, none was out on the market as we went to press, so parent feedback is not available. Given Fisher Price's track record, we expect each to be good quality and worth a look, especially the Space Saver, Close to Me and Easy Clean. We're not as sure about the Custom Ultra— for this money, we expect to be wowed with both features and fashion. That last point is not Fisher Price's strong suit and true to form, the initial colors we saw for the Custom Ultra were not that impressive. So we'll have to wait and see on this one. But meanwhile, if you don't mind the blue fabric of the Fisher Price Healthy Care, that model is a great affordable pick. ***Rating: A***

Graco *Rt. 23, Main St., Elverson, PA 19520. For a dealer near you, call (800) 345-4109, (610) 286-5951. Web: www.gracobaby.com* Graco is probably the biggest player in the under $100 high chair market. Their two main offerings: the Easy Chair and the Harmony. The Easy Chair is a bare-bones model that sells for as little as $35 at Wal-Mart (a good buy for  Grandma's house) with a simple tray, three-position recline and vinyl pad. The Harmony comes in several versions, ranging from a stripped-down version for $70 at Wal-Mart to a $90 model sold at Babies R Us with a few more bells and whistles. The Harmony's key selling point: a contoured design lets you pull baby up to the table easier than other models. The Harmony also features a one-hand height adjustment and seat recline, plus a "baby booster" insert that provides head and neck support for younger babies.

FEEDING

The cushy padded vinyl seat and storage basket are nice features, as is the snap-off dinner tray. What's the quality like? Parents give the Harmony decent marks, but quite a few complain about difficult assembly, wheels that don't roll and cheap, plastic construction. Like many Graco products, the Harmony is packed with good features and design but is hobbled by cut corners when it comes to quality. So, we'll give this chair a mid-tier rating. Not as good as our top pick (The Fisher Price Healthy Care), but better than Graco's past efforts and other low-end competitors.

New this year, Graco will debut the Contemporary high chair, which the company brags has the most compact fold of any model on the market. Completely assembled out of the box, the Contemporary will have a dishwasher-safe tray liner, six height adjustments and three-position recline (similar to the Harmony). It will sell for $100 to $130, which is a bit pricey. We only saw a prototype of this chair, so without any real-world parent feedback, we are reluctant to recommend it. *Rating: B*

John Lennon. These chairs are made by Kolcraft, see below.

Kolcraft *3455 West 31st Pl., Chicago, IL 60623. For a dealer near you, call (773) 247-4494. Web: www.kolcraft.com* Kolcraft's emphasis in this category is being the low price leader and their current offerings are a case in point. The Recline N Dine is just $29! What do you get for that? Well, a rather basic high chair with one-hand tray release, vinyl pad and storage basket (but no wheels). The Recline N Dine also comes in a $39 version that adds a more fancy pad, wheels and dishwasher-safe snap-off tray. Finally, a "Deluxe" version of this chair sells for $50, adding locking wheels and other bells and whistles. We also should note that Kolcraft markets their high chairs under the Carter's and Lennon Baby names at higher prices (basically, it's the same chair but with cuter fabric). What about the quality? Let's be honest: these would be a great idea for grandma's house, where occasional use wouldn't tax it too much, but not as an everyday high chair. In the past, we heard many gripes about Kolcraft's previous high chairs . . . seat pads that ripped too easily, straps that were hard to adjust and more. *Rating: C+*

Lennon Baby. Kolcraft makes this high chair, see above.

Martinelli. Peg Perego used to market their products in some specialty stores under the name Martinelli, but has since discontinued the line.

Peg Perego *3625 Independence Dr., Ft. Wayne, IN 46808. For a dealer near you, call (260) 482-8191. Web: www.perego.com* Yes, the Prima Pappa has been a best seller but its day has come and gone. Sure, it looks stylish and features a four-position reclining seat, seven height adjustments, a dishwasher-safe dinner tray, five-point restraint and compact fold. And the fabrics! Very chic. But let's look at the chair's key flaw: the tray. It sits a whopping 9″ above the seat, making it too tall except perhaps for Shaq's kids. Another problem: the tray sits 8″ from the back seat, creating a gap the size of the Grand Canyon between your baby and her food. Then let's talk about this chair's cleanability—it's notorious for collecting food in every little nook and cranny. All this for $160 to $180! Wow, what a deal. Perego hasn't really changed this seat much in recent years, besides adding a rocking feature to the chair. And a parent needs a high chair that rocks . . . because? We don't see the point. Ditto for the Dondolino Prima Pappa, a version of the Pappa that runs on C batteries and has music for $250.

New this year, Perego will release a new high chair model dubbed the Mirenda. This model will be a scaled down version of the Pappa, which will feature a reclining seat, dishwasher-safe tray liner and more compact fold. The Mirenda will sell for $130. Interesting side note: the Mirenda is being produced in Brazil (all other Perego products are still made in Italy).

So, we're not wild on this brand for high chairs. Instead of innovating in this category, Perego has been content to rest on its laurels . . . while competitors have knocked it off with better products at a lower price. Bottom line: if you like the looks of the Perego, save yourself $50 and get the Chicco Polly instead—same styling, just easier to use and clean. **Rating: C+**

Safety 1st. These high chairs are made by Cosco, reviewed earlier in this chapter.

Svan of Sweden *For a dealer near you, call 866-782-6222; web: www. scandinavianchild.com* Svan is the latest multi-function high chair imported from Europe. But, the Svan Chair is unique for a couple of reasons: first, it  is all wood, including the tray. Second, the high chair converts to a toddler chair and finally a chair for older kids. Clever, but we worry about the clean up with that wood tray. On the plus side, it is available in three finishes (natural, cherry and whitewash) as well as three

HIGH CHAIRS

High chairs, compared

NAME	RATING	PRICE	TRAY HEIGHT	TRAY DEPTH
BABY TREND	B-	$90	8″	7.5
CHICCO POLLY	A-	$100-$130	8	7.5
COMBI BREEZE	C	$90	7.5	7.5
EDDIE BAUER	A-	$100	9″	8
EVENFLO ENVISION	D	$50	6.5	5
EVENFLO SIMPLICITY	D	$80-$100	7.5	5.5
FISHER PRICE HEALTHY CARE	A	$90	8	5
FISHER PRICE SPACE SAVER	A	$50	*	*
GRACO HARMONY	B	$70-$90	8.5	8
GRACO CONTEMPORARY	B	$100-$130	*	*
KOLCRAFT RECLINE DINE	C+	$30-$50	8.5	6
PEG PEREGO PRIMA PAPPA	C+	$160-$180	9	8
ZOOPER PEAS CARROTS	B-	$150	9	8.5

KEY

TRAY HEIGHT: Distance from the seat to the top of the tray. Any measurement under 8″ is acceptable. Above 8″ is too tall.
DEPTH (tray to seat): Distance from the back of the seat to the tray. 5″ to 7″ is acceptable.
KICK? Can the tray be kicked off by a child? Thanks to poorly-designed one-hand tray releases, trays with pull releases and without kick guards can be trouble. If this is "yes," we judge that the tray can be kicked off by a toddler. Note: this isn't a safety hazard; more like a hassle for parents, as you might guess.
SUB?: Most high chairs have a special guard to prevent a child from submarining under the tray. Some chairs attach this to the

colors (red, blue and black). We know some folks will go for this chair for the looks alone . . . but be prepared to lay out some serious cash. The basic chair (18 months and up) goes for $160. But if you want to use it has a high chair for babies six months and up, you have to pay another $50 for an "infant kit." A matching cushion to make that wood seat more comfortable will run another $30. Total price: $240. As a result, this chair has rather limited appeal. That said, parent reviews of the Svan are favorable, so we will give it a good rating. ***Rating: A-***

Kick?	Sub?	Pad	Comment
No	Seat	Cloth	Pad should be air dried
No	Tray	Vinyl	$120 version has double pad
No	Seat	Vinyl	Tray doesn't fold flat
No	Seat	Cloth	Wood with plastic tray
No	Seat	Vinyl	Low price but flimsy seat pad
Yes	Seat	Cloth	Swing out snack tray
No	Seat	Vinyl**	Best bet; comes in 3 versions
No	Seat	Vinyl	Attaches to chair
No	Seat	Vinyl	Contoured design
No	Seat	*	Narrowest fold on market
No	Tray	Cloth	Lowest price; Grandma option?
Yes	Seat	Vinyl	Style leader; many colors
No	Tray	Vinyl	Stylish, but doesn't fold compact

chair; others to tray. A better bet: those that attach to the seat. See discussion earlier in this chapter.

Pad: Is the seat made of cloth or vinyl? We prefer vinyl for easier clean up. Cloth seats must be laundered and some can't be thrown in the drier (requiring a long wait for it to line dry). Of course, this feature isn't black and white—some vinyl seats have cloth edging/piping.

* These models were new as of press time, so we didn't have these specs yet.

** This model has a vinyl seat with cloth piping.

Zooper For a dealer near you, call 503-248-9469; web: www.zooperstrollers.com. Following Combi from the stroller world to the planet of high chairs, Zooper recently introduced their own spin on this category with the cutesy name "Peas & Carrots." Its ultra-cool look (black leatherette vinyl cover and brushed aluminum frame; it also comes in  several other colors) has had a few of our readers buzzing. It features four height positions, mesh basket, five-point harness and locking wheels. Unfortunately, it is quite pricey ($150 retail, although readers have spied it on sale for less). Another bummer: the chair doesn't fold as flat as the Italian chairs and, when folded, the basket sticks out a good four inches from the chair. The result: when folded, the Peas & Carrots doesn't stand because it isn't balanced. And we aren't wild about the tray height (too tall at 9″) nor the seat depth (8.5″ from the back of the seat to the tray). The passive restraint is on the tray instead of the seat, which is another negative. That said, parents who've used this chair say it functions well and is easy to clean. The seat is vinyl "leatherette," which is washable (but not machine dryable). Yes, it is hard to find (no chain stores carry it as of this writing), but it might be worth a look if you see it at a specialty store. **Rating: B-**

◆ **Other Brands**. Looking for a wood high chair? Once common, wooden high chairs were just about hunted to extinction in the 1990's, as plastic and metal models took over the category. But today, wood is creeping back. We discussed the **Eddie Bauer** model earlier (which is a good bet), but here are several other options.

Kettler is a brand better known in this country for their tricycles, but their Tipp Topp high chair (pictured) has won fans for its simple design. We found it for $170 at BabyUniverse.com, which also carried wooden high chairs by **DaVinci** (Million Dollar Baby) for $85 to $100 and **Rochelle** for $180. Parents who like these wood high chairs seem to value the aesthetic of the chair over func-  tionality. But if have your heart set on wood, those chairs (especially the Eddie Bauer) will do the trick!

Our Picks: Brand Recommendations

Here is our round up of the best high chair bets.

Good. The Fisher-Price Close to Me ($60) or Easy to Clean ($80) are good buys that are well-designed and durable.

Better. Chicco's "Polly" high chair is an improvement over their last effort and lands a spot as number two on our recommended list. Chicco has lowered the tray, added a compact fold and re-designed the tray for easy one-hand removal. Yep, the price is more than the Fisher Price pick we discuss next ($100 to $130, depending on the version) . . . but we'd bet many folks will view this chair's styling and fashion as worthy of the upgrade.

Best. The Fisher-Price Aquarium Healthy Care has got it all—great safety features, easy of use, cleanability and more. We like the snap-off dishwasher-safe tray, good design and easy-to-clean vinyl pad. A decent buy at $90. The only drawback: you have to like the like the cutesy blue fashion.

Grandma's house. For grandma's house, a simple Kolcraft Recline and Dine ($30) should do the trick. No, it doesn't have casters or other fancy features, but Grandma doesn't need all that.

The Bottom Line:
A Wrap-Up of Our Best Buy Picks

What's the more affordable way to feed baby? Breastfeeding, by a mile. We estimate you can save $500 in just the first six months alone by choosing to breast instead of bottle-feed.

Of course, that's easy for us to say—breastfeeding takes some practice, for both you and baby. One product that can help: a breast pump, to relieve engorgement or provide a long-term solution to baby's feeding if you go back to work. Which pumps are best? For manual pumps, we like the Avent Isis ($45) for that occasional bottle. If you plan to pump so you can go back to work, a professional-grade pump works best. Tip: rent one first before you buy. If you like it and decide you are serious about pumping, we liked the Medela Pump In Style Advanced ($270 to $300) or Ameda Purely Yours (about $150 to $180).

If you decide to bottle feed or need to wean your baby off breast milk, the most affordable formulas are the generic brands like BabyMil sold in discount stores under various private-label names. You'll save up to 40% by choosing generic over name brands, but your baby gets the exact same nutrition.

Who makes the best bottles? Our readers say Avent is tops, but others find cheaper options like Playtex and Munchkin Health Flow work just was well at half the price. A dark horse brand: Dr. Brown's bottles, which help eliminate colic.

Let's talk baby food—besides the ubiquitous Gerber, there are several other brands that are good alternatives. One of the best is Earth's Best, although it is more pricey than affordable brands like Del Monte's Nature's Goodness and Beechnut. How can you save? Make your own baby food for pennies or buy jarred baby food in bulk at discount stores. And skip the toddler meals, which are a waste of money.

Finally, consider that quintessential piece of baby gear—the high chair. We felt the best bets were those that were easiest to clean (go for a vinyl, not cloth pad) and had snap-off dishwasher-safe trays. Our top pick is the Fisher Price Aquarium Healthy Care ($90), although the Chicco "Polly" ($100 to $130) is a stylish alternative.

Now that you've got the food and kitchen covered, what about the rest of your house? We'll explore all the other baby gear you might need for your home next.

CHAPTER 7

Around the House: Monitors, Diaper Pails, Safety & More

Inside this chapter

W hat's the best bathtub for baby? Which baby monitor can save you $40 a year in batteries? What's the
best—and least stinky—diaper pail? In this chapter, we
explore everything for baby that's around the house. From
bouncer seats to the best baby monitors, we'll give you
tricks and tips to saving money. You'll learn about playpens
and swings. Finally, let's talk safety—we'll give you tips and
advice on affordable baby proofing. So let's get cracking.

Getting Started: When Do You Need This Stuff?

The good news is you don't need all this stuff right away. While
you'll probably purchase a monitor before the baby is born, other
items like high chairs, activity seats, and even bath-time products
aren't necessary immediately (you'll give the baby sponge baths for
the first few weeks, until the belly button area heals). Of course, you
still might want to register for these items before baby is born. In
each section of this chapter, we'll be more specific about when you
need certain items.

What Are You Buying?

Here is a selection of items that you can use when your baby is
three to six months of age. Of course, these ideas are merely suggestions—none of these items are "mandatory." We've divided
them into two categories: bath-time and the baby's room.

Bath

1 **TOYS/BOOKS.** What fun is taking a bath without toys? Many stores sell inexpensive plastic tub toys, but you can use other items like stacking cups in the tub as well. And don't forget about tub safety items, which can also double as toys. For example, Safety 1st (800) 739-7233 (www.safety1st.com) makes a **Bath Pal Thermometer**, a yellow duck or tugboat with attached thermometer (to make sure the water isn't too hot) for $1.50 at Kmart. *Tubbly Bubbly* by Kel-Gar (972) 250-3838 (web: www.kelgar.com) is a $10 elephant or hippo spout cover that protects against scalding, bumps and bruises. In fact, Kel-Gar makes an entire line of innovative bath toys and accessories.

2 **TOILETRIES**. Basic baby shampoo like the famous brand made by Johnson & Johnson works just fine, and you'll probably need some lotion as well. The best tip: first try lotion that is unscented in case your baby has any allergies. Also, never use talcum powder on your baby—it's a health hazard. If you need to use an absorbent powder, good old cornstarch will do the trick.

What about those natural baby products that are all the rage, like Mustela or Calidou? We got a gift basket of an expensive boutique's natural baby potions and didn't see what the big deal was. Worse yet, the $20-a-bottle shampoo dried out our baby's scalp so much he had scratching fits. We suppose the biggest advantage of these products is that they don't contain extraneous chemicals or petroleum by-products. Also, most don't have perfumes, but then, many low-price products now come in unscented versions. The bottom line: it's your comfort level. If you want to try them out without making a big investment, register for them as a shower gift.

If you have a history of allergies or skin problems in your family, consider washing baby's skin and hair with Dove or Ivory bar soap. Cetaphil is also a good mild soap. These do not contain detergents that you find in even the most basic baby shampoo.

3 **BABY BATHTUB.** While not a necessity, a baby bathtub is a nice convenience (especially if you are bathing baby solo). See the section below for more info on bathtubs.

4 **POTTY SEAT.** Since this book focuses on products for babies age birth to 2, we have put this topic in our other book *Toddler Bargains,* now in bookstores. You'll find an entire chapter devoted to reviews and ratings of the best potty seats!

Safe & Sound

◆ **BATH SEATS SHOULD NOT BE USED.** It looks innocuous—the baby bath seat—but it can be a disaster waiting to happen. These seats suction to the bottom of a tub, holding baby in place while she takes a bath. The problem? Parents get a false sense of security from such items and often leave the bathroom to answer the phone, etc. We've seen several tragic reports of babies who've drowned when they fell out of the seats (or the seats became un-suctioned from the tub). The best advice: AVOID these seats and NEVER leave baby alone in the tub, even for just a few seconds.

Baby Bathtubs

Sometimes, it is the simplest products that are the best. Take baby bathtubs—if you take a look at the offerings in this category, you'll note tubs that have "4 in 1" uses, fold up and convert to small compact cars. Okay, just kidding on the car, but these products are a good example of brand manager overkill—companies think the way to success with baby bath tubs is to make them work from birth to college.

So, it is a bit of a surprise that our top pick for a baby bathtub is, well, just a bathtub. The *EuroBath by Primo* ($25; web: www.primob-aby.com; see right) is a sturdy tub for babies age birth to two. It weighs less than two pounds and is easy to use—just add baby, water and poof! Clean baby. The EuroBath is well designed, although it is big—almost three feet from end to end. It may be a tight fit if you have a small bathroom. In that case, you might want to consider the *Comfy Duck Bath Center* by Safety 1st ($20; pictured). Nothing fancy, but it does have a foam liner and (as the name implies) a "ducky" sling to cra-dle a newborn. This might be a good choice for Grandma's house.

Got a big baby? Some parents tell us reg-ular bathtubs (like the Safety 1st tub mentioned above) don't work as well when Junior is a line-backer in training. So, try out the *First Years Sure Comfort Deluxe* tub ($15; see at right). It's no frills but does have an anti-slip backrest.

A baby bathtub is a great item to pick up second-hand or at a garage sale. Or borrow from a friend. Readers say they've snagged baby bath tubs for $2 or so at garage sales—with a little cleaning, they are just fine. What if you want to give baby a bath in a regular tub or kitchen sink? One reader writes with kudos for the **EZ Bather Deluxe** by Dex Products ($12, 800-546-1996; www.dex-products.com), an L-shaped vinyl frame that keeps babies head above water in the bathtub or kitchen sink.

Baby's Room

1   **A DIAPER PAIL.** Yes, there are dozens of diaper pails on the market. We'll review and rate the offerings in the next section.

2   **BABY MONITOR.** Later in this chapter, we have a special section devoted to monitors, including some creative money-saving tips. Of course, if you have a small house or apartment, you may not even need a baby monitor.

3   **THE CHANGING AREA.** The well-stocked changing area features much more than just diapers. Nope, you need wipes and lots of them. We discussed our recommendations for wipe brands in Chapter 4, the Reality Layette. We should note that we've heard from some thrifty parents who've made their own diaper wipes—they use old washcloths or cut-up cloth diapers and warm water.

What about wipe warmers? In previous editions of this book, we've recommended these $20 devices, which keep wipes at 99 degrees (and lessen the cold shock on baby's bottom at three in the morning). However, we've been concerned with safety issues about wipe warmers that have arisen in recent years.

First, Dex recalled a half million of their wipe warmers in 1997 after one fire was allegedly caused by the unit (there were six additional instances "involving melting of the product," says the CPSC). While Dex fixed the problem in January 1997, we were so miffed about how the company handled the recall, we won't recommend them again. (See the box on the next page).

Then, we started getting complaints from readers about another brand of wipe warmers (Prince Lionheart) that damaged dresser tops. Prince Lionheart blamed the problem on the little feet under the warmer, which were apparently leaving marks on the dresser tops when the unit warmed up. The company claims it has now fixed the problem (and denies that wipe warmers "burn" wipes—they say the heat discolors the chemicals in the wipes), but we're still leery of these products in general.

If you still want a wipe warmer, we'd go for a newer model

How NOT to Run a Recall

If we had to give an award for the Worst Recall of a Baby Product, the winner would have to be Dex, the California-based maker of wipe warmers and other baby products. In 1997, Dex recalled a popular wipe warmer, instructing parents to call a toll-free number. First, it took FOREVER to get through to Dex's hotline after the recall was announced. Then, after reaching a human, we were instructed to call Halcyon, Dex's supplier in Canada (who actually manufactured the wipe warmer). At Halcyon, a not-too-helpful person who answered the phone told us we had to send our request for a replacement wipe warmer to Canada. The piece de resistance: the Halcyon folks didn't tell us to keep the warmer COVER, which we sent back with the recalled unit. So, the heating element they sent back *sans cover* was useless. Dex is a textbook case of how NOT to run a recall. Having your customers call your supplier in another country to fix a defective product you sold is a new low in customer service.

instead of a hand-me-down because of past safety recalls. Also: newer models from makers like Prince Lionheart work better to keep wipes moist and avoid discoloration. Better yet: just skip it.

Other products to consider for the diaper changing station include diaper rash ointment (A & D, Desitin, etc.), lotion or cream, cotton swabs, petroleum jelly (for rectal thermometers) and rubbing alcohol to care for the belly button area (immediately remove this item from the changing area once you finish belly button care—it's poisonous!). If you have a Container Store nearby (800) 733-3532 (www.containerstore.com), we noticed they sell simple plastic storage containers for $4 to $20 for all those diaper changing station items. Target has also expanded their storage departments.

4 **PORTABLE CRIBS/PLAYPENS**. While this item doesn't necessarily go in your baby's room, many folks have found portable cribs/playpens to be indispensable in other parts of the house (or when visiting grandma). Later in this chapter, we have a special section devoted to this topic (see "playpens" on page 322).

5 **WHITE NOISE**. In the past, we noted that some parents swear they'd never survive without the ceiling fan in their baby's room—the "white noise" made by a whirling fan soothed their fussy baby (and quieted sounds from the rest of the house). We even recommended a white noise generator for babies who needed calming. However, in a study published in the journal *Science* (April 18, 2003), researchers say using white noise can be dangerous to your child's developing hearing. Our advice now is to avoid those white noise generators and find other ways to sooth your baby to sleep.

6 **HUMIDIFIER.** See our web page (babybargains.com; click on bonus material) for advice on buying a humidifier for baby's room.

Diaper Pails

Pop quiz! Remember our discussion of how many diapers you will change in your baby's first year? What was the amount?

Pencils down—yes, it is 2300 diapers! A staggering figure . . . only made more staggering by figuring out what do with the dirty ones once you've changed baby. Yes, we can hear first-time parents raising their hands right now and saying "Duh! They go in the trash!" Oh, not so fast, new parental one. Stick a dirty diaper in a regular trashcan and you will quickly perfume your home—not to mention draw a curious pet and we won't even go there.

So, most parents use a diaper pail, that specialized trashcan designed by trained scientists to limit stink and keep out babies, pets and stray relatives. But which diaper pail? Here's our Diaper Pail 411:

Diaper pails fall into two camps: those that use cartridges to wrap diapers in deodorized plastic and pails that use regular kitchen trash bags. As you'd guess, those plastic refill canisters are more expensive to use (they cost $4 to $8, depending on the size) and wrap about 140 or so diapers. The pail can hold 20-25 diapers at a time, which is about three days worth of diapers.

So, should you just get a diaper pail that uses regular kitchen trash bags? Yes, they are less expensive to use—but there is sometimes a major trade-off. Stink. These pails tend to stink more and hence, have to be emptied more frequently than the diaper pails that use special deodorized plastic—perhaps daily or every other day.

Obviously, the decision on which diaper pail is right for you and your baby's nursery depends on several factors. What is the distance to the trash? If you live in a house with easy access to an outside trashcan, it might be easier to go with the lower-cost alternatives and just take out the diapers more frequently. If you live in an apartment where the nearest dumpster is down three flights of stairs and a long walk across a parking lot, well, it might make sense to go with an option that requires less work. Another factor: how sensitive are you to the smell? Some folks don't have a major problem with this, while moms who are pregnant again with a second child may need an industrial strength diaper pail to keep from losing it when walking into baby's nursery.

Whatever your decision, remember you'll live with this diaper pail for three or more YEARS (that's how long before most children potty train). And it's a fact of life: diapers get stinkier as your baby gets older . . . so the diaper removal strategy that works for a newborn may have to be chucked for a toddler. Yes, you may be able to use a plain trashcan with liner when your newborn is breast-feeding . . . but after you start solid foods, it will be time to buy a diaper pail.

Given those caveats, here is an overview of what's out there:

DIAPER CHAMP BY BABY TREND

Type: Kitchen trash bag.

Price: $30. Web: www.BabyTrend.com.

Pros: Did we mention no expensive refills? The Diaper Champ uses regular ol' kitchen bags, yet the contraption works to seal out odor by using a flip handle design. Very easy to use. Taller design means it holds more diapers than the Genie.

Cons: Not as stink-free as the Genie or Dekor, but close. Enterprising toddlers can learn how to put their toys into the diaper slot.

Comments: And in this corner. . . let's crown a new champ for diaper pails—the Diaper Champ by Baby Trend. It's simple design and ease of use wins fans, although a few detractors note it isn't as stink-free as the Genie or Dekor. And you do have to empty it every few days (more often than the Genie or Dekor), despite the large capacity. That could be a hassle for apartment dwellers or those without handy access to an outside trashcan. We should also mention that one mom emailed us with a Diaper Champ tale of woe—her toddler figured out how to put toys into the top slot (which is uncovered), plopping them into the pail. Not pretty. We realize a cover might defeat the advantage of the one-hand feature, but perhaps Baby Trend could offer this as an accessory in the future. Despite the drawbacks, the vast majority of parents we interviewed felt this was the best diaper pail on the market and we agree.

Bottom line: Best pick if you want to go the kitchen trash bag route.

Rating: A

DIAPER DEKOR

Type: Refill canister

Price: $30 to $40. Refill packs are $17 and wrap 480 newborn diapers. Web: www.regallager.com

Pros: Hands free operation—you hit the foot petal and drop in a diaper. Large size can hold 5+ days worth of diapers. Converts to a regular trashcan after baby is done with diapers. Parents say it is much easier to use than the Diaper Genie,

diaper pails

reviewed below. And refills cost half as much as the Genie, on a per diaper basis. More attractive design than the Genie.

Cons: Still have to buy those expensive refill canisters.

Comments: The Diaper Dekor debuted in 2002 and is giving the Diaper Genie a good run for its money. It comes in two versions: a regular model and a "plus" version that is a few inches bigger/taller and holds more diapers. As for the stink factor, the jury is still out on this one—some parents say it is just as good as the Genie at odor control, while others think it isn't quite as effective. Overall, the Dekor does seem to get better marks for ease of use (love the foot petal idea) so we'll give it a slightly higher rating than the Genie. Plus we like the fact it can convert to a regular trashcan later after the diaper days are over.

Bottom line: A worthy alternative to the Genie.

Rating: A-

DIAPER GENIE BY PLATYEX

Type: Refill canister

Price: $25 to $30. Refill cartridges are $4 to $8 and wrap about 140 diapers (although this varies by size). Web: www.playtexbaby.com

Pros: Tops at stink control. Wraps each diaper in deodorized plastic; dirty diapers plop out the bottom like a chain of sausages. That makes it easier to carry them to the trash. Used properly, there is very little odor from the Genie. Newer Genies feature a wider-mouth opening, making it easier to use. Playtex also offers special refills for toddlers (they have a green top) with more odor control.

Cons: Expensive, since you have to keep buying those refills. Some parents complain it is difficult to use—you have to twist the top to seal the diaper, etc. Since the Genie can hold several days' worth of diapers, parents complain when they OPEN it to remove the diapers, the smell is overwhelming.

Comments: Yes, the Diaper Genie is the #1 best-selling diaper pail in the country and we did recommend it in the past several editions of this book. But, the competition has caught up with the Genie and now there are several credible alternatives. When you talk to parents about the Diaper Genie, you get strong love/hate reactions. Fans think it is the best thing since sliced bread. Detractors complain bitterly about the extra cost of those refill cartridges and some parents find it hard to use (yes, it does have detailed instructions with pictures, but it still confounds some folks). And we've been disappointed that Playtex hasn't made any improvements to this product in the last few years—it could stand a re-design to keep up with the competition.

Bottom line: A favorite that is showing its age. We still recommend the Diaper Genie, although we will give the Diaper Dekor and Diaper Champ slightly higher ratings for their ease of use and lower cost.
Rating: B+

Neat! Diaper disposal system by Safety 1st
Type: Refill canister.
Price: $20 to $25 for the pail; $5 for refills.
Pros: Seven-layer bag and double clamp system really keeps out the stink. Easier to use than the Diaper Genie. The pail holds about 20 diapers, which means you'll have to empty it out every 2-3 days.
Cons: No hand-free operation—you have to push the dirty diaper down beyond the clamp. And you'll be shelling out $5 for those refill canisters for a long while. Some parents complain that the Neat wastes refill bags due to poor design.
Comments: The Neat! diaper disposal system by Safety 1st replaces Cosco's last effort at this category, the Diaper Nanny. The Neat pail, while an improvement over the awful Diaper Nanny, is still hobbled by complaints, according to our research. Parents gripe about several problems (noted above), but chief among them is the lack of hand-free operation like the Dekor. And that can get rather gross, as you might expect. Another problem: several parents told us their Neat broke after just a few months, which echoes quality woes that dog other Dorel/Cosco products (the Safety 1st moniker is one of Dorel's brands). So, with more comprehensive feedback on this pail, we will lower the Neat's rating this time out.
Rating: B-

◆ **Other brands**. We should also mention that Cosco makes a simple diaper pail under its own name (model 09-108-WHO; pictured at left). This no-frills pail has a foot petal and built-in deodorizer, which is a joke. On the plus side, it is cheap: $9.

Fisher Price made an "Odor Free" diaper pail that was anything but—fortunately, it is now discontinued. If you see one online or in a discount store, we'd suggest skipping it.

Bonus Material Online: Humidifiers, Toys, Pets

We've got more advice than we've got room in this chapter. On our web site, BabyBargains.com, click on Bonus Material to read more:

◆ *Humidifiers.* What's the best choice for baby's room? We will give you a buyer's guide.

◆ *Toys.* Read our top 8 picks for toys (including crib mobiles) online. Also online: toy money saving tips, wastes of money and the best mail-order catalogs for toys.

◆ *Pet Meets Baby.* Got a pet? How do you introduce your dog or cat to baby? We've got tips and advice on smoothing the transition.

◆ *Baby Announcements.* We've got affordable baby announcement sites, advice for adopting parents and more.

Bouncer Seat/Activity Gyms

◆ **ACTIVITY GYM.** Among our favorites is the *Gymini by Tiny Love* (for a dealer near you, call 800-843-6292; web: www.tinylove.com). The Gymini is a three-foot square blanket that has two criss-cross arches. You clip rattles, mirrors and other toys onto the arches, providing endless fun for baby as she
lies on her back and reaches for the fun items. The Gymini comes in four different versions: a basic version in black, white and red is $40 and the "super deluxe" model (a Noah's Ark Design) is about $60. The more expensive versions have more toys, including ones with sound and lights. Another plus for the Gymini: it folds up quickly and easily for trips to Grandma's.

◆ **ACTIVITY SEAT/BOUNCER WITH TOY BAR.** An activity seat (also called a bouncer) provides a comfy place for baby while you eat dinner, and the toy bar adds some mild amusement. The latest twist to these products is a "Magic Fingers" vibration feature—the bouncer basically vibrates, simu-
lating a car ride. Parents who have these bouncers tell us they'd rather have a kidney removed than give up their vibrating bouncer, as it appears the last line of defense in soothing a fussy baby short of checking into a mental institution.

What features should you look for in a bouncer? Readers say a carrying handle is a big plus. Also: get a neutral fabric pattern, says another parent, since you'll probably be taking lots of photos of baby and a garish pattern may grate on your nerves.

Coupon deals cut the cost of online shopping

How do baby product web sites generate traffic and sales? One tried and true method is the online coupon—a special discount, either in dollars or percentage off deals. Sites offer these as come-ons for new customers, returning customers . . . just about anyone. Coupons enable sites to give discounts without actually lowering the prices of merchandise. You enter the coupon code when you place the order and zap! You've saved big.

How big? Well, when the Internet gold rush was on in the late 90's, some sites were going nuts with coupons—like $50 off a $60 purchase for first-time customers! Or 30% off and free shipping. Those steals are gone, but good deals are still out there. How do you find them? You don't have to spend hours surfing; instead just visit coupon web sites—these sites track deals on other sites.

A good example for baby products is DotDeals (www.dotdeals.com). Their special section on "Kids & Toys" lets you see all the current deals at a glance. A recent scan of the site revealed $10 off a $30 purchase at a big baby products web site, 30% off any purchase at another site and even 25% off a purchase at a toy web site if you use American Express. Some deals are for first-time customers; others are for anyone. Just note the coupon code (a series of letters and numbers) and the expiration date and you're on your way.

"But," you say, "Alan and Denise, please give us more coupon sites!" Okay, check out: Flamingo World (www.flamingoworld. com), Just Wright Gifts (www.justwrightgifts.com), and It's Raining Bargains (www.itsrainingbargains.com).

Readers have recommended Deal of the Day (www.DealOfDay.com), eDealFinder (www. eDealFinder.com), ImegaDeals (www.ImegaDeals.com), Big Big Savings (www.BigBigSavings. com), Fat Wallet (www.FatWallet.com), and Clever Moms (www.CleverMoms.com).

One reader's favorite site for coupon deals is MomsView.com, if you can get past the text-heavy graphic design. "I have subscribed to their email newsletters," she told us. "It's great for a quick 20% off coupon, free shipping and so on while shopping online." If you'd like more organization, try CurrentCodes.com. That site lets you sort deals by merchant, alphabetically or by category. Before you place an order line, give this site a quick look to make sure you aren't missing out on any deals or coupons!

Finally, check our message boards at BabyBargains.com. There you'll find a special board on coupon deals found by our readers. Now, go fire up the browser and start saving!

What is the best brand for bouncers? Fisher Price (www.fisher-price.com) makes the most popular one in the category; most are about $20 to $60, depending on the version. A good choice: the **Linkadoos bouncer** ($25) for basic duty or the **Baby Papasan Infant Seat** ($45 to $60) if you want something more plush. Yes, other companies make similar products (Summer makes one for $35, Combi has some ranging in price from $40 to $80 version, etc.) but the feedback we get from parents is that Fisher-Price is the best.

The only caveat: most bouncer seats have a 25 pounds weight limit. If you want something that will last longer, consider the **Baby Bjorn Babysitter 1-2-3**. Yes, it is more pricey (anywhere from $85 to $150, depending on the store) and lacks a vibrating feature . . . but you can use it up to 29 lbs. Fisher-Price does have a bouncer that can even be used up to 40 lbs—the **Learning Patterns Infant-to-Toddler** rocker (pictured). It's a great deal at $30. Parent feedback on that model (as with most Fisher Price bouncers) is very positive.

Here's another money-saving tip: turn your infant car seat into an activity center with an attachable toy bar. Tiny Love makes a toy bar with soft steering wheel, phone and airplane toys for $30. Infantino's car seat toy bar has detachable toys for $20. Lamaze also has a car seat toy that velcros to the seat. It includes crinkle and jingle toys, as well as a teether for $20. Another plus: your baby is safer in an infant car seat carrier than in other activity seats, thanks to that industrial-strength harness safety system. Safety warning: only use these toy bars when the car seat is NOT inside a vehicle (that is, at home, etc.). Toy bars are not safe in a vehicle as they can be a hazard/projectile in an accident.

Monitors

For her first nine months, your baby is tethered to you via the umbilical cord. After that, it's the baby monitor that becomes your surrogate umbilical cord—enabling you to work in the garden, wander about the house, and do many things that other, childless human beings do, while still keeping tabs on a sleeping baby. Hence, this is a pretty important piece of equipment you'll use every day—a good one will make your life easier . . . and a bad one will be a never-ending source of irritation.

Smart Shopper Tips for Monitors

Smart Shopper Tip #1
Bugging your house

"My neighbor and I both have babies and baby monitors. No matter what we do, I can still pick up my neighbor's monitor on my receiver. Can they hear our conversations too?"

You better bet. Let's consider what a baby monitor really is: a radio transmitter. The base unit is the transmitter and the receiver is, well, a receiver. So anyone with another baby monitor can often pick up your monitor—not just the sound of your baby crying, but also *any* conversations you have with your mate in the nursery.

You'll notice that many monitors have two channels "to reduce interference," and some even have high and low range settings—do they help reduce eavesdropping? No, not in our opinion. In densely populated areas, you can still have problems.

We should note that you can also pick up baby monitors on many cordless phones—even police scanners can pick up signals as far as one or two miles away. The best advice: remember that your house (or at least, your baby's room) is bugged. If you want to protect your privacy, don't have any sensitive conversations within earshot of the baby monitor. You never know who might be listening.

Are there any monitors on the market that scramble their signal for privacy? Until just recently, the answer was no. But there is good news: several new models debuting this year feature "digital" technology—their signals can't be intercepted, unlike older analog monitors. See later in this chapter for details.

What about higher frequency monitors—are they harder to intercept? Well, yes and no. A 900 MHz or 2.4 GHz monitor may be a bit harder to snoop on with a police scanner, but if your neighbor has the exact same model, guess what? They can probably hear everything in your house (that is, unless you have one of the newer digital models, as discussed earlier).

The best advice: only turn on your monitor when baby is napping. Leaving it on all day means others can listen in to every noise and sound.

Smart Shopper Tip #2
Battery woes

"Boy, we should have bought stock in Duracell when our baby was born! We go through dozens of batteries each month to feed our very hungry baby monitor."

Most baby monitors have the option of running on batteries or on regular current (by plugging it into a wall outlet). Our advice: use the wall outlet as often as possible. Batteries don't last long—as little as eight to ten hours with continual use. Another idea: you can buy another AC adapter from a source like Radio Shack for $10 or less—you can leave one AC adapter in your bedroom and have another one available in a different part of the house. (Warning: make sure you get the correct AC adapter for your monitor, in terms of voltage and polarity. Take your existing AC adapter to Radio Shack and ask for help to make sure you are getting the correct unit. If not, you can fry your monitor).

Another solution: several new baby monitors (reviewed later in this chapter) feature rechargeable receivers! You'll never buy a set of batteries for these units—you just plug them into an outlet to recharge it.

Smart Shopper Tip #3
Cordless compatibility

"We have a cordless phone and a baby monitor. Boy, it took us two weeks to figure out how to use both without having a nervous breakdown."

If we could take a rocket launcher and zap one person in this world, it would have to be the idiot who decided that baby monitors and cordless phones should share the same radio frequency. What were they thinking? Gee, let's take two people who are already dangerously short of sleep and make them real frustrated!

So, here are our tips to avoid frustration:

First, realize the higher the frequency, the longer the range of the monitor. Basic baby monitors work on the 49 MHz frequency—these will work for a few hundred feet. Step up to a 900 MHz monitor and you can double the distance the monitor will work (some makers claim up to 1000 feet). Finally, there are baby monitors that work on the 2.4 GHz frequency, where you can pick up your baby in Brazil. Ok, not that far, but you get the idea. Of course, "range" estimates are just that—your real-life range will probably be much less than what's touted on the box.

Now here's the rub: cordless phones can often interfere with your baby monitor. Old cordless phones worked on the 49 MHz frequency, but modern models are more likely to be found in the 900 MHz or the 2.4 GHz (or even 5.8 GHz) bands. If you've got a baby monitor at 900 MHz and a cordless phone on the same frequency, expect trouble. Ironically, as more and more devices use the higher frequency, the old 49 MHz for baby monitors now seems to be the most trouble free when it comes to interference.

So, to sum up, here is our advice: first, try to buy a baby monitor on a different frequency than your cordless phone. Second, always keep the receipt. Baby monitors have one of the biggest complaint rates of all products we review. We suspect all the electronic equipment in people's homes today (cell phones, wireless computer networks, fax machines, large-screen TV's the size of a Sony Jumbotron), not to mention all the interference sources near your home (cell phone towers, etc.) must account for some of the problems folks have with baby monitors. Common complaints include static, lack of range, buzzing sounds and worse—and those problems can happen with a baby monitor in any price range.

So, read our monitor recommendations later with a grain of salt. ANY monitor (even those we rate the highest) can still run into static and interference problems, based on what electronics are in your home.

Again, the best advice: always keep the receipt for any baby monitor you buy—you may have to take it back and exchange it for another brand if problems develop.

Smart Shopper Tip #4
The one-way dilemma

"Our baby monitor is nice, but it would be great to be able to buzz my husband so he could bring me something to drink while I'm feeding the baby. Are there any monitors out there that let you communicate two ways?"

Yep, Evenflo, Graco and Safety 1st have models that do just that (see reviews later in this chapter). Of course, there is another alternative: you can always go to Radio Shack and buy a basic intercom for about $40. Most also have a "lock" feature that you can leave on to listen to the baby when he's sleeping. Another advantage to intercoms: you can always deploy the unit to another part of your house after you're done monitoring the baby. Of course, the only disadvantage to intercoms is that they aren't portable—most must be plugged into a wall outlet.

Here are other features to consider when shopping for monitors:

◆ **Out of range indicators.** If you plan to wander from the house and visit your garden, you may want to go for a monitor that warns you when you've strayed too far from its transmitter. Some models have a visual out of range indicator, while others beep at you. Of course, even if your monitor doesn't offer this feature, you'll probably realize when you're out of range—the background noise you hear in your home will disappear from the receiver.

◆ *Low battery indicator.* Considering how quickly monitors can eat batteries, you'd think this would be a standard feature for monitors. Nope—very few current models actually warn you when you're running out of juice. Most units will just die. At this writing, only the Phillips monitors (reviewed later) have this feature.

◆ *What's the frequency?* As we discussed above, the right or wrong frequency can make a world of difference. Before selecting a monitor, think about the wireless gadgets you have in your home (particularly cordless phones). Then look carefully at packages . . . not all monitors put that info up front.

◆ *Extra receivers.* It is convenient to leave one receiver in your bedroom and then tote around another receiver when wandering in the house.

◆ *Digital technology.* New models use digital technology to prevent easedropping by your neighbors.

◆ *Great, but not necessary.* Some monitors have a read-out of the temperature in the nursery, which might help you spot a nursery that's too warm. Others have an intercom feature . . . but we doubt the usefulness of this for most folks. And you'll see several new video monitors in the baby stores today—but the quality of the video is hardly HDTV, which limits its usefulness.

 More Money Buys You

Basic baby monitors are just that—an audio monitor and transmitter. No-frills monitors start at $20 or $25. More money buys you a sound/light display (helpful in noisy environments, since the lights indicate if your baby is crying) and rechargeable batteries (you can go through $50 a year in 9-volts with regular monitors). More expensive monitors even have transmitters that also work on batteries (so you could take it outside if you wish) or dual receivers (helpful if you want to leave the main unit inside the house and take the second one outside if you need to work in the garage, etc.). Finally, the top-end monitors either have 900 MHz technology (which extends range) or intercom features, where you can use the receiver to talk to your baby as you walk back to the room. In the last year or so, the most expensive monitors have added features to soothe a fussy baby—a sound and light show displayed on the nursery ceiling, for example. At the top end of the monitor market are units that monitor a baby's "movement" and sound an alarm if baby stops breathing.

And let's not forget the baby VIDEO monitor, as a slew of new entrants have debuted in the past year. Running $100 to $150, these models send a grainy picture of baby to a little TV monitor (or LCD screen) receiver. As we mentioned above, however, the quality of the video is so poor, the usefulness of these monitors is very limited.

The Name Game: Reviews of Selected Manufacturers

If you've ever looked at monitors, you might ask yourself, "What's the difference?" Most models have all the neat features that you want—belt clips, flexible antennas, two switchable channels. But, there are some differences as we mentioned above. We'll try to make some sense of these choices in the following reviews.

Major caveat to these reviews: ANY baby monitor, even those that earn our highest ratings, can have problems with static, poor reception or interference. Why? As we discussed earlier, houses today have a myriad of radio equipment (wireless computer network, anyone?), cell phones and other interference-causing sources. The best advice: keep your receipt and buy a monitor from a store with a good return policy. You may have to try a few different models/brands before finding one that works.

Shopping 'Bots

Okay, you know there are deals on the 'net. But where do you find them, short of searching for hours on baby product web sites? One idea: DealTime (www.dealtime.com). This free service (a shopping robot, or 'bot) has a special baby section. Click on this web site's "Babies & Kids" tab and do a search for monitors. Whamo! 30 prices for different baby monitors from a slew of different sites. Among the steals: a Wamsutta three piece cotton crib bedding set on Overstock.com for $50 a savings of 61%. DealTime lists sites that have free shipping with corresponding quick links.

Don't forget Google's Froogle search option. You can google an item, then hit the Froogle button. The search engine will display all the items that match your search along with prices. You can then arrange them from lowest to highest or highest to lowest and even display it in grid format. Put in your price range and Froogle will spit out matches that meet the criteria.

The Ratings

A **EXCELLENT**—*our top pick!*
B **GOOD**— *above average quality, prices, and creativity.*
C **FAIR**—*could stand some improvement.*
D **POOR**—*yuck! Could stand some major improvement.*

Evenflo *For a dealer near you, call (800) 233-5921 or (937) 415-3300. Web: www.evenflo.com* Evenflo's Whisper Connect monitors are well-designed and packed with features: all have rechargeable batteries, out-of-range indicators, low battery warnings and sound/light display. Evenflo makes three versions of these models: a basic monitor with one receiver ($22), a dual receiver model ($40) and a 900mhz "pro" version ($35 at Target). And there's even a "pet detection" version of this monitor (the Sensa) that "alerts consumers to unusual movement near baby." Price: $50. New this year is a model (the Tria) with dual receivers that can be used as walkie-talkies for $70. How's the quality? That's a mixed picture: *Consumer Reports* gave a previous version of the Evenflo monitor high marks, but our readers are less generous. Their complaints include static and an out-of-range beeper that goes off randomly among other gripes. And we're disappointed that Evenlfo hasn't joined the rest of the market with new digital monitors—again, the company is behind the curve. So we'll drop their rating this year and hope Evenflo joins the digital crowd shortly. ***Rating: B***

First Years *To find a dealer near you, call (800) 225-0382 or (508) 588-1220. Web: thefirstyears.com* First Years is a major player in the monitor market, with not one, not two but SEVEN models. These range from a basic 49 MHz model for $28 at Wal-Mart up to a new digital monitor for $60. First Years makes monitors in all the available frequencies: 49 MHz, 900 MHz, 2.4 GHz and digital, so picking one that won't interfere with your home tech gear should (theoretically) be easy. We like how innovative this line is. An example: the First Years 900 MHz attachable monitor ($40) can be attached to cribs, swings and other baby gear—that's unique. As mentioned, the new digital monitor is the first wave of future monitors that promise to eliminate interference (we'll have to see that to believe it). If you need a monitor with the longest range, the Clear & Near ($60, also called the Ultra Range Monitor . . . there will be a quiz on this later) boasts a 2.4 GHz signal with a 1500 range. FYI: be sure to pick a First Years model that has rechargeable batteries (not all their models have this). Our recommendation of First Years' monitors is tempered by our memories of the Great Monitor

Massacre of 2002—that year, we recommended one of First Years monitors, only to have the company run into production snafus that resulted in a flood of quality complaints. So, as always with any monitor, keep the receipt in case you need to return it. **Rating: B+**

Fisher Price *To find a dealer near you, call (800) 828-4000 or (716) 687-3000. Web: www.fisher-price.com* Fisher Price offers an impressive array of FIVE models, ranging from $20 to $50 (see a chart on this page for comparison of models/features). Our recommendation: stay with the simple units like the Sounds 'N Lights—this monitor comes in single ($20) and double ($30) receiver versions and features a sound/light display. Nothing fancy, but it does the trick. Also good: the 900 MHz Long-Range monitor ($35), which the company claims has three times the range of its regular monitors (it also has a more compact design with no bulky antenna). If you need a monitor with a longer range, Fisher Price's 2.4 GHz Ultimate Range monitor ($45) offers a 1500 foot range. We'd skip Fisher Price's most expensive monitor, the "The Aquarium Monitor with Smart Response" ($40). Like its similar predecessor (the Soothing Dreams), this monitor lets parents activate soothing music with a touch of a button on the parent's unit. The baby's unit then displays a light show on the ceiling above the crib (this turned off after a period of time). Nice idea, bad execution. The unit had a mind of its own, like something out of bad Stephen King made-for-TV movie. One mom said hers would come on in the middle of the night with the sound/light show . . . waking her sleeping baby! Others complained about static and popping noises from the receiver.

F-P's MONITORS	*An overview of Fisher Price's monitors*		
	Price	Dual Receiver	Range (in feet)
SOUND & LIGHTS	$20		400 FEET
DUAL SOUND/LIGHTS	$30	✔	400
900MHZ LONG-RANGE	$35		850
PRIVATE CONNECTION	$40		850
DUAL PRIVATE CONNECT.	$50	✔	850
AQUARIUM MONITOR	$40		400
2.4GHZ ULTIMATE	$50		1500

New this year, Fisher Price has launched a new 900 MHz model dubbed the "Private Connection" ($40 single, $50 dual). This model features rechargeable batteries and 10 channels to help eliminate interference. While that's nice, we're a bit disappointed that Fisher Price isn't debuting a digital monitor like First Years and Graco. Add this to the fact that most FP models lack rechargeable batteries and we're a bit disappointed with this year's line up. Quality of this line is good; of all the choices, we'd give the Private Connection model top billing, since it is one of the few FP models with rechargeable batteries. **Rating (for the Sound 'N Lights or 900 MHz units only): A-**

Graco *To find a dealer near you, call (800) 345-4109, (610) 286-5951. Web: www.gracobaby.com* Graco has been an also-ran in the monitor market for years, but now the brand has the chance to rocket past rivals like Fisher Price. Graco is debuting its first all-digital monitor (the iMonitor), which should be out by the time you read this. This $60 model will have a 2000 foot range and feature rechargeable batteries. Again, the key benefit is the digital technology, which will help stop interference and eavesdropping. Graco has four other monitors out now as well: an $90 dual version of the iMonitor with pager feature and out of range alarm, a $50 900 MHz monitor (the Respond) that records your voice, a $40 basic model (Décor) with temperature read out and front plates that swap out to match your nursery décor as well as a $30 49 MHz model (Ultra Clear II) with two parent units and rechargeable batteries. FYI: an older version of the Ultra Clear is still out that doesn't have rechargeable batteries. So, how's the quality? Graco's track record in this category has been rocky—parents seem to have more luck with Graco's simpler models when it comes to quality. All in all, we like the iMonitor best and think this might be the model to vault Graco back into the game here. **Rating: B+**

Mobicam *Web: www.getmobi.com* If a video baby monitor is on your wish list, we'd suggest Mobicam. This wireless 2.4 GHz camera sends a decent picture to a sharp LCD screen. It has night vision technology and is automatically voice activated (you can adjust the sensitivity). You can add three more cameras to the system (including an outdoor version for security) and there is optional PC software so you can monitor baby online if you wish. Mobicam sells for $200 in baby catalogs, but we noticed it online for $150 to $170. A reader who used Mobicam praised it overall, noting the only negative was interference when she ran her microwave. As always, buy any monitor (especially an expensive one like this) from a reputable store or web site that will let you return it if there are interference issues. **Rating: A**

Philips *This company withdrew from the monitor market in 2005.*

Safety 1st *To find a dealer near you, call (800) 962-7233 or (781) 364-3100. Web: www.safety1st.com* Safety 1st figures more is better with monitors—the company's monitor line at one point had TEN models, including several innovative combo video/audio monitors. In the last year, the company pared that back to five offerings, but you'll still see their older models sold in stores and online. You can find everything from a bare bones model with no sound and light display (Crystal Clear, $20-$25) to elaborate models with rechargeable batteries and 900 MHz technology. An example of the latter: the AnyWear Monitor whose ultra-compact receiver clips on a belt and features headphones, a vibrate feature, 900 MHz, and pager function. Price: $40.

Safety 1st has spent the last few years trying to innovate in this category and the results have been hit or miss. We like the 900 MHz Home Connection Monitor. This system lets you monitor up to THREE rooms at once, which is unique to the market. You also get two receivers—but it is pricey ($130). We had a reader test this one for us and she had positive results, but other parents told us they were less than happy (many complaints about static, clicking noises, and poor-quality reception volume).

On the other hand, Safety 1st's In-Reach Child Tracking system ($120) is for the truly paranoid. As you might guess from the name, this monitor sounds an alarm when the child strays too far from mom or dad. Isn't that what eyeballs are for?

A better bet is Safety 1st's new Digital Connection Monitor ($60), which features digital technology to stop interference and eavesdropping (as well as rechargeable batteries, LCD screen, sound/light display, low battery alarm and temperature readout). While this unit wasn't out as of this writing, we think this will be a winner.

Finally, we should note that Safety 1st has several video monitors out, including he Color-View Video monitor at a pricey $200. This monitor features a high-resolution color LCD screen and 2.4 GHz technology. We thought this (as with all video monitors) was overkill. **Rating: C**

Sony *Web: www.sonystyle.com* Sony has been a fringe player in the monitor market, thanks to prices that were always too high. But there is good news: Sony has woken up and lowered prices. The Baby Call monitor now comes in two versions: a nine channel non-rechargeable model (NTM-900, $40) and a 27-channel rechargeable model (NTM-910, $50). As you can guess from the names, the first one has nine selectable channels, the latter 27. That's rather amazing, as most monitors have at most TWO channels you can select from. The result is less chance for interference and that's what

monitors

parents seem to love about Sony's Baby Call monitors—they work without static, buzzing, clicking and all the other complaints you read about monitors. Between the two, we'd go for the $50 version with the rechargeable batteries. No, these models aren't packed with whiz-bang features, but they do have out of range indicators and an optional sound-activated mode that silences the receiver until sufficient noise activates it. Given the positive feedback for Sony's models, we'll give them our highest rating. ***Rating: A***

Summer *Web: www.summerinfant.com* Summer has come from out of nowhere to be a big player in the monitor market. Its claim to fame is video monitors, including a $100 black and white CRT version and a $170 handheld color LCD model. Both have night vision technology. While we give credit to Summer for bring down the price on video monitors (they used to run $300), we still found the video and audio quality on these units lacking. And parents seemed to agree— we received many complaints about static, poor quality reception and units that flat out broke after just a few months. Summer also

---

BABY MONITORS

A quick look at various features and brands

NAME	MODEL	PRICE
EVENFLO	WHISPER CONNECT	$22
	WHISPER CONNECT DUAL	$40
	WHISPER CONNECT PRO	$35
FIRST YEARS	CLEAR & NEAR	$60
	900 MHz ATTACHABLE	$40
GRACO	IMONITOR	$60-$90
	RESPOND	$50
	DECOR	$40
	ULTRA CLEAR II	$30
SAFETY 1ST	CRYSTAL CLEAR	$20-$25
	ANYWEAR	$40
	HOME CONNECTION	$130
SONY	BABY CALL NTM-900	$40
	BABY CALL NTM-910	$50
SUMMER	BABY'S QUIET SOUNDS	$30

✔ = Yes

SOUND/LIGHT: indicates whether the monitor has a sound and lights display. This additional visual clue helps determine if baby is crying when the receiver is in a noisy environment

makes audio-only monitors: in the past year, they've debuted three new models, including a $30 rechargeable 900 MHz model (Baby's Quiet Sounds) and a new digital 2.4 GHz model (Secure Sounds). Summers audio monitors didn't impress us. Given parent feedback, we can't give this brand more than an average rating. **Rating: C-**

◆ **Other Brands.** Breathing monitors first appeared on the market in the late 90's, pitching themselves as a way to prevent SIDS. One such model is the Angelcare ($75 at Sears and Wal-Mart). Angelcare uses a sensor pad that is slipped under the crib mattress to monitor baby's breathing. If the unit determines baby has stopped breathing for 20 seconds, the parent's unit sounds an audible alarm. There's also a function that sends an audible tick to the parent's unit with each breath baby takes (this can be turned off). It can also be used as a regular baby monitor (sound only) and features a sound/light display. So, should you rush out and buy one? We say no. The American Academy of Pediatrics says there is "no evidence" that breathing monitors are effective in stopping SIDS.

RECHARGE. BATT.	SOUND/LIGHT	900MHz	INTERCOM
✔	✔		
✔	✔		
✔	✔	✔	
✔	✔		
✔	✔	✔	
✔	✔		
✔	✔	✔	
✔			
✔	✔		
✔	✔	✔	
✔	✔	✔	✔
	✔	✔	
✔	✔	✔	
✔	✔	✔	

900MHZ: Most monitors work on the 46-49mhz frequency; some work on the 900mhz frequency, which eliminates interference with cordless phones and extended a monitor's range.

INTERCOM: Does the monitor have a two-way intercom feature?

*One version of the Graco Ultra Clear has 900mhz technology.

While your pediatrician may recommend a medical breathing monitor if you have a premature baby or a baby with series health problems, there's no evidence such gadgets help prevent Sudden Infant Death Syndrome in healthy babies, according to the AAP.

Our Picks: Brand Recommendations

Here are our picks for baby monitors, with one BIG caveat: how well a monitor will work in your house depends on interference sources (like cordless phones), the presence of other monitors in the neighborhood, etc. Since we get so many complaints about this category, it is imperative you buy a monitor from a place with a good return policy. Keep the receipts in case you have to make an exchange.

Good. The *Fisher Price "Sounds 'N Lights"* monitors are a good starting point. The basic version is $20; if you need two receivers, go for the $25 model that offers that feature. No, you don't get rechargeable batteries or fancy features like an intercom, but you do get a quality baby monitor that does its job well.

Better. Are the neighbors a bit too nosy? If so, you may want to consider a new digital monitor. Both Safety 1st and Graco will debut such models by the time you read this. Safety 1st's new *Digital Connection* monitor ($60) is loaded with all the features you expect in a high-end monitor (rechargeable batteries, low battery alarm, LCD screen, etc) but also features new digital technology to stop interference and eavesdropping. Graco's *iMontor* has similar features and the same price ($60) as the Safety 1st model. Either would be a good bet.

Best. If your house is buzzing with electronic equipment and you fear Baby Monitor Interference Hell, then it's time to check out our top-rated baby monitor, the *Sony BabyCall NTM-910*. Yea, it's a bit pricey at $50, but that

pays for a monitor with 27 selectable channels . . . odds are, one will work. Add in rechargeable batteries, an out of range indicator and very positive parent reviews and we've got a winner.

Video. *Mobicam* has the best video monitor on the market. Their wireless 2.4 GHz camera has the best quality, but you'll pay for it . . . this model runs $150 to $170. Sure, other video monitors are cheaper (prices start around $100), but considering the complaints we get about the quality of the cheapo options, better stick with Mobicam.

Twins. Need to monitor two or three different rooms in your house at once? The *Safety 1st Home Connection System* is a good, albeit pricey, solution at $130. Our tests of this monitor were positive, but we  noted other parents had less luck (hint: keep the receipt). Yet for parents of multiples, this is probably the best option out there.

Swings

You can't talk to new parents without hearing the heated debate on swings, those battery-operated or wind-up surrogate parents. Some think they're a godsend, soothing a fussy baby when nothing else seems to work. Cynics refer to them as "neglect-o-matics," sinister devices that can become far too addictive for a society that thinks parenting is like a microwave meal—the quicker, the better.

Whatever side you come down on, we do have a few shopping tips. First, ALWAYS try it before you buy. Give it a whirl in the store or borrow one from a friend. Why? Some babies love swings. Others hate 'em. Don't spend $120 on a fancy swing only to discover your little one is a swing-hater.

Should you buy a manual (wind-up) or battery operated swing? We've been impressed in the past few years with the improvements of wind-up swings. These units now work effectively with only a little effort on the part of a parent; so it's a toss-up whether you should get a manual or battery operated swing. You can save $20 with a wind-up instead of a battery-operated model, as well as the additional savings in batteries. Wind-up swings start at $45 and go up to $70; battery operated swings run $50 to $100. Second-hand stores are great places to look for deals on swings; we've seen some in good condition for just $20 (check with the CPSC at www.cpsc.gov for recalls before you buy second hand).

Remember to observe safety warnings about swings, which are close to the top ten most dangerous products as far as injuries go. You must always stay with your baby, use the safety belt, and stop using the swing once your baby reaches the weight limit (about 25 pounds in most cases). Always remember that a swing is not a baby-sitter.

Our picks: Brand recommendations

Swings today come in three flavors: full-size, compact or travel. As you might guess, the latter category folds up for easy transport. Each work fine—if you have the space, go for a full-size model. If not, try a compact or travel version.

Who makes the best swing? We'd give the award to **Graco**. This brand has a mind-numbing 28 choices in all three types. Quality-wise, these swings get the best marks from parents. The price difference usually has more to do with the amount of toys, music and other doo-dads that are added on to the models. The top of the  line Graco swing ($100 to $120) features six speeds, 15 musical tunes, and (we're not making this up) "cruise control." That last feature adjusts the swing to your baby's weight to ensure consistent speed. There's even an auto shut-off timer.

A good second bet would be the **Ocean Wonders Aquarium cradle swing by Fisher Price** with its two different motions and integrated mobile for $90. A similar model is the **Nature's Touch Baby Papasan Cradle Swing**, also by Fisher Price for about $130. (FYI: even though Fisher-Price calls these products a "cradle swing," that is really a misnomer. Baby  sits in a seat, rather than lying flat in a cradle—we do not recommend swings that incorporate a bassinet or cradle, as we believe it is not safe to have infant in a prone position in a swing).

How about a swing for Grandma's house? We like the **Take-Along Swing**, again by Fisher-Price. This cool swing folds up for portability, making it a good bet for $50 to $60.

Safety

Every parent wants to create a safe environment for their baby. And safety begins at the place where baby spends the most time—your home.

First, let's discuss the biggest safety hazards . . . and what baby products cause the most injury. Next, we'll give you our picks for that ubiquitous safety item, the baby gate. Finally, we'll discuss our tips for making your baby's toys safe.

Getting Started:
When Do You Need This Stuff?

Whatever you do, start early. It's never too soon to think about baby proofing your house. Many parents we interviewed admitted they waited until their baby "almost did something" (like playing with extension cords or dipping into the dog's dish) before they panicked and began childproofing.

Remember Murphy's Law of Baby Proofing: your baby will be instantly attracted to any object that can cause permanent harm. The more harm it will cause, the more attractive it will be to him or her. A word to the wise: start baby proofing as soon as your child begins to roll over.

Safe &Sound: Smart Baby Proofing Tips

safety

The statistics are alarming—each year, 100 children die and millions more are injured in avoidable household accidents. Obviously, no parent wants their child to be injured by a preventable accident, yet many folks are not aware of common dangers. Others think if they load up their house with safety gadgets, their baby will be safe. Yet, there is one basic truth about child safety: safety devices are no substitute for adult supervision. While this section is packed with safety must-haves like gates, keep you still have to watch your baby at all times.

Where do you start? Get down on your hands and knees and look at the house from your baby's point of view. Be sure to go room by room throughout the entire house. On our web site, BabyBargains.com (click on bonus material), we have room-by-room advice on how to baby proof on a shoestring.

Top 10 Baby Products That Should Be Banned

We asked Dr. Ari Brown, an award-winning pediatrician in Austin, TX and co-author of of our new book *Baby411* for a list of baby products that should be banned. Some are dangerous, others simply foolish and unnecessary. Here is her take:

BABY WALKERS: NEVER! There are so many cases of serious injury associated with these death traps on wheels that Canada actually banned the sale, advertising and import of baby walkers.

2 **DON'T GET YOUR KIDS HOOKED ON BABY EINSTEIN.** TV and electronic media of any type, even "educational videos" designed for babies, are bad for developing brains. Babies need active, not passive learning, and getting them used to watching TV is a bad habit to encourage.

3 **THROW AWAY THE PACIFIER AT FOUR MONTHS OR DON'T USE ONE AT ALL.** At four months, a baby needs to start learning some self-soothing behaviors. Babies who can't fall asleep or can't stop crying without a pacifier have become dependent on them. Find comforting alternatives.

4 **AVOID EAR THERMOMETERS.** They are notoriously unreliable, and since fever in infants (over 100.3 degrees) could be serious, an inaccurate reading might give parents a false sense of security. Rectal thermometers are the most accurate.

5 **DON'T FALL FOR THE BABY TOOTHPASTE HYPE.** The best way to clean your baby's teeth is to wipe them with a wet washcloth, twice daily. The sweet taste of baby toothpaste encourages your baby to suck on the toothbrush once in his mouth and you can't maneuver it around well.

6 **BEWARE OF NATURAL BABY SKIN-CARE PRODUCTS.** Over 25% of the "natural" ones contain common allergens including peanuts, which can sensitize infants to permanent food allergy.

7 **YOU DON'T NEED TEETHING TABLETS** from the health food store. Some of these contain *caffeine* as an ingredient! Save the espresso for kindergarten!

8 **FORGET SIPPY CUPS.** They promote tooth decay because the flow of liquid heads straight to the back of the top front teeth. If your baby hasn't quite mastered drinking from a cup yet, offer her a straw instead.

9 **HANGING MOBILES ARE ONLY FOR NEWBORNS.** Remove all toys and decorations hanging over your baby's crib by the time he or she is five months old. They become hazardous when babies start to pull themselves up and grab for them.

10 **ENJOY THOSE BEAUTIFUL QUILTS AS WALL HANGINGS**, not in the crib

Safety Gates: Our Picks

When you look at the options available in baby gates, you can get easily overwhelmed. KidCo, Safety 1st, Evenflo, SuperGate and First Years are just a few of the brands available. And you'll see metal, plastic, fabric padded, tall, short, wide, permanent mount, pressure mount and more. So, what to get? The temptation of many parents (including us) is to buy what's cheapest. But after buying and using at least six gates, here are our picks and tips:

What are the most dangerous baby products?

The Consumer Product Safety Commission releases yearly figures for injuries and deaths for children under five years old related to juvenile products. The latest figures from the CPSC are for 2001 and show an increase overall in the number of injuries. The following chart details the statistics:

PRODUCT CATEGORY	INJURIES	DEATHS
WALKERS/JUMPERS	3,700	2
STROLLERS/CARRIAGES	10,700	4
INFANT CARRIES/CAR SEATS*	13,200	17
CRIBS, BASSINETS, CRADLES**	10,700	63
HIGH CHAIRS	9,200	6
BABY GATES/BARRIERS	1,800	0
PLAYPENS	1,600	15
CHANGING TABLES	1,800	1
BATH SEATS	***	23
OTHER	6,300	12
TOTAL	**60,700**	**149**

Key:
Deaths: This figure is an annual average from 1997 to 2002, the latest figures available.
*excludes motor vehicle incidents
** including crib mattresses and pads
***in the CPSC's latest report bath seat injuries were not tabulated due to a low sample size

Our Comments: The large number of deaths associated with cribs almost exclusively occurs in cribs that are so old they don't meet current safety standards. We encourage parents to avoid hand-me-down, antique and second hand cribs.

Your best option from the start is to stick with the metal or wooden gates. Plastic never seems to hold up that well and looks dirty in short order from all those sticky fingerprints. Our favorite brand is **KidCo**. They make the Gateway, Safeway and Elongate models plus a variety of extensions and mounting kits. We  used the permanent mount gate (the Safeway $55-$60), which expands from 24 3/4 inches to 43 1/2 inches. We thought it was fairly easy to install and simple to use. The Gateway ($60-$80; pictured) is the pressure mounted version. The Elongate ($80) fits spaces from 44 inches to 60 inches wide. All three gates can be expanded further with inexpensive extensions.

Another interesting option for a pressure gate is the **First Years' Hands Free Gate** ($50). This metal gate has a foot pedal that adults can step on to open. If you have your hands full, this is a great way to get in and out. Soft gates have recently entered the market including the **Soft n' Wide** from Evenflo ($35 to $45). It is a stationary gate (does not swing open) with nylon covered padding at the top and bottom to protect baby from the metal frame. This is useful if you don't want

Kids in Danger

Nancy Cowles, executive director for Kids in Danger (www.kidsindanger.org) a non-profit advocacy group, offers some food for thought to parents about juvenile products and safety:

"Except for cribs, bunk beds, pacifiers, and small parts in toys meant for young children, there are NO requirements in the US that manufacturers meet standards or test their products for safety. While most parents believe that if it is on the store shelf and is a recognized brand name someone has made sure it is safe for their baby, that is not the case. Voluntary standards (like the JPMA) exist for many products, but companies are in no way required to test their products to these standards. Even the mandatory crib standard does not cover all known hazards.

"Don't forget to check the products your child uses outside your home, which you have carefully baby proofed. Don't let Grandma pull the old crib down from the attic, use a recalled portable crib at childcare, or any other hazards."

Kids In Danger has a brochure (Is My Child Safe?), which gives parents three easy steps to check their products for recalls and stay up to date on product safety. It is available on their website, KidsInDanger.org.

to move the gate often and don't need to open the gate for access. Otherwise swinging gates are a better bet.

Finally, check out the plastic **Supergate** from North State Industries ($25 to $35), a gate our readers have recommended. This gate expands up to 62 inches and slides together and swings out of the way so you can easily clear a path. It is a permanent-mounted gate so it can be used at the top

of stairs. Pictured at the top right is the Supergate Superyard. You may also notice a new gate, the **Kiddy Guard**, that opens and retracts like a window blind. At $110, however, it's a bit on the expensive side.

Most of these gates can be found at Babies R Us.

Money-Saving Secrets

1 **OUTLET COVERS ARE EXPENSIVE.** Only use them where you will be plugging in items. For unused outlets, consider a cheaper option—moving heavy furniture in front to block access. What type of outlet cover should you buy? We like the Safe-Plate ($3 from www.babyguard.com), which requires you to slide a small plate over to access the receptacle. In contrast, those that require you to rotate a dial to access the outlet are more difficult to use.

2 **MANY DISCOUNTERS LIKE TARGET, K-MART, AND WAL-MART SELL A LIMITED SELECTION OF BABY SAFETY ITEMS.** We found products like gates, outlet plugs, and more at prices about 5% to 20% less than full-priced hardware stores. For example, outlet covers at Target were an affordable $2.50. And don't forget to check home improvement stores like Home Depot. They also carry safety items.

3 **SOME OF THE MOST EFFECTIVE BABY PROOFING IS FREE.** For example, moving items to top shelves, putting dangerous chemicals away, and other common sense ideas don't cost any money and are just as effective as high-tech gadgets.

4 **CRAIGSLIST.ORG.** Many parents have discovered this online classified site as a great source for used baby gear, including safety items. When you first arrive at the site, the first page is the San Francisco portal—look to the right to select your metro area. Then go to Baby & Kid Stuff. One reader scored a plethora of baby bargains there, including a Safety 1st Swing N Lock Gate (in the box, never installed) for just $10. Yep, that sells for $30 in stores.

Bonus Material Online

For more safety tips and advice, go to our web site, BabyBargains.com (click on Bonus Material). There you'll find practical tips on baby proofing on a budget, as well as mail order sources for safety gadgets.

Safe & Sound for Toys

Walk through any toy store and the sheer variety will boggle your mind. Buying toys for an infant requires more careful planning than for older children. Here are nine tips to keep your baby safe and sound:

E-MAIL FROM THE REAL WORLD
A solution for those coffee tables

Reader Jennifer Kinkle came up with this affordable solution to expensive coffee table bumpers.

"When our son started to walk we were very worried about his head crashing into the glass top tables in our living room. We checked into the safety catalogs and found those fitted bumpers for about $80 just for the coffee table. Well, I guess being the selfish person that I am, and already removing everything else dangerous from my living room. I just didn't want to give up my tables!! Where do we put the lamps, and where do I fold the laundry?

"My mother-in-law had the perfect solution. FOAM PIPE WRAPPING!!! We bought it at a home improvement store for $3. You can cut it to fit any table. It is already sliced down the middle and has adhesive, (the gummy kind that rolls right off the glass if you need to replace it). The only disadvantage that we've come across is that our son has learned to pull it off. But at $3 a bag we keep extras in the closet for 'touch-ups'.

"Now the novelty has worn off, so I've had to replace it as often. And I'm happy to report that we've had plenty of collisions, but not one stitch!"

1 **CHECK FOR AGE APPROPRIATE LABELS.** Yes, that sounds like a no-brainer, but you'd be surprised how many times grand-parents try to give a six-month old infant a toy that is clearly marked "Ages 3 and up." One common misunderstanding about these labels: the age range has NOTHING to do with developmental ability of your baby; instead, the warning is intended to keep small parts out of the hands of infants because those parts can be a choking hazard. Be careful of toys bought at second-hand stores or hand-me-downs—a lack of packaging may mean you have to guess on the age-appropriate level. Another trouble area: "Kids Meal" toys from fast-food restaurants. Many are clearly labeled for kids three and up (although some fast food places do offer toys safe for the under-three crowd). One smart tip: use a toilet paper tube to see if small parts pose a choking hazard . . . anything that can fit through the tube can be swallowed by baby.

2 **MAKE SURE STUFFED ANIMALS HAVE SEWN EYES.** A popular gift from friends and relatives, stuffed animals can be a haz-ard if you don't take a few precautions. Buttons or other materials for eyes that could be easily removed present a choking hazard—make sure you give a stuffed animal the once over before you give it to baby. Keep all plush animals out of the crib except maybe one special toy (and that only after baby is able to roll over). While it is acceptable to have one or two stuffed animals in the crib with babies over one year of age, resist the urge to pile on. Once baby starts pulling himself up to a standing position, such stuffed animals can be used as steps to escape a crib.

3 **BEWARE OF RIBBONS.** Another common decoration on stuffed animals, remove these before giving the toy to your baby.

4 **MAKE SURE TOYS HAVE NO STRINGS LONGER THAN 12 INCH-ES**—another easily avoided strangulation hazard.

5 **WOODEN TOYS SHOULD HAVE NON-TOXIC FINISHES.** If in doubt, don't give such toys to your baby. The toy's packag-ing should specify the type of finish.

6 **BATTERY COMPARTMENTS SHOULD HAVE A SCREW CLOSURE.** Tape players (and other battery-operated toys) should not give your baby easy access to batteries—a compartment that requires a screwdriver to open is a wise precaution.

7 **BE CAREFUL OF CRIB TOYS.** Some of these toys are designed to attach to the top or sides of the crib. The best advice:

remove them after the baby is finished playing with them. Don't leave the baby to play with crib toys unsupervised, especially once she begins to pull or sit up.

8 **DO NOT USE WALKERS.** And if you get one as a gift, take it back to the store and exchange it for something that isn't a death trap. Exactly what are these invitations to disaster? A walker suspends your baby above the floor, enabling him or her to "walk" by rolling around on wheels. The only problem: babies tend to "walk" right into walls, down staircases, and into other brain damage-causing obstacles. It's a scandal that walkers haven't been banned by the Consumer Products Safety Commission. How many injuries are caused by these things? Are you sitting down? Over 8000 a year.

To be fair, we should note the baby gear industry has tried to make walkers safer—with a large amount of prodding from the CPSC. While the government decided not to ban walkers outright in 1993, the CPSC did work to strengthen the industry's voluntary standards over the past few years. The result: redesigned walkers with safety features that stop them from falling down stairs. Some have special wheels or "gripping strips" that prevent such falls.

The result of these new safety features: walker injuries have dropped 70% since 1995. But we still think 8000 injured babies is 8000 too many. Our advice: don't put your baby into a walker, no matter how many new "safety" features are built-in.

Oppenheim Toy Portfolio

While we do have a few basic baby toy recommendations on our web page (BabyBargains.com; click on bonus material), our specialty is really baby gear, not toys. As a result, we recommend this source for reviews on toys, books, video and software: The Oppenheim Toy Portfolio (web: www.toyportfolio.com). Readers concur; here's what one said about this great book:

"I got tired of driving my sleep deprived self, my wonderful but heavy daughter and her heavy carrier to the local Toys R Us to return toys she hated or was scared of. Once I bought this book, I understood better what to look for in a toy and what was skill/age appropriate—not what the manufacturers listed on the boxes! We have made many fewer return-the-toy trips and I am a much happier person. The book also includes games to play with your infants and no toy was required!"

By the way, in April 2004, Canada announced an outright ban on baby walkers due to continuing concern over serious injuries from the products. The ban on these items includes second-hand walkers as well.

9 **STATIONARY PLAY CENTERS.** What about walker alternatives? So-called "stationary" play centers have made a big splash on the baby market in recent years, led by Evenflo's Exersaucer. Most stationary play centers run $50 to $90 and are basically the same— you stick the baby into a seat in the middle and there are a bunch of toys for them to play with. (The more money you spend, the better the toys, bells and whistles). While the unit rocks and swivels, it can't move. And that's a boon to parents who need a few minutes to make dinner or take a shower.

So, should you get one? Well, our belief is these play centers are optional—and if overused, can be a problem. We're troubled by studies that have shown infants who use walkers and stationary play centers suffer from developmental delays when compared to babies who don't use them. According to a study in the October 1999 Journal of Developmental and Behavioral Pediatrics, researchers at Case Western Reserve University found "babies who were placed in walkers were slower to sit up, crawl and walk than those raised without walkers. The mental development of the children also appeared to be slowed," according to an Associated Press article on the study.

Researchers studied 109 infants, including 53 who did not use walkers. On average, babies who used the walkers were delayed at least a month in sitting up, crawling and walking. Non-walker using kids also scored 10% higher on mental development tests than walker users.

The researchers concluded that "restriction in a walker may exert its greatest influence on mental development during the 6- to 9-month age period, a time regarded as transformational in a child's intellectual development," according to the AP article. Noticeably, walker babies were able to catch up to non-walker children after they started crawling—and hence used the walker less often.

Why do walkers and stationary play centers have such a dramatic effect on a child's development? Researchers speculate that "the opaque trays placed on the newer walkers as a safety device prevent the children from seeing their legs, blocking the feedback they get from moving a limb and seeing the leg actually move," the article stated.

While this study focused on walkers, we interpreted the results to also apply to stationary play centers. Why? Because both play centers and walkers use those "opaque trays" that keep baby from seeing their feet. Another study from 2002 conducted at the University of Dublin School of Physiotherapy in Ireland concurred with the results of the Case Western study. They concluded "this study provides additional evidence that baby walkers are associated with delay in achieving normal locomotor milestones . . .The use of baby walkers should be discouraged."

Bottom line: stationary play centers should be used with great caution. If you are going to use one of these items, your child should spend no more than 15 minutes a day in them (long enough for a quick shower). As for a brand of stationary play center, we recommend the *Evenflo ExerSaucer*, based on parent feedback.

And traditional walkers should never, ever be used in our opinion.

10 JUMPERS.

These contraptions attach to a doorway and let baby bounce up and down, thanks to a large spring that acts like a bungee cord. Yet, we've been troubled by the large number of recalls and reported injuries attributed to jumpers. Unfortunately, the CPSC doesn't separately break out injuries for jumpers (it lumps them in the category with walkers—these products caused a total of 6200 injuries, according to a 2003 CPSC report). But given the large number of recalls, we would suggest parents avoid this item.

Wastes of Money

Waste of Money #1
Outlet plugs

"My friend thought she'd save a bundle by just using outlet plugs instead of fancy plate covers. Unfortunately, her toddler figured out how to remove the plugs and she had to buy the plates anyway."

It doesn't take an astrophysicist to figure out how to remove those cheap plastic outlet plugs. While the sliding outlet covers are pricier, they may be well worth the investment. Another problem: outlet plugs can be a choking hazard. If baby removes one (or an adult removes one and forgets to put it back), it can end up in baby's mouth. If you want to try plugs anyway, do a test—check your outlets to see how tight the plugs will fit. In newer homes, plugs may have a tighter fit than older homes. While we generally think the outlet cover plates are superior to plugs, we do recommend the plugs for road trips to Grandma's house or a hotel room.

Tummy Time Toys: A Waste of Money?

"Friends keep telling me that Tummy Time for my baby is a must. I've heard that my daughter might even be developmentally slower than other babies if I don't include tummy time in her day. What is it and why is it so important?"

Do babies spend too much time on their backs? That's one concern parents and child development specialists have brought up in recent years. Before the advent of the Back to Sleep campaign, the SIDS awareness program that encourages parents to put their babies to bed on their backs, babies were more likely to be placed in a variety of positions. Nowadays, however, babies spend an inordinate amount of time on their backs. And some folks wonder if that is causing a delay in creeping, crawling and walking.

The solution is a simple one: just put your baby on her tummy for a few minutes a day when she is awake. Yes, there is research that shows that extra tummy time can help your child reach developmental milestones sooner. But keep in mind that normal babies who don't participate in increased periods of tummy time typically still meet developmental milestones within the normal time period. So there is no need to panic if your baby isn't getting "15 minutes of tummy time daily."

In fact, many parents have noted that their babies hate being on their stomachs. For those babies who object to being on their tummies, you simply don't have to force them. Of course, baby products manufacturers have jumped on this new craze to come up with more stuff you can buy to make Tummy Time more fun. For example, Camp Kazoo, the makers of Boppy pillows (www.boppy.com) make a Boppy Tummy Play exercise mat for $20. This smaller version of the famous Boppy includes an attached mat and loops for favorite toys.

Don't think you need to buy extra stuff to make tummy time successful in your house, however. Save your money and just get down on the floor with your baby face to face. After all, you're the thing in her life she finds most fun, so get down there and spend some quality tummy time with her.

safety

Waste of Money #2
Plastic corner guards

"The other day I was looking through a safety catalog and saw some corner guards. It occurred to me that they don't look a whole lot softer than the actual corner they cover. Are they worth buying?"

You've hit (so to speak) on a problem we've noticed as well. Our advice: the plastic corner guards are a waste of money. They aren't very soft—and they don't have air bags that pop out when you hit them either. So what's the solution? If you're worried about Junior hitting the corner of your coffee table, you can either store it for a while or look into getting a soft bumper pad (up to $80 in catalogs—see our reader email earlier in the chapter for a more affordable alternative). Similar bumpers are available for your fireplace as well. On the other hand, you may decide that blocking off certain rooms is a more practical option.

Waste of Money #3
Appliance safety latches

"I can't imagine that my daughter is going to be able to open the refrigerator any time soon. So why do they sell those appliance latches in safety catalogs, anyway?"

There must be some super-strong kids out there who have enough torque to open a full-sized refrigerator. Most infants under a year of age don't seem to have the strength to open most appliances. However, toddlers will eventually acquire that skill. One point to remember: many appliances like stoves and dishwashers have locking mechanisms built in. And, keep all chairs and stools away from the laundry room to prevent your baby from opening the washing machine and dryer.

A Baby First Aid Kit

Wonder what should be in your baby first aid kit? As a childless couple, we were probably lucky to find a couple of plastic bandages and an ancient bottle of Bactine in our medicine cabinet. Now that you're Dr. Mom (or Nurse Dad) it's time to take a crash course on baby medicine etiquette. By the way, do not administer any of the drugs mentioned here without first checking with your doctor. He/she will know the safest dosage for your infant. Here's a run-down of essentials.

◆ *Acetaminophen* (one brand name of this drug is Tylenol). For pain relief and fever reduction. If you suspect your child may have an allergy to flavorings, you can buy a version without all the additives. You may also want to keep acetaminophen infant suppositories in your medicine cabinet in case your infant persists in vomiting up his drops. Or refuses to take them at all. Do NOT keep baby aspirin in your house. Aspirin has been linked to Reyes Syndrome in children and is no longer recommended by the medical community. Warn grandparents about this issue, as some may still think baby aspirin is OK.

◆ *Children's Ibuprofen* (one brand name of this drug is Motrin). This is another great option for pain relief and fever reduction. Typically, Ibuprofen will be a bit longer lasting than Acetaminophen.

◆ *Children's Benadryl.* To relieve minor allergic reactions.

◆ *Antibiotic ointment* to help avoid bacterial infection from cuts.

◆ *Baking soda* is great for rashes.

◆ *Calamine lotion* to relieve external itching. Some versions include Benedryl so check the label carefully.

◆ *A cough and cold remedy recommended by your pediatrician.* DO NOT use adult cough syrups. A small amount given to a small child or infant has been know to cause illness and death.

◆ *A good lotion.* Unscented and non-medicated brands are best.

◆ *Measuring spoon or cup for liquid medicine.* For small infants, you may want a medicine dropper or syringe. Droppers often come in the box with some medications.

◆ *Petroleum jelly*, which is used to lubricate rectal thermometers.

◆ *Plastic bandages like Band-Aids.*

◆ *Saline nose drops* for stuffy noses.

◆ *Tweezers*. For all kinds of fun uses.

◆ *A card with the number for poison control.* You may want to call your local poison control center and ask them what poison remedies they recommend having on hand. It used to be that everyone recommended Syrup of Ipecac to induce vomiting. However, the American Academy of Pediatrics now recommends NOT keeping ipecac in your house. Why? The AAP says ipecac may cause more harm than good and is worried about misuse. Bottom line: call poison control if your child ingests a dangerous or unknown substance. DON'T try to remedy the situation by yourself. Here is the national number for poison control: 1-800-222-1222. You can also get your local poison control number from the web site of the American Association of Poison Control Centers (www.aapcc.org).

◆ *Thermometer*. Remember the old mercury thermometers of our childhood? They were so simple and straightforward. Today, you'll find digital thermometers, ear thermometers, strip thermometers, pacifier thermometers and more. Some use infrared technology and

safety

even solar-powered alternatives to mercury and simple batteries. But in the end, the most important job of a thermometer is to take an accurate temperature. And it would be nice if it could do it fast.

So with all these options, it's no wonder parents just don't know what to buy. You've got to have one, but which is best? Quick answer: the simplest. A plain old digital thermometer available from any drugstore for about $5 or $10. But (and this is a big but—or butt), with an infant, you should use it rectally! "What," you say, "I can't do that!" You'd be surprised what you can do once you become a parent. And your pediatrician or nurse will be happy to show you exactly how to do it to avoid any problems. Just ask! Yes, you can use it under your baby's arm, it just won't be as accurate.

What about those ear thermometers? Why don't they work well? Because your baby's ear canal is just too tiny. It's a tough trick to position the device properly. So save yourself $50 and don't buy an ear thermometer.

Digital forehead thermometers are the newest thing. Do they work well? Sure, but they require a 25 minute "acclimatization." Yes, you have to let them acclimatize to the room for 25 minutes. Imagine the conversation with your screaming, feverish two month old as you explain the delay in getting him relief!

Top Ten Safety Must Haves

To sum up, here's our list of top safety items to have for your home (in no particular order).

◆ *Fire extinguishers*, rated "ABC," which means they are appropriate for any type of fire.

◆ *Outlet covers.*

◆ *Baby monitor*—unless your house or apartment is very small, and you don't think it will be useful.

◆ *Smoke alarms.* The best smoke alarms have two systems for detecting fires—a photoelectric sensor for early detection of smoldering fires and a dual chamber ionization sensor for early detection of flaming fires. An example of this is the First Alert "Dual Sensor" ($25 to $35). We'd recommend one smoke alarm for every bedroom, plus main hallways, basement and living rooms. And don't forget to replace the batteries twice a year. Both smoke alarms and carbon monoxide detectors can be found in warehouse clubs like Sam's and Costco at low prices.

◆ **Carbon monoxide detectors.** These special detectors sniff out dangerous carbon monoxide (CO) gas, which can result from a malfunctioning furnace. Put one CO detector in your baby's room and another in the main hallway of your home.

◆ **Cabinet and drawer locks.** For cabinets and drawers containing harmful cleaning supplies or utensils like knives, these are an essential investment. For fun, designate at least one unsecured cabinet or drawer as "safe" and stock it with pots and pans for baby.

◆ **Spout cover for tub.**

◆ **Bath thermometer or anti-scald device.**

◆ **Toilet locks**—so your baby doesn't visit the Tidy Bowl Man. One of the best we've seen in years is KidCo's toilet lock ($15), an award-winning gizmo that does the trick. Check their web site at www.kidcoinc.com for a store that carries it.

◆ **Baby gates.** See the section earlier for recommendations.

Playpens

The portable playpen has been so popular in recent years that many parents consider it a necessity. Compared to the old wooden playpens of years past, today's playpens are made of metal and nylon mesh, fold compactly for portability and offer such handy features as bassinets, canopies, wheels and more. Some shopping tips:

◆ **Don't buy a second-hand playpen or use a hand-me-down.** Many playpen models have been the subject of recalls in recent years. Why? Those same features that make them convenient (the collapsibility to make the playpen "portable") worked too well in the past—some playpens collapsed with babies inside. Others had protruding rivets that caught some babies who wore pacifiers on a string (a BIG no-no, but that's another subject). A slew of injuries and deaths have prompted the recall of ten million playpens over the years. Yes, you can search government recall lists (www.cpsc.gov) to see if that hand-me-down is recalled, but we'd skip the hassle and just buy new.

◆ **Go for the bassinet feature.** Some playpens feature bassinet inserts which can be used for babies under three months of age (always check the weight guidelines). This is a handy feature that we recommend. Other worthwhile features: wheels for mobility, side-rail storage compartments and a canopy (if you plan to take the playpen outside or to the beach). If you want a playpen with canopy, look for those models that have "aluminized fabric" canopies—they reflect the sun's heat and UV rays to keep baby cooler.

Our Picks: Brand Recommendations

What are the best brands for playpens? Once again, we give it to **Graco**—their **Pack 'n Play** playpens are the best designed and least-recalled. Last we looked, they had 36 models that ranged from $59 to $139.

So, which model should you get? We like the basic Pack 'n Play with bassinet attachment, which runs $50 to $75 depending on the pattern. Pictured is a $140 deluxe version of the Pack 'n Play with bassinet, changer station, canopy and more. If you plan to use the  playpen outdoors, go for one with a canopy that is aluminized to cut down on the heat ($140), or consider the new Pack 'n Play Sport (discussed below).

What if you need a no-frills playpen? Just the basics, no toys, bassinet, canopy and so on? A good basic choice is **J. Mason's Safe Surround Sport**, which is just $40 and has a non-folding rail that safety advocates cite as a  great feature. The screw-in steel posts are easy to set up. Don't expect to move this from room to room easily, however, as it lacks wheels.

What about the other playpen brands? Yes, you can find playpens by Baby Trend, Evenflo, Kolcraft and Fisher Price, but we don't think their quality or features measure up to Graco's offerings.

So, what's new for playpens this year? In a word, extra padding. Graco is upgrading their Pack 'n Plays with quilted pads and bumpers. **Chicco** will also jump on this trend, debuting their first playpen with extra cushy padding (which will be machine-washable). The Chicco Lullaby LX is a winner—it will sell in a no-frills (no toys) version for $100 and a deluxe model with toys for $150 to $160.

Chicco won't be the only new entrant in the playpen market: **Peg Perego** has launched their first playpen with a $170 offering dubbed the Vogue. It will have a bassinet and feature an extra large play area—50″ x 25″ with a 45 lb. weight limit (most playpens stop at 30 lbs). Don't plan to take this one on the road however . . . we found the sample extremely heavy to move.

For something much lighter for Grandma's house, Graco's new "Travel Lite Crib"($60) is a good bet. It is 20% smaller than a standard Pack N Play, but still has a bassinet attachment and canopy, wheels and push button fold.

Finally, let's mention **Graco's new Pack 'n Play Sport** ($110 to $140), which is billed as an indoor/outdoor play yard for both home or, say, the beach. We liked the Sport's quick set-up, tent-like protection from sun and also a lockable play hatch for toddlers to use. A great solution if you have to take baby to an older sibling's soccer game.

FYI: Be sure to check out a discussion on portable playpen sheets in Chapter 3. While most parents love their playpen, the cheap-o sheets that come with most are a bane (they slip off the mattress too easily, etc). We discuss an alternative portable playpen sheet (Mr. Bobbles Blankets) in Chapter 3 that solves that problem.

The Bottom Line: A Wrap-Up of Our Best Buy Picks

In the nursery, we highly recommend the Diaper Champ as the best diaper pail . . . but the Diaper Dekor is a stylish option worth a look. Skip wipe warmers, which have safety concerns.

An activity/bouncer seat with a toy bar is a good idea, with prices ranging from $30 to $60—we like the Fisher Price bouncers best. An affordable alternative: adding a $10 toy bar to an infant seat.

As for bathtubs, we thought the EuroBath ($25) by Primo was the best bet, although it is big. A good option for Grandma's house might be the simple Fold-Up Tub by Safety 1st ($13).

For baby monitors, a simple Fisher Price Sound 'N Lights for $20 will work for most folks. If you want rechargeable batteries (highly recommended), consider the Evenflo Whisper Connect Pro for $35 or the Sony BabyCall NTM-910 for $50. No, you don't need a video monitor for baby . . . but if you insist, the Mobicam is our pick.

For swings and playpens, Graco is the brand of choice. Graco's swings set the standard for quality and features, although Fisher-Price's cradle swings are a good second bet. For playpens, the Graco Pack 'n Play with bassinet feature is our pick.

playpens

CHAPTER 8

Car Seats: Picking the right child safety seat

Inside this chapter

W hat's the best car seat for your baby? What is the difference between an infant and a convertible seat? We'll discuss these issues and more in this chapter. You'll find complete reviews and ratings of the major car seat brands as well as informative charts that compare the best choices.

Here's a sobering figure: last year, motor vehicle crashes killed 1543 children under age 15 and injured another 227,000. While the majority of those injuries and deaths occurred to children who were not in safety seats, the toll from vehicle accidents in this country is still a statistic that can keep you awake all night. Just to make you feel a tiny bit better, the lives of 367 children under age five were saved last year because they used a child restraint.

Every state in the U.S. (and every province in Canada) requires infants and children to ride in child safety seats, so this is one of the few products that every parent must buy. In fact you may find yourself buying multiple car seats as your baby grows older—and for secondary cars, grandma's car, a caregiver's vehicle and more.

So, which seat is the safest? Easiest to use? One thing you'll learn in this chapter is that there is not one "safest" or "best" seat. Yes, we will review and rate the various car seat brands and examine their recall/safety history. BUT, remember the best seat for your child is the one that correctly fits your child's weight and size—and can be correctly installed in your vehicle.

And that's the rub: roadside safety checks by police reveal 80% to 90% of child safety seats are NOT installed or used properly. Although the exact figure isn't known, a large number of child fatalities and injuries from crashes are caused by improper use or installation of seats. Realizing that many of today's child safety seats are a failure due to complex installation and other hurdles, the federal government has rolled out a safety standard (called LATCH) for child seats and vows to fix loopholes in current crash testing. We'll discuss these changes in-depth in this chapter.

Getting Started:
When Do You Need This Stuff?

You can't leave the hospital without a car seat. By law, all states require children to be restrained in a child safety seat. You'll want to get this item early (in your sixth to eighth month of pregnancy) so you can install it in your car before baby arrives. Also: some of the best deals on car seats are found online. You'll need to leave a few weeks in shipping time to insure the seat arrives before baby does.

Sources to Find Car Seats

1 DISCOUNTERS. Car seats have become a loss leader for many discount stores. Chains like Target and Wal-Mart sell these items at small mark-ups in hopes you'll spend money elsewhere in the store. The only caveat: most discounters only carry a limited selection of seats, typically of the no-frills brands.

2 BABY SPECIALTY STORES. Independent juvenile retailers have all but abandoned car seats to the chains. With the exception of premium brands like Britax or Combi, you'll only see a few scattered offerings here.

3 THE SUPERSTORES. Chains like Babies R Us, Toys R Us and Burlington Coat Factory's Baby Depot (reviewed in depth in Chapter 2) tend to carry a wider selection of car seats than discounters. And, sometimes, that includes the better brands. Prices can be a few dollars higher than the chains, but sales often bring better deals.

4 MAIL ORDER/THE WEB. Yes, you can buy a car seat through the mail or online. More on the 'net next. A run-down of other mail order sources appears later in the chapter. Prices are usually discounted, but watch out for shipping—the cost of shipping bulky items like car seats can outweigh the discount in some cases. Use an online coupon (see the previous chapter for coupon sites) to save and look for free shipping specials.

car seats

CAR SEATS

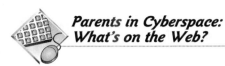

Parents in Cyberspace: What's on the Web?

The web is teeming with both information and bargains on car seats. Here's the best of what's out there.

◆ **NHTSA.** The National Highway Traffic Safety Administration site (www.nhtsa.dot.gov) is a treasure trove of car seat info—you can read about recalls, the latest news on changing standards and installation tips. The NHTSA's brochure "Buying a Safer Car For Child Passengers" is a must read (online or call 888-DASH2DOT). You can also contact the government's Auto Safety Hotline at 800-424-9393 to ask car seat related questions. Even better: the NHTSA now ranks car seats on their ease of use (assembly, instructions, securing a child, etc). The most recent report covers 67 seats, from infant to booster. See the report here: www.nhtsa.gov/cps/cssrating or by calling 888-327-4236. Note: these ratings do NOT cover how well a seat does in crash tests or compatibility with different vehicles.

◆ **The American Academy of Pediatrics** (www.aap.org, go to "Parenting Corner") is an excellent resource for buying tips.

◆ **The National Safe Kids Campaign** (www.safekids.org) has a helpful interactive "safety seat guide" that helps you determine which seat is right for the age and weight of the child.

◆ **Safety Belt Safe USA** (www.carseat.org) has a good site with tips on picking the best seat for your child, as well as the latest recalls and info on child safety seats.

◆ **CarSeatData.org** has an "interactive compatibility database" that lets you search for which seats work in which vehicles. Very cool.

◆ **ParentsPlace** (www.parentsplace.com) has a car seat FAQ, buying guide and message board dedicated to car seats. BabyCenter.com is another good site to check out.

◆ **Our web site** has a message boards dedicated to car seats. Plus: we have a brochure called "Buying a Better Car Seat Restraint" produced by a Canadian auto insurance company. This publication (downloadable as a PDF) has excellent advice on buying a seat. The institute's web site (www.icbc.com) has rating charts that compare major brands of car seats—go to "Road Safety," then "Child Seats" and then finally to "Buying a Child Seat." For a link to the brochure and the ratings web page, go to www.BabyBargains.com and click on the "Bonus Material" section for a link to this car seat guide.

◆ *Where to buy online.* Many of the large baby product web sites (and catalogs) mentioned throughout this book sell car seats at competitive prices. When you find an online coupon for these sites (see Chapter 7, Around the House, for a list of such sites), the deals can be even better. One great site: BabyCatalog.com has rock-bottom deals on car seats (and often has free shipping specials).

More Money Buys You . . .

As you'll read later in this chapter, all child safety seats are regulated by the federal government to meet minimum safety standards. So whether you buy a $50 seat from K-Mart or a $250 brand from a specialty store, your baby is equally covered. When you pay extra money, however, there are some perks. First, on the safety front, the more expensive seats have shock-absorbing foam that protects a seat from side-impact collisions. The more expensive seats are also easier to use and adjust . . . and clearly that is a major safety benefit. For infant seats, when you spend more money, you get an adjustable base (which enables a better fit in vehicles), a canopy to block the sun and plush padding.

Speaking of padding . . . the more money you spend, the more cushy the seat—some makers throw in infant head pillows, body cushions and more to jack the price of a car seat. These are not marketed as a safety benefit, but more for the baby's "comfort." The problem? Newborns and infants don't really care. They are just fine in a seat with basic padding (versus the deluxe version). Of course, if you have a super long commute or an older child (say over two years), padding and comfort becomes more of a relevant issue. But for most babies, basic padding is just fine.

Smart Shopper Tips

Smart Shopper Tip #1
So many seats, so much confusion
"I'm so confused by all the car seat options out there. For example, are infant car seats a waste of money? Or should I go with a convertible seat? Or one of those models that is good from birth to college?

CAR SEATS

Children's car seats come in three flavors: "infant," "convertible" and "boosters." Let's break it down:

◆ **Infant** car seats are just that—these rear-facing seats are designed for infants up to 22 lbs. or so and 26" in height. On average, parents get about six months of use out of an infant seat (of course that varies with the size/height of the child). Infant car seats have an internal harness (usually five-point) that holds the infant to the carrier, which is then snapped into a base. The base is secured to the car. Why the snap-in base? That way you can release the seat and use the carrier to tote your baby around.

◆ **Convertible** car seats (see right) can be used for both infants *and* older children (most seats go up to 40 lbs.)—infants ride rear facing; older kids ride facing forward. Convertible seats have different harness options (more on this later); unlike infant seats, however, they do not have snap-in bases.

◆ **Booster** seats were once used exclusively to position the vehicle's safety belt to correctly fit a young child up to 80 pounds (hence, they are called belt-positioning boosters). In recent years, some boosters have added five-point harnesses (see picture) for use by younger children weighing less than 40 pounds (after that time, the five-point harness is removed and the seat is used with the vehicle's safety belt; see lower picture). These new seats are called "transitional boosters" or "combo seats."

Since this book focuses on products for babies up to two years of age, this chapter only reviews and rates infant and convertible seats. Please see our book *Toddler Bargains* (check the back of the book for more info) for reviews of booster seats.

Of course, just to make things more confusing for you first-time parents, these neat categories have blurred somewhat in recent years. One car seat maker, Cosco/Eddie Bauer, has introduced seats that morph from a convertible seat to a booster. One such model: the Cosco Alpha Omega (also called the Eddie Bauer Three in One) can be used rear-facing from 5 to 30 pounds, then forward-facing to 40 lbs. From 40 lbs. to 80 lbs. the Alpha Omega converts to a booster seat that uses the auto safety belt to restrain an older child. We'll review this seat later in this chapter. (There will be a quiz on this later as well).

So does it make more sense to buy one car seat (that is a convertible car seat) and just skip the infant car seat? Nope. Safety experts say it's best for babies under 20 lbs. to be in an *infant* car seat—they're built to better accommodate a smaller body and baby travels in a semi-reclined position, which better supports an infant's head and neck. Yes, some convertible seats recline—but the degree of recline can be affected by the angle of your vehicle's seat back. And certain convertible seats (those with bar shields or t-shields instead of five-point restraints—more on this later) simply don't work well with infants. Furthermore, most babies don't reach the 20-pound mark until six months (and some as late as 12 months)—and that can be a very long period of time if you don't have an infant car seat.

Why? First, it's helpful to understand that an infant car seat is more than just a car seat—it's also an infant carrier when detached from its base. Big deal, you might say? Well, since infants spend much of their time sleeping (and often fall asleep in the car), this *is* a big deal. By detaching the carrier from the auto base, you don't have to wake the baby when you leave the car. Buy a convertible car seat, and you'll have to unbuckle the baby and move her into another type of carrier or stroller (and most likely wake her in the process). Take it from us: let sleeping babies lie and spend the additional $60 to $90 for an infant car seat, even if you use it for just six months.

Remember: babies should be REAR-FACING until they reach one year of age, regardless of weight. If your child outgrows their infant car seat before one year of age, be sure to use a convertible seat in rear-facing mode for as long as possible. Most convertible seats can be used rear-facing until 30 or 33 lbs.

Smart Shopper Tip #2
Infant seat versus convertible

"My friend thinks infant car seats with snap-in bases are dangerous—she thinks in a crash, the seat will detach from the base. Is it safer to just skip the infant seat car seat and go to a convertible?"

This is a common debate in car seat circles—what is the safest for newborns, an infant or convertible seat? Fueling the debate was the recall of several defective infant car seats in the 1990's that did separate from their bases in government crash tests. While those problems are now fixed, fears about infant seats linger among some parents and car seat safety advocates. Among the concerns:

infant car seats that are not correctly latched into their bases (you can hear a click) can come loose in a crash. And some safety advocates claim the government doesn't crash test infant car seats with bases at high speeds.

We hear all these concerns, but still think the infant car seat is the way to go. First, they are designed to fit infants better than larger convertible seats (more on this in a moment). Yes, the snap-in base is really a *convenience* feature, not a safety feature—but that does not make the bases *unsafe*. Reports of seats detaching from bases during high-speed crashes are so rare, we don't think this is an issue either.

And let's take a look at the alternative to the infant seat for a newborn—a convertible seat. Many seat makers advertise their seats can work from five pounds and up . . . but the real factor in determining whether a newborn will fit in these larger seats is the height of the lowest harness slot. The reality: some seats have lower slots (and hence are more newborn compatible) than others. Parents have complained to us that some of the seats we recommend don't really fit their small newborns. Convertible seats with the LOWEST slot heights are: Graco's ComfortSport, Safety 1st's Comfort Ride and Evenflo's Triumph. For example, the lowest slot of the Graco ComfortSport is 8.5"—that's a full 1.5" under the Britax Roundabout (whose lowest slot is at 10"). FYI: measurements for most car seats are online at CarSeatData.org (click on measurements).

Bottom line: your child is equally safe in an infant car seat with base as they are in a convertible seat, provided they fit the seat and the seat is correctly installed in your vehicle. If you decide to forgo the infant seat, be sure to get a convertible seat whose harness fits your newborn.

Smart Shopper Tip #3
New standards, new confusion?

"I hear the federal government has issued new car seat standards. What was wrong with old car seats anyway? And will a newer seat fit my car?"

Stop any ten cars on the road with child safety seats and we'll bet eight or nine are not installed or used correctly. That's what road-side checks by local law enforcement in many states have uncovered: a recent study by the National Highway Traffic Safety Administration stopped 4000 drivers in four states and found a whopping 80% made mistakes in installing or securing a child safety seat.

What's causing all the problems?

Our view: current child safety seats have failed parents. Installation of a car seat can be an exercise in frustration—even parents who spend hours with the instructions can still make mistakes. The number one culprit: the auto seat belt—it is great at restraining adults, but not so good at child safety seats. And those seats simply won't work well if they aren't attached to a car correctly . . . that's the crux of the problem. Simply put, thanks to the quirkiness of auto safety belts (different auto makers have different systems), putting a child safety seat in a car is like trying to fit a square peg into a round hole.

The bottom line: some child safety seats simply DON'T FIT in some vehicles. Which cars? Which seats? It's hard to tell. There is one good web site with a car seat compatibility database (www.carseatdata.org), but it doesn't cover every seat and every vehicle. Often, parents find it's trial and error to see what works.

Finally, there is good news to report, however: The federal government has rolled out new, mandated "uniform" attachments (called LATCH or ISOFIX) required for all vehicles and safety seats made after September 2002. LATCH stands for "Lower Anchors and Tethers for Children." ISOFIX stands for International Standards Organization FIX, which is the international version of LATCH. (More on ISOFIX later in this section). Instead of using the auto's seat belt, car seats attach to two anchor bars installed in the lower seatback.

The result: fewer confusing installations, no more locking clips or other apparatus needed to make sure the seat is correctly attached. (Another part of the new standard: tether straps, which are discussed later in this section.) See picture of a LATCH installed car seat at right.

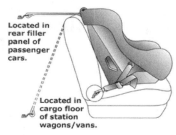

Located in rear filler panel of passenger cars.

Located in cargo floor of station wagons/vans.

As with the transition to any new standard, however, there is quite a bit of confusion about LATCH seats (judging from our reader email). Here is a sum up of frequent questions we get on LATCH seats:

◆ **Which manufacturers sell LATCH seats?** Answer: all. Every infant and convertible car seat sold now includes LATCH.

◆ **Will I have to junk my old car seat?** No. If you have an older model vehicle and an older (non-LATCH) car seat, that is fine—the law just mandates you use an appropriate safety seat, it doesn't specify a LATCH seat. FYI: car seat safety advocates do NOT recommend using a seat that is over five years old. Why? Belts, clips and interior parts in car seats wear out over time . . . hence, seats five years old or older may no longer be safe to use.

◆ **I just bought a new car that has LATCH attachments but I**

CAR
SEATS

got a hand-me-down seat from my sister that does not have LATCH. Can I use an old seat in the new vehicle? Yes . . . but here is our advice: if you have a vehicle that has the new attachments, get a seat that takes advantage of the system.

◆ **I've seen two different LATCH systems, straps/clips and a rigid bar. Which is best?** We discuss this issue in depth in the following box.

◆ **My car does not have LATCH. What is the safest seat I can buy?** Remember the safest seat is the one that best fits your car *and* your child. There is no one "safest" seat. Get the best seat you can afford (we'll have recommendations later in this chapter) and use it with a tether strap. And get your car seat safety checked to make sure you have the best installation and fit.

Which flavor of LATCH is best?

The party line on LATCH from child passenger safety experts is that LATCH is supposed to be a more convenient option for installing a car seat—and this will curb the incorrect installation of non-LATCH seats that has been so prevalent. While we see that point, we're going to wade into the deep end of the controversy pool with some observations about test results of LATCH versus non-LATCH installed seats.

Fact: LATCH seats perform better in crash tests than seats just belted in the old way (with the auto safety belt and a locking clip), even when the latter uses a snug tether strap. We base that opinion on the results of crash tests by Ford Motor Company. What about government data showing little difference between LATCH and non-LATCH crash tests? The problem is that the government used non-LATCH car seats that were tightly installed with less than one-eighth of an inch of lateral movement—yes, that is possible in a lab, but most parents can't or don't install a seat that tight in the real world.

So, you're sold on the idea that LATCH is the safest option. Now, which type of LATCH seat should you get? Yes, it is confusing, but there is no one standard "LATCH" attachment. LATCH seats now come in three flavors:

◆ **Single Flexible strap:** These seats have one strap that loops through the seat and attaches to the anchors. Examples of these seats include the Cosco and Eddie Bauer seats.

◆ **Double flexible strap:** As the name implies, these seats have two

---

◆ *I need to move my LATCH seat to a second car that does-n't have the new attachments. Will it work?* Yes, you should be able to secure a LATCH seat in an older car using the auto's safety belt. But always check the car seat's instructions to make sure this installation is possible.

◆ *I know the safest place for a baby is in the middle of the back seat. But my car doesn't have LATCH anchors there, just in the outboard positions! Where should I put the seat?* Our advice: use the LATCH positions, even if they are just in the side positions. Now, some car seat and vehicle makers say it is okay to use a LATCH seat in the middle of the back seat if you use the LATCH anchors in the outboard positions—check with your car seat and vehicle owner's manual to see if this is permissible.

separate belts that attach to LATCH anchors. Examples of these seats include the Britax Roundabout.

◆ *Rigid ISOFIX:* These seats have rigid connectors (called ISOFIX) that snap into LATCH anchors. An example of this: the Baby Trend Latch-Loc infant seat.

ISOFIX flexible (belt) mount system

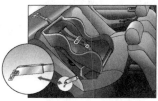

ISOFIX rigid mount system

So, which is best? According to crash tests (again, by Ford), the double flexible strap seats or rigid ISOFIX were the safest options. This was especially true for side-impact crash-es. No, that does not mean a single flexible strap LATCH seat is *unsafe*—those seats still meet federal safety requirements. It just means the former seats have an extra measure of safety, as judged by per-formance in crash tests.

We like the rigid ISOFIX seats better than the flexible strap LATCH seats for another reason—they are easier to install. There is no tight-ening of straps, just snap and go! The problem: there are few rigid ISOFIX seats on the market. At this writing, only the Baby Trend infant seat has this type of attachment. A convertible seat with rigid ISOFIX (the Britax Expressway) is discontinued. A good second bet are the double flexible strap LATCH seats like the Britax Roundabout.

CAR SEATS

◆ **I got a LATCH seat that doesn't fit in my vehicle! I thought this was supposed to be universal.** LATCH has been sold the public as some kind of magic pill that will instantly make all seats fit all vehicles. Hardly. Because of the wide variety of vehicles and seats (a SUV versus a compact, minivan versus pickup), it is unreasonable to expect any system would make this happen. While LATCH helps, it is not the cure-all.

Smart Shopper Tip #4
Strap Me In
"What is a tether strap? Do I want one?"

Back in 1999, the federal government mandated that all convertible child safety seats be sold with a tether strap—these prevent a car seat from moving forward in the event of a crash. How? One end of the tether strap attaches to top of the car seat; the other is hooked to an "anchor bolt" that is permanently installed on the back of the back seat or on the floor in your vehicle.

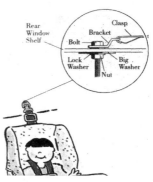

Most newer vehicles already have installed anchor bolts, making the use of a tether strap a snap. (Hint: check your vehicle's owner's manual to find instructions on using tether straps). Older vehicles may have pre-drilled anchorage points—just ask your car dealer for the "anchor bolt installation kit" (a part number that's listed in your owner's manual in the section on installing child safety seats). You can install the bolt or have the dealer do it.

Of course, really old cars are trickier since they lack anchor bolts or even pre-drilled holes—to install the anchor bolt, you may need to drill through your car's sub floor (a job for the car dealer, as you can guess). And just finding out the part number for the anchor bolt can be a challenge; some car dealers are clueless about this issue.

(One tip: call a CANADIAN dealer to find out the part number of the anchor bolt for child safety seats. Why? Tether straps have been required for years in Canada. Hence, car dealers there are more familiar with this request. You can find a Canadian dealer's phone number on most automobile maker's web sites.)

A side note: most car seats can only use tether straps when they are FORWARD-FACING. Only four models (the Britax Roundabout, Marathon and Wizard plus the Combi Avatar, reviewed later) have a tether which can be used in either the rear or forward-facing positions. Note: tether straps are typically not used with infant seats or booster seats (but always consult your seat's directions for specific advice on this).

So, is the tether strap worth all the hassle? Yes—crash tests show car seats are SAFER when used with a tether strap. The strap keeps the car seat (and hence, your baby's head) from moving forward in a crash, lowering the chance of injury. So are seats used without tethers unsafe? No, the federal government requires seats to be safe even when a tether is not in use. Of course, the tether adds that extra measure of safety and is always preferable to a tether-less installation.

Smart Shopper Tip #5
One Size Does Not Fit All

"My friend has a car seat that just doesn't fit very well into her car. Does anyone put out a rating system that says which seats are most compatible? Easiest to use? Safest?"

There is good news on this front. In 2000, Congress passed a law (the Transportation Recall Enhancement, Accountability and Documentation (TREAD) Act) that instructed the Department of Transportation to come up with a rating system for car seats. (What a concept!) After years of complaining from safety advocates, we have to give Congress a hand for passing this legislation (particular thanks to Senator John Fitzgerald R-Ill. and his aide, Evelyn Fortier, for seeing this to fruition).

The new rating system is now online: you can see it at www.nhtsa.gov/cps/cssrating or by calling 888-327-4236. Note: these rankings cover ease of use (assembly, etc.), not how well the seats do in crash tests. Nor do the rankings cover how compatible seats are with different vehicles. On the plus side, the NHTSA did rank 67 seats, which covers about 98% of what's out there on the market. And there is more on the way: in 2005, the NHTSA will release star-ratings for seats based on crash tests.

We should also point out the new car seat law requires the federal government to develop new crash tests for car seats that simulate rear-impact and side-impact crashes, a long overdue change.

Smart Shopper Tip #6
Recalls

"I saw in the paper that a particular car seat is being recalled. Should I be skeptical of other seats by that manufacturer?"

Here's a sobering fact of car seat shopping: most major brands of car seats has had a recall over the past five years. We've seen recalls on cheap seats sold in Wal-Mart and $200 car seats sold in

CAR
SEATS

specialty stores, so recalls are a fact of life no matter what brand you consider. So, how can pick among the different brands, even if all have had recalls?

First, realize that some recalls are more serious than others. Some car seats are recalled for minor problems, like incorrect warning labels. Other companies do voluntary recalls when their own testing reveals a problem. The key issue: look to see if there are any deaths or injuries associated with the defective product. Obviously, car seats that are so defective as to cause injury to babies are much

Registering a Complaint: Do Some Seat Makers Ignore Registered Users During Recalls?

As a new parent, you try to do everything you can to make sure your baby is safe. Besides researching which products are safe, many parents also diligently fill out warranty and registration cards with the expectation they will be contacted in case of a future safety recall.

Yet many parents are surprised to learn that baby product companies fail to mail out notices of defective products to registered users. Why? Companies complain that mailing costs are too high—instead they issue a press release to the media, hoping local newspapers, radio and TV will spread the word about a defective product.

Case in point: the March 2002 recall of the Graco SnugRide infant seat. Graco discovered that over 900,000 units of the popular infant car seat were defective. The problem: a number of the bases had missing components that were used to attach the carrier to the base (Graco has subsequently fixed the problem and we still recommend that seat).

Registered users of the SnugRide probably expected Graco to drop them a note about the problem. If so, they were sorely disappointed. Graco did send a press release to the media regarding the recall, but made no effort to contact registered users directly.

Hello? Is this insane or what? Parents take the time to fill out and mail those registration cards that manufacturers include in product boxes, but for what? Instead of receiving a courtesy call or postcard that the car seat they are using might be a death trap, you are supposed to be watching the local news at exactly the right moment to hear your car seat is recalled? Or see page 16A of the local paper?

Companies like Graco should be ashamed. Let's do the math—assuming only one-third of all SnugRide users actually registered their seats (and that is a conservative guess), Graco would have to send out notices to 300,000 parents. What does a postcard cost to mail these days? A whopping 23¢. So, Graco's total costs would be about $75,000 (assuming some printing costs). That seems a small price to pay for a company with $600 million in annual sales.

And what about email? Last we looked, most of the world used

more serious than minor labeling recalls.

Another issue: how does a company handle a recall? Do they fight the government, forcing regulators to order a recall? Or do they voluntarily recall the item and set up an efficient process (toll-free phone number) to get replacements or retrofit kits to consumers? In the past, we lowered the rating for one major car seat maker (Evenflo) for the abysmal way they handled a recall for their On My Way infant seat.

When a company announces a recall, the product is typically

the 'net to communicate. Yet some baby manufacturers (including Cosco and Evenflo) still don't allow parents to register online. Emailed recall notices? Forget about it. Here is a partial list of companies that do allow online registration: Combi, Graco and Kolcraft.

Last year, the Consumer Products Safety Commission (CPSC) issued 71 recalls of children's' products, including toys. That's more than one per week! So, what can a parent do to keep up with what's safe and what's recalled? Here are our tips:

◆ *Track your purchases.* In order to know whether you have a recalled product, you first have to know what you got to begin with. One parent told us she kept a spreadsheet with the following info for all her baby products; manufacturer, model, serial #, date manufactured, company phone number/web site, where purchased and price paid. Okay, perhaps that's a bit overboard for most parents. But at least put all your receipts and product manuals into a file or shoebox. The goal: create ONE place you go to when a recall is announced.

◆ *Stay informed.* Register for free email alerts about recalls. Our web page (BabyBargains.com) has a free newsletter that sends out email alerts to readers whenever a baby product is recalled. Of course, the Consumer Products Safety Commission also sends out recall notices—sign up at www.cpsc.gov.

◆ *Consider buying products from web sites that will inform you of recalls.* Case in point: Amazon/Babies R Us does a good job of letting customers know of recalled products. One reader was amazed when Amazon sent her a recall notice (with detailed instructions on what to do) for a bassinet she bought over a year ago.

◆ *Be careful with eBay and other second-hand purchases.* Yes, eBay has great deals, but be sure you aren't buying a recalled product. Do a search of the CPSC's web site (www.cpsc.gov) to find whether that car seat deal is really a dud.

removed from store shelves (if the recall is for the current production run). If the recall is for a product's previous production run, you may still see it on store shelves (since the defect may have been corrected months before). That's why it is key to see WHEN the recalled product was manufactured. Of course, different car seats in the same manufacturer's line may be totally unaffected by a recall.

Another tip: make sure to fill out the registration card that comes with any car seat you buy . . . and send it in! In theory, this will get you expedited recall info and repair kits. Also: sign up for a recall list like the free e-newsletter on our web site (see the back of the book for details). Unfortunately, with some car seat makers, even if you fill out a registration card you may not get a recall notice. For more on this problem, see the following box.

Smart Shopper Tip #7
Watch the height limit
"My son isn't anywhere near the 20 lb. limit for his infant seat, but he's so tall I don't think it is safe anymore—he has to bend his legs when we put him in!"

Here's a little known fact about most infant seats: in addition to WEIGHT limits, all infant car seats also have HEIGHT limits. And like everything in the car seat world, each seat has different limits (check the sticker on the side of the carrier—by law, the manufacturer must list both height and weight limits). Once your baby exceeds EITHER the height or weight limit, you should move him to a convertible seat.

One note on this: while the weight limit is important, do one other test if your child is approaching the height limit—is there less than an inch of seat left above baby's head? If so, then move your baby to a convertible seat (facing the rear of the vehicle until they pass one year of age).

With the bigger babies everyone seems to be having these days (credit more breastfeeding? Genetically modified foods?), this isn't a moot point. A large infant might exceed the height limit BEFORE he or she passes the weight limit. Here's the scoop: height limits range from 26" for the Graco SnugRide to 29" for the Eddie Bauer (Cosco) infant car seat and one version of the Baby Trend Latch-Loc. Most infant seats have weight limits in the 20lb to 22lb range (FYI: in 2005, the government is changing the safety standard, requiring all infant seats to work to 22 lbs.). Later in this section, we'll have a chart that lists the height and weight limits of all major infant car seats. See the box "How Big is Normal?" later in this chapter for more on this topic.

Finally, remember WEIGHT limits are more relevant than height limits with seats. Why? Some babies have longer legs, while others have longer torsos. Babies that have longer legs may technically surpass the height limit, even though you still have more than an inch of space above their head to the top of the seat. In that case, leave them in the infant seat until they outgrow it by weight.

Smart Shopper Tip #8
Do I have to buy THREE seats?
"My baby has outgrown his infant seat. Can I buy a combo seat that converts to a booster?"

The short answer: yes. Do we recommend it? No. Why? We think the safest place for an infant who has outgrown an infant seat is in a CONVERTIBLE seat in rear-facing mode. Leave them there until they are AT LEAST a year of age—longer if they still are under the weight limit. Note: all "combo" seats with five-point harnesses that convert to a belt-positioning booster are FORWARD-FACING only seats. Examples of combo seats include the Cosco Summit, Graco CarGo, Evenflo Vision and so on.

So, what is best? When your child outgrows their convertible seat, THEN we recommend a booster seat (combo or regular). Now, we realize what you are thinking: have we lost our minds? We are recommending you buy THREE seats for your child: infant, convertible, and then a booster. Wouldn't it be cheaper to get one of those all-in-one seats or at least one that combines the convertible/booster function? No, not in our opinion. The all-in-one-seats (like the Eddie Bauer Three-In-One or Cosco Alpha Omega) are a poor choice; see review later in this chapter. And while those combo boosters are a good choice for a three or four year old child who has outgrown his convertible seat but is not mature enough to sit in a belt-positioning booster, combo seats are NOT good for infants—they often don't recline and have less sleeping support than convertibles.

That's why you won't see reviews of combo seats in this book—they are best for children over two years of age. We review combo seats and regular boosters in our *Toddler Bargains* book.

Smart Shopper Tip #9
Holding Your Baby Back: Safety Harness Advice
"Which safety harness is best—the 5-point, bar-shield, or T-shield?

Car Seat Lesson 101: understanding the different harness systems available on the market. For INFANT seats, you have two choices: three point or five-point belts (although nearly all infant seats now have five-point harnesses). For CONVERTIBLE seats, you have three choices: five-point, bar-shield or t-shield.

Three (or five) point belts refer to the number of points in which the belt attaches to the car seat. A t-shield is a plastic shield that buckles in below baby's crotch. A bar shield lowers over the baby's head and snaps into a buckle.

Our recommendations: for INFANT seats, in past editions, we thought three-point systems were just fine, based on crash test data we reviewed. Today, with most infant car seats in the market sporting five-point harnesses, that has become the de facto standard. Yes, you will see an occasional three-point harness on a cheap infant car seat sold at Wal-Mart, but that is the exception to the rule. Our advice: go for the five-point harness.

For CONVERTIBLE seats, we also recommend the five-point version. Why? Safety experts say it's the best choice because you can tighten the belts to securely hold your baby in her seat. T-shields are second in preference (but don't work well for small infants). And bar shields have another problem—some don't adjust well to growing children. Even those expensive models that feature *adjustable* shields only adjust so much—if your child grows quickly, they still might outgrow the car seat. The result? You'll have to move them into a booster seat (making an extra purchase) sooner than you want to.

Another major problem with bar shields: wiggling toddlers can get out of them way too easily. One mom told us she was horrified to look in her rear view mirror one day and find her 18 month-old child STANDING in his car seat while the vehicle was moving. We

Are higher price seats better?

When you shell out $200 instead of $100 for a car seat, do you get a car seat that is twice as safe? Answer: no, price is not always an indicator of quality. For example, some expensive seats have leather-like covers. Yes, they cost $200, but often you are paying for a fancy pad or designer name, not the safety features of a seat.

Now, that said, we should note that in some cases you DO get better safety features when you spend more. Example: Britax seats are pricey ($200 or so), but they have extra EPS foam for crash protection, no-twist straps and a slew of other safety and convenience features. Plus you can tether these seats either forward OR rear facing, unlike most of the competition, which is just forward-facing. The tether has been shown to greatly reduce seat movement in a crash. Now, THAT is a safety feature. And if a seat is loaded with features that make it easier to use, you could argue that parents would be less likely to miss-use the seat—and that makes it safer.

think five point harnesses are safer since it is very difficult for baby to wiggle out when the belts are tightened correctly.

Let's be honest, however: the five-point harness is the *least convenient* to use. You have to put each strap around baby's arms, find the lower buckle (which always seems to disappear under their rump) and then snap them in. Bar-shields and t-shields slip over the baby's head in one motion and are easier to buckle.

The fact that the five-point harness is inconvenient is just the way it goes. Simply put, it's the safest choice for your baby. And sometimes as a parent you have to do what's best for your child, even if that makes your life less convenient.

Here are ten more shopping tips for car seats:

◆ *How easily does it recline?* All convertible seats are supposed to have a recline feature to make sure baby is at a proper angle. Of course, how easily the seat reclines varies from model to model—and reaching that lever in a rear-facing seat may be a challenge. Check it out in the store before you buy.

◆ *No-twist straps.* Better car seats have thicker straps that don't twist. The result: it is easier to get a child in and out of a seat. Cheaper seats have cheaper webbing that can be a nightmare—"twisty straps" are a key reason why parents hate their car seats. Later in this chapter, we'll point out which seats have this problem.

◆ *Check the belt adjustments.* You don't merely adjust the car seat's belts just when your baby gets bigger—if you put Junior in a coat, you'll need to loosen the belts as well. As a result, it's important to check how easily they adjust. Of course, every car seat maker seems to have a different idea on how to do this. The best car seats let you adjust the belts from the *front*. Those models that require you to access the back of the seat to adjust the belts are more hassle. FYI: do not put your child in a bulky coat or snowsuit when sitting in a safety seat. In the case of an accident, the bulky coat might compress, compromising the safety of the seat. At most, only put a child in a thin coat (like a polar fleece) when they are riding in a child safety seat. (To keep an infant warm, consider a seat cover-up, which goes on the outside of the seat. We'll discuss examples of these products later in this chapter).

◆ *Change the harness height.* Some seats require you to re-thread the belts when you change harness heights. Try this in the store to see how easy/difficult it is. Note: the best seats have automatic harness height adjusters that require no re-threading.

◆ *Look at the chest clip.* The chest clip or harness tie holds the two belts in place. Lower-quality seats have a simple "slide-in" clip—you slip the belt under a tab. That's OK, but some older toddlers can slip out from this type of chest clip. A better bet: a chest clip that SNAPS the two belts together like a seat belt. This is more kid-proof.

◆ *Are the instructions in Greek?* Before you buy the car seat, take a minute to look at the set-up and use instructions. Make sure you can make sense of the seat's documentation. Another tip: if possible, ask the store for any installation tips and advice.

◆ *Is the pad cover machine-washable?* You'd think this would be a "no-brainer," but a surprising number of seats (both convertible and infant) have covers that aren't removable or machine washable. Considering how grimy these covers can get, it's smart to look for this feature. Also check to see if you can wash the harness.

◆ *Will the seat be a sauna in the summer?* Speaking of the seat pad, check the material. Plush, velvet-like covers might seem nice in the store, but think about next August. Will your baby be sitting in a mini-sauna? Cotton or cotton-blend fabric pads are better than heavier weight, non-breathable fabrics.

◆ *Does the seat need to be installed with each use?* The best car seats are "permanently" installed in your car. When you put baby in, all you do is buckle them in the seat's harness system. Yet some infant car seats and even a few convertible models need to be installed with each use—that means you have to belt the thing into your car every time you use it. Suffice it to say, that's a major drawback.

◆ *Watch out for hot buckles.* Some inexpensive car seats have exposed metal buckles and hardware. In the hot sun, these buckles can get toasty and possibly burn a child. Yes, you can cover these buckles with a blanket when you leave the car, but that's a hassle. A better bet is to buy a seat with a buckle cover or no exposed metal.

◆ *Is it shopping cart compatible?* Some infant car seats are better at this than others. One simple test: while you are in a store like Babies R Us, Target or Wal-Mart, take the infant carrier and try snapping it into shopping cart. You'll find some fit better than others. Now, we should point out that many safety advocates cringe when they see infant seats snapped into the upper part of a shopping cart—they say this makes the cart top-heavy, which could cause it to tip over. Advocates say the safest place for baby is in their infant seat in the *main* part of the basket or carried by mom or dad. Some stores now realize this problem and have shopping carts with integrated infant seats, eliminating the need for you to bring your own. However, they can get rather grimy from the last passenger.

◆ *How heavy is it?* This is a critical factor for infant car seats, but also important for convertibles. Why? First, remember you are lugging that infant seat WITH a baby that will weigh 7 to 10 lbs. *to start.* When your baby outgrows the infant seat, she will weigh 20 to 22 lbs. *in addition to the seat weight!* To help you shop, we list the weights for major infant car seat brands later in this chapter. What about convertible seats? If you buy one seat and plan to move it from car to car, realize weight may be a factor here as well.

◆ *Buying a new car?* Consider getting a built-in (also called integrated) child safety seat. The cost varies from car maker to maker, but is about $200 to $400. Remember that most built-in seats can only be used with children one year or older in a FORWARD-FACING position; you'll still need to buy an infant car seat for babies under one year of age. And if your child outgrows their infant seat before a year of age, you will need to use a convertible seat in rear-facing mode. That obviously eliminates some of the advantages of an integrated seat; that said, since the built-in seat is designed as part of the vehicle, you are getting a very safe seat. Note: the limits for integrated seats vary by vehicle maker, so check before purchasing.

Safe & Sound

I **NEVER BUY A USED CAR SEAT.** If the seat has been in an accident, it may be damaged and no longer safe to use. Bottom line: used seats are a big risk unless you know their history. And the technology of car seats improves every year; a seat that is just five years old may lack important safety features compared to today's models. (And, as we discussed earlier, seats older than five years old also have parts that may wear out and fail . . . a big reason not to use an old seat). Another tip: make sure the seat has not been recalled (see the contact info below for the National Highway Traffic Safety Administration). Safety seats made before 1981 may not meet current safety standards (unfortunately, most seats aren't stamped with their year of manufacture, so this may be difficult to determine). The bottom line: risky hand-me-downs aren't worth it. Brand new car seats (which start at $50) aren't that huge of an investment to ensure your child's safety.

2 **GET YOUR SEAT SAFETY CHECKED.** No matter how hard you try to buy and install the best seat for your child, mistakes with installation can still occur. There's nothing like the added peace of mind of having your car seat safety checked by an expert. Such checks are free and widely available. The National Highway Traffic Safety Administration's web site (www.nhtsa.dot.gov) has a national listing of fitting/inspection stations. Another cool program: Daimler Chrysler has a FREE car seat inspection—just take your car to a Chrysler dealer and they'll check your seat to see if it is safely installed. No, you don't need to have an appointment, nor do you have to own a Chrysler. Call 877-FIT-4-A-KID or web: www.FitForAKid.org to find a local participating Chrysler, Jeep or Dodge near you.

3 DON'T TRUST THE LEVEL INDICATOR. Yes, many infant car seats come with "level indicators" and instructions to make sure the seat is installed so the indicator is in the "green" area. When in the green, the seat is supposedly at the correct angle to protect your baby in case of a crash. Nice idea, but thanks to the myriad of back seat designs in dozens of cars, the seat may be incorrectly installed even if the indicator says it is fine. At car seat safety checks, many techs ignore the level indicator and instead use this test: They take a piece of paper and fold one corner to form a 45-degree angle. Then they place the side of the paper against the back of the infant car seat where the baby's back would lie. When the folded corner is level with the horizon, the seat is at the correct angle—even if the indicator says it ain't so. If you aren't sure your seat is installed to the correct angle, take it to a car seat safety check.

4 FORGET CAR SEAT ADD-ONS. We've seen all manner of travel "accessories" for kid's in car seats, including bottle holders, activity trays and so on. The problem: all these objects are potential hazards in an accident, flying around the car and possibly striking you (the adult) or your child.

5 HOW TALL IS TOO TALL? You'll notice that most child safety seats utilize two types of limits: weight and height. It's the latter limit that creates some confusion among parents. Convertible seats have both a rear and forward facing height limit—this is required by federal law (for those inquiring minds, the standard is FMVSS 213). Most safety techs say the maximum height for a child is when their head is one inch below the top of the shell (the 1″ rule) or if your child's shoulders exceed the height of the top harness slot. The problem: some car seat makers have more strict height limits than the 1″ rule. Here's the frustrating part: kids often outgrow the seat's stated height limit *before* they reach that 1″ rule or their shoulders are taller than the top harness slot, leaving some parents to wonder if they should continue using the seat. The problem is one of interpretation: while the federal law requires every seat to have height limits, car seat makers are free to interpret this rule (and usage of the seat). Some seat makers just interpret the rules more strictly than other car seat makers. Bottom line: while we understand seat makers might have their own take on federal safety standards, it is generally safe to use a seat until your child's head is 1″ below the top of the seat or their shoulders exceed the top harness slot—even if their height is slightly above the stated limit for the seat.

6 **READ THE DIRECTIONS VERY CAREFULLY.** Many car accidents end in tragedy because a car seat was installed improperly. If you have any questions about the directions, call the company or return the car seat for a model that is easier to use. Another tip: read your vehicle's owner's manual for any special installation instructions. Consult with your auto dealer if you have any additional questions.

What's the number-one problem with car seat installation? In the past, figuring out what to do with that darn locking clip was perhaps the most misunderstood part of your child's car seat. Vehicles made before September 1, 1995 typically require the use of a locking clip, a small piece of metal that "locks" the safety belt. The locking clip attaches right above the buckle. Newer vehicles made after that date may have safety-belt locking features that eliminate the need for locking clips—check your owner's manual for details. Without a locking clip in older cars, the seat could become a projectile, injuring or killing your child. Make sure the safety seat is held firmly against the back of the car seat and doesn't wobble from side to side (or front to back).

Thankfully, some child safety seat makers have woken up to the locking clip problem—two models we'll review later actually have built-in locking clips. Also, the new LATCH or ISO-FIX car seats eliminate the locking clip as well.

Finally, it's always good to put your knee on the seat and push down with your full weight while you tighten the seat belt. This eliminates belt slack and ensures a snug installation.

7 **USE YOUR CAR SEAT.** Don't make the mistake of being in a hurry and forgetting to (or just not wanting to) attach the restraints. Many parents merely put their child in the seat without hooking up the harness. It is more dangerous to leave your child in a car seat unrestrained by the safety harness than it is to put him or her in a regular seat belt. And always observe weight limits. As we mentioned earlier, children should ride REAR-FACING to one year of age, regardless of weight. Make sure your child's safety seat is able to accommodate her weight in that position.

8 **PUT THE CAR SEAT IN THE BACK SEAT.** Air bags and car seats don't mix—several reports of injuries and deaths have been attributed to passenger side air bags that deployed when a car seat was in the front seat. As a result, the safest place for kids is the back seat. In fact, whether the car has an air bag or not, the back is always safer—federal government statistics say putting a child in the back seat instead of the front reduces the risk of death by 27%.

And where is the safest part of the back seat? Safety experts say it's the middle—it is the furthest away from side-impact risks. The only

Baby's Away: Vacation Rentals

Just because you're a parent doesn't mean you'll never take a vacation again. Yet, how do you travel with baby . . . or more importantly, with all baby's stuff? Well, the good news is you don't have to lug all that baby equipment with you on the plane (or in the car). Baby's Away (800) 571-0077 (web: www. BabysAway. com) rents everything you need at many resort and vacation spots in the U.S. You can rent name-brand cribs, strollers, high chairs, safety gates, potty seats, toys and more at reasonable rates (either by the day or week).

problem with that advice is that some cars have a raised hump in the middle of the back seat that makes it difficult/impossible to safely install a car seat. Another problem: safety seats are best held against the car's back seat by a three-point belt—and many middle seats just have a two-point belt. Finally, consider the LATCH problem we noted above (where many vehicles have no LATCH anchors in the middle of the back seat, only the sides). Bottom line: while the middle of the back seat is the safest spot, sometimes you just can't install a seat there. The next best place is in an outboard position with a lap/shoulder belt.

What about side curtain air bags you see in the back seats of some cars? Many new cars come equipped with side-impact air bags or curtains. These air bags are NOT as dangerous as front air bags, as they deploy with much less force in the event of a side impact crash. Therefore, putting a car seat next to a door that has a side curtain air bag is not a danger.

9 **REGISTER YOUR SEAT.** Don't forget to send the registration card back to the manufacturer. Yes, earlier we discussed how some manufacturers ignore sending notice to registered users when a car seat is recalled (instead, relying on a media announcement), but others will send notice.

10 **DON'T USE A SEAT OVER FIVE YEARS OLD.** Car seats don't last forever—parts wear out, extreme heat and cold in a vehicle takes a toll on a seat's internal mechanics and more. And safety standards change and improve over time. That's why experts say don't use a seat that is over five years old. What about seats sold on eBay that might have been sitting in a warehouse for several years? Again, don't take the risk. Finally, let's talk about those seats that promise you can use them for kids up to 65 or 80 pounds? Britax makes one (the Marathon) which can be used up to 65 pounds with a five point harness (or about six to seven years

car seats

of age), while Eddie Bauer/Cosco claims their Three-in-One (or Alpha Omega) seat will last up to 80 pounds as a belt-positioning booster. 80 pounds is equivalent to an 8 to 10 year old child. Notice a problem here? If it is unsafe to use a seat up older than five years, does it make sense to go for that Eddie Bauer seat? No, not in our opinion.

While we do recommend the Britax seat (as 65 pounds or six/seven years would be the outer limit of any seat use), remember the PRACTICAL limits of any seat. Car seats can get pretty gross after a few years of use. Even if you are diligent about keeping the cover clean, you still might have to replace it after three to four years of use (and not all car seat makers sell replacement covers as an accessory).

Recalls

The National Highway Traffic Safety Administration (NHTSA) has a toll-free hot line to check for recalls or to report a safety problem. For info, call (800) 424-9393 or (202) 366-0123 (web: www.nhtsa.dot.gov). You can have a list of recalled car seats automatically faxed to you at no charge. Note that this is a different governmental agency than the Consumer Product Safety Commission, which regulates and recalls other juvenile products. (For Canadian recalls and safety seat rules, see the special section at the end of this book for more info).

Money-Saving Secrets

GET A FREE SEAT! A reader emailed in this great tip—her health insurance carrier provides free infant car seats to parents who complete a parenting class. No specific class is required . . . you just provide proof of completion. And health insurance providers aren't the only ones with car seat deals—check with your auto insurance provider as well. Plus, some employers may have negotiated deals, so check there as well. Of course, it is in insurance carriers' best interest to hand out free seats or rebates—each child safety seat used today saves auto insurers $100, private health insurers $45 and the government $45 in costs that would otherwise be incurred from unrestrained kids in auto crashes. Insurers pay out a whopping $175 million in claims annually resulting from crashes in which children age birth to four were traveling unrestrained in motor vehicles (source: "Child Safety Seats: How Large are the Benefits and Who Should Pay?" The Children's Safety Network). The take-home message: CALL your health and auto insurance providers to see what freebies, rebates and other deals they have for new parents.

2 **IF YOU HAVE TWO CARS, YOU DON'T NEED TO BUY TWO INFANT SEATS.** Instead, just buy one seat and then get an extra stay-in-the-car base. While it's not widely known, major infant seat makers like Graco and Evenflo sell their auto bases separately for $40 to $60. If you can't find them in stores likes Babies R Us, check out baby web sites that stock them.

3 **WEB SHOPPING 'BOTS AND COUPONS TO CUT PRICES.** Who has the lowest prices on car seats? It depends—stores like Babies R Us and Baby Depot are very competitive on car seat prices. But, the web may have even better deals, especially if you use an online coupon or find a free shipping offer. Again, using a shopping 'bot like Shopping.com (go to the Kids & Family section) or Froogle (www.froogle.google.com) is a good way to compare prices for a model or brand across several sites at once. Look for the free shipping deals for the best bargains, since bulky car seats can be expensive to ship. Before you order, check which sites have coupons (see Chapter 7 for a list of such sites like DotDeals.com and FlamingoWorld.com).

4 **EXPENSIVE MODELS AREN'T NECESSARILY BETTER.** If you spend $100 on a car seat, are you getting one that's twice as safe as a seat that's $50? Not necessarily. Often, all you get for that additional money is plush padding and extras like pillows. Do infants notice the extra padding? No, not in our opinion. Sure, you need SOME padding, but the minimum is fine for most infants. We do agree that this becomes more of an issue as a baby gets older—toddlers may be uncomfortable in less-padded seats for longer car trips. But since infants sleep most of the time, we think babies under a year of age don't notice the quilted upgraded fabric you paid an extra bucks for. Bottom line: the $50 seat may be just as safe and probably as comfortable for baby.

The Name Game: Reviews of Selected Manufacturers

Here are our reviews of the major car seat makers sold in the U.S. and Canada. Many of the infant seats reviewed here are sold as part of stroller/car seat combo products; the strollers are reviewed separately in the next chapter. Of course, you don't have to buy a travel system—nearly all these seats are sold separately.

Special note: this section gives you an overview of each brand;

CAR SEATS

we now review each model seat separately later in this chapter! All seats are LATCH-compatible, unless otherwise noted.

The Ratings

A **EXCELLENT**—*our top pick!*
B **GOOD**— *above average quality, prices, and creativity.*
C **FAIR**—*could stand some improvement.*
D **POOR**—*yuck! Could stand some major improvement.*

Baby Trend *For a dealer near you, call (800) 328-7363, (909) 902-5568, Web: www.babytrend.com.* Better known for their strollers and other baby products, Baby Trend entered the car seat market in 2002. Their main offering is the Latch-Loc infant seat which is the only infant seat at this writing that has a "rigid" ISOFIX-type LATCH attachment system. This seat sells for $90. Baby Trend also makes a flexible LATCH version of their seat called the Flex-Loc. FYI: The Latch-Loc is sold as a stand-alone seat online and in some stores, while the Flex-Loc is sold as part of a travel system at Babies R Us for $140 to $180.

Safety Track Record. There have been no recalls on these seats as of this writing.

Baby Trend's infant seats are reviewed on page 369.

Britax *460 Greenway Industrial Dr., Ft. Mill SC 29715. For a dealer near you, call (888) 4-BRITAX or (704) 409-1700. Web: www.britax.com* European-based Britax came to the U.S. car seat market in 1996 and immediately made a big splash—their convertible seats (particularly the Roundabout) became best sellers thanks to their innovative features. Britax got its start providing child seats for Mercedes and Porsche and translated that Euro safety-know-how into innovative features not seen before in the U.S. and Canada. The Roundabout is one of the few car seats on the market that can use a tether in either the front or rear-facing position (Britax calls this their Versa Tether feature). Britax seats also use a patented "lock-off" clamp (for use in cars that don't have LATCH) that securely attaches the seat to the car's belt. Finally, we're impressed that Britax is the only child seat manufacturer with its own state-of-the-art crash test sleds that can certify seats to various government safety requirements.

That said, Britax did hit some speed bumps in the past few years. The company has been hit with several recalls, including 2004's recall of 350,000 Marathon and Wizard car seats for a faulty adjuster strap. While recalls are a fact of life in the car seat biz, we were not happy with how Britax handled (or more accurately, mis-handled)

the recall. We received many complaints from parents who couldn't get through on Britax's recall hotline and others said their repair kits took weeks to arrive. We expected better customer service from a company that charges top-shelf prices for its products.

Britax has also struggled to keep up with demand for some of their popular seats; the result has been waits of several weeks for certain models. Another frustration: the company often announces new models (including plugging them on their web site), only to miss their targeted release dates by *months* (and, in one case, two years). Britax blames this on their extensive safety testing, which of course is understandable—but it is still frustrating. The company should stop promising new product until it is ready to deliver.

This year, Britax is trying to widen its market reach by selling scaling downed versions of its seats under the Fisher Price label. As you'll read later in this section, these are re-packaged versions of Britax car seats that will carry a lower price tag.

Safety track record: Yes, there have been recalls on Britax's car seats, including the big Marathon/Wizard recall from 2004. So, is all this talk about Britax's safety just sales hype? No, we still think these are among the best seats on the market. None of the recalled products were associated with injuries (Britax caught the problems

Seat cover-ups provide warmth

Okay, you aren't supposed to put baby in a car seat with a bulky coat. But what if you live in, say, Maine and its currently 10 degrees outside as you read this? Try a cover-up that fits OVER the car seat and hence doesn't compromise the seat's safety. One of our favorites: **Kiddopotamus's "Great Baby Cover Up" Fleece Warmer** ($26), a multi-purpose cover-up that can be used as a front carrier warmer, stroller warmer . . . or for car seats. The same company also offers several other innovative travel products, including the Baby Shade (a cover for infant seats and strollers). For more details, call (800) 772-8339 or web: www.kiddopotamus.com.

What about other infant body pillows or warmers? If it does not come in the box with your infant or convertible car seat, we wouldn't use it. Add-on or after-market products that are not manufacturer-tested may compromise the seat safety. The same thing goes for car seat toy bars or special mirrors so you can see baby from the front seat. We say don't use them. They could come loose in an accident, becoming a dangerous projectile.

in time) and Britax seats continue to score well on crash-tests.

Britax's infant seats are reviewed on page 371. Britax's convertible seat reviews begin on page 379.

Century. This brand, owned by Graco, was discontinued in 2002.

Combi *1962 Hwy 160 West #100, Ft. Mill, SC 29708. For a dealer near you, call (800) 992-6624, (803) 802-8416; Web: www. combi-intl.com.* While better known for its strollers, Combi has branched out with a line of car seats in recent years. The main emphasis here is on infant seats that pair with Combi strollers to form travel systems, although Combi does sell a couple of convertible and booster seats as well.

As of this writing, Combi's infant car seat line up includes the Tyro, Connection and Centre DX. The Tyro works with Combi's Urban Life Series (Savona, Tetra and Ultra Savvy), while the Connection infant seat works with Combi's City Life Series (City Savvy, Soho DX, Savvy EX and Select DK5). The new Combi Centre DX will work with the Metro Life Series strollers, including the Cosmo ST, Cosmo DX and Combi 4. FYI: The convertible Avatar is being phased out for a new offering later in 2006 (no word yet on what that is).

Safety track record. In 2005, Combi recalled the Avatar convertible seat after the model failed a Consumer Reports crash test. Combi fixed the problem and a re-tested Avatar scored well in CR's tests.

Combi's infant seats are reviewed on page 372. Combi's convertible seats are reviewed on page 383.

What is the lightest infant car seat carrier?

Here at BABY BARGAINS we have Ivy League-trained scientists who help us determine important stuff like which infant car seat weighs the least (and hence, is easiest to lug around). Oh, we're just kidding. Actually, we the authors just went to our local baby store and stood there in the aisles lifting each infant seat and saying things like "Yep, this one is lighter!" For this edition, we actually employed a scale to get accurate readings (and you thought only the folks in lab coats at *Consumer Reports* got to play with such toys). Our official results: the lightest seat is the Evenflo Discovery (5.5 lbs.) followed by the Evenflo Portabout (6.5 lbs.) and Graco SnugRide (7 lbs.). The heaviest seats? That crown goes to the Eddie Bauer (Cosco) seat, as well as the Baby Trend Latch-Loc—both weighed in at 9 lbs. We list the weights for infant car seat carriers in a chart later in this chapter. Of course, the weight of an infant seat isn't the only factor we used to decide which was best, but it certainly is important.

Compass *For a dealer near you, call (888) 899-2229. Web: www.compassbaby.com* Ohio-based Compass is a new player in the car seat market. Founded by former Evenflo employees, Compass first debuted on the market in 2004 with a booster seat. In the past year, Compass launched their first infant seat (the I400) and companion stroller. Compass' niche seems to be car seats that are a step up in features, safety and design from the cheap stuff you see in Wal-Mart . . . but are priced below the premium that Britax charges. We're talking seats with extra EPS foam for crash protection, plusher padding and so on.

Safety track record. Compass is so new, we don't have any safety data on their seats. They have not been crash-tested by *Consumer Reports* yet, nor have there been any recalls as of this writing.

Compass' infant seat is reviewed on page 373.

Cosco *For a dealer near you, call (812) 372-0141 or 514-323-5701 for a dealer in Canada). Web: www.djgusa.com* Owned by Canadian conglomerate Dorel Industries, Cosco has staged a comeback in the car seat market in recent years. Previously an also-ran, Cosco had big success with their Alpha Omega seat (described later) and Eddie Bauer-licensed products. Yet, we are still troubled by Cosco's poor safety track record, which we'll discuss at the end of this review.

Before we get to the models, let us point out that Cosco makes three versions of their car seats: one under their own name and as well as versions under the "Eddie Bauer" and "NASCAR" names. Note that in all cases, the seats are just the same, only the colors/fab-

---

Consumer Reports crash tests vs our ratings

Every time *Consumer Reports* comes out with a report on car seats, our phones and email light up—many readers want to know how we sometimes come to different conclusions as to which are the best car seats. It's quite simple: *Consumer Reports* actually crash tests car seats, something we don't have the budget to do here at *Baby Bargains*. When we rate a car seat, we look at the seat's overall features, ease of use and value based on parent feedback and our own hands-on inspections. We also look at the company's recall track record and (if they are available) any *Consumer Report's* crash test reports. Even though we might use different rating methodologies, most of the time we agree with *Consumer Reports*. In the case of a major discrepancy, we'll often comment on this on our web page at BabyBargains.com. For more on this topic, see the discussion in Chapter 1.

car seats

ric patterns have changed. Of course, you will pay extra for the name. Cosco also makes car seats under their Safety 1st brand.

FYI: Cosco used to import a series of car seats from their European subsidiary, Maxi Cosi. These seats were discontinued in 2002.

Safety track record: Cosco's safety track record has been marred by recalls—12 at last count since 1990. Among the worst was a 1999 recall involving 670,000 Arriva and Turnabout infant car

The NYC Taxi Dilemma

Here's a common email we get from parents in New York and other urban areas: are there any portable car seats that can be used in taxis? Something that is lightweight, easy to install and collapses to fit inside a small purse when not in use? Well, the answer is no—there's no perfect solution. But we have a few ideas. Let's break out our advice for New Yorkers by age:

◆ *Infant* (birth to six months). The safest way for an infant to ride in a taxi is in an infant car seat. Most (but not all) can be strapped in without the stay-in-the-car base. An exception: the Peg Perego Primo Viaggio. This seat CANNOT be strapped into a taxi just without its base, making it a poor choice for this use.

◆ *Older baby* (six months to four years). This is where it gets trickier. Our advice here would be the *Cosco Tote 'N Go* (formerly called the Travel Vest)—basically a small seat with a five-point harness for babies 25 to 40 pounds. It can only used forward facing. Best of all, it weighs just 4 pounds—we can hear those parents on the way to Zabar's cheering  right now. Is it safe? Yes, for that occasional taxi ride. Would we use it every day in a vehicle? No—while the Cosco Tote 'N Go meets federal safety standards, parent testers we've interviewed say it is hard to get a good, tight fit with it, no matter whether they installed it with just a lap belt or with a lap and shoulder belt.

What about belt-positioning devices? The jury is still out on these products (lightweight devices that simply adjust a vehicle's belts to better fit a child). Some safety advocates say they don't provide any protection and the government has no data on them—yet. The National Highway Traffic Safety Administration has pledged to study belt-positioners, but we're unsure when they'll announce the findings. Stay tuned.

seats. The seats' handles unexpectedly released in some cases, causing the seats to flip forward and dump out the occupants. 29 children were injured due to this defect. And the problems for Cosco continued—in 2002, the company was investigated by Transport Canada (the Canadian equivalent of the NHTSA) for "omitting" foam padding in several car seats. Sears of Canada then removed Cosco seats from their shelves pending the investigation. There was no formal recall, but Cosco quietly asked Canadian retailers to stop selling several models. And in 2005, Cosco recalled 190,000 infant car seats (Designer 22 model) for defective harnesses.

To Cosco's credit, however, we should note the company has rolled out several innovative models that convert from infant to toddler and then to booster seats. This extra value pitch (use the seat from birth to college) explains Cosco's success in chains stores like Babies R Us, where the brand runs a strong second to Britax.

Reviews of Cosco's infant seats start on page 374, while Cosco's convertible seat reviews start on page 384.

Eddie Bauer. These seats are made by Cosco; see the previous review for details.

Evenflo *1801 Commerce Dr., Piqua, OH 45356. For a dealer near you, call (800) 233-5921 or (937) 415-3300. In Canada, PO Box 1598, Brantford, Ontario, N3T 5V7. (905) 337-2229. Web: www.evenflo.com* Evenflo is like the Avis of car seats—they try harder because they are number two (or three or four, in terms of car seat market share). In the last few years, the company has tried to put several disastrous recalls behind them and add innovative features to their car seats. The results? Mixed—seats like their Triumph convertible seat (reviewed later in this chapter) have been modest successes, with innovative features such as the Memory Harness. However, Evenflo's infant seat (Portabout) usually scores below category leaders Graco and Perego in crash tests and parent reviews. All in all, Evenflo often seems outflanked in the car seat market; Britax trumps them on safety features and Graco outguns them in the lower-price points. Even downscale Cosco has a hotter license (Eddie Bauer) than Evenflo, whose OshKosh line seems dated fashion-wise. FYI: The OshKosh seats are exactly the same as Evenflo's offerings, just different fabric.

And despite the fact that Evenflo's convertible seats score closer to the top of the pack in crash tests by *Consumer Reports*, we still get many parent complaints about Evenflo. Ease of use (or lack thereof) is a common gripe, with seats that have difficult-to-adjust belts and other frustrations.

Safety track record: In 1998, Evenflo was forced to recall 800,000

On My Way infant seats after 89 children were injured when the seat's handle failed to lock and the seat tipped forward. Yeah, that was several years ago, but what still bothers us to this day was how Evenflo handled this situation—while we realize car seat recalls are an all-too-frequent fact of life, we were miffed that Evenflo first blamed parents for misusing the product when reports of the problem first surfaced. Only after arm-twisting by the federal government did Evenflo reluctantly recall the seat and admit the production defect. A top safety regulator heavily criticized Evenflo's foot-dragging, calling the company one of "the most difficult to work with" in the industry. That kind of behavior is inexcusable; as a result, we gave Evenflo poor ratings in the last few editions of our book.

So, what's up with Evenflo now? The company has tried to mend its ways. The entire management team that was in charge in the 1998 infant seat fiasco is now gone, replaced by a new crew that seems to care more about safety. So, we have slowly warmed to Evenflo seats in the recent years, as you'll read in the reviews later in this chapter.

Reviews of Evenflo's infant seats start on page 375, while Evenflo's convertible seat reviews start on page 386.

Fisher-Price Fisher Price car seats are re-packaged Britax seats—scaled down with fewer features but with lower prices. These seats were launched in 2006, so we don't have crash test or parent feedback on them yet. *See info on FP's infant seat on page 376 and convertible model on page 387,*

Graco *Rt. 23, Main St., Elverson, PA 19520. For a dealer near you, call (800) 345-4109, (610) 286-5951. Web: www.gracobaby.com.* In recent years, Graco kept their car seat line simple—they offered just

---

Leaving On a Jet Plane

Which car seats can be taken on an airplane? All of the seats reviewed in this section are certified for use in an airplane. But will they fit? That's a tougher question—each airline has different size seats. Hence, wide car seats like the Evenflo Triumph may not fit (especially if you're required to keep the armrests down for take-off). Check with the airline before you get to the airport if you have questions about car seat compatibility. A better bet: simple seats like the Graco ComfortSport (which is narrow and light in weight) usually do the trick.

Here's a listing of convertible car seats with the narrowest bases: Graco ComfortSport (17.0"), Safety 1st Intera (16.5") and Cosco Touriva (16.3").

one infant car seat (the SnugRide) and one convertible seat (the ComfortSport). No, these seats don't have a fancy look, but they are excellent offerings with good features at decent prices.

Graco plans to launch a new collection of car seats, out by the time you read this. The "Safe Seat" collection will feature an infant seat, "toddler" seat (forward facing only for kids 20 to 40 lbs.) and a convertible. Graco has also inked a deal with Laura Ashley to create Ashley-themed versions of their car seats and strollers.

Safety track record: In 2003, Graco recalled 650,000 SnugRide infant seats for missing hardware used to attach the carrier to the base.

Graco's infant seat is reviewed on page 377. Graco's convertible seat is reviewed on page 388.

Laura Ashley. These seats are made by Graco; see review above.

OshKosh. These seats are made by Evenflo. See their review earlier for details.

Peg Perego *3625 Independence Dr., Ft. Wayne, IN 46808. For a dealer near you, call (260) 482-8191. Web: www.perego.com* After seeing their stroller sales eaten away by travel systems for years, Peg Perego finally decided to address this shortcoming with the debut of an infant seat (and travel system). The infant seat has since gone on to be quite a success, despite two recalls (see below).

Safety track record: Underscoring how difficult it is to crack the car seat market, Peg Perego has had not one but TWO recalls since its release. While no children were injured by the recalls, the misfires made us question whether Perego's infant seat was really ready for prime time in our last edition. Since then, however, Perego has worked out the kinks in this seat and we now recommend it.

Peg Perego's Primo Viaggio is reviewed on page 378.

Safety 1st. These seats are made by Cosco; see earlier review.

Strolee. These seats are made by Combi; see earlier review.

Infant Car Seats (model by model reviews)

BABY TREND LATCH-LOC ADJUSTABLE BACK

Price: Latch-Lock Adjustable Back: $90. Extra bases $40.

Type: Infant seat, five-point harness.

Limits: 22 lbs. and 29".

CAR SEATS

Pros: Only infant seat on the market that uses the rigid or ISOFIX version of LATCH. 29" height limit.

Cons: Carrier is WAY heavier than competitors; may not work well in non-LATCH cars. A bit hard to find in stores.

Comments: We love this seat's rigid or ISOFIX version of LATCH—the result is a rock-solid installation in cars that have LATCH. The seat itself has nice features . . . you get two harness slots, an adjustable crotch strap, EPS foam for head protection and a machine washable

Mighty Big Controversy

In a past edition of this book, we recommended the Mighty-Tite car seat belt tightener, which removes slack and provides for a tighter car seat installation. It's $20 at Babies R Us and other stores, (web: www.mighty-tite.com). Similar belt-tighteners are made by other companies. However, since our last edition, we noticed belt-tighteners like the Mighty-Tite are a bit controversial among safety advocates.

Their biggest concern about the Mighty-Tite: it might mislead parents into thinking the add-on belt tightener will make any car seat fit in any vehicle. As you've read in this chapter, there are simply some seats that don't work in some vehicles. Yes, you can check a web site like Car Seat Data (www.CarSeatData.org) to see what might work in your vehicle, but sometimes you have to buy a seat on faith. The Mighty-Tite sort of promises to let you cheat car seat installation—enabling a tight fit even if you can't get the seat to work in a vehicle. Not true, say safety advocates—if a seat is incompatible with the back seat of a vehicle, no add-on product will fix it.

Safety advocates also blast the company's marketing tactics, which claim the Mighty-Tite passes federal crash standards. But those standard are written for seats, not add-on products, say advocates. And even Mighty-Tite's instructions say you should install your car seat according to the manufacturer's guidelines . . . which of course, should provide for a rock-solid fit, even without the Mighty-Tite. Car seat techs would rather parents learn how to correctly install a seat (or take it to a safety check) instead of using add-on products to shortcut the installation process.

So, what's the verdict on the Mighty-Tite? Well, we'd like to see some more testing on this product, preferably from a third-party to confirm add-on belt tighteners are truly safe. So, until that happens, we'll take a pass on recommending the Mighty-Tite.

FYI: The new LATCH system eliminates the need for any add-on belt tighteners like the Mighty-Tite—so if your vehicle is equipped with this system and you use a LATCH seat, this debate is moot for you!

pad. The base is adjustable and uses an all-steel connection for the seat—all that steel provides great safety, but makes the BASE quite heavy (in fact, the carrier is also heavy, weighing nine lbs.). You can buy a separate base for $40 for a second car or use the seat without the base in a car by strapping it in with the auto safety belt. All in all, this is a great seat—we like the fact you can use it in grocery shopping carts and the large canopy is nice. The downsides? The somewhat cheesy level indicator can get stuck, giving false readings. And the strange triangle handle takes a bit of getting used to. *Consumer Reports* knocked the Baby Trend infant seat as difficult to install with its rigid LATCH system and one parent emailed us that the seat did NOT work well in a non-LATCH car with a small backseat (the seat's size made it hang over the seat edge). On the other hand, the government gave this seat an A for ease of use; *Consumer Reports* says it performed "very good" in crash tests with or without LATCH. Our readers gave this seat a B+ in reviews on BabyBargains.com. FYI: the Latch-Loc is a bit hard to find—it is sold as stand-alone seat online and in some specialty stores. **Rating: A-**

BABY TREND FLEX-LOC ADJUSTABLE BACK

Comments: This seat is the same as the Latch-Loc above, but features a flexible webbing-based LATCH system like you see on most other infant car seats. FYI: The Flex-Loc is only sold as part of Baby Trend's travel systems, which combine a car seat and stroller. Since the seat is virtually the same as the Latch-Loc, we will give it the same rating. **Rating: A-**

BRITAX COMPANION

Price: $170; extra base: $45.
Type: Infant seat, five-point harness.
Limits: 22 lbs., 30".
Pros: Top crash test ratings.
Cons: Heavy carrier, price.

Comments: This seat came out in 2003 but is now just catching on, thanks to a price drop and favorable crash test result in *Consumer Reports*. In fact, CR rated Britax's Companion as their top pick and we agree that the features (enhanced side impact protection and an anti-rebound bar, which keeps baby from hitting the front seat in an accident) are impressive. The downside? The carrier is among the heaviest in the market, weighing in at a whopping TEN pounds. Add in a baby and you have a nice upper-body work out toting this thing around. Now that the price is lower (it used to be over $200), we can see the Companion as a good alternative to the Peg Primo Viaggio, which is similar in price.
Rating: A-

BRITAX BABY SAFE

Price: $300.

Type: Infant seat, five-point harness.

Limits: 22 lbs., 30".

Comments: So, what is Britax thinking with this seat? We love the features, including the narrow base and rigid LATCH attachment, like the Baby Trend Latch-Loc. And the carrier is much lighter than the Companion (7.5 lbs. versus 10 lbs.), plus you get a similar anti-rebound bar. But what's with the $300 price tag? We don't see why you should pay 75% more than the Companion for this model.

Rating: C (sorry, the price is too high to be considered seriously).

CHICCO KEYFIT

Price: $150, extra base $60.

Type: Infant seat, five-point harness.

Limits: 22 lbs., 30".

Pros: Lined with EPS foam, Italian look.

Cons: Not crash tested yet by CR.

Comments: Chicco's first infant car seat in the U.S. just debuted and boasts a nice list of features: a seat lined with EPS foam for improved side impact protection, thick seat padding, multi-position canopy and comfort grip handle. Chicco hired a former Graco engineer who worked on the SnugRide to design the KeyFit and it shows in the details . . . the base has a "single-pull" LATCH adjustment, leveling foot to account for uneven back seats and even a smooth underside to keep from damaging your back seat upholstery. As you'd expect from Chicco, the fashion of this seat boasts Italian flair and there is even a newborn insert for a better fit. The downsides? The seat is so new it has not yet been crash-tested by *Consumer Reports* (as of this writing). And while the KeyFit works in Chicco's C1 and Cortina strollers (which are winners, by the way), we are unsure how compatible it is with other stroller frames out the market. So we'll give this a cautious recommendation, pending more parent feedback and further crash test data.

Rating: A

COMBI TYRO

Price: $130; extra base $50.

Type: Infant seat, five-point harness

Limits: 22 lbs., 29".

Comments: Combi plans to phase out this seat in 2006; you can read an archived review of the Tyro on our web page (BabyBargains.com, click on Bonus Material).

COMBI CONNECTION & CENTRE

Price: $150 (Connection), $130 (Centre).
Type: Infant seat, five-point harness
Limits: 22 lbs., 29".

Comments: The Combi Connection (top) and Centre (bottom) infant car seats have similar features: while the bases are slightly different, both have carriers with EPS foam for crash protection, comfort pads on the harness and one-pull harness adjustment. The Connection costs about $20 more than the Centre, but the Connection does add a bit more padding (Combi's "egg shock" foam in the head area) and an infant body pillow.

The big difference between the seats is which Combi stroller they work with. The Connection works with the Combi City Life series strollers (Savvy EX, DK-5 and all the City Savvy models, including the basic, Select and All Weather).

Meanwhile, the Combi Centre infant seat works with Combi's Metro Life series strollers, including the Cosmo ST and Cosmo DX. FYI: The Centre has three different models: ST, DX and EX. All are the same, just different fabric colors (the Centre DX is a Babies R Us exclusive). Just to confuse you, the Combi Tyro (mentioned on the pervious page) works only with the Savona stroller. Confusing, no?

Unfortunately, parent feedback on the Connection and Centre models is sparse; both are new and have not been crash tested by *Consumer Reports*. The only data we have is on the Tyro, which our readers gave a B+ and *Consumer Reports* said scored "excellent" on crash protection with a belt and "good" with LATCH (yet overall, it ranked just seventh out of eight seats tested). So, we will go with a conservative rating here until we get more feedback on both seats.
Rating: B

COMPASS 1400

Price: $140
Type: Infant seat, five-point harness.
Limits: 22 lbs., 30".
Pros: Carrier is completely lined with foam. Widest, deepest carrier.
Cons: Must use carrier with base. Compass is new to the market, so little safety track record.

Comments: Based in Ohio, Compass is a new entrant to the car seat world, debuting in 2004 with a booster seat that has been well received. While Compass itself is new, the folks behind it are all ex-

Evenflo engineers and hence have many combined years of car seat experience. The company's offerings are positioned above the cheapest seats you see in discount stores, with added features and safety . . . but priced below that of Britax. The impressive 1400 is a case in point. It features a carrier entirely lined in EPS foam (yet still weighing only 8.4 lbs.), a padded handle, up front belt adjustment, washable pad, height adjustable base and more. We liked the built-in belt lock-off for non-LATCH installations and steel-on-steel construction for latching the carrier to the base (some cheaper seats use plastic hooks, which can break and have led to past recalls). Compass has priced this seat slightly below Peg Perego and Britax's infant seats, making it a good value.

Rating: A

COSCO DESIGNER 22. See the Eddie Bauer infant seat review later in this section. The Cosco Designer 22 is the same as this seat.

EDDIE BAUER INFANT CAR SEAT (AKA COMFORT OR SAFETY 1ST DESIGNER 22)

Price: $90 to $100; extra base: $35.
Type: Infant seat, five-point harness
Limits: 22 lbs., 29".
Pros: Adjustable base. Three crotch belt positions. Front belt adjuster. Scored well in crash tests.

Cons: Handle and straps are hard to adjust. Carrier is heavy. Made by Cosco.

Comments: This seat is sold in two versions: Eddie Bauer and Safety 1st, but the features are the same. Basically, this is a simple infant seat with the same features you see in most other seats on the market: an adjustable base, five-point harness, canopy, etc. What's missing? Side-impact protection, for one. EPS foam for additional crash protection (which is almost now a standard feature) isn't here either. Of course, this seat is on sale for as little as $90—that's about 30% to 50% less than seats with those features, so we guess you can call that a trade-off.

On the plus side, this seat scored "excellent" in *Consumer Reports* latest crash tests. Oddly, *Consumer Reports* decided the seat was "very good" for ease of use in their 2005 report . . . that compares with a "fair" rating for easy of use in 2004. Since the seat didn't change, we can only wonder if CR's testers were drinking smoothies with a brain boost during the past year. Meanwhile, our real world parent feedback on this seat has been mixed: parents have complained the harness and handle are hard to adjust and the carrier is heavy (about two pounds more than the Graco Snug Ride). So, all in

Chocolate donuts with sprinkles?

Here's a confusing thing about car seat shopping: most car seat makers offer their models in a plethora of versions. At one point a couple of years ago, one infant seat maker had FIVE different versions of the same seat: the Classic, Plus, Elite, Supreme and the Extra Crispy. Okay, there wasn't an Extra Crispy, but you get the point. The key thing to remember: the seat was basically the very same seat in each configuration, just with minor cosmetic variations (an extra bit of padding here, a pillow there, etc). Yes, sometimes there are more significant variations like a five-point harness (versus three-point) or an adjustable base. But often there isn't much difference. Think of it this way: car seat makers produce a chocolate donut and top it with different color sprinkles—the rainbow sprinkle version goes to Wal-Mart, the green sprinkle donut goes to Target, etc. That way the companies can offer "exclusives" on certain "models" to large retailers, so the chains don't have the same exact offerings. But remember this: basically, it's the same donut. Bottom line: don't get caught up in all the version stuff. If the basic seat has the features you want, it doesn't really matter whether you buy the Plus or the Elite. Or the Extra Crispy.

all, we will raise our rating of this seat to reflect the better crash-test results. But Cosco's track record (numerous safety recalls, including one on this very model in 2005) gives us pause.
Rating: B

EVENFLO DISCOVERY
Price: $40 to $50; extra base $25.
Type: Infant car seat, three-point harness.
Limits: 22 lbs., 26".
Pros: Lightweight carrier, canopy, low price. Z-shaped handle is easy to carry.
Cons: Non-adjustable base, three-point harness, must adjust belts from the back.

Comments: This bare-bones seat is sold in discount stores like Wal-Mart. The carrier (at 5.5 lbs.) is among the lightest on the market. You don't get many features with this seat—the base doesn't adjust, there is just one crotch strap position and the harness is only three-point (most on the market today are five-point). Want to adjust the straps? You'll have to do that from the back of the seat, a major pain. And this seat received only average marks in *Consumer Report's* crash tests. Our advice: spend a few extra bucks and get an Evenflo Embrace if you want an Evenflo infant seat.
Rating: C+

EVENFLO EMBRACE
Price: $69-$99.

Type: Infant car seat, five-point harness.

Pros: Three-position adjustable base, easier to release base and handle.

Cons: Last Evenflo seat failed crash test.

Limits: 22 lbs., 26".

Comments: The Evenflo Embrace replaces the ill-fated PortAbout, which failed a *Consumer Reports* crash test in 2005. The PortAbout snapped off its base when tested at a speed just above the federal limit, CR reported. Well, that wasn't good news for Evenflo, which has struggled in this category ever since its On My Way infant seat was the subject of a massive recall back in the late 90's.

So, the Embrace is Evenflo's attempt at a fresh start. The Embrace features a new, easier release mechanism for the carrier (this was a gripe for past models). The seat also has a three-position adjustable base and Z-handle with the "Press 'n' Go" system that releases the handle with one hand.

As usual, Evenflo makes several versions of the Embrace, so you'll see it priced from $70 to as much as $100. The difference? Just fancier fabric. That's nice, but the Embrace is missing several features seen in other seats, including EPS foam and side impact protection. We were also disappointed to note the 26" height limit (most other seats are 29").

The Embrace was so new as we went to press, we have little parent feedback and *Consumer Reports* hasn't crash tested it yet. As we look at our reader reviews for the PortAbout, however, it's clear Evenflo still has some learning to do in this category. So, we'll pass on this seat.

Rating: C-

EVENFLO PORTABOUT
Comments: While still for sale in some stores, this seat is being phased and replaced by the Evenflo Embrace (see above). For an archived review of the Evenflo PortAbout, click on "Bonus Material" at BabyBargains.com.

FISHER PRICE SAFE VOYAGE INFANT SEAT
Price: $120

Type: Infant car seat, five-point harness.

Comments: Out by the time you read this, the Fisher Price Safe Voyage infant seat is part of the company's new venture to re-package Britax car seats at a lower price. The Safe Voyage will be based on the Britax Companion . . . but will omit the Companion's headrest with enhanced side impact protection. We suppose if your vehicle already has side-curtain air bags that the the watered-down Fisher Price version of the Companion would be just be as safe.

Given the prototype we saw at a trade show, we expect the Safe Voyage to include the Companion's anti-rebound bar—and the carrier will be just as heavy at ten pounds. We don't have a rating for this seat yet, as the specs are in flux. We'd like to see the final version before we recommend it as highly as the Companion. **Rating: Not yet.**

GRACO SAFE SEAT
Price: $130 to $170.
Type: Infant car seat, five-point harness.
Comments: Graco is launching an entire new car seat line, dubbed Safe Seat, which should be out by the time you read this. The Safe Seat line will include an infant, forward-facing and booster seat. Graco said the Safe Seat collection will feature easier installation and enhanced side impact protection—the company says this will allow the seats to pass crash tests at twice the speed required by the federal government.

We got a sneak at the new infant car seat and thought it looked impressive: it will fit babies up to 30 pounds, enabling most one year olds to stay rear-facing in their infant seat. The carrier will weigh about eight pounds (which is reasonable) and will feature an over-molded handle for easier carrying. The base will have a dial adjustment and integrated belt lock-off for a tighter fit (if you aren't using LATCH).

Of course, the final specs aren't in yet so we don't have any more details, such as if the seat is lined with EPS foam. And without any crash test data or parent feedback, we'll have to wait and see on this one.
Rating: Not yet.

GRACO SNUGRIDE
Price: $70 to $150; extra base $35.
Type: Infant seat; comes in both three-point and five-point harness versions.
Limits: 22 lbs., 29".
Pros: Our top choice for infant seats. Lightweight carrier (seven lbs.), level indicator, canopy, easy to use. Front belt adjuster on some models.
Cons: Only one crotch position. Watch out for older models with rear harness adjustments.
Comments: Here it is folks—our top pick for infant seats. Now, before we rave about this seat, let us point out that Graco makes 26 versions of the SnugRide. There is one version that has a three-point

harness, while the rest feature a five-point (as always, we suggest the latter). Most of the difference is fashion—there are fancier versions of this seat with a foot warmer (boot) and extra foam padding that can cost $150. A basic SnugRide is $70. While we don't have a preference as to which version is best (the basic model should do fine for most folks), we do suggest you get one with a front-belt adjuster. A few older models (called DX) had back adjusters, which are a pain to use. All in all, however, this is an excellent seat—you get a lightweight carrier (seven lbs.), adjustable base, level indicator, nice canopy and straps that don't twist. Best of all, parents say the seat is easy to use. As for crash tests, *Consumer Reports* said this seat scored "excellent" with a belt and "very good" for LATCH. The only thing missing? Side-impact protection, which Graco will offer with their new Safe Seat (see earlier review). All in all, however, we think this is an excellent seat and affordable to boot.

Rating: A

PEG PEREGO PRIMO VIAGGIO SIP

Price: $230 extra base: $60.

Limits: 22 lbs., 30".

Pros: Matches Perego's hot-selling strollers. Side impact protection, auto harness adjustment, improved canopy, luxe fabrics.

Cons: Did we mention it is $230?

Comments: Peg Perego has had much success in this category, despite its high price tag and an earlier model that had some noticeable flaws. Peg is back with a revised version of the Viaggio this year (note the added SIP tag) and they have aimed to fix the first seat's shortcomings. The new seat features side impact protection, an automatic adjustable harness and better canopy, which are all welcome improvements. The seat now can be used up to 22 lbs. and 30", two pounds and three inches more than the previous version. Also new: the Viaggio can be used with or without the car base. Like the old seat, the Viaggio features plush padding, luxe fabrics and an adjustable base. As for crash tests, the Peg seat scored "very good" and third overall according to *Consumer Reports* most recent crash tests. Obviously, the price of the Viaggio is its biggest drawback—at $230 retail, it is nearly *three times* the price of Graco's excellent seat, although we expect chain stores to sell the Viaggio SIP for a bit less. One caveat: be sure to get the most recent version of this seat (ask for the Peg Perego Viaggio SIP), as the old version goes by the same basic model name (Viaggio) but lacks all the improvements we mentioned above.

Rating: A-

SAFETY 1ST DESIGNER 22. This is the same as the Eddie Bauer seat, reviewed earlier in this section.

◆ *Other infant car seats and car beds.* Cosco has two other infant seats that are a bit hard to find. Example: the bare bones *Arriva* infant seat (rating: C). This entry-level seat ($30 to $50; rear-facing to 22 pounds) is sold in versions with and without a stay-in-the-car base. The simplest Arriva has a three-point harness and no base. Next up, is a version that adds a canopy that wraps around the handle. We think this is a rather lousy design, since you then can't carry the carrier under your arm. Cosco also makes an Arriva version with an "adjustable canopy," which is better.

The *Cosco Dream Ride SE* ($65, rating: A) is one of the few "travel beds" for premature infants and other babies that must travel lying down. A similar product: *Graco Cherish Car Bed* ($60, rating: A) is designed for preemies (up to nine pounds) that must ride lying down. Graco's car bed is now discontinued and hard to find.

Convertible and Forward Facing-Only Car Seats (model by model reviews)

BRITAX BOULEVARD
Price: $290.
Type: Convertible, five-point harness.
Limits: 5 to 33 lbs. rear facing, 20 to 65 lbs. forward facing, 49" tall.
Pros: Same as the Marathon (see 381), but seat adds a height adjuster knob. Additional side impact protection with headrest.
Cons: Price; is it really necessary to keep a child in a five-point harness up to 65 pounds?
Comments: This seat is virtually the same as the Marathon, with two significant differences. First, you get a height adjuster knob that lets you make numerous adjustments to the harness heights (instead of being stuck with the four positions you see in the Marathon). Hence, you don't have to re-thread the belts every time your child grows. The second difference is what Britax calls "true impact protection." Basically, this is a reinforced headrest lined with EPS foam that protects your child in a side-impact collision. The first version of this seat (called the Wizard) had a headrest that many felt was too restrictive, so Britax revised the headrest to make it wider. Britax also added an infant pillow, like the Decathlon.

So, should you shell out nearly $300 for the Boulevard. Well, this debate is much like the one for the Marathon . . . that is, is the 65

convertible seats

pounds weight limit for this seat really necessary? See that review for a discussion. This is a good seat, but the ultra-high price leads us to dock the rating below Britax's Roundabout.

Rating: B

BRITAX DECATHLON
Price: $270
Type: Convertible, five-point harness.
Limits: 5 to 33 lbs. rear facing. 20 to 40 lbs. forward facing. 49″ tall.
Pros: Use up to 65 pounds, can be tethered rear- or forward-facing, adjustable crotch strap, plush padding.

Cons: Expensive. Very tall seat, which can block rear view in some cars. Some complain the harness is hard to adjust.

Comments: The Decathlon is a slight evolution of the more widely available Britax Marathon. Like the Marathon, the Decathlon works up to 65 pounds, can be tethered front or rear facing and has the HUGS strap system (read the Marathon review for the pros and cons of HUGS). So, what's different? And why is this seat about $20 more than the Marathon? Well, the Decathlon includes an infant body pillow, which the Marathon omits. So if you plan to use this seat from birth or you have a small infant that is graduating from their infant seat, the pillow may make for a better fit. The other key difference: the Decathlon has an automatic harness adjustment—basically a button you push to adjust the straps. While that sounds like a plus (the Marathon has a manual strap you pull on), parents give mixed reviews to the push-button harness adjustment. Some find it difficult to use (the button is stiff to press), while others say it is fine. Spend a few minutes with it in the store to see what you think before buying this seat.

Other than that, the Decathlon and Marathon are twins—and that means the Decathlon is just as tall as the Marathon. It may not fit well into the back seat of a small car . . . or your rear-view may be obstructed by the seat (depending on the vehicle).

Rating: B

BRITAX ROUNDABOUT
Price: $180 to $200.
Type: Convertible, five-point harness.
Limits: 5 to 33 lbs. rear facing. 20 to 40 lbs. forward facing. 40″ tall.
Pros: Excellent features—EPS foam, no-twist straps, can be tethered rear- or forward-facing, easy to adjust harness, double-strap LATCH, nice colors.

Cons: Harness slot a bit too high for smallest infants.

Comments: Here it is, folks—our pick once again as one of the best convertible seats. Yes, it is expensive, but you get a boatload of extras that make the seat easy to use . . . if the seat is easy to use and adjust, odds are folks will use it correctly.

Britax sells the Roundabout (and all its seats) on its safety record. Part of that safety advantage is rock-solid installation and this is where Britax excels—the lock-off clips provide snug belt install and Britax's double-strap LATCH connectors are among the best in the business. We also found Britax's harness to be easy to use and the straps don't twist. Finally, we should mention that you can tether the Roundabout either rear or forward-facing, a key safety advantage. Crash tests bear that out—*Consumer Reports* recently rated this seat as second overall, scoring this seat as "very good" in their tests.

So, what are the downsides? These are mostly minor quibbles. The lowest harness slot (10″) is too tall for the smallest infants, even though this seat is rated for use from five pounds and up. Other seats like the Evenflo Triumph (8.0″) and the Graco ComfortSport (8.5″) have lower harness slots and hence would be a better choice if you decide to forgo the infant seat and just buy one convertible. Another slight problem: the Roundabout is a bit wide—1″ to 3″ inches wider than other competing seats. Not a big deal . . . except if you try to take this seat on an airplane. While the Roundabout is approved by the FAA for aircraft use, we think it is probably too wide to fit into some airline seats. (See our recommendation earlier for the best convertible seat for aircraft use). Finally, we should note that Roundabout uses a push-button harness adjustment, similar to the Decathlon. . . but for some reason, we don't get as many complaints about this for the Roundabout compared to the Decathlon (see earlier review).

All in all, this is an excellent seat. Parents laud its comfort features and safety (EPS foam lines the child's head and torso area, while the seat has an extra layer of "comfort foam"). We give the Britax Roundabout our highest rating.

Rating: A

BRITAX MARATHON
Price: $250.
Type: Convertible, five-point harness.
Limits: 5 to 33 lbs. rear facing, 20 to 65 lbs. forward facing, 49″ tall.
Pros: Up to 65 pounds with a five-point harness. Plush pad, EPS foam, same pros as Roundabout.

Cons: Did we mention it is $250? Taller, wider than the Roundabout—hence sometimes doesn't fit in smaller cars. Some parents don't like the HUGS harness system. And do you really need a seat

convertible seats

that goes to 65 lbs.?

Comments: The Britax Marathon is one of the few convertible seats on the market that goes to 65 pounds—the pitch here is that older kids are safest when left in a five-point harness, versus a belt-positioning booster.

While we like this seat, there are several flaws with the 65 pound pitch. First, when does the average child hit 65 pounds in weight? The answer: between ages nine and ten. If you think you can use this seat until your child is in the fourth grade, don't kid yourself. A child will not want to ride in a "baby seat" at that age.

There are more practical limits to the Britax Marathon. First the top harness slot is just 18", only two inches higher than the Roundabout. Odds are, your child may outgrow this seat by HEIGHT long before they hit anywhere near 65 pounds. In fact, Britax limits the Marathon's use to kids under 48 inches tall, which undercuts their own 65 pound pitch.

We suspect parents pick a Marathon based on the false perception of how fast their child will grow. Babies triple their birth weight in the first year—hence a seven pound newborn should be a hefty 21 lbs. by their first birthday. By age two, that same child will be 28 lbs. You can forgive parents for thinking that a 40 lb seat might be too restrictive for junior . . . yet the fear their child will continue to grow fast is misplaced. After age two, most kids only gain four pounds a year.

Bottom line: most kids will outgrow a 40 lb convertible seat around age four—that is about the best time to transition to a belt-positioning booster, as the child is mature enough (both physically and emotionally) to sit in a booster held by the auto safety belt.

So, do most babies need a Marathon? No, in our opinion. If your child is truly at the top of the growth curve at age one, the Marathon may have value. But it still won't prevent you from having to buy a belt-positioning booster when your child outgrows it, as most states now require a booster seat up to age eight.

And let's talk about the HUGS system, which appears on the Marathon. Britax says this harness system is designed to "better distribute webbing loads to reduce head movement and minimize the chance for webbing edge loading on the child's neck in the case of an impact. In addition, it is designed to reduce the chance of improper positioning of the chest clip." Parents complained that the first version of HUGS didn't fit larger children well—the chest clip was above the armpits and couldn't be adjusted down. Others gripe that the whole HUGS thing is confusing to use. Britax responded to this by coming out with a larger HUGS strap and attempting to clarify use of the seat. Most of the problems we heard about this seat were probably due to the "version 1.0" nature of any new model—since it debuted in 2002, Britax has made improvements to the Marathon, including the adding of an EPS foam insert to increase shoulder width room by another 1.5 inches. Finally, let us warn parents that the Marathon is bigger/wider (it's 19.5″ wide and 28″ tall) than the Roundabout and hence may not fit into some smaller cars (go to www.carseatdata.org to see which vehicles work and which ones don't).

As for crash tests, the Marathon earned lower marks than the Roundabout in *Consumer Reports*, notably scoring only a "good" for infant LATCH. So, it is mixed review for the Marathon. While we understand Britax's pitch for a 65 lb seat, the number of folks who truly need this seat is limited.

Rating: B

Note: The Marathon is the only Britax seat available in Canada as of this writing.

◆ *More Britax models:* The **Britax Regent** ($240, rating: B+), which used to be called the Husky or Super Elite, is a forward-only facing seat that can use a five-point harness up to an amazing 80 pounds. Great, but this seat is a monster—21.5″ wide and 28″ tall! That means it won't fit into smaller vehicles (heck, even some mid-size ones). Yes, it does have an extra, fourth harness slot at 19″, but the risk with this seat is the same as the Marathon—your child may outgrow it by height before weight. Along the lines of the Regent, Britax also makes a "special-needs" seat called "Traveller Plus" ($450, rating: B) that goes to 105 pounds with a five-point harness. This seat is designed for disabled children who need the protection of a five-point harness.

Britax's booster seats are reviewed in our book, *Toddler Bargains*. See back of this book for details.

COMBI AVATAR
Price: $160 to $200.
Type: Convertible, five-point harness.
Limits: 5 to 30 lbs. rear-facing, 20 to 40 lbs. front-facing.
Pros: Tether works in forward or rear-facing position. Excellent padding. Can recline with child sitting in seat.

Booster seats

As you read this section, you might wonder where are the reviews for booster seats, those seats for older children who've outgrown their convertible seats? Since these seats are designed for older children (most of whom are three or four years of age), we've included this topic as a large chapter in our book *Toddler Bargains*. See the back of this book for details.

convertible seats

Cons: Expensive, rocky safety history. Bigger shell may not fit in smaller vehicles.

Comments: This seat has had a rocky history—we gave it an A- in our last book, lauding its safety features (the reversible tether is a key feature) and plush padding. Then Combi recalled the Avatar, after failing a *Consumer Reports* crash test (the Avatar's latch attachment broke). So, Combi fixed the strap and CR re-tested it—this time, the Avatar did very well, earning "excellent" marks. So, we'll continue to recommend this seat. We like the fact that the Avatar is bigger than the Britax Roundabout, which means kids won't outgrow it as quickly. The Avatar also reclines while the child is seated, which is also a plus. The downside? The Avatar is hard to see in person, with limited distribution. It is also larger than most other seats, making it a tougher fit in smaller vehicles. Despite this, we will still give the Avatar an A-, reflecting the seat's strong crash test results.

Rating: A-

COMBI VICTORIA

Price: $130 to $150.

Type: Convertible, five-point harness.

Limits: 5 to 30 lbs. rear-facing, 20 to 40 lbs. front-facing.

Pros: Multi-position recline. Less expensive than the Avatar.

Cons: Even harder to find than the Avatar.

Comments: Even though this seat is made by Combi, it is quite different than the Avatar (which was designed by an Italian company). You'll note the difference by looking at the bases. Frankly, we prefer the Avatar's design to the Victoria's—the Victoria lacks the Avatar's reversible tether, one-pull harness adjustment, and cushy padding. You still get a multi-position recline, but this seat is priced about twice that of competitors with similar features.

Rating: B

COSCO ALPHA OMEGA. See Eddie Bauer Three in One.

COSCO APEX 65. This combo seat is reviewed in *Toddler Bargains*.

EDDIE BAUER THREE IN ONE

(a.k.a. Cosco Alpha Omega)

Price: $150 to $180.

Type: Convertible, five-point harness.

Limits: 5 to 33 lbs. rear-facing, 20 to 40 lbs. front-facing, 30 to 80 lbs. as a booster. Up to 100 pounds as a booster with the Elite version.

Pros: It's an infant seat! It's a convertible! It's a booster!

Cons: Twisty straps. Poor recline. And much more!

Comments: This best-selling seat also is known as the Cosco Alpha Omega. The big pitch: buy just one seat, as this one is good from infant through college (okay, just 100 pounds or eight years of age). The problem: it just doesn't live up to the hype. It is poorly designed, hard to use and expensive. Our reader feedback hasn't been kind to this seat: readers knock the instructions as "vague and confusing," the belts are hard to adjust in the rear-facing mode and the straps are so thin they constantly get twisted and snagged. Yet another problem: the highest harness slot in this seat (14.5") is a full inch lower than other seats like the Britax Roundabout. Why is this a problem? That low slot means some parents will be forced to convert this seat to booster mode too soon for larger children.

As for safety, this seat scored better in crash tests with LATCH than just with a safety belt. *Consumer Reports* latest tests pegged this seat as only "good" (most other seats in this price range scored "very good" or "excellent") for crash protection with a safety belt. And we're disappointed that this seat doesn't have EPS foam or side impact protection. Considering this seat costs nearly as much as a Britax Roundabout, you clearly aren't getting the same value or ease of use.

FYI: This seat is sold in several versions; we saw a bare bones $100 model in Costco, while the Eddie Bauer versions can sell for $180 (basically, it is just fancier fabric). At that price, it would be better to just go for a Britax Roundabout or Combi Avatar.

Rating: D

◆ *Other Cosco models:* Besides the more famous Alpha Omega (a.k.a. Eddie Bauer Three in One), Cosco does make a handful of other less expensive seats. Example: the entry-level *Touriva* ($50 to $75, rating: C) comes in five-point and bar-shield (which is not adjustable) versions and is sold in stores like K-Mart. It suffers from the same twisty straps as the Eddie Bauer/Alpha Omega. The plusher *Regal Ride* car seat ($50, rating: C) also comes in five-point and adjustable bar-shield versions. We were not impressed with these car seats, which lacked features and the ease-of-use you see in similarly priced seats. As for crash tests, *Consumer Reports* gave both these seats lower marks in a belt test compared to LATCH (much like the Alpha Omega).

New this year, Cosco debuted an opening-price point convertible seat called the *Scenera* ($50). This bare bones seat works from five to 35 lbs. rear-facing and 20 to 40 lbs. front-facing—it will have an up-front harness adjustment and recline feature. This seat was not out as of this writing, so no rating yet. FYI: The *Cosco Summit* and *Safety 1st Vantage Point* are combo boosters that are reviewed in our other book, *Toddler Bargains*. Also: the *Cosco Tote 'N Go*, a portable seat for taxis, is discussed on page 366.

convertible seats

CAR SEATS

EVENFLO TRIUMPH

Price: $100 to $130.

Type: Convertible seat; five-point harness

Limits: 5 to 30 lbs. rear-facing, 20 to 40 lbs. forward-facing.

Pros: Special harness "remembers" last setting, EPS foam, up-front five-position recline and harness adjustment (no re-threading).

Cons: Tension knob is hard to adjust when seat is in rear-facing mode. Wide base may not fit in smaller cars. Only can use the top harness slot when forward facing, making the seat difficult to use for larger (but young) infants. A litany of gripes from parents about this seat's usability.

Comments: We gave high marks to this Evenflo seat in our last edition, but a steady stream of complaints from parents have had us revaluate our rating. Yes, it is feature-packed and a good value (it costs about $50 less than a Britax Roundabout). This well-padded seat has several innovative features: among them, a cool "Memory Harness" that lets you "let out" the belts and then returns them to their original tension, so it is easier to move baby in and out of this seat. Also neat: the "HeightRight" harness system that lets you adjust the height of the harness without threading the belts. Yep, that is the same feature you see on the Britax Wizard . . . for $150 less here.

So, what's not to like? While most parent reviews on the Triumph are positive, there is a sizeable minority that are not happy. First, this is a BIG seat—19.5" in width. That's 2-3" bigger than most other car seats and as wide as the Britax Marathon (but that seat can be used up to 65 lbs.; the Triumph stops at 40 lbs.). As a result, you may not be able to fit it in smaller vehicles. Another problem: the neat-o adjustment knobs that are placed up front. When the seat is placed in rear-facing mode, these neat-o knobs are impossible to access (as you might guess).

In fact, all this seat's whiz-bang features (Memory Harness, HeightRight) frustrate a good many parents, who find them hard to use or master. And the seat is quirky . . . when forward-facing, you can only use the top harness slot. Hence we received several complaints about this seat from parents of young (but big) babies, who didn't fit well in the Triumph. And removing the seat pad requires a screwdriver?! What is Evenflo thinking? So, this seat is hard to rate—on the upside, when it works for parents, it does well. And the Triumph scored very well in *Consumer Reports* crash tests. Yet it is hard to ignore all the parent complaints about using the seat in the real world. Our advice: if you buy it, keep the receipt and make sure the store has a good return policy.

Rating: B

EVENFLO TITAN 5

Price: $60 to $90

Type: Convertible; comes in five-point and bar-shield versions.

Limits: 5 to 30 lbs. rear-facing, 20 to 40 lbs. forward-facing.

Pros: Value, excellent crash tests.

Cons: Hard to clean cover or adjust straps.

Comments: Here's a great seat for grandma's car—the Evenflo Titan is a bare-bones seat where the price ($60) is right. Nothing fancy here: you get a five-point seat, four shoulder positions and simple padding. While we weren't wild about Evenflo's Triumph, the Titan shows how sometimes simpler is better.

FYI: Evenflo makes several versions of the Titan, including a Titan Deluxe that adds more padding, a head pillow, cup holders and so on. But at $100, it is too pricey. If you plan to use this as a secondary car seat, save the $40 and just get the basic version.

The crash tests on the Titan were "excellent" for LATCH and "very good" for belt, according to *Consumer Reports*. And this seat's smaller footprint gives it a good fit in just about every type of vehicle. No, there is no side-impact protection, fancy padding or EPS foam, but, hey, it only costs about $60. The big gripe we heard from parents on the Titan were the straps—some found the harness hard to adjust, especially when the seat is rear-facing. So we will caveat our review: the Titan is probably best as a seat for kids over a year (and not riding rear-facing). In that case, this seat would be great for that little-used second car, the nanny's wheels or grandma's Hummer.

Rating: B+

◆ *Other Evenflo models:* The Evenflo *Vanguard* ($100, rating: D) is an upgraded version of the Titan—same basic seat as the Titan, but with added padding, pillow, etc. It is much like the Titan Deluxe. But the Vanguard is dogged by the same problems as the Titan, including straps that are very difficult to adjust, especially when the seat is rear-facing. While that annoyance might be a worthy trade-off for the $60 Titan, you deserve more if you spend $100.

The Evenflo *Tribute I* ($60 to $75, rating: C-) is an overhead bar shield seat sold at chain stores like Sears and Baby Depot. We don't recommend bar shields (they aren't as safe as five-point harnesses, in our opinion), so we won't recommend this seat. We did notice that Wal-Mart has a five-point version of the Tribute for $60.

FISHER PRICE SAFE VOYAGE CONVERTIBLE SEATS

Comments: As mentioned earlier in this chapter, Fisher-Price has teamed with Britax to launch a new car seat line dubbed "Safe

Voyage." There will be two Fisher Price Safe Voyage convertible seats, basically stripped-down versions of the Britax Roundabout and Decathlon. The Roundabout-like seat with a 40 lb. limit will sell for $160 and a Decathlon-like seat with a 55 lb limit with be $180—both will be out by the time you read this. We saw prototypes of these seats and noticed they had re-designed bases and less-fancy features (a manual recline, etc.) than the Britax seats. Since the specs weren't final yet as we went to press, we will have to wait and see on a rating for this new venture.

Graco ComfortSport

Price: $80 to $140.

Type: Convertible, five-point harness. (Wal-Mart has a version with an overhead bar shield, which we don't recommend).

Limits: up to 30 lbs. rear-facing, 20 to 40 lbs. forward-facing.

Pros: Great low-end seat—nice features, good price. Front belt-adjuster, level adjuster, easy to use. Most expensive versions have more plush pads and cup holders.

Cons: Cheaper versions have skimpy padding; average crash tests.

Comments: This seat is our recommendation for a bare bones seat, a good choice if you are on a tight budget or need a seat for a second (or Grandma's) car. Be forewarned, however: the cheapest ComfortSports ($80) have skimpy padding, not good if you plan to take a long trip. Spend an extra $20 and you get plusher padding. All in all, Graco offers 16 versions of this seat, including three that are bar-shields (we don't recommend this type). The other 13 versions have five-point harnesses and feature front belt adjustments. Best of all, parent find the seat easy to use. No, you don't get all the gee-whiz features of seats like the Britax Roundabout or Evenflo Triumph—but then again, you are spending $50 to $150 less. This is the seat for that second car or for airline travel—its narrow width (17") should make it work in most airline seats and its light weight (11 pounds) make carrying it through an airport easier than others seats that can weigh 20+ pounds.

The only negative: the ComfortSport received only average marks in *Consumer Reports'* most recent crash tests; other bare-bones seats (like the Evenflo Titan) scored better. BUT, parents tell us the ComfortSport is much easier to use than the Titan. Example: the belts are easier to adjust and the ComfortSport comes with an easy-to-wash pad that doesn't require you to rethread the belts. We also like the fact that the seat is lined with EPS foam for additional crash protection. Our recommendation: if you need a simple seat for grandma or that little-used second car, the basic $80 ComfortSport is a good bet.

Rating: B+

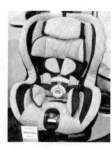

GRACO SAFE SEAT FOR TODDLERS
Price: $129-169

Type: Forward-facing only, five-point harness.

Limits: 20 to 40 lbs. forward-facing.

Pros: EPS foam, five-position easy recline, deep side wings.

Cons: Can't use rear-facing, so baby must be a year old.

Comments: Graco plans to launch this seat as part of their new Safe Seat grouping and it should be out by the time you read this. This is a forward-facing only seat, designed for kids at least one year of age. Why do a forward-facing seat instead of a convertible? Well, since Graco's new Safe Seat infant seat will work up to 30 pounds, your baby should be over a year by the time they can graduate to the toddler seat. We see the logic here, but we wonder if parents will pass over this seat for the lack of convertibility. Nonetheless, we thought Graco got most of the features right: EPS foam, deep side wings, plush padding and an easy-install belt path. Graco seems to be positioning the Safe Seat in the middle of the market: more than the bare-bones Graco ComfortSport but below the Britax Roundabout. Since this seat was not out as of this writing, we will have to wait on a rating.

Rating: Not yet.

◆ *More Graco models: Graco CarGo* is a combo booster seat line that is reviewed in our other book, *Toddler Bargains*. Ditto for the Century NextStep and Century Breverra models.

SAFETY 1ST COMFORT RIDE
(also known as the Forerunner)

Comments: This seat is being phased out; read an archived review of it on our web page at BabyBargains.com (click on Bonus Material).

SAFETY 1ST ENSPIRA
Price: $100

Type: Convertible, comes in both bar shield and five-point harness versions. Converts to a belt-positioning booster.

Limits: 5 to 35 lbs. rear-facing, 22 to 40 lbs. forward-facing. 30 to 100 pounds as a belt-positioning booster.

Pros: Two position recline. Converts to a belt-positioning booster for use up to 100 pounds.

Cons: Hard to install. Huge size may not work in some vehicles. LATCH hard to install.

convertible seats

Comments: Basically, this seat is a new twist on Cosco/Eddie Bauer's 3-in-1—the Enspira adds a two-position recline and extra padding. The Enspira comes both in a five-point harness and over-head bar-shield. You also get a few extras like a cup holder and removable harness pads plus a four-position adjustable headrest. Parent feedback on this seat is not very positive—many noted this seat's huge size and (as a result) difficult installation; threading the belt in a rear-facing position vexed several parents. Again, Safety 1st/Cosco's poorly designed LATCH attachments make this seat difficult to install with LATCH. Yes, this seat converts to a belt-positioning booster, but as you read earlier in our review of the Eddie Bauer 3-in-1, we think this pitch is a bit overblown.

Rating: C

SAFETY 1ST INTERA

Price: $140

Type: Convertible, five-point harness. Converts to a belt-positioning booster.

Limits: 5 to 35 lbs. rear-facing, 22 to 40 lbs. forward-facing. 30 to 100 pounds as a belt-positioning booster and backless booster.

Pros: Back removes, making it a backless booster for even longer use.

Cons: Cosco's poorly designed LATCH attachments strike again!

Comments: The Safety 1st Intera's claim to fame is its conversion first to a belt-positioning booster and then a backless booster (the back removes). That is helpful when a child is at the end of their child seat days (around years seven to eight), when they just need a boost to sit correctly in an auto safety belt. Hence, Safety 1st now claims this is their first four-in-one seat (infant, convertible, belt-positioning booster and then backless booster). Safety 1st throws in a bunch of extras you'd expect at this price point (removable infant body insert and pillow, cup holder, cushioned pad, three-position recline and adjustable headrest). The puzzle buckle takes a bit of getting used to. We had a reader road test this seat with her one year old and the report was positive, for the most part. Like the Enspira, the Intera is a big seat—the back is 24.5" tall, about an inch shy of the Britax Marathon. Here's a unique feature: the Intera can be installed with or without its base . . . and that's a good thing, since with the base, the seat clocks in at a huge 19" width. It took our reader 90 minutes to wrestle it into the back of a Subaru Outback. As for day-to-day use, our reader's one year old looked like he was swimming in this seat, designed extra-large to morph into all those future uses. Little things didn't work well—the cup holder was just out of reach for that one year old, the straps tended to twist (a Cosco/Safety 1st problem overall) and Cosco/Safety 1st's notorious LATCH hooks make it tough to install. Other parents echoed these complaints. Despite all this, we will give this seat a better grade than Safety 1st and Cosco/Eddie Bauer's other offerings. No, we would not recommend it for newborns (we'd suggest waiting until at least six to eight months of age), nor would it work for parents with small vehicles.

Rating: B

STROLEE CASPIAN

Comments: This seat is very similar to the Combi Victoria, reviewed earlier. Strolee is a Combi sub-brand.

STROLEX SIT ´ N´ STROLL

Price: $200

Type: Holy convertible baby product, Batman! It's a car seat! And a stroller!

Limits: birth to 40 pounds.

Pros: The only car seat that morphs into a stroller.

Cons: Doesn't function well either as a car seat or a stroller. Top harness slot is only 14".

Comments: The Sit 'n' Stroll is made by Strolex Corporation (web: www.strolex.com), formerly known as Safeline, and has won a small but loyal fan base for its innovative car seat/stroller. With one flick of the hand, this convertible car seat morphs into a stroller. Like the Batmobile, a handle pops up from the back and wheels appear from the bottom. Presto! You've got a stroller without having to remove baby from the seat.

We've seen a few parents wheel this thing around, and though it looks somewhat strange, they told us they've been happy with its operation. We have some doubts, however. First, unlike the travel systems reviewed in the next chapter, the Sit 'n' Stroll's use as a stroller is quite limited—it doesn't have a full basket (only a small storage compartment) or a canopy (a "sunshade" is an option). We'd prefer a seat that reclines (it doesn't) and you've got to belt the seat in each time you use it in a car—even if you don't take it along as a stroller. Not only is installation a hassle, but the Sit 'n' Stroll's wide base (17.5") may also not fit some vehicles with short safety belts or contoured seats. Plus, lifting the 14-pound car seat with a full-size child out of a car to put on the ground is quite a workout. Finally, we should note the seat's top harness slot is only 14", much lower than other seats on the market today (that means baby will outgrow it that much quicker). So, we're not sure we can wholeheartedly recommend this seat. On the other hand, we did hear from a flight attendant who loved her Sit 'n' Stroll—it wheels down those narrow plane aisles. So, it's a mixed bag for the Sit 'n'

car seats

Stroll. For frequent fliers, the Sit 'n' Stroll is probably heaven-sent. Yet, like many hybrid products, it is not great at being either a car seat or a stroller.
Rating: C+

As you can imagine, the child safety seat world changes quickly—read our blog (BabyBargains.com) for the latest news, recalls and more with car seats.

Our Picks: Brand Recommendations

Here are our top picks for infant and convertible seats. Are these seats safer than others? No—all child safety seats sold in the U.S. and Canada must meet minimum safety standards. These seats are our top picks because they combine the best features, usability (including ease of installation) and value. Remember the safest and best seat for your baby is the one that best fits your child and vehicle. Finding the right car seat can be a bit of trial and error; you may find a seat CANNOT be installed safely in your vehicle because of the quirks of the seat or your vehicle's safety belt system. All seats do NOT fit all cars. Hence it is always wise to buy a seat from a store or web site with a good return policy.

FYI: See the chart on pages 394-395 for a comparison of features for both infant and convertible/front-facing car seats.

Best Bets: Infant car seats

Good. Let's be honest: if you're on a super-tight budget, consider not buying an infant car seat at all. A good five-point, convertible car seat (see below for recommendations) will work for both infants and children.

Better. The *Peg Perego Primo Viaggio SIP* has two key advantages: first, it snaps into most Perego strollers for a slick looking travel system. Second, it's a decent enough infant seat that scored well in *Consumer Reports* most recent crash tests. If you can get past the heavy carrier—not to mention the $200+ price—this is a decent runner-up to our top pick reviewed next.

Best. For $70 to $150, the *Graco SnugRide* impressed us with its ease of use, lightweight carrier and adjustable base. If you go for a SnugRide, make sure you get a version that has up-front adjustments for the harness (a few older models had back adjusters). This is our top recommendation.

Dark Horses. If you are willing to take a look at a new infant seat that doesn't have the long track record of the above picks, check out the **Compass 1400** ($140) and **Chicco KeyFit** ($150). We were impressed by the Compass' wide and deep carrier, as well as the rock-solid design of the base. The Chicco Key Fit is also well-designed (lined with EPS foam for example), but sports a snazzy Italian fashion look, similar to the Peg infant seat . . .but $80 less.

Best Bets: Convertible & Forward-Facing car seats

Good. For a decent, no-frills car seat, we recommend the **Graco ComfortSport**. This seat ranges from $80 to $140, depending on how plush the pad is. Nothing fancy, just a good five-point harness seat and up-front belt-adjustment. (FYI: Wal-Mart sells a version of this seat with a bar shield, which we don't recommend). The Graco ComfortSport is a great choice for that less-used second car, Grandma's Mini Cooper or for airline travel. Another good bet for Grandma: the **Evenflo Titan 5**.

Better. The **Combi Avatar** is a step up from the Graco ComfortSport, both in price (the Avatar starts at $160) and features. The Avatar's tether works either in forward or rear-facing mode, which is a key safety benefit. You can even recline this seat while the child is sitting in it. And the plush padding earns special kudos. One caveat: this seat's larger shell may make installation in smaller vehicles a challenge.

Best. So, what is our top recommendation for convertible car seats? The crown goes to the **Britax Roundabout**. This excellent five-point harness seat has EPS foam, no-twist traps, easy-to-adjust harness and a "double strap" LATCH system. Best of all, you can tether this seat either rear OR forward facing, for an extra measure of safety. Yes, it is expensive ($180 to $200), but you are getting a top-notch seat that is well designed and easy to use.

Flying the unfriendly skies: Survival Tips & Advice

Most parents know the safest place for any child (newborn, infant, toddler) onboard a plane is buckled into an approved child safety seat. Reports of passengers injured during in-flight turbulence only serve to reinforce this recommendation.

Continued on page 396

CAR SEATS

INFANT SEATS

The following is a selection of the better infant car seats and how they compare on features:

Maker	Model	Price	Weight/ Height Limits
Baby Trend	Latch-Loc Adj. Back	$90	22 lbs./29"
Britax	Companion	$170	22 lbs./30"
	Baby Safe	$300	22 lbs./30"
Chicco	KeyFit	$150	22 lbs/30"
Combi	Connection/Centre	$130-150	22 lbs./29"
Compass	1400	$140	22 lbs./30"
Eddie Bauer	Comfort/Designer 22	$90-$100	22 lbs./29"
Evenflo	Discovery	$40-50	22 lbs./26"
	Embrace	$70-100	22 lbs./26"
Graco	SnugRide	$70-$150	22 lbs./29"
Peg Perego	Primo Viaggio SIP	$230	22 lbs./30"

CONVERTIBLE SEATS

The following is a selection of popular convertible car seats and how they compare on features:

Maker	Model	Price	Weight Limits (in pounds) Rear	Forward
Britax	Boulevard	$290	33 lbs.	65 lbs.
	Roundabout	$180-$200	33	40
	Marathon	$250	33	65
Combi	Avatar	$160-200	30	40
Eddie Bauer*	3-in-1	$150-180	33	100
Evenflo	Triumph	$100-130	30	40
	Titan 5	$60-90	30	40
Graco	ComfortSport	$80-$140	30	40
Safety 1st	Enspira	$100	35	100
	Intera	$140	35	100

Infant seat chart:

Side Impact: Does the seat have side-impact protection?

Harness Type: Does the seat have a 3 or 5-point harness? "Both" means either type is available, depending on the model.

Level Ind.: Does the seat have a level indicator for easier installation?

Carrier Weight: This is the weight of the carrier only (not the base).

Side Impact	Level Ind.	Harness Type	Base Width	Carrier Weight	Our Rating
Yes	Yes	5 point	16.5"	9 lbs.	A-
Yes	No	5 point	18.5	10 lbs.	A-
Yes	No	5 point	16.5"	7.5 lbs.	C
Yes	Yes	5 Point	15.25"	9 lbs.	A
No	Yes	5 point	18.5	8 lbs.	B
Yes	No	5 point	16.5	7.5 lbs.	A
No	No	5-point	18	9 lbs.	B
No	No	3-Point	17.5	5.5 lbs.	C+
No	Yes	5-point	18	N/A	C-
No	Yes	Both	17	7 lbs.	A
Yes	Yes	5-point	17	8 lbs.	A-

Rating	Comment
B	Harness Height Adjuster Knob is nice, but the price
A	EPS foam, no-twist straps, Tether rear or forward
B	Highest weight limit on market with 5 pt harness
A-	Excellent padding, Tether rear or forward
D	Converts to booster seat, but straps are twisty
B	Memory Harness; can adjust belts without rethread
B+	Good Bare-Bones seat, but harness hard to adjust
B+	Best buy for bare-bones model; good for planes
C	Converts to booster, huge seat can be hard to install
B	Converts to booster, but harness hard to adjust

Convertible seat chart: All of these seats have five-point harnesses.

Model: These are the company's flagship models. See reviews earlier in this chapter for other models.

Recline: Most seats recline, but the reclines are not equal—some recline more than others. Generally, the more positions, the more the recline. "3-pos" means a three position recline.

Notes:

* The Eddie Bauer 3-in-1 is also known as the Cosco Alpha Omega.

Yet, have you actually tried to use a car seat on a plane? Get ready for a torture test, thanks to a myriad of FAA and airlines rules that are at best family-unfriendly . . . at worst, downright cruel.

First, consider the car seat itself—most are *not* designed to be carried through a long airport terminal. You aren't suppose to carry any seat by the harness straps, so that involves finding a place on the back of the seat to grip . . . plus your child, luggage, sanity and so on. Yes, infant seats are easier (since your newborn can obviously ride in the seat), but life gets more complicated when you move to a convertible seat.

Then, let's talk about boarding. Many airlines have eliminated the courtesy pre-board for families, forcing parents to struggle with car seat installation while corralling a wayward child . . . this takes skill—and the ability to withstand the icy stares of fellow passengers waiting in line behind you. (Fortunately, a few airlines do still allow families to pre-board—check with the airline ahead of time to determine their current policy. And you can always beg the gate agent to let you pre-board . . . if they are in a good mood, some will bend the rules.

What about seats? FAA rules require child safety seats to be put next to the window. If you are traveling alone, that means you (the parent) gets stuck with a middle seat. And, inevitably, you'll have to use the restroom during the flight . . . requiring you to climb over the passenger in the aisle seat. Want the bulkhead for extra room? Tough luck, say some airlines. Example: United saves those seats for big-dollar business travelers (read: not you). Of course, when you get to the airport, you can again beg the gate agent for bulkhead if it isn't already taken.

Changing planes is another major hassle—requiring you to go through the trauma of boarding and securing a car seat all over again.

So, how can you can travel by plane with baby without losing your sanity? We've taken our hard-earned experiences along with other parents' advice and put together a brief primer on air travel with kids. Read it for free online on our site, BabyBargains (click on Bonus Material.).

 ## *The Bottom Line*

Now that you've got the car seat covered, let's move on to that next great mystery of baby transportation—the stroller. Close your eyes and click your heels three times. It's off to Stroller Land.

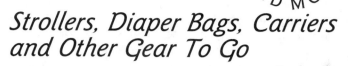

CHAPTER 9

Strollers, Diaper Bags, Carriers and Other Gear To Go

Inside this chapter

W*hat are the best strollers? Which brands are the most durable AND affordable? We'll discuss this plus other tips on how to make your baby portable—from front carriers to diaper bags and more. And what do you put in that diaper bag anyway? We've got nine suggestions, plus advice on dining out with baby.*

Getting Started: When Do You Need This Stuff?

While you don't need a stroller, diaper bag or carrier immediately after baby is born, most parents purchase them before baby arrives anyway. Another point to remember: some stroller models have to be special-ordered with at least two to four weeks lead time. And some of the best deals for strollers and other to-go gear are found online, which necessitates leaving a week or more lead-time for shipping.

Sources to Find Strollers, Carriers

Strollers and carriers are found at similar sources as we mentioned for car seats in the previous chapter. Once again, the discounters like Target and Wal-Mart tend to specialize in just a handful of models from the mass-market companies like Cosco, Kolcraft, Graco and so on. The baby superstores like Babies R Us and Baby Depot have a wider selection and (sometimes) better brands like Peg Perego and Combi. Meanwhile, juvenile specialty stores almost always carry the more exclusive brands like Maclaren, Zooper and other upscale options.

Yet perhaps the best deals for strollers, carriers and diaper bags are found online—for some reason, this seems to be one area the web covers very well. This is because strollers are relatively easy to ship (compared to other more bulky juvenile items). Of course, more competition often means lower prices, so you'll see many deals online. Another plus: the web may be the only way to find certain premium-brand strollers if you live in less-populous parts of the U.S. and Canada (most of their dealers are concentrated on the East and West coasts).

Beware of shipping costs when ordering online or from a catalog—many strollers may run 20 or 30 pounds, which can translate into hefty shipping fees. Use an online coupon (see Chapter 7 for coupon sites) to save and look for free shipping specials.

Parents in Cyberspace: What's on the Web?

Online info on strollers, diaper bags and carriers falls into two categories: manufacturer sites and discounters who sell online. Here's a brief overview:

◆ *Most manufacturers do not sell online, but you can find a wealth of info on their sites in some cases.* With stroller makers, you may find fabric swatches and other technical info about different models. This is helpful since most stores don't carry every available fabric, accessory or model. Among the better sites is Combi (www.combi-intl.com), which includes detailed info on their models and even comparison charts so you can analyze several models at once.

◆ *Discounters.* Besides previously mentioned web sites like BabyCatalog.com (which has excellent stroller deals), readers say they've had luck with smaller sites like TravelingTikes (www. travelingtikes.com). Another site to check out for stroller deals: BabyCenter (www. babycenter.com). This site's sale area often has deals with up to 30% off and free shipping. Readers also praise Net Kids Wear (www.netkidswear.com) for their stroller deals as well.

Of course, any mention of online bargains for strollers wouldn't be complete without discussion of eBay (www.eBay.com), the massive bargain bazaar. Go to eBay's baby section and choose both the "general" and "stroller" categories for deals (see Figure 1 on the next page). Sure, there are some dogs here (like Graco or Evenflo models that are virtually worthless at resale), but you'll also find

Figure 1: We found 1343 strollers for auction on eBay during a recent visit—most at prices way below retail.

new-in-the-box Perego models as well as jogging strollers by the score. Do your price research up front (know what things really sell for at retail) and you'll find many 50% off bargains.

Strollers

Baby stores offer a bewildering array of strollers for parents. Do you want the model that converts from a car seat to a stroller? What about a stroller that would work for a quick trip to the mall? Or do you want a stroller for jogging? Hiking trails? The urban jungle of New York City or beaches of LA?

And what about all the different brand names? Will a basic brand found at a discount store work? Or do you need a higher-quality brand from Europe? What about strollers with anti-lock brakes and air bags? (Just kidding on that last one).

The $180 million dollar stroller industry is not dominated by one or two players, like you might see in car seats or high chairs. Instead, you'll find a couple *dozen* stroller makers offering just about anything on wheels, ranging from $30 for a bare-bones model to $750 for a Dutch-designed uber stroller. A recent trend: tri-wheel strollers that are hybrids between joggers and traditional strollers.

We hope this section takes some of the mystery out of the stroller

strollers

buying process. First, we'll look at the six different types of strollers on the market today. Next, we'll zero in on features and help you decided what's important and what's not. Then, it's brand ratings and our picks as the best recommendations for different lifestyles. Finally, we'll go over several safety tips, money saving hints, wastes of money and a couple of mail order sources that sell strollers.

Whew! Take a deep breath and let's go.

What Are You Buying?

There are six types of strollers you can buy:

◆ **Umbrella Strollers.** The name comes from the appearance of the stroller when it's folded, similar to an umbrella.

WHAT'S COOL: They're lightweight and generally cheap—that is, low in price (about $25 to $35). We should note that a handful of premium stroller makers (Maclaren and Peg Perego) also offer pricey umbrella strollers that sell for $150 to $250. Pictured here is a no-frills Kolcraft umbrella stroller.

WHAT'S NOT: They're cheap—that is, low in quality (well, with the exception of Maclaren and Peg Perego). You typically don't get any fancy features like canopies, storage baskets, reclining seats, and so on. Another problem: most umbrella strollers have hammock-style seats with little head support, so they won't work well for babies under six months of age.

◆ **Carriage Strollers.** A carriage (also called a pram) is like a bed on wheels—most are similar in style to a bassinet. Since this feature is most useful when a baby is young (and less helpful when baby is older), most companies make carriages that convert to strollers. Pictured here is the Peg Perego Venezia carriage stroller.

WHAT'S COOL: Full recline is great for newborns, which spend most of their time sleeping. Most combo carriage/strollers have lots of high-end features like plush seats, quilted canopies and other accessories to keep the weather out. The best carriage strollers and prams have a dreamy ride, with amazing suspensions and big wheels.

WHAT'S NOT: Hefty weight (not easy to transport or set up) and hefty price tags. Another negative: most Euro-style "prams" have fixed front wheels, which make maneuvering difficult on quick trips. Some carriage/stroller models can top $300 and $400. These strollers once dominated the market but have lost favor as more parents opt for "travel systems" that combine an infant seat and stroller (see below).

◆ **Lightweight Strollers.** These strollers are our top recommendation: they're basically souped-up umbrella strollers with many convenience features.

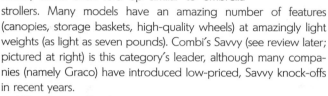

WHAT'S COOL: Most offer easy set-up and fold-down; some even fold up similar to umbrella strollers. Many models have an amazing number of features (canopies, storage baskets, high-quality wheels) at amazingly light weights (as light as seven pounds). Combi's Savvy (see review later; pictured at right) is this category's leader, although many companies (namely Graco) have introduced low-priced, Savvy knock-offs in recent years.

WHAT'S NOT: Can be expensive—most high-quality brands run $200 to $300. The smaller wheels on lightweight strollers make maneuvering in the mall or stores easy . . . but those same wheels don't perform well on uneven surfaces or on gravel trails. Skimpy baskets are another trade-off.

◆ **Jogging (or Sport) Strollers.** These strollers feature three big bicycle-tire wheels and lightweight frames—perfect for jogging or walking on rough roads.

WHAT'S COOL: How many other strollers can do 15 mph on a jogging trail? Some have plush features like padded seats and canopies—and the best fold up quickly for easy storage in the trunk. This category has boomed in recent years; now it seems like every stroller maker is rolling out a jogger model.

WHAT'S NOT: They can be darn expensive, topping $200 or even $300. Jogging strollers are a single-purpose item—thanks to their sheer bulk and a lack of steering, you can't use one in a mall or other location. On the plus side, the flood of new models is helping lower prices. New, low-end jogging strollers run $100 to $150. The trade-offs to the new bargain price models: heavier steel frames and a lack of features.

◆ **All-terrain Strollers.** The baby equivalent of four-wheel drive sport-utility vehicles, these strollers are pitched to parents who want to go on hikes or other outdoor adventures.

WHAT'S COOL: Big air-filled tires and high clearances work better on gravel trails/roads than standard strollers. These strollers are great for neighborhoods with broken or rough sidewalks. All-terrain strollers still have convenience features (baskets, canopies, etc.), yet don't cost as much as jogging strollers (most are under $100). Besides, they look cool. Pictured here is the Zooper Boogie (reviewed later in this chapter).

WHAT'S NOT: A few models have fixed front wheels, making them a hassle to use—when you want to turn the stroller, you have to lift the entire front half off the ground. Even if the front wheels swivel (which is more common these days), the larger wheels make the stroller less maneuverable in tight spaces. All-terrain strollers are wider than other strollers, which could make them troublesome in stores with narrow aisles. Another caveat: many models now boast "pneumatic" (inflated) wheels for a smoother ride. The only bummer—what if you get a flat? Look for brands that include a pump. While pneumatic-tire strollers seem to be the new hot trend, most folks who really want to go on a hike will opt for a jogging stroller instead of an all-terrain.

◆ **Travel systems.** It's the current rage among stroller makers—models that combine infant car seats and strollers (also called "travel systems"). Century (now part of Graco) kicked off this craze way back in 1994 with its "4-in-1" model that featured four uses (infant carrier, infant car seat, carriage and toddler stroller). Since then, just about every major stroller maker has jumped into the travel system market. Travel systems have just about killed sales of carriage strollers; now even carriage stroller king Peg Perego has bowed to the travel system trend. Pictured here is the Graco MetroLite travel system.

WHAT'S COOL: Great convenience—you can take the infant car seat out of the car and then snap it into the stroller frame. Voila! Instant baby carriage, complete with canopy and basket. Later, you can use the stroller as, well, just a stroller.

WHAT'S NOT: The strollers are often junk—especially those by mass market makers Cosco and Evenflo. Quality problems plague this category, as does something we call "feature bloat." Popular travel systems from Graco, for example, are so loaded with features that they tip the scales at nearly 30 pounds! The result: many parents abandon their travel system strollers for lighter weight models after baby outgrows his infant seat. And considering these puppies can cost $150 to $250 (some even more), that's a big investment for such short use. On the plus side, quality stroller makers Peg Perego, Maclaren and Combi have jumped into the travel system market, albeit with different solutions (see reviews later in this chapter).

Safe & Sound

Next to defective car seats, the most dangerous juvenile product on the market today is the stroller. That's according to the U.S. Consumer Product Safety Commission, which estimates that over 10,000 injuries a year occur from improper use or defects. The problems? Babies can slide out of the stroller (falling to the ground) and small parts can be a choking hazard. Seat belts have broken in some models, while other babies are injured when a stroller's brakes fail on a slope. Serious mishaps with strollers have involved entanglements and entrapments (where an unrestrained baby slides down and gets caught in a leg opening). Here are some safety tips:

1 **NEVER HANG BAGS FROM THE STROLLER HANDLE**—it's a tipping hazard.

2 **DON'T LEAVE YOUR BABY ASLEEP UNATTENDED IN A STROLLER.** Many injuries happen when infants who are lying down in a stroller roll or creep and then manage to get their head stuck in the stroller's leg openings. Be safe: take a sleeping baby out of a stroller and move them to a crib or bassinet.

3 **THE BRAKES SHOULDN'T BE TRUSTED.** The best stroller models have brakes on two wheels; cheaper ones just have one wheel that brakes. Even with the best brakes, don't leave the stroller unattended on an incline.

4 **FOLLOW THE WEIGHT LIMITS.** Most strollers shouldn't be used for children over 35 pounds.

5 **CHECK FOR THE JPMA CERTIFICATION.** The JPMA (the Juvenile Products Manufacturers Association) has a pretty good safety certification program for strollers. They require that strollers must have a locking device to prevent accidental folding and meet other safety standards, such as those for brakes. You can contact the JPMA for a list of certified strollers at (856) 231-8500 or www.jpma.org.

6 **JOGGING STROLLERS ARE BEST FOR BABIES OVER ONE YEAR OF AGE.** Yes, some stroller makers tout their joggers for babies as young as six weeks (or six months) of age. But we think the neck

strollers

muscles of such small infants can't take the shocks of jogging or walking on rough paths (or going over curbs). Ask your pediatrician if you need more advice on when it is safe to use a jogger.

Recalls: Where to Find Information

The U.S. Consumer Product Safety Commission has a toll-free hotline at (800) 638-2772 (web: www.cpsc.gov) for the latest recall information on strollers and other juvenile products. It's easy

---

Guaranteed Frustration:
Baby gear warranties can leave you fuming

It's a fact of life: sometimes you buy a product that breaks only days after purchase. So, you pick up the phone and call the manufacturer and ask about their warranty. "Sure, we'll help," says the customer service rep. In no time, you have a replacement product and a happy parent.

Fast forward to real life. Most parents find warranties only guarantee frustration—especially with baby products like strollers and other travel gear. Numerous hassles confront parents who find they have a defective product, from endless waits on hold to speak with a customer service rep (on a non-toll free line) to the actual process of returning a product.

First, consider the process of actually registering an item. Filling out a warranty card often requires information that you can only find on the product box or carton. Some parents find this out the hard way . . . after they've hauled all the boxes off to the trash. Even worse: some baby product makers like Peg Perego actually request a copy of the sales receipt for their warranty form. Hello? What about gifts?

Then, let's say something goes wrong. Your new stroller breaks a wheel. That brand new baby monitor goes on the fritz after one week. If it is a gift or you lost the receipt, the store you bought it from may say "tough luck"—call the manufacturer. With many warranties, you have to return the defective item to the manufacturer *at your expense*. And then you wait a few more weeks while they decide to fix or replace the item. Typically you have to pay for return shipping—and that can be expensive for a bulky item like a stroller. And then you must do without the product for weeks.

Dealing with the customer service departments at some baby product makers can add insult to injury. It seems like some companies can count their customer service staff with one hand—or one finger, in some cases. The result: long waits on hold. Or it takes days to get responses to emails. The U.S. offices of foreign baby product companies seem to be the worst at customer service staffing (Chicco, Perego), while giant firms such as Graco and Evenflo have better customer service.

---

to use—the hotline is a series of recorded voice mail messages that you access by following the prompts. The same info is online. You can also report any potential hazard you've discovered or an injury to your child caused by a product. If you prefer, you can write to the U.S. Consumer Products Safety Commission, Washington, D.C. 20207.

And customer service can go from good to bad in the blink of an eye. Combi was known for its good customer service until a meltdown back in 2001—then a large influx of calls from a recall and a staff shortage created long waits on hold, unreturned emails and frustrated consumers. Combi has long since the fixed the problem, but other companies (notably Fisher Price, Chicco, Peg Perego) continue to struggle with providing decent customer service.

The bottom line: it's no wonder that when something goes wrong, consumers just consider trashing the product and buying a new one. And let's be realistic: paying $20 in shipping to send back a broken $39 stroller doesn't make much sense. Here's our advice:

◆ **Keep your receipts.** It doesn't have to be fancy—a shoebox will do. That way you can prove you bought that defective product. If the item was a gift, keep the product manual and serial number.

◆ **If something goes wrong, call the manufacturer.** We're always surprised at how frustrated consumers forget to first call the company—you might be surprised at how responsive some companies are at fixing an issue.

◆ **If the problem is a safety defect, immediately stop using the product and file a complaint with the Consumer Product Safety Commission** (www.cpsc.gov). Also contact the company.

◆ **Attack the problem multiple ways.** Don't just call; also send an email and perhaps a written letter. Be reasonable: allow the company 1-2 business days to reply to a phone call or email.

◆ **Let other parents know about your experiences.** The best way to fix lousy customer service? Shame companies into doing it better. Post your experiences to the message boards on our site (BabyBargains.com) and other parenting sites. Trust us, companies are sensitive to such criticism.

strollers

Smart Shopper Tips

Smart Shopper Tip #1
Give it a Test Drive

"My friend was thinking of buying a stroller online, sight unseen. Should you really buy a stroller without trying it first?"

It's best to try before you buy. Most stores have at least one stroller set up as a floor model. Give it a whirl, practice folding it up, and check the steering. One smart tip: put some weight in the stroller seat (borrow a friend's toddler or use a backpack full of books that weighs about 15 pounds is good). The steering and maneuverability will feel different if the stroller is loaded then empty—obviously, that's a more real world test-drive.

Once you've tried it out, shop for price through 'net or mail order sources. Ask retailers if they will meet or beat prices quoted to you online (many quietly do so). What if you live in Kansas and the nearest dealer for a stroller you want is in, say, Texas? Then you may have no choice but to buy sight unseen—but just make sure the web site or catalog has a good return policy. Another tip: use message boards like those on our web site (www.BabyBargains.com) to quiz other parents about stroller models.

If you buy a stroller from a store, we strongly recommend opening the box and making sure everything is in there BEFORE you leave the store!

Smart Shopper Tip #2
What Features Really Matter?

"Let's cut through the clutter here. Do I really need a stroller that has deluxe shock absorbers and four-wheel drive? What features are really important?"

Walk into any baby store and you'll encounter a blizzard of strollers. Do you want a stroller with a full recline? Boot and retractable canopy? What the heck is a boot, anyway? Here's a look at the features in the stroller market today:

Features for baby:

◆ **Reclining seat.** Since babies less than six months of age sleep most of the time and can't hold their heads up, strollers that have reclining seats are a plus. Yet, the *extent* of a stroller's seat recline varies by model. Some have full reclines, a few recline part of the way (120 degrees) and some don't recline at all. FYI: just because a stroller has a "full recline" does NOT mean it reclines to 180 degrees. It may recline slightly less than that for safety reasons.

◆ *Front (or napper) bar.* As a safety precaution, many strollers have a front bar (also called a napper bar) that keeps baby secure (though you should always use the stroller's safety harness). Better strollers have a bar that's padded and removable. Why removable? Later, when your baby gets to toddler hood, you may need to remove the bar to make it easier for the older child to access the stroller. FYI: Some strollers have a kid snack tray, which serves much the same function as a napper bar.

◆ *Seat padding.* You'll find every possible padding option out there, from bare bones models with a single piece of fabric to strollers with deluxe-quilted padding made from fine fabrics hand woven by monks in Luxembourg. (Okay, just kidding—the monks actually live in Switzerland). For seating, some strollers have card-board platforms (these can be uncomfortable for long rides) and other models have fabric that isn't removable or machine washable (see below for more on this).

◆ *Shock absorbers or suspension systems.* Yes, a few strollers do have wheels equipped with shock absorbers for a smoother ride. We're unsure how effective this feature really is—it's not like you could wheel baby over potholes without waking her up. On the other hand, if you live in a neighborhood with uneven or rough sidewalks, they might be worth a look.

◆ *Wheels.* In reality, how smooth a stroller rides is more related to the type of wheels. The general rule: the more the better. Strollers with double wheels on each leg ride smoother than single wheels. Most strollers have plastic wheels. In recent years, some stroller makers have rolled out models with "pneumatic" or inflated wheels. These offer a smoother ride.

◆ *Weather protection.* Yes you can buy a stroller that's outfitted for battle with a winter in New England, for example. The options include retractable hoods/canopies and "boots" (which protect a child's feet) to block out wind, rain or cold. Fabrics play a role here too—some strollers feature quilted hoods to keep baby warm and others claim they are water repellent. While a boot is an option some may not need, hoods/canopies are rather important, even if just to keep the sun out of baby's eyes. Some strollers only have a canopy (or "sunshade") that partially covers baby, while other models have a full hood that can completely cover the stroller. Look for canopies that have lots of adjustments (to block a setting sun) and have "peak-a-boo" windows that let you see baby even when closed.

What if your stroller doesn't have a rain cover? One option is the Protect a Bub Rain & Wind Cover, which comes in both single ($20) and double versions ($30). An Australian company makes it (web:protect-a-bubusa.com).

Features for parents:

◆ **Storage baskets.** Many strollers have deep, under-seat baskets for storage of coats, purses, bags, etc. Yet, the amount of storage can vary sharply from model to model. Inexpensive umbrella strollers may have no basket at all, while other models have tiny baskets. Mass-market strollers (Graco, etc.) typically have the most storage; other stroller makers have been playing catch-up in the basket game. Combi, for example, has added new models with bigger storage baskets. One tip: it's not just the size of the storage basket but the *access* to it that counts. Some strollers have big baskets but are practically inaccessible when the seat is reclined. A support bar blocks others.

◆ **Removable seat cushion for washing.** Let's be honest: strollers can get icky real fast. Crushed-in cookies, spilt juice and the usual grime can make a stroller a mobile dirt-fest. Some strollers have removable seat cushions that are machine washable—other models let you remove *all* of the fabric for a washing. Watch out for those models with non-removable fabric/seat cushions—while you can clean these strollers in one of those manual car washes (with a high-pressure nozzle), it's definitely a hassle (especially in the winter).

◆ **Lockable wheels.** Some strollers have front wheels that can be locked in a forward position—this enables you to more quickly push the stroller in a straight line.

◆ **Wheel size.** You'll see just about every conceivable size wheel out there on strollers today. As you might guess, the smaller wheels are good for maneuverability in the mall, but larger wheels handle rough sidewalks (or gravel paths) much better.

◆ **Handle/Steering.** This is an important area to consider—most strollers have a single bar handle, which enables one-handed steering. Other strollers have two handles (example: Maclarens as well as Perego's Pliko line). Two handles require two hands to push, but enable a stroller to fold up compactly, like an umbrella. It's sort of a trade-off—steer ability versus easier fold. There are other handle issues to consider as well. A handful of strollers feature a "reversible" handle. Why would you want that? By reversing the handle, you can push the stroller while the baby faces you (better for small infants). Later, you can reverse the handle so an older child can look out while being pushed from behind. (Note: models with reversible handles seem increasingly rare in recent years; we'll note which models still have this feature later in this chapter). Another important factor: consider the handle *height*. Some handles have adjustable heights to better accommodate taller parents (more on this later). However, just because a stroller touts this feature doesn't mean it adjusts to accommodate a seven-foot tall parent (at most, you get an extra inch or two of height). Finally, a few stroller makers offer "one-touch fold" handles. Hit a button on the stroller and it can be folded up with one motion. On our web site BabyBargains.com (click on Bonus Material), we have a chart that lists strollers with height-adjustable handles and one-touch folds.

◆ **Compact fold.** We call it the trunk factor—when a stroller is folded, will it fit in your trunk? Some strollers fold compactly and can fit in a narrow trunk or airline overhead cabin, which is great if you plan to do much traveling. Other strollers are still quite bulky when folded—think about your trunk space before buying. Unfortunately, we are not aware of any web site that lists the size/footprint of strollers when folded. You are on your own to size up models when folded in a store, compared to your trunk (hint: take measurements before you hit the baby store). Not only should you consider how compactly a stroller folds, but also how it folds in general. The best strollers fold with just one or two quick motions; others require you to hit 17 levers and latches. The latest stroller fold fad: strollers that fold standing UP instead of down. Why is this better? Because strollers that fold down to the ground can get dirty/scratched in a parking lot.

◆ **Durability.** Should you go for a lower-price stroller or a premium brand? Let's be honest: the lower-priced strollers (say, under $100) have nowhere near the durability of the models that cost $200 to $400. Levers that break, reclining seats which stop reclining and other glitches can make you hate a cheap stroller mighty quick. Yet, some parents don't need a stroller that will make it through the next world war. If all you do is a couple of quick trips to the mall every week or so, then a less expensive stroller will probably be fine. However, if you plan to use the stroller for more than one child, live in an urban environment with rough sidewalks, or plan extensive outdoor adventures with baby, then invest in a better stroller. Later in this chapter, we'll go over specific models and give you brand recommendations for certain lifestyles.

◆ **Overall weight.** Yes, it's a dilemma: the more feature-laden the stroller, the more it weighs. Yet it doesn't take lugging a 30-pound stroller in and out of a car trunk more than a few times to justify the expense of a lighter-weight design. Carefully consider a stroller's weight before purchase. Some parents end up with two strollers—a lightweight/umbrella-type stroller for quick trips (or air travel) and then a more feature-intensive model for extensive outdoor outings.

One factor to consider with weight: steel vs. aluminum frames. Steel is heavier than aluminum, but some parents prefer steel because it gives the stroller a stiffer feel. Along the same lines, sometimes we get complaints from parents who own aluminum strollers because they feel the stroller is too "wobbly"—while it's lightweight, one of aluminum's disadvantages is its flexibility. One tip for dealing with a wobbly stroller: lock the front wheels so you can push the stroller in a straight line. That helps to smooth the ride.

Smart Shopper Tip #3
The Cadillac Escalade or Ford Focus Dilemma

"This is nuts! I see cheap umbrella strollers that sell for $30 on one hand and then fancy designer brands for $300 on the other. Do I really need to spend a fortune on a stroller?"

Whether you drive a Cadillac Escalade or Ford Focus, you'll still get to your destination. And that fact pretty much applies to strollers too—most function well enough to get you and baby from point A to point B, not matter what the price.

So, should you buy the cheapest stroller you can find? Well, no. There *is* a significant difference in quality between a cheap $30 umbrella stroller and a name brand that costs $100, $200 or more. Unless you want the endless headaches of a cheap stroller (wheels that break, parts that fall off), it's important to invest in a stroller that will make it through the long haul.

The real question is: do you need a fancy stroller loaded with features or will a simple model do? To answer that, you need to consider *how* you will use the stroller. Do you live in the suburbs and just need the stroller once a week for a quick spin at the mall? Or do you live in an urban environment where a stroller is your primary vehicle, taking all the abuse that a big city can dish out? Climate plays another factor—in the Northeast, strollers have to be winterized to handle the cold and snow. Meanwhile, in Southern California, full canopies are helpful for shading baby's eyes from late afternoon sunshine.

Figuring out how different stroller options fit your lifestyle/climate is the key to stroller happiness. Later in this chapter, we'll recommend several specific strollers for certain lifestyles and climates.

One final note: quality, name-brand strollers actually have resale value. You can sell that $300 stroller on eBay, at a second-hand store, or via the classifieds and recoup some of your investment. The better the brand name (Peg Perego, Bugaboo, Maclaren, Zooper, Mountain Buggy), the more the resale value. Unfortunately, the cheap brands like Graco, Evenflo and Kolcraft are worth little or nothing on the second-hand market—there is a reason for that (beyond snob appeal). Take a quick look at eBay's stroller section to see what we mean.

What if you buy a stroller that is great, except for a skimpy canopy? You can fix that with a cool sunshade from Australia called the Pepeny (web: www.pepeny.com). This shade screens out the weather, sunlight and UV . . . and is all the rage in New York City. The Pepeny comes in several colors and fits most stroller models. It's about $50 and available in stores and on web sites like OneStopBabyShop.com. This would also be a good idea for California parents to screen out low-angle sun.

Smart Shopper Tip #4
Too tall for their own good

"I love our stroller, but my husband hates it. He's six feet tall and has to stoop over to push it. Even worse, when he walks, he hits the back of the stroller with his feet."

Strollers are made for women of average height. What's that? About 5'6". If you (or your spouse) are taller than that, you'll find certain stroller models will be a pain to use.

This is probably one of the biggest complaints we get from parents about strollers. Unfortunately, just a few stroller models have height-adjustable handles that let a six-foot tall person comfortably push a stroller without stooping over or hitting the back of the stroller with his feet. (See box later in this section for such models). One smart shopping tip: if you have a tall spouse, make sure you take him or her stroller shopping with you. Checking out handle heights in person is the only way to avoid this problem.

Smart Shopper Tip #5
The Myth of the Magic Bullet Stroller

"I'd like to buy just one stroller—a model that works with an infant car seat and then converts to full-featured pram and then finally a jogger for kids up to age 4. And I want it to weigh less than 10 pounds. And sell for just under $50. What model do you suggest?"

Boy, that sounds like our email some days! We hear from parents all the time looking for that one model that will do it all. We call it the Myth of the Magic Bullet Stroller—an affordable product that morphs into seven different uses for children from birth to college. Sorry, we haven't found one yet.

The reality: most parents own more than one stroller. A typical set-up: one stroller that holds an infant car seat (or a stroller frame) and then a lightweight stroller that folds compactly for the mall/travel. Of course, we hear from parents who own four, five or six strollers, including specialty models like joggers, tandem units for two kids and more. First-time parents wonder if these folks have lost their minds, investing the equivalent of the gross national product of Aruba on baby transportation. Alas, most parents realize that as their baby grows and their needs change, so must their stroller. Far be it from us to suggest you buy multiple strollers, but at the same time, it is hard to recommend just one model that works for everyone. That's why the recommendations later in this chapter are organized by lifestyle and use.

Wastes of Money

1 **GIVE THE "BOOT" THE BOOT.** Some expensive strollers offer a "boot" or apron that fits over the baby's feet. This padded cover is supposed to keep the baby's feet dry and warm when it rains or snows. Sometimes you have to spend an extra $50 to $75 to get a stroller with this accessory. But how many parents walk their baby in the rain or snow anyway? We say save the extra cost and use a blanket instead. Or try a product like the Cozy Rosie or Bundle Me (mentioned later in this chapter), which are made of fleece and provide more warmth than a typical stroller boot. Or, if you decide you need a boot, buy a stroller model that includes this feature—several models now include a boot as standard equipment.

2 **SILLY ACCESSORIES.** Entrepreneurs have worked overtime to invent all kinds of silly accessories that you "must have" for your stroller. We've seen stroller "snack trays" ($15) for babies who like to eat on the run. Another company made a clip-on bug repellent, which allegedly used sound waves to scare away insects. Yet another money-waster: extra seat cushions or head supports for infants made in your stroller's matching fabric. You can find these same items in solid colors at discount stores for 40% less.

So which stroller accessories are worth the money? One accessory we do recommend is a toy bar (about $10 to $20), which attaches to the stroller. Why is this a good buy? If toys are not attached, your baby will probably punt them out the stroller. We also like Kelgar's Stroll'r Hold'r cup holder ($7, call 972-250-3838 or web: www.kelgar.com).

What about stroller handle extensions? If you find yourself kicking the back of the stroller as you walk, you might want to invest in one of these $20 devices (sold online at sites like HappyBabyProducts.com). They add up to 8" in height to your stroller handle.

3 **"NEW" OLD STOCK.** A reader alerted us to this online scam—the problem of "new" old stock. She ordered from a small web site what was described as a "new Chicco stroller" in 2001. Turns out, the stroller she got was from 1994. Yes, technically it was "new," as in "not previously used" and still in its original box. Unfortunately, since it was sitting in a warehouse for seven years, it had a cracked canopy, torn fabric and other problems. Apparently, there must be warehouses full of "new" old baby products out there, perhaps left over from the dot-com bust. Our advice: if you see a great online deal, ask what MODEL YEAR the stroller or other product is from. While previous year models can be a great deal, we wouldn't buy anything over three years old. . . even if a web site says it is "new."

 ## Money-Saving Tips

1 CHECK OUT THE DISCOUNTERS. As we discussed earlier, the web is a great source for stroller bargains. But don't forget stores like Babies R Us and Baby Depot. They sell quality brands (including Peg Perego) and have frequent specials.

2 WHY NOT A BASIC UMBRELLA STROLLER? If you only plan to use a stroller on infrequent trips to the mall, then a plain umbrella stroller for $30 to $40 will suffice. One caveat: make sure you get one that is JPMA certified (see the Safe & Sounds section earlier). Some cheap umbrella strollers have been involved in safety recalls. Second caveat: most plain umbrella strollers do NOT recline—you will not be able to use it until your baby is able to hold up his head (around six months).

3 CONSIDER THE ALTERNATIVES TO BULKY (AND EXPENSIVE) TRAVEL SYSTEMS. Among the best bets: the Kolcraft Universal Car Seat Carrier stroller frame ($50), the Snap N Go (also called Kar Seat Karriage, $50 to $60) from Baby Trend (800-328-7363 or web: www.babytrend.com) or Combi's Strolee Streak or Combi Flash ($50; www.combi-intl.com). You pop just about any name-brand infant car seat carrier into these strollers and voila! Instant travel system at half the price. Another idea: consider a front carrier or backpack instead of a bulky stroller. Later in this section, we'll discuss our picks for carriers and backpacks.

4 CHECK FOR SALES. We're always amazed by the number of sales on strollers. We've seen frequent sales at the Burlington Coat Factory's Baby Depot, with good markdowns on even premium brand strollers. And just the other week we received a coupon booklet from Toys R Us that featured a $10 off coupon on any Graco stroller over $70. That's nearly a 15% savings. Another reason strollers go on sale: the manufacturers are constantly coming out with new models and have to clear out the old. Which leads us to the next tip.

5 LOOK FOR LAST YEAR'S MODELS. Every year, manufacturers roll out new models. In some cases, they add features; other times, they just change the fabric. What do they do with last year's stock? They discontinue it—and then it's sale time. You'll see these

E-MAIL FROM THE REAL WORLD
Last year's fashion, 50% off

A reader emailed her tip on how she saved $100 on a stroller:
"When looking for strollers you can often get last year's version for half the price. I purchased the 2001 Maclaren Vogue from dmartstores.com for $135 versus the Babies R Us price for the 2002 model of $250. As far as my research could tell, the models are identical except for the color pattern. I just typed in 2001 Maclaren Vogue into the Google search engine and found a number of sources that were selling them, colors are limited (dmartstores.com had the widest selection) but it is a great way to save $100 for a very nice stroller."

models on sale for as much as 50% off in stores and on the web. And it's not like stroller fabric fashion varies much from year to year—is there really much difference between "navy pin dot" and "navy with a raspberry diamond"? We say go for last year's fabric and save a bundle. See the Email from the Real World on the next page for a mom's story on her last year model deal.

6 SCOPE OUT FACTORY SECONDS. Believe it or not, some stroller manufacturers sell "factory seconds" at good discounts—these "cosmetically imperfect" models might have a few blemishes, but are otherwise fine. An example: one reader told us Peg Perego occasionally has factory sales from their Indiana headquarters. See Peg's contact info later in this chapter to find the latest schedule.

7 DON'T FALL VICTIM TO STROLLER OVERKILL. Seriously evaluate how you'll use the stroller and don't over buy. If a Toyota Camry will do, why buy a Lexus? You don't really need an all-terrain stroller or full-feature pram for mall trips. Flashy strollers can be status symbols for some parents—try to avoid "stroller envy" if at all possible.

8 SELL YOUR STROLLER TO RECOUP YOUR INVESTMENT. When you're done with the stroller, consign it at a second-hand store or sell it in the classifieds or on eBay. You'd be surprised how much it can fetch. The best brands for resale are, not surprisingly, the better names we recommend in this chapter.

9 WAREHOUSE CLUB DEALS. Yes, Sam's and Costco periodically sell strollers, including joggers. At one point before going to press, Costco was selling Schwinn jogging strollers from their web site (Costco.com) at 30% under retail. Of course, these deals come and go—and like anything you see at the warehouse clubs, you have to snap it up quickly or it will be gone.

10 eBay. It's highly addictive and for good reason—the site is more than just folks trying to unload a junky stroller they bought at K-Mart. Increasingly, baby gear retailers are using eBay to discreetly clear out overstock. Better to unload online the stuff that isn't moving then risk the wrath of local customers who bought the model for full price last week. An example: a reader scored a brand new Peg Perego for HALF the stroller's retail price through an eBay auction. Other readers regularly report saving $100 to $200 through eBay. Hint: many strollers sold online are last year's model or fashion. Be sure to confirm what you are buying (is it in an original box? No damage? Which model year?) before bidding.

The Name Game: Reviews of Selected Manufacturers

Here's a wrap-up of many of the stroller brands on the market today. We evaluated strollers based on hands-on inspections, interviews with recent parents, and conversations with juvenile product retailers. For us, the most important attributes for strollers were safety, convenience and durability. Of course, price to value (as reflected in the number of features) was an important factor as well.

One key point to remember: the ratings in this section apply to the ENTIRE line of a company's strollers. No, we don't assign ratings to individual strollers, but we will comment on what we think are a company's best models. Following this section, we will give you several "lifestyle recommendations"—specific models of strollers to fit different parent lifestyles.

The prices quoted here are street prices—that is prices we saw in stores or on the 'net. In other cases, we used manufacturer's estimated retail prices. Yet, prices can fluctuate widely: in areas with heavy competition among stores (like the Northeast or West Coast), prices are lower. In more isolated communities, however, you may find prices in stores to be higher than what's quoted here.

The Ratings

A Excellent—our top pick!
B Good— above average quality, prices, and creativity.
C Fair—could stand some improvement.
D Poor—yuck! Could stand some major improvement.

Aprica *400 W. Artesia Blvd., Compton, CA 90004. For a dealer near you, call (310) 639-6387 or (201) 883-9800 (web: www.apri-causa.com).* Aprica has all but disappeared from the U.S. market in recent years, but you'll still see a few of their models in some stores. As a result, we've moved their former review to our web site (BabyBargains.com and click on Bonus Material).

Baby Trend *For a dealer near you, call (800) 328-7363, (909) 902-5568, Web: www.babytrend.com.* Baby Trend's biggest selling stroller isn't really a stroller at all—it's a stroller *frame*. Here's an overview of the line:

The models. The Snap N Go is such a simple concept it's amazing someone else didn't think of this years ago—basically it's a stroller frame that lets you snap in most major-brand infant car seats. Presto! Instant travel system at a fraction of the price. The original Snap N Go was just a frame and wheels and sat low to the ground. Newer model Snap & Go's ($50) now have a big basket and sit higher. And memo to parents of twins: there's even a double version of the Snap N Go that holds two car seats ($100 on BabiesRUS.com). New this year, Baby Trend will launch a Snap & Go that converts to a stroller (with a snap-on tray and fabric sling seat). Be aware that the Snap N Go doesn't work with ALL infant car seats (but most major brands will fit). Consult Baby Trend's web site (FAQ's) for a current list.

The Snap N Go has been so successful it has spawned knock-offs

Who's who?

A big trend in recent years in strollers are licensed names—stroller makers try to add cache to their strollers by slapping a better-known company's name on it. Here's a run-down of the major licenses and who to look up in this chapter for a review of their parent company:

LICENSE	MADE BY
CARTER'S	KOLCRAFT
EDDIE BAUER	COSCO
JEEP	KOLCRAFT
MARTINELLI	PEG PEREGO
OSHKOSH	EVENFLO
REEBOK	BABY TREND
SAFETY 1ST	COSCO
SWAN	BABY TREND
SCHWINN	INSTEP

from several competitors, namely Kolcraft and Combi. We will review those options later. All in all, we think the Snap & Go is a winner.

Besides the stroller frame, Baby Trend also offers travel systems, double strollers and joggers.

Baby Trend's travel systems combine their Flex-Loc infant seat (see review in last chapter) with basic low-end strollers. Example: the Trendsport Traveler system for $140 (car seat plus stroller). That's a great price, but the stroller (18 lbs.) is nothing fancy—steel frame, three-point harness and two-position recline. You do get a decent canopy, one-hand fold and a big basket, but the recline is only to 145 degrees (not a full recline). Baby Trend sells two more expensive travel systems, the Shuttle ($150) and the Profile ($150). Compared to the Trendsport, the Shuttle and Profile offer bigger canopies, larger wheels and more plush padding.

Baby Trend is a big player in the jogging stroller market (we'll discuss these models later in this chapter in the "Exercise This" section). Baby Trend now has a jogging stroller travel system (the Expedition LE, $189), which pairs the Baby Trend infant seat with a jogger. In the past year, Baby Trend has rolled out upgraded joggers under the Reebok label.

Finally, we should also note that Baby Trend markets their products under the name "Swan" for specialty stores. Basically, these are the same products/models as Baby Trend makes, albeit with a few cosmetic differences (fabric color, etc.). For example, the Swan Excursion jogger travel system features a removable snack tray, parent tray and ratcheting canopy. Price: $160 for a single, $200 for a double.

FYI: Baby Trend has lost the license to sell the Sit N Stand (an innovative "pushcart" that combined a stroller with a jump seat for an older child)—that has been picked up by upstart Joovy (see review later in this chapter). And while the company has promised to debut a new tandem to replace its Caravan Lite, there has been no release as of this writing.

Our view. We're not sure what to make of Baby Trend—parents seem to love some of their products (particularly the Snap N Go) and loathe others (basically, most of their other strollers). Yes, the jogging strollers get good marks for value, but Baby Trend has been dogged by numerous quality problems when it comes to their regular strollers. Parents say parts break, wheels fall off and worse—"bad engineering" was how one parent put it. Example, with the Shuttle stroller: you can't open the canopy and have a drink in the holder at the same time! Doh! And before you buy a Baby Trend travel system, be sure to read the caveats to their infant car seat in our last chapter. So, it's hard to assign a rating. If we were just looking at the Snap N Go or the joggers, we'd give them an A. Yet, the other models would barely earn a C. So, we'll compromise. **Rating: B-**

Britax *Web: www.britaxusa.com* Best-known for its well-made car seats, Britax launched a stroller line in 2005 so it could compete in the travel system market.

The Models. Britax offers three stroller options: the Esprit, Forerunner and Preview. A fourth model, dubbed the Global, will be out sometime this year. The Esprit ($99, 12 lbs.) is positioned as a lightweight umbrella stroller with aluminum frame, foam grip handles and partial reclining seat. The Esprit does NOT work with any Britax car seat, however. For that, you have to upgrade to the Forerunner or Preview. The Forerunner ($160, 16 lbs.) has a more traditional design with height adjustable handle and child snack tray. The Forerunner works with the Britax Companion infant seat, as does the Preview ($130, 17 lbs.). The Preview is similar to the Forerunner, but has two separate handles (like the Esprit).

Britax plans to debut the Global Travel System ($300 to $350) in the coming months. This travel system will feature a full-size stroller similar to the Peg Perego Venezia: it will have a removable, reversible seat, full recline, parent and child tray, full enclosing canopy and full suspension. The 24 lb. Global will come in a basic and deluxe model . . . the basic will omit the parent tray, boot or extended canopy.

Our View. "Underwhelming" would be our sum-up for Britax's strollers. For a company that made its name on a slew of innovative car seats, Britax strollers are strangely lacking in both design and features. Let's get real: who comes out with a stroller today WITHOUT a parent cup holder? Britax, apparently, as the Preview omits this key feature that is standard on just about every other stroller on the market today.

Little details about these strollers show Britax's inexperience in this category. Examples: when you recline the seat on the Preview or Forerunner (and when you have the car seat attached), you can't access the basket. You'll need two hands to fold up the stroller . . . or even to recline seat. While you might expect to see those flaws on a cheap-o $50 stroller sold at Wal-Mart, Britax owes its customers more at this price point.

All in all, these strollers are let-downs. Given the Britax name, we expect to be wowed with innovation, features and fashion. Instead, we got me-too models that are missing key features. ***Rating: B-***

Bugaboo *For a dealer near you, call 800-460-2922. Web: www.bugaboo.nl.* Bugaboo. It's Dutch for "priced as if from a hotel mini-bar."

The Models. Here's an unlikely recipe for success in the stroller biz. Take a Dutch-designed stroller, attach a $700 price tag and voila! Instant hit, right? Well, chalk this one up to some creative

Different versions spark confusion

Here's a common question we get at the home office: readers go into a chain store like Babies R Us and see a major brand stroller they like. Then, they visit a specialty store and see a similar model, but with some cosmetic differences . . . and a higher price tag. What's up with that? Big stroller makers like Graco have to serve two masters—chain stores and specialty retailers. Here's a little trick of the baby biz: stroller makers often take the same basic model of stroller and make various versions for different retailers. Hence, you'll see a Graco stroller with basic fabric in Babies R Us—and then the same model sold as a Laura Ashley stroller with fancier fabric in specialty stores. So is there any real difference besides the fabric color to justify the increase in price? No, not in our research. The strollers are almost exactly the same. Our advice: if you can live with the basic version, go for it.

marketing (or at least, lucky timing).

Bugaboo's breakthrough success was the Frog, named as such for its small wheels in front that give it a frog-like look. The Frog was a clever hybrid between an all-terrain and carriage stroller, pitched to parents for its multiple uses. The Frog was comprised of three parts: an aluminum frame and bassinet that could later be replaced by a stroller seat (included with canopy and basket). It weighed about 19 to 22 lbs., depending on how it was configured.

So, how did the Bugaboo become so hot? Sure, it was fashionable, but that doesn't quite explain it. The Bugaboo had one of the great product placements of all time . . . it was the featured stroller on HBO's series *Sex in the City*. The rest is stroller history. In no time, celebs like Gwyneth Paltrow were swishing their Bugaboos across the pages of *People* magazine.

Figuring a $700 stroller was a bit bourgeois, Bugaboo's sequel to the Frog—the aptly named Cameleon—now costs $880. The Cameleon adds a more springy suspension on the front wheels, plus a slightly larger seat frame and higher chassis. Unlike the Frog, the Cameleon will be available in a wide range of color combinations—you can choose from four base colors and eight top colors, mix and match. Also new: a height adjustable handle.

If that is too much, the stripped down Gecko also joins the Bugaboo line. The Gecko omits the front suspension and is lighter (15 lbs. versus 20 lbs. for the Cameleon). It sells for $680. We suppose the Gecko is for B-list celebrities.

FYI: Bugaboo sells a raft of accessories for its strollers (what? you thought that would be included?). Add in these extras and you could be out $1000 or more. Example: a $45 car seat adapter lets you attach most major brand infant car seats to the frame.

Our view. Well, on the plus side, parents who have purchased Bugaboo strollers universally praise their quality and ease of ease—fans love the smooth steering, cozy bassinet, reversible seat and so on. On the other hand . . . it's insane to spend this much on a stroller. And shhh! Don't tell anyone, but the Bugaboo is actually made in Taiwan, not Europe. ***Rating: You're kidding, right?***

BumbleRide *For a dealer near you, call 800-530-3930. Web: www.bumbleride.com.* BumbleRide's mission is to inject a bit of fashion into stroller market often marked by models that are dull and duller. Started by a husband and wife team in San Diego, BumbleRide's bright colors have set our message boards buzzing with parents who have been impressed with the brand.

The Models. The Flyer (in "pumpkin"—yep, it is orange) is a good place to start and BumbleRide's most popular stroller. This $300 carriage stroller weighs 19 lbs. and features a five-point harness, reversible handle (which is nice), four-position recline, adjustable footrest and mesh basket. Best of all, it is compatible with several major infant car seats. The only negative: it is quite bulky when folded, so you'll need a large trunk to haul it around. New this year, BumbleRide made the rear wheels of the Flyer unlock and swivel, which makes pushing easier when the handle is reversed. Also new: the strollers is three pounds lighter than last year's model and now has a cup holder.

The Rocket is a tri-wheel stroller with quick release 12" inflated tires, boot, adjustable handle, deep storage basket and an optional carrycot. It weighs 25 lbs. and runs $300. Basically, this is a more stylish (albeit slightly heavier) version of the Mountain Buggy Urban Single. Of all Bumbleride's models, this one is our favorite.

BumbleRide's most expensive model is the Queen B ($380, 31 lbs.), a pram-style stroller with wire basket. Yes, it comes with plush padding, reclining seat, boot and more. Good news: this year's Queen B has front swivel wheels, replacing the fixed wheels of last year's model.

Our view. We will give BumbleRide its due—they have helped brighten an otherwise navy blue world. And Bumbleride has tried to improve the line's initial shortcomings—we like the fact the company has shaved some weight off the Flyer and added swivel wheels to the Queen B. Yet, the company has raised prices this year, eliminating some of the price advantage the Rocket had over, say, Mountain Buggy. And readers still gripe somewhat about how bulky these strollers are when folded (better have a SUV to haul them around). Finally, we'd still like Bumbleride to throw in extras like rain covers at this price point (Zooper does that). All in all, however, quality is good and we will give BumbleRide our recommendation. ***Rating: A-***

Carter's These strollers are made by Kolcraft; see their review at the end of this section in "Other Brands."

Chicco *4E Easy Street, Bound Brook, NJ 08805. For a store near you, call (877) 4-CHICCO or (732) 805-9200. Web: www.chiccousa.com* Chicco (pronounced Kee-ko) has a 50-year history as one of Europe's leading juvenile products makers. Along with Peg Perego, Chicco is Europe's biggest producer of strollers and other baby products and toys. In the U.S. and Canada, however, Chicco was always an also-ran while Perego was a top-seller. Chicco has tried to turn that around in recent years by emphasizing their lightweight stroller models instead of full-featured carriage models. Here's an overview:

The models. Despite the Italian pedigree, most Chicco strollers sold in the U.S. are made in China. The entry-level Caddy ($50, 11 lbs.) has a five-point harness, two-position recline and a rather skimpy sunshade (but no basket). Parents love the included rain cover and bright colors—the quality is very good and the handle height is great for taller moms.

A step-up in terms of features is the London ($70, 15 lbs.). It has a five-position recline, adjustable leg rest, padded handles, canopy. . . and basket. No, it doesn't push as smoothly as a Maclaren—but it is half the price!

Not many changes with the Caddy and London this year—the Caddy gets upgraded fabric and a slightly bigger canopy that drops down in front.

E-Mail from The Real World
The Weight Game

"I saw the same stroller listed with two different weights online. How can the same model weigh five pounds less on one site?"

Good question—call it the weight shell game. We've noticed some web sites play fast and loose with the weights of strollers listed on their sites. Why? Many sellers know what parents want most is a LIGHTWEIGHT stroller. So, why not list a stroller's weight, minus a few items like a canopy, basket or other amenities? Other times stroller makers add features to newer versions of stroller models. This adds weight, but web sites "mistakenly" still list the old model's weight. Yes, it is deceptive—but there are ways around the problem. First, this book lists the true weight for most models. If in doubt, check the manufacturer's web site, which almost always lists the correct weight.

FYI: Babies R Us sells its own version of the Caddy, which is called the Capri. Basically, the Capri is the same as the Caddy but includes a basket. This year Chicco plans to add a better canopy to the Capri.

Among Chicco's better new offerings is the lightweight C5 ($90, 13.7 lbs.). This stroller features a multi-position reclining seat, decent size basket and nice canopy. Combine this with a compact, umbrella-style fold and Chicco has a winner. FYI: a twin version of the C5

Shopping Cart Covers: Advice & Picks

Grocery store carts aren't exactly the cleanest form of transportation—yet once your baby outgrows her infant car seat, you will put likely baby in the little seat up front . . . and quickly realize that keeping the carts clean doesn't seem to be a high priority for most stores.

To the rescue comes the shopping cart cover, basically a fabric seat that provides a clean and safe space for baby while you shop. If you decide one is for you, there are surprisingly quite a few options to chose from in a variety of price ranges. Here's what to look for in a shopping cart cover:

◆ **Washability**. Well, that sounds like a no-brainer, but be sure to check the cover's washing instructions. Machine washable and dryable are key.

◆ **Side coverage**. Cheaper cart covers don't cover the entire cart seat—some leave the sides of the cart exposed, etc. Make sure the ENTIRE cart seat is covered.

◆ **Pockets and toy loops.** The best covers have pockets for toys, diapers, wipes, etc. Make sure the pockets have zipper or Velcro closures—and are located on the back of the cover, so they are out of baby's reach. Toy loops are great for attaching toys.

◆ **Flexibility**. Can the cover also work on restaurant high chairs? Will the cover work on those super-sized carts you see at Costco or Sam's? Make sure the cover has large enough leg holes to accommodate a growing child.

◆ **Safety**. Make sure the cover has enough padding for smaller infants. Seat belts are a must—the cover should have its own seat

sells for $189 and weighs 25 lbs.

New this year, Chicco has debuted a travel system that matches a stroller (the Cortina) with their new infant car seat (the KeyFit). This system sells for about $300 at Babies R Us. As for the stroller, the Cortina is a more traditional design with height-adjustable handles and decent size basket. We thought it was well-designed—we liked the one-hand fold and fully reclining seat.

belt to secure baby AND securely attach the cover to the cart. Of course, the cover should be easy to install and remove.

Speaking of safety, that's another reason to have a cart cover—falls from shopping carts are the leading cause of head injuries to young children, according to the Consumer Products Safety Commission. Every year, 12,800 kids under age five are taken to the hospital emergency room each after falling from shopping carts. A key reason: carts with broken or missing safety belts. Having a shopping cart cover with a secure belt is a smart way to avoid such injuries.

Here are our top picks for shopping cart covers:

◆ **SewCuteBoutique.com** is queen of the cart cover world, based on reader feedback from our message boards. Their $40 cover (pictured on the previous page) is all cotton with one-inch thick quilt batting, storage pocket, toy loops, matching pillow and adjustable safety belt. It fits all carts, including the ones at warehouse clubs. Best of all, SewCuteBoutique will customize a cover for you, from a myriad of fabric choices.

◆ **ChubbySeats.com** is another great choice, with thick batting and customized fabric options. Their $35 cover includes two bungee bands for toys and cups, two pockets an attached tote bag and more. There is also a version for twins ($50).

◆ **The SnazzySeat** by SnazzyBaby.com is a good candidate as a shower gift. Their reversible cart cover features silky fabric on one side, warm fuzzy fabric on the other. You get three pockets (including a large mom pocket), key chain hook plus fabric that can stand up to multiple washings without bunching. Yea, it's pricey ($100), but this is probably the most fashionable of the cart covers.

Our readers also recommended the Kangaroodle.com cover ($45) with its matching storage bag, the BuggyBagg ($70), and the Clean Shopper ($30). The latter just has quilted cotton fabric, no batting— it is no frills, but does the job. Readers gave much lower marks to the cart covers from Infantino and Nojo, which we would avoid.

Finally, let's mention the C1, Chicco's only stroller sold here that is made in Italy. The C1 is a like a C5 on steroids—22 lbs. and $280, the C1 features handles that rotate 180 degrees (for more compact storage), a fully reclining seat and aluminum frame.

Our view. While it took a few years, Chicco finally has a winning line-up here in the states. Parents particularly like the Caddy and London models—we think they combine the best of both worlds: light weight, decent features and great prices. These strollers are good alternatives to the massive travel system strollers you see out there that weigh in at 30 lbs. Quality is good, so we'll raise Chicco's rating this year. If you like the look of Maclaren but don't have a Maclaren bank account, Chicco is a good alternative.

Two caveats: first, don't go to Chicco's web site to find additional information about their strollers. It doesn't exist. Chicco promises to have an online presence sometime before 2011, but as of this writing, no dice. And second, be aware that Chicco has struggled with customer service issues in the past (although they have improved in recent years). So, our rating is somewhat discounted to reflect those problems. **Rating: B+**

Combi *1962 Hwy 160 West #100, Ft. Mill, SC 29708. For a dealer near you, call (800) 992-6624, (803) 802-8416; Web: www. combi-intl.com.* Japanese-owned Combi came to the U.S. in the late 80's and staked out a claim as a leader in lightweight strollers. Their famous Savvy Z was a seven-pound wonder that was often imitated. But Combi has had its ups and downs in recent years; it has shifted strategies more often than Italy changes governments. Here's an overview of their current offerings.

The models. Combi offers a bewildering array of 20 models, so it can be hard to get your head around their offerings. The basics: Combi breaks their line into two parts: the City Life and Metro Life series. The difference? Each series works with a different Combi infant car seat. The City Life is paired with the new Combi Connection; the Metro Life works with the Combi Centre car seat (see previous chapter for reviews of Combi infant seats).

The City Life series features mostly lightweight models with aluminum frames; models include the City Savvy Select ($150, 13 lbs.), Soho DX ($120, 12 lbs.), Savvy EX ($200, 18 lbs.) and Select DK5 travel system ($400 for both infant seat and stroller, 13 lbs.). The City Savvy Select is a new model that features a taller handle, bigger wheels and a side cup holder. If you live in a cold climate, Combi also makes a version of this stroller (City Savvy All Weather) with zippered boot, rain cover and expanded canopy for $200.

The City Savvy and Soho DX are very similar (both have a drawstring recline, five point harness, boot and compact fold) . . . the main difference is the Soho DX has an infant head pillow and cup holder/storage pack. A step up is the Savvy EX, which is heavier but adds an extended canopy visor, push-button recline and removable guardrail with cup holders. Finally, the Select DK5 (sold only as a travel system) has a one-hand fold, shock absorbers and a heavily padded seat. All City Life strollers work with the Combi Connection car seat and have a full recline.

The Metro Life Series features two main strollers: the Cosmo ST and DX. The Cosmo ST ($60, 12 lbs.) is affordable, yet features a full recline and compact fold. The Cosmo DX ($100, 13 lbs.) adds more plush padding and a fancier canopy. Again, both of these seats can be paired with the Combi Centre infant car seat to make a travel system.

Also in the Metro Life series: the Combi 4 stroller, a hybrid tri-wheel stroller that has two small front fixed wheels. The Combi 4 ($300) features a full recline, large basket and height adjustable handle. This stroller isn't designed for jogging (walks or hikes would be fine), but is probably too big for the mall.

In the premium price segment, Combi's I-Thru is a $300 16 lbs. plush carriage stroller whose bassinet turns around. The I-Thru also features a boot, large canopy that unzips for even more coverage and foam-padded seat. FYI: The I-Thru is the only Combi that will NOT work with Combi's infant car seat; it is marketed as a second stroller for older children that have outgrown the infant seat.

To hedge its bets in the travel system market, Combi has a stroller frame that holds other brand infant car seats. The Flash ($60) is much like the Baby Trend Snap & Go, but adds a stroller back with two bottle holders. FYI: Combi also sells this stroller frame sans the bottle holders as the Strollee Streak. Trivia note: Strollee is a defunct stroller brand name from the 80's; Combi has revived it to sell low end strollers to chain stores. Combi's Strollee STS-11 (11 lbs.) is an entry-level stroller with basket and canopy for $30. It is sold on Target.com.

Got twins? Combi offers both side-by-side and tandem models for parents of multiples (or a toddler and infant). The Combi Twin Savvy is a side-by-side model that weighs 21 pounds and sports a removable napper bar, machine washable cushions, a 165-degree reclining seat, a separate canopy and a stroller pack with two insulated bottle holders. At 30″ wide, this side by side should fit through most doors. New this year, the Twin Savvy EX will accommodate one infant car seat (the Combi Connection) on one side of the stroller, which is a plus. The price, however, is a bit steep: $300. Also new: the Combi Counterpart Tandem, Combi's first front/back stroller in several years. This 23.5 lb. stroller includes a third set of wheels for easy turning, push-button recline and the ability to hold one infant seat. It sells for $300 as well.

strollers

Whew! Is that overwhelming or what? There is good news: Combi has comparison charts on their web site that help point out differences between all the models. Combi's web site also includes a "virtual showroom" where you can view how stroller models fold via Flash animation.

Our view. Combi's strategy of throwing many models out at the marketplace to see what sticks makes it hard to judge this line. The company had numerous strategy shifts in the past few years; Combi can't seem to decide if it wants to be a high-end premium brand a la Perego or a clone of bulky travel system maker Graco. This has muddied Combi's brand in the minds of many parents.

In reviewing our parent feedback, Combi has more success when it sticks to its roots: lightweight, premium strollers like the City Savvy or Soho DX. Parents like these strollers for the mall, although the low handle bar height irks taller moms (that is, anyone over 5'5"). Combi also

And now, from Europe . . .

Ah, you've got to love the web. Today you can zip over to European baby product web sites and ogle the latest strollers swishing down the streets of Milan or Paris. Many of these strollers are discussed on our message boards at BabyBargains.com, as parents scheme to find ways to import them to the U.S.

The biggest cross-ocean import in recent years was the Bugaboo, that legendary stroller designed in the Netherlands (but made in Taiwan). So why don't we see more European strollers here? And why are U.S. stores instead filled with cheap Chinese-made models, invariably in navy blue?

Let's take a look at the biggest trends for strollers in Europe . . . and why many of these strollers fail to make a splash here in North America (special thanks to "American Mama," a member of our message boards for sharing these insights after living and travelling extensively in Europe).

◆ ***Pram madness***. Europeans live a much different lifestyle than your average American—they walk more places, take public transport and don't drive as much. Hence, strollers tend to be heavier since you aren't lifting the thing in and out of a trunk. European strollers feature big wheels, the better to ride over cobblestones and rough sidewalks. Prams are common—these combine a stroller and bassinet. Again, nice when walking from your flat to a café in Rome. Prices for prams run $450 to $700 in Europe—-the bassinets alone can cost $170 or more! An odd contradiction: big strollers are popular in Europe, despite the fact that their apartments, elevators and shops are small. And public transport is so crowded.

has a winner with their stroller frames (the Flash or Streak); parents like the compact fold but find the storage basket hard to access.

Combi could improve its line by doing one thing: better storage baskets. By "better" we mean BIGGER and easy to access, especially when the stroller is in a reclined position. **Rating A-**

Cosco *2525 State St., Columbus, IN 47201. Call (812) 372-0141 for a dealer near you (or 514-323-5701 for a dealer in Canada;. Web: www.coscoinc.com* Dorel (the parent of Cosco), the baby products powerhouse, has struggled in the stroller market for years. Why? The key driver of stroller sales in discount stores are travel systems . . . yet, Dorel/Cosco's main offering for infant car seats (the Designer 22) has failed to win many fans. That has undercut their momentum in this category, forcing the company to come up with several alternatives. Key among these: licensed brand names. Dorel is probably better

◆ *My stroller, my country.* Imagine if every state had its own stroller brand—Texas joggers, Utah umbrella strollers, etc. Europe is like that, with many countries boasting their own stroller brands (Emmaljunga in Sweden, Jane in Spain, Bebe Confort in France, etc). Europeans are often loyal to their own country's stroller maker (thanks to good distribution and marketing), but what sells in Portugal doesn't necessary translate across the border. Or the ocean.

◆ *Cup holder, what cup holder?* Here's one key reason many European strollers fail in the U.S.—no cup holders. Europeans don't understand why mom needs a place to put that Starbucks cup; or why baby would need to have a snack tray. When Europeans want coffee, they go to a café, sit down and drink coffee. The whole concept of toting a beverage with you is alien. As a result, many European stroller makers fail to include this crucial feature in their models.

◆ *Colors.* Europeans love bright colors—strollers come in bright orange, plaids, two contrasting (clashing?) colors and more. Those larger prams let Europeans show off strollers with lots of chrome. Why are dull colors so common here in the U.S.? Hard to say, but we wonder if it has something to do with the chains, which dominate retailing here. There seems to be a mindset among chain store buyers that unless it is dull and blue, it won't sell in South Dakota. Chains must stock one model nationwide, so they play it safe. And stroller makers simply respond to what the chain store buyers say they want.

strollers

known for its alter egos, Eddie Bauer and Safety 1st. Dorel has tried to buttress its weakness in travel systems by entering other hot stroller categories, like joggers and (new this year) stroller frames.

Dorel also owns several European brands of strollers and, from time to time, has imported these to the U.S. (Quinny is the best example).

The models. We will give Dorel its due—they are trying to innovate here. Examples: the new Safety 1st Acella Sport Travel System. This hybrid jogger features a tri-wheel stroller with turnable front wheel and one-hand standing fold. Price: $140 at Wal-Mart. That includes the Designer 22 car seat. (There's an Eddie Bauer version of this stroller, called the Vector).

Recently, Cosco has tried to freshen their stroller offerings with a new Euro look and aluminum frames, one-hand fold and a standing fold feature. Example: the Safety 1st Alumilite for $100 and the Eddie Bauer Euro Z travel system ($200).

New this year: the Eddie Bauer Integrated Travel System, which combines the new Eddie Bauer Comfort Car seat with a stroller that features a one-hand fold and large storage basket. Price: $220.

Also new, the Roo stroller ($60 at Target) is a funky tri-wheel that combines a simple umbrella stroller with a triangle-like frame that is popular now in Europe. The low weight (9 lbs.) is amazing, but the lack of a basket (the Roo has a mesh storage pouch) and optional skimpy canopy are turn-offs.

Cosco is a big player in the double stroller market—their Transit tandem folds flat and weighs about 22 lbs. for $130. And let's not forget low-end joggers, where Cosco offers several models. Cosco's flagship jogging stroller (The Safety 1st Two Ways Jogger, $150) features a reversible seat—a first in the jogger market. The telescoping handle is quite cool, as is the infant seat attachment system (another first). The steel frame for this model is a bit heavy, but the five-point harness is nice as are the full size (16") rear wheels.

Our view. We will raise our rating of Cosco this time out, reflecting improved parent feedback and several innovative models.

That said, Cosco still has a way to go when it comes to quality and durability. We still get emails and message board posts from parents who fall for the cool Eddie Bauer colors . . . and then the regrets start. Complaints about wheels that squeak within the first month, hard-to-adjust harnesses, and other quality woes still dog these strollers.

Yes, the feedback on Eddie Bauer travel systems has improved (the Euro Z models sold at Babies R Us, for example), but Cosco is still dogged by that Designer 22 infant seat that gets, at best, mixed reviews. It is possible the new Eddie Bauer Comfort infant seat will fare better, but it wasn't out yet as we went to press.

Cosco has struggled with safety issues in the past, but has been recall-free with strollers since 1999 (when the company had to recall

57,000 tandem strollers which collapsed suddenly, injuring more than 200 children). Even though that was several years ago, Cosco still struggles with its brand image.

The take home message: Cosco/Safety 1st/Eddie Bauer have made strides in recent years, but if you really want one of these, keep your expectations in check. These strollers are still at the lower-end of the quality pool, no matter how fancy they are dressed up. **Rating: C+**

Eddie Bauer These strollers and travel systems are made by Cosco. See the above review for more info.

Emmaljunga Web: www.emmaljunga.com This Swedish stroller brand withdrew from the U.S. market in 2001.

Evenflo 1801 Commerce Dr., Piqua, OH 45356. For a dealer near you, call (800) 233-5921 or (937) 415-3300. In Canada, PO Box 1598, Brantford, Ontario, N3T 5V7. (519) 756-0210; Web: www.evenflo.com Evenflo's claim to fame, stroller-wise, is their one-hand steering. All of Evenflo's strollers and travel systems have this feature. Here is a breakdown:

The models. Evenflo's flagship stroller is the Ellipsa, whose elliptical tubing design gives the brand a much-needed boost in style. You'll see Ellipsa strollers both as travel systems ($229 to $249) and as stand-alone models for $129. Ellipsas weigh 22 to 24 lbs.

The Ellipsa features a bigger footrest than past Evenflo strollers, as well as a removable dishwasher-safe snack tray and infinite recline settings (up to 180 degrees). The Ellipsa's "ArcFold" is a unique, one-hand system that folds the stroller down flat.

Evenflo is a major player in the tandem stroller segment with their Take Me Too. This 29 lb. double stroller has a couple of unique features—a side entry step for toddlers lets them get in and out of the back seat better than other models and an extra large basket. Yes, this unit can hold TWO infant seats (including non-Evenflo seats) and the one-hand fold feature is good. Price: $90 for a stripped down version in discount stores to $120 for an upgraded version at places like Baby Depot.

As with its other products, Evenflo also makes Osh Kosh versions of their strollers and travel systems—these have the exact same features, just denim fabric and a different name. And the price is about $20 higher.

Our view. One-handed steering is Evenflo's strongest feature—why every other stroller maker hasn't copied this yet is a mystery. Fans of Evenflo love how these strollers push.

Quality and durability, however, is another story. If you've been reading our blog (BabyBargains.com), you'll recall our discussion of quality woes that dogged the Ellipsa launch in 2005. Parent feed-back on this stroller line has been quite negative, with complaints about parts that break and worse. As a side note, we should mention that the feedback on the Aura, however, has been more positive than the Ellipsa.

Another problem for Evenflo is what we call feature bloat. Like Graco, Evenflo is trying to appeal to first-time parents who think their stroller should be outfitted with every last gizmo . . . but that tends to add weight. Example: the Ellipsa stroller clocks in at nearly 25 lbs. empty! Add an infant seat and you've got 35 pounds even before you've added a baby.

So, it's a mixed bag for Evenflo. We give them bonus points for trying to freshen up the line with innovative models, especially the Take Me Too tandem. We also like their customer service department, which earns good marks from our readers for promptly taking care of problems. Yet, the bottom line for us is quality and durability. And on that score, Evenflo falls short. ***Rating: C+***

Fisher Price. *See J. Mason. Web: www.fisher-price.com* Fisher-Price is a bit player in the stroller market, but their offerings are sold at discounters like Wal-Mart so they have quite a bit of exposure. (All FP strollers are made by J. Mason). A typical offering: the Go & Play ($70). This stroller has a toy tray, one hand fold and multi-position reclining seat. Basically, it is similar to the Graco LiteRider. Fisher-Price also has one of the cheapest tandems on the market, the Comfort Tandem LX. For $75 (at Wal-Mart), you get a one-hand fold, large storage basket, parent tray and front swivel wheels that can lock in position. Yes, that is a quite a deal, considering most tandems are twice the amount. But what about the quality? These are very cheap strollers that are short on padding and features. If you don't have any high expectations for durability, you won't be disappointed. We'd put them on par with Cosco's offerings. ***Rating: C-***

Graco *Rt. 23, Main St., Elverson, PA 19520. For a dealer near you, call (800) 345-4109, (610) 286-5951; Web: www.gracobaby.com* Graco is a great example of what's right (and wrong) with the stroller biz today. The company (a division of Rubbermaid) is probably the market-leader in strollers, with affordable models that are packed with features like oversized baskets. You'll find Graco everywhere: discount stores, baby superstores, specialty shops and more.

Graco's primary target market is first-time parents, who want a SUV-like stroller (that is, one packed with tons of features and gizmos). Unlike years past, Graco is now more of a mid-priced brand. Gone are the super-cheap low-end strollers . . . Graco seems to have ceded this market to Cosco.

...troller with two handles, deep basket and partial *recline*. This stroller has a "three-dimensional" fold—that basically means it folds down to the ground but doesn't scrape or dirty the stroller in the process. The Mosaic sells for $99 to $149 as a stand-along model or $199 as a travel system.

We thought Graco did an impressive job designing the Mosaic—the compact fold means it will fit in most trunks and the high handles make it a comfortable push for parents of most heights. If we had to criticize anything about the Mosaic, it would have to be the two-hand fold and somewhat skimpy storage.

The LiteRider and MetroLite are Graco's other lightweight offerings. The LiteRider (20 to 22 lbs.) runs about $60 to $70 as a stand-alone model or $140 as a travel system and features a one-hand fold. The MetroLite ($100 to $130 stand-alone, $200 travel system) is an 18 lb. stroller with rubber tires for a smooth ride, three-position reclining seat and plush padding. The Metrolite also has a full recline and height adjustable handle. We've heard very good feedback on both of Graco's lightweight strollers, which combine decent features and an affordable price.

FYI: All Graco travel systems include their excellent infant seat, the SnugRide (see review in the last chapter).

Graco's "standard-size" strollers are anchored by the Quattro, a ...k-like stroller that weighs nearly 30 pounds empty. The Quattro ... runs $100 separately or $200 to $230 as a travel system. Graco ...s just about everything into this model, including a fully ...ng hood, all weather boot, one-hand gravity fold, four-posi-...eclining seat, plush padding and more.

...something heavier? The Graco CoachRider is Graco's ...roller, weighing 29.5 pounds and featuring a two-in-one ...iage seat. This runs $250 as a travel system or $150 as ...model. FYI: The CoachRider is being phased out.

...as two other standard-size strollers: the Passage ...Passage is a 20 lb. stroller ($80 to $100) which fea-...ng fold, added locks to secure an infant seat, ...for access when the stroller is reclined and a ...r five-points. The new Vienna ($100 stand alone ...system) is a bit heaver at 24 lbs. but adds a ...dle, huge basket and full recline.

...llers are Graco's last major forte—the Duo-

STROLLERS AND MORE

Rider ($130) is Graco's side-by-*side model, while the DuoGlider*
($150) is a front/back tandem. Graco's claim to fame in the tandem
market is their "stadium seating," where the rear seat is elevated. Of
ger basket a... in the stroller fra...

Graco's entry in the stroller fra... Graco ...
winner—this $60 frame holds the (what else?) Graco ...
infant car seat with a secure lock-in feature and has a one-hand fold
and basket. FYI: The Snug Rider will also work with Graco's new
infant seat, the Safe Seat.

FYI: Graco sells its strollers under the Laura Ashley banner—
same models and features as Graco, just a fancier fabric (and higher price, naturally).

Our view. Graco has come a long way and now sits atop the
mountain as the top-selling mass market brand for strollers. That's in
no small part due to the success of their SnugRide infant seat, which
is paired with strollers in their travel systems. Our favorite in this line
is the Mosaic, which combines a lightweight stroller that doesn't
skimp on features.

We don't fault Graco for focusing on the lucrative first-time parent niche, but we can't help but point out to folks that NO, you do
not need a 30 pound stroller to push around baby. In fact, many parents end up cursing their Graco Hummers as impossible to wrestle in
and out of a trunk, among other sins. Stick with the lighter-weight
models (Mosaic, LiteRider, MetroLite) and you'll be happier here.

Little annoyances frustrate Graco owners. Look at how th
LiteRider folds up . . . when folded, the front tray hits the groun
inevitably damaging or scratching it in a parking lot. Parents compla
about other quality woes, like canopies that break or reclining se
that stop reclining. But most gripes focus on Graco's low-end mod
so you have to align your expectations with what you are paying

And we will give Graco props for its safety record—33 years
not one recall on its strollers. Now, that's impressive. **Rating: B-**

Inglesina (877) 486-5112 or (973) 746-5112; web: www.ingle
com. Inglesina has always played second fiddle to its Italian c
Peg Perego and Chicco in the stroller market. While other
players have had significant success peddling their wares to
American parents, Inglesina always seemed stuck in low gea

Not any more. Inglesina has hot-sellers with the Zip
Espresso, which have lit up our product review section on c

Graco's line is huge, so let's get to the highlights:

The models. Graco divides their stroller line into four areas: light-weight (Mosaic, MetroLite), standard-size (Quattro), travel systems and double models (mostly tandems like DuoGlider).

In the lightweight category, Graco has three models: the Mosaic, LiteRider and MetroLite. The Mosaic is Graco's flagship stroller—an 18 lb. umbrella stroller with two handles, deep basket and partial recline. This stroller has a "three-dimensional" fold—that basically means it folds down to the ground but doesn't scrape or dirty the stroller in the process. The Mosaic sells for $99 to $149 as a stand-along model or $199 as a travel system.

We thought Graco did an impressive job designing the Mosaic—the compact fold means it will fit in most trunks and the high handles make it a comfortable push for parents of most heights. If we had to criticize anything about the Mosaic, it would have to be the two-hand fold and somewhat skimpy storage.

The LiteRider and MetroLite are Graco's other lightweight offerings. The LiteRider (20 to 22 lbs.) runs about $60 to $70 as a stand-alone model or $140 as a travel system and features a one-hand fold. The MetroLite ($100 to $130 stand-alone, $200 travel system) is an 18 lb. stroller with rubber tires for a smooth ride, three-position reclining seat and plush padding. The Metrolite also has a full recline and height adjustable handle. We've heard very good feedback on both of Graco's lightweight strollers, which combine decent features and an affordable price.

FYI: All Graco travel systems include their excellent infant seat, the SnugRide (see review in the last chapter).

Graco's "standard-size" strollers are anchored by the Quattro, a tank-like stroller that weighs nearly 30 pounds empty. The Quattro Tour runs $100 separately or $200 to $230 as a travel system. Graco throws just about everything into this model, including a fully enclosing hood, all weather boot, one-hand gravity fold, four-position full reclining seat, plush padding and more.

Need something heavier? The Graco CoachRider is Graco's super-size stroller, weighing 29.5 pounds and featuring a two-in-one reversible carriage seat. This runs $250 as a travel system or $150 as a stand-alone model. FYI: The CoachRider is being phased out.

Graco also has two other standard-size strollers: the Passage and Vienna. The Passage is a 20 lb. stroller ($80 to $100) which features a self-standing fold, added locks to secure an infant seat, drop-down basket for access when the stroller is reclined and a harness with three or five-points. The new Vienna ($100 stand alone or $200 for a travel system) is a bit heaver at 24 lbs. but adds a height adjustable handle, huge basket and full recline.

Finally, double strollers are Graco's last major forte—the Duo-

Rider ($130) is Graco's side-by-side model, while the DuoGlider ($150) is a front/back tandem. Graco's claim to fame in the tandem market is their "stadium seating," where the rear seat is elevated. Of course, you get all the standard features: huge storage baskets, removable canopies, etc. Graco also offers the DuoGlider in a travel system that will now accept two infant car seats (note to parents of twins) for $240, but that price just includes one infant seat. New in the past year: the DuoGlider LXI features a one-hand fold, bigger basket and improved parent organizer tray.

Graco's entry in the stroller frame category, the Snug Rider, is a winner—this $60 frame holds the (what else?) Graco Snug Ride infant car seat with a secure lock-in feature and has a one-hand fold and basket. FYI: The Snug Rider will also work with Graco's new infant seat, the Safe Seat.

FYI: Graco sells its strollers under the Laura Ashley banner—same models and features as Graco, just a fancier fabric (and higher price, naturally).

Our view. Graco has come a long way and now sits atop the mountain as the top-selling mass market brand for strollers. That's in no small part due to the success of their SnugRide infant seat, which is paired with strollers in their travel systems. Our favorite in this line is the Mosaic, which combines a lightweight stroller that doesn't skimp on features.

We don't fault Graco for focusing on the lucrative first-time parent niche, but we can't help but point out to folks that NO, you do not need a 30 pound stroller to push around baby. In fact, many parents end up cursing their Graco Hummers as impossible to wrestle in and out of a trunk, among other sins. Stick with the lighter-weight models (Mosaic, LiteRider, MetroLite) and you'll be happier here.

Little annoyances frustrate Graco owners. Look at how the LiteRider folds up . . . when folded, the front tray hits the ground, inevitably damaging or scratching it in a parking lot. Parents complain about other quality woes, like canopies that break or reclining seats that stop reclining. But most gripes focus on Graco's low-end models, so you have to align your expectations with what you are paying.

And we will give Graco props for its safety record—33 years and not one recall on its strollers. Now, that's impressive. ***Rating: B-***

Inglesina *(877) 486-5112 or (973) 746-5112; web: www.inglesina. com.* Inglesina has always played second fiddle to its Italian cousins Peg Perego and Chicco in the stroller market. While other Italian players have had significant success peddling their wares to North American parents, Inglesina always seemed stuck in low gear.

Not any more. Inglesina has hot-sellers with the Zippy and Espresso, which have lit up our product review section on our web

> ## *Stroller overload?*
>
> Whoa! Finding yourself overwhelmed with all this stroller stuff? Take a break for a minute. We realize making a stroller choice can seem daunting. Here's our advice: first, read our specific recommendations by lifestyle later in this chapter. We boil down all the options to our top picks, whether you live in Suburbia or in downtown Giant Metropolis. Second, realize that you don't have to make all these stroller decisions BEFORE baby is born. Most parents will buy an infant car seat—pair this with an inexpensive stroller *frame* from Kolcraft, Combi or Baby Trend ($50) and you've got an affordable alternative to those pricey travel systems. This will last you for your baby's first six months . . . or longer. That will give you plenty of time to think about/research your next stroller.

site with glowing reviews. Here's an overview of Inglesina's models:

The models. So, what's cool about the Zippy? Check out the one-hand fold—you lift up on a lever on the back of the stroller and poof! Instant folded stroller. This 17 lbs. model has all the cool features most urban moms want—full recline, adjustable backrest, removable front bumper and storage basket. Best of all: the Zippy has a universal car seat adapter that lets you secure an infant car seat to the stroller (yes, the Graco SnugRide works well with it).

So what's not to love? First, the Zippy is darn expensive: $240 to $290, depending on the store. Second, when the Zippy first debuted, we complained it came in two colors (dull and duller). Fortunately, that's now been fixed, with new Zippy hues that are, well, more zippy. Basically, the Zippy is much like the Peg Perego Pliko, but costs $50 more for that much easier fold. Inglesina has made some nice improvements to the Zippy over the past couple of years, including a extended canopy and front snack tray. New this year, Inglesina has teamed with Compass to do matching fabrics, so you can use the Compass infant seat as a travel system with the Zippy.

The Inglesina Espresso is basically Inglesina's take on the Peg Perego Aria. The Espresso is a 16 lb. aluminum stroller that has a one hand fold (the Aria lacks that), boot, rain cover, standing fold and height adjustable handle. Okay, it lacks a cup holder for mom/dad and only has a partial recline. If you can over look all that (and ignore the skimpy sunshade), the Espresso still has a lot to offer for its $150 to $200 price.

The Espresso also comes in a plethora of fashionable colors, including bright red, electric blue, pink, yellow and more. What's the difference between the Espresso and the Aria? The Espresso has

strollers

slightly larger wheels and a height adjustable handle, but the Aria has a more compact fold and is about three pounds lighter. You also get thicker padding (one of the Aria's flaws), larger hood and shock absorbers with the Espresso. The Aria's advantages over the Espresso are a child snack tray and a slightly deeper seat recline, plus an adjustable strap on the five-point harness. New this year, Inglesina made the Espresso compatible with the Graco Snug Ride infant car seat—and the Espresso will omit the previously included rain cover and boot . . . but the price will drop to around $150 at retail.

Inglesina's other single stroller is the Swift (11 lbs., $100), a super-lightweight stroller with four-position reclining seat, detachable storage basket and two handle design (like the Peg Pliko). The downside? A rather skimpy canopy and no cup holder. We should note that Inglesina plans to debut a new version of the Swift (dubbed the Trip) by the time you read this. The Trip is like the Swift on steroids—a $180 stroller with bigger wheels, adjustable leg rest and cup holder.

FYI: All of Inglesina's strollers bound for the American market are made in China; in Europe, Inglesina sells a wide variety of prams and carriages made in Italy.

Parents of twins and triplets may want to give Inglesina's double and triple strollers a look-see. The Twin Swift is a side-by-side model weighing just 22 lbs. which features dual-operating canopies for $199. Inglesina's Domino is a pram-like stroller that comes in both double and triple versions ($600 to $770).

Our view. The feedback on these strollers is very positive—reviews by parents on our web site give Inglesina good marks overall for quality, durability and function. *Rating: A*

i´coo/Traxx This German stroller brand is reviewed on our web site, BabyBargains.com (click on Bonus Material).

Jane Call 866-355-2630 for a dealer near you. Web: janeusa.com. Spanish baby products maker Jane (pronounced HA-nay) traces its roots back to 1932 in Barcelona and now has decided to give the U.S. market a try.

Jane's PowerTwin is a good example of how European stroller companies just don't get this market. This innovative tri-wheel stroller with a turnable front wheels is impressive: it boasts two seats (the rear fully reclines), quick release wheels, hand break and cushy suspension. Cool, eh? Except the price is $540 and it weighs 41 lbs. And there are no cup holders. Whoops.

And there, in a nutshell, is why so many European stroller companies wash out here in the U.S. The fashion is right, the quality is good (Jane strollers are made in Hong Kong) but the price blows most folks out of the water. While Jane may some day break through in America, its first offerings are disappointing. ***Rating: Not Yet.***

Jeep These strollers are made by Kolcraft, reviewed on the next page.

Joovy *Call 214-761-1809 for a dealer near you. Web: joovy.com*
Newcomer Joovy is headed by a former Baby Trend executive. In
fact, Joovy scored its first big coup by winning the license to the
English push cart better known as the Baby Trend Sit N Stand.
Joovy has re-christened this model as the Caboose Stand-on
Tandem ($150, 24 lbs.). Compared to the old Sit N Stand, Joovy's
Caboose features a higher handle height, foam handle, improved
car seat attachment (most brands will work) and nicer canopy. The
company also brightened up the fashion.

While the Caboose is Joovy's flagship model, the company also
launched three other models. The Groove ($200, 16 lbs.) is a high-
end umbrella with aluminum frame, adjustable footrest, drawstring
seat recline, extended canopy and two up holders. It also comes in
a twin version (Groove 2, $200, 26 lbs.). Joovy's Easy Rider ($250)
is a jogger with no rear axle (so you can run without kicking the
back), fully canopy and parent tray. The Easy Rider also comes with
a sun filter and rain/wind cover.

Our View. Joovy is so new, we don't have much parent feedback yet, but the initial word on the Caboose is positive. We liked
the thoughtful design touches through out this line (a jogger with
parent cup holders–what a concept!) and the bright yet simple fashion is a nice alternative to navy blue. Yet we thought the Groove was
over-priced–if Joovy plans to compete with Maclaren in this segment, they better come up with something more innovative than this.
So, we'll give them good marks for a good initial effort . . . but we'd
like to see what they have planned for an encore. ***Rating: B+***

J. Mason *(818) 993-6800; web: www.jmason.com*. This company
was best known for the cheap-o umbrellas that are sold for $20 or
$30 in discount stores like Wal-Mart. But in recent years J. Mason
has tried to move beyond that niche. Their key weapon: license
deals with Sesame Street and Fisher Price to give their offerings
more brand clout. The company has also expanded its offerings,
with models in different segments from umbrella to joggers.

Among the more interesting models: the J. Mason Freedom Trail
jogger sold in the One Step Ahead catalog for $150. This model is
the first jogger that includes a bassinet so it is safe (allegedly) for
newborns, claims the catalog. Later the bassinet detaches and you
can use the stroller as a regular jogger. We'll give J Mason bonus
points for creativity with this one, but we still don't like the idea of
a newborn in a jogging stroller–their neck muscles just aren't up to

strollers

the jostling if you really plan to run with this model. Yes, it would be fine for occasional walks, but that's not how it is pitched. And we wouldn't recommend this stroller for serious exercise anyway, since the smallish 12" wheels won't really work for runners.

As for the rest of J Mason's strollers, these Chinese-made models are basically duplicates of what Graco and Baby Trend offer. Quality is only average. If J Mason wants to be a serious player in this market, it will need more innovative offerings like the Freedom Trail and fewer of the $20 throwaway umbrella models. **Rating: C**

Kolcraft *3455 West 31st Pl., Chicago, IL 60623. For a dealer near you, call (800) 453-7673. Web: www.kolcraft.com.* Kolcraft has always been an also-ran in the stroller market—that is, until their recent hot selling Jeep-branded strollers took off. Since Kolcraft exited the car seat business in 2001, the company has no travel systems to offer. That's good in a way: many Kolcraft models hold other major brands of car seats, giving parents more flexibility.

The models. Kolcraft divides its stroller business into three areas: its namesake strollers are designed as entry-level options at chains like Wal-Mart. The Carter's line offers slightly upgraded fabrics. But the real story here is the success of Kolcraft's Jeep line—Kolcraft has an entire line of Jeep strollers, complete with SUV-like knobby wheels, beefed up suspension, and sporty fabrics at affordable prices ($30 to $150). Clever touches like simulated lug nuts on the wheels and a toy steering wheel for baby have made these models quite popular.

The best-selling Jeep is the Liberty SE Terrain—a three-wheel stroller with turnable front wheel that can be locked in a forward position. This hybrid between jogging and sport strollers features one-hand fold, child snack tray with the aforementioned toy steering wheel and parent tray. At $118 at Wal-Mart, it's no surprise this one has been a hot seller. And surprise: parent reviews have been very positive on this model, albeit with a stray complaint that the handle is too low for very tall parents. In the past year, Kolcraft rolled out an upgraded version of the Liberty (dubbed the Limited), with extra storage (a bag on the side of the basket), fancier padding and an electronic baby toy steering wheel. It is $140 at Target.com.

Kolcraft also makes a raft of other Jeep models, including an umbrella style (Wrangler, 12 lbs., $30) and a more traditional lightweight model, the Cherokee ($70). There is also a tandem, the Jeep Wagoneer ($140 to $190, depending on the version). This affordable tandem has won kudos from readers for its basket, which is the size of Montana. It also holds any brand infant car seat, which is another nice plus. The Wrangler Twin Sport is a new side-by-side model for $80.

Finally, we should mention Kolcraft's knock-off of the Baby Trend's Snap & Go: the Universal Car Seat Carrier (13 lbs.) for $40 to $50. This stroller frame will accommodate most car seats and has a large basket and one-hand fold.

In the past year, Kolcraft has invaded the jogger category with their Jeep Overland Limited ($160), a 25 lb. aluminum jogger with one-hand fold, 16" wheels and height adjustable canopy.

Our view. Kolcraft has improved its quality in recent years and we've upped their rating this time out. Dollar for dollar, these are the best affordable strollers on the market—the Jeep Liberty Urban Terrain is a great example and the pick of the litter. Compared to other low-end brands (Graco, Cosco), Kolcraft shines. That said, you can't compare these to models to high end models like Mountain Buggy or Maclaren . . . Kolcraft still has a way to go to match their quality. But for suburbanites who need a sturdy stroller with lots of storage and decent looks for the mall and occasional outing, Kolcraft's Jeep line fits the bill. **Rating: B+**

Laura Ashley These strollers are made by Graco, reviewed earlier.

Maclaren *4 Testa Place, S. Norwalk, CT 06854. For a dealer near you, call (877) 504-8809 or (203) 354-4400; Web: www.maclaren-baby.com* Maclaren is the brand with British roots that sells 500,000 strollers each year in 30 countries worldwide. Their specialty? High-quality umbrella strollers made from lightweight aluminum. Maclaren is most popular on the East Coast and the brand has many fans in New York City and Boston. You might wonder whether these parents (who fork over $200 to $300 for a Maclaren) have lost their minds—can't they just go down to a discount store and buy an umbrella stroller for $30? Well, unlike the cheap-o umbrella strollers you find at Toys R Us, Maclaren strollers are packed with good features and are ultra lightweight. Plus, they look oh so stylish, which is important when you're zipping around the Upper West Side.

The models. Okay, let's take a deep breath. Maclaren offers ELEVEN models, so there is much to cover. There will be a quiz at the end of this review.

Maclaren's entry-level model, the Volo (9.2 lb., $100) is a super light, stripped down stroller (this year's version does have a canopy). You get a five-point harness and a mesh seat and basket but that's about it. A "Volo Accessory Pack" includes rain cover, seat liner and carry bag . . . for another $40.

A more full-featured model from Maclaren is their Triumph, ($140 to $150) which weighs 12.2 pounds and features a fully enclosed protective hood and one-hand fold. This seat does have a two-position recline, which is a new feature for this price point.

Next up is the Quest (13.4 lbs.), which adds more padding, a four-position partial seat recline and an extendable footrest. Price: $200. The Quest comes in three versions: the Quest Sport (basic colors), Quest Mod (fancy retro look with circular design fabric) or Kate Spade Quest (polka dots with a green accent, $300).

An upgraded version of the Quest is called the Ryder (14.8 lbs.)—it adds even more padding and front/rear suspension for $250.

The Techno XT (17 lbs., $289) is the top of the line Maclaren—it features the most padding, a new flip-down sun visor and three-position adjusting handles that can be extended to a height of 42 inches. The Techno also has upgraded wheels and reflective trim; a "classic" version of the Techno was released last year with similar features but a "softer" look, the company says. And yes, Maclaren throws in a cup holder for the Techno.

Want to use a Maclaren with an infant car set? Until recently, you were out of luck. Fortunately, Maclaren now has a model (the Global, 19.5 lbs., $260 to $300), which lets you attach any major brand infant car seat. The Global does have a fully reclining seat and is similar to the Techno in terms of plushness.

Finally, we have to talk about Maclaren's top-selling side-by-side strollers, the Rally Twin (26.8 lbs., $300) and the Twin Traveller (32.4 lbs., $350). The basic difference between these models is the Twin Traveller has fully reclining seats; the Rally Twin has a partial recline. Parents of twins rave about these strollers, which are among the best made side-by-side models on the market. Maclaren's doubles are good for older child/infant needs as well.

So, what's new for Maclaren this year? Maclaren plans to debut the first carbon fiber stroller in 2006. Carbon fiber? Yes, that's the same material used in tennis rackets for its strength and lightweight. The Maclaren Carbon Fiber CF6506 stroller will boast leather seats and go for $1000.

Maclaren will give the three-wheel stroller niche another try with the MX3, due out in March 2006. It features a swivel front wheel and quick release tires. Price: $400. Also new for 2006: a stroller frame a la the Snap & Go. Mac's version will be $90 and features a large basket with an easy fold similar the Volo.

Maclaren continues to offer a slew of accessories, including foot muffs (in coordinating fabric, naturally, darling), plus a $20 universal stroller organizer that fits on the back handles—it includes two bottle pockets that can hold drinks, a cell phone pocket and a mesh storage bag. This helps address parent complaints that Maclarens lack adequate storage.

One important caveat to this line: all Maclaren strollers (with the exception of the Global) lack napper or bumper bars on the front of the seat. Yes, these models all have five-point harnesses to keep baby securely inside the strollers, but the absence of a napper bar will turn off some parents.

Our view. While we still think Maclaren is one of the best quality stroller brands on the market, there are a couple of caveats. First, while this brand stakes its reputation on its British heritage, Maclaren switched all its production to China back in 2001. The result? A revolt among some Mac fans, who noticed that quality slipped with the new Chinese-made models. Maclaren quietly admitted it made some misssteps with this transition, but now says it has worked out the kinks (and parent feedback in the past year or so has been much more positive).

On a more serious note, Maclaren got a major black eye in 2004 when it was forced to fix a large batch of Technos whose wheel housings cracked in cold temperatures. This problem was exposed by the *New York Post*, which portrayed Maclaren as unresponsive and trying to hide the problem. Maclaren says the company learned from that PR melt down and promises to be more forthcoming in the future about quality glitches. We hope so.

And let's talk frankly about Maclaren. Yes, the darling of the East Coast crowd, but the truth is these strollers are quite fragile. Retailers who sell huge quantities of Maclarens tell us the brand is the most frequently repaired. A sample problem: if you don't fold up a Mac correctly, it may never be the same (you have to make sure the backrest is completely upright and the canopy is back before folding). Reports of malfunctioning brakes are another quality glitch Maclaren needs to fix pronto.

And while the company irons out its quality issues, it could fix those skimpy canopies—the coverage is a joke.

Despite all these faults, we will still give Maclaren a good rating. If you understand the caveats and take care with the fragile fold, then this is still among the better brands on the stroller market. ***Rating: A-***

Martinelli These strollers are made Peg Perego. See their review later in this section.

Mountain Buggy *Web: www.mountainbuggy.com.* This little company from New Zealand has a hot seller in its rugged, all-terrain strollers, which have won fans in both urban areas and the 'burbs. These tri-wheel strollers feature lightweight aluminum frames (17-19 lbs. depending on the model), 12" air-filled wheels with polymer rims (great for use near the beach), full reclining seats, height adjustable handles, one step folds and large two-position sun canopies.

The models. The key model is their Urban Single, which has a front wheel that can swivel or be fixed. The result is great maneuverability, unlike other joggers with fixed wheels (which limits their appeal for more urban uses). If you don't need the swivel front wheel, Mountain Buggy offers a model with a fixed front wheel (the Terrain Single). Mountain Buggy also sells two double models (the Urban Double with swivel front wheels and the Terrain Double with fixed wheels).

Are these strollers too big? Check out the Breeze, a mini-version of the Terrain with a fixed front wheel, wire basket, fully reclining seat. It features 10″ tires and weighs just 14 lbs.

So, how much is this going to cost you? Here's the bummer: Mountain Buggies are darn expensive. The Urban Single is $430, the Terrain Single $350, the Breeze Single $300. The Urban Double is $650; the Terrain Double $420-$480. There are even TRIPLE versions of the Urban and Terrain that run about $700 to $800.

New in 2006, Mountain Buggy adds some improvements to the Urban, including shock absorbers, a new scratch-resistant finish for the frame and an extended sun canopy with extra storage.

Our view. Okay, those prices are high. BUT, Mountain Buggies have a weight limit of 100 pounds, so you can use this stroller for a LONG time. And parents love the slew of optional accessories, including bug shield and full sun cover . . . AND a clip that lets you attach an infant car seat to their single stroller models. Too tall for most strollers? Mountain Buggy also sells a "handlebar extender" that adds 3″ of height for taller parents.

And we can't forget Mountain Buggy's recent brush with fame: after an Urban Double saved a toddler from a building collapse in New York City, Mountain Buggy was featured on TV news shows around the world.

So, we'll give this brand our top rating despite the stiff prices. Positive parent reviews and added flexibility from all those accessories make these strollers worth the price. FYI: Mountain Buggy is so new to North America that these strollers are hard to see in person. Nonetheless, if you have a dealer near by, they are worth a look. ***Rating: A***

Osh Kosh These strollers are made by Evenflo. See their review earlier in this chapter for more details.

Peg Perego *3625 Independence Dr., Ft. Wayne, IN 46808. For a dealer, call (260) 482-8191;. Web: www.perego.com* Perego is among the most popular stroller brands in America and that's no small feat. Most European stroller makers have either failed here (Emmaljunga, Teutonia) or moved their production to China (Maclaren, Inglesina) . . . Perego still makes its strollers in Italy. And sells them by the boatload here in America, despite premium prices.

Yet for all their success, Perego has stumbled in recent years and lost its momentum. The company has completely missed out on the all-terrain and tri-wheel stroller craze, only belatedly adding one such model to its line this year. Meanwhile, Perego has been content to rest on its laurels and occasionally roll out a novelty model that invariably never ships (exhibit number one: the Dinamico self-propelled stroller for $700).

No wonder all the buzz on our stroller message boards omits Perego. You can't stand still in this biz, or else the Bugaboos (and a host of smart competitors) will roll right over you. Perego has also lost a bit of its cache as it began selling strollers in chains stores like Babies R Us (and, in closeout, at places like Marshalls), although many parents still think Perego's European pedigree and fashion are superior to strollers from China.

Let's take a look at Perego's current lineup.

The models. Perego's best-selling models are their lightweight strollers, including the Pliko P3 and Aria MT. The Pliko features a five-point safety harness, storage basket, 150 degree reclining seat, adjustable leg rest, adjustable height handle and removable/washable seat cushions. This year's version (the Pliko P3 Classico, $240 to $270, 17 lbs.) has changed little from last year's model, which added ergonomic handles, cup holder, removable tray and easier fold. One new feature: a one-hand fold, which was sorely lacking in the previous Pliko. No, the Pliko is not as easy to fold up as the Zippy (it takes a few more motions), but at least they are moving in the right direction.

New this year, Peg has debuted the Pliko Lite: similar to the P3, but without the arm rests and front tray. It sheds three pounds in the process. Price: $230, 14 lbs.

Realizing the Pliko P3 is a bit heavy, Peg Perego rolled out an even lighter weight model, dubbed the Aria ($160 to $200, 12 lbs.). It features a seat that reclines to 150 degrees (same as the Pliko), decent storage basket, canopy and a five-point restraint. What's missing? The Aria lacks an umbrella-style fold like the Combi Savvy or a one-hand fold like the Inglesina Zippy (it also lacks a fully enclosing hood and the padding is a bit skimpy)—but parents seem to love it anyway, thanks to that light weight. Yes, the Aria does hold the Perego infant car seat and there is also a twin (side-by-side) version of the Aria that is 32" wide and sells for $330. Parents of twins give the Aria twin high marks (the only complaint, again, is the skimpy seat padding). Bargain alert: readers have spied Arias (previous year models) on sale for as little as $50 to $100 at discounters like Value City and Big Lots.

FYI: All Peg strollers (with the exception of the Aria twin) can hold Perego's infant car seat, the Primo Viaggio. And you can find the same matching fabric for the car seat in the stroller line, for most models. No, Peg doesn't sell them together as a "travel system" per se, but same difference; just buy them a la carte.

Will the Perego strollers work with other brand infant seats? No.

In the past, Perego did offer an adapter bar, but it is now discontinued. Peg seems to change its mind on this issue frequently, so check their web site for the latest word.

Peg has de-emphasized its large carriage strollers in recent years, but still has the Venezia as its main offering in this category. The Venezia MT (21 lbs., $350) features a fully reclining seat, reversible handle, and removable boot that snaps and folds back plus a height adjustable handle. Like all Pegs, the Venezia has a decent size storage basket and stylish fabrics. In the past year, Perego added a new split boot for the Venezia that will let you remove just the top part.

Besides the Venezia in the carriage stroller category, Peg also offers the A3 Pramette ($300, 17 lbs.). The A3 lets you reverse the seat so you can use it as a carriage for newborns and then a regular stroller for older babies. The A3 is much like the Pliko P3, but has one handle (instead of the P3's two separate handles). On the plus side, the A3 has a one-hand fold and one-hand steering.

So, what's new at Perego? The GT3 (aka Grand Tourismo) is Peg's first tri-wheel stroller that should be out by the time you read this. With inflated tires, this 28 lbs. stroller features a swivel front wheel with lock, big canopy, boot, rain cover and adjustable suspension. At $550, it is a hefty investment.

Also new: Peg plans to refresh its Duette tandem (32 lbs., $540) with front wheels that can turn with the aid of a steering wheel mounted on the back handle bar. Nope, we are not making that up. The Duette can hold two infant seats (you remove the stroller seats to lock the infant seats into the chassis) and the seats can face in or out.

The Duette joins Peg's other tandem, the Tender XL ($470) for parents of twins. The big difference between the Tender XL and the Duette is the Duette has seats that can face each other, while the Tender XL does not. And yes, Perego even has a Triplette stroller for a whopping $770.

Our view. As we discussed above, Perego has lost a bit of its mojo. The prices continue to creep up and the company is missing out on hot multi-use designs like the Bugaboo. Yes, the new GT3 is a step in the right direction, but is too pricey.

On the other hand, let's talk quality. Peg still makes a darn good quality stroller. Yes, true Peg fans gripe that the company has cheapened its models with more plastic trim in the past years . . . but we rarely get emails from parents who say they are unhappy with their Pegs.

So, what's the best stroller in the Peg line? We'd go for the lightweight Aria or Pliko. **Rating: A**

Phil & Ted Most Excellent Buggy Company Web: www.philandteds.com Phil & Ted followed their fellow kiwis Mountain Buggy to the U.S. stroller market in 2000, but haven't quite had the same market success. Yet Phil & Ted have quietly plodded along, making improvements to their strollers and now they have a winner: the e3 ($380, 22 lbs.). Like Mountain Buggy and Valco, Phil & Ted's flag-ship stroller is a tri-wheel with a swivel front wheel and air-filled tires. What sets Phil & Ted apart is their toddler seat ($90 extra), which attaches to the BACK of the stroller (for comparison, Valco's toddler seat attaches to the front). Yep, that's a funky configuration that turns off some parents (safety hint: the child in the backseat has to be removed first to prevent tipping). And if you put a larger tod-dler in the back seat, the access to the stroller's storage basket is limited. But that caveat aside, folks seem to love the e3 (which descended from an earlier model called the Kiwi Explorer). Parents tell us the all-terrain 12" air-filled wheels are perfect for both the mall and hiking trails, plus the wide seat accommodates children for many years. All in all, we recommend Phil & Ted—their excellent cus-tomer service, wide range of accessories and good quality overall make this a good choice for parents who want an all-terrain at a decent price. ***Rating: A-***

Quinny *Web: www.quinny.com.* This Dutch brand of strollers was bought by Cosco's parent Dorel in 2001 and made its debut (as jogging strollers) in the U.S. in 2003. They quickly disappeared. As of this writing, Dorel has no plans to re-launch the brand in the U.S. FYI: We did from our Canadian readers that Dorel does sell Quinny joggers at Sears in Canada. And some Quinny fans have ordered models from Euro web sites; see our message boards for more info.

Safety 1st These strollers and travel systems are made by Cosco. See the earlier review for more info.

Schwinn These jogging strollers are made by InStep, which is part of Dorel/Cosco. We will discuss these strollers later in this chapter (under "Green Acres").

Silver Cross *This brand withdrew from the North American market in 2005. For an archive of our review of Silver Cross, see our web page BabyBargains.com (click on Bonus Material).*

Stokke *For a dealer near you, call (877) 978-6553. Web: www.stokkeusa.com* And now for something totally different: the Stokke Xplory, a stroller so bizarre we have to show you a picture just to explain it. Yea, it looks like something George Jetson might have pushed Elroy around in, but it's more than a museum piece about what strollers might look like in the year 2050. We will give Stokke bonus points for creativity (they've tried to push it as the next Bugaboo), but the $750 Xplory is a bit too funky for its own good. Like the Bugaboo, you get a modular system that includes a frame with rubber tires and a seat that can attach to the frame either forward or rear facing. The baby's seat can ride high on the frame, which gives the Xplory a weird mobile high chair look. The pitch, according to Stokke, is to keep baby higher off the ground so they are away from exhaust fumes, etc. (the target market is urban parents). So why haven't you seen the über rich pushing the Stokke Xplory around Greenwich Village? That's because for the most part, the Xplory has been a bust sales-wise. First, most of the Xplory's frame and handle is injection-molded plastic, not something you'd expect for a $750 stroller. The "plastic-y" feel turns off many, while the lack of a basket is another major negative. Instead the Xplory has a "carriage bag" with zipper that attaches to the frame . . . wrong answer! Add the lack of a car seat adapter (even Bugaboo has this) and inadequate padding for the seat and you've got stroller that looks like it will be assigned to the dust bin of baby product history. **Rating: D+**

Stroll Air *For a dealer near you, call (519) 579-4534. Web: www.stroll-air.com* Polish-made Stroll Air is another European stroller company hoping to become the next Bugaboo. Debuting this year, Stroll Air's modular stroller systems come with both bassinet and stroller seat, for use on an aluminum chassis. An example: the Driver 3XL, a tri-wheel stroller with two larger inflated tires and a front double wheel that can lock or swivel. You also get a decent size basket, height adjustable handle and a nice series of extras (foot muff, wind cover, diaper bag, umbrella, mosquito net). Price: $669. Okay, that's not cheap, but at least Stroll Air isn't charging you those big bucks for a stroller and then expecting you to shell out $40 for an umbrella or $120 for a foot muff (ahem, Bugaboo). The only negatives: the weight of these strollers (the Driver 3XL is 26-28 lbs., depending on how you configure it) and the relatively drab fashion (three colors, red, blue or black—although a limited edition pink is a popular). Stroll Air also makes a four-wheel version of the Driver (dubbed the 4XL) and a double stroller (the Spider Twin).

New this year, Stroller Air is debuting the Driver NV—a tri-wheel stroller chassis that comes with both a bassinet and stroller seat. At $700, it clearly is aiming at the Bugaboo crowd, yet it is quite heavy (22 lbs. for the chassis alone; add another 8 lbs. for the bassinet or stroller seat). But like its other models, Stroll Air does roll out all the stops for this model: you get a reversible seat, multi-position foot and backrest, adjustable handle, plush padding, air tires, adjustable suspension, rain cover and more. And yes, the Driver NV includes a diaper bag and umbrella. We liked the Driver NV's mini-front wheel, which should give the model more maneuverability in the supermarket than the Driver 3XL or 4XL models.

Our View. Parent feedback on Stroller Air is limited, but the few reports we've received are positive. One reader loved her Driver 4XL, especially the reversible seats, smooth ride and numerous adjustments for the seat, handlebar and so on. The downside: the front wheels on that model only pivot, they don't rotate 360 degrees—that makes tight turns hard to do. Hence this model is best for outdoor walks and off-road trials, not the mall (the new Driver NV might be a better urban stroller). Another bummer: Stroller Air is only sold in a handful of stores and online sites. Yet the quality is excellent and the value (with all the included extras) make this brand a contender. **Rating: B+**

Strolee See Combi.

Swan This brand is made by Baby Trend. See their review earlier in this section.

Traxx See i'coo review earlier in this section.

Valco For a dealer near you, call (800) 610-7850. Web: www. valcobaby.com Australian-based Valco has made a splash in the all-terrain stroller market with their recently released Runabout, a tri-wheel stroller whose key selling point is its expandability. The basic Runabout comes in both a single ($375) and double ($550) version and features a five-position, fully reclining seat, large storage basket, aluminum frame, newborn insert and swivel front wheel that can be locked in a fixed position. That's nice, but what really has parents jazzed is Valco's add-ons: a bassinet ($90) and toddler seat ($80) that extend the use of this stroller. The bassinet is very nice, but the toddler seat is really cool, turning the Valco into a double stroller. Valco's other accessories include a car seat adapter ($40, which holds a Graco seat) and foot muff ($50). Valco's key competitors in this market would be the Zooper Zydeco or Mountain Buggy Urban Single. Valco is nice, but the Mountain Buggy is much lighter (19 lbs. versus the Valco at 25 lbs.), while the Zooper throws in more goodies (boot, carry cot and more for $425). And the colors for the Valco are a bit on the dull side (red, black, navy, green, although ice pink and blue are coming). Yet parents who've purchased a Valco give it an enthusiastic thumbs-up, saying the ride is smooth and the compact fold makes it an easy fit in most trunks. Yes, we'd like to see a button on the handle that releases and locks the front wheel, but perhaps that can be on version 2.0.

New this year, Valco will launch several new models, including the Roadie ($140, 14 lbs.), a Pliko-like stroller with two handles. Also new: the Everest, a $200 28 lb. stroller that is basically a less-fancy version

strollers

of the Runabout with a one-hand hold (but it omits the ability to pop on the toddler seat). In the double category, Valco will debut the Twin Sportz this year—this 22 lb. side-by-side stroller will have full reclining seats for $275. There will be subtle changes for the Runabout this year, including a bigger canopy and the ability to lock the front wheel in one of three modes (lock, full swivel and 45 degree pivot). The basket on the Runabout will also be easier to access.

All in all, Valco is a winner. ***Rating: A***

Zooper *(503) 248-9469; Web: www.zooperstrollers.com* Zooper is one of the few stroller brands to break out of the pack in recent years. Zooper fans love their smartly designed models, combined with rugged sporty looks and high-quality features. Most Zooper models fit in the all-terrain category, with air-filled wheels (although a few have plastic wheels). An overview:

The models. The Boogie (26 lbs., $360) is Zooper's flagship tri-wheel stroller. No, it isn't cheap, but check the specs: it has a four-position full reclining plush seat that reverses so you can see baby when pushing it, full canopy, boot, rain cover, decent size basket and (drum roll) it holds an infant car seat. Note: all those features are usually pricey extras with other brands—that is Zooper's secret sauce. Best of all, the Boogie has a swivel front wheel that can be locked plus better access to its basket.

At first glance, you might think the Zooper Waltz (16 lbs., $200) was really a Peg Aria. But this stroller offers a napper bar, ergonomic handle and is compatible with most infant car seats—Peg only works with its own infant seat. And Zooper again throws in all the extras (full boot, rain cover, basket) that make it a much better deal. The Zooper Waltz has a four position, full seat recline.

While the Boogie and Waltz are Zooper's best-sellers, the company offers a plethora of different models in three categories: Elite, Everyday and Escape.

The Boogie is in the Everyday category, along with the Waltz and three other models: the Disco, Twist and Tango. The Disco (formerly the Jazz) is a 22 lb. stroller that runs $300. Similar to the Boogie, the Disco is a tri-wheel stroller that holds an infant car seat and features a swivel front wheel that can be locked from a simple button on the handlebar. Very cool. This seat also has a partial (155 degree) recline. The Twist ($160, 13 lbs.) is a bit like the Peg Perego Pliko, with two handles and a compact fold.

Zooper's most expensive strollers are the "Elite" models: the Hula and Zydeco. The Hula (16 lbs., $290) is a plush version of the Twist, adding height adjustable handles, one-hand recline and an extra sunshade. FYI: The Hula used to be called the Swing. The top of the line Zooper is the Zydeco ($425, 29 lbs.). This funky three-wheel stroller looks like one of those concept cars you see at auto shows. It has a "magnesium encased multi-direction suspension system," height adjustable handle and is infant car seat compatible. The Zydeco has a reversible seat, large basket and full recline. You also get a carrycot, rain cover, boot and (new this year) a "sleeping bag" (basically a souped-up additional boot).

The most bare bones Zooper is the Salsa (the Escape category), a super-lightweight mesh model that is nine lbs. It includes a canopy, basket and rain cover for $120. The Zooper Salsa is much like the Mac Volo (but Maclaren charges $40 extra for a rain cover in an accessory pack that also includes a seat liner).

Need a double? The Zooper Tango is a side-by-side stroller (26 lbs., $270) with a 30" width and newborn-friendly reclining seats.

Our view. Good and bad news on Zooper this year. Good news: Zooper put all its strollers on a diet this year—as a result, most models dropped about 20% in weight (including the Boogie, which shed six pounds). Bad news: Zooper has raised prices 20% or more to cover the increased cost of the lightweight frames.

Yet, still Zooper offers decent value despite the higher prices: all the extras (rain cover, boot, etc) make these strollers standout when compared with competitors. Best of all, Zooper has great customer service. And the manly fabric choices mean Dad won't be embarrassed to push this stroller.

We'd recommend the Hula or Twist for urban environs; the Zooper Boogie is a good suburban bet for neighborhood walks and hiking trails. And the Waltz would work well for mall crawlers. ***Rating: A***

◆ ***Other brands to consider.*** Several brands of strollers have washed out in the past year, so we've moved these to our web site: Allo, Simo and Bebecar. You'll also find reviews of smaller players Bertini and Kidco there as well. Go to BabyBargains.com and click on Bonus Material.

Our Picks: Brand Recommendations by Lifestyle

Unlike other chapters, we've broken up our stroller recommendations into several "lifestyle" categories. Since many parents end up with two strollers (one that's full-featured and another that's lighter for quick trips), we'll recommend a primary stroller and a secondary option. For more specifics on the models mentioned below, read each manufacturer's review earlier in this chapter. Let's break it down:

··

Mall Crawler

You live in the suburbs and drive just about everywhere you go. A stroller needs to be packed with features, yet convenient enough to haul in and out of a trunk. Mostly the stroller is used for the mall or for quick trips around the block for fresh air.

In the past, we recommended buying a travel system that combined an infant seat and stroller. This time we have one word of advice when it comes to travel systems: DON'T. Don't waste your money on those huge, bulky systems from mass-market brands like Graco, Eddie Bauer/Cosco, or Evenflo. Why? Parents repeatedly tell us the strollers in these travel systems are aggravating to use, thanks to low quality and hefty weight. Many readers tell us they usually chuck the stroller when their baby outgrows the infant seat.

Instead, consider one of the great new alternatives to the massive travel system—first, look at stroller frames like the **Baby Trend Snap & Go** $50 (pictured), **Kolcraft Universal Car Seat Carrier** ($40 to $50), **Combi Flash** ($60) or **Strolee Streak** ($50). Heck, even **Graco** has a stroller frame (the **SnugRider**) for $60.

All these stroller frames work the same way: snap or strap in any major brand car seat and you've got a "travel system" without the expense. Of course, if you go this route, you'll have to buy a second stroller after baby outgrows the infant seat (we'll have some thoughts on this in just a second).

Which stroller frame is best? The Baby Trend or Graco models are probably the best, but the best one for you depends on the infant car seat you get. Take a second and snap your favorite infant car seat into the various stroller frames in a store before purchasing. Check the instructions, as some stroller frames have bars that have to be adjusted into a certain position to accommodate different brands.

Another idea: go for a stroller that has a car seat attachment bar. Many of the top-rated stroller brands we reviewed earlier (Combi, Peg Perego, Inglesina, Maclaren Mountain Buggy, Zooper) have certain models with the ability to attach an infant car seat. Yes, sometimes you have to buy an optional accessory to make this work, but it is an alternative.

"But really, Denise and Alan, which travel system do you like?" No matter how much we editorialize against pre-packaged travel systems, we still get emails from parents who want to go this route. Okay, if you want to ignore the above advice, we'd suggest one of Graco's more affordable offerings, such as the **Graco Mosaic or MetroLite** travel systems (about $200). At least then you are getting a decent infant seat (the Graco SnugRide).

··

Please don't email us, however, when you decide you hate the stroller after three months . . . or when the wheels fall off. Yes, Graco has improved the MetroLite over the years and the Mosaic is a new model with good reviews, but you can't expect the same durability here as with the better-quality brands. Above all, stay away from the travel systems with heavy strollers—if the stroller is over 20 lbs., don't do it.

Second stroller. If you buy a stroller with a car seat attachment bar, you won't need a second stroller. But if you decide to add a second stroller to your collection, go for something that is ultra lightweight and folds compactly. At the budget end, the **Graco LiteRider** ($60-$70) boasts a large number of features at an affordable price. We also like the **Chicco London** (aka **Tuscany**)— for $70 to $80, you get a 15 lb. stroller that includes lots of extras (rain cover, bigger canopy, adjustable leg rest). Finally, the **Chicco C5** for $90 is a smart choice—feature packed, but just 13.7 lbs.

The best mid-price lightweight stroller for suburbanites is probably the **Peg Perego Aria** ($170, 12 lbs., pictured), with a partially reclining seat, decent size basket and five-point restraint. Yea, the padding is a bit skimpy and the canopy could have more coverage, but in general the Aria is a winner.

A bit harder to find, but worth a look is the **Inglesina's Espresso**. This 16 lb. stroller does weigh a few more pounds than the Aria, but has larger wheels, nicer padding and a height-adjustable handle. An Espresso runs $150 to $200, but includes a rain cover and boot.

Is Grandma paying for your second stroller? The best options at the top of the market for suburban parents are probably the **Inglesina Zippy** ($240 to $290), the **Maclaren Techno XT** ($290) or the **Peg Perego Pliko P3 Classico** ($240 to $270). We also like the **Combi I-Thru** from ($300) in this category.

If you live in a rainy climate (read: Seattle), consider the **Zooper Waltz**, a $200 stroller that includes rain cover, boot and more.

A dark horse for the Mall Crawler: a tri-wheel all-terrain stroller with an air-filled front wheel that either swivels or locks. We'll review those strollers in the Green Acres section later because most of those strollers are pitched for hiking or gravel roads. You can use these strollers in the mall, but beware: they are heavier and somewhat less maneuverable than the strollers discussed above.

Urban Jungle

When you live in a city like New York, Boston or Washington D.C., your stroller is more than just baby transportation—it's your primary vehicle. You stroll to the market, on outings to a park or longer trips on weekend getaways.

Weight is crucial for these parents as well. While you are not lugging a stroller in or out of a trunk like a suburbanite, you may find yourself climbing up subway stairs or trudging up to a fourth-floor walk-up apartment. It's a major trade-off here: full-featured strollers that are outfitted for the weather (full boot, rain cover) can weigh more than lightweight models designed for the mall. Basically, you want a rugged stroller that can take all the abuse a big city can dish out—giant potholes, uneven sidewalks, the winter from Hell . . . without the weight of a bulldozer.

In the past, carriage strollers or prams were the primary "urban jungle" stroller, but these have fallen out of favor for their bulky weight and other disadvantages (prams typically have front wheels that don't turn).

This year we will crown a new entrant to the stroller biz as the best urban jungle stroller: meet the **Valco Runabout**. This tri-wheel stroller ($375, 25 lbs., designed in Australia) has 12" inch air-filled wheels and all the comforts you need for the city: five-position fully reclining seat, decent size storage basket, five-point harness, cushy padding, reflective trim for nighttime visibility and more. The front wheel swivels . . . or can be locked for a little exercise in the park.

But here's the best part: Valco offers a variety of accessories to extend the use of the Runabout. First is a bassinet ($90) that snaps into the aluminum frame. Second, check out the innovative toddler seat ($80) that turns the Runabout into a double stroller. There's also a car seat adapter ($40), footmuff ($50) and full rain cover ($20). All in all, Valco is a great hybrid, combining the plushness of carriage strollers of the past with the flexibility of all-terrain models that can be used both for shopping and the park.

A good second bet for the Urban Jungle is the **Zooper Zydeco** ($425, 29 lbs). The great thing about Zooper is all the extras you get for the price: carrycot, rain cover, boot and more. Yes, it is four pounds heavier than the Valco, but the quality is excellent and the price is less (when you factor in all the extras).

Finally, let's talk about the 800-lb. gorilla in this category: the **Bugaboo Cameleon**. Dutch-designed (but made in Asia), the Bugaboo's claim to fame is its flexibility. You get an aluminum frame that can hold either a bassinet or stroller seat (both included). It pushes like a dream and most parents who have a Bugaboo absolutely adore it . . . but there is a catch. The price: $880. Add in accessories and you can easily see the total soar past $1100. Even a Valco with an added bassinet is 40% less than a Bugaboo. So unless you have a rich uncle, we say pass.

Second stroller. While full-featured strollers are nice, they do have one disadvantage. They're heavy (many are 20 to 40 lbs.) and most don't fold compactly. Sometimes, all you need is a lightweight stroller that can withstand big-city abuse YET quickly folds like an umbrella so you can get in a taxi or down a set of subway stairs. (Just try lugging a Perego Venezia up the stairs at a T stop in Boston).

The solution: Maclaren—their strollers weigh just ten to 14 pounds and fold compactly. The entry-level ***Maclaren Triumph*** ($140; pictured) has all the features you'd need (including a partially reclining seat) yet weighs a mere 12 lbs. For another $50 to $100, you can get a plusher seat and other upgrades with the Maclaren Quest, Ryder or Techno XT—with the caveat of added weight.

Another recommendation for a lightweight stroller for urban parents would be the ***Chicco London/Tuscany*** ($70, 15 lbs.), which has a five-position recline, adjustable leg rest, padded handles, canopy, rain cover and basket. The ***Chicco C5*** model ($90) is also worth a look-see.

Is your apartment some distance from the subway stop? If so, consider a ***Zooper Twist*** ($160), similar to the Peg Pliko but lighter at 13 lbs.—and the Twist includes a rain cover, sun/UV cover and foot muff.

If a stroller with an one-hand fold is a must, the ***Inglesina Zippy*** ($230 to $270) is pricey but very cool at 17 lbs.

While it's easy to spend less money than one of these recommendations, don't be penny-wise and pound-foolish. Less-expensive strollers lack the durability and weatherproofing that living in an East Coast city requires. And since baby spends more time in the stroller than tots in the suburbs, weatherized fabrics and padding are more of a necessity than a luxury.

Green Acres

If you live on a dirt or gravel road or in a neighborhood with no sidewalks, you need a stroller to do double duty. First, it must handle rough surfaces without bouncing baby all over the place. Second, it must be able to "go to town," folding easily to fit into a trunk for a trip to a mall or other store.

This is a tough category to recommend a stroller for—there are many so-called "all-terrain" strollers on the market. Yet, we found those made by the big guys (Cosco, Evenflo) were just pretenders. Yeah, the box says "all-terrain" and they have larger wheels and shock absorbing suspensions, but we just don't think most of them really cut it. Like faux-SUV's that couldn't handle two inches of snow, these strollers are long on promise and short on delivery.

There is good news on the Green Acres front: in the past year, more "all terrain" models have debuted, providing parents more choice. Now, the best choices for this lifestyle would probably be the Zooper Boogie or Mountain Buggy Urban Single.

The **Zooper Boogie** (pictured on page 402) is a hybrid between a jogging stroller and an all-terrain—you still get the tri-wheel configuration and 12" air-filled wheels (as with joggers), but the Boogie has a real stroller seat (no sling or mesh seat) with nice padding and other features. Yes, the Boogie is pricey ($360), but you get a raft of included extras such as a rain canopy, boot, basket and (this is important) the ability to snap in an infant car seat. Even better news: the Boogie's turnable front wheel can be locked into a forward position from a lever on the handle (now that's cool).

All right, the Boogie is great, but what if you want a simpler all-terrain stroller with a swivel front wheel that costs less than $120? The **Jeep Liberty SE Terrain** is an excellent choice: it features one-hand fold, child snack tray with a cute toy steering wheel, and parent tray.

STROLLER ROUND-UP

Here's our round-up of popular models by the major stroller manufacturers.

MAKER	MODEL	WEIGHT	PRICE	RECLINE
CHICCO	C5	13.7 LBS.	$90	PARTIAL
COMBI	CITY SAVVY SELECT	13	$150	FULL
	SAVVY EX	18	$200	FULL
GRACO	MOSAIC	18	$100-150	PARTIAL
INGLESINA	ESPRESSO	16	$150-200	FULL
	ZIPPY	17	$240-290	FULL
JEEP/KOLCRAFT	LIBERTY SE TERRAIN	26	$118	FULL
MACLAREN	TRIUMPH	12	$140-150	PARTIAL
PEG PEREGO	ARIA	12	$160-200	PARTIAL
	PLIKO P3	17	$240-270	FULL
VALCO	RUNABOUT	25	$375	FULL
ZOOPER	BOOGIE	26	$360	FULL

Target sells a slightly upgraded version of the Liberty for $140.

At the upper end, we'd also recommend the **Mountain Buggy Urban Single** from New Zealand (pictured). Nope, it isn't cheap at $430 but it is built to last with quality features like polymer wheels that won't rust (memo to parents who live near an ocean).

Fellow kiwis Phil & Ted also have a great entry in this category that is worth checking out: the **e3** ($380, 22 lbs.). Yep, it is 50 bucks cheaper than the Mountain Buggy, but you get much the same features (tri-wheel stroller with swivel front wheel) plus the ability to add a second toddler seat for $80.

Okay, let's say that all those strollers are overkill. If you want to go more on the budget end for Green Acres, we'd suggest an entry-level jogging stroller like those by **Baby Trend** or **InStep** (discussed in the next section). These run about $100. The only disadvantage to these joggers: the front wheel is fixed and their heavy steel frames don't make them very trunk-friendly.

Exercise This: Jogging and Sport Strollers

How times have changed. When the first edition of this book appeared in 1994, there were just a handful of jogging or "sport"

strollers

Frame	Best For	Comments
Aluminum	Mall/Urban	Compact Umbrella Fold
Aluminum	Mall Crawl	Taller handle than in past
Aluminum	Mall Crawl	Push button recline
Aluminum	Mall Crawl	3-D fold, two handles
Aluminum	Urban Jungle	1-hand fold, boot
Aluminum	Urban Jungle	1-hand fold, car seat adapt.
Steel	Green Acres	Turnable front wheel
Aluminum	Urban Jungle	Fully enclosed hood
Aluminum	Urban Jungle	Lightest weight peg
Steel	Mall Crawl	Adjustable handle, 1-hand fold
Aluminum	Urban Jungle	Swivel Wheel, Toddler seat
Aluminum	Green Acres	Includes Boot, Rain Cover

strollers on the market, most of which cost $200 or more. Today, the number of offerings in this category has exploded—over 30 jogging strollers are offered on the market at last count, with prices as low as $100. And it's not just the small companies . . . the big boys like Cosco/Safety 1st are busy rolling out joggers and sport strollers as well.

So, what's all the fuss about? Most jogging or sport strollers have three wheels and are built like bicycles—they boast large rubber wheels with rugged tread that can handle any terrain, yet move smoothly along at a fast clip. Folks who like to jog or even walk for fitness favor joggers over regular strollers for that reason.

How young can you put a baby in a jogger? First, determine

Three mistakes to avoid when buying a jogging stroller

With jogging strollers available everywhere from Target to high-end bike stores, it is easy to get confused by all the options. Keep in mind these traps when shopping for a jogger:

◆ **Rust.** Warning: cheaper jogging strollers are made of steel—rust can turn your pricey jogging stroller into junk in short order. This is especially a problem on the coasts, but can happen anywhere. Hint: the best joggers have ALUMINUM frames. And make sure the wheels rims are alloy, not steel. All-terrain strollers like Mountain Buggy use polymer wheels to get around the rust problem.

◆ **Suspended animation.** The latest rage with joggers is those with cushiony suspensions, which smooth out bumps but can add to the price. But do you really need it? Most jogging strollers give a smooth ride by design, no added suspension is necessary. And some babies actually LIKE small bumps or jostling—it helps them fall asleep in the stroller.

◆ **Too narrow seats**. Unlike other baby products, a good jogging stroller could last you until your child is five years old—that is, if you pick one with a wide enough seat to accommodate an older child. The problem: some joggers (specifically, Baby Jogger and Kelty) have rather narrow seats. Great for infants, not good for older kids. We noticed this issue after our neighbors stopped using their Baby Jogger when their child hit age 3, but our son kept riding in his until five and beyond. Brands with bigger seats include Kool Stop, Dreamer Design and BOB. (As always, confirm seat dimensions before committing to a specific stroller; seats can vary in one brand from model to model).

whether the seat reclines (not all models do). If it doesn't, wait until baby is at least six months old and can hold his or her head up. If you want to jog or run with the stroller, it might be best to wait until baby is at least a year old since all the jostling can be dangerous for a younger infant (their neck muscles can't handle the bumps). Ask your pediatrician for advice if you are unsure.

The prime time to use a jogger is when your baby is a toddler (18 months or two years and up), as those children seem more suited to longer outings. Hence, we have decided to put an expanded discussion of joggers in our other book, *Toddler Bargains*. (We also have more room there, as the explosion of options is out-stripping the room we have here). In the *Toddler Bargains* book, you'll find in-depth analysis of jogging stroller brands and detailed model-by-model reviews. Meanwhile, in this book, we'll give you a brief overview of the major players and a sum-up of our top choices.

Before heading out to buy a jogging stroller, consider how you'll use it. Despite their name, few parents actually use a jogging stroller for jogging. If you just plan to use the stroller for walks in the neighborhood, a lower price model (we'll have specific recommendations below) with 12" wheels will do fine. If you really plan to run with a jogger, go for 16" or 20" wheels for a smoother glide and a higher-quality brand name for durability.

Another decision area: frame material. The cheapest strollers (under $200) have steel frames—they're strong but also heavy (and that could be a drawback for serious runners). The most expensive models ($200 to $350) have aluminum frames, which are the lightest in weight. Once again, if you plan casual walks, a steel frame is fine. Runners should go for aluminum.

Check the seat fabric carefully. The best strollers use Dupont Cordura, which is also used in backpacks for its durability and strength. As for other features, go for a model that has a hand brake on the handle (the cheapest models omit this). The brake is used to slow the stroller when you are going down a steep incline. And always check the folding feature: some are easier than others.

Finally, remember the Trunk Rule. A great jogger is a lousy choice if you can't get it easily in your trunk. Check the DEPTH of the jogger when it is folded—compared this to your vehicle's trunk. Many joggers are rather bulky even when folded. Yes, quick release wheels help reduce the bulk, so check for that option.

A good web site with detailed jogging stroller info: JoggingStroller.com. The site has user reviews and even editorial opinions from the owner about which stroller has the best fold, etc.

Here's an overview of the key players (in alphabetical order).:

Baby Jogger (web: www.babyjogger.com; Rating: A) literally invented this category 20 years ago, but recently went through a bankruptcy and now has new owners. Their new emphasis: all-terrain models with swivel front wheels like the City Series (single, $350, double $550). The City Series has the easiest fold we've seen for such models: one-hand and zip! It's done. Baby Jogger seems to be moving away from its long-time emphasis on models for serious runners—now only one style features 20″ wheels while the others have 16″ wheels. Baby Jogger's running strollers now include the Performance series ($320 single, $430 double) and Q-series, the latter with a quick-fold feature ($300 to $350 for a single, $480 for a double). Quality is good, despite the move of all the production move to China and the ownership upheaval.

BOB Strollers (web: bobgear.com, Rating: A) have won awards and accolades for their innovative joggers—you can tell these were designed by runners for runners. (Trivia note: BOB stands for Beast of Burden trailers—they decided BOB was easier to spell). BOB's strollers are billed as "sport utility" strollers and that's an apt moniker, as their rugged design (polymer wheels to prevent rust, for example) and plush ride make these stroller best-sellers despite their $300+ price tags. In recent years, BOB has branched out to strollers with turnable front wheels (the Revolution model).

Chariot (web: www.ChariotCarriers.com; Rating: A) is an impressive jogging stroller brand from Canada. Their Cavalier jogger features an aluminum frame, wide seat, adjustable handlebars, reclining seat, decent storage, reflective trim and a lifetime warranty. The Cavalier comes in both single ($300) and double ($400) versions and is sold in both specialty stores and in chains like REI. We were also impressed with the Chariot Cabriolet, which combines both a jogger and bike trailer ($360 to $460). Parents tell us the quality of Chariot is excellent; if you want both a jogger and bike trailer, this brand should

SPORT STROLLERS

How top sport/jogging strollers compare:

MODEL	CAPACITY	PRICE	HARNESS
BABY TREND EXPEDITION	50 LBS.	$100	5-POINT
BOB SPORT UTILITY	70 LBS.	$300	5-POINT
CHARIOT CAVALIER	75 LBS.	$300	5-POINT
DREAMER REBOUND GST	80 LBS.	$240	5-POINT
GOZO 1x2	55 LBS.	$350	5-POINT
KELTY SPEEDSTER DELUXE	N/A	$325	5-POINT
KOOL STRIDE SR 16″	75 LBS.	$290	5-POINT
REEBOK VELOCITY EXTREME	50 LBS.	$200	5-POINT

on the top of your shopping list.

Dreamer Design (formerly Fitness First, 509-574-8085; web: www.dreamerdesign.net, Rating: A-) is best known for their great bubble canopies that provide more coverage than most joggers. Most Dreamers have aluminum frames and run $200 to $300—that's about $100 less than competitors. Among the standouts here: the Manhattan for $230, Dreamer's first design with a turnable front wheel and optional infant car seat adapter. New this year, the Dreamer Design Rebound Deluxe sports a "refined suspension" and upgraded styling for $325.

GoGo Babyz's (web: www.GoGoBabyZ.com, Rating: A-) Urban Advantage Swivel Wheel Stroller is positioned as an affordable tri-wheel stroller with a swivel front wheel—at $190, it is less than the Mountain Buggy and Zoopers, but still more than the Kolcraft/Jeep models at Wal-Mart. Unique features for this model include a removable front child tray and brake-activated kickstand (to keep it from tipping when a toddler climbs in). The Urban Advantage is designed less for running and more for gravel trails or neighborhood walks.

Gozo (415-388-1814; web: www.getgozo.com; Rating A-) offers the only tandem (front/back) jogging stroller on the market—their stroller frame can be configured to carry one or two seats. The strollers (21 lbs. with one seat, 26 lbs. for two) feature quick-release 16" wheels, three-position reclining seats, sun canopies, five-point harness, removable/washable seat covers, and a storage basket and aluminum chassis. The stroller itself is $350, while the second seat is $135. We were very impressed with these innovative strollers.

InStep is better known by their alter ego, Schwinn—see review on the next page.

Kelty (303-530-7670, web: www.kelty.com, Rating: B+) is best known for their backpacks, but jumped into the jogger market in 2001. Their re-designed line won kudos when it was launched last

Suspension	Seat Recline	Sun Shade	Pin-free folding
	✔	✔	
✔	✔	✔	✔
	✔	✔	✔
✔	✔	✔	✔
	✔	✔	✔
	✔	✔	✔
	✔	✔	
✔	✔	✔	✔

year: the Speedster is $235 or in a "deluxe" version for $325 that adds an easier fold, height adjustable handle, hand break and reclining seat. A double version (Speedster Deuce 16) runs $400. An older model (the Joyrider) is still sold online for $320, although its funky handle bars are an acquired taste. Quality is very good, although the canopy coverage is a bit skimpy.

Motobecane (web: motobecane.com; Rating: B) is better known for their bicycles, but they also make a jogger (the Tot to Trot) for $350 and a double for $600. We occasionally see them pop up on eBay and other sites, but distribution is sparse. We've had very little feedback on these models, but the few parents we found who bought one seem pleased.

Safetech (Rating: C-) these cheap jogging strollers have been sold on eBay and elsewhere online for as little as $90, but we aren't impressed with their quality.

Schwinn (web: instep.net; Rating: C) is made by InStep, which is in turn part of the Dorel/Cosco stroller empire. Basically, Schwinn models are the same as InStep, with upgraded fabric and additional accessories (insulated cooler bag, etc). A single Schwinn is $200, while a double is $290. Frankly, we'd suggest cheaper InStep models if the fabric upgrade doesn't jazz you. New this year: the Schwinn Free Runner LT ($200) designed for runners, with aluminum frame, alloy hubs, adjustable handle and integrated weather shield. (FYI: Schwinn's rating is lower than InStep because we think it represents a lower value for the dollar.)

Tike Tech by X-Tech Outdoors' (web: www.xtechoutdoors.com, Rating: B-) claim to fame is their Double Trouble jogger—at $300, it is the cheapest double jogger on the market. Of course, they do singles too: the ATX All Terrain with 16" wheels ($200) has a height-adjustable handle and removable safety bar for kids (which is unique). All in all, these are mid-price joggers made of aluminum, sold online at BabiesRUs.com as well as other web sites. Parent feedback on this brand is mixed: some complain about quality glitches and most are unimpressed with the canopy, which doesn't offer as much coverage as the competition. Tike Tech strollers can be prone to tipping because the weight of the child is so far back in the stroller. Fans of Tike Tech like the mountain bike-like tires and overall value—these strollers fill a niche between the ultra-cheap joggers you see in chain stores and pricey $300+ models. We're impressed with new features Tike Tech has rolled out this year, including a removable sun visors and a fully reclining seat. As a result, we've upped their rating a bit.

Zooper (web: www.zooperstrollers.com) is reviewed in depth earlier in this chapter. Their models are hybrids between true joggers and regular strollers and more appropriate for the walking crowd than runners.

Whew! Just a few choices, eh? So, which jogging stroller do we recommend? Let's break that down into two categories: low-end and high-end. Note that all these strollers have fixed front wheels; if you want a stroller with a turnable front wheel (more suited to the mall or light duty outdoor activities), see the Green Acres section on page 451.

Low end (walks, hikes). Baby Trend's affordable joggers (see earlier review for more background on Baby Trend) are sold in Babies R Us and other chain stores. The entry-level **Baby Trend Expedition** ($100-$150 stand alone, or $200 as a travel system with infant car seat) has a five-point harness, canopy and two-position seat recline. These steel frame strollers will do fine for occasional walks and other light-duty use.

Want something a bit more deluxe? Baby Trend's upgraded joggers are sold under the Reebok name (a la InStep's license with Schwinn). The **Reebok Velocity Extreme** ($200) has an aluminum frame with spring suspension, alloy rims on the 16″ wheels, no rear axle (for runners with longer strides), multi-position reclining padded seat, reflective trim and a two-trigger fold. A good value, considering you also get an included rain cover and boot.

High end (serious runners). What if you really want to jog or run with a sport stroller? Or you plan to use it intensively for exercise (say more than two times a week)? Or go for hikes? Then we suggest investing in a top-quality stroller from Dreamer Design.

Dreamer this year captures the top spot in our jogger review. Our favorite model is the **Dreamer Rebound GST**—for runners, we suggest the 20″ wheel version for $240 to $280 (pictured is the 16″ wheel version). The Rebound features all you want in a jogger (height adjustable handle, one-step fold, five point harness, reclining seat). Dreamer's key advantage is their cool bubble-style canopy, which provides among the best sun coverage in this category. The Rebound also has Dreamer's patented suspension system, which cushions baby from bumps. New this year, the Rebound Deluxe model will feature a "refined" suspension for $325. If you think you just need a 16″ wheel stroller without the suspension (you plan to jog on smooth surfaces), then Dreamer's Slingshot is a good bet at $200.

Tall parents who are serious runners should give **Kelty's Speedster Deluxe** ($325) a test drive. The height adjustable handle will let both a shorter and taller parent use this model with equal ease.

Does Dad need a manly jogger? Then **BOB's Sport Utility Deluxe** stroller should do the trick ($300). BOB's polymer wheels are more suited for near-ocean environs, as they won't rust. The Deluxe features a cushy suspension and among the easiest folds on the mar-

strollers

ket. BOB's Ironman strollers ($350) add adjustable tracking, stainless steel wheel spokes, new smooth tires and bright yellow fabric. This jogger weighs just 20 pounds.

Finally, let's give a recommendation for **Kool Stop's** joggers (800-586-3332, 714-738-4973; www.koolstop.com; rating: A). Each Kool Stride has a five-point safety harness, reclining seat, and giant, retractable hood. Another plus: Kool Stop's rear wheels are angled by five degrees for improved tracking. Quick release wheels and simple fold up make the stroller easy to transport. Their flagship mode is the "Senior" ($290, 19 lbs.) with an alloy frame, reclining seat and quick release wheels. Yes, Kool Stop may be a bit harder to find, but we think it's worth the effort. New in the past year, Kool Stride has a "Kool Fold" feature for their models—basically, this is an easier one-step fold process, which is indeed rather cool. FYI: In mid 2006, Kool Stop plans a re-vamp for their entire line, but we didn't have any details as of press time.

So, let's sum it up. For high-end joggers for serious runners, we give Dreamer Design's Rebound GST top honors, although Kelty's Speedster and BOB's Sport Utility Deluxe are close runners-up. Each of these strollers is in the $250 to $350 range. On the low end, Baby Trend's Expedition ($100) is good for occasional walks and hikes. A step up would be Baby Trend's Reebok strollers, with suspension and other goodies for about $200.

The same advice for brands applies to double joggers—the better brands for single joggers are the same as the ones for doubles.

Plan to take your jogger out in the cold weather? Instead of bundling up baby, consider a stroller blanket. **The Cozy Rosie** by Sew Beautiful ($50-$55, 877-744-6367 or 914-244-6367; web: www.cozyrosie.com) fits over the stroller and is made of washable polar fleece with Velcro fasteners. A similar product is the **JJ Cole Bundle Me** (web: www.bundleme.com) for $40 to $50. We also like the **Buggy Bagg**—pricey at $75 to $115 (web: www.buggybag.com) but readers love it.

Double The Fun: Strollers for two

There are two types of strollers that can transport two tikes: tandem models and side-by-side styles. For the uninitiated, a tandem stroller has a "front-back" configuration, where the younger child rides in back while the older child gets the view. These strollers are best for parents with a toddler/older child and a new baby.

Side-by-side strollers, on the other hand, are best for parents of twins. In this case, there's never any competition for the view seat. The only downside: some of these strollers are so wide, they can't fit through narrow doorways or store aisles. (Hint: make sure the stroller is not wider than 30" to insure door capability). Another bummer: few have napper bars or fully reclining seats, making them impractical for infants.

So, what to buy—a tandem or side by side? Our reader feedback shows parents are much happier with their side-by-side models than tandems. Why? The tandems can get darn near impossible to push when weighted down with two kids, due to their length-wise design. Yes, side by sides may not be able to fit through some narrow shopping aisles, but they seem to work better overall.

Double strollers can be frustrating—your basic choices are low-price (and low-quality) duos from Graco, Cosco or Baby Trend or high-price doubles like those from Perego, Maclaren or Combi. There doesn't seem to be much in between the low-price ones (at $150) and the high-end ($300 and up).

Given the choices on the low end for tandems, we like the **Graco DuoGlider** best (37 lbs., $150). Yes, this one accepts not one but TWO infant car seats, but probably most parents who buy this will have an older/younger child configuration. The DuoGlider has stadium seating (the rear seat is

E-MAIL FROM THE REAL WORLD
Biting the bullet on a pricey twin stroller

Cheapo twin strollers sound like a good deal for parents of twins, but listen to this mother of multiples:

"Twins tend to ride in their strollers more often and longer, and having an unreliable, bulky or inconvenient stroller is a big mistake. As you suggest, it's a false economy to buy an inexpensive Graco or other model, as these most likely will break down before you're done with the stroller. My husband and I couldn't believe that we'd have to spend $400 on a stroller, but after talking to parents of multiples we understand why it's best to just bite the bullet on this one. We've heard universally positive feedback about the Maclaren side-by-side for its maneuverability, durability and practicality. It fits through most doorways and the higher end model (Twin Traveler) also has seats that fully recline for infants. We've heard much less positive things about front-back tandems for twins. These often are less versatile, as only one seat reclines, so you can't use them when both babies are small (or tired). And when the babies get bigger, they're more likely to get into mischief by pulling each others' hair and stuff."."

higher than the front)) and the rear seat fully reclines for infants. Plus, you get a giant basket.

Another good bet on the low end: the ***Joovy Caboose Stand-on Tandem*** ($150, 24 lbs.). It really isn't a tandem, but a pushcart—the younger child sits in front while an older child stands in back (there is also a jump seat for the older child to sit on).

If grandma is paying the bill for a double stroller, then we'd recommend the ***Peg Perego Duette*** ($540), a superb tandem stroller complete with steering wheel that can also hold two infant car seats.

What about side-by-side strollers? For parents of twins on a tight budget, we suggest the ***Jeep Twin All Weather Twin Sport Umbrella*** (27 lbs., pictured.) for $72 at Wal-Mart. It's bare bones (no basket) but will get the job done with reclining seats and a compact fold. If you've got a bit more budget, the ***Inglesina Double Swift*** ($200, 28 lbs., pictured) gets rave reviews from our readers, as does the ***Maclaren Twin Traveler*** ($350, 25 lbs.) with its full reclining seats. Another good bet: the ***Zooper Tango*** ($270, 26 lbs.), stylish yet still packed with extras. Finally, for outdoor treks with twins, we like the
Mountain Buggy's side-by-side all-terrain strollers—very pricey at $420 to $650 but built to last.

Do It By Mail

THE BABY CATALOG OF AMERICA.

To Order Call: (800) PLAYPEN or (203) 931-7760; Fax (203) 933-1147
Web: www.babycatalog.com

This web site won't win any design awards (the main stroller section is just a few paragraphs of advice on buying strollers), but they've added more thumbnail graphics to each category. And the selection is still great. Baby Catalog has it all—over three-dozen models from such brand names as Peg Perego, Combi, Baby Jogger and more. Prices are rock bottom, about 20% to 30% below retail. Once you click to each stroller's page, you'll find detailed pictures and fabric swatches that make shopping easy.

Baby Catalog has been in business since 1992, first as a printed catalog and now primarily a web site (don't waste your time with the printed catalog as it is only produced sporadically and the web site has more up-to-date stuff). The company has a good record when it comes to customer service. The site does offer a baby registry as well.

Of course, this site sells much more than strollers—they also discount Avent bottles, Dutailier gliders, designer bedding and more.

One tip: you can save an additional 10% off the site's prices by purchasing a membership, $25 for a year (or $49.95 for three years). With each membership, you also get three "associate" memberships for friends/relatives to purchase items for you at the same discount. Interestingly, this is a clever way to get a premium brand that is rarely discounted online—for some reason, manufacturers who don't allow sites to discount their products don't seem to mind when Baby Catalog offers their members that 10% discount.

Top 7 Tips for Traveling with Baby

1 AIRLINE-PROOF YOUR STROLLER. Even if you have a stroller that folds as compact as an umbrella, you may still find the airline will ask you to "gate check" it if the plane is full (read: 98% of the time). That means before you board the plane, you leave it outside the aircraft door . . . and pray you'll see it again in one piece. It's the ugly part of traveling with baby—having an airline baggage handler manhandle your stroller. We've heard numerous stories of strollers that disappeared into cargo holds, only to reappear damaged, trashed and worse. Our advice: take an affordable umbrella-type stroller on the road (prices start at $30 to $50), not that $200 model. That way, if the airline trashes it, you don't take that big of a financial hit.

2 PACK FOOD AND DIAPERS, TIMES THREE. Ever try to buy diapers at a major airport? While airports are great at catering to business travelers, families stuck with a three-hour delay are often out of luck when it comes to finding baby necessities. A word to the wise: calculate how many diapers and formula/snacks you need for a trip and then triple it to deal with delays. Yes, if you are breastfeeding, you have that part covered, but other supplies can be hard to track down (and very expensive) if you run out.

3 ALWAYS GET THAT KID'S MEAL. Airlines keep shrinking the meals they give all passengers (if they give any at all), so it is wise to always request a child's meal on a flight that still serves food. Yes, request that kid's meal even if your child is still breastfeeding. Why? You can always eat the meal if you are still hungry. And trust us, hauling all those diapers from tip #2 through the airport requires a significant amount of energy. Moment of irony: kid's meals often taste better than what airlines serve adults.

strollers

4 **THINK "SHERPA."** Those expert mountain guides in Nepal know how to pack smart and you should too. Always consider the WEIGHT of any item when you travel. Buy a lightweight, simple car seat like the Graco ComfortSport for the airplane and leave that heavy Britax at home. Ditto for the stroller.

5 **USE A CARRIER.** The best way to move through an airport is with a front carrier like the Baby Bjorn, reviewed in this chapter. That way, you have two hands free to carry everything else. Yes, we still recommend buying a baby a separate seat and bringing/using a child safety seat. But if you use a carrier like the Bjorn, you won't need a stroller when shuttling between gates, etc.

6 **PACK YOUR OWN CRIB SHEETS.** Yes, most hotels have cribs, but some try to cheat when it comes to bedding—attempting to wrap a crib mattress with a twin sheet or worse. Be safe: pack your own crib sheets just in case.

7 **VACATION RENTALS: BABY'S AWAY.** As we mentioned in the previous chapter, Baby's Away rents baby gear at many vacation destinations nationwide. See page 359 for more.

Bike Trailers, Seats & Helmets

Bike Trailers. Yes, lots of companies make bike trailers, but the gold standard is **Burley** (866-248-5634; web: www.burley.com). Their trailers (sold in bicycle stores) are considered the best in the industry. A good example is the  **Burley "d'Lite."** It features a multi-point safety harness, built-in rear storage, 100 lb. carrying capacity and compact fold (to store in a trunk). Okay, it's expensive at $430 but check around for second-hand bargains. All Burley trailers have a conversion kit that enables you to turn a trailer into a jogging stroller (although we hear mixed reviews on the Burley as a jogging stroller for its wobbly steering).

A close runner-up to Burley in the bike trailer race is Canada's **Chariot** (www.chariotcarriers.com). "These are the best engineered bike trailers I've ever seen," opined a reader and we agree. Sold at REI, they run $250 to $350 (although one pricey version that combines a stroller and bike trailer runs $550).

Kool Stop's (the jogger company reviewed earlier in this chapter) new trailer, the Koolite, is a departure from the usual design. The towing bar in the center rather than to the right or left as with Burley

(Burley then bends the bar so the trailer stays centered behind the bike). Kool Stop claims the center bar helps "enhance towing, tracking, turning and control." These new trailers sell for a whopping $450 on sites like BicycleMall.com The original Kool Stop trailer retails for a bit less: $350.

What about the "discount" bike trailers you see for $150 to $200? *InStep* makes a few of these models: the Quick N Lite ($145), the Rocket Aluminum ($180), the Ride N Stride ($170) and the Quick N EZ ($105). InStep also makes the Schwinn bike trailer, which is an upgraded version of their regular line. The Schwinn has 20" quick release alloy wheels, five-point restraints, extra storage and a carrying capacity of 100 lbs. Cost: about $250.

What do you give up for the price? In general, lower priced bike trailers have steel frames and are heavier than the Burleys (which are made of aluminum). And the cheaper bike trailers don't fold as easily or compactly as the Burleys, nor do they attach as easily to a bike.

The key feature to look for with any bike trailer is the ease (or lack thereof) of attaching the stroller to a bike. Quick, compact fold is important as well. Look for the total carrying capacity and the quality of the nylon fabric.

So, should you spring for an expensive bike trailer or one of the $150 ones? Like jogging strollers, consider how much you'll use it. For an occasional (once a week?) bike trip, we'd recommend the cheaper models. Plan to do more serious cycling, say two or three times a week? Then go for a Burley, Schwinn or Kool Stop. Yes, they are expensive but worth it if you really plan to use the trailer extensively.

Hint: this might be a great item to buy second-hand on eBay or Craigslist. We saw several used Burley trailers for sale on eBay (www.eBay.com) for $50 to $200, or 30% to 60% off retail.

Safety information: you should wait on using a bike trailer until your child is OVER one year of age. Why? Infants under age one don't have neck muscles to withstand the jolts and bumps they'll hit with bike trailers, which don't have shock absorbers. Remember you might hit a pothole at 15+ mph—that's not something that is safe for an infant to ride out. Be sure your child is able to hold his head up while wearing a helmet as well. Your child should always wear a helmet while riding in a bike trailer—no exceptions. And, no, there is no bike trailer on the market that safely holds an infant car seat, which might cushion the bumps. Most trailers will accommodate children up to about age six. Check the instruction manual for individual trailers.

Bike seats. When shopping for a bike seat, consider how well padded the seat is and what type of safety harness the unit has (the best are five-points with bar shields; less expensive seats just have three-point harnesses). The more expensive models have seats that recline and adjust to make a child more comfortable.

One good model is the *CoPilot Limo Child Seat* ($110-$135) by CoPilot (formerly called Rhode Gear), which has a florescent orange safety bar, three-point harness and four-position reclining seat. A simpler version of this seat is called the CoPilot Taxi for $90, which lacks the reclining seat. Another option is the *Topeak BabySitter*. It has a spring suspension system to cushion bumps. They also include dual safety latches to lock the seat to the rack, adjustable foot rests, a quick release padded safety bar, and four-way safety harness. Cost: $120.

We've not seen any safety problems with the cheaper bike seats sold in discount stores; they just tend to lack some of the fancier features (padding, reclining seats) that make riding more comfortable for a child.

Safety advice: as with a bike trailer, your child should be able to hold her head up easily while wearing a bike helmet to ride in a bike seat. We think it's best to use a bike seat for children two or over. They can accommodate children up to 40 pounds.

Bike helmets. Consumer Reports tested kids bike helmets in 2002 and recommended options from *Bell* (who also makes *Giro*). CR noted that all toddler models were a bit lacking in ventilation, but the Bell Boomerang ($30) did a very good job at impact absorption and scored best for ease of use. Although Bell makes other models of toddler bike helmets, they didn't all score the same. We would agree with Consumer Reports, as their research matches feedback from parents on Bell. We'd recommend avoiding the really cheap helmets under $20.

Safety advice: many states are requiring all children to wear bike helmets when riding in a bike seat or trailer. That makes sense, but it is sometimes hard to find a helmet to fit such small heads. One tip: add in thick pads (sold with some bike helmets) to give a better fit. Don't glue pads on top of pads, however—and adding a thick hat isn't a safety solution either. If your child cannot wear a bike helmet safely, put off those bike adventures until they are older. Be sure your child wears the helmet well forward on his head. If a helmet is pushed back and your child hits the ground face first, there is no protection for the forehead.

The Well-Stocked Diaper Bag

We consider ourselves experts at diaper bags—we got five of them as gifts. While you don't need five, this important piece of luggage may feel like an extra appendage after your baby's first year. And diaper bags are for more than just holding diapers—many include compartments for baby bottles, clothes, and changing pads. With that in mind, let's take a look at what separates great diaper bags from the rest of the pack. In addition, we'll give you our list of nine items for a well-stocked diaper bag.

Parents in Cyberspace: What's on the Web

Just because you have a new baby doesn't mean you have to lose all sense of style. And there is good news: an entire cottage industry of custom diaper-bag makers has sprung up to help fill the style gap. One good place to start: our message boards. Go to BabyBargains.com, click on the message boards and then to Places to Go (All Other Gear, Diaper Bags, etc). There you'll find dozens of moms swapping tips on the best and most fashionable diaper bags. Here's a round up of our readers' favorite custom diaper bag makers (most sell direct off their sites, but a few also sell on other sites):

Amy Michelle	amymichellebags.com
Cherry Pie	cherrypieinc.com
Chester Handbags	chesterhandbags.com
Dobre Goods	dobregoods.com
Ella	ella-bags.com
Fleurville	fleurville.com
Haiku Diaper Bags	haikubags.com
Holly Aiken	hollyaiken.com
I'm Still Me!	blueberrybabies.com
Kate Spade	katespade.com
Kecci	kecci.com
Oi Oi	oioi.com
One Cool Chick	onecoolchick.com
Reese Li	reeseli.com
Skip Hop	skiphop.com
Timbuk2	timbuk2.com
Tumi	tumi.com
Vera Bradley	verabradley.com

diaper bags

No doubt there are dozens more, but that's a great starting point. You can expect prices to be commensurate with style. Kate Spade can cost over $300 for some styles. But there are some great looking options for under a $100 too. One caveat: many of these manufacturers are small boutique companies. Often it may be the owner who's taking the order. . . and also sewing the bag! While we admire the entrepreneurship of these companies, many are so small that a minor event can put them off kilter. All it takes is one hurricane or a deluge of orders to turn a reputable company into a customer service nightmare. Check the feedback on these companies on our message boards before ordering.

 Smart Shopper Tips

Smart Shopper Tip #1
Diaper Bag Science

"I was in a store the other day, and they had about one zillion different diaper bags. Some had cute prints and others were plainer. Should I buy the cheapest one or invest a little more money?"

The best diaper bags are made of tear-resistant fabric and have all sorts of useful pockets, features and gizmos. Contrast that with low-quality brands that lack many pockets and are made of cheap, thin vinyl—after a couple of uses, they start to split and crack. Yes, high-quality diaper bags will cost more ($30 to $75 versus $15 to $20), but you'll be much happier in the long run. High-end diaper bags (like those made by Kate Spade and other designers) can reach the $300 mark or more. Of course, many of our readers have found deals on these bags, so check out our message boards for shopping tips.

Here's our best piece of advice: buy a diaper bag that doesn't *look* like a diaper bag. Sure those bags with dinosaurs and pastel animal prints look cute now, but what are you going to do with it when your baby gets older? A well-made diaper bag that doesn't look like a diaper bag will make a great piece of carry-on luggage later in life. The best bets: Lands' End's or Eddie Bauer's high-quality diaper bags (see reviews later).

What's the hip new fabric for diaper bags this year? Two words: micro fiber. You'll see more of this super-soft fabric appearing as diaper bags in the months to come.

Smart Shopper Tip #2
Make your own

"Who needs a fancy diaper bag? I just put all the necessary changing items into my favorite backpack."

That's a good point. Most folks have a favorite bag or backpack that can double as a diaper bag. Besides the obvious (wipes and diapers), put in a large zip-lock bag as a holder for dirty/wet items. Add a couple of receiving blankets (as changing pads) plus the key items listed below, and you have a complete diaper bag.

Another idea: check out the "Diaper Bag Essentials" from Mommy's Helper (call 800-371-3509 or 316-684-2229 for a dealer near you; web: www.mommyshelperinc.com). This $20 to $30 kit is basically everything for a diaper bag but the bag—you get an insulated bottle holder, changing pad, dirty duds bag, toiletry kit, etc. That way you can transform your favorite bag or backpack into a diaper bag. We found it on Target.com for $20.

Top 9 Items for a Well-Stocked Diaper Bag

After much scientific experimentation, we believe we have perfected the exact mix of ingredients for the best-equipped diaper bag. Here's our recipe:

1 TWO DIAPER BAGS—one that is a full-size, all-option big hummer for longer trips (or overnight stays) and the other that is a mini-bag for a short hop to dinner or the shopping mall. Here's what each should have:

The full-size bag: This needs a waterproof changing pad that folds up, waterproof pouch or pocket for wet clothes, a couple compartments for diapers, blankets/clothes, etc. Super-deluxe brands have bottle compartments with Thinsulate (a type of insulation) to keep bottles warm or cold. Another plus: outside pockets for books and small toys. A zippered outside pocket is good for change or your wallet. A cell phone pockets is also a plus.

The small bag: This has enough room for a couple diapers, travel wipe package, keys, wallet and/or cell phone. Some models have a bottle pocket and room for one change of clothes. If money is tight, just go for the small bag. To be honest, the full-size bag is often just a security blanket for first-time parents—they think they need to lug around every possible item in case of a diaper catastrophe. But, in the real world, you'll quickly discover schlepping that big full-size bag everywhere isn't practical. While a big bag is nice for overnight or long trips, we'll bet you will be using the small bag much more often.

2 **EXTRA DIAPERS.** Put a dozen in the big bag, two or three in the small one. Why so many? Babies can go through quite a few in a very short time. Of course, when baby gets older (say over a year), you can cut back on the number of diapers you need for a trip. Another wise tip: put whole packages of diapers and wipes in your car(s). We did this after we forgot our diaper bag one too many times and needed an emergency diaper. (The only bummer: here in Colorado, the wipes we keep in the car sometimes freeze in the winter! As they say, you don't know cold. . .)

3 **A TRAVEL-SIZE WIPE PACKAGE.** A good idea: a plastic Tupperware container that holds a small stack of wipes. You can also use a Ziplock bag to hold wipes. Some wipe makers sell travel packs that are allegedly "re-sealable"; we found that they aren't. And they are expensive.

4 **BLANKET AND CHANGE OF CLOTHES.** Despite the reams of scientists who work on diapers, they still aren't leak-proof—plan for it. A change of clothes is most useful for babies under six months of age, when leaks are more common. After that point, this becomes less necessary.

5 **A HAT OR CAP.** We like the safari-type hats that have flaps to cover your baby's ears (about $10 to $20). Warmer caps are helpful to chase away a chill, since the head is where babies lose the most heat.

6 **BABY TOILETRIES.** Babies can't take much direct exposure to sunlight—sunscreen is a good bet for most infants. Besides sunscreen, other optional accessories include bottles of lotion and diaper rash cream. The best bet: buy these in small travel or trial sizes.

7 **DON'T FORGET THE TOYS.** We like compact rattles, board books, teethers, etc.

8 **SNACKS.** When baby starts to eat solid foods, having a few snacks in the diaper bag (a bottle of water or milk, crackers, a small box of cereal) is a smart move. But don't bring them in plastic bags. Instead bring reusable plastic containers. Plastic bags are a suffocation hazard and should be kept far away from babies and toddlers.

9 **YOUR OWN PERSONAL STUFF.** Be careful of putting your wallet or checkbook into the diaper bag—we advise against it. We've left our diaper bag behind one too many times before we learned this lesson. Put your name and phone number in the bag in case it is lost.

Our Picks: Brand Recommendations

We've looked the world over and have come up with two top choices for diaper bags: Lands End and Eddie Bauer (plus a couple of other smaller brands worthy of consideration). They both meet our criteria for a great diaper bag—each offers both full-size and smaller bags, they don't look like diaper bags, each uses high-quality materials and, best of all, they are affordably priced. Let's take a look at each:

Lands End (800) 356-4444 (web: www.landsend.com) sells not one but five diaper bags: The Do-It-All Diaper bag ($30), the Triple Compartment Bag ($40), the Little Tripper ($20) and a diaper bag tote for $40.

The Do-It-All features a wide mouth (like a doctor's bag) that lets you see the large main compartment for diapers and wipes. There is also a parent pocket for your stuff, extra long changing pad and exterior bottle pockets. Then there's another zippered compartment for a blanket or change of clothes, a waterproof changing pad and an expandable outside pocket for books and small toys. In the past we praised the bag's long carry straps but one parent pointed out that the new design leaves only about 17" of strap meaning the bag rides right under her armpit. Another parent complained that the new design of the bag now makes it very heavy too.

E-MAIL FROM THE REAL WORLD
Diaper Bag Find

This reader found a great diaper bag from California Innovations (web: www.ca-innovations.com) for $25. FYI: These bags are sold from time to time in Costco warehouse clubs.

"I got a fantastic diaper bag by a company called California Innovations. They have several different types but they all seem to be made from black or navy blue microfibre with insulated bottle compartments, plastic lined interiors, and lots of special pockets. The one I purchased has a removable plastic liner (for easy cleaning), a portable padded changing station, plastic "dirty bag", one insulated bottle pocket that holds two bottles, one outside bottle pocket, a separate insulated section that attaches to the bottom of the bag, a side zipper pocket for a wallet/keys/other small stuff, and snap on cell phone and pacifier holders on the outside. The straps are set up so it can be carried with a small handle like a shopping bag, used as a single or double strap backpack. A great find for $20!"

Beside those drawbacks, the bag does seem to hold a lot of stuff. After all these years of recommending the Do-It-All, it's still a winner with most parents. Readers have hauled this thing on cross-country airline trips, on major treks to the mountains, and more. At $30, it's a good buy considering the extra features and durability. (Don't forget to check Lands End's outlet stores for diaper bag bargains).

How about those quick trips to the store? We bought the Little Tripper ($20) for this purpose and have been quite happy. It has a changing pad and two exterior pockets. With just enough room for a few diapers, wipes and other personal items, it's perfect for short outings.

This might be a good place to plug the "Overstocks" page on Lands End's web site (www.landsend.com). This regularly updated section has some fantastic bargains (up to 50% off) on all sorts of Lands End items, including their kids clothing, bedding, diaper bags and more. You can also sign up for their newsletter, which updates you on the site.

Not to be outdone, **Eddie Bauer** (800) 426-8020 (web: www. eddiebauer.com) offers four diaper bags—a backpack ($50), case bag ($50), sling bag ($40) and even a men's Down Diaper Bag ($150). Each is made of fabric that's easy to clean and contains a removable changing pad, bottle pockets, and a detachable wet/dry pouch for damp items (except for the smaller day pouch). The *Wall Street Journal* called Bauer's offerings "the most manly diaper bag available" and we have to agree—the look does not scream baby.

Just to confuse you, we should note that Eddie Bauer has a SEPARATE line of diaper bags that are in Babies R Us: these options range from $18 to $35. Parents we interviewed gave these bags a thumbs up, but not as high as the ones Eddie Bauer sells from its web site and catalog (they come from different suppliers apparently).

Besides Lands End and Eddie Bauer, readers say they've had success with **Baby Bjorn's Diaper Backpack** ($50), but it looked a bit bulky and cumbersome to us. Baby Bjorn also makes a traditional diaper bag style for $80. See it on Target.com.

A dark horse contender in the diaper bag wars is **Combi**, the stroller maker mentioned earlier in this chapter. Their main offering is the Urban Sling, a well-designed bag with nice features (cell phone pocket, insulated bottle pocket, etc) and fashionable colors (Pink Diva, Keylime). Price: $45. FYI: Combi did make a slew of other diaper bag styles that are now discontinued, but you may see them on clearance online.

If you're looking for more fashion forward, less utilitarian designs, check out our list above in the CyberSpace section for custom diaper bag makers. What about the fancy pants designers? Kenneth

Cole, Kate Spade and Nicole Miller top the list of designers that get the highest marks from our readers. But some of the more obscure options are worth checking out to.

In the end we recommend Lands End, Eddie Bauer or Combi as your best bets for the money. They may be basic in the fashion department but they do the job for a good price.

Carriers

Got chores to do? Looking for a way to free yourself up from carrying your little one everywhere? Carriers seem to be the products that parents turn to. Carriers free up your hands, help you keep track of your baby, even get a little exercise for yourself. But what kind of carrier is best for you? Let's take a look.

Parents in Cyberspace: What's on the Web

The Baby Wearer
Web Site: www.thebabywearer.com
What It Is: A resource for parents interested in "baby wearing"
What's Cool: This site is extensive. You'll find articles, reviews, product listings, ads, you name it. The main emphasis seems to be on sling-type carriers, not so much front carriers. There are a couple of great charts that offer detailed comparisons for carriers. In fact, there is so much here, you could spend days on the site. If you're a newbie to baby wearing, be sure to start with the basic articles as well as the glossary of terms. Then you can join chats and message boards or click on product links.
Needs Work: There's a lot of advertising here. And the site is very jumbled. You're probably smart to take their recommendations with a grain of salt and verify reviews with other sites before you buy.

What Are You Buying?

Carriers come in several flavors: slings, hip carriers, front carriers and frame or backpack carriers. Let's take a look at each type:

◆ **Slings.** Slings allow you to hold your baby horizontally or upright. Made of soft fabric with an adjustable strap, slings drape your baby across your body (see picture). The most famous sling, made with input from Dr. Sears (the father of "baby wearing"), is made by NoJo (pictured), but many other manufacturers have jumped into the sling market. Whichever brand you choose, devoted sling user Darien Wilson from Austin, Texas has a great tip for new moms: "The trick for avoiding backache when using a sling is to have the bulk of the baby's weight at the parent's waist or above."

Weight Limit: 20 pounds. *(Note: weight limits may vary by manufacturer. This is only an approximate weight limit. Please check the directions for each item you purchase.)*

Recommendations: While NoJo was the first, we don't really think they're the best slings out there. Readers complain that they hang too low and hurt their backs. Instead, our readers recommend the **Maya Wrap Sling** ($48-$53; www.mayawrap.com) citing its flexibility and comfort. Others praise the **Over the Shoulder Baby Holder** ($45; web: www.otsbh.net).

If you're looking for unusual fabrics so you can be a "stylish" baby wearer, go no further than the **ZoLo** sling (www.zolowear.com). The silk version (it's machine washable) will set you back a hefty $160 but wow, is it beautiful! And they'll send you fabric swatches if you have trouble deciding from one of their 20 fabrics (other fabrics start at $60). Another parent recommended the **Moms in Mind** sarong carrier (www.momsinmind.com, $40 to $50) saying it had a simpler buckle and enough support to allow for hands free nursing. **Mamma's Milk** (www. mammasmilk.com) offers a streamlined sling with "invisibly adjustable pouches." These slings use Aplix (a stronger version of Velcro), to allow for adjustments without using zippers or snaps. Prices range from $45 to $85 depending on fabric. They even make a Shower Pouch which can be used in the shower or the pool ($30).

New Native Baby carriers are yet another option in the sling department (www.newnativebaby.com, $40 to $50). They tout their streamline design, which allows you to stuff it into a diaper bag for on-the-go convenience.

Kangaroo Korner makes adjustable "pouches" in fleece, cotton and solarveil. They're the first we've seen to use a UV barrier fabric. And their unpadded pouches can be used in water as well. Prices range from $55 to $60. Finally, we liked the **Sling Baby** from Walking Rock Farm (www.walkingrockfarm.com) the well-padded strap plus soft knit fabrics make this a great option for $64 to $67.

Where to buy: Most sites sell their slings directly, but **Kangaroo Korner** (www.kangarookorner.com) is a web site recommended by readers for their wide selection. They carry several brands and will even custom design a sling for you. Best of all, they offer tips and advice for using a sling.

◆ **Hip Carriers.** Hip carriers like the **Cuddle Karrier** (pictured; www.cuddlekarrier.com) are a minimalist version of the sling. With less fabric to cradle baby, they generally work better for older babies (over six months). Baby is in a more upright position all the time, rather than lying horizontally. And like a sling, the hip carrier fits across your body with baby resting on your hip.

Weight/Age Limit: Manufacturers claim hip carriers can be used up to three years of age. *(Note: weight/age limits may vary by manufacturer. This is only an approximate limit. Please check the directions for each item you purchase.)*

Recommendations: Hip Hammock ($40 to $60; web: www. hiphammock.com) was recommended by a reader who had back problems—she said this was the most comfortable carrier. And the Hip Hammock (made by Playtex) can be used up to age three. FYI: As we went to press, the Hip Hammock was being recalled for a defective strap, which the company is fixing. If you use a hand-me-down, make sure it was made after this was corrected.

The Cuddle Karrier mentioned earlier runs about $75 and claims to do everything but make toast. It converts from a carrier to a shopping cart restraint, high chair restraint, even a car seat carrier.

◆ **Front Carriers.** The most famous of all carriers is the **Baby Bjorn** (pictured), that Scandinavian wonder worn by celeb moms and even yours truly. Yep, we used the Bjorn and we loved it. Front carriers like the Bjorn are basically a fabric bag worn on your chest. Your baby sort of dangles there either looking in at you (when they're very young) or out at the world (when they gain more head control).

carriers

Weight Limit: 25 to 30 pounds. *(Note: weight limits may vary by manufacturer. This is only an approximate weight limit. Please check the directions for each item you purchase.)*

Recommendations: So why is Baby Bjorn our top recommended front carrier? In a Bjorn, baby can face forward or backward and is positioned for easy carrying. Adjusting the straps is also easy, since everything is up front. And best of all, you can snap off the front of the Bjorn to put a sleeping baby down. Imported from Europe (www.babybjorn.com), the Baby Bjorn isn't cheap (about $90 retail) but it's vastly superior to other carriers on the market. There is also a "tall" version of the Bjorn for vertically-blessed parents.

In the past year, Baby Bjorn has debuted two new versions of the Bjorn: the "Active" ($120) adds lumbar support for longer walks and the "Air" ($100), a mesh version to keep baby cool in warmer climates.

A word of safety advice on the Bjorn: a recall back in 1999 fixed a design problem with the Bjorn's leg openings. Bjorns made between 1991 and October 1998 had leg openings that were too large; as a result, a small infant (under two months) could slip out of the carrier. The company fixed the problem with a redesign and offered a retrofit kit for parents with the older model. If you get a hand-me-down Bjorn, make sure you have this kit (call toll-free 877-242-5676 to get one). Finally, we should note Bjorn also issued a recall on the Bjorn Active in the past year for a defective latch. This has been corrected and all the Actives on the shelves today are fine.

Theodore Bean front carriers were bought out by stroller-maker **Maclaren** in 2004, which continues to make them under its own name. We still see older Theodore Bean carriers sold online for $50 to $70. Meanwhile, Maclaren continues to improve the line with an enclosed harness system, new one-handed buckle release and an infant insert. The Maclaren baby carrier sells for about $60 to $70.

Canadian parents write to us with kudos for the **Baby Trekker** (800-665-3957; web: www.babytrekker.com). This 100% washable cotton carrier has straps that wrap around the waist for support. Canucks like the fact a baby can be dressed in a snowsuit and still fit in the Baby Trekker. The carrier ($90 U.S., $125 Canada) is available in baby stores in Canada or via the company's web site for folks in the U.S.

One mom wrote to us extolling the virtues of the **MaxiMom** carrier (www.4coolkids.com). "It does everything short of making dinner. It can be used as a front carrier facing forward or backward, backpack facing forward or backward, emergency high chair, sling and can be used for a child up to 35 pounds. Here's the great part: MaxiMom is designed to also be used with multiples!" The cost: $55 to $125 depending on how many children you'll be using it for.

Looking for a front carrier that can also be used as a soft back carrier? Walking Rock Farm's **Hip Baby** ($72 to $84; web: www.walkingrockfarm.com) can be worn in front, on your hip or in back but only for kids 6 months up to 45 pounds.

We also recommend taking a look at the **Kelty Kangaroo** ($80; web: www.kelty.com). This soft carrier is high quality and well designed. Sort of like an outdoor version of the Baby Bjorn. They also offer a stripped down soft carrier called the Wallaby for $60.

Finally, what about a carrier so you can get into a swimming pool with your older kids and not worry about baby? **WaterTot** makes a "water friendly baby carrier" which allows babies to face forward and play in the water (www.watertot.com, $60). Made of neoprene, the carrier can also be used on the hip.

What about those low-end carriers like **Snugli, Infantino, Eddie**

Bauer? We don't recommend them. Let's be honest here: yes, you can spend $20 on a carrier at a discount store. And that is much less than a Bjorn. But take a second to read parent reviews of carriers, whether on our site or other baby message boards. Most parents quickly realize a bargain carrier can be a pain to use . . . literally. Cheap-o carriers are more complicated to put on and adjust as well as just being darn painful on the back.

Of all the cheaper carriers, Infantino's models are probably the most well-known. And we will give Infantino kudos for trying to innovate here: their *SmartRider Baby Carrier with Intelligel* ($50) has straps with gel cushions. Yet if you're going to spend $50 on an Infantino, you might as well pony up another $20 to $40 and get something that is even better-designed.

Where to buy: Most of these carriers are only available on their manufacturers' web sites. Baby Bjorn, however, is everywhere. One reader recommended Best Baby Store (www.bestbabystore.com) online. They offer last year's Bjorns at good discounts.

◆ *Frame (or backpack) Carriers.* Need to get some fresh air? Just because you have a baby doesn't mean you can never go hiking again. Backpack manufacturers have responded to parents' wish to find a way to take their small children with them on hikes and long walks. The good news is that most of these frame carriers  are made with lightweight aluminum, high quality fabrics and well-positioned straps. Accessories abound with some models including sunshades, diaper packs that Velcro on, and adjustable seating so Junior gets a good view.

Weight Limit: 45 to 50 pounds. (Note: weight limits may vary by manufacturer. This is only an approximate weight limit. Please check the directions for each item you purchase.)

Recommendations: Kelty (web: www.kelty.com) and *Sherpani Alpina (*www.sherpanipacks.com) have come to the rescue of parents with full lines of high-quality backpack carriers. If you want a frame carrier, Kelty offers six models, including the Adventure ($235) that has all the bells and whistles. Kelty still offers its combo backpack stroller, the Convertible (basically a Tour pack with wheels) for $160 that weighs just nine lbs.

Sherpani offers frame carriers built specifically to accommodate women's bodies. The Rumba (pictured above) is their flagship full feature carrier. This carrier ($210) has an aluminum frame and suspension system to take the strain off your back. It's also the only backpack carrier that can be adjusted while on your back. It has a five-point safety harness and padded chest plate among other features. New this year is a "super light" version of the Rumba for $150 (4.5 lbs.).

What most impressed us with Kelty and Sherpani is their quality—these are real backpack makers who don't skimp on details. Backpack carriers made by juvenile product companies are wimpy by comparison.

If those prices are a bit hard to swallow, check out the **Tough Traveler Kid Carrier** ($167, www.toughtraveler.com). Adjustable for just the right fit, the Tough Traveler features cushioned pads, tough nylon cloth, and two-shoulder harnesses for baby. A comfortable seat provides head and neck protection for smaller children—you even get a zippered pouch for storage. Tough Traveler has several other models that combine great quality and decent pricing. Check out their web site recommendations regarding the best pack for your height.

So, what's the best backpack among Kelty, Sherpani or Tough Traveler? That's a tough one—each has great features. Readers give the slight edge to the Tough Traveler for its quick and easy adjustments, lightweight and great storage. Sherpani, however, is technically amazing, made to fit a woman's body structure better. And the prices are lower this year than in the past.

Our readers also recommend a couple dark horse backpack carriers. The first is by **Outbound**, a Canadian manufacturer (www.outbound.ca) that offers four frame carriers: the Kiddie Carrier, Toddler Tote (versions 1 and 2) and Cub Carrier with prices ranging from $139 Canadian to $219 Canadian. Readers also praise the **Tatonka Baby Carrier** ($190) from another Canadian manufacturer, Sherpa Mountain (www.sherpa-mtn.com).

Where to buy: A good source for outdoor baby gear is the **Campmor** catalog (800) 226-7667 (web: campmor.com). You can also find this gear at outdoor retailers like REI. There are discounts on Tough Traveler's web site if you don't mind last year's models or factory seconds.

◆ **Other designs.** The Lillebaby 5-in-1 Soft Travel System (www.lillebaby.com) is a new item that doesn't quite fit into the other categories above. It's a five-function soft carrier that can be slung over your shoulder, used in a stroller or as a play blanket or travel bedding. It works as a carrier until your child is 20 pounds (with a back board to keep the carrier stable), then use it for the other functions. Bonus: Lillebaby has a  feature to swaddle baby, a plus for very young babies and it's adjustable and washable. Cost: $80. We don't recommend using the Lillebaby in a car seat, however, as it could compromise the safety of your baby in a crash (see Chapter 8 for more info).

So, how do you decide which carrier is best for you and your baby? The best advice is to borrow different models from your friends and give them a test drive. For most parents, a front carrier is all one really needs, although some parents like slings.

The Bottom Line: A Wrap-Up of Our Best Buy Picks

Strollers are a world unto themselves, with prices ranging from $30 for a cheap umbrella style to $500 or more for a deluxe foreign model with all the bells and whistles. The key message here is to buy the right stroller for your lifestyle (see specific recommendations earlier in this chapter). No one model works best for all situations.

In general, the best stroller brands are Peg Perego, Combi and Maclaren. For jogging strollers, Dreamer Design and Kelty are our top pick while we liked Burley bike trailers best in that category.

Who's got the best deals on strollers? We use web sites and online coupons for the best pricing. But we have to give it to stores like Babies R Us and Baby Depot—their prices are competitive and the sales can't be beat.

For diaper bags, we love Lands End and Eddie Bauer best, although Combi offers a decent alternative.

Baby Bjorn runs away with the crown for best front carrier; for outdoor enthusiasts, check out the offerings from Kelty, Tough Traveler and Sherpani.

carriers

CHAPTER 10

Childcare: Options, Costs and More

Inside this chapter

E ven stay-at-home moms agree there are days when you need a break. So whether you're a full time executive or a full time diaper changer, childcare will be an issue after your baby arrives. And your choices run from Mom's Day Out services at the local church to full time in-home care and everything in between. In this chapter we'll explain a few of the different options, scare you with the costs of day care and advise you where to look to find the best quality childcare in the best setting for your child.

Childcare

"It's expensive, hard to find and your need for it is constantly changing. Welcome to the world of child care," said a recent *Wall Street Journal* article—and we agree. There's nothing more difficult than trying to find the best childcare for your baby.

With 59% of moms with children under age one back in the workforce today, wrestling with the choices, costs and availability of childcare is a stark reality. Here's a brief overview of the different types of childcare available, questions to ask when hiring a provider and money saving tips.

What are you buying?

On average, parents pay 7.5% of their pre-tax income for child-care. And if you live in a high-cost city, expect to shell out even more. As you'll read below, some parents spend $20,000 or more per year.

Whatever your budget, there are three basic types of child care:

◆ **Family Daycare.** In this setting, one adult takes care of a small number of children in her home. Sometimes the children are of mixed ages. Parents who like this option prefer the lower ratio of children to providers and the consistent caregiver. Of course, you'll want to make sure the facility is licensed and ask all the questions we outline later. One drawback to family daycare: if there is only one caregiver, you might have to scramble if that person becomes ill. How much does it cost? Family daycare typically runs $6000 to $15,000 per year—with bigger cities running closer to the top figure.

◆ **Center Care.** Most folks are familiar with this type of daycare—commercial facilities that offer a wide variety of childcare options. Convenience is one major factor for center care; you can often find a center that is near your (or your spouse's) place of work. Other parents like the fact that their children are grouped with and exposed to more kids their own age. Centers usually give you a written report each day that details your baby's day (naps, diaper changes, mood). On the downside, turnover can be a problem—some centers lose 40% or more of their employees each year. A lack of consistency can upset your child. Yet center care offers parents the most flexibility: unlike nannies or family care, the day care center doesn't take sick or vacation days. Many centers offer drop-off care, in case you need help in a pinch. The cost: $3000 to $15,000 per year, yet some pricey centers can cost over $20,000 in the biggest cities. As with family daycare, the cost varies depending on how many days a week your baby needs care.

◆ **Nanny Care.** No, you don't have to be super-rich to afford a nanny. Many "nanny-referral" services have popped up in most major cities, offering to refer you to a pre-screened nanny for $200 to $400 or so. Parents who prefer nannies like the one-to-one attention, plus baby is taken care of in your own home. The cost varies depending on whether you provide the nanny with room and board. Generally, most nannies who don't live in run $8 to $17.50 per hour. Hence, the yearly cost would be $10,000 to $22,000. And the nanny's salary is just the beginning—you also must pay social security and Medicare taxes, federal unemployment insurance, plus any state-mandated taxes like disability insurance or employment-training taxes. All this may increase the cost of your $20,000 nanny by another $4500 or more per year. And the paperwork hassle for all the tax reporting can be onerous. The other downside to nannies? You're dependent on one person for childcare. If she gets sick, needs time off or quits, you're on your own.

Money Saving Tips

1 **ASK YOUR EMPLOYER ABOUT DEPENDENT CARE ACCOUNTS.** Many corporations offer this great benefit to employees. Basically, you can set aside pretax dollars to pay for child-care. The maximum set aside is $5000 (total per couple; single parents can put away $2500). Both parents can contribute to that amount. If you're in the 31% tax bracket, that means you'll save $1550 in taxes by paying for childcare with a dependent care account. Consult with your employer for the latest rules and limits to this option.

2 **SHARE A NANNY.** As we noted in the above example, a nanny can be expensive. But many parents find they can halve that cost by sharing a nanny with another family. While this might require some juggling of schedules to make everyone happy, it can work out beautifully.

3 **GO FOR A CULTURAL EXCHANGE.** The U.S. government authorizes a foreign nanny exchange program, referred to as "au pair." Through this program, you can hire a foreign-born young adult for up to 45 hours a week of childcare. Your kids get exposure to another language and culture, your au pair gets to hang out in the US to learn about our culture and language. What's the catch? See our box on Au Pairs for more information and costs.

4 **TAKE A TAX CREDIT.** The current tax code gives parents a tax credit for childcare expenses. The amount, which varies based on your income, equals about 20% to 30% of childcare costs up to a certain limit. The credit equals about $500 to $1500, depending on your income. Another tax break: some states also give credits or deductions for child care expenses. Consult your tax preparer to make sure you're taking the maximum allowable credit/deduction. New in recent years, the federal government expanded the adoption credit up to $10,000 for "qualified" expenses related to adoption.

Questions to Ask

Here are questions to ask a daycare center:

1 **WHAT ARE THE CREDENTIALS OF THE PROVIDER(S)?** Obviously, a college degree in education and/or child development is preferred. Additional post-college training is also a plus.

Au Pair Child Care

Au pairs have become more popular recently for one big reason: last year, the federal government (which regulates au pair programs) changed its rules to allow au pairs, or nannies from other countries, to stay in the U.S. as long as two years. That's up from only one year in the past. So if you find just the right nanny, you won't have to send him or her home in just 12 months and look for another childcare provider.

But how does the au pair idea work? First, only six organizations are allowed by the U.S. government to place au pairs with American families. These agencies must provide the au pair 32 hours of child safety classes and training. Au pairs are also required to have at least 200 hours of infant care experience if they are caring for children under two, be able to speak English proficiently, have a secondary school education and pass both reference and background checks. Whew! That's a lot of work you won't have to do as a parent. The age range of au pairs is 18 to 26 years.

If you're interested in hiring an au pair, you contact one of these six agencies (see below for a list). There is typically an application and program fee. The program fee is about $6000 and includes all the screening and prep of the au pair, as well as airfare, medical and travel insurance, training materials and support from the agency itself for the period of employment. Families must pay an au pair a $140 per week stipend and an educational allowance of $500. All these fees work out to about $14,000 per year, comparable to the high end of the family care childcare option (discussed earlier).

So how do you decide if an au pair is for your family? The *Wall St. Journal*, in a February 10, 2005 article on au pairs, noted that you should "choose an au pair only if you: can limit her work week to 45 hours a week, 10 hours a day, have a private bedroom available, value cross cultural experiences, can care for the emotions of a teen or young adult, can help and train an inexperienced caregiver, will treat her like a member of the family, (and) don't mind changing caregivers after two years."

Here's a partial list of au pair agencies:

AuPairCare	aupaircare.com
Au Pair in America	aupairinamerica.com
Cultural Care Au Pair	culturalcare.com
EurAuPair	euraupair.com
InterExchange	interexchange.org

2 **WHAT IS THE TURNOVER?** High turnover is a concern since consistency of care is one of the keys to successful childcare. Any turnover approaching 40% is cause for concern.

3 **WHAT IS THE RATIO OF CHILDREN TO CARE PROVIDERS?** The recommended national standard is one adult to three babies (age birth to 12 months). After that, the ratios vary depending on a child's age and state regulations. With some day care centers, there is one primary teacher and a couple of assistants (depending on the age of the children and size of class). Compare the ratio to that of other centers to gain an understanding of what's high and low.

4 **DO YOU HAVE A LICENSE?** All states (and many municipalities) require childcare providers to be licensed. Yet, that's no guarantee of quality—the standards vary so much from locale to locale that a license may be meaningless. Another point to remember: the standards for family daycare may be lower than those for center daycare. Educate yourself on the various rules and regulations by

Does your nanny have a past?

Yes, it sounds like the plot of a bad Hollywood thriller—the nanny WITH A PAST! Still, many parents want to feel secure that the person they trust to take care of their child hasn't had any run-ins with the police. In the past, this required laborious background checks with local police or numerous calls to past employers. Today, the web can help. Several web sites now let you screen a nanny's background with a simple point and click. Examples: MyBackgroundCheck.com offers a range of searches for $25 to $77. ChoiceTrust.com has a proprietary criminal records database and court records search for $64. Wonder if the background checking service you found online is legit? Ask the International Nanny Association (www.nanny.org), a non-profit group, which keeps tabs on such agencies. Of course, you can hire someone else to do the checking—most high-quality nanny employment agencies do those background checks, but of course you pay . . . about 10% of the nanny's first year salary as a fee. One note: while criminal background checks are relatively easy, drivers' records are another story. You may need to contact your state motor vehicle's bureau and have the nanny ask for a copy of her own report.

One smart tip: when asking for references from a nanny, get a LANDLINE phone number to call. Why? Some dishonest nannies have faked their references by having friends pose as references. That's easier to do with a cell phone versus a landline.

spending a few minutes on the phone with your state's child care regulatory body. Check on the center's file with the state to make sure there are no complaints or violations on record. Many states are putting this info on the web.

5 **MAY I VISIT YOU DURING BUSINESS HOURS?** The only way you can truly evaluate a childcare provider is an on-site visit. Try to time your visit during the late morning, typically the time when the most children are being cared for. Trust your instincts—if the facility seems chaotic, disorganized or poorly run, take the hint. One sign of a good childcare center: facilities that allow unannounced drop-in visits.

6 **DISCUSS YOUR CARE PHILOSOPHY.** Sit down for a half-hour interview with the care provider and make sure they clearly define their attitudes on breast-feeding, diapers, naps, feeding schedules, discipline and any other issues of importance to you. The center should have established, written procedures to deal with children who have certain allergies or other medical conditions. Let's be honest: child-rearing philosophies will vary from center to center. Make sure you see eye to eye on key issues.

7 **DO YOU HAVE LIABILITY INSURANCE?** Don't just take their word on it—have them provide written documentation or the phone number of an insurance provider for you to call to confirm coverage.

8 **DOES THE CENTER CONDUCT POLICE BACKGROUND CHECKS ON EMPLOYEES?** It's naive to assume that just because employees have good references, they've never been in trouble with the law.

9 **IS THE CENTER CLEAN, HOME-LIKE AND CHEERFUL?** While it's impossible to expect a childcare facility to be spotless, it is important to check for basic cleanliness. Diaper changing stations shouldn't be overflowing with dirty diapers, play areas shouldn't be strewn with a zillion toys, etc. Another tip: check their diaper changing procedures. The best centers should use rubber gloves when changing diapers and wipe down the diapering area with a disinfectant after each change. Finally, ask how often toys are cleaned. Is there a regular schedule for washing children's hands?

10 **WHAT TYPE OF ADJUSTMENT PERIOD DOES THE CENTER OFFER?** Phasing in daycare isn't easy—your child may have to have time to adjust to the new situation. Experienced providers should have plans to ease the transition.

childcare

Sources For The Best Child Care Facilities. Which childcare centers have the highest standards? The National Association of Family Childcare (800) 359-3817 (web: www.nafcc.org) and the National Association for the Education of Young Children (800) 424-2460 (www.naeyc.org) offers lists of such facilities to parents in every state.

Bottom Line

Whew! We're almost done. You've learned about cribs, pondered the car seat choice and now even pondered the best choices in childcare. But how much can you really save using our advice? The next chapter provides a summary of our budget versus the national averages.

CHAPTER 11

CONCLUSION

What Does it All Mean?

How much money can you save if you follow all the tips and suggestions in this book? Let's take a look at the average cost of having a baby from the introduction and compare it with our Baby Bargains budget.

Your Baby's First Year

ITEM	AVERAGE	BABY BARGAINS BUDGET
Crib, mattress, dresser, rocker	$1500	$1180
Bedding / Decor	$300	$200
Baby Clothes	$500	$340
Disposable Diapers	$600	$300
Maternity/Nursing Clothes	$1200	$540
Nursery items, high chair, toys	$400	$225
Baby Food/Formula	$900	$350
Stroller, Car Seat, Carrier	$400	$250
Miscellaneous	$500	$500
TOTAL	$6300	$3885
TOTAL SAVINGS:		***$2415***

WOW! YOU CAN SAVE OVER $2400! We hope the savings makes it worth the price of this book. We'd love to hear from you on how much you saved with our book—feel free to email, write or call us. See the "How to Reach Us" page at the back of this book.

What does it all mean?

At this point, we usually have something pithy to say as we end the book. But, as parents of two boys, we're just too tired. We're going to bed, so feel free to make up your own ending.

And thanks for reading *Baby Bargains*.

APPENDIX A
Canada

$20,612.

Yes, that's the average cost of raising a child to age two in Canada (see chart on the next page). With those costs, Canadian parents need bargains just as much as parents in the U.S.!

Here's an overview of our best bargains sources for Canada.

Recap of Canadian sources

Many of the brands reviewed earlier are based in Canada. For example, crib makers AP, Cara Mia, Morigeau, Ragazzi and others are reviewed in Chapter 2. Glider-rockers brands Shermag and Dutailier also are Canadian brands, of course.

In this section, we will focus on Canada's best bargains, baby stores and outlets. But be sure to read earlier sections of this book to find general reviews of Canadian baby product brands.

Layette Items and Diapers

If you're looking for great shoes for your little one, reader Teri Dunsworth recommends Canadian-made **Robeez** (800) 929-2623 or (604) 929-6818; web: www.robeez.com. "They are the most AWESOME shoes—I highly recommend them," she said in an email. Robeez are made of leather, have soft skid-resistant soles and are machine washable. They start at $22 for a basic pair. "My baby wears nothing else! They have infant and toddler sizes and oh-so-cute patterns." Another reader recommended New Zealand made **Bobux** shoes (www.bobuxusa.com). These cute leather soft soles "do the trick" by staying on extremely well according to our reader.

A Canadian clothing manufacturer to look for in stores near you is **Baby's Own** by St. Lawrence Textiles (613) 632-8565.

The Mercedes of the cloth diaper category is Canada-made **Mother-Ease** (www.mother-ease.com), a brand that has a fanatical following among cloth diaper devotees. Suffice it to say, they ain't cheap but the quality is excellent. Mother-Ease sells both fitted diapers and covers; the diapers run $9 to $10 a pop, while the covers are about $9.75. Before you invest $73 to $375 in one of Mother-Ease's special package deals, consider trying their "introductory offer" (see details below in our money-saving tips section).

Other parents like **Kushies** (800) 841-5330 (web: www.kushies.com), another Canadian product. This brand offers several models.

One note: both Kushies and Mother-Ease are sold via mail-order only. Yes, you can sometimes find these diapers at second-hand or thrift stores, but most parents buy them via a catalog or on the 'net. Kushies are trying to branch out into retail stores—check your local baby specialty shop.

TC KidCo (888) 825-4326 is another Canadian catalog that sells "Indisposables" all-in-one cloth diapers and diaper covers. You can buy from the catalog or from their direct representative. The catalog also has nursing bras, blankets, bibs and more.

Maternity

Toronto-based *Breast is Best* catalog sells a wide variety of nursing tops, blouses and dresses as well as maternity wear. For a free catalog and fabric swatches, call (877) 837-5439 toll free or check out their web site at www.breastisbest.com.

Looking for plus-size maternity or petites? Canadian maternity maker *Maternal Instinct* has a catalog and web site (www.maternal-instinct.com; 877-MATERNAL). The line is also sold in a dozen stores in Canada (and another dozen or so in the U.S.). "They don't have a huge catalog inventory," writes one Vancouver mom, "but it's a nice, simple selection of plus-size and petite work and casual maternity clothes with a few pieces of formalwear thrown in."

CANADA FIGURES

What does it cost to raise a child in Canada? These figures are from Manitoba, but are a good general guide for most Canadian parents. Costs of raising a child to age two (total cost for two years):

FOOD	$2,311
CLOTHING	2,119
HEATH CARE	282
PERSONAL CARE	112
RECREATION	571
CHILD CARE	10,768
SHELTER	4,451
TOTAL	**$20,612**

Figures are for 2004 in Canadian dollars. Source: Manitoba government web page (http://www.gov.mb.ca/agriculture/homeec/).

Carriers

Mountain Equipment Co-operative (MEC; web: www.mac.ca) is a unique, not-for-profit member owned co-op that sells baby carriers (among other outdoor products). A reader in Ottawa emailed us a rave for their "excellent" backpack carriers that are "renown for their excellent quality." At C$159, the MEC backpack carrier "clearly beats Kelty Kids and other U.S.-made carriers" at a much lower price. MEC has stores in major cities in Canada; call 800-747-7704 for details.

Canadian parents also write to us with kudos for the *Baby Trekker* (800) 665-3957; web: www.babytrekker.com. This 100% washable cotton carrier has straps around the waist for support. Canucks like the fact a baby can be dressed in a snowsuit and still fit in the Baby Trekker. The carrier ($80 US, $102 Canada) is available in baby stores in Canada.

Our readers also recommend *Outbound*, a Canadian manufacturer (www.outbound.ca) that offers three frame carriers, the Kiddie Carrier, the Toddler Tote and the Cub Carrier with prices ranging from $139 Canadian to $219 Readers also praise the *Tatonka Baby Carrier* ($136) from another Canadian manufacturer, Sherpa Mountain (www.sherpa-mtn.com).

Web Resources

Canadian Parents Online (www.canadianparents.com) is a great resource, with advice columns, chat/discussion areas and recall info for Canadian parents. We liked their "Ask an Expert" areas, which included advice on childbirth, lactation and even fitness.

The *Childcare Resources and Research Unit* (www.childcare-canada.org) has great info and statistics on childcare costs in Canada.

Sears may not have a catalog any more in the U.S., but the Canadian version of *Sears* (www.sears.ca) has both a web site and printed catalog with baby products and clothes. A reader said the catalog has a nice selection of products and is a great resource for Canadian parents who might live outside the major metro areas.

Baby gear shopping in Canada

Toronto mom Rhonda Lewis scouted the best baby stores and bargain sources in Canada for us (and did a great job, we must say). Here's her report:

Toronto

Macklem's *416-531-7188, www.macklems.com.* Family run business in Downtown area. Well known for stroller/pram repairs. Friendly and knowledgeable staff. Good selection of strollers, including Zooper Zydeco, Jazz, Boogie ($550), Swing ($249), Waltz ($239), Tango, Rhumba, Maclaren (Triumph $260, Techno $425, Global $475 and other models), Peg (high chairs, double strollers, umbrellas, travel systems), Bertini. They also carry products by Baby Bjorn, Britax and Dutailier to name a few. Good selection of bedding (four, five, and six piece sets from $99) and cribs including: AP, EG, Morigeau Lepine. Parking is available on the street nearby.

Dearborn Baby Express *72 Doncaster Avenue, Thornhill 905-881-3334.* Small store, crammed with merchandise. Wide selection of strollers, car seats, gliders and furniture. Infant car seats range from $159 to $239 and toddler car seats (rear and front facing) range from $189 to $350. Brands include Peg, Graco, Kidco, Evenflo, Inglesina. For furniture, brands include Pali, Morigeau Lepine, Generations and Cara Mia. If you're looking for double strollers they do have a few Peg & Baby Trend. However, it is very hard to maneuver strollers around store as it is so full. Bargains are limited, usually on end of year models. Lots of toys, layette accessories. The parking lot does get very busy, but you can usually find a spot.

Nestings' Kids *418 Eglinton Avenue W, 416-322-0511. 2835 W. Fourth Avenue, Vancouver, 604-734-5437. www.nestingskids.com* If you want exceptional furnishings, bedding, furniture, look no further than Nestings. They carry Morigeau-Lepine, EP and AG cribs. Their windows are always gorgeous and they carry great, unique items, but at a steep price. Cribs range from $848 to $2695. Lamps can be purchased for up to $395. They have very cute, whimsical lampshade nightlights which are $40 and custom bedding is priced around $1000. Parking is available on the street, or at a lot just to the west of the building.

Baby's Room Warehouse *Hwy 400 & 89, in Cookstown Outlet Mall (705) 458- 8050* Specializing in baby bedding, accessories, cribs and furnishings at wholesale prices. Cribs range from $189 to $649. Brands include Little Angel, EG and Cara Mia. They also offer discount packages consisting of a crib, mattress and bedding. There are many kinds of fabric to choose from for bedding ($99-$289), or if you cannot find something you like, simply bring your fabric of choice to them, and they'll create the bedding, typically 5-6 piece sets. Mattresses are $50, $60 or $100. Store is open Monday-Friday 10-9, Saturday and Sunday from 9-6.

Wal-mart. Great place to stock up on accessories and toys Difficult to see car seats and strollers as they are tied down and above eye level for safety reasons. Good place to go if you've done your research elsewhere and are shopping for the lowest prices. Example: Diaper Genie ($35.95 at Wal-mart compared to $49.95 elsewhere, $42.95 at Toys R Us).

Costco often has excellent products at great prices. They have carried highchairs, jogging strollers, gliders and other products. The only problem is that you never know what they will have and once it is out of stock, they typically do not reorder. Check often and ask anyone you know who is going there to check too. Items tend to sell quickly as their prices are superb.

Some **Toys R Us** locations also have **Babies R Us** stores where you can register. Prices relatively competitive, watch for flyers for sales. You receive a free gift package just for registering which is great.

Sears has a wonderful registry program called "Waiting Game" where you can guess the date that your baby will be born. You can change that date twice before you are seven months pregnant. If you guess the correct date, you get gift certificates in the amount of money you and your friends spent on your registry. It is free to join and you also receive a gift package just for taking the time to register.

Toronto Outlets

DIAPERS ETC. OUTLET STORE

734 Kipling Avenue, Etobicoke (416) 503-0313; 90 Northline Rd, North York (416) 752-0222; 7 Stafford Dr., Brampton (905) 450-1955; Ann Street, Barrie, (705) 721-9555

Save up to 45% on baby supplies from cribs, car seats, strollers and playpens to smaller items such as bottles, creams and soothers. A Luna crib is $179. Brands for strollers and car seats include Evenflo, Graco and Eddie Bauer. There are great deals on bulk packages of diapers (generic brand) and baby wipes. Parents of twins can save an extra 10% on purchases. Call store for hours.

ROOTS OUTLET STORE

120 Orfus Rd., (416) 781-8729

Great savings on Roots fashions for babies and the whole family including pajamas, sweats, jeans, hats, jackets. Discounts vary, but items have been seen at 80% off. Call for store hours. Parking is available at the back of the store.

SNUGABYE FACTORY OUTLET

188 Bentworth Ave. (416) 783-0300

Save up to 50% on Canadian-made, brand-name baby clothing and sleepwear ranging in sizes from newborn to 6X. They have great prices on items like crib sheets ($5.99 to $9.99). Bedding choices change seasonally and they do sell the occasional mobile. Hours are 10-5, Monday to Saturday.

And more: Mattel Outlet *Mississauga Outlet 905-501-5147 Cookstown Outlet Mall 705-458-4144. Southworks Mall 519-620-4211. www.mattdoutletonline.com* offers a range of discontinued, closeout and excess product stock for toys at value prices, 50% savings on many toy items. Check the web site for monthly specials on toys and baby baskets. In fact, the Cookstown Outlet Mall has many other stores, offering a wide selection of accessories, clothing, footwear, gifts for the whole family. It's worth it to drive up and spend a few hours, you can save hundreds off regular retail prices!

Toronto Maternity Clothing

There are many maternity shops in Toronto which are excellent.

Rhonda Maternity *(416) 921-3116 www.rhondamaternity.com* offers a wide range of career wear. Prices are high ($100+ for pants), but quality and service are excellent and they have a wide selection of merchandise including bathing suits in season and evening dresses. Another store that recently opened, ***Kick****, 454 Eglinton Avenue West* has the latest trends in maternity wear. Or, try ***Modern Maternity****, 3329 Yonge Street, 416-322-6565 www.modernmaternity.com* for casual clothes (Bathing suits $75, long black skirt $105 and tank dresses for fancier outings at $189 plus wrap $49).

Secrets from your sister *476 Bloor St. W. Telephone: 416-538-1234.* Beautiful lingerie in realistic sizes for all women. Bra fitting experts can fit you in maternity, nursing, sports or everyday bras.

Old Navy has four stores in Canada that sell maternity wear, a few of which are in the Greater Toronto Area (Promenade Mall and Mississauga Square One Mall). They have a great return policy so if you stock up at the beginning of your pregnancy and don't end up needing some items, you can return them at any time with your receipt. Watch for great sales as their merchandise often goes on sale.

If you happen to be near Thunder Bay, there is a store called ***Moms To Be Factory Outlet*** where they sell breast pumps, maternity clothes, strollers and bedding (800) 524-6973.

Thyme Maternity is the largest maternity chain in Canada and they have locations in every province. Their fabric choices are at times clingy, but their merchandise turnover is high and they receive new shipments often. The location at Yorkdale Mall probably has the best selection. The prices are a bit high, but often you can find merchandise on sale at the end of season and during promotions. Sweater prices are $30 to $50, pants were on sale at $25 to $60. They also sell bras, underwear, swimwear, pajamas and formal wear.

Bravado Designs www.bravadodesigns.com, a Toronto based company, has an excellent selection of funky, great quality bras ($37) for both pregnancy and breast-feeding, and underwear ($15). This company encourages women to maintain their style during pregnancy with funky, unique prints.

Toronto Resources & More

Help! We've Got Kids www.helpwevegotkids.com is a unique Children's Reference Directory book for Toronto which was put together over 10 years ago by two young mothers. It is updated yearly. There are many coupons in the back, valued at over $4000.

Cuddle Karrier. www.cuddlekarrier.com 1-877-283-3535 A popular carrier from newborn to toddler. There are eight ways to use it. $60.

BabySteps Children's Fund www.babystepsgiftshop.com or call 905-707-1030. Personalized gifts for all. Puzzle stools, coat racks & more. Baby's 1st Year/School Frames for monthly baby/annual school photos. Funky hairbrushes and much more. All proceeds to Hospital for Sick Children. They offer a wonderful selection of great gifts at reasonable prices and the money supports the hospital.

Today's Parent Magazine www.todaysparent.com is available monthly at a price of $18.14 including GST (savings of 65% off newsstand if you order for one-year). It's an excellent national magazine, offering insight into parenting issues, nutrition, holidays, activities, etc.

Mothering 'n more www.motheringnmore.com is a new organization dedicated to providing education, preparation and support to women in their mothering years. They offer pre- and post-natal courses designed women to come while pregnant and then after with their newborns. Topics include nutrition, CPR, strollers, baby massage, and more.

Vancouver

Crocodile *1946 West 4th Avenue, Vancouver, 604-730-0232 www.crocodilebaby.com* They carry a wide range of strollers, including the Peg Pliko ($319), Maclaren Techno ($489), Maclaren Triumph ($279), Mountain Buddy Urban Jogger ($499) and the Bugaboo Frog ($1050). They sell cribs (the number one seller is $439), change tables, gliders with ottomans ($529). Peg Perego high chairs are sold from $219-$239. They sell car seats too including Graco, Peg Perego and Britax. You can find toys, videos and other child-friendly items. Parking is available at the back of the store.

Baby's World *6-1300 Woolridge Street, Coquitlam, BC 604-515-0888 www.itsababysworld.com* Furniture lines include AP and EG. They have a large selection of strollers including Inglesina and Peg Perego. Sample prices include: Peg Atlantico $449, Peg Pliko $369, Peg Pliko Pramette $519, Snap 'n Go $129, Inglesina Zippy $399 and Inglesina Swift $209. They also have a Chicco Caddy umbrella stroller with tall handles, a rain cover and carrying bag for sale at $129. Peg car seats are $239 and Graco infant car seats are $189. They have Baby Bjorns from $129.

Vancouver Maternity Clothing

Hazel & Company *3190 Cambie St 604-730-8689* They carry a wide selection of their own brands and other well-known brands. Offer casual and dressy clothes (mix & match two-piece set, tops run from $65 to $75 and skirts $59). Jean brands include Rebel, Tummyline, Duet and range from $50 to $95 (low-rise are more expensive). They do carry Bravado undergarments, maternity bras $37 and underwear $15. Open seven days a week. There are two parking spots behind the store, otherwise look for lot parking nearby.

Thyme Maternity *www.thymematernity.com* has several locations in British Columbia including: Burnaby, Richmond, Victoria, Surrey, Coquitlam, Abbotsford.

Formes *www.formesvancouver.com* They have locations in Toronto, Montreal and Vancouver. Their merchandise is very expensive ($170 for sweaters, $140 bathing suits) but quality and styles are excellent. If you are looking for something for a special event, you may want to check this stores out.

Maternal Instinct *3673 W.4th Avenue, 604-738-8300 www.maternal-instinct.com* This company has a retail location in Vancouver and a comprehensive web site. They sell dresses for all occasions, ranging from $65-$135, pants from $29 to $79, a wide range of skirts in many styles from $29 to $70. Excellent quality and fashionable merchandise at a wide range of prices. They also carry yoga wear, bathing suits, hosiery and underwear and breast pumps.

Kid Clothing & Consignment

Boomers & Echoes Kid's & Maternity, *1985 Lonsdale Ave. (at 20th) 604-984-6163* Boomers and Echoes carries: new and consigned quality items; new maternity including Rebel, Ripe, Duet, Bravado & Gem (jeans from $15, tops from $9.95 including tanks, nursing tops); seasonal clothing such as capris, shorts, sweaters is always available. New kids' wear including Robeez, Kushies, Baby Byon, Jelly Beans, Vals Kids & more; consignment including maternity and kids wear (by appointment only); car seats, strollers, furniture. Boomers and Echoes takes great pride in re-merchandising the store with new and consignment and ensures stock reflects current fashions. Large turnover of inventory but items such as a Chariot Jogger ($375) and Peg Perego Pliko ($149) have been seen there. Plenty of parking in back.

Little Critters Outfitters *5631-176A St., Cloverdale (604) 575-2500* is children's store carrying new and nearly new clothing, toys, furniture and accessories at a fraction of the original price. They offer the style and quality of brand names such as Gap, Oshkosh, Tommy, Gymboree, V-tech, Fisher Price, Little Tikes and Discovery Toys. Examples of prices include a Gap Fleece Hoody ($15), Girls Cardigan ($18-$20) and toys are for sale at approximately 50% off original prices. They also feature a great selection of new and consigned dance wear. Their Critter Card program gives you 10%-20% back on all your purchases and there is no fee to join.

Trendy Tots: *22344 Dewdney Trunk Rd, Maple Ridge, (604) 467-0330* Name-brand clothing, books, videos, toys and infant care items! Trendy Tots offers a great alternative to consignment. The store buys your items outright. All seasons of clothing from newborn to teen and maternity wear are accepted, as are baby equipment, furniture and toys. Trendy Tots only accepts items in excellent condition. No appointment is necessary.

Online Resources

◆ Don't want to leave the comfort of your home? Visit *www.canadaretail.ca/Babies.html* for Canadian baby products, priced in Canadian dollars. Tons of links and resources for local and national shopping.

◆ Here are some web sites that offer discounts for parents of multiples: *http://www.multiplebirthscanada.org/~vimba/discounts.html*. Brand offerings include: Huggies, Pampers, Diaper Genie, Similac, Evenflo

◆ For you crafty people out there who are looking to document the first years of their babies lives, check out **Scrapbook Warehouse** *www.scrapbookwarehouse.com* for the latest in scrapbooks, accessories, cutters, stickers. They carry over 5000 products and have over 100 scrapbooks ranging from $12 to $60. They will teach you how to use the products you buy (i.e. cutters and scissors) so that you will have no problems when you get home. (604) 266-4433. They also offer classes. 8932 Oak St. @ Marine Dr. They are located about 5 minutes from the Vancouver Airport.

◆ *Local Guides to Pregnancy and Parenting Resources.* There are interesting articles/sections on topics including: coupons and freebies, classes for kids, summer camps, pregnancy, breastfeeding, vacation guide, etc. You can also track your pregnancy with a daily journal. *toronto.babyzone.com. vancouver.babyzone.com, montreal.babyzone.com*

Vancouver Parenting Support Groups

Kerrisdale Parent-Infant Group—Pacific Spirit Community Health Centre *2110 West 43rd Avenue* 261-6366 New moms and their babies (0-8 months) meet on Wednesdays at 10:30 am at the community centre. Phone for more information.

New Parents Group—Langley Health Unit *22033 Fraser Highway, Langley,* 604-532-2300 New parents and their babies (up to 9 months) are welcome to drop in on Wednesdays from 10 to 11:30 am to discuss parenting, infant development, nutrition, dental and safety concerns.

Parent-Infant Drop In—Coal Harbour Community Center *480 Broughton Street, Vancouver* 604-718-8222 Parents and their babies from birth to 6 months meet every Tuesday from 1:30 to 3 pm in Activity Room 103 to discuss development, growth, feeding, sleeping and much more. No appointment necessary.

Parent-Infant Drop In—False Creek Community Centre *1318 Cartwright Street, Vancouver, BC* 604-257-8195 Parents and their babies meet every Thursday from 1:30 to 3 pm to discuss development, growth, feeding, sleeping and much more. Parents of newborns to 4 months meet upstairs and parents of babies 4 to 6 months meet downstairs. No appointment necessary.

Dial-a-Dietitian *www.dialadietitian.org (604) 732-9191; 1-800-663-3438* A registered dietician available to answer your general and medical nutrition questions over the phone from 9 am to 5 pm Monday to Friday. Service available in English, Punjabi or Chinese. *Free to residents of BC.*

Montreal

Bambino 6572 Papineau, Mtl (514) 729-2901 www.bambinofurni-ture.com A family run business since 1985, they offer service in both English and French. There are a variety of coupons offered on their web site including $100 off purchase of any three-piece furniture set, $15 off rocking chair and $20 off any stroller. They carry products by Peg, Evenflo, Dutailier, Graco and Safety First including swings, highchairs, Graco Pack 'n Plays, baby baths, etc.

La Mere Helene 7577A Edouard, Ville LaSalle, 514-368-2959 www.merehelene.com This store offers maternity wear as well as items for your baby. Maternity items include: tops & skirts $95 for combo, jeans $60 and skirts from $25. They also sell Graco double strollers $209-$269, car seat with duo travel systems, or car seats only $145. Graco Metro Lite travel system is $299. Graco swings are $154-$159. Diaper bags are available too $30-$50, Baby Carrier $65. There are also lots of stuffed animals and whimsical items for sale.

Jeunes d'ici 134 Laurier St. West, Montreal, 514-270-5512 www.jeunesdici.com In business since 1979, this store offers furniture, exclusive bedding and decorative accessories. Cribs start at $725 and brands include Ragazzi, Generation, EG, Natart. Bedding starts at $498 for five-piece sets, lamps $160 and drawer pulls $13.50.

Junior Furniture 9520 Maurice-Duplessis, Riviere-des-Prairies, Montreal (514) 643-1450 www.juniorbaby.com Established in 1998 by two fathers who did not have a good experience when they themselves were shopping for baby furniture/items for their own children. The focus of the store is on customer service and an enjoyable shopping experience. They carry many strollers, high chairs, accessories including Peg Perego Venezia $429, Graco Metro Lite $249, Inglesina Swift, Zippy. Other brands include Manhattan Baby, Avent, Morigeau Lepine, EG, Status Furniture. They have liquidation sales on their floor models of furniture and can put together packages including a crib, change table and armoire at discounted prices.

Bummis 123 Mont-Royal ouest Montreal, Quebec, Canada (514) 289-9855 www.bummis.com Nursing/maternity bras and underwear by Bravado Designs, nursing pillows, and nursing clothes. Herbal products by Clef des Champs, Lunar Eclipse and Substance Company for pregnancy, nursing, postpartum, and beyond. Coming soon—a line of funky and comfortable maternity clothes.

Additional resources for Montreal are on our web site, BabyBargains.com (click on Bonus Material).

APPENDIX B

Sample registry

Here's the coolest thing about registering for baby products at Babies R Us—that neato bar code scanner gun. You're supposed to walk (waddle?) around the store and zap the bar codes of products you want to add to the registry. This is cool for about 15 seconds, until you realize you have to make DECISIONS about WHAT to zap.

What to do? Yes, you could page through this book as you do the registry, but that's a bit of a pain, no? To help speed the process, here's a list of what stuff you need and what to avoid. Consider it *Baby Bargains* in a nutshell:

The order of these recommendations follows the Babies R Us Registry form:

Car Seats/Strollers/Carriers/Accessories

◆ **Full Size Convertible Car Seat.** Basically, we urge waiting on this one—most babies don't need to go into a full-size convertible seat until they outgrow an infant seat (that could be in four to six months or as much as a year). In the meantime, new models are always coming out with better safety features. Hence, don't register for this and wait to buy it later.

If want to ignore this advice, go for the **Britax Roundabout** ($180 to $200). Two other good choices for less money: the **Graco ComfortSport** ($80 to $140) or the **Combi Avatar** ($160).

◆ **Infant car seat.** Best bet: the **Graco "SnugRide"** ($70 to $150).

◆ **Strollers.** There is no "one size fits all" recommendation in this section. Read the lifestyle recommendations in Chapter 8 to find a stroller that best fits your needs. In general, stay away from the pre-packaged "travel systems"—remember that many of the better stroller brands now can be used with infant seats.

◆ **Baby Carriers.** *Baby Bjorn* ($90). You really don't need another carrier (like a backpack) unless you plan to do serious outdoor hikes. If that is the case, check Chapter 8 for suggestions.

◆ **Misc.** Yes, your infant car seat should come with an infant head support pillow, so if you buy one of these separately, use it in your stroller. There really isn't a specific brand preference in this category (all basically do the same thing). Any other stroller accessories are purely optional.

Travel Yards/High Chairs/Exercisers/Accessories

◆ **Gates.** The best brand is **KidCo** (which makes the Gateway, Safeway and Elongate). But this is something you can do later—most babies aren't mobile until at least six months of age.

◆ **Travel Yard/Playard.** Graco's **Pack 'N Play** is the best bet. Go for one with a bassinet feature.

◆ **High Chair.** The best high chair is the Fisher Price Healthy Care ($90)—go for the Deluxe or Linkadoos version.

◆ **Walker/Exerciser.** Skip the walker; an excerciser is optional. Good model: ExerSaucer Classic Activity Center. See Chapter 7 for details.

◆ **Swing.** We like Graco's swings ($70 to $120) best.

◆ **Hook on high chair.** Not really necessary; if you want one, get it later. We review hook-on chairs in our other book, *Toddler Bargains*.

◆ **Infant jumper.** Too many injuries with this product category; pass on it.

◆ **Bed rail.** Don't need this either.

◆ **Bouncer.** Fisher Price (www.fisher-price.com) makes the most popular one in the category—their basic bouncer is about $25.

Cribs/Furniture

◆ **Crib.** For cribs, you've got two basic choices: a simple model that is, well, just a crib or a "convertible" model that eventually morphs into a twin or full size bed. In the simple category for best buys, **Child Craft's 10171** is a basic hardwood crib with single-drop side for just $200. Other features that are nice (but not necessary) for cribs include a double drop side, a quiet rail release and hidden hardware. If you fancy an imported crib, there are few bargains but we found that **Sorelle/C&T** has reasonable prices ($200 to start) for above average quality.

◆ **Bassinet.** Skip it. See Chapter 2 for details. If you buy a playpen with bassinet feature, you don't need a separate bassinet.

◆ **Dressing/changing table.** Skip it. Just use the top of your dresser as a changing area. (See dresser recommendation below.)

◆ **Glider/rocker and ottoman.** In a word: *Dutailier*. Whatever style/fabric you chose, you can't go wrong with that brand. Hint: this is a great product to buy online at a discount, so you might want to skip registering for one. **Shermag** is another great brand.

◆ **Dresser.** Dressers and other case pieces by **Rumble Tuff** were great deals—they exactly match the finishes of Child Craft and Simmons, but at prices 10% to 25% less than the competition. We liked their three-drawer combo unit that combines a changing table and a dresser for $500 to $600. Unfortunately, Rumble Tuff isn't sold in chain stores like Babies R Us (see chapter 2 for details). Another good brand: Munire.

◆ **Misc.** Babies R Us recommends registering for all sorts of miscellaneous items like cradles, toy boxes and the like. Obviously, these are clearly optional.

Bedding/Room Décor/Crib Accessories

◆ **Crib set.** Don't—don't register for this waste of money. Instead, just get two or three good crib sheets and a nice cotton blanket or the Halo Sleep Sack. See Chapter 3 for brands.

◆ **Bumper pads, dust ruffle, diaper stacker.** Ditto—a waste.

◆ **Lamp, mobile.** These are optional, of course. We don't have any specific brand preferences.

◆ **Mattress.** We like the foam mattresses from **Colgate** ($120 for the Classica I). Or, for coil, go for **Simmons** Super Maxipedic 160 coil mattress for $100 at Babies R Us. Unfortunately, Babies R Us and other chains don't sell foam mattresses but you can find them online.

◆ **Misc.** Babies R Us has lots of miscellaneous items in this area like rugs, wallpaper border, bassinet skirts and so on. We have ideas for décor on the cheap in Chapter 3.

Infant Toys, Care & Feeding

◆ **Toys:** All of this (crib toys, bath toys, blocks) is truly optional. We have ideas for this in Chapter 6.

◆ **Nursery monitor.** In general, *Fisher Price* and *Sony* are the best bets but keep the receipt—many baby monitors don't work well because of electronic interference in the home.

◆ **Humidifier.** The *Holmes/Duracraft* line sold in Target is best. Avoid the "baby" humidifiers sold in baby stores, as they are overpriced.

◆ **Diaper pail.** The *Baby Trend Diaper Champ* is best.

◆ **Bathtub.** While not a necessity, a baby bath tub is a nice convenience—try to borrow one or buy it second hand to save. As a best bet, we suggest the *EuroBath by Primo*—it's a $25 bath tub that works well.

◆ **Bottles.** *Avent* is the best bet, according to our readers.

◆ **Bottle Warmer.** Also optional. Avent's *Express Bottle and Baby Food Warmer* ($40) can heat a bottle in four minutes. *The First Years "Night & Day Bottle Warmer System"* ($30) is an alternative. It steam heats two 8 oz. bottles in under five minutes (one reader said its more like three minutes). For night-time feedings, it can keep two bottles cool for up to eight hours (so there's no need to run to the kitchen).

◆ **Sterilizer.** Also optional, *Avent's "Microwave Steam Sterilizer"* ($25-30) is a good choice. It holds four bottles of any type and is easy to use—just put in water and nuke for eight minutes.

◆ **Thermometer.** Don't register for a fancy thermometer—the cheap options at the drug store work just as well. *First Years* has a high-speed digital thermometer ($10) that gives a rectal temp in 20 seconds and an underarm in 30 seconds. Ear thermometers are not recommended, as they are not accurate.

◆ **Breast pump.** There isn't a "one size fits all" recommendation here. Read Chapter 5 Maternity/Nursing for details.

◆ **Misc.** In this category, Babies R Us throws in items like bibs, hooded towels, washcloths, pacifiers and so on. See Chapter 4 "Reality Layette" for ideas in this category.

Diapers/Wipes

◆ **Diapers.** For disposables, the best deals are in warehouse clubs like *Sam's* and *Costco*. Generic diapers at *Wal-Mart* and *Target* are also good deals. We have a slew of deals on cloth diapers in Chapter 4.

◆ **Wipes.** Brands like *Pampers Baby Fresh* and *Huggies* are the better bets, although some parents love the generic wipes that Costco stocks.

Clothing/Layette

◆ See the "Reality Layette" list (Ch. 4) for suggestions on quantities/brands.

APPENDIX C

Multiples advice

Yes, this year, one in 35 births in the US is to twins. As a parent-to-be of twins and that can mean double the fun when it comes to buying for baby. Here's our round-up of what products are best for parents of multiples:

Cribs

Since twins tend to be smaller than most infants, parents of multiples can use bassinets or cradles for an extended period of time. We discuss this category in depth in Chapter 2, but generally recommend looking at a portable playpen (Graco Pak N Play is one popular choice) with a bassinet feature as an alternative. A nice splurge if your budget allows it: the *Arm's Reach Co-Sleeper*.

Cool idea: a mom of twins emailed us about a crib divider for $25 that lets you use one crib for twins. Available on MoreThanOne.com.

Nursing help

Check out *EZ-2-NURSE's pillow* (800-584-TWIN; we saw it on www.doubleblessings.com). A mom told us this was the "absolute best" for her twins, adding "I could not successfully nurse my girls together without this pillow. It was wonderful." This pillow comes in both foam and inflatable versions (including a pump). Cost: $40 to $48.

Wal-Mart has a breastfeeding collection with *Lansinoh* products (including their amazing nipple cream). Check the special displays in the store or on their web site at www.walmart.com.

Yes, nursing one baby can be a challenge, but two? You might need some help. To the rescue comes *Mothering Multiples: Breastfeeding & Caring for Twins and More* by Karen Kerkoff Gromada ($14.95; available on the La Leche League web site, www. lalecheleague.com). This book was recommend to us by more than one mother of twins for its clear and concise advice.

FYI: Skip buying a glider-rocker if you plan to nurse your twins. The large nursing pillows won't fit! Instead, go for a loveseat.

Car seats

Most multiples are born before their due date. The smallest infants may have to ride in special "car beds" that enable them to lie flat (instead of car seats that require an infant to be at least five or six pounds and ride in a sitting position). The car beds then rotate to become regular infant car seats so older infants can ride in a sitting position.

The **Cosco's Ultra Dream Ride** ($50–$55, www.coscoinc.com) can be used up to 20 pounds and 26 inches. The only criticism we heard of the Cosco bed: sometimes it is a bit difficult to put in a smaller car when in the car bed position. For years, the Cosco Dream Ride was the only choice in this category. Now, a new company, **Angel Guard**, is selling a Preemie Infant Car Bed for $100. The key feature: a wrap-around harness to protect a preemie in an accident. See it online at ShowerYourBaby.com

Another idea: check with your hospital to see if you can RENT a car bed until your baby is large enough to fit in a regular infant car seat.

Strollers

Our complete wrap-up of recommendations for double strollers is in Chapter 8 (see Double the Fun in the lifestyle recommendations). In brief, we should mention that the **Graco DuoGlider** accepts two infant seats ($250 for a travel system that includes one infant seat). Evenflo sells a similar travel system with their Take Me Too tandem ($225).

If Grandma is paying for a stroller as a gift, Perego's **Duette** double stroller ($540) allows parents of twins to attach TWO infant car seats (included) to the G-matic frame. (And there is also a **"Triplette"** version of this stroller).

Those strollers are great since they can handle two infant car seats, but most parents of twins find that side-by-side strollers do better for them than tandem (front/back) models. Why? Tandem strollers typically only have one seat that fully reclines (when parents of twins find they need two reclining seats). And the front/back configuration seems to invite more trouble when the twins get older—the back passenger pulling the front passenger's hair, etc.

Here are our picks for side by side strollers. For parents of twins on a tight budget, we suggest the **Jeep Twin All Weather Twin Sport Umbrella** (27 lbs.) for $72 at Wal-Mart. It's bare bones (no basket) but will get the job done with reclining seats and a compact fold. If you've got a bit more budget, the **Inglesina Double Swift** ($200, 28 lbs.) gets rave reviews from our readers, as does the **Maclaren Twin Traveler** ($350, 25 lbs.) with its full reclining seats. Another good bet: the **Zooper Tango** ($270, 26 lbs.), stylish yet still packed with extras. Finally, for outdoor treks with twins, we like the **Mountain Buggy's** side-by-side all-terrain strollers—very pricey at $420 to $650 but built to last.

In the dark horse category, consider the **Double Decker Stroller** (941-543-1582; www.doubledeckerstroller.com), a jogging stroller than can accommodate two infant car seats. It runs $260. New this year is the "Triple Decker," a model that will hold three babies!

As for other jogging strollers, the side-by-side versions of **Dreamer Design** and **Kool Stop** are probably best if you really plan to exercise with a sport stroller. The tandem jogger by **Gozo** (again, see Chapter 8) is an interesting alternative as well.

Carrier

A mom of twins emailed us to rave about the *MaxiMom* carrier. She found it easier to use and adjust. The best feature: you adjust it to be a sling and nurse a baby in it. We saw this carrier on 4CoolKids (4coolkids.com) for $100 for twins; a triplet version is $125.

Deals/Freebies

◆ Chain stores like Babies R Us and Baby Depot offer a 10% discount if you buy multiples of identical items like cribs.

◆ Get a *$7 off coupon for the Diaper Genie from Playtex* when you send proof of multiple births to Playtex (800) 222-0453; www.playtex.com.

◆ *Kimberly Clark Twins Program:* Get a gift of "high-value coupons" for Huggies diapers by submitting birth certificates or published birth announcements. (800) 544-1847).

◆ *The First Years* offers free rattles for parents of multiples when you send in copies of birth certificates. Web: www.thefirstyears.com.

◆ *The National Mothers of Twins Clubs* (www.nomotc.org) has fantastic yard/garage sales. Check their web page for a club near you.

Source: Twins Magazine is a bi-monthly, full-color magazine published by The Business Word (800) 328-3211 or (303) 290-8500 (www.twinsmagazine.com). Remember that offers can change at any time. Check with the companies first before sending any info.

Miscellaneous

For clothes, make sure you get "preemie" sizes instead of the suggestions in our layette chapter—twins are smaller at birth than singleton babies.

BabyBeat is a fetal monitoring device that lets you listen to your babies' heartbeats as early as 10-12 weeks. Best of all, BabyBeat lets you rent the device instead of buying—$30 to $50 per month depending on the model. You can also buy the unit at $450 to $549. For details, call 888-758-8822 or www.babybeat.com. Unlike cheaper ultrasound monitors that are low-quality, BabyBeat is similar to the Doppler instruments found in doctor's offices. FYI: You must have a prescription from your doctor before purchasing a fetal monitor; be sure to check with your OB before any purchase.

APPENDIX D
Phone/Web Sites

Contract Name	Toll-Free	Phone	Web Site
General Baby Product Manufacturers			
Baby Trend	(800) 328-7363	(909) 773-0018	babytrend.com
Chicco	(877) 4-CHICCO		chiccousa.com
Cosco	(800) 457-5276	(812) 372-0141	coscoinc.com
Evenflo	(800) 233-5921	(937) 415-3229	evenflo.com
First Years	(800) 225-0382	(508) 588-1220	thefirstyears.com
Fisher Price	(800) 828-4000	(716) 687-3000	fisher-price.com
Graco	(800) 345-4109	(610) 286-5951	gracobaby.com
Peg Perego		(260) 482-8191	perego.com
Safety 1st	(800) 962-7233	(781) 364-3100	safety1st.com
Introduction			
Alan & Denise Fields (authors)		(303) 442-8792	babybargains.com
Chapter 2: Nursery Necessities			
JCPenney	(800) 222-6161		jcpenney.com
CPSC	(800) 638-2772		cpsc.gov
Baby Furniture Plus			babyfurnitureplus.com
Baby News			babynewsstores.com
NINFRA			ninfra.com
USA Baby			usababy.com
EcoBaby			ecobaby.com
Hoot Judkins			hootjudkins.com
Crib N Carriage			cribncarriage.com
Baby Furniture Outlet	(800) 613-9280	(519) 649-2590	babyfurnitureoutlet.com
Buy Buy Baby			buybuybaby.com
Babies R Us	(888) BABYRUS		babiesrus.com
Baby Depot	(800) 444-COAT		coat.com
Room & Board			roomandboard.com
Baby Furniture Warehouse			babyfurniturewarehouse.com
Fun Rugs			funrugs.com
Decorate Today			decoratetoday.com
Rugs USA			rugsusa.com
NetKidsWear			netkidswear.com
Baby Bunk			babybunk.com
Cosco (outlet)		(812) 526-0860	
Child Craft (outlet)		(812) 524-1999	
Kiddie Kastle (outlet)		(502) 499-9667	
Baby Boudoir (outlet)	(800) 272-2293	(508) 998-2166	
Pottery Barn (outlet)		(901) 763-1500	potterybarnkids.com
Baby Catalog America		(800) PLAY-PEN	babycatalog.com
Baby Style			babystyle.com
Pottery Barn Kids			PotteryBarnKids.com
Danny Foundation			dannyfoundation.org
Great Beginnings	(800) 886-9077	(301) 417-9702	childrensfurniture.com
Rocking Chair Outlet			rockingchairoutlet.com
Crib manufacturers			
Alta Baby	(888) 891-1489		altababyweb.com

Amby Baby Bed			AmbyBaby.com
Angel Line	(800) 889-8158	(856) 863-8009	angelline.com
AP Industries	(800) 463-0145	(418) 728-2145	apindustries.com
Baby's Dream	(800) TEL-CRIB	(912) 649-4404	babysdream.com
Bassett		(540) 629-6000	bassettfurniture.com
Bellini	(800) 332-BABY	(516) 234-7716	bellini.com
Berg		(908) 354-5252	bergfurniture.com
Bonavita	(888) 266-2848	(732) 346-5150	bonavita-cribs.com
Bratt Décor	(888) 24-BRATT	(410) 327-4600	brattedecor.com
Canalli		(973) 247-7222	canallifurniture.com
Cara Mia	(877) 728-0342	(705) 328-0342	caramiafurniture.com
Chanderic	(800) 363-2635	(819) 566-1515	www.shermag.com
Child Craft		(812) 883-3111	childcraftind.com
Corsican Kids	(800) 421-6247	(323) 587-3101	corsican.com
Generation 2	(800) 736-1140	(334) 792-1144	childdesigns.com
Delta		(718) 385-1000	deltaenterprise.com
Domusindo			domusindo.com
Ethan Allen	(888) EAHELP-1		ethanallen.com
Forever Mine	(800) 356-2742	(819) 297-2000	forevermine.com
Kinderkraft			kinderkraft.com
Luna	(888) 346-5862		lunaproducts.com
Million Dollar Baby		(323) 728-9988	milliondollarbaby.com
Morigeau/Lepine	(800) 326-2121	(724) 941-7475	morigeau.com
Mother Hubbard		(416) 661-8201	mhcfurniture.com
Munire	(973) 574-1040		MunireFurniture.com
Natart		(819) 364-2052	natartfurniture.com
Pali	(877) 725-4772		paliltaly.com
Petite Cheris	(800) 363-9817	(450) 772-2403	dutailier.com
PJ Kids	(800) 935-5060		pjkids.com
Pottery Barn	(800) 430-7373		potterybarnkids.com
Ragazzi		(514) 324-7886	ragazzi.com
Relics		(612) 374-0861	relicsfurniture.com
Sauder			sauder.com
Simmons		(920) 982-2140	simmonsjp.com.
Simplicity	(800) 448-4308		simplicityforchildren.com
Sorelle	(888) 470-1260	(201) 461-9444	sorellefurniture.com
Stanley	(888) 839-6822		stanleyfurniture.com
Stokke/Sleepi	(877) 978-6553		stokkeusa.com
Stork Craft		(604) 274-5121	storkcraft.com
Vermont Precision		(802) 888-7974	vtprecision.com
Babies Boutique			babiesboutique.com
IKEA		(610) 834-0180	ikea.com
JPMA		(856) 439-0500	jpma.org
Arm's Reach	(800) 954-9353		armsreach.com
Colgate		(404) 681-2121	colgatekids.com
Halo Innovations	(888) 999-4256	(218) 525-5158	halosleep.com
SIDS Alliance			SidsAlliance.org
Jupiter Industries			bopeepnurseryproducts.com
Sleep Tight Soother	(800) NO-COLIC		colic.com
Burlington Basket Co.	(800) 553-2300	(319) 754-6508	
Container Store	(800) 733-3532		containerstore.com
Rumble Tuff	(800) 524-9607	(801) 226-2648	rumbletuff.com
Camelot Furniture		(714) 283-4194	
Dutailier	(800) 363-9817	(450) 772-2403	dutailier.com
Rocking Chairs 100%	(800) 4-ROCKER		rocking-chairs.com
Brooks	(800) 427-6657	(423) 626-1111	
Conant Ball	(800) 363-2635	(819) 566-1515	
Relax-R	(800) 850-2909		

web/phone directory

Towne Square	(800) 356-1663		gliderrocker.com
American Health	(800) 327-4382		foryourbaby.com
Closet Maid	(800) 874-0008		closetmaid.com
Storage Pride	(800) 441-0337		
Lee Rowan	(800) 325-6150		leerowan.com
Hold Everything	(800) 421-2264		holdeverything.com
Closet Factory	(800) 692-5673		closetfactory.com
California Closets	(800) 274-6754		californiaclosets.com
Shades of Light	(800) 262-6612		shades-of-light.com

Chapter 3: Bedding & Décor

Baby Bedding Online			babybeddingonline.com
Baby's Best Buy			babiesbestbuy.com
Country Lane			countrylane.com
Basic Comfort	(800) 456-8687		basiccomfort.com
Kiddopotamus	(800) 772-8339		kiddopotamus.com
Clouds & Stars			cloudsandstars.com
Michaels Arts/Crafts	(800) MICHAELS		michaels.com
Bumpa Bed	(800) 241-1848	(509) 457-0925	babyjogger.com
Stay Put safety sheet			babysheets.com
Baby-Be-Safe			baby-be-safe.com
Wall Nutz			wallnutz.com
Creative Images artwork			crimages.com

Outlets

| Garnet Hill | (802) 362-6198 |
| The Interior Alternative | (413) 743-1986 |

Bedding Manufacturers

Amy Coe		(203) 221-3050	amycoe.com
Baby Guess	(714) 895-2250		crowncraftsinfantproducts.com
Bananafish	(800) 899-8689	(818) 727-1645	
Beautiful Baby		(903) 295-2229	bbaby.com
Blueberry Lane		(413) 528-9633	blueberrylanehome.com
Blue Moon Baby		(626) 455-0014	bluebaby.com
Brandee Danielle	(800) 720-5656	(714) 957-1240	brandeedanielle.com
California Kids	(800) 548-5214	(650) 637-9054	
Carters	(800) 845-3251	(803) 275-2541	carters.com
Celebrations		(310) 532-2499	baby-celebrations.com
Cotton Tale	(800) 628-2621	(714) 435-9558	
CoCaLo		(714) 434-7200	cocalo.com
Crown Crafts	(714) 895-9200		crowncraftsinfantproducts.com
Fleece Baby			fleecebaby.com
Gerber	(800) 4-GERBER		gerber.com
Glenna Jean	(800) 446-6018	(804) 561-0687	
Hoohobbers		(773) 890-1466	hoohobbers.com
KidsLine		(310) 660-0110	kidslineinc.com
Kimberly Grant		(714) 546-4411	kimberlygrant.com
Lambs & Ivy	(800) 345-2627	(310) 839-5155	lambsivy.com
Luv Stuff	(800) 825-BABY	(972) 278-BABY	luvstuffbedding.com
Martha Stewart			kmart.com
Mr. Bobbles Blankets			MrBobblesBlankets.com
Nava's Design		(818) 988-9050	navasdesigns.com
Nojo	(800) 854-8760	(310) 763-8100	nojo.com
Patchkraft	(800) 866-2229	(973) 340-3300	patchkraft.com
Picci			picci.it
Pine Creek		(503) 266-6275	pinecreekbedding.com
Quiltex	(800) 237-3636	(212) 594-2205	quiltex.com
Red Calliope	(800) 421-0526	(310) 763-8100	redcalliope.com

Sleeping Partners		(212) 254-1515	sleepingpartners.com
Sweet Kyla	(800) 265-2229		sweetkyla.com
Sumersault	(800) 232-3006	(201) 768-7890	sumersault.com
Sweet Pea		(626) 578-0866	
Wendy Bellissimo		(818) 348-3682	wendybellissimo.com
Uhula			uhula.com
Riegel	(800) 845-3251	(803) 275-2541	parentinformation.com
Springs		(212) 556-6300	springs.com
Bebe Chic		(201) 941-5414	bebechic.com
Creative Images	(800) 784-5415	(904) 825-6700	crimages.com
Eddie Bauer	(800) 426-8020		eddiebauer.com
The Company Store	(800) 323-8000		companykids.com
Garnet Hill	(800) 622-6216		garnethill.com
Graham Kracker	(800) 489-2820		grahamkracker.com
The Land of Nod	(800) 933-9904		landofnod.com
Lands' End	(800) 345-3696		landsend.com
Pottery Barn Kids	(800) 430-7373		potterybarnkids.com

Chapter 4: Reality Layette

Bella Kids			bellakids.com
One of a Kind Kid			oneofakindkids.com
Preemie.com			preemie.com
SuddenlyMommies			suddenlymommies.com
Kids Surplus			kidssurplus.com
Internet Resale Directory			secondhand.com
Nat'l Assoc. Resale & Thrift			narts.org
Minnetonka Moccasins		(718) 365-7033	minnetonka-by-mail.com
Robeez shoes	(800) 929-2623	(604) 435-9074	robeez.com
Bobux shoes			bobuxusa.com
Scootees			scootees.com
Once Upon a Child		(614) 791-0000	onceuponachild.com

Outlets

Carter's	(888) 782-9548	(770) 961-8722	
Flapdoodles		(970) 262-9351	
Hanna Andersson		(503) 697-1953	
Hartstrings		(610) 687-6900	
Health-Tex	(800) 772-8336	(914) 428-7551	vfc.com
JcPenney outlet	(800) 222-6161		jcpenney.com
Osh Kosh		(920) 231-8800	oshkoshbgosh.com
Talbot's Kids	(800) 543-7123	(781) 740-8888	talbots.com
Outlet Bound mag	(800) 336-8853		outletbound.com

Clothing Manufacturers

Alexis	(800) 253-9476		alexisusa.com
Baby Gap	(800) GAPSTYLE		babygap.com
Cotton Tale Originals	(800) 628-2621		cottontaledesigns.com
Flap Happy	(800) 234-3527		flaphappy.com
Flapdoodles		(302) 731-9793	flapdoodles.com
Florence Eisman		(414) 272-3222	florenceeiseman.com
Gymboree	(800) 990-5060		gymboree.com
Hartstrings		(610) 687-6900	hartstrings.com
Jake and Me		(970) 352-8802	jakeandme.com
Little Me			littleme.com
Mother-Maid		(770) 479-7558	jordanmarie.com
Mulberri Bush (Tumbleweed too)			mulberribush.com
OshKosh B'Gosh			oshkoshbgosh.com
Patsy Aiken		(919) 872-8789	patsyaiken.com
Pingorama			pingorama.com
Sarah's Prints	(888) 4-PRINTS		sarasprints.com
Skivvydoodles		(212) 967-2918	skivvydoodles.com

web/phone directory

Sweet Potatoes and Spudz	(510) 527-7633	sweetpotatoesinc.com
Wes & Willy		wesandwilly.com
Carter's	(770) 961-8722	carters.com
Fisher Price	(800) 747-8697	fisher-price.com
Good Lad of Philadelphia	(215) 739-0200	
Le Top	(800) 333-2257	

Catalogs

Childrens Wear	(800) 242-5437	cwdkids.com
Hanna Andersson	(800) 222-0544	hannaandersson.com
Lands End	(800) 963-4816	landsend.com
LL Kids	(800) 552-5437	llbean.com
Patagonia Kids	(800) 638-6464	patagonia.com
Talbot's Kids	(800) 543-7123	talbots.com
Wooden Soldier	(800) 375-6002	(603) 356-7041	disneystore.com
Disney Catalog	(800) 237-5751	disneystore.com
Fitigues	(800) 235-9005	fitigues.com
Campmor	(800) 226-7667	campmor.com
Sierra Trading Post	(800) 713-4534	sierratradingpost.com

Diapers

BioKleen		biokleen.com
All Together Diaper Company		clothdiaper.com
Baby Lane		thebabylane.com
Diapers 4 Less		diapers4less.com
Drug Emporium		drugemporium.com
CVS Pharmacy		cvspharmacy.com
Baby's Heaven		babysheaven.com
Diaper Site		diapersite.com
Costco		costco.com
Weebees		weebees.com
Baby J		babyj.com
BarefootBaby		Barefootbaby.com
Kelly's Closet		kellyscloset.com
Jardine Diapers		jardinediapers.com
Baby Bunz	(800) 676-4559	babybunz.com
Organic Bebe		organicbebe.com
Huggies		huggies.com
Luvs		luvs.com
Diaper Wraps		diaperaps.com
Tushies		tushies.com
Nature Boy & Girl		natureboyandgirl.com

Cloth Diaper Resources

Diaper Changes book	(800) 572-1826	
homekeepers.com		
Mother-Ease		motherease.com
Kushies	(800) 841-5330	kushies.com
DiaperDance		diaperdance.com
Daisy Diapers		diasydiapers.com
All Together	(801) 566-7579	clothdiaper.com
Bumkins	(800) 338-7581	bumkins.com
Indisposables	(800) 663-1730	
Baby Town		eskimo.com/~babytown
Sams Club		samsclub.com
BJ's		bjswholesale.com
Baby Works	(800) 422-2910	babyworks.com
Nurtured Baby	(888) 564-BABY	nurturedbaby.com
TC Kidco	(888) 825-4326	

Chapter 5: Maternity/Nursing

Expressiva			expressive.com
Playtex	(800) 537-9955		playtex.com
Motherwear	(800) 950-2500		motherwear.com
Anna Cris Maternity			annacris.com
Little Koala			littlekoala.com
Maternity 4 Less			maternity4less.com
Mom Shop			momshop.com
One Hot Mama			onehotmama.com
Fit Maternity			fitmaternity.com
Birth&Baby			birthandbaby.com
Mommy Gear			mommygear.com
From Here to Eternity			fromheretomaternity.com
Just Babies			justbabies.com
Lattesa			lattesa.com
Liz Lange Maternity			lizlange.com
Mothers In Motion			mothers-in-motion.com
Naissance Maternity			naissancematernity.com
Pumpkin Maternity			pumpkinmaternity.com
Style Maternity			stylematernity.com
Thyme Maternity			maternity.ca
Twinkle Little Star			twinklelittlestar.com

Plus maternity sources

Baby Becoming			babybecoming.com
Expecting Style			expectingstyle.com
Imaternity			imaternity.com
JCPenney			jcpenney.com
Maternal Instinct			maternal-instinct.com
MomShop			momshop.com
Motherhood			maternitymall.com
One Hot Mama			onehotmama.com
Plus Maternity			plusmaternity.com
About Babies Inc			aboutbabiesinc.com
Plus Size Mommies			plussizemommies.com
Majamas			majamas.com
Bravado Designs	(800) 590-7802	(416) 466-8652	bravadodesigns.com
One Hanes Place	(800) 300-2600		onehanesplace.com
Decent Exposures	(800) 524-4949		decentexposures.com
Fit Maternity		(530) 938-4530	fitmaternity.com
Title 9 Sports		(510) 655-5999	titleninesports.com
Hue		(212) 947-3666	
Motherwear	(800) 950-2500		motherwear.com
Breast is Best	(877) 837-5439		breastisbest.com
Elizabeth Lee Designs		(435) 454-3350	elizabethlee.com
Danish Wool			danishwool.com
Breast Feeding Styles			breastfeedingstyles.com
Sierra Blue			sierrablue.com
Wears the Baby			wearsthebaby.com
Leading Lady			leadinglady.com
Raising a Racquet			raisingaracquet.com
BoeBabyBiz			boebabybiz.com

Outlets

No Nonsense			nononsense.com

Maternity Chains

Japanese Weekend	(800) 808-0555	(415) 621-0555	japaneseweekend.com
Motherhood	(800) 4MOM2BE		maternitymall.com

Chapter 6: Feeding

Breastfeeding

La Leche League	(800) LALECHE		lalecheleague.org

Nursing Mothers' Council		(408) 272-1448	nursingmothers.org
Int'l Lactation Consultants Assoc		(703) 560-7330	iblce.org
Bosom Buddies	(888) 860-0041	(720) 482-0109	bosombuddies.com
Avent	(800) 542-8368		aventamerica.com
Medela	(800) 435-8316		medela.com
White River Concepts		(800) 824-6351	
Ameda Egnell	(800) 323-4060		hollister.com
My Brest Friend	(800) 555-5522		zenoffproducts.com
EZ-2-Nurse	(800) 584-TWIN		everythingmom.com
MedRino			breastpumps-breastfeeding.com
Nursing Mothers Supplies			nursingmotherssupplies.com
Baily Medical			bailymed.com
Affordable Medela Pumps			affordable-medela-pumps.com
Mother's Milk			mothersmilkbreastfeeding.com

Baby Formula

Baby's Only Organic		babyorganic.com
BabyMil	(800) 344-1358	storebrandformulas.com
Mothers Milk Mate	(800) 499-3506	mothersmilkmate.com
Bottle Burper	(800) 699-BURP	

Bottles

Dr Brown's			babyfree.com
Munchkin	(800) 344-2229	(818) 893-5000	munchkininc.com
BreastBottle			breastbottle.com

Baby Food

Beech-Nut	(800) BEECHNUT	beechnut.com
Earth's Best	(800) 442-4221	earthsbest.com
Gerber		gerber.com
Well Fed Baby	(888) 935-5333	wellfedbaby.com
Super Baby Food book		superbabyfood.com

Chapter 7: Around the House

Kel-Gar		(972) 250-3838	kelgar.com
EuroBath			primobaby.com
Pure White Noise			purewhitenoise.com
Ear Plug Store			earplugstore.com
Comfy Kids	(888) 529-4934		comfykids.com
BabySmart	(800) 756-5590	(908) 766-4900	baby-smart.com
Nature Company			naturecompany.com
Container Store	(800) 733-3532		containerstore.com
Diaper Genie	(800) 843-6430		playtexbaby.com
Learning Curve	(800) 704-8697		learningtoys.com
Dolly mobiles	(800) 758-7520		dolly.com
Toy Portfolio			toyportfolio.com
Buffoodles			marymeyer.com
Infantino	(800) 365-8182		infantino.com
Gymini	(800) 843-6292		tinylove.com
Children on the Go	(800) 345-4109		gracobaby.com
Neurosmith		(562) 296-1100	neurosmith.com
North American Bear	(800) 682-3427	(312) 329-0020	nabear.com
EZ Bather Deluxe	(800) 546-1996		dexproducts.com
Discovery Toys	(800) 426-4777		discoverytoysinc.com

Coupon sites

BabyDollar	babydollar.com		
Deal of the Day	dealoftheday.com	EDealFinde	eDealFinder.com
ImegaDeals	imegadeals.com	Big Big Savings	bigbigsavings.com
Fat Wallet	fatwallet.com	Clever Moms	clevermoms.com
Image Deals	imagedeals.com	DotDeals	dotdeals.com
It's Raining Bargains	itsrainingbargains.com		

Catalogs

Back to Basics Toys	(800) 356-5360		backtobasicstoys.com
Constructive Play.	(800) 832-0572	(816) 761-5900	constplay.com
Edutainment	(800) 338-3844		mattelinteractive.com
Kaplan Co	(800) 533-2166		kaplanco.com
Playfair Toys	(800) 824-7255		playfairtoys.com
Sensational Begin.	(800) 444-2147		sensationalkids.com
Toys to Grow On	(800) 542-8338		toystogrowon.com
Totally Thomas' Toy	(800) 30-THOMAS		totallythomas.com
Thomas The Tank Engine			thomasthetankengine.com
FAO Schwarz	(800) 426-8697		faoschwarz.com
Hearthsong	(800) 325-2502		heathsong.com
Imagine/Challenge	(888) 777-1493		imaginetoys.com
Leaps & Bounds	(800) 477-2189		leapsandboundscatalog.com
Smarter Kids			smarterkids.com
Earthwise Toys			naturaltoys.com
Cozy Crib Tent	(800) 626-0339		totsinmind.com
DealTime			dealtime.com
Overstock			overstock.com
Mobicam			getmobi.com
Philips Baby Monitors			consumer.Philips.com
BeBe Sounds			unisar.com
Summer Infant Products			summerinfant.com

Chapter 8: Car Seats

NHTSA	(888) DASH2DOT	(202) 366-0123	nhtsa.dot.gov
American Academy of Pediatrics			aap.org
National Safe Kids Campaign			safekids.org
Safety Belt Safe USA			carseat.org
Car Seat Data			carseatdata.org
Fit for a Kid			fitforakid.org
Safety Alerts			safetyalerts.com
ParentsPlace			parentsplace.com
Auto Safety Hotline	(800) 424-9393		
Might Tite	(888) 336-7909		might-tite.com
Fit for a Kid	(877) FIT4AKID		fit4akid.com
Britax	(888) 4-BRITAX	(704) 409-1700	childseat.com
Safeline SitNStroll	(800) 829-1625	(303) 457-4440	safelinecorp.com
Baby's Away	(800) 571-0077		babysaway.com
Kiddopotamus	(800) 772-8339		kiddopotamus.com
InMotion Pictures			inmotionpictures.com

Chapter 9: Strollers & To-Go Gear

Traveling Tikes			travelingtikes.com
Lots4Tots			lots4tots.com
PePeny canopies			pepeny.com
Dmart Stores			dmartstores.com
Aprica		(310) 639-6387	apricausa.com
Baby Trend	(800) 328-7363		babytrend.com
Bugaboo	(800)460-2922		bugaboo.nl
Combi	(800) 752-6624	(630) 871-0404	combi-intl.com
J Mason		(818) 993-6800	jmason.com
i'coo/Traxx		(214) 761-5661	i-coo.com.
Ingelsina	(877) 486-5112	(973) 746-5112	ingelsina.com
Maclaren	(877) 504-8809	(203) 354-4400	maclarenbaby.com
Mountain Buggy			mountainbuggy.com
Phil & Ted Most Excellent Buggy Company			philandteds.com
Silver Cross	(866) 887-9642		silvercrossbaby.com
Stroll Air		(519) 579-4534	www.stroll-air.com
Valco			valcobaby.com
Zooper		(503) 248-9469	zooperstrollers.com

web/phone directory

Simo	(800) SIMO4ME	(203) 348-SIMO	simostrollers.com
Bertini			bertinistrollers.com
Kidco	(800) 553-5529	(847) 970-9100	kidcoinc.com
Safety 1st		(718) 385-1000	
Baby Jogger		(509) 457-0925	babyjogger.com
Kool Stop	(800) 586-3332	(714) 738-4973	koolstop.com
Dreamer Design		(509) 574-8085	dreamerdesign.net
Gozo		(415) 388-1814	getgozo.com
InStep	(800) 242-6110		instep.net
BOB		(805) 541-2554	bobtrailers.com
Tike Tech			xtechoutdoors.com
Yakima			Yakima.com
Cozy Rosie	(877) 744-6367	(914) 244-6367	CozyRosie.com
Bundle Me			bundleme.com
Buggy Bagg			buggybagg.com
Burley	(800) 311-5294		burley.com
Schwinn	(800) SCHWINN		schwinn.com
Tanjor			lodrag.com
Rhode Gear			rhodegear.com

Diaper Bags

Mommy's Helper	(800) 371-3509	(316) 684-2229	mommyshelperinc.com
California Innovations			ca-innovations.com

Carriers

Maya Wrap			mayawrap.com
Over the Shoulder Baby Holder			otsbh.net
ZoloWear			zolowear.com
Walking Rock Farm			walkingrockfarm.com
Kangeroo Korner			kangerookorner.com
Cuddle Karrier			cuddlekarrier.com
Hip Hammock			hiphammock.com
Baby Bjorn	(800) 593-5522		babybjorn.com
Theodore Bean	(877) 68-TBEAN		theodorebean.com
Baby Trekker	(800) 665-3957		babytrekker.com
Kelty		(303) 530-7670	kelty.com
Tough Traveler	(800) GO-TOUGH	(518) 377-8526	toughtraveller.com
Sherpa Mountain			sherpa-mtn.com
Pathfinder Outdoors			pathfindersoutdoor.com
Great Escpaes			greatescapes.com

Chapter 10: Childcare

Nat'l Parenting Ctr	(800) 753-6667	(818) 225-8990	tnpc.com
Au Pair in America	(800) 727-2437 x6188		
Nat'l Assoc Family Child Care	(800) 359-3817		nafcc.org
Nat'l Assoc Educ Young Child.	(800) 424-2460		naeyc.org
My Background Check			mybackgroundcheck.com
Choice Trust	choicetrust.com	US Search	ussearch.com

More Resources
Baby Announcement Sources

Babies N Bells			babiesnbells.com
Celebrate Invitations			celebrateinvitations.com
Stork Avenue	storkavenue.com	E-Invite	evinte.com
Card Creations	cardcreations.com	AlphaBit Soup	alphabitsoup.com
FairyGodmother	thefairygodmother.com	Angel Bars	angelbars.com
Announcements by Jeannette			announcingit.com
Celebrating Children			celebratingchildren.com
Paper Direct	(800) 272-7377		paperdirect.com

Hershey's wrappers	(800) 544-1347		hersheys.com
Homestead wrappers	(800) 995-2288		carsonenterprises.com

Announcement Printers

Carlson Craft	(800) 328-1782		carlsoncraft.com
Chase		(508) 478-9220	
NRN Designs		(714) 898-6363	
William Arthur	(800) 985-6581	(207) 985-6581	williamarthur.com
Elite	(800) 354-8321		
Encore	(800) 526-0497		encorestudios.com
Invitations Hotline	(800) 800-4355		invitationhotline.com
Heart Thoughts	(800) 524-2229		heart-thoughts.com
Artitudes	(800) 741-0711		miracleofadoption.com
Adoption World			adoptionstuff.com

Catalogs

One Step Ahead	(800) 274-8440	onestepahead.com
Right Start Catalog	(800) LITTLE-1	rightstart.com

BabyNames

Babynames	babynames.com	Alphabette Zoope	zoope.com
Parentsoup	parentsoup.com	Baby Zone	babyzone.com

Shopping Bots

My Simon	mysimon.com	PriceScan	pricescan.com
Shop Best	shopbest.com		

Baby Products Web Sites

Babycenter	babycenter.com	Planet Feedback	planetfeedback.com
BabyStyle	babystyle.com	Baby Ant	babyant.com
Baby Super Center	babysupercenter.com	Smart Bargains	smartbargains.com
Baby Bundle	babybundle	Baby Super Mall	babysupermall
Just Babies	justbabies.com	Baby Universe	babyuniverse.com
Baby Age	babyage.com	UrbanBaby	urbanbaby.com
Baby P.C.	babypressconference.com		
Overstock	overstock.com		

Nat'l Parenting Ctr	(800) 753-6667	(818) 225-8990	tnpc.com
Au Pair in America	(800) 727-2437 x6188		
Nat'l Assoc Family Child Care	(800) 359-3817		nafcc.org
Nat'l Assoc Educ Young Child.	(800) 424-2460		naeyc.org
My Background Check			mybackgroundcheck.com
Choice Trust	choicetrust.com	US Search	ussearch.com

Appendix A: Canada

Transport Canada	(613) 990-2309	tc.gc.ca
Canadian Auto. Assoc		caa.ca
British Columbia AAA	(604) 268-5000	bcaa.bc.ca
Canadian Parents Online	(877) 325-8888	canadianparents.com
Maternal Instinct	(877) MATERNAL	maternal-instinct.com
Mountain Equip Coop		mac.ca
Child Resources		childcarecanada.org

Appendix C: Twins

Twins Magazine	(800) 328-3211	(303) 290-8500	twinsmagazine.com
Baby Beat	(888) 758-8822		babybeat.com
Kimberly Clark Twins	(800) 544-1847		
Double Decker Stroller		(941) 543-1582	doubledecker.com
Maxi Mom Carrier			twinsstuff.com

web/phone directory

How to Reach the Authors

Have a question about

Baby Bargains?

Want to make a suggestion?

Discovered a great bargain
you'd like to share?

Contact the Authors, Denise & Alan Fields
in one of five flavorful ways:

1. By phone:
(303) 442-8792

2. By mail:
436 Pine Street, Suite 600,
Boulder, CO 80302

3. By fax:
(303) 442-3744

4. By email:
authors@BabyBargains.com

5. On our web page:
www.BabyBargains.com

If this address isn't active, try one of our other URL's:
www.DeniseAndAlan.com or www.WindsorPeak.com.
Or call our office at 1-800-888-0385
if you're having problems accessing the page.

What's on our web page?
◆ *Parent product reviews.*
◆ *Sign up for a FREE E-NEWSLETTER!*
◆ *MESSAGE BOARDS with in-depth reader feedback.*
◆ *CORRECTIONS and clarifications.*

If this book doesn't save you at least

$250

off your baby expenses, we'll give you a complete refund on the cost of this book!

NO QUESTIONS ASKED!

Just send the book and your mailing address to

Windsor Peak Press • 436 Pine Street, Suite T Boulder, CO, 80302.

If you have any questions, please call
(303) 442-8792.

Look at all those other baby books in the bookstore—no other author or publisher is willing to put their money where their mouth is! We are so confident that *Baby Bargains* will save you money that we guarantee it in writing!